Social and Labour Market Aspects of
North American Linkages

GENERAL EDITORS:
RICHARD G. HARRIS & THOMAS LEMIEUX

Social and Labour Market Aspects of North American Linkages

University of Calgary Press

HF
1766
.S57
2005
M

ISBN 1-55238-145-5
ISSN 1700-2001

University of Calgary Press
2500 University Dr. N.W.
Calgary, Alberta, Canada T2N 1N4

Library and Archives Canada Cataloguing in Publication

Social and labour market aspects of North American linkages /
General editors, Richard G. Harris & Thomas Lemieux.

(Industry Canada Research Series, ISSN 1700-2001 ; v. XII)
Issued also in French under title: Les liens en Amérique du Nord.
Proceedings of a conference held in Montreal, Quebec, on Nov. 22, 2002.
Co-published by Industry Canada.
Includes bibliographical references.
ISBN 1-55238-145-5

54240B (Industry Canada)
SP-614-05-05 (Human Resources and Skills Development Canada)

1. North America – Economic integration – Congresses.
2. Free trade – North America – Congresses.
3. Labor market – North America – Congresses.
4. North America – Social policy – Congresses.
5. Canada – Economic conditions – 1991- – Congresses.
I. Harris, Richard G.
II. Lemieux, Thomas
III. Canada. Industry Canada.
IV. Series

HF1766.S63 2005   382'.917   C2005-900717-6

Canada We acknowledge the financial support of the Government of Canada through the Book Publishing Industry Development Program (BPIDP) for our publishing activities.

We acknowledge the support of the Alberta Foundation for the Arts for this published work.

Published by the University of Calgary Press in cooperation with Industry Canada, Human Resources and Skills Development Canada and Public Works and Government Services Canada.

Catalogue Number: ID53-11/12-2005E

EDITORIAL AND TYPESETTING SERVICES: CIGC Services conseils inc.
COVER DESIGN: Paul Payer/ArtPlus Limited

Printed and bound in Canada
∞ This book is printed on acid-free paper.

Table of Contents

Acknowledgments

THE GENERAL EDITORS WOULD LIKE TO THANK all those involved in the preparation of this volume and of the conference. Richard Roy (Acting Director-General, Micro-Economic Policy Analysis, Industry Canada) conceived and organized the conference at which the papers published here were initially presented. Wendy Salmon, Aaron Sydor, Leslie Krukoff and Sarah Fisher provided invaluable assistance in the organization of the conference. Joanne Fleming coordinated the publication of the volume with the assistance of Varsa Kuniyal, who also prepared the contributors' biographies. Daniel Boothby and Jeff Waring also contributed to the preparation of the volume. Jean-Pierre Toupin assisted with English editing and provided French translation; Marie-Claude Faubert did the page setting; and Véronique Dewez proofread the French version. Finally, we would like to thank Walter Hildebrandt and John King of the University of Calgary Press for their support in the publication of this volume.

y>o

Book Title:

Preface

T HE DEEPENING OF REGIONAL ECONOMIC INTEGRATION in North America over the past twenty years has taken many forms, such as increased trade and investment flows, the strategic location of plants within North America to supply an integrated market, and growing movements of people across borders. This strengthening of integration is in part driven by policy initiatives such as the North American Free Trade Agreement (NAFTA), but also by fundamental factors that include advances in information technology and their dissemination, the globalization of trade flows and economic competition, and a unique political geography. As a result of increased integration, businesses and individuals in North America are increasingly developing continental strategies in their decision-making, which encompasses the location of production facilities, the location and intensity of research and development spending and the organization of production for firms, and skills acquisition and work-location decisions for highly skilled individuals.

The effects of economic integration are pervasive, but we know little about how integration affects such aspects of our economic life as the organization of workplaces or the functioning of the labour market. While there is wide agreement that North American economic integration offers opportunities to Canadians and has increased their standard of living, there are concerns that deeper integration may restrict Canada's ability to pursue a number of important domestic policy goals. For example, greater mobility of professionals between Canada and the United States is thought to create fiscal competition that may force policy convergence in areas such as taxation and the financing of post-secondary education. Policy research on North American linkages must address the extent to which further economic integration could restrict options for social and labour market policies and might lead to convergence in these areas.

To explore these issues, Industry Canada and Human Resources Development Canada (now Human Resources and Skills Development Canada) jointly organized a workshop on Social and Labour Market Aspects of North American Linkages, held in Montreal on November 20-22, 2002. The workshop was organized around four themes: obstacles to and opportunities of further economic integration; integration and the domestic labour market; integration and social programs; and potential benefits and costs of further easing labour mobility between Canada and the United States. This volume includes the studies commissioned for the workshop, discussants' comments on these studies, a summary of the panel discussions held at the workshop, and an Overview prepared by the general editors. The research assembled in the volume should contribute to an improved understanding of the implications of North American economic integration for social programs and labour markets.

Professors Richard Harris, of Simon Fraser University, and Thomas Lemieux, of the University of British Columbia, served as general editors for this volume. We would like to thank them for their diligent work in reviewing and preparing this material, as well as all the authors, discussants and panelists for their contribution to the workshop and to our understanding of these issues.

LUCIENNE ROBILLARD
PRESIDENT OF THE QUEEN'S PRIVY COUNCIL OF CANADA,
MINISTER OF INTERGOVERNMENTAL AFFAIRS AND
MINISTER OF HUMAN RESOURCES AND SKILLS DEVELOPMENT

DAVID L. EMERSON
MINISTER OF INDUSTRY

Richard G. Harris   &   *Thomas Lemieux*
Simon Fraser University   *University of British Columbia*

Book Title:
Canada, USA NAFTA

Overview

F15
F16 F22 J61
J24 D72 P16

INTRODUCTION

THIS RESEARCH VOLUME IS THE OUTGROWTH of a workshop organized by Human Resources Development Canada and Industry Canada in November of 2002 on issues related to the "Social and Labour Market Aspects of North American Linkages." In this overview, we attempt to provide the contextual backdrop for the questions addressed in the volume, an outline of the various studies and their conclusions, and implications for future policy-related research. The volume represents the collaboration of a large number of people across a wide range of disciplines. It offers a rich set of history, facts and conceptual ideas in what is a rapidly evolving policy area.

There is probably no single policy issue that has attracted as much public interest as the social and labour market implications of globalization generally, and of North American linkages in the case of Canada. The basic reasons for this are well known. Canada's economic integration with the United States as measured by trade and investment data has increased steadily since the signing of the Canada-U.S. Free Trade Agreement (FTA) in 1988. While the exact role of the FTA in this regard is still debated, the 'reality' of the Canada-U.S. economic integration is perhaps the key structural shift in the Canadian economy over the last 15 years.[1] Increased trade integration has also occurred in other countries, and the costs and benefits of globalization are subjects of active debate in virtually all countries. In addition to globalization, other trends have also fuelled debates on labour markets and social policy. In a number of countries, income inequality and, more specifically, wage inequality have risen quite significantly. As measured, for example, by the earnings of people with a college degree against those of less-educated workers, there has been a substantial increase in skill premiums. Moreover, some countries have had very different unemployment experiences. In North America, Canadian unemployment rates persistently remain above U.S. levels. An extensive literature, both international and country-specific, has tried to attribute the source of the trends in inequality and employment to trends in technology, increasing globalization and shifts in economic policy. A number of studies presented in this volume are motivated either directly or indirectly by this set of issues. While most studies suggest that income inequality trends in Canada have been less pronounced than in the United States, the tendency toward greater income inequality is attributed by many to Canada's stronger linkages with the U.S. economy. This can be viewed as a necessary consequence of more efficient markets. On the other hand, greater inequality leads to increased demands for social policy interventions. The tension between these two perspectives is an important policy driver linking North American integration to domestic social and labour market trends.

A second development of the 1990s which had a very large impact on the policy debate in Canada was the larger flows of high-technology workers and professionals to the United States. This has led to the perception that Canada was suffering from a significant *brain drain* among its best and brightest during the latter part of that decade. Whether this trend was policy-induced or was simply a consequence of the U.S. technology boom is a crucial issue. This debate provides the background for a number of studies in the volume, and it interacts with virtually all of the other themes. It raises significant issues about public subsidies to education, the underlying sources of the rising skill premium, and Canada's ability to retain and employ its most highly skilled individuals. The brain drain debate is itself part of the larger debate on the possible sources and potential cures for the growing gap between Canadian and U.S. living standards. The higher levels of market income available to Canadians who can get jobs in the United States are an important competitive constraint on Canadian firms, educational institutions, and health care systems. Social policy advocates argue that the brain drain is quantitatively insignificant, and seriously biases public policies due to an overly narrow definition of 'standard of living' — one which does not pay enough attention to social services. While this debate is now somewhat muted, given the post-2000 technology bust, it remains a durable element of the overall perception of Canadians about the constraints that U.S. labour markets exert on Canadian labour markets and policies.

Closely related to this theme is the extent to which increased North American linkages have reduced Canada's *room to manoeuvre* in setting its own economic and social policies. This is a theme running through a number of studies, both from a positive and a normative perspective. Some would argue that there has been a significant reduction in the ability of Canada to pursue a social policy distinct from that of its large neighbour to the South; moreover, they argue that it is reducing the overall level of the welfare state in Canada.

Others claim that there is little evidence to suggest this has happened. If there are pressures for economic integration, it is natural to look for other mechanisms to sustain national differences. Evidence on whether Canada can maintain national differences with the United States has become an important contextual element in this debate. A strand of the economics literature has put forward the hypothesis that trade within countries is much larger than trade between countries — what has been dubbed the *border effect*[2]; this is used to support the notion that national linkages are in fact stronger than international linkages, and that despite globalization national institutions have not weakened and policy differences can be sustained. A number of studies deal directly with the measurement and interpretation of border effects.

The European Union (EU) as a model of economic integration continues to attract policy attention in North America. Should Canada push a policy agenda focused on deeper economic integration with the United States, perhaps using the North American Free Trade Agreement (NAFTA) as the institutional vehicle? This issue has prompted an animated debate and was given yet more impetus by the September 11 terrorist attacks, with both contributing to add security to the list of objectives and highlighting Canada's vulnerability to disruptions at the U.S. border. At this point, there is little policy consensus on deepening NAFTA. A number of proposals put forward on the notion of closer Canada-U.S. economic integration include more formalized labour mobility provisions within NAFTA. Free movement of labour across the Canada-U.S. border would have significant consequences for Canada. Until quite recently, this issue had attracted little attention. However, the European common market and both the Canadian and U.S. experiences with regard to national labour mobility (between provinces and between states) provide interesting case studies on the consequences of increased cross-border labour mobility. A number of studies take up this theme. The range of potential questions is large. Would the elimination of restrictions to cross-border labour flows lead to a convergence of wages and unemployment rates? Would Canadian trade and industry patterns change as a result? Would the forces currently sustaining Canada-U.S. differences in living standards be weakened or strengthened? Would cross-border labour mobility lead to greater regional inequality in Canada? The research agenda is both long and, thus far, largely unexplored. A number of studies offer some initial probing of these questions.

We now turn to a summary of the studies and their main messages. Part I addresses the issue of measuring trade integration and assesses the current state of the border effect debate. Parts II and III deal with measuring the impact on the domestic labour market of the increased economic integration that occurred during the 1990s. Part IV deals explicitly with social policy convergence or divergence within North America. Parts V and VI examine research and policy issues motivated by changes in Canada-U.S. cross-border labour mobility, both in the recent past and, possibly, in the future as a result of more formal changes in the policy regime. In addition, we summarize the three panel discussions that took place during the workshop. They covered several themes closely related to the topics addressed in the studies.

PANEL I – NORTH AMERICAN LINKAGES: SOCIAL AND LABOUR MARKET ISSUES FOR CANADA

THIS FIRST PANEL dealt with the issues of continental economic integration and policy convergence between Canada and the United States. The two panelists, Stephen Clarkson and Keith Banting, are distinguished political scientists who bring a wealth of experience and range of views to these issues. They also provide a useful contrast to the economic perspective of most of the other studies. Are social policies converging as a result of increased economic integration? Keith Banting contends that there is little evidence of convergence of social policy either globally, within the EU or within NAFTA, despite strong claims to the contrary. As for Canada and the United States, both countries spend about equally on social policy, but produce quite different outcomes — evidence he claims in support of divergence and the existence of real policy choice at the national level. A very different view is presented by Stephen Clarkson, who focuses on the impact of NAFTA on workers and labour market conditions. He claims that NAFTA has a) reduced employment opportunities; b) increased social dumping with greater divergence between high- and low-skill labour; and c) led to poorer working conditions as labour standards were weakened by the forces of globalization and trade integration. Overall, the panelist sees the process of continental integration as having expanded the relative power of capital over labour. Clarkson is sceptical about the prospects on any further increases in continental labour mobility. Political action to preserve jobs and income within the United States will limit access of Canadian and Mexican workers to the U.S. labour market. Faced with the political realities of U.S. protectionism, Canadian governments will thus continue to preserve as much room-to-manoeuvre as possible with respect to domestic labour market policy instruments.

PART I – THE EXTENT AND EVOLUTION OF CANADA-U.S. ECONOMIC INTEGRATION

THE FIRST SET OF STUDIES deals with issues raised in measuring the extent and implications of Canada-U.S. economic integration using trade data. Much of this literature has been driven recently by new data tracking trade between and amongst provinces and states. John McCallum (1995) originally used this data to show that, as of the mid-1980s, there was a significant border effect on Canadian trade — suggesting Canadian provinces traded much more between themselves than internationally based on distance and income variables. There is now an extensive literature on this issue and the Coulombe and Helliwell studies cover two alternative views of these developments. While trade integration does not impact directly on cross-border labour mobility, it does factor importantly into the overall position one takes on the economic pressures toward future labour market integration. If borders are still strong trade inhibitors, then these pressures are likely to remain weak. On the other hand, if the border is losing its effectiveness as a means of segmenting Canadian and U.S. markets, labour market integration may follow trends in goods markets.

John Helliwell's study and James Anderson's comment provide a useful overview of the current research of the impact of national borders and distance on economic linkages, primarily trade flows, from alternative perspectives. Helliwell reviews some of his well-known work in this area, and presents some new estimates based on Canadian and U.S. province-state trade data, within a gravity equation model of trade. He also offers an extensive discussion and critique of the Anderson and van Wincoop (2003) study on border effects. For those who have an interest in these matters, this study is an excellent starting point. Going through the logic and details of the theory, data, and interpretation of econometric results leaves one confused as to the state of the literature despite Helliwell's best efforts. He carefully documents the work that has shown the overwhelming significance of border effects in a large number of studies on internal versus international trade, price variability between cities, research and development effects on productivity and migration flows. There is virtually no doubt that national borders matter and, apparently, they matter quite a lot. For example, on the trade issue, the consensus estimate seems to be that internal Canadian trade is 10.6 times greater than international trade, while U.S. internal trade is 2.6 times greater. Moreover, distance has a very significant impact in reducing trade. It is not possible to cover all the material reviewed by Helliwell. He and Anderson clearly have some unresolved methodological differences, with the latter arguing strongly that we can only use gravity models derived from an explicit theoretical framework in order to draw policy conclusions.

It appears that much of the disagreement hinges upon how one interprets the estimated border effect. Helliwell claims that borders and distance matter much more because of a loss of network density and shared norms as one moves across the national border, than of formal trade or regulatory barriers originating in national policies. He then uses these ideas to defend two major policy positions. First, that further trade integration within North America, and in particular with the United States, will not lead to any significant welfare gains for Canada. This, of course, is a powerful idea in Canada and runs against the notion that further economic integration with the United States is economically beneficial. A corollary of this view is that investment in national institutions that serve to deepen Canadian networks and shared norms will improve welfare in Canada and trade between Canadian provinces. His second set of arguments pertains to the issue of a possible Canada-U.S. monetary union. Here, he stands firmly opposed to the idea on the grounds that national sovereignty would inevitably be compromised by such a move. However, he goes on to contend, based on the border effect observed in trade regressions, that the existing level of economic integration of Canada with the United States is not sufficient to justify a Canada-U.S. currency union.

Serge Coulombe offers an extremely useful overview and criticism of the theoretical and empirical literature on the border effect as estimated with a gravity-based model of trade. As he points out, both the size of the estimated border effect and its interpretation are extremely sensitive to a number of factors. He starts by noting that McCallum's border effect based on the use of Canadian interprovincial trade data and state-province trade data is more than 10 times the border effect estimated for the United States using interstate and international trade data. He points to two important reasons why this is the case. First, the border effect is the ratio of weighted interprovincial trade to weighted international trade. Trade is weighted by income and distance so that economic size has a large effect on the estimated border effect. Small countries will, *ceteris paribus*, have larger intranational trade when weighted by the inverse of income. His second point is that the estimated border effects using this type of data suffer from an omitted-variable bias — in particular, the absence of data on trade with third countries implies that multilateral resistance to trade is missing from the analysis. In the Canadian case, given geography and the distance to external markets, multilateral resistance to trade is greater than it is in the United States, again leading to larger interprovincial trade flows and over-estimates of the border effect. He goes on to emphasize what he sees as a crucial missing element of the gravity equation-economic density system. Not only is Canada small, but it is not economically dense relative to the United States. Again, this tends to induce greater internal trade. He goes on to discuss time-series estimates of the McCallum border effect, and notes that they have been steadily falling. First, because interprovincial trade had been falling relative to gross domestic product from 1981 to 1991. Second, because there was a dramatic expansion of international trade after 1991. He concludes his study with a call for considerable caution in interpreting the policy significance of the border effect estimated from cross-section regressions. First, it does not necessarily reflect accurately the role of unmeasured international trade barriers, in the sense that the estimated parameter tells you something about what would happen to trade if all border costs could be removed in some way. Second, in his view, it does not provide an accurate assessment of the trade-generating power of a particular set of national institutions, as emphasized in Helliwell's work. He generally argues that, without a more detailed structural model of regional trade that pays careful attention to geography, both of these questions are difficult to answer.

Upon reading these studies, one is left with quite different assessments of the past and current significance of the border as a barrier to economic integration. It is certain that this debate will continue and readers will find these contributions extremely useful in forming their own opinions on the issue.

PART II – LABOUR MARKET IMPACTS OF CANADA-U.S. ECONOMIC INTEGRATION

THE SECOND SET OF STUDIES looks directly at the impact of trade integration on wages and employment. Thomas Lemieux examines the effect of integration on workers' wages for different skill groups in Canada and the United States. Beaulieu and Joy push the analysis further by looking at whether the groups of workers who have the most to gain from North American integration are also the ones who tend to support free trade agreements.

Lemieux seeks to determine whether free trade between Canada and the United States has lead to a convergence in both the level and distribution of wages in the two countries. He points out that it would be unrealistic to expect wages to be equalized between two countries when systematic wage differences persist across regions of the same country. In other words, differences in both the level and the dispersion of wages across regions of the same country provide a useful benchmark for interpreting the magnitude of Canada-U.S. wage differences. Lemieux first shows that while wage levels were comparable in Canada and the United States prior to free trade in 1984, Canadian wages are now substantially lower than south of the border. However, this emerging gap is substantially smaller than existing differences between regions of Canada (e.g. Ontario and the Atlantic provinces). By contrast, wage dispersion as measured by the university-high school wage gap has increased much more in the United States than in Canada between 1984 and 2001. As a result, this gap is now essentially larger in every single region of the United States than in the six regions of Canada examined in the study. This suggests that, if anything, Canada-U.S. differences in wage levels and dispersion are larger now than prior to free trade between the two countries.

Lemieux's findings indicate that economic integration between Canada and the United States has little impact on Canadian wages. This result confirms previous work by Gaston and Trefler (1997) and Beaulieu (2000), who also found, using different data and methodologies, that Canadian wages were not much affected by free trade between Canada and the United States.

Beaulieu and Joy examine the distributional impact within Canada of Canada-U.S. free trade, an area that remains relatively unexplored by comparison with other aspects of free trade. As the authors note, this is somewhat surprising since, historically, arguments as to who supports trade liberalization have hinged on how incomes were likely to be impacted. Two polar case economic models that look at this issue are the specific-factors model and the Heckscher-Ohlin-Vanek (HOV) model. The specific-factors model assumes that factors of production are not mobile across industries; therefore, support or opposition to trade liberalization can be predicted based on whether a given industry is likely to gain or lose. Industries with high protective tariffs in particular are most likely to oppose free trade. The HOV model assumes that factors are mobile across industries, at least in the longer run, and support or opposition to trade liberalization is based upon the factor of production supplied by an individual voter, not the industry in which this factor is based.

Beaulieu and Joy first look at data from the Canadian federal election of 1988, which is generally viewed as a form of referendum on free trade with the United States — the key election issue. Using this data, they attempt to explain what motivated voters to support, or not, the FTA. In a statistical model, they find that industry of employment does not predict voter behaviour but that skill level does. This supports the view that voters consider the factors they supply as mobile in the longer run and, furthermore, that it was unskilled workers who were most opposed to the FTA because they feared they had the most to lose. Both findings are somewhat consistent with the HOV interpretation of the Canadian economic structure at that time.

The authors go on to examine the actual consequences of the FTA as opposed to the factors determining voter preferences. Did the voters get it right, and if so, why? It is well known that during that period, the wages of unskilled workers stagnated generally across all Organisation for Economic Co-operation and Development countries, including Canada, and the wages of skilled workers improved. In Canada's case, however, one needs to determine the degree to which the FTA has changed the wage structure. In previous work based on a control-treatment framework, Beaulieu (2000) concluded that the FTA had no effect on wages, although it did increase the employment of skilled workers and lowered the employment of unskilled workers. Using a Mincer wage regression framework, the authors check whether the earlier predictions of the HOV model of trade policy preferences were consistent with the changes in wages observed after the FTA. The results were rather mixed and, in some cases, clearly contrary to the HOV model, which is more or less consistent with Lemieux's findings. Lastly, Beaulieu and Joy review the impact of the FTA on plant closures. They find that high-tariff industries had higher rates of closures relative to low-tariff industries.

Two broad conclusions can be drawn from this study. First, to some degree, voters can rationally anticipate the long-run impact of shifts in economic policy; secondly, economic adjustments to a basic phenomenon such as trade liberalization tend to be greater for workers with low skill levels. To the extent that further economic integration imposes additional adjustments, these results support policies that focus on increasing education and skill levels among low-skill workers. Moreover, if one wants to anticipate or reduce political barriers to such adjustments, it is policies of these types which are most likely to work, rather than support measures focusing on specific industries.

PART III – ADJUSTMENTS BY FIRMS AND WORKERS TO CANADA-U.S. ECONOMIC INTEGRATION

THE TWO STUDIES IN THIS PART cover a different angle of the effects of economic integration on the labour market. A common theme of these studies is that they examine the micro level to see how specific workers and firms adjust to closer integration. Ross Finnie looks at how particular workers may "vote with their feet" and leave Canada because of better economic opportunities elsewhere. By contrast, the firms considered by Richard Chaykowski and George Slotsve do not leave Canada, but they have to be more innovative to remain competitive in an increasingly integrated economic environment.

Finnie uses income tax data from the Longitudinal Administrative Database (LAD) to estimate the extent of migration out of Canada and of return migration back to Canada. In the LAD, it is possible to identify three potential groups of people who have left Canada: those who declare (on their tax return) that they left Canada, those who declare to be non-resident for tax purposes, and those who can provide a foreign mailing address on their tax return. Using these various tax-based definitions of migration, Finnie finds that about 0.1 percent of Canadians emigrate from Canada every year. He also finds that only a relatively small fraction of these migrants eventually return to Canada (less than 20 percent after 10 years). Finnie's results support the view that the brain drain problem became more important during the 1990s. Throughout the 1980s and 1990s, high-income earners have been substantially more likely to leave Canada than lower- and middle-income earners. By the 1990s, the fraction of high-income earners (those with annual earnings of $100,000 or more) leaving Canada had reached close to 1 percent per year. Overall out-migration rates also increased steadily throughout the 1990s. The empirical findings also confirm that younger individuals are more likely to leave Canada, while Quebec Francophones are much less likely to depart than other taxpayers.

What is the impact of economic integration on firms' workplace and industrial relations practices? Richard Chaykowski and George Slotsve use the recently released Workplace and Employee Survey (WES) to answer this question.

After reviewing the existing literature on the adoption of innovative workplace practices, Chaykowski and Slotsve develop a formal model showing the conditions under which firms will introduce these practices when trade is liberalized between two countries. Key predictions of the model are then confronted to the WES data. That survey provides invaluable information on the extent of competition faced by firms (local, national and international) and on detailed workplace practices introduced by firms such as organizational change, work organization, employee involvement, flexible compensation and training. The empirical results show that firms that only compete locally are less likely to adopt these innovative practices. By contrast, firms competing at the national level are more likely to introduce some of these new workplace practices. Further competition from the United States or the rest of the world has little impact on the adoption of most of these practices. The only exception is training intensity, which was found to be higher in firms that compete at the international level than in other firms.

PANEL II – ASSESSING THE EXTENT OF CURRENT CANADA-U.S. ECONOMIC LINKAGES AND THEIR COSTS AND BENEFITS

THE SECOND PANEL addressed the current state of Canada-U.S. economic linkages. Two very different set of views were presented. Glen Hodgson argues that what has transformed international trade, and trade relations, is the emergence of global supply chains in manufacturing. Countries have specialized in these vertical supply chains. This has been especially good for small countries and the developing world. Moreover, foreign direct investment (FDI) is the important complementary factor to this process, as evidenced by the trends of both outward and inward FDI. Hodgson claims that the Canada-U.S. FTA had a very large impact on Canadian trade patterns, and he provides a back-of-the-envelope calculation that Canada's trade ratio would be about 60 percent instead of the current 80 percent (or more) if the FTA and NAFTA had not been implemented. He argues that the most important item on the agenda today is to keep the Canada-U.S. border open. Andrew Jackson offers a quite different perspective. He reiterates his well-known views that the FTA benefits have been overstated, and he cites as evidence the growing Canada-U.S. manufacturing productivity gap and the increased trade dependence of Canada on resource exports. He goes on to suggest that closer integration of Canada with the United States, for example in the form of a customs union or other common market arrangements, is a bad idea. He claims that any further loss of sovereignty on a wide range of issues, such as social policy and foreign affairs, is highly undesirable. In his view, Canada needs to preserve its options on industrial policy for purposes of economic development and must actively use social policy as a means to avoid the inequality trends observed in the United States.

PART IV – IMPLICATIONS OF CANADA-U.S. INTEGRATION FOR SOCIAL POLICY: IS THERE A RACE TO THE BOTTOM?

IN THIS PART OF THE VOLUME, the studies by Rafael Gomez and Morley Gunderson and by Gerard Boychuk both consider whether increased North American economic and labour market integration leads to a convergence of social policies across regions and countries. Gomez and Gunderson provide a broad overview of the existing literature, while Boychuk looks explicitly at the case of redistribution policies across Canadian provinces and U.S. states.

Gomez and Gunderson first review the existing theory and evidence on the determinants of social policies in an integrated economic environment. They then consider whether Canada and the United States have introduced increasingly similar laws and regulations in the 1990s. They look at a broad range of legislations and regulations in areas such as labour relations, labour standards, unemployment insurance, workers' compensation, health and safety, human rights and anti-discrimination rules, pension policy, welfare and family benefits, and taxes. Overall, they conclude that social policies have generally converged over the last decade, though considerable divergence is sustained.

The study is a highly useful source of reference on how a broad array of Canadian social and economic policies compare to those of the United States and other countries. Given the wide range of policies and programs considered, it is difficult to provide a clear and encompassing answer to the question of whether labour market integration leads to the convergence of social policies across countries. In this sense, Gomez and Gunderson set the stage for a further round of more specialized research that should look in more detail at how integration affects specific policies and programs.

Gerard Boychuk's study provides a good example of how a more focused approach can be used to answer a similar question: what are Canada's prospects for maintaining distinct social policies in an increasingly integrated North American labour market? The study first looks at whether different U.S. states have been able to maintain distinct social policies despite the high level of labour market integration within the United States. This provides a useful benchmark for assessing the extent to which Canada may be able to maintain distinct social and redistribution policies in an increasingly integrated North American labour market. If even U.S. states can maintain distinct policies, surely Canada should be able to do so. Boychuk looks at a broad measure of social protection — share gains — to show that different U.S. states have indeed maintained distinct social policies over time. Share gains measure the extent to which social programs increase (decrease) the share of income accruing to different income classes, particularly the lowest quintile of the income distribution. Boychuk then compares share gains in Canadian provinces and U.S. states. He finds that, if anything, there has been a divergence in social policies, as measured by share gains, between Canadian provinces and U.S. states. Boychuk concludes that there is no evidence that labour market integration leads to a race to the bottom in social policies.

The conclusions of the two studies are somewhat contradictory. Gomez and Gunderson find that social policies have generally converged over the last decade while Boychuk comes to the opposite conclusion. It remains to be seen whether this discrepancy simply reflects the different perspectives taken by the researchers or a more fundamental methodological difference. In the meantime, the two studies, along with the comments by Smith and Noël, provide a very useful reference for readers interested in the important issue of social policy convergence in an increasingly integrated economic environment.

PART V – ASSESSING THE EXTENT AND CONSEQUENCES OF CANADA-U.S. LABOUR MOBILITY

THE NEXT PART OF THE VOLUME addresses directly the issue of cross-border labour mobility. One study looks at new and old econometric evidence on the extent of cross-border labour mobility between Canada and the United States, while another uses counterfactual general equilibrium methods to assess the consequences that increased labour mobility might have on the two economies. Literature in both areas is relatively sparse, so these are welcome contributions.

DeVoretz and Coulombe try to explain why Canadian mobility toward the United States appears moderate despite the existence of special access provisions under NAFTA (TN visas). They first develop the concept of a "home bias" in mobility between Canada and the United States. In the absence of a home bias, all Canadians who have an economic incentive to migrate to the United States would do so. The determinants of the decision to move south of the border would be exactly the same as the determinants of the decision to move to another province in Canada (e.g. higher wages or better employment prospects). Based on econometric estimates from previous studies, DeVoretz and Coulombe argue that there is no home bias for highly skilled workers. Using a variety of legal and economic evidence, they find that TN visas introduced as part of NAFTA have greatly facilitated cross-border movements for the groups of (highly skilled) workers covered by this type of visa. They also point out, however, that the September 11 attacks have fundamentally changed the dynamics of Canada-U.S. mobility. Increased scrutiny at the border has raised the transaction costs of obtaining a visa and could potentially segment the Canadian labour market between Canadians born in Canada and Canadians born elsewhere (particularly in the Middle East). DeVoretz and Coulombe conclude that North American integration has halted and is in a process of reversal.

Jean Mercenier and Nicolas Schmitt attempt the difficult task of providing an assessment of the impact of increased labour mobility of entrepreneurs between Canada and the United States within a quantitative general equilibrium framework. They note that some fundamental theoretical problems need to be resolved in an appropriate model of the process by which firms are created. Despite the fact that trade and migration are substitutes in the most renowned international trade theory, the Heckscher-Ohlin model, the data and most of the subsequent work point to a complementarity between migration and trade. The authors review some of the recent theory based on models of economic geography and discuss some of the channels through which trade and migration interact. It appears that the results of these theories are often quite sensitive to assumptions about parameter values, but generally the *new economic geography* theme seems to be that mobility of highly skilled individuals in the presence of free trade for goods and capital tends to exacerbate inequality among regions.

Mercenier and Schmitt argue that, in looking at the migration of highly skilled entrepreneurs, we need to deal with both skill heterogeneity and increasing returns to ability — the Sherwin-Rosen *superstar* effect. Very talented entrepreneurs (superstars) can benefit from being in larger markets either by attracting more customers or by lowering the costs of production at all levels of output. With open international markets, however, these entrepreneurs can also get the benefit of a large market by staying at home and selling both locally and abroad. Heterogeneity of ability levels is important because it implies heterogeneity in returns to ability. When labour is mobile, this may induce additional migration, with individuals leaving one country to become entrepreneurs in another. The authors cast their model of firm formation and entrepreneurship within a model of trade with vertical and horizontal product differentiation. In this set-up, more able entrepreneurs produce higher-quality goods, and thus the location and skill of entrepreneurs across countries impact on the pattern of trade in vertically differentiated goods.

Given the overall complexity of the theory, Mercenier and Schmitt move to a simulation version of the general equilibrium model and examine how the introduction of mobility of entrepreneurs affects outcomes given some exogenous asymmetries between countries. The results are quite interesting and lead to rather counterintuitive observations. For example, if countries differ only in their endowment of skilled labour and thus the potential supply of entrepreneurs, upon introducing mobility the larger country will tend to export entrepreneurs. If, alternatively, the latter has a larger endowment of unskilled labour, mobility will tend to reduce the pool of entrepreneurs in the small country as they move to the large country markets. Interestingly, the authors find that it is mid-skilled entrepreneurs who sometimes move. Real superstars do not need to migrate in order to capture the full gains of exceptional abilities —they can always use the export market as a way to achieve size. Mercenier and Schmitt further argue that the pattern of trade in vertically differentiated goods is the most impacted by changes in mobility, and this may be an important channel that has been overlooked in welfare analyses of labour mobility, which have focused on factor endowment-based trade.

Part VI – Analytical and Policy Implications of Cross-Border Labour Market Integration

DAVID WILDASIN AND RICHARD HARRIS present overviews of the broader issues surrounding the integration of previously segmented national labour markets. Wildasin focuses on some of the fiscal issues and lessons that can be drawn from the experience of U.S. states as national labour markets become more fully integrated. It is clear that government tax and expenditure policies cannot be viewed as either exogenous or non-responsive to this process. Harris is concerned with the possible relevance of a number of global trends among the determinants of economic growth and technology to the question of the costs and benefits of cross-border labour market integration. He argues that, ultimately, it will be necessary to demonstrate the positive impact on productivity growth in Canada of policies aimed at increasing labour mobility, and he suggests some channels through which this might occur.

Wildasin examines the complex linkages between trade integration, migration and the fiscal policy framework as impacted by the state of labour mobility between states, regions, and nations. Much of his analysis is motivated by the existing literature on labour economics and local public finances, which uses data on Canadian provinces and U.S. states, as well as on local governments. He begins by noting that the integration of national markets with respect to both goods and labour has been accompanied by simultaneous growth in trade flows and labour movements. He thus concludes that trade and migration are most likely complements rather than substitutes. He argues that, should Canada-U.S. labour mobility be improved, it is also most likely that both trade and labour flows would increase. Wildasin argues that increased labour mobility, both internally and internationally, is likely to improve overall efficiency by moving labour from low-productivity jurisdictions to high-productivity ones. Income differences among regions are still one of the most important factors driving migration. However, he also notes that, by deepening the labour market for any particular form of human capital, increased labour mobility substantially reduces the income risk from investment in that human capital. Increased mobility thus lowers risk and encourages specialization, both of which stimulate economic growth. While this has been observed in national labour markets, the argument is general and clearly applicable to broader cross-border labour mobility.

Wildasin goes on to examine some policy issues — fiscal competition generally and the financing of higher education more specifically. Labour mobility across provinces or states implies that the location where one receives an education is not necessarily the same as the one in which subsequent employment and taxation occur. This de-linking of individuals benefiting from the expenditure function of governments from individuals who pay taxes creates fiscal competition among state and provincial governments. Lower-level governments would like to attract highly educated workers through lower taxes, but at the same time their residents want better education for their children. In reviewing the literature on this complex issue, the author comes to the conclusion that, while there is not much evidence of a race to the bottom between states, there is an increasingly stronger case for shifting the responsibility for higher education to the federal level. He argues that, in fact, data on the financing of higher education in the United States confirm this trend. This is true under the existing state of labour mobility, and the forces pushing in this direction are likely to be strengthened by increased international labour mobility. The key implication of his study is that changes in the degree of North American labour mobility could have important consequences for relations between different levels of government, and taxation and expenditure policies.

One of the most compelling facts driving the Canadian policy research agenda over the last decade has been the growing disparity between Canadian and U.S. living standards. It is generally agreed that much of this disparity is due to differences in productivity levels between the two countries. In his study, Harris reviews the evidence on this and argues that policy toward North American labour mobility must be viewed within an analytical approach that effectively deals with the determinants of international productivity differences and how these differences react to changes in cross-border labour mobility. He argues that there are four analytical approaches that offer some interesting insights on the possible link between productivity growth and labour mobility.

The first of these is associated with the human capital approach to endogenous growth developed by Lucas. If economic growth (in per capita terms) is driven by human capital accumulation, then mobility of people across borders with different levels of human capital become a powerful force for convergence of income levels. One such theory carries with it the implication that free trade in goods and capital is not sufficient to guarantee that national income levels will converge. The economic integration agenda based on free trade and open capital markets as a means to reduce international income inequality without addressing labour mobility is therefore incomplete.

A second set of theories links labour mobility to international knowledge spillovers. A model is developed where the labour force becomes segmented between those who are globally mobile and those who are not, where knowledge is diffused through interactions among global workers, and where policies aimed at improving either the demand for, or supply of, global workers will contribute to productivity growth. Small countries can benefit by having more mobile global workers who facilitate knowledge diffusion. The third set of theories is a variant on the first but focuses on the practical importance of the service sector and of service exports. Increased cross-border labour mobility should foster the growth of Canadian service exports and thus Canadian productivity growth in the service sector.

The last set of theories deals with the information and communications technologies (ICT) revolution as an explanation for the observed acceleration of productivity growth in the United States. If ICTs are a type of general purpose technologies that are the root cause of the observed trends in productivity and wage inequality, then they have implications for changes in international labour mobility regimes. One possibility is that ICTs are closely linked to the phenomena of multi-tasking and the increased skill requirements of jobs due to the adoption of more flexible production methods and flatter organizational structures associated with ICT use. On the other hand, closer trade integration is increasing product-line specialization in small countries through outsourcing and vertical industry specialization. These two trends are working in opposite directions on task specialization within firms, and thus matching demand and supply in heterogeneous labour markets. Improving cross-border labour mobility can mitigate the tensions between these two forces by effectively deepening the market for highly specialized occupations available to the citizens of small countries without foregoing the benefits from free trade in goods and services.

PANEL III − ASSESSING THE MERIT OF EASING FURTHER THE MOVEMENTS OF WORKERS BETWEEN CANADA AND THE UNITED STATES

THE SPEAKERS ON THE THIRD PANEL, Jean-Christophe Dumont, Robert Lacroix, and Marc Van Audenrode, discussed possible opportunities for liberalizing worker mobility between Canada and the United States. Dumont presents an interesting comparison between the experiences of Europe and North America. He first cautions that the EU is a much more ambitious political, social, and economic venture than NAFTA, which mostly focused on economic issues like trade barriers. Nonetheless, he argues that North American countries can draw useful lessons from the European experience. One is that trade liberalization is not sufficient for stemming the flow of migrants from poorer to richer countries. For example, a large number of workers migrated from Southern Europe (Spain, Italy, etc.) to Northern Europe even after trade within the region was substantially liberalized. These flows only came to a halt when average incomes in Spain and Italy had substantially caught up with those of countries like France and Germany. Based on this experience, it is likely that a large number of Mexican workers will keep migrating to Canada and the United States despite the liberalization of trade under NAFTA.

Robert Lacroix discusses the case of Canadian universities, which have a long tradition of recruiting highly trained personnel from other countries. Throughout the 1960s and 1970s, Canadian universities hired a large number of academics from Europe, the United States and other countries to meet the needs of the baby-boom generation entering university classrooms. Lacroix views the next 10 years as presenting a similar, or even greater, challenge for Canadian universities. With the upcoming retirement of a large number of professors and ever-growing enrolments, these institutions will have no choice but to hire many foreign PhDs in an extremely competitive world context. In his view, providing newly hired faculty with world-class research facilities will be key to succeed in this massive recruitment endeavour. Flexible immigration policies and competitive salary and taxation levels are also important factors.

Marc Van Audenrode presents some personal and general observations on the changing role of border effects in migration decisions. He notes that while most barriers to mobility have been removed in Europe, movements across rich European countries remain limited, as also noted by Dumont. Van Audenrode points out that moving remains a costly and difficult option, even in a context where barriers to international mobility have been removed, as TN visas did for Canadian professionals interested in taking up jobs in the United States. In concluding, he discusses how demographic changes and taxes may increasingly pose a challenge to migration policies between Canada and the United States.

CONCLUSION

WHAT ARE THE MAIN POLICY LESSONS TO DRAW from the collection of studies contained in this volume? What key research issues remain to be addressed? In this final part of our overview of the volume, we attempt to answer these questions in the context of the four main themes outlined in the Introduction.

The first theme was how economic integration and globalization are often blamed for the growing income inequality experienced by most countries over the last two decades. Should we be worried about the consequences on inequality of further integration with the United States? On the one hand, both the study by Beaulieu and Joy and that by Lemieux show that the labour market for less-skilled workers in Canada has deteriorated over the last 10 to 20 years. However, these studies also show that the adverse changes are at best loosely linked to economic integration with the United States. For example, Beaulieu and Joy do not generally find that wages declined in the occupations that should have been the most adversely affected by free trade. Lemieux looks at the issue from a different angle and points out that inequality increased even more in the United States than in Canada. Taken together, the two studies suggest that free trade and economic integration had relatively little adverse effects on inequality in Canada. These conclusions are also broadly consistent with the Chaykowski and Slotsve study, which concludes that free trade only had a limited impact on workplace and industrial relations practices. This further limits the number of channels through which free trade can result in increased inequality.

The issue of growing inequality is also closely linked to the brain drain debate. The studies by Finnie and by DeVoretz and Coulombe show that Canadians who recently moved to the United States (or elsewhere) tend to be at the upper end of the income distribution. DeVoretz and Coulombe find that workers who took advantage of TN visas to go work in the United States are generally highly educated individuals employed in professional and other well-paying occupations. Similarly, Finnie shows that taxpayers earning more than $100,000 a year are much more likely than others to emigrate (to the United States or another country). The lower level of inequality in Canada makes the United States particularly attractive to high-income Canadians who typically earn substantially less than their U.S. counterparts. If free trade and economic integration had pushed Canadian income inequality in Canada to the U.S. level, we would likely not have seen this systematic migration of highly skilled and high-income Canadians to the United States. In their panel discussion, Dumont, Lacroix and Van Audenrode also note the growing importance of workers' mobility in an increasingly integrated North American economy.

Growing inequality is also linked to the third theme mentioned in the Introduction, the *room to manoeuvre* of national governments in an increasingly integrated economic environment. As was just mentioned, growing inequality and other policy challenges may or may not be the consequences of economic integration. But even if inequality was not a consequence of economic integration, policy responses to growing inequality may be increasingly limited by growing integration. Boychuk addresses this squarely in the context of the policies of different U.S. states. He concludes that even in this highly integrated environment, governments are able to sustain distinct redistribution policies. This finding is echoed by Banting in his panel discussion. Like Boychuk and Banting, Wildasin concludes that there is not much evidence of a race to the bottom between U.S. states. He nonetheless stresses that in a context of increased labour mobility, there is a stronger case for shifting the responsibility of higher education to the federal government. This is a problem in the context of Canada-U.S. labour mobility since there is no supra-national level of government to provide for higher education. This may result in fiscal competition, where each country reduces taxes to attract highly educated workers, leaving it short of resources for financing higher education. Gomez and Gunderson are not quite as positive as Boychuk on the prospect for distinct national policies when they look at a broader set of policies and programs. They conclude that Canada and the United States have adopted increasingly similar policies and programs during the post-FTA period and that there is, to some extent, a race to the bottom. In his panel discussion, Clarkson also strongly argues that there is indeed a race to the bottom.

The fourth and last theme mentioned in the Introduction explores the consequences of increased cross-border labour mobility. From a purely analytical point of view, it is not clear why labour needs to move across borders once trade in goods (and services) has been fully liberalized. However, Harris points out several channels through which labour mobility can improve the economic performance and living standards of countries. Mercenier and Schmitt add to the analysis by focusing on the mobility of highly skilled workers in a computable general equilibrium (CGE) model. Their approach reveals interesting, and sometimes counterintuitive, mechanisms through which mobility can impact on the income distribution. This is an important and relatively unexplored research area and the two studies offer interesting avenues for future research.

In the end, most of the issues addressed in the studies can be linked to two basic questions: 1) Can policies that promote further integration improve economic performance and (average) standards of living in Canada? and 2) If so, would these policies have adverse social consequences? The studies just discussed all provide, in one way or another, partial answers to these questions. In all cases, they more or less start from the premise that integration is good from an economic standpoint but can be bad from a social point of view because of increased inequality, less room to manoeuvre for governments, etc. This is also the position taken by Hodgson and Jackson in their panel discussions. Hodgson focuses on the beneficial effects of integration on economic performance, while Jackson warns us about its adverse social consequences.

By contrast, Helliwell points out that a large border effect may well be an indication that further integration would be a "lose-lose" option. It would have adverse consequences both on the social and economic fronts. The study by Coulombe provides alternative interpretations of the border effect that lead to very different policy implications. It is clear that the alternative interpretations given to border effects indicate that further research is essential for sorting out the economic and social consequences of closer integration.

Overall, the studies published in the volume probably raise more questions than they answer. Some studies use an empirical approach to document the social and economic effects of previous rounds of integration (Canada-U.S. FTA and NAFTA). Others use more analytical approaches to forecast what would be the consequences of further rounds of integration. From a policy perspective, it is useful to view the studies' findings in light of what has happened in the 15 years since Canada-U.S. free trade was first enacted. As is well known, there is little doubt that the FTA and NAFTA have intensified the volume of trade between Canada and the United States. Labour mobility as measured by the number of Canadians going to work in the United States has also intensified during the 1990s, thanks in part to new labour mobility provisions in the FTA and NAFTA.

But beyond trade and migration flows, it is fair to say that the studies featured in this volume show that the views of the most vocal supporters and opponents of free trade have not materialized. Looking more broadly at economic performance, Canada is not doing any better relative to the United States than it was 15 years ago. The unemployment rate remains higher than in the United States, productivity gains have not kept pace with those experienced south of the border, and Canadian living standards as measured by average incomes have declined relative to the United States. So, if free trade yielded substantial economic benefits, those were more than offset by other developments.

While large and systematic economic gains from free trade have not been observed, the dire predictions about how free trade would ruin Canada's social fabric have not materialized either. Unlike economic outcomes that are relatively easy to quantify, several important social outcomes are difficult to track down in a systematic fashion over time. But these measurement issues aside, it is clear that Canada has not just become a "U.S.A. of the North", as some vocal opponents of free trade argued it would. One simply needs to look at the current social legislative agenda of the Canadian and U.S. governments to see that this is certainly not the case after 15 years of free trade. As in the case of economic performance, the true social consequences of free trade may be confounded by other developments that have little to do with economic integration. One nonetheless comes away with the impression that beyond trade flows, the economic and social consequences of 15 years of North American integration have been relatively modest.

Many things have happened over the past 15 years and economic integration is only one of many factors that have reshaped Canada's economic and social landscape. On balance, the studies assembled in the volume suggest that if further integration cannot solve Canada's productivity problem, it will not turn Canada into a U.S.A. of the North either. The volume illustrates how research can provide the starting point of a careful reflection on the impacts of Canada-U.S. free trade and economic integration, and on how lessons from past experiences can be used to improve policies in the future.

ENDNOTES

1   These issues are discussed extensively in the first Industry Canada research volume on North American linkages. See Harris, 2003.
2   The border effect was first identified in John McCallum, 1995.

BIBLIOGRAPHY

Anderson, James, and Eric van Wincoop. "Gravity with Gravitas: A Solution to the Border Puzzle." *American Economic Review* 93, 1 (March 2003): 170-192.

Beaulieu, Eugene. "The Canada-U.S. Free Trade Agreement and Labour Market Adjustment in Canada." *Canadian Journal of Economics* 33, 2 (May 2000): 540-563.

Gaston, Noël, and Daniel Trefler. "The Labour Market Consequences of the Canada-U.S. Free Trade Agreement." *Canadian Journal of Economics* 30, 1 (February 1997): 18-41.

Harris, Richard G., (ed.) *North American Linkages: Opportunities and Challenges for Canada*. The Industry Canada Research Series. Calgary: University of Calgary Press, 2003.

McCallum, John. "National Borders Matter: Canada-US Regional Trade Patterns." *American Economic Review* 85, 3 (September 1995): 615-623.

Panel I

North American Linkages: Social and Labour Market Issues for Canada

F15 F16 J81 F22

J53

The Political Economy of Labour under North American Integration[1]

J23

J08

Stephen Clarkson
University of Toronto

NAFTA Canada,
USA, Mexico

B EYOND APPRECIATING THE HONOUR of being invited to take part in the opening panel of this select conference, I am also experiencing the uncomfortable sensation of barging in upon an epistemic community which speaks a different dialect.

In reading the material prepared for this conference, I find myself plunged into the humanly neutered discourse of labour economics. Some passages refer to the 'functioning of the labour market' and its 'labour supply' without using the word 'jobs'. Others cite 'access to employment', 'flexibility' and 'labour mobility' without mentioning 'unemployment'. The closest the text comes to addressing citizens' concerns about their work world is where it mentions 'compensation' (not 'wages'), the 'standard of living' (not the 'social wage') and 'daily life' (not 'working conditions'). The paper invokes 'governance structures underpinning the labour market' without a single mention of 'labour union'.

This language generates a linguistic landscape where one might not suspect that human beings exist as working men and women. It depicts a largely apolitical world that is undisturbed by struggles of social or economic or cultural groups for control and advantage.

These are not idle ruminations. Language bears values, and assuming that the values expressed in this background paper represent the conference's values, then I need more than a translator into the other official language to address it. For I speak not the language of *neoclassical economics* with its concern for liberating the market from 'barriers' to maximize its efficiencies, but that of *political economy* with its concern for the state's interaction with the market as rule maker and adjudicator. Other differences are contained within its linguistic signals:

- In contrast with economists' scepticism being directed at government failures to achieve market efficiency, a political economist's scepticism is directed at market failures to achieve goals of social equity.

- Actual power relations among societal actors comprise our concern, rather than imagined equilibrium points among competing market players.

- Different methodologies favour different access points into common material. Where *ceteris paribus* signals the economist's simplifying commitment to testing hypothesized relationships among a limited number of factors, the political economist's oyster is the whole world in all its complexity as context for the forces under investigation.

I should not exaggerate the differences, since there is much that is common in our discourse, as one can also see in the background paper.

- The presence of the state, for instance. Canada is mentioned as a nation state at one place, and the existence of the United States as a territorial state is acknowledged by the prominence of the 'border effect' on the conference's agenda.

- The issue of state autonomy is implicitly addressed by wording about "our ability to pursue domestic goals" and an interest in "the capacity of Canadian governments to carry out their social objectives such as maintaining income through social insurance programs," or their capacity to use income or wealth redistribution to meet their social objectives.

- Other policy issues are flagged in terms of "convergence in areas such as taxation or the financing of post-secondary education."

- North American economic integration is the subject of our deliberations, specifically in terms of the undesired convergence of social policies and the mobility of production factors such as capital and highly skilled labour.

- The conference's analytical problematic is highlighted as two types of "linkages". First, there is the connection between continental economic integration and domestic social and labour market outcomes (health care, education, and employment levels). Second, there is the relationship between labour mobility (attacking collective bargaining norms) and the efficiency gains resulting from trade liberalization (de-skilling, job shedding). What the paper calls barriers to labour mobility, whether legislative or non-legislative, a political economist may see as state actions to protect workers' rights or to provide them with a social wage.

My own relationship to labour policy questions is that of a generalist who is seeking to understand the impact on the Canadian state over the past two decades of the complex interplay between exogenous forces of change (such as economic globalization and global governance) and endogenous factors (such as the ideological shift to neo-conservatism and the continuing role of institutions inherited from the past like the Charter of Rights and Freedoms). Understanding continental integration is thus just one part of the larger picture that requires us to look also at changes taking place at the global level and domestic transformations that may be partially disconnected from external phenomena.

LABOUR AND THE STATE

BEFORE EXPLORING THE IMPACT of North American integration on the situation of Canadian workers, we need to identify the three key areas — working conditions, industrial relations, and job creation — where the state has addressed labour in order to regulate the unequal relationship between capital and labour.

These three types of interactions are closely related. For example, if governments fail to create jobs, higher unemployment makes businesses more reluctant to concede better labour contracts. Other types of public policy can also affect the labour market: if the Bank of Canada raises interest rates to curb inflation, any resulting rise in unemployment helps businesses resist wage increases.

CONTINENTAL RESTRUCTURING AND LABOUR

ECONOMISTS SUPPORTING NAFTA (North American Free Trade Agreement) have argued that free trade would stimulate an automatic increase in Canadian employment and living standards. They also anticipated that any job losses from the closure of uncompetitive firms would be offset by increases in productivity and high-end work, but they did not promise more jobs or more job security.

Canadian manufacturers would achieve greater economies of scale in their high-value-added facilities and become more competitive by using Mexico's low-cost labour in their production plants (Gagnon, 1998).

As tariff barriers fell, Canadian businesses did become subject to more competition from the south. They reacted by pressing the federal and provincial governments to lighten or lift regulations of working conditions and industrial relations. The fact that it is helping to release transnational corporations (TNCs) from high labour standards shows NAFTA's primary, though indirect, impact on Canadian labour. By cutting back national systems of regulation — at least in Canada and Mexico — but not replacing them with enforceable continental regulations, NAFTA created space for freer capital accumulation on a continental basis.

Industrial Relations

Labour has become a competitive tool in a continentally integrated market, where NAFTA increased corporations' ability to insulate themselves from trade-union pressures. The Canadian Labour Congress documented many bargaining situations where "companies make it clear that production and new investments can be shifted if rates of return do not match those in the United States or Mexico."[2] To the extent that it constitutionalizes a new regime of capital accumulation in which labour has lost bargaining power, NAFTA has entrenched, rather than mitigated, the phenomenon of social dumping.

NAFTA also acts to aggravate social divisions within its peripheral members by discriminating between high- and low-paid labour. American unions' fear that Mexican immigrants would drive down U.S. wages led to North American economic integration denying mobility to most workers. In response to the needs of continental TNCs to have key personnel move unhindered within their corporate domain, NAFTA allows corporate executives, managers and skilled workers to move among a company's affiliates. In addition, professional workers in a specified list of occupations can obtain renewable *temporary* work permits on proof of citizenship. From 2,677 Canadian temporary professional workers migrating to the United States in 1989, the flow had increased to 26,987 by 1996.[3] Beyond facilitating the *brain drain*, this mobility enhances the market value of those who already earn the most. This is just one of the ways in which NAFTA increases class divisions in Canada.

Working Conditions

Once thought crucial to running an economy based on Fordist methods, high labour standards have come to be viewed as costly rigidities imposing unnecessary and anti-competitive expenditures on both government and business. Competing with less regulated economies, businesses announced that they could no longer survive under Canadian labour regulations (which raised their costs) and industrial relations rules (which empowered unions to bargain for more benefits). Quite the opposite: they needed to cut costs by using labour more *flexibly* and by becoming more efficient. Canadian policy makers (and much of the public) have generally condoned this argument for lowering labour norms.

Beyond pushing down domestic labour standards, governments are undermining previous methods of mitigating social and gendered inequalities. As Canada competes against the United States and Mexico for investments, it has become less able to tax corporations in order to fund national expenditures that maintain a social wage. Most provinces have significantly cut social assistance measures since 1992.[4] The North American Agreement on Labour Cooperation does not provide any means for redressing these inequalities or offsetting the erosion of labour's position. NAFTA rules ensure *market effectiveness* as the most powerful stratifier of labour and social relations and obstruct any equalizing redistribution of the gains derived from continentalization. In sum, the Commission on Labour Cooperation cannot offset the asymmetry caused by capital's great increase of power and by growing labour insecurity in North America.

CONCLUSION

CONCEPTUALIZING THE LABOUR POLICY PROBLEMS raised by continentalism solely in terms of North American economic integration risks diverting our attention from the whole forest to a number of its individual trees. Three rounds of trade liberalization — the bilateral Canada-U.S. Free Trade Agreement (FTA), the North American Free Trade Agreement, and the World Trade Organization — have created and imposed on the Canadian state an external constitution.

Once we realize that these bilateral, trilateral and multilateral institutions are having a constitutional effect, it becomes easier to see that blithe talk about removing barriers to labour mobility comes as easily in the classroom as it is unrealistic in the real world. With the FTA virtually obliterated by NAFTA, in which Mexico is an equal partner, any substantial policy change in the rules governing Canada's border treatment by Washington will have to be assented to by Mexico City.

The creation of greater capital mobility while leaving labour largely immobile across the two national borders means that labour market inefficiencies are bound to persist at the continental level. There being no continental institutions to address such a problem, neither Canada nor Mexico can expect to achieve some *nirvana* of labour mobility until the American Federation of Labor and Congress of Industrial Organizations (AFL/CIO) gives up its protectionism and the congressional lion decides to lie down with its neighbouring lambs.

By refusing to give up its contingency trade measures, and so rejecting genuine continental free trade, the U.S. government compels the Canadian and Mexican states to stay in business as the political institutions legitimately responsible for determining the standards governing conditions in the workplace, mediating relations between employees and their employers, and promoting job creation.

Condemned to survive, federal, provincial, and municipal governments retain considerable room for political manoeuvre in the context of increased constraints imposed on them by global governance. This means that politicians and their civil-service advisers can still decide where their policy mix should be on the spectrum between raising quality and promoting their economy's competitiveness through cost-cutting. Increased levels of North American integration may have moved the goal posts somewhat. It has not changed the game.

ENDNOTES

1   Parts of this text, reprinted with permission, draw on chapter 16, entitled "The Working State: Labour Relations under Stress," in my earlier book: *Uncle Sam and Us: Globalization, Neoconservatism, and the Canadian State.* Toronto and Washington, DC: University of Toronto Press and Woodrow Wilson Center Press, 2002, 535 pages.
2   See Jackson and Baldwin, 1997, p. 16.
3   See Globerman, 1999, p. 17, cited in Gabriel and Macdonald.
4   See Statistics Canada, cited in Gabriel and Macdonald.

BIBLIOGRAPHY

Gabriel, Christina, and Laura Macdonald. "Beyond the Continentalist/Nationalist Divide: Canada in North America." In *Changing Canada: Political Economy as Transformation.* Edited by Wallace Clement and Leah Vosko. Montreal: McGill-Queen's University Press. Forthcoming.

Gagnon, Éric. *Free Trade in North America: The Impact on Labour-management Relations and Human Resources Management in Canada.* Kingston, Ont.: Queen's University, 1998.

Globerman, Steven. *Trade Liberalization and the Migration of Skilled Workers.* Perspectives on North American Free Trade Series, Document No. 3, Ottawa: Industry Canada, 1999.

Jackson, Andrew, and Bob Baldwin. *The Lessons of Free Trade: A View from Canadian Labour.* Research Paper No. 6, Ottawa: Canadian Labour Congress, 1997.

What's a Country For? Canadian Social Policy in the New North America[1]

Keith G. Banting
Queen's University

SINCE THE DAWN OF THE STATE SYSTEM IN EUROPE in the 17th and 18th centuries, states have existed at the intersection between the international order and their domestic societies. In the words of Theda Skocpol, the state "is fundamentally Janus-faced, with intrinsically dual anchorage in domestic society and the international system" (1979, p. 32). Inevitably, therefore, the role of governments has been to balance pressures from these two domains. In part, governments seek to protect domestic society from external threats and nudge as best they can the international system in directions consistent with domestic interests and concerns. But, in part, governments also convey pressures emanating from the wider global context to domestic society, adapting internal policies to international conditions they cannot alter and helping domestic interests adjust to the world beyond the nation's borders.

In the contemporary period, there is an intense debate over whether the balance has shifted decisively. Some commentators argue that global pressures are narrowing the degrees of freedom enjoyed by the state, and that pressures for harmonization or convergence are slowly but inevitably leading advanced democracies to converge toward common transnational policy models over a wider and wider range of policy areas. Such arguments raise important issues for our basic understanding of the political realm. If there is considerably less scope for domestic policy autonomy, what is the role of domestic politics and governance processes, which still dominate the front pages in our newspapers and the lead stories in our newscasts? What imprint can distinctive national cultures leave on the structure of public programs? Or, to put the question more colloquially, "What's a country for?"

This presentation highlights the continuing importance of domestic political choices in the design of social policy. Countries everywhere have had to adjust to a new global economy. But distinctive political and cultural structures of different countries continue to shape the ways in which countries adjust. The international constraints may be somewhat tighter than in the past, the costs of distinctiveness somewhat greater. But governments still enjoy significant room for manoeuvre in the modern era, and political choices still matter.

Implicit in this analysis is a compelling message for our own country. During the postwar decades, Canada charted a distinctive social trajectory on the northern half of the North American continent. And although the country is coming to grips with a wider and deeper set of linkages in the new North American economy, there is little evidence that these linkages necessarily require convergence to U.S. social norms. Our two countries have been adapting to a changing world in distinctive ways. If, in the decades ahead, Canadians abandon the social aspirations that underpinned the social contract they inherited from the postwar generation, if they evolve toward social programs that increasingly resemble those prevailing south of the border, the transition will represent the product of political choices, not the inexorable unfolding of economic imperatives.

GLOBALIZATION AND SOCIAL POLICY: THE GENERAL PATTERN

THE POLICY REGIME THAT EMERGED in advanced democracies in the postwar period can be characterized in musical terms: it was a policy composition with a powerful common theme and rich national variations. The central theme was a policy package that combined the liberalization of the international trading regime with an expansion of social security protections, a package which John Ruggie has labelled "embedded liberalism" (Ruggie, 1983, 1994). Under the General Agreement on Tariffs and Trade and other initiatives, a steady process of economic liberalization broke down the barriers to international trade and many of the detailed regulatory regimes created during the depression and war years. However, this liberalization was accompanied by the development of social protections which provided greater security for citizens and populations as a whole. In Ruggie's words, "governments asked their publics to embrace the change and dislocation that comes with liberalization in return for the promise of help in containing and socializing the adjustment costs" (1994, pp. 4-5). Thus, the postwar welfare state developed together with greater openness in the international economy and eased the consequent adjustment processes. In this sense, the social contract was a buffer against the kinds of social and political backlashes that undermined openness in the first half of the 20th century: protectionism, nationalism and international conflict.

Within this central theme of embedded liberalism, however, countries enjoyed a considerable degree of freedom to design their social contracts in accordance with national cultures and domestic political interests, and different countries built quite different systems of social protection. Some countries invested heavily, designing comprehensive security systems; others devoted less of their resources to the task. In 1974, which probably represented the high point of this era, the proportion of gross domestic product (GDP) represented by social spending among the Organization for Economic Co-operation and Development (OECD) countries ranged from 8 percent in Japan to 27 percent in the Netherlands. Moreover, program design, in terms of eligibility, comprehensiveness, benefit levels and so on, varied remarkably. There was no single, transnational model of the welfare state during the postwar era.

Fast forward to the contemporary period. We have clearly entered a new era of economic liberalization, and virtually all western nations are redesigning their systems of social protection. Out of this process are emerging new common themes which, taken together, represent an attempt to re-embed another wave of economic liberalization in a system of social security that is appropriate to a global and knowledge-based economy. These common themes include the importance of flexible labour markets, the centrality of investment in human capital, and the need to reduce social exclusion. These themes reverberate in social policy debates in virtually all advanced industrial countries.

However, pressure to adapt social policy to a new economy is not, in itself, evidence of the erosion of the autonomy of states. The critical issue for our purposes is whether there is still scope for significant national variations around the new common themes. Are countries free to chart distinctive social futures, or does economic integration compel movement toward some transnational social policy model? What's a country for in the global era?

In fact, there is remarkably little evidence of a general convergence of social policy regimes. Nancy Olewiler's analysis of taxation trends and Geoffrey Garrett's analysis of both taxation and expenditures found no evidence of significant convergence across OECD nations (Olewiler, 1999; Garrett, 1998). These findings have been confirmed again and again, and now represent a consensus position in the research literature. (For a sample from a much larger literature, see Iverson, 2001; Swank, 1998, 2002; Reiger and Leibfried, 1998). For additional evidence, some analysts point to the durability of significant differentials in workers' compensation and labour standards across U.S. states despite a common currency and unrestricted mobility of labour, capital, goods and services. Dani Rodrik probably has it about right when he argues that "while the trade-offs facing policy makers have been rendered steeper by the increased trade and capital flows, there exists plenty of room for nation-states to maintain their own distinctive domestic social arrangements" (1997, p. 13).

This conclusion does extend automatically to a second form of economic integration — regional trading blocs. The European Union (EU) reveals interesting cross-currents. During the postwar era, different European countries built quite different welfare states, and each of Esping-Andersen's three worlds of welfare capitalism has deep roots in the continent (Esping-Andersen, 1990). Now however, these historic variations confront a determined integrative project. The political determination to build an ever closer union and the decision to establish a common monetary regime generate pressures on domestic choices that go well beyond those implicit in the global economy alone. The result has been a pattern of convergence in social spending as a proportion of GDP over the last two decades. Yet underlying this trend is the continuing reality of distinctive national responses. Convergence in social spending has been due as much to the considerable increases witnessed in southern countries such as Portugal, Spain and Greece as to a slowing of spending growth in northern Europe. Moreover, the actual design of social programs is marked by national variations. Despite the adoption by member states of a formal resolution in favour of a voluntary strategy of convergence in social protection policies in the early 1980s, a study by the European Commission could find no consistent pattern of convergence: "There has certainly been convergence of the problems to be solved ... (but) there is no clear evidence of convergence of social protection systems in the Community of the 1980s" (Commission of the European Communities, 1994, p. 9). The EU is trying again with a new strategy of encouraging convergence, known as the "Open Method of Coordination," but the process is focused on ends, not means, and still leaves final policy choices firmly in the hands of member states. There seems to be little reason to assume that European welfare states are morphing into a common model.

CANADA AND THE UNITED STATES

WHAT THEN OF THE NORTH AMERICAN CASE? On the one hand, NAFTA does not create the same depth of economic integration as the EU and there is no prospect of supranational political integration on the horizon. On the other hand, the deeply asymmetrical nature of the relationship and Canada's stunningly high level of trade dependence on the U.S. economy might still create real pressures for convergence. To date, however, the Canadian experience is consistent with the broader international trend. There have been some shifts toward U.S. norms, with employment insurance and child benefits being the most dramatic examples. But the larger story remains the persistence of traditional differences in the social trajectory of the two countries (Banting, 1996, 1997; Hoberg, Banting and Simeon, 2002; Boychuk, 1997; Boychuk and Banting, 2003). In areas such as health care and pensions, historic differences have persisted or even grown, and Canada has maintained a distinctive pattern of social outcomes. Whereas the United States has seen a significant increase in inequality over the last 20 years, especially in the 1980s, the trend has been much more muted in Canada.

But can we sustain this pattern in the future? To understand whether we can continue to chart a separate trajectory, it is useful to ask which instruments have been most important to preserving a distinctive Canadian model so far. Is it the overall levels of social spending? Is it the design of social programs? Is it the patterns of taxation? Once we have identified the key instruments, we can ask whether they are likely to be subject to tightening constraints in the future, as the long-term consequences of integration into the North American economy unfold.

FIGURE 1

PUBLIC SOCIAL EXPENDITURES IN CANADA AND THE UNITED STATES,
1980-99 (PERCENT OF GDP)

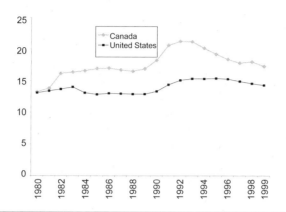

Source: OECD Social Expenditures data set.

The difference between Canada and the United States does not primarily reside in the level of social spending. As Figure 1 shows, total social spending in the two countries is much closer than most Canadians realize. Moreover, an analysis of 1995 data reported in Table 1 suggests that the gap in gross public expenditures is reduced considerably when differences in the tax treatment of social benefits are taken into account. It is hard to believe that the different social outcomes in the two countries are sustained primarily by such small differences in spending levels. (As an aside, it is worth noting the final column of

TABLE 1

SOCIAL EXPENDITURES IN CANADA AND THE UNITED STATES,
1995 (AS A PROPORTION OF GDP)

	GROSS PUBLIC EXPENDITURES	PUBLIC EXPENDITURES NET OF TAXES	PUBLIC AND PRIVATE EXPENDITURES NET OF TAXES
Canada	24.6	22.1	25.0
United States	19.1	19.5	26.0

Note: The numbers differ from those published by the OECD because they are adjusted to exclude the value of U.S. public employee pensions, include public education expenditures, and are based on GDP at market prices rather than GDP at factor cost.

Sources: OECD with data from Human Resources Development Canada and the U.S. Social Security Administration. Calculations provided by Statistics Canada.

Table 1, which shows that when private expenditures on social needs such as health and education are added to the tally, Americans outspend Canadians.)

If *how much* we spend is not the full answer, perhaps it is *how* we spend. Here, we are on to something, as our two biggest social programs — health care and pensions — illustrate. Figures 2 and 3 confirm that expenditures as a percent of GDP are lower in Canada, but social outcomes are better. Clearly, program design matters a lot.

What about the bigger picture? Figure 4 confirms that the tax-transfer system continues to offset the level of inequality in market incomes much more in Canada than in the United States. And Figure 5 makes it clear that most of the redistributive effort in Canada takes place on the expenditure side. The difference between the level of inequality in market income and inequality in total income (which includes the impact of government transfers) is much greater than the difference between total income and after-tax income (which takes into account both transfers and taxes). The tax system is critical in raising the resources to sustain the expenditure side; and direct taxes do play a role in redistribution, but a secondary one.

What does this imply for the future? The good news on the spending side is that design matters and that the design of social programs is not particularly constrained by economic integration. There seems to be little reason to assume that we will lose our room for manoeuvre here. Admittedly, there is more debate about the revenue side, with some analysts insisting that global economic competition requires lower income tax rates. I am convinced that this argument is wrong. But even if it were true, we could preserve our social contract if we wished to do so by altering the tax mix. We have traditionally relied less on social security taxes than other countries in the world, including the United States, depriving ourselves of the higher political durability of these dedicated forms of taxation. The expansive welfare states built by social democrats in northern Europe rely more heavily on such taxes; and in the United Kingdom, the Chancellor, Gordon Brown, is relying on increased national insurance premiums to finance his commitment to raise British social spending to the European average. Canadian evidence points in the same direction. The lack of public resistance to the steady increase in Canada Pension Plan contribution rates each year is telling; and Alberta and Ontario have recently moved to adopt health-care premiums. Admittedly, there was a negative reaction from the Ontario public, but it seems to have been generated by the fact that the government broke its electoral promise not to raise taxes. Greater reliance on social security taxes may make our tax system slightly less progressive, depending on their design. If so, we would still have the option of pursuing our redistributive goals even more heavily on the expenditure side. In the end, it is the bottom line, not the middle line, in Figure 5 that counts.

FIGURE 2

HEALTH EXPENDITURES AND HEALTH OUTCOMES, CANADA AND UNITED STATES, 1960-2000 (PERCENT OF GDP)

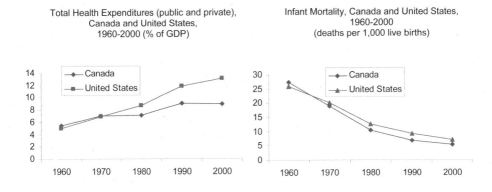

Sources: Left panel: OECD, Social Expenditures data set.
Right panel: OECD, Health Data 2004.

FIGURE 3

PENSION EXPENDITURES AND OUTCOMES

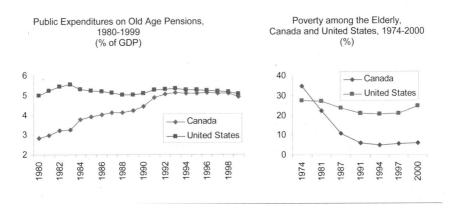

Note: Poverty is defined as 50 percent of median disposable income.
Sources: Left panel: OECD, Social Expenditures data set.
Right panel: Luxembourg Income Study.

FIGURE 4

CHANGE IN THE REDISTRIBUTIVE IMPACT OF TAXES AND TRANSFERS, CANADA AND UNITED STATES, 1974-95

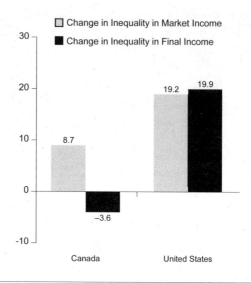

Note: Figures represent percentage change in Gini coefficients between 1974 and 1995.
Source: Calculations by Statistics Canada.

FIGURE 5

INCOME INEQUALITY IN CANADA, ALL FAMILIES, 1971-2001

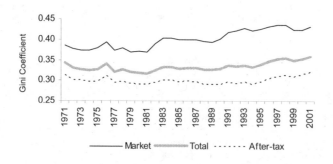

Source: Statistics Canada, *Income Trends in Canada* , on CD-ROM.

What are the implications for the future of our social programs? The most important message is that our social future is still in our hands. Our domestic politics remain important to the ways in which we navigate in, and adapt to, the global era. This does not mean that Canadians will automatically make the same choices they have made in the past. Faith in the effectiveness of government programs and in the capacity of governments to manage public funds with probity has taken a beating in recent years. The electorate might choose to move onto a new path, giving priority to tax cuts over social programs. But if Canadians opt for a less generous social contract, if they increasingly adopt an American conception of the obligations we owe to each other, it will represent a political choice, not an economic necessity. For myself, I hope that Canadians will continue to express distinctive cultural traditions through their social programs. After all, what's a country for?

ENDNOTE

1   This text represents an updated version of my presentation at the Conference on Social and Labour Market Aspects of North American Linkages. A revised version was later incorporated as part of my Donald Gow Memorial Lecture, delivered at the School of Policy Studies, Queen's University, April 25, 2003.

BIBLIOGRAPHY

Banting, Keith. "Social Policy." In *Border Crossings: The Internationalization of Canadian Public Policy*. Edited by G. Bruce Doern, Leslie Pal and Brian Tomlin. Toronto: Oxford
University Press, 1996.

———. "The Social Policy Divide: The Welfare State in Canada and the United States." In *Degrees of Freedom: Canada and the United States in a Changing World*. Edited by Keith Banting, George Hoberg and Richard Simeon. Montreal: McGill-Queen's University Press, 1997.

Boychuk, Gerard. "Are Canadian and U.S. Social Assistance Policies Converging?" *Canadian-American Public Policy*. Discussion Paper Series, No. 30, Canadian-American Center, University of Maine, 1997.

Boychuk, Gerard and Keith Banting. "The Paradox of Convergence: National versus Sub-national Patterns of Convergence in Canadian and U.S. Income Maintenance Policy." In *North American Linkages: Opportunities and Challenges for Canada*. Edited by Richard G. Harris. The Industry Canada Research Series. Calgary: University of Calgary Press, 2003, pp. 533-572.

Commission of the European Communities. *Social Protection in Europe: 1993*. Directorate-General for Employment, Industrial Relations and Social Affairs. Luxembourg: Office for the Official Publications of the European Communities, 1994.

Esping-Andersen, Gosta. *The Three Worlds of Welfare Capitalism*. Princeton, NJ: Princeton University Press, 1990.

Garrett, Geoffrey. "Global Markets and National Politics: Collision Course or Virtuous Circle?" *International Organization* 52 (1998): 787-824.

Hoberg, George, Keith Banting and Richard Simeon. "North American Integration and the Scope for Domestic Choice: Canada and Policy Autonomy in a Globalized World." In *Capacity for Choice: Canada in the New North America*. Edited by George Hoberg. Toronto: University of Toronto Press, 2002.

Iverson, Thorben. "The Dynamics of Welfare State Expansion: Trade, Openness, Deindustrialization and Partisan Politics." In *The New Politics of the Welfare State*. Edited by Paul Pierson. Oxford: Oxford University Press, 2001.

Olewiler, Nancy. "National Tax Policy for an International Economy: Divergence in a Converging World." In *Room for Manoeuvre? Globalization and Policy Convergence*. Edited by Thomas Courchene. Kingston, Ont.: John Deutsch Institute for the Study of Economic Policy, Queen's University, 1999.

Rieger, Elmar and Stephan Leibfried. "Welfare State Limits to Globalization." *Politics & Society* 26, 3 (1998): 363-390.

Rodrik, Dani. *Has Globalization Gone Too Far?* Washington, DC: Institute for International Economics, 1997.

Ruggie, J. "International Regimes, Transactions and Change: Embedded Liberalism in the Postwar Order." In *International Regimes*. Edited by S. Krasner. Ithaca, NY: Cornell University Press, 1983.

——. "Trade Protection and the Future of Welfare Capitalism." *Journal of International Affairs* 48 (1994): 1-12.

Skocpol, Theda. *States and Social Revolutions*. Cambridge: Cambridge University Press, 1979.

Swank, Duane. "Funding the Welfare State: Globalization and the Taxation of Business in Advanced Market Economies." *Political Studies* 46, 4 (1998): 671-692.

——. *Global Capital, Political Institutions and Policy Change in Developed Welfare States*. Cambridge: Cambridge University Press, 2002.

Part I

*The Extent and Evolution of Canada-U.S.
Economic Integration*

John F. Helliwell
University of British Columbia

Canada
USA
F15
R12
F14
L14
F22
Z13

1

Border Effects: Assessing Their Implications for Canadian Policy in a North American Context

INTRODUCTION

THIS STUDY SUMMARIZES THE CURRENT EVIDENCE on the extent to which distance and national borders lessen the intensity of a variety of economic and social linkages, analyzes a range of possible explanations for the current border effects, and finally considers the implications for Canadian policy in a North American context. Although there is still considerable uncertainty, and even some controversy, about the past, present and likely future values of border effects, their prevalence has led analysts to investigate the reasons for their existence, and policy-makers to ask what they might mean for policy. To a great extent, the answer for policy-makers depends on the answers to the analysts' puzzle. For example, if trade or other policy barriers are responsible for the border effects, and if there are likely large gains from further trade expansion, then large border effects are a signal that there is much left to be done in completing the North American free trade agenda. On the other hand, if the surprisingly local and national structure of economies and societies is a response to the lower costs of dealing with those close at hand, and reflects the sharing of a variety of common institutions, tastes, values, norms and networks, then border effects could represent an optimal outcome. If this were the case, then there would be no presumption that further economic integration between Canada and the United States would provide net economic advantages to either country.

A particular policy issue inviting special attention is that of the advantages and disadvantages of having a separate national currency. Since currency boundaries and political boundaries are generally co-extensive for the OECD (Organisation for Economic Co-operation and Development) countries, with the important new exception of the Euro zone, some part of existing border effects is likely to be due to the presence of currency differences. The use of a separate national currency is not a trade barrier in the usual sense, and it may indeed permit countries to have more open trade policies that they would otherwise choose, but if currency differences are a large part of the reason for border effects, and if border effects are bad, then the adoption by Canada of the U.S. currency might be viewed as an alternative means of increasing trade, at least between Canada and the United States. The debate on that issue is covered by a companion study (Helliwell, 2002c).

The analysis presented in this study will be linked with others prepared for the conference by considering the extent to which there are welfare trade-offs between the economic gains that are the focus of increased North American economic integration and a variety of other individual and community-level outcomes. Studies by other authors are considering the extent to which increased economic integration might or might not lead to increased parallelism in other policies and institutions. The early-stage welfare analysis in this study can then be used to evaluate, at least in an indicative way, the overall net changes in Canadian well-being likely to flow from policies aimed at increasing North American integration. The second and third sections, entitled *Borders Matter, for Trade and Much More* and *Why Do Borders Matter?*, are largely drawn from Helliwell (2002c), while the fourth and fifth sections, entitled *Gravity with Gravitas: A Solution to the Border Puzzle?* and *Updated Results and Policy Implications*, describe more recent research, and the last section, entitled *Policy Implications for Canada*, spells out some policy implications.

BORDERS MATTER, FOR TRADE AND MUCH MORE

I WAS NOT THE ONLY ONE SURPRISED by McCallum's finding that 1988 interprovincial merchandise trade flows were more than 20 times more intense than those between Canadian provinces and U.S. states. In light of some recent criticisms of the way in which McCallum estimated the gravity model underlying this result, it should be noted at the outset that the raw data for distance-matched comparisons of province-province and state-state trading pairs showed much the same result. For example, Ontario is about the same distance from California as it is from British Columbia, and California's population and gross domestic product (GDP) are about 10 times larger than those of British Columbia. Thus, if there were no systematic differences between interprovincial and province-state trade, one would expect to find that two-way movements of goods between Ontario and California are 10 times larger than those between Ontario and British Columbia. But actual merchandise flows between British Columbia and Ontario are more than twice as large as those between California and Ontario, or 20 times greater than expected. Of course,

McCallum's result related to 1988, the year before the Canada-U.S. Free Trade Agreement (FTA) was signed. In the aftermath of that agreement, there have been large increases in north-south merchandise trade flows. These were sufficient to reduce the border effect from 14.7 in 1991 to 10.2 in 1996 (Helliwell and Verdier, 2001, p. 1037). Indeed, these increases have been so large, and the associated productivity gains so small, as to raise puzzles in their own right. Economic models of the expected future consequences of the FTA projected that Canadian exports to the United States would increase by one-third, and imports would rise by 12 percent, in both cases holding income unchanged. The associated gains in Canadian productivity were projected to be equivalent to 8 percent of GDP per capita. But the actual trade increases, even after adjusting for the effects of rising incomes in the two countries, were more than three times as large as projected (Helliwell, Lee and Messinger, 1999), while GDP per capita grew more slowly in Canada than in the United States, with no evidence of a narrowing of the productivity gap. To some extent, the pattern of productivity changes is what would be expected, with industries facing the largest increases in international competition and market opportunities having larger productivity gains (Trefler, 1999). However, there is still a puzzle about why increases in trade were larger than expected based on the size of tariff reductions, but little or no sign of any narrowing of the long-standing manufacturing productivity gap between the two countries. I'll return to this puzzle later. But first, here is a summary of more recent evidence on the extent and consequences of the border effects.

McCallum's result suggests strongly that national economies have a much tighter internal structure than previously thought, and hence that the extent of globalization is much less than commonly supposed. First, it was necessary to verify if this result applies more generally in other places, other times and other markets. This seems a simple enough research strategy, but it turns out to be not so easy to follow, for reasons that may also help to explain why perceptions were so far from the evidence uncovered by McCallum. It was not by accident that McCallum's research related to 1988, and only to that year. Statistics Canada had developed full estimates of bilateral merchandise trade for the years 1984 through 1988, based on surveys of manufacturers and prepared as part of a consistent estimation of provincial and national accounts. There are yet no other countries that have such fully developed measures of internal trade. Second, in anticipation of post-FTA interest in a more detailed monitoring of trade flows between Canada and the United States, Statistics Canada started publishing, from 1988, bilateral merchandise imports and exports between Canadian provinces and U.S. states.

McCallum realized that these two data sources could be combined so as to provide for the first time a direct comparison of the domestic and international trade intensities. He also realized the necessity of making the comparisons in a way that permitted trade intensity to be measured separately from the effects of size and distance. By choosing comparison pairs of equal distance, as when trade between Ontario and California is compared to that between Ontario and British Columbia, it is possible to make allowance for distance. But the gravity model is a better bet, as it permits all trading pairs to be used together to give a single average size for the border effect. So the gravity model is what he used to produce his startling result, backed up by enough specific examples to convince readers that the statistical result was not flowing from some extreme and unrepresentative observations.

One of the general difficulties in separating the effects of distance from those of borders is that, almost by definition, the borders of a country contain cities or provincial economies that are closer to each other than they are to cities or provinces in some other country. However, the unusual economic and political geography of Canada and the United States, with most of the Canadian population perched along the northern border of the United States and the border itself swooping south into the heartland of the United States, means that the average bilateral distance between Canadian provinces is almost exactly the same as the average distance between Canadian provinces and the 30 major trading states used in McCallum's analysis. Furthermore, each Canadian province has both provincial and state trading partners that are near and far, so that there is no correlation between the border variable (used to denote province-state trading pairs) and the distance variable. Thus, it was possible for McCallum to obtain strong and easily distinguishable effects of both distance and the national border. Much attention has been paid to the size of the border effects he discovered. Also important, and more easily replicated in other studies of international trade, is the large size of the distance effects. National borders greatly reduce trade intensities, but so does distance and to a far greater extent than can be explained by transport costs. I shall argue later that these two results can and should be explained in similar ways.

The unique nature of the Canadian data exposes a fundamental difficulty in replicating McCallum's research for other countries, other types of economic linkages, and earlier decades. It also helps to explain why everyone was surprised by McCallum's result. Even if earlier researchers had been interested in comparing intra-national and international economic linkages, they had no data that would easily yield straightforward results. In the absence of data, researchers and commentators were inclined to assume, given all the talk of globalization and the widespread reporting of large and growing volumes of international trade, that domestic and international economic linkages were comparably close.

Once I knew that my previous assumption was wrong, a multi-pronged research strategy was indicated: to prod the province-state merchandise trade results to see how they were concentrated by product and by region; to make comparable estimates for services; to trace the evolution of border effects in the wake of the FTA; to establish some methods of producing comparable estimates for other countries; and, finally, to see to what extent there are comparable border effects for movements of capital and population. At the same time, a full review of the international trade and linkages literature might help to reveal earlier studies that contained either direct or implicit evidence of border effects.

One very comparable study was that of Engel and Rogers (1996), who were studying the co-variability of prices across city pairs, using a large number of Canadian and U.S. cities. They showed that prices changed more in concert if cities were closer, or if they were in the same country. This is, of course, just what one would expect after seeing McCallum's result, since one of the classic motivations for trade is to arbitrage price differences arising between markets in different locations. Buy bananas where they are cheap and sell them where they are expensive. If there is a greater volume of this type of trading, then one would expect to find prices moving in a more concerted way in the two markets. Since trade between provinces is much denser than that between provinces and states, one would expect prices to be more closely aligned for city pairs that are in the same country. So they found, reporting that the Canada-U.S. border was over 2,500 miles wide, in the sense that it lowered price co-variability by as much as 2,500 miles of within-country distance. This estimate was based on their more conservative estimate of the effect of the border. Subsequent research showed that the effect of the border on price co-variability is far higher than they had estimated. One obvious thing to check is whether the effect of distance on trade flows is the same for cross-border as for internal linkages. I did this for province-state and interprovincial trade flows, and found that the distance effect was the same in the two cases. However, when I re-estimated the Engel and Rogers equation, I found that the distance effect was significant for internal city pairs, but that there was no effect for cross-border pairs. Since the width of the border is calculated from the relative sizes of the border and distance effects, this means that the implied width of the border is infinite. Furthermore, I discovered (Helliwell, 2002a) that even using their estimated distance effect as though it applied equally to cross-border pairs, the method of computation was not appropriate. Using the correct method raises the estimated width of the border to distances that have been described in parallel studies as intergalactic.

Using the correct method to compute the distance equivalent of the border effect, the estimated width of the Canada-U.S. border is about 10,000 miles based on merchandise trade flows, but many millions of miles, or even infinity, based on the co-variability of prices among city pairs (Helliwell, 2002a). Thus, the Engel and Rogers study strongly confirms the trade-based results. Indeed, their result appears even more extreme when the two results are expressed in somewhat comparable terms. The contrast between the trade and price results is even more striking when province-state trade densities are compared to inter-state rather than interprovincial trade densities, for reasons that will be explored in the fourth and fifth sections below. What explains the sharp difference between these results?

Three reasons explain why there is so little cross-border price arbitrage in the data used by Engel and Rogers. The first and most important is that, in the short term, most consumer prices are rather stable, while foreign exchange rates are not. Thus, by far, the greatest source of cross-border discrepancy in two-month price changes (those studied by Engel and Rogers) is changes in the exchange rate. The second reason is that these authors are using two-month price changes, which is probably too short-term to trigger much in the way of transborder shipments. Finally, Engel and Rogers are using components of the consumer price index for their comparison, including both goods and services, and including in both cases the retail margins. By contrast, the trade results are based only on goods and exclude local retail margins. Other research has shown that services have substantially higher border effects, in some cases two to three times greater than for merchandise trade (Helliwell, 1998, p. 38), and local retail margins are less tradable than most other services. The three reasons together provide powerful grounds for explaining the almost complete lack of cross-border price arbitrage of short-term changes in consumer prices. Most of this variability comes from the exchange rate, and would in any event be arbitraged, if at all, by some cheaper means than changing cities for monthly haircuts, or buying bananas in Toronto for consumption in Seattle.

Putting the Engel and Rogers study into a broader context, there have been scores of studies focusing on whether and when prices and exchange rates move so as to maintain purchasing power parity. As already noted, standard economic models of trade have long assumed that purchasing power parity would hold for so-called *tradable goods*, reflecting the *law of one price*. In this setup, any international differences in prices were to be explained by differences in the prices of *non-tradables*, with labour-intensive services being the typical examples. Studies of purchasing power parity, especially those done since the generalized move towards flexible exchange rates started in the early 1970s, showed that the world is at odds with the standard assumption. Three results proved of general application. First, foreign exchange rates are subject to short-term changes that are not immediately reflected in the prices of goods and services on either side of the border. Thus, just as found by Engel and Rogers, short-term changes in nominal exchange rates lead to equivalent departures from purchasing power parity.

Put slightly differently, changes in nominal exchange rates are generally matched, in the short run, by equivalent changes in real exchange rates. Second, if there is a move in prices or exchange rates towards purchasing power parity, it happens slowly, with the adjustment spread out over a period better measured in years than in months. Third, departures from purchasing power parity are as much in evidence for goods as for services, thus removing the possibility of explaining the lack of purchasing power parity as being simply due to the presence of non-tradable goods and services. These results have been accumulating for many years. The Engel and Rogers study was the first to put them in contrast with domestic price movements, thus showing the extent to which international market linkages are not as tight as domestic linkages.

There is another strand of the empirical trade literature that can be more easily understood in the light of strong border effects for trade. Tests of the standard theoretical model for international trade, the so-called Heckscher-Ohlin model, have consistently failed to find international trade patterns that reflect comparative advantages. However, more recent tests of the predictions of the model using regional trade flows within Japan show that Japanese regions do indeed specialize in industries where the theory suggests they have a comparative advantage (Davis, Weinstein, Bradford and Shimpo, 1997). This was thought to pose a puzzle: Why should international trade models that have failed to predict the patterns of international trade nonetheless succeed at explaining the patterns of specialization of production within an economy? The reason, as suggested by the size and pervasiveness of border effects, is that the mobility assumptions underlying the classical trade theory do apply reasonably well within the Japanese economy, but are a long way from being met for trade between countries. Perhaps the only thing wrong with traditional international trade theory is the word *international*. It does work to explain domestic trade, but fails to explain international trade because it neglects the variety of factors that separate markets, especially national markets: costly information, diverging knowledge and tastes, and transaction costs that grow substantially with distance and when one attempts to operate in a society with different norms and institutions. Since many institutions and networks are national in scope, this reasoning suggests that market separation will increase with both distance and movement from one national market to another.

Are there border effects also in capital markets? The answer is complicated and the evidence often seems to say one thing while really indicating something else. The economic literature has tended to accept the assumption that there is a single world capital market for interest-bearing securities of equivalent risk, so that international differences in interest rates would represent either a risk premium or an expected change in the exchange rate. This fairly tight form of capital market integration is known as "uncovered interest parity" to distinguish it from "covered interest parity". Covered interest parity reflects a situation where international differences in nominal interest rates are exactly offset by a forward foreign exchange premium or discount. It is possible to test whether or not covered interest parity holds, since it is often possible to obtain market prices for interest-bearing securities and for matching forward exchange contracts that permit an exact offset of the foreign exchange risk. Research has long shown that while the covered interest parity condition is not met exactly, it does tend to hold, except in times of market turbulence, within bounds that could reasonably be ascribed to transaction costs. The uncovered interest parity condition cannot be tested directly, since it states only that the interest differential is equal to the expected change in the foreign exchange rate plus some allowance for the costs of carrying foreign exchange risk. Since neither the expected future exchange rate nor the risk premium can be directly measured, the theory itself is not directly verifiable.

Given evidence supporting the covered interest parity condition, it has long been common for economists to assume that both the covered and the uncovered interest rate parity conditions hold. This implies that capital markets are perfectly linked internationally, and that the forward exchange differential represents the expected rate of change in the exchange rate. Any difference between the forward exchange differential and the actual future price of foreign exchange represents some measure of foreign exchange risk, plus of course random influences arising between now and then. The empirical fly in this theoretical ointment is that the forward exchange differential is typically a very bad predictor of the actual future change in the exchange rate. Indeed, the forward exchange rate is such a bad predictor of the future spot rate that it is beaten in the betting sweepstakes by the current value of the exchange rate. Thus, the assumption that next year's exchange rate will be the same as today's is more accurate than the forward exchange rate. In my view, this long-standing result makes it a mistake to assume that the uncovered interest parity condition holds. I have tended to argue that the forward exchange rate differential is actually determined by the difference between the two national interest rates, so that the covered interest parity condition tends to hold fairly closely. But the fact that the forward exchange rate differential is such a bad predictor of the future spot rate shows that the uncovered interest parity condition is a dangerous assumption. After all, if international capital markets were perfectly linked, then there would be many speculators willing to bet against the forward rate when it is a long way off base, thus making it a better predictor of the future spot rate. But there is no easy test of that presumption either, and the bulk of the exchange rate literature continued to treat international capital markets as completely integrated, at least for short-term financial capital.

Given the general assumption of tightly linked international capital markets, there was considerable scepticism when Feldstein and Horioka (1980) claimed that capital markets were still national rather than international in scope. They based their conclusion on a study of cross-country correlations between national savings rates and domestic investment rates. They reasoned that if there were a single global capital market, then savings arising randomly in one country would equally likely be invested in any country, and investment booms in one country would be met from the global savings pool, so that there would be no reason for countries with high savings rates to also have high investment rates. Sceptical theorists were quick to point out that domestic investment booms might lead to increases in national incomes and, through that route, to simultaneous increases in national savings even if international capital markets were perfectly linked. I was inclined towards that view myself, since I was operating an empirical open-economy macro model with just these features: investment booms would lead to increases in income and national savings even if the model operated under the assumption of uncovered interest parity, and hence of perfect international linkage of capital markets.

Fortunately, the same Statistics Canada efforts that gave rise to interprovincial trade data also provide provincial accounts that allow savings and investment to be defined on a provincial basis, just as they are in the national accounts for OECD countries. Thus, it was possible to combine Canadian provinces and OECD national data in a single sample to obtain a more definitive test of the Feldstein and Horioka proposition. If these authors were right to conclude that their results reflected international separation of national capital markets, then the correlation they found between national savings and domestic investment using country data would be markedly less for the Canadian provincial data. On the other hand, if the correlation was unrelated to national border effects and if there was a single global capital market, the correlation between savings and investment rates would be as equally likely to arise among provinces as among countries. The research provided strong support for the Feldstein and Horioka interpretation. In the pooled sample, there remains a strong correlation of savings and investment rates across countries, but none across Canadian provinces (Helliwell and McKitrick, 1999). Other studies using less complete savings and investment data for regions in other countries show the same pattern.[1] Many repetitions of the Feldstein and Horioka tests, which tend to show some reduction in correlations as capital markets became more integrated over the past 20 years, have combined with the evidence showing no correlation within national economies to convince a growing number of economists that Feldstein and Horioka's interpretation of their results is correct, and that capital markets remain largely national in scope. This conclusion has been supported by studies of portfolio structure showing that investors routinely prefer to hold home-country rather than foreign equities (French and Poterba, 1991; Baxter and Jermann, 1997) and by other studies showing no evidence that consumers borrow or lend abroad to smooth their consumption in the face of temporary income fluctuations.

Thus far, we have confirmed that border effects for trade remain large in Canada and are matched by price linkages that are much tighter between national than international city pairs. Border effects for services are even larger than those for merchandise trade, and they show less evidence of a post-FTA reduction (Helliwell, 1998, p. 38). Canadian and international evidence also indicates that capital markets are primarily national in scope. What can be done to get international evidence of border effects for merchandise trade? The key problem, as has been noted already, is that other countries do not have internal trade data as complete and comparable as those available for Canadian provinces. Two alternative approaches have been adopted in the face of this difficulty. One direct approach has been to use less complete internal trade data, and using different means of making them comparable to international trade statistics. For example, this has been done by Nitsch (2001) for German landers, and by Wolf (2000), Hillberry (1998, 1999) and Anderson and van Wincoop (2003) for U.S. states. The results depend a great deal on the assumptions made to establish the comparability of internal and external trade data, so that Hillberry obtains much higher estimates of border effects for the United States than do Anderson and van Wincoop. Indeed, the latter argue convincingly that large countries like the United States should be expected to have much smaller border effects than are economies counting for a smaller fraction of world GDP. Since their analysis has many other implications for the study of the size and consequences of border effects, it will be the focus of the section entitled *Gravity with Gravitas: A Solution to the Border Puzzle?* below in this study.

The other way of proceeding, initiated by Wei (1996) for OECD countries, and since applied by Helliwell (1997; 1998, chapter 3), Nitsch (2000a, 2000b) and Chen (2004) for OECD countries, by Helliwell (1998, p. 57) for larger global samples of countries, and by Helliwell and Verdier (2001) to compare Canadian intra-provincial and interprovincial trade, is to make use of input-output data to establish total final sales of merchandise, then subtracting exports to obtain a residual estimate of goods sold domestically. This provides a reasonable estimate of goods sold within the country, but application of the gravity model also requires an estimate of potential trading distances. The original method adopted by Wei (1996) and Helliwell (1997, 1998) was to use one-quarter the distance separating a country from its international trading partner. As noted by Nitsch (2000a), this method relies too much on the geography of the neighbouring countries, and too little on the geography of the home country.

Later studies have tended to move towards measures based on internal distance estimates that combine the theoretical structure of the gravity model with information about the distribution of the population and economic activity within the country (Helliwell and Verdier, 2001; Nitsch, 2000b; Chen, 2004; Helliwell, 2002a). These more accurate estimates of internal distances are on average greater than those assumed by Wei, and thus give larger estimates of border effects. However, more recent estimates of border effects also generally improve on the basic bilateral gravity model by including measures of each country's alternatives to trading with each of its bilateral trading partners, and this extension sometimes results in lower estimates of border effects. All of the studies have shown significant border effects for the industrialized countries, and very much higher effects for developing countries. These effects are still large and significant even for trade between pairs of countries that have long been members of the European Union (EU). For example, even in the 1990s, trade within typical EU members not sharing a common language was six times as intense as international trade between them (Nitsch, 2000b; Helliwell, 1998, p. 51). Merchandise trade densities within developing countries were up to 50 or 100 times greater than trade across national borders (Helliwell, 1998, p. 56). Studies of trade flows by industry show that border effects tend to pervade all industries (Chen, 2004; Helliwell, 1998, p. 31). Furthermore, studies have shown that the inter-industry pattern of border effects is not explained by differences in the extent of non-tariff barriers (Head and Mayer, 2000), so that any general explanation of border effects cannot just be based on the extent of remaining official barriers to trade.

Within Canada, much attention has been paid to the existence and possible effects of barriers to interprovincial trade. Recently improved measures of intra-provincial trade distances permit more useful estimates of the relative size of interprovincial and international border effects, which were previously found to be insignificant for all provinces (Helliwell, 1998, pp. 23-26). The new data show that, for the four largest provinces, there is no evidence that interprovincial trade is less dense than intra-provincial trade, and for none of the provinces are the interprovincial border effects more than a fraction as large as the international ones (Helliwell and Verdier, 2001). Thus, even interprovincial differences in language, networks and regulations have very little importance compared to such differences across national borders.

WHY DO BORDERS MATTER?

WHAT ARE THE LIKELY CAUSES of the separation of national markets? Until we have at least some preliminary answer to this question, we cannot make any judgements about whether this pooling of markets by nation is a good thing or a bad one, and what may be the implications for public policies.

Because studies have revealed that policy barriers are not an important cause of the remaining border effects among industrial countries, the reasons must lie elsewhere. I have long been convinced that the underlying explanation must deal simultaneously with border effects and the very large market-separating effects of distance. What happens to trade as distance grows, as borders are crossed, and as one moves from the known into the unknown, or at least the less familiar? Being further from home usually means being less well-connected to local networks, less able to understand local norms, and less able to be sure how much to trust what people may say. These changes occur as one gets further from familiar territory, and are especially likely as one crosses national boundaries, since many institutions and legal systems are national in scope and differ much from one country to another. Also, as will be reported later on, migration is much more likely within than across national borders, and migration and travel are primary means for extending knowledge and networks.

In order for the loss of network density and shared norms to be a primary cause of the very large border effects discovered, one, or both, of two conditions must hold: i) the costs of trading over less dense networks are high, and ii) the gains from additional long-distance international trade are modest. Let's look first at the importance of shared norms and networks, and the extent to which they are likely to decline with distance and as one crosses national borders. Consider an extreme case of what happens to trade and economic activity in the absence of a shared framework of rules and institutions. After the fall of the Berlin Wall in 1989, most students of economic development thought that the high levels of education and the generally widespread desire for democracy and open markets would lead to rapidly expanding trade and to a convergence of living standards between the parts of Europe that had been divided by the Iron Curtain. Yet, in the following decade, the largest parts of the former Union of Soviet Socialist Republics (U.S.S.R.), including Russia, Ukraine and many smaller republics, saw not convergence towards western European living standards, but a halving of their real GDP per capita. At the time, reliable institutions, widely accepted norms, and high levels of mutual trust were seen to be important (Marer and Zecchini, 1991), but no one foresaw the extent and costliness of their absence, or suspected how rapidly and successfully the Mafia would dominate legitimate business in an institutional vacuum.

Admittedly, the U.S.S.R. experience is an extreme example, but nonetheless useful for being dramatic. Smaller scale studies of the cost-reducing effects of shared norms and networks and of the effects of national boundaries and distance are available. For example, studies have shown that the spillover effects of research and development (R&D) depend considerably on the strength and structure of networks of association and trust, and that these effects decline strongly with distance (Keller, 2002) and national borders (Helliwell,

1998, p. 105). Similarly, international networks of high-tech workers migrating from India to Silicon Valley have been able to establish, through a process of *reputational intermediation* (Kapur, 2001), long-distance business relations that would have been implausible in the absence of the mutual trust embodied in these personal networks. The importance of mutual trust as a less costly and more effective substitute for complicated contracts and legal enforcement has also long been recognized. The cost-reducing importance of informal networks and repeated contacts in building trust and validating informal contracts has been emphasized in studies as diverse as explanations of the existence of the modern corporation (Hart, 1995), the success of northern Italian industrial districts, and the development of historical trade patterns and routes (Greif, 1992).

If networks and trust are important in facilitating trade, and if the strength of these networks diminishes with distance and as borders are crossed, then this would be sufficient to explain why both distance and national borders mark steep reductions in the intensity of trade linkages. This explanation seems increasingly accepted. If so, what does it imply? Should individuals and governments concentrate their efforts on increasing the density of international networks, working towards homogeneous institutions and cultures, in the hope that trade will thereby increase, with resulting improvements in national and global living standards?

What is the evidence on the effects of expanded trade on growth and real incomes? One well-known study by Sachs and Warner (1995) divided developing countries into a closed group and an open group, and found that the open group showed significant convergence towards the higher living standards of industrial countries, while on average less open countries showed no sign of closing the gap in living standards. In addition, Frankel and Rose (2000) have recently argued that countries that trade more have significantly higher levels of GDP per capita. My interpretation of the Sachs and Warner evidence is that some degree of openness is likely to be required to permit the residents of a country to learn valuable lessons from abroad, and to make the most of their own resources and talents. However, as the comparison of China and the former U.S.S.R. in the 1990s illustrates starkly, openness is neither necessary nor sufficient to produce growth or stability. Greater openness in the absence of robust domestic institutions may well hurt more than it helps. My own results are consistent with the finding of Frankel and Rose that richer countries are more open to trade, since I have noted that border effects tend to be smaller for rich than for poor countries (Helliwell, 1998). However, subsequent tests reported in the next section suggest that most of this relation between richness and the size of the border effect disappears if one accounts separately for the expected inverse relation between country size and the size of the border effect.

In order to decide whether the rich industrial countries would be richer still if they were to change their policies so as to encourage international trade over domestic trade, it would perhaps be most helpful to see whether the larger industrial countries are significantly richer than the small ones. Why is it a useful exercise? Because the importance of national border effects means that larger countries already have larger and denser trading networks than countries with lower levels of GDP. The evidence shows no tendency for large OECD countries to have per-capita incomes higher than those of smaller countries. This suggests that for these countries, the major gains from comparative advantage trade have already been reaped, and that further expansions of trade are likely to be based on increasing product variety, as represented by the number of brands on the shelves. Indeed, many of the modern theories of international trade build on the fact that much of the recent trade growth is due to intra-industry rather than inter-industry exports, and thus focused on product variety. Psychological studies show that widening the range of product choice becomes costly to buyers at a fairly early stage — they find it harder to make decisions when faced with many alternatives, take longer to reach their decisions, and are more likely to later regret the decisions they made (Iyengar and Lepper, 1999). Thus, in the absence of demonstrated welfare benefits from trade densities beyond those already available among industrial countries, it seems plausible to infer that the extra denseness of national over international networks may reflect a desirable state of affairs. If local networks have their own value, and are not causing highly advantageous trading opportunities to be ignored, then the fact that the resulting least-cost trading patterns have a high local and national content may well be just what the doctor ordered. As will be noted in the next section, the welfare analysis that flows from the Anderson and van Wincoop model is just the reverse, since the model hypothesizes that increasing product variety, which is assumed to increase with a region's GDP, is the sole motivation for, and benefit of, trade.

The core of my favourite explanation of border effects is that it is cheaper and easier to operate within networks of shared norms and trust, and that the density of such networks declines with distance, especially as one crosses national borders. An important corollary is that local producers are better placed to cater to local tastes, so that consumers are correspondingly more likely to be attracted by the characteristics of local production. If this is the case, and local goods and services are therefore better tailored to meet local conditions and tastes, then it would be a mistake to assume that consumers value goods and services from afar as much as they like local products.

What evidence is there that networks and shared norms have important local and national features? Two main dimensions may be worth exploring. One is the movements of people, since personal contacts are all-important in the establishment and maintenance of networks and trust. The other relates to the formal institutions that supplement and sometimes substitute for more informal personal networks. These include laws and the administration of justice, the design and implementation of standards, and the efficiency and quality of essential services, especially health and education, but including also the classic utilities — water, heat, light, power and communications. If unfamiliar institutions and lack of trusted connections underlie the decay of trading and other densities with distance and across borders, we would expect to find evidence of weaker personal contacts and more variety of institutional structure and quality where communities are separated by distance and borders.

Two strands of the migration literature help to shed light on the effects of distance and borders on network density. The first looks at the extent to which migration is altered by distance and national borders. Using data from Canadian and U.S. censuses, it is possible to model how both distance and national borders influence the probability of migration. The results are striking. The effects of distance are large, just as was observed for trade flows. There are only half as many migrants from a province twice as far away. The effects of national borders are even greater for migration than for trade in goods and services. For example, there are only one-hundredth as many Canadian residents who were born in a U.S. state as were born in another Canadian province, after taking due account of differences in size and distance (Helliwell, 1998, pp. 85-86). This border effect of 100 applies to residents of Canada. The bilateral national border effect is much smaller for individuals resident in the United States, reflecting the fact that over the past 100 years there have been three times as many Canadian-born individuals moving to the United States as U.S.-born individuals moving to Canada. It is noteworthy that these bilateral border effects have been increasing rather the decreasing over the century, since the fraction of the residents of one country who were born in the other has been on a fairly steady downward trajectory over the past 100 years. For example, in 1910 the number of Canadian-born individuals living in the United States was 20 percent as large as the remaining population of Canada, while by 1990 this fraction had dropped to about 3 percent (Helliwell, 2000, p. 17). In the reverse direction, in 1920 the number of U.S.-born individuals living in Canada was about 4 percent as large as the total U.S.-resident population, dropping to slightly more than 1 percent by 1990. Thus, border effects on migration have grown substantially over the past century, coincident with the rising importance of the nation state during the 20th century. No doubt some of the decline of international migration between the two countries has been due to policies adopted in both countries to control the pace and structure of immigration; but these periodic policy changes cannot easily explain the long downward trend in international mobility between the two countries. There have been periods of higher mobility over the century, with net migration north during the Vietnam War period, large southbound movements of professionals during the 1950s and 1960s, and much talk in Canada during the late 1990s of new southbound flows. As has been noted elsewhere (Finnie, 2001; Frank and Bélair, 1999; Helliwell, 2000; Helliwell and Helliwell, 2000, 2001), the 1990s data provide scant support for the talk.

The second relevant strand of the migration literature documents the importance of networks as a determinant of the scale and patterns of migration, and demonstrates the importance of migration to subsequent patterns of trade, investment, and migration. Migrants follow established pathways, since those who precede pass back information about the possibilities and prospects, provide contacts for the newcomers, and offer a community into which to settle on arrival. Thus it is that there comes to be dense pockets of migrants originating from the same village many thousands of kilometres away. These clusters are more apparent, and denser, where the immigrants come from further, and cross more linguistic, political and cultural divides. Migrants bring more migrants in their wake, and the transnational networks they create generate in turn matching patterns of international trade and investment. For example, the country mix of immigrants to Canada helps to predict the patterns of subsequent changes in Canadian trade with the countries of origin. These changes are more apparent for Canadian imports than exports, suggesting that at least part of the effect relates to maintained tastes for goods from the home country (Head and Ries, 1998).[2] The migration literature thus shows strong border effects and illustrates that human migration both depends upon and provides international networks of information and support.

There is a burgeoning field of research into the scope, density, causes and consequences of social norms and networks. Although such studies go back many years in a number of disciplines and under different names, they have had a resurgence in the past decade under the name of *social capital*. A recent OECD report defines social capital as "networks together with shared norms, values and understandings that facilitate co-operation within or among groups." (2001, p. 41) This definition encompasses almost exactly the same factors suggested above as important determinants of the density of trade and other economic and social interactions. If the evidence on social capital show that the strength of networks generally decreases with distance and across national borders, then this would provide further support to the notion that differences in network densities explain differences in trade and other economic transactions.

One early piece of research into the effects of borders on networks was a study of the relative intensity of long-distance telephone calls between cities in Ontario, Quebec and the United States. Using a gravity framework to model the expected effects of size and distance, the study (Mackay, 1958) found that call frequencies were highest within the home province, lower between cities with different principal languages, and by far the lowest across the international boundary; the size- and distance-adjusted intensity of calls was 50 times greater between Ontario cities than between Ontario and nearby U.S. cities.

The path-breaking recent research into the nature and consequences of norms and networks was the long-term study of democracy in the regions of modern Italy by Putnam (1993) and his associates. Putnam was studying the efficiency of regional governments, especially how they developed in different regions in the aftermath of reforms that devolved important powers to regional governments in the 1980s. He developed numerous measures of the quality of norms and shared networks within the 20 regions studied, and found that those with the highest quality of social capital delivered higher quality services to their citizens and made the best use of the newly devolved powers. Indeed, there is some evidence that the better use made of these new powers by regions with more social capital was responsible for a reversal of what had been a repli-cation in Italy of the post-war convergence of income per capita in Europe (Helliwell and Putnam, 1995). Putnam found, importantly for the study of *in-ternational* differences in norms and networks, that there were large and long-sustained *interregional* differences in norms and networks, despite large migration flows among regions. However, for Italy, as for most other countries, the vast majority of people stayed close to where they were born, and their networks and norms were similarly local.

When Putnam turned his research to the United States, he found that many measures of social capital had been growing for the first 60 years of the 20th century, and falling thereafter at about the same rate as they had previously been increasing. Since his U.S. and Italian studies had shown that communities with high levels of his social capital measures tended to rank high on many indicators of economic, physical and community welfare, he sounded widely-heeded warnings about the possible risks to the fabric of U.S. communities (Putnam, 1995, 2000). Earlier research (Almond and Verba, 1963) on the quality of mid-century civic life found large differences among countries in many measures and consequences of social capital, and especially in the level of interpersonal trust. Three features of these international differences must be noted here: they are of long standing and persist for decades, they are transported from one country to another as migration takes place, and they are in some cases traceable to specific events or government policies. The extent to which these international differences are transported with migration has been studied by Rice and Feldman (1997), who found that a strong predictor of inter-state differences in U.S. interpersonal trust was differences in the number of residents whose parents or grandparents were born in countries with high levels of trust. In the same vein, Putnam (2000) has found that one of the best predictors of interstate differences in trust levels is the share of the population with Scandinavian ancestors. To understand the latter point, one needs to know that measures of interpersonal trust are significantly higher in Scandinavian countries than elsewhere. Finally, a link between trust levels and events has been revealed by the study of social capital in post-1990 Russia (Raiser, 1997), while a link with policies has been made by Worms (2002), who suggests that the unusually low levels of interpersonal trust in France (relative to those in other countries, and to trust in governments) may be partly due to the fact that pre- and post-revolutionary governments in France have systematically suppressed various non-state networks, seeing them as potential threats to the status and legitimacy of the state.

I have been arguing thus far that the quality of networks is an important determinant of many other forms of economic and social contact, and that networks are much tighter close to home, and within the same country. The latter point was made in part by showing the existence of long-sustained international and interstate differences in various measures of social capital. The existence of these differences may be sufficient to show that networks decay with distance and borders, but it is not necessary. For example, it is possible that several countries show the same aggregate levels and distributions of various measures of social capital, but still have networks that are largely unconnected with one another. Indeed, that is almost surely the case. However, study of the radius of trust and networks, and the extent to which individuals are involved in many different types of networks, for different purposes and with different implications for their behaviour and attitudes, is still in its infancy. Thus, it would be premature to make firm conclusions about the extent to which various overlapping networks decay with distance and across borders. It is likely that changes in the types and patterns of communication, ranging from the jet plane in the 1960s to e-mail and the Internet in the 1980s and 1990s, are altering the nature and costs of developing and maintaining different types of networks.

GRAVITY WITH GRAVITAS: A SOLUTION TO THE BORDER PUZZLE?

ANDERSON AND VAN WINCOOP'S (A&vW, 2003) important study bearing this title is an empirical application of the earlier influential theoretical model of Anderson (1979). The A&vW proposed solution to the border puzzle is that taking the theory of the gravity model seriously leads to a quite different set of results: removal of the border effect would lead to only a 44-percent increase in trade between Canada and the United States, accompanied by a six-fold drop in interprovincial trade. If this result is found to be of general application, to what extent does it solve the border puzzle? That depends on what one thinks the border puzzle is, or was. I have always thought that the main border puzzle is *why*? A&vW answer this question in two ways. First, they argue that for countries larger than Canada (in terms of GDP), the border effect is materially smaller, and even for Canada it is likely to be up to one-third smaller than would be indicated by the estimation procedure used by McCallum (1995). Their results suggest a 1993 border effect of 10.6 for Canada and 2.6 for the United States. But the link between border effect and size, which has increasing support from both theory and data, would then suggest that the border effects for typical countries are larger than those for either Canada or the United States. World Bank data comparing national GDPs at purchasing power parity put the United States in first place by a fairly large margin, followed by China, Japan and India, with Canada arriving in 12th position in the World Bank's list of 164 countries. The median country on the list has a GDP that is 3 percent of Canada's GDP and about 0.25 percent of the U.S. GDP. Thus, if 2.6 is the smallest border effect, and if these effects rise with falling size to the extent suggested by the A&vW results, then we should expect typical border effects to be much larger than those found by McCallum.[3]

Second, A&vW assume that the cause of the border effect is rooted in national policies. This assumption is common among international economists. For example, Paul Krugman argued "All of which leads us to the real reason why national boundaries matter and to the proper notion of a nation for our analysis. Nations matter — they exist in a modeling sense — because they have governments whose policies affect the movements of goods and factors." (1991, pp. 71-72) If the determinants of regional and national distributions of economic activity are anything like those I have outlined in earlier sections, then Krugman's inference is likely to be seriously misleading. I used to think rather similarly myself, but in the past 10 years I have seen so much evidence of border effects, and so little success from attempts to explain their size by government policies, that I have come to believe that these effects arise principally because tastes, markets, resources, institutions and societies differ across space within countries and even more across borders. In a context, much emphasized by Krugman in terms of industrial location, where past patterns determine future ones, and where investment decisions are costly to reverse, the fact that local producers have, through their immediacy, an advantage in spotting and exploiting local opportunities means that markets are likely to remain local and national in scope even in the absence of national policies designed to restrict international mobility.

If solving the border puzzle means showing why border effects exist, then the A&vW model does not provide a solution, since its authors assume the cause to be policies but provide no evidence bearing on the validity of that assumption.

Indeed, as they are careful to point out — and as Balistreri and Hillberry (2002) illustrate very clearly —, there is nothing in the A&vW model that permits their estimation to discriminate between their assumption that border effects are due to policies (that keep consumers from getting full access to foreign goods, which they like as much as local goods) and an alternative in which border effects exist because local products more closely match local tastes. As will be seen later, these two quite different interpretations, which cannot be distinguished by the current A&vW model, have very different implications for the policy consequences of border effects.

When I wrote the first version of this study, I was only part-way through my efforts to replicate the A&vW results and to understand if and why their model and results differed from those reported in Helliwell (1998). As noted by James Anderson in his careful comments on that version, my understanding of what they were doing, and of the implications of alternative estimation procedures, was incomplete and confused. It may be still, but at least now, as students are fond of saying, I am confused at a higher level. In reaching this higher level, I have benefited from data and advice from both Eric van Wincoop and James Anderson, and also from the parallel research work of others, most especially Ed Balistreri and Russell Hillberry (2002, 2003) and Robert Feenstra (2003). To save space, it might be best to report in point form what I think I have learned thus far, recognizing that changes are still being made in the data, estimation and theory, so that some of these conclusions may themselves have to be revised. But here is a start.

1. In my first version, I noted that the two-country border effect for Canada estimated by A&vW was 10.6 for 1993, which is in the same range as the estimate of 12.3 reported in Helliwell (1998, p. 22) based on the same dependent variable and applying to the same year, but making much more rudimentary efforts to situate the bilateral trading data into a multilateral context. Much effort was devoted to explaining why these estimates differed. They were both much lower than the estimate in McCallum (1995), mainly because the effects of the FTA were important between 1988 (the year of McCallum's data) and 1993, and also because of data refinements and revisions. For a long time, I thought that the much lower explanatory power of the A&vW equation, relative to the equations we had been estimating, was due to some implausible restriction imposed by their model. I eventually discovered that the main reason for the low A&vW explanatory power, as measured by the adjusted R^2, was merely a consequence of redefining the dependent variable as a means of imposing their assumed unitary income elasticities. In the course of replicating their work, I also discovered that significant revisions were made to GDP data since our earlier work, and that we

and A&vW had been using different data sources. I also discovered some mechanical data errors in our earlier data sample, and eventually developed a preferred data set that is better than either our earlier data set or that used by A&vW, but that is also closer to theirs than to ours. In particular:

2. The preferred data set uses GDP at factor cost for both U.S. states and Canadian provinces (instead of GDP at market prices). This is the only way to get strict comparability, since only factor-cost data are available for states, while both are available for provinces. Tests comparing results based on GDP at market prices with those based on GDP at factor cost favour the latter, which was the choice made by A&vW.

3. For interprovincial and province-state distances, A&vW used distances between capital cities, while we used distances between major cities, sometimes using a geographically weighted average of major cities, as was done by McCallum (1995). The latter approach is more consistent with the gravity framework, and gives slightly stronger empirical results, and thus is probably to be preferred. The impact on the size of border effects is minimal.

4. For internal trading distances, which are important for the multilateral resistance variables defined by A&vW, but not needed either for our own work or for the alternative simpler framework proposed by Feenstra (2003), A&vW used one-quarter of the distance between a state's capital city and that of its nearest neighbour, as first proposed by Wei (1996). Using instead the population-weighted average of internal distances for each unit (as proposed by Helliwell and Verdier, 2001) materially increases the explanatory power of the A&vW model, and raises the distance coefficient closer to that found by other studies. Since the latter method is also more coherent with the logic of all versions of the gravity model, it is probably to be preferred.

5. A&vW show that it is theoretically and empirically important to include the border effect, as well as the opportunity of trading within the same state or province, in the relevant definition of alternatives to each bilateral trade observation. At some stage, I thought that this was implied only by their particular version of the gravity model, and that it was possibly responsible for the apparently worse fit of their model. I am now convinced that they are exactly right on this issue, and thus that their 10.5 estimate of the Canadian border effect in 1993 is to be preferred to any that does not incorporate these adjustments. Several lines of research have come together to make me reasonably confident about this conclusion. First, by the time fully comparable data and

specifications are used, the fit of the A&vW equation and that of the equation based on the simpler version of alternative trading opportunities used in Helliwell and Verdier (2001) are essentially the same. Second, as A&vW show convincingly, any application of the gravity model must include the possibility of greater internal trade within the larger country if it is to be applied to countries of different sizes and structures. Third, the border effects belong in the definition of alternative trading opportunities even if the underlying theoretical model explains the border effects by taste differences rather than by policy obstacles. As will be seen later, the difference only comes in when one tries to simulate the effects of changes in policy. Fourth, the theory and empirical work of Feenstra (2003), which we have also replicated and slightly extended here, show that by using an appropriately defined set of country fixed effects instead of the more complicated A&vW estimation procedure, we can obtain a consistent and empirically very similar estimate of the average of Canadian and U.S. border effects.

UPDATED RESULTS AND POLICY IMPLICATIONS

TABLE 1 REPORTS SOME UPDATED ALTERNATIVE ESTIMATES of border effects for Canada and the United States, consistent with the summary of findings reported in the previous section. It includes earlier McCallum-type results, the A&vW results, followed by the results of the re-estimation with the revised set of data, and parallel estimates using Feenstra's alternative strategy. The results are quite consistent in showing an average border effect of about 5 for Canada and the United States, with the A&vW model implying component values of 10.5 for Canada and 2.6 for the United States. The Feenstra estimation method is valuable in providing a consistent estimate of the geometric mean of the Canadian and U.S. border effects. It provides an estimate that is quite close to the geometric mean of the separate estimates for Canada and the United States produced by the A&vW model. This helps to strengthen the confidence with which the A&vW results can be assumed to follow from models more general than theirs, since Feenstra's equation imposes no theoretical structure, achieving consistency in its estimation of the border effects by the use of importer and exporter fixed effects for each state and province. The higher R^2 obtained by Feenstra does not therefore suggest a more successful model, since the coefficients for the country fixed effects (which are, on average, more than significant enough to cover their cost in terms of degrees of freedom) are really just a way of showing the puzzle yet to be explained. Why do different states and provinces have such different trading intensities? The significant fixed effects are just highlighting that these differences are large. Supplementary tests

TABLE 1

CANADIAN BORDER EFFECTS FOR 1993, ESTIMATED WITH INTERPROVINCIAL AND
PROVINCE-STATE MERCHANDISE TRADE DATA

| | | BORDER EFFECTS | | ADJUSTED R² |
	CANADA	UNITED STATES	GEOMETRIC MEAN	OF EQUATION
(1) McCallum-type equation estimated in 1997 (taken from Helliwell, 1998, Table 2-2) using remoteness variables	12.3			0.764
(2) Same equation estimated in 2002 using updated and corrected data and alternative trading opportunities, as in Helliwell and Verdier (2001)	14.3			0.766
(3) A&vW theoretically consistent estimate (their Table 5)	10.5	2.6	5.2	0.430
(4) A&vW re-estimated using Helliwell and Verdier (2001) internal distances	10.5	2.6	5.2	0.490
(5) Feenstra (2003) equation with importer and exporter fixed effects			4.7	0.640

Notes: All equations are estimated by OLS. There are 676 observations used for equation (1), which is
quoted directly from Helliwell (1998, Table 2-2), and has a smaller sample so as to have the same
trading pairs represented for all years between 1991 and 1996. Equation (2) follows A&vW in using
679 observations for interprovincial and province-state trade, the maximum number available for
1993. If equation (1) is re-estimated with 679 observations, the border effect rises to 12.6, while if
equation (2) is re-estimated with 676 observations the border effect drops to 13.7. Equations (3)
and subsequent are estimated with 1,511 observations, comprising the 679 observations of (2) and
832 observations for interstate trade.

suggest that this split reflects the data and is not due to theoretical restrictions
imposed on unwilling data. The raw data show interstate trading relations that
are far less intense than interprovincial trading relations. For example, if we
take a pure form of the bilateral gravity model, in which trade would be equal
to some constant multiplied by the product of the GDPs and divided by the
bilateral distance, the implied constant for 1993 is more than 10 times greater
for interprovincial trade than for interstate trade. This is even greater than the
difference in border effects implied by the A&vW model. I am inclined to
think that some of this may be due to non-comparability of data on interprovincial and interstate shipments. Statistics Canada has just completed major
improvements to the interprovincial and province-state trade data, and these
should permit better analysis of the 1992-2001 period, for which the data will

be available. As for the state-state data, however, there is the possibility of a new data set for 1997 but no chance of a full time series, and no great likelihood of getting data that are properly comparable to the interprovincial data. Thus, although it will be possible to study the trends in the Canadian border effect, the analysis of the relation between country size and border effects will be hard to conduct in the same way.

In the meantime, are there any ways of using other evidence to shed light on the extent to which the A&vW assumptions about the causes of the border effect are realistic? The most obvious solution is to examine the extent to which the model predicted the consequences of the FTA for interprovincial and international trade. Another is to analyze the implications of the model for transport costs, as suggested by Balistreri and Hillberry (2002). I shall do both in this and the following section.

First, as already noted earlier, the FTA between Canada and the United States provided something very close to a controlled experiment for a policy-driven reduction in the border effect. The A&vW model makes a striking forecast about what will happen in a country of Canada's size following a reduction in the border effect. A&vW's comparative statics analysis starts with a border effect for Canada very close in size to that based on the more general McCallum-type gravity model and concludes that removal of the border effect would increase Canada-U.S. trade by only a small fraction of the extent to which interprovincial trade would be reduced. The FTA triggered a reduction of the border effect, which provides a semi-experimental test of the comparative statics analysis of A&vW. According to their model, a reduction of the border effect that increases Canada-U.S. trade by 70 percent will also lead to a six-fold reduction in the density of interprovincial trade. But the facts of the matter are rather different. In the wake of the FTA, the reduction in the density of interprovincial trade was only a small fraction of the increase in Canada-U.S. trade. The proximate reason for the false forecast in this case has already been presented. A&vW assume that consumers on both sides of the border value greater product variety and have identical preferences for domestic and foreign goods. Put slightly differently, domestic producers are no better able than foreign producers to design and deliver products that match local tastes. The A&vW model cannot distinguish that interpretation from an alternative embodying systematically closer matching between local goods and local preferences. The post-FTA experience suggests that there are taste differences along national borders, as well as over geographic distance. This alternative would also show much smaller decreases in interprovincial trade than does the A&vW model in response to any measure that reduces the size of the border effect.

Second, it is possible to evaluate the A&vW model with respect to its analysis of the effects of distance on the density of trade linkages. They attribute the reduction of trade densities with distance as being due to transport costs. The problem is that the decay of trade densities with distance is so great as to imply transport costs that are impossibly high relative to actual transport costs. For example, Balistreri and Hillberry (2002) calculate that in the A&vW model the estimated decrease in trade with distance implies that almost half of output is devoted to transportation in the aggregate — and an even greater share for goods that travel longer than average distances within North America. I suspect that the nature of the border and distance puzzles is very similar at heart. In both cases, trade densities fall far faster than can be rationalized by any reasonable estimates of the costs of moving goods across distance or borders. Any satisfactory resolution of either puzzle is likely, in my view, to depend on many of the same features of economic and social life: that networks facilitate information, trust, and exchanges of all sorts; that the density of networks decay with distance; that tastes change with distance and borders, and that producers located close to consumers can more effectively predict and meet local needs. Full answers to the border and distance puzzles are likely to rely on several of these influences.

My summary judgement is that the A&vW analysis has provided two major contributions to the understanding of border effects. First, these authors have clearly spelled out the negative correlation between country size and border effects implied by any application of the gravity model in a multilateral trading environment. Second, they have strongly made the case for embedding border effects in alternative models of international trade. However, they have not yet provided a solution to the border puzzle, in two main respects: They have provided no explanation of what underlies border effects, and their own specific varieties-based endowment model produces conditional forecasts for the consequences of the FTA that seem at variance with what actually happened. In particular, in their setup, the impact of the FTA should have been a small proportionate increase in province-state trade coupled with a much larger proportionate decrease in interprovincial trade. If anything, the actual results seem to be the reverse of this pattern, with much greater increases in north-south trade than reductions in east-west trade. This alternative pattern suggests the need for more general models.

What more general models are likely to be required? First, it would be useful to develop some empirical means for determining the extent to which local products and local tastes are consistent. The A&vW model is silent on this matter — nonetheless crucial for deriving any policy implications.

Second, the endowment plus trade model ignores key classical determinants of trade, especially comparative advantage and economies of scale. Depending on how endowments are distributed, both types of classical trade will result in trade flows that are well-fitted by the gravity equation, although it becomes very difficult to find precise means for modelling trading opportunities with third parties.

Third, the A&vW and many other models of the geographic distribution of production and trade ignore trade in intermediate products. This issue is of critical importance even for interpreting the data. When analysts use ratios of trade to GDP as measures of globalization, they risk comparing apples and oranges. In the A&vW theoretical model, final output originates in each state or province, and is subsequently consumed either there or elsewhere. There are only different brands of apples. But to a large and growing extent the modern economy involves vertical decomposition of the production chain, so that much of the growth in the volume of trade within the same industry is based on shipments of parts and assemblies. This vertical decomposition can be based either on economies of scale or on comparative advantage. As an example of the latter, it is common to perform labour-intensive stages in locations where labour is abundant and real wage rates are low.

An extreme form of international intra-industry trade dominated by vertical disaggregation is provided by the North American automobile industry, which is divided amongst Michigan, Ontario and Quebec in such a way that the border is best seen as a line passing through the middle of an auto plant whose assembly line snakes back and forth across the border line as production proceeds. Thus, although typical border effects are as large for cars and parts as for other industries, they disappear entirely for flows among Michigan, Ontario and Quebec (Helliwell, 1998, Table 2-4).

The large and growing nature of trade in intermediate products raises problems even for the measurement of trade intensities. Ratios of trade to GDP are used as though they represent shares of production that might sum up to 100 percent. Yet, the latest Canadian data show that total shipments of goods and services (defined consistently for domestic and foreign shipments) are more than twice as large as GDP, so that the often-quoted trade/GDP ratios overstate the trade share of shipments by a factor of more than 2.0. There has also been an upward trend in the ratio of shipments to GDP, rising from about 2.0 in 1992 to 2.3 in 2001, so that part of what is seen as a trend towards greater globalization is in fact a more general trend, in both domestic and international markets, towards increased trade in intermediate goods and services. It is also likely that the FTA would have led to increasing cross-border trade of just this type, thus helping to clarify the puzzles left unexplained by both the computable general equilibrium (CGE) model and the A&vW predictions of the likely impacts of the FTA. There was much more international trade but much less GDP growth generated than predicted by the CGE models, and there was much less reduction in interprovincial shipments than predicted by the A&vW model. These results could easily be explained in the context of a model incorporating endogenous trade in intermediates. Such a model would permit the FTA to increase substantially province-state shipments, to reduce slightly interprovincial shipments, and to increase the ratio of total shipments to GDP.

There is clearly a full research agenda facing both theorists and empirical researchers before firm conclusions can be formulated about the causes and welfare implications of border effects. The latest results continue to show that these effects remain significant for all countries, are significantly greater for smaller than for larger countries, and are much smaller for goods than for services, although with some signs of downward trends in all cases. However, as noted above, even the measurement of such trends is complicated by the fact that trend and GDP are conceptually different, so that some of the increase in the trade-to-GDP ratio does not represent a growing international focus of shipments, but rather an upward trend in the ratio of total shipments to GDP. Models are needed to embody and explain these empirically and theoretically important conceptual differences, and to explain their trends.

POLICY IMPLICATIONS FOR CANADA

MUCH OF CANADA'S HISTORY IS BASED ON the military, cultural, linguistic and economic causes and consequences of borders. The study of border effects is thus a serious matter, with far-reaching implications for politics, economics and welfare. How can the recent empirical research on the size and consequences of border effects be used to enrich and extend the traditional debates? The first wave of new results, triggered by McCallum (1995), exposed the continuing economic importance of national borders, but left open for future research the key policy-related questions: What is the cause of these effects? and What would be the consequences of removing borders? More recent work has attempted to answer these questions in quite different ways, and with divergent evaluations of the policy implications. One strand of the subsequent empirical literature has addressed the 'why?' by looking at disaggregated data for different industries, different provinces, and different aspects of economic and social life.[4] This includes attempts to explain the extent to which inter-industry differences in border effects can be traced to differences in border-related policies. There are some cases (e.g. agricultural commodities, autos and parts, and tobacco products) where the size and pattern of border effects have been clearly linked to trade policies. In general, however, it has been found that border effects are so pervasive across industries and aspects of economic life as to make trade policies a small part of the story.

A quite different approach, adopted by Anderson and van Wincoop (2001; hereafter A&vWb) in their welfare analysis of border effects, is to use a specific model with a clearly defined role (but no explanation) for border effects, including some proxies for welfare effects, and do comparative statics exercises by removing border effects on a bilateral or multilateral basis. As noted in A&vWb, this has some parallels with the earlier use of CGE models to evaluate the possible consequences of the Canada-U.S. FTA. A&vW argue that their new analysis is superior in placing greater reliance on empirical estimation of the model structure, and in the simplicity of this structure, thus making it easier to see where the results are coming from. However, those who developed and used CGE models would say that when A&vW set up a model with no role for output-enhancing specialization and economies of scale they are ruling out the most important likely sources of benefits from trade enhancing policies. In addition, by including a large range of industries in a model structure with particular roles for industry-specific tariffs, CGE models were able to produce a specific analysis of many different variants of tariff reductions. The CGE modellers would also mention that they used a wide range of empirical estimates for the key model parameters.

A&vWb argue that the CGE models are unable to explain why the post-FTA trade increases were as large as they turned out to be. They contend that their model, by showing large trade increases in response to the removal of border effects, overcomes this shortcoming. However, as noted in previous sections, this claim is not well supported by the post-FTA experience, and the comparison with CGE exercises is inappropriate. Taking the latter point first, the CGE models were forecasting the consequences of reducing the levels of identified tariff barriers, and found what were then thought to be substantial trade expansion effects, even if smaller than what actually transpired.[5] However, the GDP-enhancing effects were smaller than forecasted by the CGE models. The CGE modellers made no claim that the tariff reductions in question would make interprovincial and province-state merchandise trade flows equally intense. Indeed, their studies preceded the discovery of the size and prevalence of border effects. The A&vWb comparative statics exercise is quite different. These authors assume that all border effects are directly or indirectly due to policies, and then remove them entirely. Since they suppose a much larger reduction in border effects than did the CGE modellers, it is no surprise, in some sense, that they show larger trade effects. However, it must be remembered that all of the extra trade in the CGE models comes from increased specialization to exploit economies of scale, and there are consequently increases in total GDP. By contrast, as already noted in previous sections, the A&vWb results are entirely due to consumers switching from domestic to foreign sources of goods, the supply of which remains unchanged. Hence, there are no

GDP gains in the A&vW case, but there is the potential for changes in welfare if consumers are more satisfied.

The A&vWb welfare analysis predicts that Canadians would enjoy substantial welfare gains in the absence of border effects. They argue that if borders were removed (starting from the 1990s border effect levels, not those of 1988), there would be an increase in Canadian welfare of more than 50 percent, compared to an increase of about 6 percent in the United States (Anderson and van Wincoop, 2001b, Table 2). In their model, this huge welfare gain in Canada is attributed, in roughly equal parts, to a resource effect (lower transport costs),[6] to expanded trade and to an improvement in the terms of trade. This is far more than was ever promised by the CGE analysis that provided the economic underpinning for the FTA. Does it constitute a clarion call for a new North American agenda, or even for an aggressive new move towards political and economic globalization? A&vW argue that one cannot do sensible policy analysis without using a specific theoretical model that shows how and why policies have a welfare effect. By the same token, the policy results are only as relevant as the model applied to obtain them. How do the A&vWb results measure up?

In both their studies, A&vW argue that by taking theory seriously (with *gravitas*), they are able to simultaneously solve the border puzzle and derive policy implications for the removal of border effects. As I have already noted, the A&vW *gravitas* study is, in my view, a highly valuable and important contribution to border-related research. It makes two primary contributions, first by explaining clearly the link between border effects and country size, and second by providing an example of how border effects can be represented in the context of a specific theoretical model of the determination of trade and welfare. But to proceed from their specific model to the analysis of the effects of policies requires not just that the theory be taken seriously, but that it is shown to be consistent with the evidence. In the first version of this study, our partially finished efforts suggested that the A&vW model and its assumptions were rejected by the data. I am now convinced that their model fits the data as well as any of the alternatives thus far proposed. The problem with their welfare conclusions is not that they come from a model rejected by the data, but that their model also contains an alternative interpretation in which border effects are the result of differences in tastes. If the latter were the whole story, and if policies were adopted with the objective of increasing north-south trade flows (rather than simply reducing artificial barriers), they would be more likely to lead to decreases than to increases in welfare, for all of the reasons that economists use to establish the consequences of trade distortions.

Is it possible to look more broadly for evidence that would lead us to prefer the identical tastes assumption to the alternative taste-differences approach? If the A&vW assumption is correct, with consumer welfare being
driven heavily by product variety, and with consumers being indifferent between domestic and foreign products (and desiring 10 times more goods from a
country 10 times as large), then current levels of well-being would be much
higher in larger economies, given the existence of large border effects, especially in smaller countries. The implied difference is very large, as indicated by
the welfare calculations presented in Table 2 of A&vWb. They calculate that
welfare would rise by more than 50 percent in Canada if border effects were
removed, compared to an increase of 6 percent in the United States. According
to the A&vW analysis, Canadians apparently have welfare levels far below
those of Americans, because border effects imply, in the A&vW setup, more
limited variety than is available to consumers in larger countries, particularly
the United States. Countries smaller than Canada, which as noted earlier includes most, would be even worse off in the current state of affairs. Fortunately,
systematic comparable data on subjective well-being in fifty countries (Inglehart
et al., 2000) are available to test the A&vW presumption about the effects of borders on welfare. I have already noted in earlier sections that there is psychological
evidence to the effect that increasing product variety quickly leads to situations
where consumers feel worse off than with lesser variety, since they are required
to spend more time making decisions and are subsequently more likely to regret
their decisions (Iyengar and Lepper, 1999). This suggests that the varieties-
based model of trade and welfare employed by A&vW may be counterfactual.

If those living in smaller countries already have sufficient product variety
or if locally-made products are more suitable in any event to their idiosyncratic
tastes, then life would be no better in larger economies. On the other hand, if
the A&vW theory has any relevance, we would expect to find that well-being
is higher in larger countries. I have done a number of direct tests of this hypothesis and found that among OECD countries, subjective well-being is systematically higher in the smaller than in the larger countries. When total
economic size is divided into GDP per capita and total population, GDP
per capita has positive but heavily truncated effects, while population size has a
negative effect. This negative effect of population size on average well-being
shows up in simple equations as well as when the size variables are added to the
fully specified model used in Helliwell (2002b).[7] The negative effect of size is
smaller when account is taken of the positive effect of government quality on
subjective well-being, since government quality (using the average of the measures in Kaufmann, Kraay and Zoido-Lobatoni, 1999a, 1999b) is negatively correlated with the size of a country's population. Thus, the data on subjective
well-being, increasingly used by economists as a measure of welfare[8], provides

no support at all for the idea that a reduction of border effects would raise well-being through increases in product variety.

A simple inspection of the raw data on subjective well-being serves to reject the notion that welfare is higher in larger countries, as subjective well-being is highest in Scandinavian countries and Switzerland. Subjective well-being in Canada, even with border effects in operation, is significantly higher on average than in the United States, but below that in Scandinavia. Thus, the idea that welfare in Canada could rise by more than one-third relative to the United States simply by offering Canadian consumers more direct access to U.S. products has less than no support in the well-being data. If anything, the data support the notion that people living in smaller countries have a greater capacity to create goods, services and governments that match their preferences and respond to their needs. The full linkages between the presence of border effects and the levels of well-being remain to be spelled out, as does the complex web of factors that lie behind border effects. Although research is still at a preliminary stage, it is already convincing, at least in my view, that there simply cannot be large unreaped welfare gains to be derived through systematic efforts to make international and national trading relations equally intense.

Now that formal trade barriers have reached the low levels currently observed among industrial countries, remaining border effects likely signal segmentation of those that have differing institutions, tastes and networks, with residents of small countries at no systematic disadvantage, in terms of quality of life measured by subjective well-being, relative to residents of larger countries. Only further research will show where greater co-ordination and harmonization of global efforts will have their highest payoffs. For Canadian policy, the preferred alternative is not likely to involve a stronger focus on North American integration. This is because Canada's higher average measures of subjective well-being are supported by institutional differences that would be threatened by closer harmonization with U.S. institutions. Moreover, Canada's ability to use its good offices to help other countries and to assist in the development of global institutions that are especially important to those in smaller countries requires perceived policy independence.[9]

ENDNOTES

1   See Dekle (1996) for Japan, Sinn (1992) for the United States, and Bayoumi and Rose (1993) for the United Kingdom.

2   If one asks how much of world trade is among countries with border effects of different sizes, then the midpoint could be at a country size closer to that of Canada, or perhaps even larger. Such calculations are complicated by the finding of earlier

research that border effects are higher in poorer countries. China and India both have low per capita incomes and together comprise more than one-third of the global population.

3   Gould (1994) provides a comparable study of the trade effects of U.S. immigration.

4   For example, Chen (2004) and Head and Mayer (2000).

5   The predictions and results are compared in Helliwell, Lee and Messinger, 1999.

6   Readers might wonder where the resource savings are coming from in an endowment economy. Even though total output is unchanged, much less is absorbed by transport costs when Canadian consumers are able to satisfy their tastes for variety from closer U.S. sources. These presumed savings are so large because of the very high coefficient on transport costs. As already noted by Balistreri and Hillberry (2002), this coefficient implies impossibly high transport costs. Indeed, the 18 percent Canadian resource savings on transport costs calculated by A&vWb (Table 2) are far higher than total resources devoted to transportation in Canada. As I have already argued, the reason for the high distance coefficient in the trade equations is not that transport costs are that high, but that markets and tastes are separated by distance as well as by national borders. By neglecting this possibility, A&vW are then driven to the necessarily counterfactual conclusion that if there were no border effects, transport costs would be reduced by far more than their total initial size.

7   If the log of either national GDP or national population is added to the final equation (5) of Helliwell (2002b), it attracts a small and insignificant negative coefficient. If the size variables are included separately for the OECD and developing countries, they show a small positive effect in the developing countries (which include a number of struggling new small states) and a larger and significant negative effect in OECD countries. The coefficient is –0.055 for the log of population (t=3.3) or –0.050 (t=2.8) for the log of aggregate GDP.

8   See, for example, Alesina, Di Tella and MacCulloch (2001), Blanchflower and Oswald (2000), Di Tella, MacCulloch and Oswald (2000), Easterlin (1974, 1995), Frey and Stutzer (2000, 2002), Helliwell (2001a, 2001b, 2002b), Gardner and Oswald (2001), Offer (2000) and Oswald (1997).

9   The reasons for this are spelled out more fully in Chapter 3 of Helliwell (2002c).

Acknowledgments

THIS REVISED VERSION DIFFERS SUBSTANTIALLY from the conference paper, especially in the fourth and fifth sections — entitled *Gravity with Gravitas: A Solution to the Border Puzzle?* and *Updated Results and Policy Implications* — , for several reasons. First, our efforts to understand the differences between the Anderson and van Wincoop results and our own were still underway when the conference version was prepared. Our now successful efforts to reconcile the two sets of results depended heavily on the data and advice of Eric van Wincoop, Jim Anderson, Russell Hillberry, Ed Balistreri, and Rob Feenstra. In addition, discussions with Jim Anderson at and after the conference, and heavy reliance on the parallel research activities of Balistreri and Hillberry, and Rob Feenstra have clarified my understanding (about time, some might say) of the nature and consequences of alternative ways of formulating and testing the gravity equation. In this overdue lurching towards a better understanding of the theories and results, I have been greatly aided by the research assistance and collaboration of Martin Berka, Aneta Bonikowska, Nikola Gradojevic, and Christy Leung. The internal distance estimates are derived from joint research with Aneta Bonikowska, Genevieve Verdier, Martin Berka and Volker Nitsch.

BIBLIOGRAPHY

Alesina, Alberto, Rafael Di Tella and Robert MacCulloch. *Inequality and Happiness: Are Europeans and Americans Different?* NBER Working Paper No. 8198. Cambridge (Mass.): National Bureau of Economic Research, 2001.

Almond, Gabriel A., and Sidney Verba. *The Civic Culture: Political Attitudes and Democracy in Five Nations.* Princeton: Princeton University Press, 1963.

Anderson, James E. "A Theoretical Foundation for the Gravity Equation." *American Economic Review* 69, 1 (1979): 106-116.

Anderson, James E., and Eric van Wincoop. *Borders, Trade and Welfare.* NBER Working Paper No. 8515. Cambridge (Mass.): National Bureau of Economic Research, 2001.

———. "Gravity with Gravitas: A Solution to the Border Puzzle." *American Economic Review* 93, 1 (2003): 170-192.

Balistreri, Edward J., and Russell H. Hillberry. "Trade Frictions and Welfare in the Gravity Model: How Much of the Iceberg Melts?" U.S. International Trade Commission, 2002.

———. "Gravity with Gravitas: A Solution to the Border Puzzle: Comment." U.S. International Trade Commission, 2003.

Baxter, Marianne, and Urban J. Jermann. "The International Diversification Puzzle is Worse than You Think." *American Economic Review* 87, 1 (1997): 170-180.

Bayoumi, Tamim, and Andrew Rose. "Domestic Saving and Intra-National Capital Flows." *European Economic Review* 37, 6 (1993): 1197-1202.

Blanchflower, David G., and Andrew J. Oswald. *Well-Being over Time in Britain and the USA.* NBER Working Paper No. 7487. Cambridge (Mass.): National Bureau of Economic Research, 2000.

Chen, Natalie. "Intra-National Versus International Trade in the European Union: Why Do National Borders Matter?" *Journal of International Economics* 63, 1 (2004): 93-118.

Davis, Donald R., David E. Weinstein, Scott C. Bradford and Kazushige Shimpo. "Using International and Japanese Regional Data to Determine When the Factor

Abundance Theory of Trade Works." *American Economic Review* 87, 3 (1997): 421-446.

Dekle, Robert. "Savings-Investment Associations and Capital Mobility: On the Evidence from Japanese Regional Data." *Journal of International Economics* 41, 1-2 (1996): 53-72.

Di Tella, R., R.J. MacCulloch and A.J. Oswald. "Preferences over Inflation and Unemployment: Evidence from Surveys of Happiness." Working Paper. 2000.

Easterlin, R.A. "Does Economic Growth Improve the Human Lot? Some Empirical Evidence." In *Nations and Households in Economic Growth*. Edited by P.A. David and M.W. Reder. New York: Academic Press, 1974, pp. 89-125.

——. "Will Raising the Incomes of All Increase the Happiness of All?" *Journal of Economic Behaviour and Organization* 27, 1 (1995): 35-48.

Engel, Charles, and John H. Rogers. "How Wide Is the Border?" *American Economic Review* 86 (December 1996): 1112-1125.

Feenstra, Robert. *Advanced International Trade: Theory and Evidence*. Princeton: Princeton University Press, 2003.

Feldstein, Martin S., and Charles Horioka. "Domestic Savings and International Capital Flows." *Economic Journal* 90 (June 1980): 314-329.

Finnie, Ross. *The Brain Drain: Myth and Reality – What It Is and What Should Be Done*. IRPP Policy Paper. Montreal: Institute for Research on Public Policy, 2001.

Frank, Jeff, and Éric Bélair. *South of the Border: An Analysis of Results from the Survey of 1995 Graduates Who Moved to the United States*. Ottawa: Human Resources Development Canada and Statistics Canada, 1999.

Frankel, Jeffrey, and Andrew Rose. *Estimating the Effect of Currency Unions on Trade and Output*. NBER Working Paper No. 7857. Cambridge (Mass.): National Bureau of Economic Research, 2000.

French, Kenneth R., and James M. Poterba. "Investor Diversification and International Equity Markets." *American Economic Review* 81, 2 (1991): 222-226.

Frey, Bruno S., and Alois Stutzer. "Happiness, Economy and Institutions." *Economic Journal* 110, 466 (2000): 918-938.

——. *Happiness and Economics*. Princeton: Princeton University Press, 2002.

Gardner, Jonathan, and Andrew Oswald. *Does Money Buy Happiness? A Longitudinal Study Using Data on Windfalls*. University of Warwick Working Paper. Coventry: University of Warwick, 2001.

Gould, David M. "Immigrant Links to the Home Country: Implications for U.S. Bilateral Trade Flows." *Review of Economics and Statistics* 76, 2 (1994): 302-316.

Greif, Avner. "Institutions and International Trade: Lessons from the Commercial Revolution." *American Economic Review* 82, 2 (1992): 128-133.

Hart, Oliver. *Firms, Contracts and Financial Structure*. Oxford: Clarendon Press, 1995.

Head, Keith, and Thierry Mayer. "Non-Europe: The Magnitude and Causes of Market Fragmentation in the EU." *Weltwirtschaftliches Archiv* 136, 2 (2000): 284-314.

Head, Keith, and John Ries. "Immigration and Trade Creation: Evidence from Canada." *Canadian Journal of Economics* 31, 1 (1998): 47-62.

Helliwell, John F. "National Borders, Trade and Migration." *Pacific Economic Review* 2 (1997): 165-185.

——. *How Much Do National Borders Matter?* Washington (D.C.): Brookings Institution Press, 1998.

——. *Globalization: Myths, Facts and Consequences.* Benefactors Lecture. Toronto: C.D. Howe Institute, 2000. (Available at www.CDHowe.org).

——. "Social Capital, the Economy and Well-Being." In *The Review of Economic Performance and Social Progress.* Edited by Keith Banting, Andrew Sharpe and France St-Hilaire. Montreal and Ottawa: Institute for Research on Public Policy and Centre for the Study of Living Standards, 2001a, pp. 43-60.

——, (ed. and contrib.) "The Contribution of Human and Social Capital to Sustained Economic Growth and Well-Being." Proceedings of an OECD/HRDC conference held in Quebec, March 19-21, 2000. Ottawa: Human Resources and Development Canada, 2001b.

——. "Measuring the Width of National Borders." *Review of International Economics* 10, 3 (2002a): 517-524.

——. *How's Life?: Combining Individual and National Variables to Explain Subjective Well-Being.* NBER Working Paper No. 9065. Cambridge (Mass.): National Bureau of Economic Research, 2002b; *Economic Modelling* 20, 2 (March 2003): 331-360.

——. *Globalization and Well-Being.* Vancouver: UBC Press, 2002c.

Helliwell, John F., and David F. Helliwell. "Tracking UBC Graduates: Trends and Explanations." *ISUMA: Canadian Journal of Policy Research* 1, 1 (Spring 2000): 101-110. (Available at www.isuma.net).

——. "Where Are They Now? Migration Patterns for Graduates of the University of British Columbia." In *The State of Canadian Economics: Essays in Honour of David Slater.* Edited by Patrick Grady and Andrew Sharpe. Montreal: McGill-Queen's University Press, 2001, pp. 291-322.

Helliwell, John F., Frank C. Lee and Hans Messinger. *Effects of the Canada-United States Free Trade Agreement on Interprovincial Trade.* Perspectives on North American Free Trade Series No. 5. Ottawa: Industry Canada, 1999.

Helliwell, John F., and Ross McKitrick. "Comparing Capital Mobility Across Provincial and National Borders." *Canadian Journal of Economics* 32, 5 (November 1999): 1164-1173.

Helliwell, John F., and Robert D. Putnam. "Economic Growth and Social Capital in Italy." *Eastern Economic Journal* 21, 3 (1995): 295-307.

Helliwell, John F., and Geneviève Verdier. "Measuring International Trade Distances: A New Method Applied to Estimate Provincial Border Effects in Canada." *Canadian Journal of Economics* 34, 5 (November 2001): 1024-1041.

Hillberry, Russell. "Regional Trade and the Medicine Line: The National Border Effect in U.S. Commodity Flow Data." *Journal of Borderland Studies* 8, 2 (Fall 1998): 1-17.

——. "Explaining the Border Effect: What Can We Learn from Disaggregated Commodity Flow Data?" Washington (D.C.), 1999. Mimeo.

Inglehart, Ronald, et al. "World Values Surveys and European Values Surveys, 1981-1984, 1990-1993, and 1995-1997." Ann Arbor, Michigan: Inter-university Consortium for Political and Social Research, 2000. (Computer File) ICPSR Version.

Iyengar S.S., and M.R. Lepper. "Rethinking the Value of Choice: A Cultural Perspective on Intrinsic Motivation." *Journal of Personality and Social Psychology* 76 (1999): 349-366.

Kapur, Devesh. "Diasporas and Technology Transfer." *Journal of Human Development* 2, 2 (2001): 265-286.

Kaufmann, Daniel, Aart Kraay and Pablo Zoido-Lobatoni. *Aggregating Governance Indicators.* Working Paper No. 2195. World Bank Policy Research Department, 1999a.

——. *Governance Matters.* Working Paper No. 2196. World Bank Policy Research Department, 1999b.

Keller, Wolfgang. "Geographic Localization of International Technology Diffusion." *American Economic Review* 92, 1 (2002): 120-142.

Krugman, Paul. *Geography and Trade.* Cambridge (Mass.): MIT Press, 1991.

Mackay, J. Ross. "The Interactance Hypothesis and Boundaries in Canada: A Preliminary Study." *The Canadian Geographer* 11 (1958): 1-8.

Marer, Paul, and Salvatore Zecchini (eds.) *The Transition to a Market Economy: Volume 1 – The Broad Issues.* Paris: Organisation for Economic Co-operation and Development, 1991.

McCallum, John. "National Borders Matter: Canada-U.S. Regional Trade Patterns." *American Economic Review* 85 (June 1995): 615-623.

Nitsch, Volker. "National Borders and International Trade: Evidence from the European Union." *Canadian Journal of Economics* 33 (2000a): 1091-1105.

——. "It's Not Right but It's Okay: On the Measurement of Intra- and International Trade Distances." Berlin: Bank Gesselschaft, 2000b.

——. "Statistics Canada 2, Statistisches Bundesamt 1: What Does German Data Tell Us About the Home Bias in International Trade?" Berlin: Bank Gesselschaft, 2001.

Offer, Avner. *Economic Welfare Measurements and Human Well-Being.* Discussion Papers in Economic and Social History No. 34. Oxford: University of Oxford, 2000.

Organisation for Economic Co-operation and Development. *The Well-Being of Nations: The Role of Human and Social Capital.* Paris: Organisation for Economic Co-operation and Development, Centre for Educational Research and Innovation, 2001.

Oswald, A.J. "Happiness and Economic Performance." *Economic Journal* 107, 445 (1997): 1815-1831.

Putnam, Robert D. *Making Democracy Work: Civic Traditions in Modern Italy.* Princeton: Princeton University Press, 1993.

——. "Tuning In, Tuning Out: The Strange Disappearance of Social Capital in America." *PS: Political Science and Politics* 28 (December 1995): 664-683.

——. *Bowling Alone: The Collapse and Revival of American Community.* New York: Simon & Schuster, 2000.

Raiser, Martin. *Informal Institutions, Social Capital and Economic Transition: Reflections on a Neglected Dimension.* Working Paper No. 25. London: European Bank for Reconstruction and Development, 1997.

Rice, Tom W., and Jan L. Feldman. "Civic Culture and Democracy from Europe to America." *Journal of Politics* 59, 4 (1997): 1143-1172.

Sachs, Jeffrey D., and Andrew Warner. "Economic Reform and the Process of Global Integration." *Brookings Papers on Economic Activity* 1 (1995): 1-118.

Sinn, Stefan. "Saving-Investment Correlations and Capital Mobility: On the Evidence from Annual Data." *Economic Journal* 102 (September 1992): 1162-1170.

Trefler, Daniel. *The Long and Short of the Canada-U.S. Free Trade Agreement.* Perspectives on North American Free Trade Series, No. 6. Ottawa: Industry Canada, 1999.

Wei, Shang-Jin. *Intra-national versus International Trade: How Stubborn Are Nations in Global Integration?* NBER Working Paper No. 5531. Cambridge (Mass.): National Bureau of Economic Research, 1996.

Wolf, Holger. "Intranational Home Bias in Trade." *Review of Economics and Statistics* 82, 4 (2000): 555-563.

Worms, Jean-Pierre. "Old and New Civic and Social Ties in France." In *Democracies in Flux.* Edited by Robert Putnam. New York: Oxford University Press, 2002, pp. 137-188.

Comment

James E. Anderson
Boston College and National Bureau of Economic Research

JOHN HELLIWELL'S PAPER SURVEYS AND COMMENTS on a wide variety of border effect literature. I will pass over much of this to concentrate on his regression analysis of trade flows and particularly on methodological arguments he joins with two recent papers of mine. These comments are part of a continuing conversation in both a narrow and a broad sense. In the narrow sense, the conversation began with Helliwell's first draft, delivered to the conference. In reaction, he substantially changed his paper, so my comments necessarily must change. In the broad sense, Helliwell's work and my own are part of the large recent and continuing research program into the shape and determinants of trade costs. We have benefited from each other's work and the work of many others in this program. Some of Helliwell's survey covers ground I have surveyed elsewhere (Anderson and van Wincoop, 2003b) with somewhat different emphasis and conclusions.

Part of the conversation is another iteration of an old methodological debate between structuralism and inductionism. All participants in the research program seek to infer trade costs from data. Which approach yields more useful progress is open to debate, but I stand with the structuralists while Helliwell stands with the inductionists. The shortcoming of the former is that many plausible insights are very difficult to embed in a feasible structural econometric model. So much energy is spent on the development of theory that discovery of suggestive patterns in the data is secondary, and econometric model specifications often are not tested against sufficiently broad alternatives for their fit to be convincing. The inductive approach reverses the priority. The shortcoming of the latter is that seemingly plausible econometric models can often implicitly embed very implausible or even impossible economic structures (implicit theorizing in Leontief's famous criticism). The history of the border effect literature and the Anderson *vs.* Helliwell part of it on display here illustrates both the usefulness of structural methods and the usefulness of inductive methods to turn up puzzling anomalies and regularities in the data ahead of their satisfactory explanation.

HELLIWELL ON A&VW

HELLIWELL ARGUES THAT ANDERSON AND VAN WINCOOP'S (2003a) work is inconsistent with the data, hence unreliable for policy conclusions. His conclusion is to move to theoretical regression models which do not support general-equilibrium comparative statics or welfare analysis. My alternative is to move to methodologically appropriate refinements of A&vW. I am sure that this will yield border effects that differ quantitatively from those we report, but that the qualitative conclusions will be robust.

Let me start with the important anomaly Helliwell points to. While all theories are false, as Ed Leamer says, some degree of inaccuracy is tolerable. Helliwell argues that the experience of the FTA in Canada falsifies our model's predictions because Canada-U.S. trade rose while within-Canada trade did not change much. We did not attempt to calculate an FTA experiment, but presumably if we had, Helliwell reasons that we would have reproduced the large bilateral trade changes actually observed, and found a larger than credible change in internal trade flows. We cannot straightforwardly draw such an inference from the exercises of A&vW because an FTA is preferential (frictions are reduced with members only) and also partial (not all frictions are removed). Nevertheless, since the two-country version of our model is based on treating Canada and the United States as if they were the only two countries in the world, where border removal is equivalent to frictionless trade, it is pretty clear that Helliwell's objection will apply to a general-equilibrium comparative statics FTA analysis: internal trade flow changes will look excessive in light of the history of NAFTA. Of course, the actual historical data are driven by other changes that are not being controlled for in the simple comparative statics experiments described, which could give rise to the pattern seen while maintaining consistency with the model. A full analysis should consider this. In the end, the implications for internal trade will probably be too large an anomaly to ignore.

The methodologically appropriate line of response to this finding is to extend the model in some parsimonious way. I suggest extension to incorporate substitution between traded and nontraded goods. Adding this Salter Swan dimension of the simple exchange model gains a big increase in realism while maintaining tractability. Note that with much of GDP being nontraded, the impact of external trade barrier changes on intra-national trade is damped by the presence of the nontraded good which is an inferior substitute for a region's exportables than are other traded goods. The extended model with a nontraded good in each region can allow for less response in intra-national activity than the simple model allows for. I have done this in unpublished notes. The modeling effort may benefit from a further extension to goods which are intra-nationally, but not internationally, traded. This I have not done, but it may be tractable and would make for an interesting development. The sequence of posing a simple model, finding anomaly and then extending the model is normal science.

My basic suggestion to allow for nontraded goods was actually in my 1979 paper. I suggested interpreting deviations of income elasticities from one along with the non-zero population elasticities as elements of a reduced-form function representing the trade expenditure share, with the reduced form embedding nontraded goods market clearance. The profession chose to ignore this suggestion, perhaps for good reasons. I speculate that a structural approach may pay off here.

HOME BIAS VS. BORDER BARRIERS

HELLIWELL SUGGESTS THAT THE MODEL BE EXTENDED to allow for home bias in tastes as well as border barriers. The problem is that these are not separately identifiable in the CES (constant elasticity of substitution) preferences/technology model which yields the gravity equation under Anderson's derivation. Some careful thinking about structure and imaginative use of data may reveal a way to disentangle the two.

Helliwell's interpretation is that border effects represent the effects of cultural affinity and social networks, a plausible statement which incorporates both trade costs and elements of taste differences. My methodological preference, reflected in the emphasis of my work on interpreting the border effect as a cost, is to use differences in tastes or technology only as a last resort. I suspect that, at the end of the quest, we may find that different tastes matter, but regularities in many investigators' measures of implicit trade costs suggest that border effects incorporate significant cost elements. See Anderson and van Wincoop (2003b) for a full development.

Helliwell concludes from his examination of the FTA period not only that the A&vW model is rejected (which I accept, but with different conclusions as to the next step, as noted above), but also that the taste differences explanation of border effects is indicated. I can not make sense of this, because taste changes that have driven the very large international trade changes observed since the FTA should equally drive counterfactual changes in interprovincial trade, at least if these changes are constrained to operate in the CES framework yielding the gravity equation. Indeed, this point is obvious in the observational equivalence of taste differences and border barriers in the theoretical model. I guess what Helliwell has in mind is a departure from the structural model — A&vW is rejected, so some non-structural model possibly reflecting taste differences which change after the FTA can 'explain' the pattern of the data.

Helliwell buttresses his taste differences argument by citing Balistreri and Hillberry's observation that the distance elasticity and border effects in A&vW yield cost differences too large to be explained by transport costs and conventional border barriers. My conclusion on Balistreri and Hillberry is that non conventional elements of trade costs (information, insecurity of contract and so forth) seem to be very large. See Anderson and van Wincoop (2003b) for more discussion.

WELFARE ANALYSIS

IN THE A&vW BROOKINGS STUDY (2002), we show that the gravity model is a complete computable general equilibrium model (CGE). We take full advantage of this to conduct a number of welfare evaluations of various types of border barrier removals. We were reasonably up front about the limitations of these experiments: no role for specialization is allowed, no dynamics of trade liberalization is admitted, and the non-rent border barriers are treated as completely exogenous resource costs following the iceberg trade-costs tradition. Objections to each of these simplifications are quite legitimate and were admitted by us already in the Brookings study.

Helliwell labels the gravity model based on the CES preferences a "love-of-variety" approach. This is a label based on the monopolistic competition application of the CES preferences, a label which emphasizes the potential for trade to expand the number of goods consumed. Helliwell questions the usefulness of the love-of-variety model in welfare analysis, citing psychological studies showing that increases in options can initially reduce some measure of well-being, presumably due to the processing cost of new information. For comparative statics experiments where new goods enter trade, there may be something in this critique. It resonates with the fixed cost explanation of why some bilateral trade flows are absent while suggesting that fixed costs are present for both seller and buyer. But in the applications of Anderson and van Wincoop, the focus is entirely on comparative statics, which change the magnitude of existing trade flows. The welfare analysis here is a completely conventional analysis of the exchange gain from trade and has nothing whatever to say about gains from variety.

The value of our results, I think, is to point to potential large gains still to be earned from economic integration. The list of qualifications above include some that make this potential a lower bound (no specialization, no dynamic gains) and some that make it an upper bound (border removal entails costs as well as benefits, some part of the border effect may be due to taste differences which are immutable). Seeing the size of the stakes implied by the simple gravity model is nevertheless quite interesting in light of the rather small stakes implied by conventional CGE models. Secondarily, I found it surprising in our NAFTA exercise to see that terms-of-trade effects are so powerful in the model. I think there may be a valuable lesson of some generality here.

WHERE ARE WE NOW? WHERE ARE WE GOING?

DESPITE SEVEN YEARS OF SUBSEQUENT ANALYSIS, we are still unsure about how large border barriers are and what their welfare significance is. We know that border barriers are much less than appears to be suggested by McCallum's study. We have made progress in how to model trade resistance and how to estimate gravity models. We have clues from empirical studies as to how the gravity model should be improved. We are able to draw at least simple welfare conclusions based on the gravity model.

I conjecture that the main reasons for border effects come under the heading of insecurity on the one hand, and information on the other hand. In theoretical work, I have been building models of trade and insecurity which endogenize the quality of institutions to support trade, while James Rauch and Vitor Trindade (forthcoming) have modeled trade with asymmetric information. These models at least start on the road to a deeper understanding of the welfare significance of border effects, which appear as exogenous resistance in the border literature. An interesting aspect of these models is that there can be knock-on effects of liberalization, as a fall in trade costs of one type induces reductions in other costs as institutions improve. Nevertheless, I am uneasy about this line of research leading to an understanding of the Canadian border effect. It seems to eat a large volume of trade (40 percent according to the A&vW calculations in the *American Economic Review* study), and it is hard to believe that insecurity and asymmetric information bite so hard on this border.

Conventional CGE models did a very poor job of predicting the actual changes in trade flow observed after NAFTA. This is consistent with the folklore about CGE models that they perform very poorly 'out of sample'. I found it quite interesting that our rather ad hoc NAFTA exercise in the Brookings study was able to come much closer to the changes seen in the bilateral trade of NAFTA partners in the 1990s. This is consistent with the goodness-of-fit and stability of the gravity model of course, but NAFTA presents a much sterner test because it is a large parametric change imposed on a model which, until our efforts to take the theory seriously, was taken only as an empirical regularity in reduced form. I think that small scale CGE models in the future may benefit from attempting to adapt to the empirical approach of the gravity model.

We have an exciting prospect before us as economic scientists. The border effect literature and its offshoots inform us that the profession's understanding of how markets actually work over space is quite deficient, both qualitatively and quantitatively. We have the tools to make progress.

BIBLIOGRAPHY

Anderson, James E. "A Theoretical Foundation for the Gravity Equation." *American Economic Review* 69, 1 (1979): 106-116.

Anderson, James E., and Eric van Wincoop. "Borders, Trade and Welfare." In *Brookings Trade Policy Forum 2001*. Edited by Dani Rodrik and Susan Collins, Washington (D.C.): Brookings Institution, 2002.

———. "Gravity with Gravitas: A Solution to the Border Puzzle." *American Economic Review* 93, 1 (2003a): 170-192. Revised version of NBER Working Paper No. 8079.

———. "Trade Costs." Survey draft under preparation for the *Journal of Economic Literature*, 2003b.

Rauch, James E., and Vitor Trindade. "Information, International Substitutability, and Globalization." *American Economic Review* (June 2003).

Serge Coulombe
University of Ottawa

2

Border Effects and North American Economic Integration: Where Are We Now?

F 15
F 14
R 12

ABSTRACT

IN THE FIRST PART OF THE STUDY, we review and discuss the recent evolution of the literature on border effects in light of Anderson and van Wincoop's (2001) proposed solution to the border puzzle. We argue that these authors have taken a critical step forward regarding the information contained in border effect estimates. In the second part of the study, we estimate border effects for Canada and the ten provinces with a sample spanning the years 1981-2001. For most provinces and for Canada as a whole, the border effect on goods trade appears to have been declining steadily over the 1981-2000 period.

INTRODUCTION

WITH GLOBALIZATION and the gradual elimination of trade barriers, especially among trading blocs of industrialized countries, the phlegmatic observer might have been tempted to anticipate the emergence of a borderless world. The Canada-U.S. situation might even have been at the top of a list of case studies documenting this forecast. The two economies share many institutional, political, social, and cultural features. Goods and capital should flow freely across this border, a large part of which appears to be an artificial straight line drawn over the 49th parallel by an unimaginative geographer.

This is basically why McCallum's 1995 study — stating that national borders *do* matter *a lot* — drew so much attention from economists and policy makers. That result was very surprising and, for some, embarrassing. Some saw it as an economic puzzle that needed solving (Obstfeld and Rogoff, 2000;

Grossman, 1998). Others took that conclusion very seriously and put in a lot of productive effort to illustrate its robustness and to document and analyze its policy implications (Helliwell, 1998).

The purpose of this study is twofold. First, we propose to look at the recent evolution of the literature on the border effect from the viewpoint of an outsider, a Canadian regional economist. We will argue that the recent trend of research in this area (Brown, 2003; Brown and Anderson, 2002; and particularly Anderson and van Wincoop, 2001) is likely to change the direction of the economic and policy debate on the subject. Recent studies use a newly released U.S. interstate trade database that unveils, in our view, a crucial new stylized fact: the effect of the Canada-U.S. border is a magnitude larger when measured with interprovincial trade data than with interstate trade data. The theoretical explanation for this stylized fact proposed by Anderson and van Wincoop (2001) is a decisive step toward solving the border effect puzzle. Using the theoretical model of resistance to trade developed by Anderson in 1979,[1] Anderson and van Wincoop explain that most of the differences in border effect estimates calculated from the two databases can be attributed to the fact that the Canadian economy is considerably smaller than the U.S. economy [as measured by the gross domestic product (GDP)]. We will show, however, that this explanation of the border puzzle is incomplete because it does not incorporate the concepts of distance and density. As Brown (2003) phrased it, spatial structure matters. Second, we make use of well-known aggregate provincial data on trade flows to indirectly estimate Canadian border effects for the 1981-2000 period. Border effects are usually estimated using (more or less compatible) detailed North American regional data, but only for the 1988-96 period. Extending the period under study gives new insight into the time-trend evolution of Canadian border effects. For most provinces and for Canada as a whole, the border effect on goods trade appears to have been declining over the entire 1981-2000 period. This finding is likely to challenge the common wisdom (Helliwell, 1998) that the decline of the border effect in the 1990s is observed only in the period following the introduction of the Free Trade Agreement (FTA) and that border effects have been stable ever since. This is not the case, however, for the border effects on services trade for which the FTA story appears to adequately capture time-series evidence.

In the second section, we briefly synthesize the origin and meaning of the border effect, starting from the gravity model of trade. In the third section, we analyze recent contributions that use the new interstate trade data and we closely examine the critical theoretical analysis proposed by Anderson and van Wincoop (2001). In the next section, we show how and why these authors' focus on economic size is a shortcut that does not take into account other important factors such as distance and density. Brown (2003) has recognized the possible role of distance and density (the spatial structure) in explaining the differences in border effect estimates derived from interprovincial trade data and from interstate trade data. In the fifth section, we revisit two dominant interpretations of the border effect in the light of the recent analysis. The sixth section contains our time-series extension on Canadian border effects for goods and for services. We conclude with a policy discussion in the final section.

THE BORDER EFFECT STORY

THE GRAVITY EQUATION

THE STARTING POINT FOR THE BORDER EFFECT DISCUSSION is the gravity equation, which has long been known for its strong fit with cross-country international trade data (Tinbergen, 1962; Linneman, 1966). The simple form of the gravity equation relates trade between two countries i and j to the product of the GDP (Y) of both countries, divided by the distance between the two. More specifically, in the following gravity equation,

$$(1) \qquad trade(ij) = \frac{A Y(i)^b Y(j)^c}{dist(ij)^d},$$

b and c are the income elasticities of trade and d is the distance elasticity. Other variables, including the participation in trade blocs, might enter the gravity equation in a multiplicative way through parameter A. Equation (1) is usually tested with a multiplicative error term in the following linear logarithmic form:

$$(2) \qquad \ln trade(ij) = a + b \ln Y_i + c \ln Y_j - d \ln dist_{ij} + \varepsilon_{ij}.$$

The gravity relation was originally an empirical regularity, before it became an economic model. Anderson (1979) proposed a theoretical foundation for the gravity relation based on goods differenced by place of origin, a CES (constant elasticity of substitution) utility function, and distance being a proxy for transportation costs. Other theoretical frameworks were developed for gravity in the 1980s, notably works by Bergstrand (1985) and Helpman (1984).

The empirical regularity was slowly becoming the gravity model but it was not yet famous. It was the work of a Canadian economist, using newly released, unique Canadian regional trade data, that put the gravity model in the headlines in 1995. McCallum (1995) used the gravity model to compare interprovincial trade data with province-state trade data. He asked the question: Do borders matter? His answer was: Yes.

McCallum's Border Effect

THE CENTRAL FINDING OF MCCALLUM'S FAMOUS STUDY is that testing regression equation (2) with interprovincial trade data and province-state trade data for the year 1988 clearly underpredicts interprovincial trade by a substantial multiplicative factor. He estimated the following gravity equation:

$$(3) \qquad \ln trade(ij) = a + b \ln Y_i + c \ln Y_j - d \ln dist_{ij} + e\, DUMMY_{ij} + \varepsilon_{ij},$$

where the dummy variable takes the value 1 for interprovincial trade and the value 0 for province-state trade. The point estimate of parameter e was around 3 and McCallum interpreted this as:

> Other things equal, trade between two provinces is more than 20 times larger than trade between a province and a state [exp(3.09) = 22]. (p. 616)

The original Canadian data were the only ones for which the effect of borders on trade could be tested directly, and only data for the year 1988 (pre-FTA) were available at the time. McCallum anticipated correctly at the end of his study that the FTA and NAFTA (North American Free Trade Agreement) would lead to a radical shift in regional and international trade patterns. The uniqueness of Canadian trade data made replication of McCallum's findings with other detailed data banks impossible at the time. Nevertheless, McCallum concluded his famous study with a statement that suggests his results could be extended to borders in general:

> The fact that even the relatively innocuous Canada-U.S. border continues to have a decisive effect on continental trade patterns suggests that national borders in general continue to matter. (p. 622)

The border effect was born.

Further Estimates of McCallum's Border Effects

JOHN HELLIWELL TOOK MCCALLUM'S RESULT very seriously and subsequently produced a series of studies documenting, analyzing, and extending the border effect story of Canada-U.S. trade (Helliwell and McCallum, 1995; Helliwell, 1996, 1998). Overall, Helliwell's research illustrates the robustness of McCallum's finding, but it highlights the fact that the border effect tended to decrease rapidly following the FTA. Nevertheless, the parameter $\exp(e)$ in regression equation (3), using Statistics Canada data banks on interprovincial trade and province-state trade, remains large. There is no trick, no cheating.

A good part of Helliwell's contribution is methodological. He showed (1998) that using better data from a more accurate reconciliation of inter-provincial and international trade data — the trade data from two different Statistics Canada data banks, data that are available only for years after 1990 — decreased the McCallum border effect by 20 percent (from 25.3 to 19.5). Furthermore, he showed that, between 1990 and 1996, the border effect dropped from 19.5 to 11.9, with most of the decrease occurring prior to 1994. He attributed this decrease to the FTA. Using gravity equations, he estimated border effects for provinces, industries, imports and exports. He produced a rough estimate of the border effect for trade in services. The border effect for services was much more significant than for goods, ranging from 42 to 29 in the 1988-96 period. He used a remoteness measure to be more consistent with Anderson's (1979) model, but this variable does not have much effect on the point estimate of parameter e.

MEASURES OF THE BORDER EFFECT USING OTHER DATA BANKS

AS WAS POINTED OUT ABOVE, until the very recent development of interstate trade data, Canadian provincial data were the only real intranational trade data with which a McCallum-type border effect could be estimated. Furthermore, province-state trade data exist only since 1988.

However, there were attempts to estimate the border effect using other data banks for developed countries with rough estimates of distances for in-tranational trade. The usual rule followed to proxy internal distance in studies was proposed by Wei (1996). Internal trade distance for a given country is assumed to be one fourth of the distance between the capital of the country and the nearest capital of another country. Wei's estimate of the border effect for OECD countries using this rather rough ad hoc estimate of distance was considerably smaller (just over 2) than McCallum's estimate. Helliwell (1998) reports similar findings, with an estimated border effect of 5.6 for OECD countries sharing the same language compared to a 15.2 estimate for the inter-provincial/province-state trade for the year 1992. Helliwell (1998) shows that the border effect estimates for the OECD countries were very sensitive to the (ad hoc) definition of internal distance. He then concludes:

> In the meantime, it is probably appropriate to place more weight on the evidence from the province-state trade flows, with the results for the OECD countries being taken to represent the lower end of the likely range. (p. 62)

As for McCallum (1995), Helliwell assumes implicitly that a McCallum-type border effect estimated using the ratio of interprovincial trade to Canada-U.S. states trade was an observable phenomenon of a magnitude that could apply to border effects between countries. It was then assumed that the magnitude of border effects, in general, could be approximated by the point estimate of $\exp(e)$ in the regression equation (3) using a McCallum-type data bank. This point of view, however, is likely to change with the recent studies using interstate trade data (Brown, 2003; Brown and Anderson, 2002; Anderson and van Wincoop, 2001).

WHAT DOES THE PARAMETER EXP(E) MEASURE?

BEFORE GOING FURTHER, it is important to describe exactly what is the McCallum-type border effect [parameter $\exp(e)$]. What exactly does the high value measure? To this end, we return to the gravity equation (1) in its multiplicative form and process it in a non-formal way to get a simple stylized result. With a border effect like the one modelled in equation (3), equation (1) becomes:

$$(4) \qquad trade(ij) = \frac{AY(i)^b Y(j)^c \exp(e \bullet DUMMY)}{dist(ij)^d}.$$

To simplify the discussion, assume we are estimating the border effect for only one province, say, Quebec (as in Helliwell, 1996), which is province q. In this example, i takes the value q for Quebec and j is either p for the other nine provinces or s for the U.S. states. Using solutions to equation (4) for which the DUMMY takes the value 1 for Quebec-province (qp) trade and the value 0 for Quebec-state (qs) trade (for the 30 largest states used in McCallum's analysis), we get the following expression after manipulations:

$$(5) \qquad \exp(e) = \sum_{p=1}^{9} \frac{\dfrac{trade(qp) \bullet dist(qp)^d}{Y(p)^b}}{\displaystyle\sum_{s=1}^{30} \frac{trade(qs) \bullet dist(qs)^d}{Y(s)^c}}.$$

McCallum's border effect estimate of 22, from his study published in the *American Economic Review* (1995), is a linear least-squares estimation using cross-sectional data. The border effect parameter is the ratio of interprovincial *weighted* trade to international *weighted* trade. The trade between Quebec (or all other Canadian provinces in the general case) and its trading partners is weighted by distance (multiplied) and GDP (divided). The typical point estimate of the distance parameter is 1.4 and the parameter estimates for GDP elasticity are often very close to unity. Some studies (such as Anderson and van Wincoop, 2001), in their replication of the McCallum border effect parameter estimate for the year 1993, show that imposing income elasticities equal to unity, as suggested by Anderson's gravity model, does not change much the estimated value of exp(e).

The bottom line here is: What is really meant by "after controlling for scale and distance" is that interprovincial trade is 16.4 times more important than province-state trade. The number 16.4 is a ratio of weighted trade. Given the multiplicative form of the gravity model, in border effect estimates, trade is weighted by the reverse of GDP and multiplied by distance exponent 1.4. In the rest of this study, we will use the term "weighted trade" to indicate that we are not talking about trade in its usual sense. Precision is needed in the following discussion of Anderson and van Wincoop's (2001) study since the exact understanding of their contribution, and its limits, is related to the notion of weighted trade.

SIZE AND RESISTANCE TO TRADE: A PROPOSED SOLUTION TO THE BORDER PUZZLE

WE NOW LOOK AT RECENT CONTRIBUTIONS to the border effect literature and focus on the key issues related to this topic in the rest of the study. We believe that these issues are not related to the estimation of exp(e), but instead to the interpretation of the result. Discussion of the significance of the border effect in the Canadian context was fundamentally changed following the publication of Anderson and van Wincoop's (2001) NBER Working Paper. To directly outline the issues raised in this important study, let us just quote from its abstract:

> McCallum's spectacular headline number is the result of omitted variable bias and the small size of the Canadian economy.

Two major points are made in their study: the size effect and the omitted variable bias. Both could be addressed separately even if, as we will show later, they are partly related. But before we get to them, we will briefly discuss a key stylized fact revealed in recent contributions to the literature, a fact intrinsically related to Anderson and van Wincoop's important analysis.

THE CANADA-U.S. BORDER EFFECT IS NOT SYMMETRIC

THREE RECENT STUDIES ON THE BORDER EFFECT (Anderson and van Wincoop, 2001; Brown 2003; Brown and Anderson, 2002) have prepared the ground for a new interpretation of the border effect. The border effect is a magnitude smaller (between six and twelve times) when measured as the ratio of interstate to U.S. cross-border weighted trade rather than using McCallum's method, which is the ratio of interprovincial weighted trade to Canadian cross-border weighted trade. In itself, this point is very important since it shows that the border does not have an equal effect on all countries in terms of weighted trade. The border matters much more — an order of magnitude more — for Canadian weighted trade patterns than for U.S. weighted trade patterns.

Interestingly, Brown (2003) and Brown and Anderson (2002) used a disaggregated database by sector, unlike Anderson and van Wincoop (2001), and arrived at very comparable results. Their econometric methodology is also markedly different since they control for wages, productivity, and spatial factors in estimating the gravity equation. Overall, the result of a non-symmetrical border effect that emerges from the new interstate trade data appears very robust and should now be considered a stylized fact.

Following McCallum's conclusion in his 1995 study, many have suggested that McCallum's border effect estimate was the only reliable estimate of a general phenomenon (the importance of a country's borders for trade). The three recent studies demonstrate that the McCallum-type border effect estimates were extremely sensitive to whether one compared international weighted trade to *interprovincial* or to *interstate* weighted trade in a gravity equation. This finding has to be explained. Anderson and van Wincoop (2001) have taken a decisive step in this direction.

THE SIZE EFFECT

THE PARADOX REVEALED BY ESTIMATING THE BORDER EFFECT with interstate trade data is the starting point of Anderson and van Wincoop's analysis. Using a McCallum gravity equation with 1993 data from various sources (for interprovincial trade, state-province trade, and interstate trade), they estimate a McCallum-type border effect of 16.4 for Canadian interprovincial trade and a McCallum-type border effect of only 1.6 for U.S. states trade. Anderson and van Wincoop focus on this point and claim to have a very simple and convincing explanation for the apparent paradox. The large numbers found by McCallum and in subsequent studies, and the small number found for the border effect based on U.S. states data, follow mainly from the fact that the Canadian economy is small compared to the U.S. economy. The explanation of the size effect in Anderson and van Wincoop (2001) is set in the framework of an

Anderson-type (1979) theoretical gravity model. We will return to the theoretical aspect of the gravity model developed in Anderson and van Wincoop's study when discussing the omitted variable bias problem since the relevance of the size effect is general and not specific to a given theoretical framework.

The best way to explain the size effect is to use the example put forward in Anderson and van Wincoop (2001). Let us suppose the world economy consists of two countries, a large one with 100 regions (states), and a small one with only two regions (provinces). Distance does not matter in this example as it does not matter in the formal demonstration of the size effect in the framework of Anderson and van Wincoop's theoretical model. Let us assume also an endowment economy of regions of equal economic size. Initially, there is no trade barrier between the two countries and all regions trade one (divisible) unit of goods with each other. This assumption is equivalent to weighting trade by size with an elasticity of one as in the gravity model, since the ratio of intranational to international trade is proportional to economic size. Now, suppose that a small trade barrier is imposed, which reduces trade between the two countries by 20 percent. The effect of this shock is much larger for the provinces of the small economy than for the states of the large economy. Province 1 in the small economy sees its exports to the large country decrease by twenty units. Under the pure diversion hypothesis, province 1 will now sell ten more units of goods to itself and ten more to the other province. Interregional trade in the small country is multiplied by a factor of 11 whereas it is multiplied by only 1.004 in the large country. If you analyze the new situation with McCallum's border-gravity model, you find that interprovincial trade, after adjustment for size, is 13.75 times larger than international trade, whereas interstate trade is only 1.255 larger than international trade.

Thus, even a modest trade barrier between a small country and a large one could generate a substantial border effect as measured by the ratio of interprovincial to international trade in a McCallum exercise where trade is weighted with size. Anderson and van Wincoop's solution to the border puzzle might be summarized by the following question and answer: Do national borders matter? Yes, but much more for a small country than for a large one. For a small country, the border increases trading costs with most of its trading partners. This is not the case for a large economy like the United States, for which the border does not increase the cost of interstate trade.

The size effect of the Canada-U.S. case study is even more convincing when used in conjunction with the gravity model. Let us assume that trade is proportional to GDP and inversely proportional to distance. Given that North America is far from other wealthy regions of the world (Europe and Japan), a substantial proportion of state and provincial potential trade opportunities (weighted by size and distance) are situated in North America. Even a modest trade barrier such as one associated with a currency transaction cost or an exchange rate risk premium can potentially generate a substantial McCallum border effect, measured as the ratio of interprovincial to international weighted trade. The U.S. economy represents a very substantial proportion of trading opportunities for any single Canadian province and there is a border between them. This is not the case for U.S. states for which the large majority of trading opportunities are found among neighbouring states.

THE OMITTED VARIABLE BIAS PROBLEM

ANDERSON'S 1979 STUDY published in the *American Economic Review* is often cited as one of the theoretical building blocks of the gravity model. Not surprisingly, Anderson and van Wincoop's (2001) analysis employs a theoretical framework derived from Anderson's previous work. The two building blocks of Anderson and van Wincoop (2001) are the same as in Anderson (1979): (1) goods are differentiated by place of origin; and (2) homothetic preferences are approximated by a CES utility function. The key theoretical aspect of the study is that it breaks down trade resistance between regions i and j into three components: (1) the bilateral trade barrier between regions i and j; (2) the multilateral resistance to trade of a given region i with all regions i; and (3) j's multilateral resistance to trade. A region's multilateral resistance to trade is a function of the distance from its potential trading partners *and* of trade barriers. The central result of Anderson and van Wincoop's gravity model is that *size-adjusted* trade between two economies is a function of the ratio of the bilateral trade resistance between the two economies and the product of their multilateral trade resistance.

Compared with a borderless trading world, the Canada-U.S. border increases the three components of trade resistance for provinces and states. The effect of the border on the ratio of interprovincial trade to international trade is computed by Anderson and van Wincoop in a multi-step exercise and is a function of the changes in multilateral resistance terms. This "theoretically consistent estimate" of the border effect is calculated at 10.7. It is possible for Anderson and van Wincoop to compute a "McCallum parameter implied by theory," which is a function of the ratio (not the change) of the multilateral resistance terms. This parameter is estimated at 14.8. According to Anderson and van Wincoop, McCallum-type estimations of the border effect for Canada based on the ratio of interprovincial trade to the ratio of international trade overestimate the border effect by 38 percent due to the omitted variable bias. The omitted variables are the multilateral resistance terms, which are not modelled in a McCallum gravity regression.

It is important to note that the bias translates into an overestimation of the border effect because the multilateral resistance term is higher for Canadian provinces than for U.S. states. This is not surprising because the Canada-U.S. border increases the multilateral resistance of Canadian provinces much more than for U.S. states because of the size effect, as discussed earlier. Conversely, Anderson and van Wincoop show that a McCallum-type regression estimating the border effect from the ratio of interstate trade to (U.S.) international trade underestimates the true border effect. They find that the theoretically consistent estimate of the border effect is 2.24, compared to a McCallum parameter value of 1.63.

REFLECTIONS ON LOCATION IN ANDERSON AND VAN WINCOOP'S ANALYSIS

INTERESTINGLY, ANDERSON AND VAN WINCOOP REPORT that a McCallum-type regression will estimate a positive border effect for the ratio of interprovincial weighted trade to (Canadian) international weighted trade even in a borderless world. According to them, it is only because of distance that the borderless estimate of multilateral resistance is, on average, higher for Canadian provinces than for U.S. states. This has nothing to do with the (economic) size effect but is instead related to geographic location. Canadian provinces are, on average, further from their (weighted) potential trading partners than U.S. states because of the provinces' non-central location. Canada is not only a small country compared to the United States; it is located on the periphery of the North American economy.

To illustrate the impact of location on multilateral resistance and standard border effect estimates, consider the following alternative to the real world. Suppose that the Canadian economy lies between the United States and the European Union (EU) economies, at the same distance from each. Suppose again that trade flows among the three economies (and their regions) follow the law of a gravity model with national border effect. In Anderson and van Wincoop's framework, a McCallum-type estimate of the Canada-U.S. border effect would be much smaller than the usual value of 16. Why? Because Canada's multilateral resistance would be relatively smaller than it is in reality because Canada would be closer to Europe. In this hypothetical world, the effect of the U.S. border on Canadian potential trade opportunities is smaller than in the real world because the Canada-U.S. border does not increase trade barriers between Canadian regions and their EU neighbours. The United States' multilateral resistance to trade would be smaller as well. However, the difference would be more important for Canada because its economy is smaller than that of the United States and because Canada is located, in this hypothetical world, between the United States and the European Union.

Given that McCallum border effect estimates are proportional to the ratio of multilateral resistance in Anderson and van Wincoop's theoretical analysis, the border effect estimates might be much smaller in the hypothetical world. This point illustrates another aspect of Anderson and van Wincoop's omitted variable bias.

In summary, Anderson and van Wincoop's contribution is likely to change the dominant view of the interpretation and significance of the border effect. The study shows that the effect of the border on weighted trade ratios between two countries is not symmetric. The analysis highlights the role of multilateral resistance and helps to explain why the weighted ratio of inter-provincial trade to Canada-U.S. trade is so high compared to the weighted ratio of interstate trade to international trade. As we will see in the next section, however, the analysis pertaining to the relative size of the two economies does not take into consideration the role of distance and location. These two factors are at the centre of the omitted variable bias analysis but they should also be part of the size effect analysis.

What Ultimately Matters? Size and Density

ANDERSON AND VAN WINCOOP EMPHASIZE the importance of (economic) size for the effect of trade barriers on multilateral resistance. This is the first important contribution of their study, the second being the econometric analysis and estimation of the omitted variable bias. However, we think that their analysis is incomplete when it comes to the theoretical relationship between economic size and weighted (by size and distance) trade flows. It follows that the link they make between the McCallum headline number and the small size of the Canadian economy might be somewhat misleading. This is because Anderson and van Wincoop do not include distance when deriving their results on size. But we will show that distance does matter, especially in a gravity model. When coupling (economic) size with distance, we illustrate that economic density (economic size divided by distance) is another determinant of the McCallum headline number (along with the omitted variable bias).

Could Anderson and van Wincoop's Theoretical Analysis of Size Be Transposed to a Gravity Model?

IN THEIR DEMONSTRATION OF THE EFFECT OF TRADE BARRIERS on size-adjusted trade between large and small countries, Anderson and van Wincoop (2001, pp. 11-12) do not take distance into account. Distance enters the analysis only on page 12 in equation (16). They are well aware of it since the three implications of their section 3 analysis are formulated in terms of the relationship between trade barriers and *size-adjusted trade*. Prior to the formal introduction of distance — in equations (12) to (15) — they isolate the effect of changing trade barriers t across all countries on intranational and international trade flows as a function of the economic size of countries. For example, the structure of their equation (15), on page 11, is:

$$d(\text{interprovincial}(ii)/\text{international}(ij) \text{ weighted trade ratio}) =$$
$$F[\text{economic size}(ij)] \bullet dt \,,$$

where dt is the differential of trade barriers. This comparative exercise is based on the assumption that the borderless initial equilibrium implies $t = 1$ for all economies and that the effect of the increase in trade barriers is dt for all economies. This crucial assumption is done just prior to the set-up of equation (16).

Generally speaking, *this analysis could not be directly transposed to a gravity model in which trade barrier is a function of distance.* This clearly follows from Anderson and van Wincoop's analysis, since in the following equation (16), as they put it,

> We follow other authors in hypothesizing that t_{ij} is a loglinear function of observables: bilateral distance and whether there is an international border between i and j:

$$t_{ij} = b_{ij} \, D_{ij}^{\rho}.$$

Consequently, taken in a gravity model, the dt in equations (12) to (15) should be proportional to the distance factor D_{ij}^{ρ}. Here, ρ is the distance parameter of equation (3). In a complete analysis, both internal distance and external distance would appear in the results linking trade ratios to economic size. Therefore, their analysis is based on the special assumption that internal and external distances are the same for a small and a large economy! This is valid only in a gravity model under the assumption that economic density is proportional to economic size.

MORE DETAIL ON THE McCALLUM HEADLINE NUMBER

EVEN IF CANADA IS A SMALL COUNTRY compared to the United States from the standpoint of population and GDP, typical distances for Canadian interprovincial trade are rather large and of the same order of magnitude as typical distances for Canada-U.S. trade. As shown by Helliwell (1998, p. 18), the mean distance between Canadian provinces is 7 percent greater than between provinces and U.S. states. Wei (1996) and Helliwell (1998) also show that a standard estimate of the border effect is very sensitive to the measure of internal distance.

Broadly speaking, with a distance elasticity d in equation (3) close to 1, the McCallum-type border effect is proportional to the measure of internal distance for a given country.

Now, consider the following hypothetical experiment. Suppose that the internal distance in Canada, compared to the United States, becomes proportional to the Canada-U.S. GDP ratio; that internal distance does not change within the United States; and that the distance for province-state trade does not change. In other words, economic density (GDP/internal distance) is the same within Canada and the United States. Since internal distance in Canada is cut by a factor of 10, a McCallum-type border effect estimate based on weighted interprovincial trade in this hypothetical case would be highly comparable to an estimate based on weighted interstate trade.

In the preceding example, economic density is the same in the two countries. To illustrate this concept, let us compare the following alternative versions of a two-country world. In the first case, the world consists of the United States and Canada; in the second, the world consists of the United States and Belgium. The typical distance between Canada and Belgium on the one side, and the United States on the other side, is the same. The economic size of the U.S. economy is ten times the size of the Canadian and Belgium economies. The geographic size of Canada equals the size of the United States and is ten times larger than Belgium. To put it another way, Belgium and the United States have identical economic densities whereas Canada's density is ten times smaller. What would be the McCallum-type border effect estimates based on ratios of intranational weighted trade data for Canada and Belgium to international weighted trade with the United States in these two versions of the world? The answer will depend on numerous things, but one of the key determinants of the relative border effect estimates for Canada and Belgium would be the point estimate of the distance parameter in equation (3). If the point estimate is zero, both border effects would be of the same order of magnitude. But if the point estimate is around 1, the border effect would be a magnitude larger for Canada than for Belgium (such as 16 to 1.6). This is because internal trade and external trade are weighted by distance in a McCallum-type border effect estimate. With a point estimate of 1 for the distance parameter, trade between regions that are 1,000 miles apart (as in Canada) is worth ten times the trade between regions that are separated by only 100 miles (as in Belgium). In other words, Anderson and van Wincoop are right: economic size matters, but geographic size matters as well. What ultimately matters is the ratio between the two, or economic density.

What Anderson and van Wincoop demonstrate in their analysis of the multilateral resistance is that *trade barriers increase size-adjusted trade within small countries more than within large countries* (the second implication of their analysis).

But that does not imply that trade barriers increase *size-and-distance*-adjusted trade within small countries more than within large countries. This, essentially, is our contribution. If a small (economic) country is also small from a geographic standpoint, internal distance will be smaller than within a large country. The McCallum-type border effect will not necessarily be biased. But as economic density varies a great deal across countries (as does economic size), the overall consequence of the analysis is the same as in Anderson and van Wincoop (2001): McCallum-type border effects do not capture the quantitative effect of borders on trade barriers that could be compared at a cross-sectional level (across countries).

GRAVITY, SPATIAL STRUCTURE, RELATIVITY AND TOPOLOGY

IF WE RESTRICT THE ANALYSIS TO SIZE and abstract from distance, Anderson and van Wincoop's analysis appears to us perfectly correct. Their analysis could not be transposed directly to a framework where distance matters, but nevertheless, the analysis remains very revealing. But *gravity with gravitas* is not enough to solve the *border puzzle*. To maintain the analogy with physics, we have to go from gravity to relativity to solve the border puzzle. This follows from the fact that a border effect estimate based on relative weights (size and distance) in our view is extremely sensitive to relative density. We think it will be extremely difficult to isolate theoretically the relationship between size- and distance-adjusted trade in an Anderson and van Wincoop theoretical framework in a world where density varies. Such a theoretical analysis goes well beyond the scope of this study.

Two recent studies, by Brown and Anderson (2002) and Brown (2003), also highlight and discuss in a different way the importance of the specific spatial structure of the North American economies for the estimation of border effects. Of course, introducing spatial structure with variables such as distance and density into a theoretical gravity model is very complicated. It has not yet been carried out and the analysis of the spatial structure remains at the discussion level in these two studies. However, Brown (2003) clearly points out the importance of distance and density in the following discussion:

> Effectively, the Canadian economy functions over a thin, dispersed market that stretches east-west along the U.S. border, hemmed in by largely uninhabited land to the north and the U.S. border to the south. In contrast, the U.S. economy has no comparable economic or geographic limitations. Its market is larger, denser and more evenly spread over space. Therefore . . . Canadian regions encounter a higher level of multilateral resistance than their U.S. counterparts. Therefore, any measure of the border effect that uses interprovincial trade as a benchmark may be substantially biased upwards. (p. 4)

There is a "crude" (the word employed by Brown) attempt in Brown (2003) to test the significance of spatial structure for North American trade flows. However, without a theoretical gravity model that takes into account the impact of distance and density on border effect estimates, it is a very difficult hypothesis to test. Not surprisingly, Brown's (2003) exercise produces ambiguous results that are very hard to interpret. We agree completely with its conclusion that more research is needed on this topic. However, we believe that further empirical investigation should focus more specifically on the role of density of economic activity in a gravity model.

To close this discussion on the importance of distance and density, we want to highlight the role played by topology. The mean distance between trading partners within a country is determined not only by the country's geographic size. It is determined equally by the topology of trade patterns, a very complicated topic. Let us just say this: The fact that Canadian interprovincial trade follows mainly just one axis (east-west) — instead of multiple axes as in the United States — implies *ceteris paribus* that internal distances are greater on average in Canada than in the United States, for countries of equal geographic size. This point can be illustrated by a simple example. Consider two cases: (1) points A, B, and C lie on a straight line with B being equidistant from A and C; (2) points A, B, and C lie on separate points of an equilateral triangle. Let us assume that the distance between B and the other two points in the two cases is the same. In the first case, there is only one axis of trade with the distance between A and C being twice the distance AB. In the second case, there are three trade axes and the distance between A and C is equal to AB. The mean internal distance in the linear case (case 1) is 33 percent greater than in the triangular case (case 2). This result could be generalized, but what is important is that internal distances are greater, for a given country geographic size, when trade flows follow just one axis, as is the situation in Canada.

To sum up, the McCallum headline number is the result of an omitted variable bias and the typical long internal distance in Canada's interprovincial trade. Even if the Canadian economy is roughly one tenth the size of the U.S. economy, the typical internal trade distance across Canadian provinces is of the same order of magnitude as the typical trade distance between a province and a U.S. state. This follows from the geographic nature of Canada and from the fact that Canadian interprovincial trade basically follows an east-west axis in comparison with the multiple axes of Canada-U.S. trade.

INTERPRETATIONS OF THE BORDER EFFECT

A QUICK LOOK AT EQUATION (5), which specifies what a McCallum-type border effect measures, reveals why various and sometime contradictory interpretations of the border effect have been made in the economic literature and in the economic policy debate. The large value is a complicated ratio of trade weighted by size and distance. That number could be very misleading because it is not a simple question of interpreting it in terms of what really matters for economic policy: the size of unweighted trade flows and welfare. Let us suppose that Ontario redirects one unit of trade from Michigan to British Columbia. Suppose that the economic size of Michigan is four times that of British Columbia and the distance between the two Canadian provinces is ten times the distance between Ontario and Michigan. In a McCallum-type gravity model, the unit of trade between British Columbia and Ontario is worth 40 times the unit of trade between Ontario and Michigan. This large number has nothing to do with what really matters: welfare.

We now review two interpretations made in the literature on the McCallum "headline number," in light of recent studies on this topic (particularly that of Anderson and van Wincoop) and the analysis presented in the preceding section.

THE INTERNATIONAL TRADE-DIMINISHING EFFECT OF BORDERS

> National borders diminish trade volumes, in many cases by a factor of ten to twenty.

THIS IS THE VERY FIRST SENTENCE in a recent study by Evans (2000) — a spectacular way to start any publication. However, this narrow interpretation of the border effect is seriously misleading. This is one of the clear contributions of Anderson and van Wincoop (2001); in their own words:

> The lack of theoretical foundation of empirical gravity equations has two important implications. First, estimation results are biased due to omitted variables. Second, and perhaps even more important, one cannot conduct comparative statics exercises, even though this is generally the purpose of estimating gravity equations. In order to conduct a comparative statics exercise, such as asking what the effects are of removing certain trade barriers, one has to be able to solve the general equilibrium model before and after the removal of trade barriers. (p. 1)

The fact that interprovincial trade, after controlling for scale and distance, is sixteen times larger than Canada-U.S. trade does not imply that removing the border will translate into a multiplication by sixteen of our trade with the United States. For example, compared with a borderless world, the border might have multiplied (weighted) interprovincial trade by a factor of 8 and divided (weighted) international trade by a factor of 2, leading to a border effect estimate of 16. Anderson and van Wincoop (2001) estimate that the effect of removing trade barriers between Canada and the United States (for a border effect of 16 in 1993) would be to increase Canada-U.S. trade by 44 percent. The magic of weighting trade by distance and size, and the omitted bias variable, transforms a substantial effect into headline numbers.

Another way to put it into perspective is to look at the border effect estimate from the ratio of interstate trade to international trade (Anderson and van Wincoop, 2001; Brown, 2003; Brown and Anderson, 2002). These McCallum-type border effects are roughly ten times smaller than McCallum-type border effects computed from interprovincial trade, basically because of Canada's small economic density.

THE INTRANATIONAL TRADE-GENERATING EFFECT OF BORDERS

> Thus, the trade-generating powers of the Canadian federation are more than an order of magnitude larger than those of the European Union. (Helliwell, 1996, p. 508)

THE ANALYSIS UNDERLYING THE ABOVE QUOTE is based on a value of 20 estimated at the time by Helliwell for a McCallum-type border effect between Canada and the United States, and an estimate of 1.6 obtained by Frankel and Wei (1993) in a comparison of trade between EU countries and non-EU countries. Recent studies on the border effect highlight the fact that it is misleading to associate the relative size of a McCallum-type border effect (as for Canada and the European Union in the above quote) with the relative trade-generating powers of a country or an economic union.

Interestingly, the 1.6 value for the European Union is exactly equal to the McCallum-type border effect estimated recently on the basis of the ratio of interstate to international trade. If we push Helliwell's analysis further, the trade-generating powers of the Canadian federation would be more than one order of magnitude larger than that of the U.S. federation.

The post-2000 studies on border effects illustrate well why it is dangerous and often misleading to compare border effect estimates for two countries like Canada and the United States. McCallum-type border effect estimates are very sensitive to the size and density of the respective economies. The effect of a border on weighted (for distance and size) trade is much larger for a country of small economic size and low density than for the United States or the European Union. To put it differently, Helliwell's (1998, tables 3-4) own record of a border effect estimate for Zimbabwe was 232.5 in 1988. This should not be interpreted as a measure of the trade-generating power of that country's institutions.

ESTIMATED EVOLUTION OF THE BORDER EFFECT DURING THE 1981-2000 PERIOD

M CCALLUM-TYPE BORDER EFFECT ESTIMATES for Canada are based on detailed province-to-province and province-to-state trade data that are available only for the 1988-96 period, and on a consistent basis, only for the 1990-96 period. This interval is not long enough to allow serious conclusions to be drawn about the time-trend evolution of the border effect. But since that brief time period coincides with the introduction of the FTA, the short sequence of border effect estimates gave rise to conclusions that encompass time-series dimensions (Helliwell, 1998; Helliwell, Lee and Messinger, 1999); the border effect declined following the introduction of the FTA up to 1993-94, and it has been stable since.

In this section, we attempt to add to the dynamic dimension of the border effect by making the best use of the information contained in the aggregate Gross Domestic Product, Expenditure-Based (GDPEB) database of Statistics Canada on interprovincial and international trade in goods and services, for Canada as a whole and the ten provinces. This information is coupled with Helliwell's (1998) estimates based on detailed data to produce an approximation of the border effect during the 1981-2000 period. This exercise is not intended to produce border effect values to compete with Helliwell's detailed estimates. Our purpose is simply to extend the time-series dimension.

The notion of using aggregate data to compute rough estimates of Canada's border effect is not new. To our knowledge, it was first used in Helliwell (1998) to produce estimates of the border effect for the services sector. The same methodology is used below for the services sector, in the section entitled *Border Effects for Services*. In the next section, we use a more precise approximation for extending the time-series dimension of the border effect in the goods sector.

BORDER EFFECT FOR GOODS AND THE "L" CURVE

THE BASIC HYPOTHESIS FOR OUR ESTIMATION of the border effect from aggregate data is that the McCallum-type border effect [$\exp(e)$ in equation (5)] is proportional to the ratio of interprovincial trade to international trade, TR, obtained from the aggregate database. Of course, this hypothesis is based on strong assumptions that the share of Canadian trade with the United States and other Canadian trade partners is constant, that there is no trend factor in the distance and size dimensions of equation (5), and that the aggregate and detailed databases contain comparable information on trade.

The estimation is performed in two steps. First, the proportional assumption [between Helliwell's (1998) estimates and the trade ratio from aggregate data on goods] is estimated separately with OLS (ordinary least squares) without a constant for the eleven cross-sections i (the ten Canadian provinces and Canada), using the nine time-series observations t in the 1988-96 sample:

$$(6) \qquad \exp(e)_{i,t} = p_i \cdot TR_{i,t} + \varepsilon_{i,t}.$$

The error term $\varepsilon_{i,t}$ (i.i.d.) is supposed to capture stochastic shocks to the size and distance dimensions of border effect estimates and to the other factors involved in the correspondence between data banks in this exercise. The R-square for the pooled (separate) regression (eleven cross-sections) is 0.84.[2] The estimated p_i are the proportional factors and are presented in Table 1 below. Second, the estimated proportional factors are then used to compute border effect estimates with aggregate data from the 1981-2000 sample. Helliwell's (1998) border effect estimates for the years 1988-96 and our border effects computed from aggregate data for the years 1981-2000 are presented separately for Canada and the ten provinces in Figure 1.

The proportional factors reported in Table 1 range from 9.1 for Alberta to 55.7 for Ontario. They capture the effect of weighting trade flows by distance and economic size. The fact that all have large values is an indication of the small relative economic size and low density of the Canadian economy. Interestingly, the proportional factor is much larger (3.5 times) for Ontario than for the other nine provinces, on average. This might appear surprising in light of the topology argument presented earlier. Ontario being a central province, the typical distance between Ontario and another Canadian province is smaller than for British Columbia or Newfoundland. But one should not forget that Ontario is very close to its most important trading partners, like Michigan, that are located in the Great Lakes area.

The first thing to look for in Figure 1 is the general fit between Helliwell's estimates and our computations for the limited 1988-96 period, for which both series are available. The fit is very bad only for Newfoundland, British Columbia, and the small province of Prince Edward Island. For Newfoundland and British Columbia, the bad fit could be explained by the fact that the evolution of aggregate data on international trade does not capture well enough the evolution of these two provinces' trade with the United States. This is because they are located at the extreme east and west edges of the country, and are naturally more inclined to trade with the rest of the world than with other provinces.[3] The fit between the two border effect series is exceptional for New Brunswick and Saskatchewan and it is not bad for the other five provinces and Canada.

FIGURE 1

BORDER EFFECTS FOR GOODS, 1981-2000

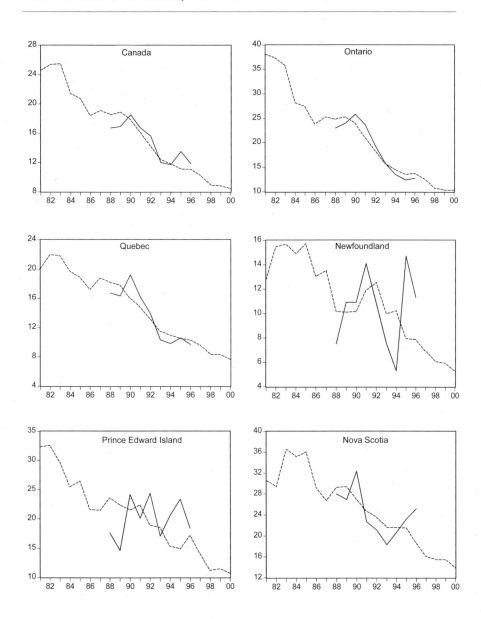

FIGURE 1 (CONT'D)

BORDER EFFECTS FOR GOODS, 1981-2000

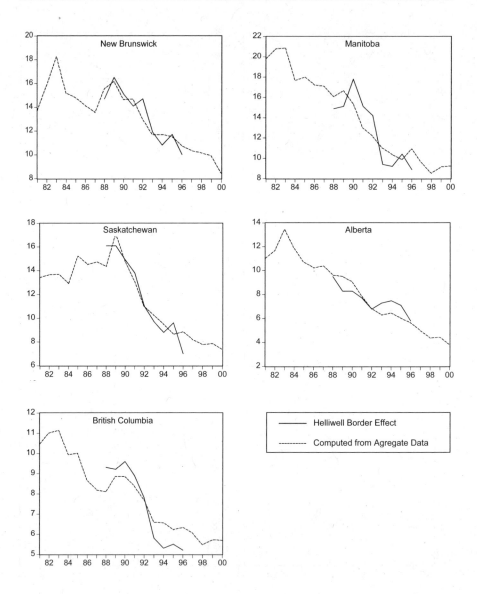

TABLE 1	
ESTIMATED PROPORTIONAL FACTORS	
Alberta	9.136889
British Columbia	17.43912
Manitoba	14.37406
New Brunswick	15.32113
Newfoundland	13.74871
Nova Scotia	26.12206
Ontario	55.72116
Prince Edward Island	10.98510
Quebec	23.13872
Saskatchewan	14.04893
Canada	28.92855

Note: OLS estimated p_i in equation (6) for the ratios between Helliwell's (1998) estimated border effects and the ratio of interprovincial to international trade for goods in the 1988-96 sample. All significant at the 1-percent level.

The second thing to look for in Figure 1 is the key point of this whole exercise. Generally speaking, border effects appear to follow a declining trend over the whole 1981-2000 sample. The border effect for goods did not wait for the introduction of the FTA to start a downward trend. The computed border effect shows a significant negative time trend in the pre-FTA 1981-89 sample period (despite the very low degree of freedom for the econometric analysis) for seven provinces and Canada as a whole.[4] The negative trend is not significant at the 5-percent level for Nova Scotia and New Brunswick. The trend is significant but positive for Saskatchewan. For the whole 1981-2000 sample, the negative time trend is not significant at the 5-percent level only for Saskatchewan.

The conclusion of this exercise is clear. It appears that the general decline of McCallum-type border effects in Canada is not a phenomenon that should be associated with the introduction of the FTA. Empirical evidence — when the period of analysis is extended to the 1981-2000 period with aggregate trade flows — strongly indicates that border effects have followed a declining trend in the whole 1981-2001 sample period and during the pre-1989 sub-period.

This result is best illustrated with the "L" curve, analyzed and documented in Coulombe (2003). In Figure 2, interprovincial and international trade shares to GDP $[(X+M)/GDP]$ for goods in Canada, using the same aggregate GDPEB data bank, are plotted in a scatter diagram. The resulting picture is stunning and reveals that the 1981-2000 sample period is clearly divided into two separate trends. From 1981 to 1991, the interprovincial trade share is

FIGURE 2

THE "L" CURVE: TRADE OF GOODS FOR CANADA

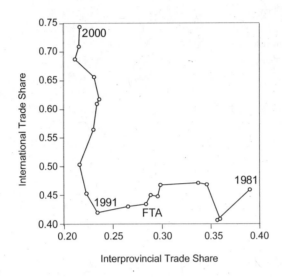

falling while the international trade share is constant. From 1991 on, the international trade share is booming while the interprovincial trade share is constant. Consequently, prior to 1991, the border effect computed from aggregate data is falling because of the decrease in the interprovincial trade share. After 1991, it continues to fall because the international trade share is increasing. The introduction of the FTA in 1989 does not appear to alter the picture much. The real break in the evolution of trade patterns occurred in 1991.

BORDER EFFECTS FOR SERVICES

BORDER EFFECTS FOR SERVICES CAN BE COMPUTED only indirectly from the aggregate GDPEB data bank, such as in Helliwell (1998). We can produce a very rough estimate based on heroic assumptions, such as interprovincial and international trade flows that follow the same pattern for services as for goods. We simply adjust the computed border effect for goods from the 1981-2000 sample by multiplying it by the ratio of two ratios: the ratio of interprovincial to international trade in services to the ratio of interprovincial to international trade in goods. This is basically what was done in Helliwell (1998).

FIGURE 3

BORDER EFFECTS FOR SERVICES

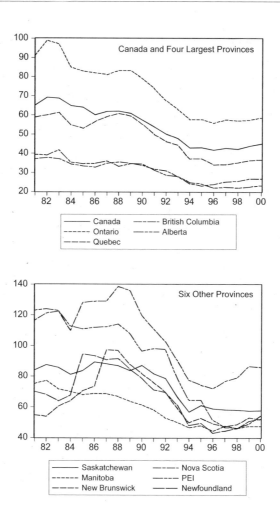

The results of this exercise are shown in Figure 3 for Canada and the ten provinces. They differ considerably from the results reported in previous sections, in two respects. First, the FTA appears to play an important role as the 1989-94 (or 1995) period is the only one where border effects for services appear to follow a clear and significant declining trend. Prior to the FTA, border effects are either stable or even increasing (Newfoundland, Nova Scotia, and New Brunswick). After 1994-95, the border effects appear stable. The standard dynamic adjustment story following the introduction of a shock (the FTA) in 1989 seems to fit the facts well in the case of services. Second, the border effect estimates for services are much larger than the estimates for goods, as in Helliwell (1998). This follows simply from the fact that the ratio of interprovincial to international trade is much larger for services than for goods. This point appears to be related to the core/periphery nature of the Canadian economy, but the analysis of this interesting fact goes well beyond the topic of border effects and the scope of this study.

CONCLUSION AND POLICY DISCUSSION

THE DEBATE SURROUNDING BORDER EFFECTS that has raged over the past century is likely to have been fundamentally changed with the wave of studies (Anderson and van Wincoop, 2001; Brown, 2003; Brown and Anderson, 2002) that came out recently to analyze the newly released interstate trade data. It should be clear by now that, for a given degree of trade diversion generated by the common border, a McCallum-type border effect is about ten times larger when measured from Canadian interprovincial trade data than from U.S. interstate trade data. This new finding is critical for the general interpretation of border effects. It clearly indicates that it is at least risky, and probably misleading, to draw conclusions about the level of trade barriers or the trade-generating power of a country or trade bloc by comparing the magnitude of border effect estimates on a cross-sectional basis. Border effect estimates do contain information that is extremely hard to interpret at the cross-sectional level. This drawback should seriously restrain future research on the topic.

Anderson and van Wincoop (2001) have taken a critical step forward as regards the information contained in border effect estimates. Thanks to the separation of the concepts of multilateral and bilateral trade resistance, they are able to show that the Canada-U.S. border has roughly an order of magnitude (about 10) greater effect on interprovincial weighted trade flows than on interstate weighted trade flows for a given degree of trade diversion between the two countries. As shown in this study, however, Anderson and van Wincoop's analysis of the role of economic size would be more revealing if it incorporated the concepts of distance and density. Those two concepts are the determinants of Anderson and van Wincoop's multilateral resistance but they clearly interfere with economic size. For us, McCallum's headline number is the joint result of the small economic size and the low density of the Canadian economy. Small size matters because of a low density. The spatial structure (Brown, 2003), associated with a low density, the topology (east-west) of trade, and the relative unique location of the Canadian economy should be a required complement to Anderson and van Wincoop's analysis in a satisfactory gravity model of trade. But all those factors are very complicated to handle in a theoretical model.

Economists are not used to working with density and topology. Gravity is not enough. We have to move to relativity.

The key findings unveiled by recent research should clearly affect the orientation of the economic policy debate on the significance of the border effect, for two reasons. First, under a pure diversion hypothesis, an increase of one unit in weighted (by size and distance) trade with the United States is accompanied by a decrease of around ten units of interprovincial weighted trade in a McCallum-type gravity equation. This follows from the relative size, density, and topology of the two economies. This spectacular arithmetic, hidden by the magic of weighting trade flows by distance and size, implies that Canada-U.S. border effect estimates should be interpreted with great care. Changes in the direction of trade links can potentially generate sharp and substantial changes in the magnitude of border effects estimated from provincial trade data.

Second, it appears that McCallum's high number has decreased since the early 1980s. Based on aggregate provincial trade flows, the remaining value is no longer in the double-digit range, and stands at around 8 for Canada overall. Consequently, what remains of the Canada-U.S. border effect in terms of bilateral resistance is quite low when measured from an international trade basis. Under the pure diversion hypothesis, following Anderson and van Wincoop's estimation of the effect of eliminating trade barriers between Canada and the United States, a 25-percent further increase (post-2001) in Canada-U.S. cross-border trade might well bring McCallum's number down to around 1. What remains of the bilateral resistance is so low that it could be largely explained by the fact that Canada and the United States are not using the same currency. As documented in Frankel and Rose (2000), the adoption of a common currency by two countries might certainly lead to a 25-percent increase in (un-weighted) trade flows! The negative impact of a separate currency on trade flows comes from the transaction costs associated with currency conversion and exchange rate variability.[5] The experience of the European Community has shown that floating exchange rates have a negative impact on trade flows (De Grauwe, 1988).

Two important points should be made to clarify the preceding analysis. First, one should not conclude from this that Canadians are losing as the orientation of trade links changes from east-west to north-south and a small amount of international trade is substituted for a huge amount of interprovincial weighted trade. This should be clarified, because what matters for welfare and employment is not weighted trade flows but unweighted trade flows. Canadians might well be better off by trading ten units of weighted interprovincial trade for one unit of international trade with the United States.

Second, the previous analysis, following the typical approach used in the now-standard theoretical gravity model such as that of Anderson and van Wincoop (2001), is based on the pure diversion hypothesis and an endowment economy. The effect of borders is restricted to a re-orientation of trade flows. However, this hypothesis clearly does not reflect the dynamic evolution of interprovincial and international trade flows of goods for Canadian regions since 1980. As shown in Coulombe (2003) and simply illustrated by the "L" curve presented in this study, interprovincial and international trade flows appear to be more complementary than substitutionary. Consequently, a 25 percent increase in international trade might not reduce McCallum's number to 1 because it would not necessarily be accompanied by a one-for-one decrease in (unweighted) interprovincial trade. A simple explanation for the non-diversion result would be that the expansion of north-south trade links increases the degree of specialization among Canadian regional economies. This is likely to stimulate trade between them. As Ontario and Quebec are exporting more manufactured products to the United States, they might import more primary products from the other provinces and from each other.

This potential change in the industrial structure of regions induced by trade goes well beyond the standard endowment economy (fixed supply of differentiated goods) assumed in theoretical gravity models, such as in Anderson and van Wincoop (2001). This characteristic is a natural limitation of gravity models to capture adequately the dynamic evolution of changing regional trade patterns in North America.

To conclude, the series of studies on the Canada-U.S. border effect initiated by McCallum (1995) and continued with the works of Helliwell has proved to be a serious challenge to the economic profession. This field of research has contributed to a substantial improvement in our understanding of the mechanics of regional trade flows. It is very important for trade policy, and for economic policy in general, to understand why and how a border barrier (such as having a separate currency) has a much larger effect on an economy like that of Canada than on the U.S. economy. But this should be common sense since we are well aware in Canada that the United States has a much larger margin in which to manoeuvre (especially when it comes to raising trade barriers) than does Canada in terms of trade policy. And the debate is not over. Despite the breakthrough following the theoretical and empirical analysis of interstate trade data, more work needs to be done to capture the real disrupting effect of trade barriers when distance and economic density are fully taken into consideration.

ENDNOTES

1   It might be useful to remember that the J.E. Anderson, who worked with van Wincoop, is the author of the theoretical study on the border effect published in 1979 in the *American Economic Review*. W.P. Anderson is another researcher on the border effect; he has worked with W.M. Brown on the 2002 study cited.

2   The Durbin-Watson for the pooled regression is 1.66 and no separate AR(1) is significant at the 10-percent critical level, indicating that serial correlation is not a problem in these simple regressions.

3   In 2000, trade with the United States represented only 56 percent and 47 percent of total international trade of goods for British Columbia and Newfoundland, respectively. For Ontario, the proportion was 83 percent. (Computed from Trade Data Online, www.strategis.ic.gc.ca.)

4   We refer in the text to a linear time trend with a constant term estimated with AR(1) on the log of computed border effect from Figure 1. We keep the econometrics very simple here, given that the secular declining trend of the border effect is so evident in Figure 1, generally speaking.

5   For a recent analysis of the benefits and costs of dollarization in Canada, with a regional perspective, see Beine and Coulombe (2003).

ACKNOWLEDGMENTS

THE AUTHOR IS GRATEFUL to John Helliwell and Richard Roy for their helpful comments and to Patricia Buchanan for English editing.

BIBLIOGRAPHY

Anderson, J.E. "A Theoretical Foundation for the Gravity Equation." *American Economic Review* 69 (1979), pp. 106-116.

Anderson, J.E., and E. van Wincoop. *Gravity with Gravitas: A Solution to the Border Puzzle*. NBER Working Paper No. 8079. Cambridge (Mass.): National Bureau of Economic Research, 2001.

Beine, M., and S. Coulombe. "Regional Perspectives on Dollarization in Canada." *Journal of Regional Science* 43, 3(2003): 541-570.

Bergstrand, J.H. "The Gravity Equation in International Trade: Some Microeconomic Foundations and Empirical Evidence." *Review of Economics and Statistics* 67 (1985), pp. 474-481.

Brown, W.M. *Overcoming Distance, Overcoming Borders: Comparing North American Regional Trade*. Ottawa: Statistics Canada (Micro-Economic Analysis Division), 2003. 11F0027, n° 008.

Brown, W.M., and W.P. Anderson. "Spatial Markets and the Potential for Economic Integration Between Canadian and U.S. Regions." *Papers in Regional Science* 81 (2002), pp. 99-120.

Coulombe, S. *International Trade, Interprovincial Trade, and Canadian Provincial Growth*. Working Paper No. 40. Ottawa: Industry Canada, 2003. Forthcoming.

De Grauwe, P. "Exchange Rate Variability and the Slowdown in Growth of International Trade." IMF Staff Papers No. 35, 1988, pp. 63-84.

Evans, C.L. *The Economic Significance of National Border Effects*. Federal Reserve Bank of New York, 2000.

Frankel, J.A., and A.K. Rose. *Estimating the Effect of Currency Unions on Trade and Output*. NBER Working Paper No. 7857. Cambridge (Mass.): National Bureau of Economic Research, 2000.

Frankel, J.A., and S.-J. Wei. *Trade Blocs and Currency Blocs*. NBER Working Paper No. 4335. Cambridge (Mass.): National Bureau of Economic Research, 1993.

Grossman, G. "Comment on Alan V. Deardorff: Determinants of Bilateral Trade: Does Gravity Work in a Neoclassical World?" In *The Regionalization of the World Economy*. Edited by J.A. Frankel, Chicago: University of Chicago Press, 1998, pp. 29-31.

Helliwell, J.F. "Do National Boundaries Matter for Quebec's Trade?" *Canadian Journal of Economics* 29 (1996), pp. 507-522.

——. *How Much Do National Borders Matter?* Washington (D.C.): The Brookings Institution, 1998.

Helliwell, J.F., F.C. Lee and H. Messinger. *Effects of the Canada-United States Free Trade Agreement on Interprovincial Trade*. Perspectives on North American Free Trade Series, No. 5. Ottawa: Industry Canada, 1999.

Helliwell, J.F., and J. McCallum. "National Borders Still Matter for Trade." *Policy Options* 16 (1995), pp. 44-48.

Helpman, E. "Increasing Returns, Imperfect Markets, and Trade Theory." In *Handbook of International Economics 1*. Edited by R. Jones and P. Kenen. Amsterdam: North-Holland, 1984, pp. 325-365.

Linneman, H. *An Econometric Study of International Trade Flows*. Amsterdam: North-Holland, 1966.

McCallum, J. "National Borders Matter: Canada-U.S. Regional Trade Patterns." *American Economic Review* 85, 3 (1995), pp. 615-623.

Obstfeld, M., and K. Rogoff. *The Six Major Puzzles in International Macroeconomics. Is there a Common Cause?* NBER Working Paper No. 7777. Cambridge (Mass.): National Bureau of Economic Research, 2000.

Tinbergen, J. *Shaping the World Economy: Suggestions for an International Economic Policy*. New York: The Twentieth Century Fund, 1962.

Wei, S.-J. *Intra-national versus International Trade: How Stubborn are Nations in Global Integration?* NBER Working Paper No. 5531. Cambridge (Mass.): National Bureau of Economic Research, 1996.

p 83:

Comment

Mark Brown
Statistics Canada

IN HIS STUDY, PROFESSOR COULOMBE PROVIDES AN INSIGHTFUL ANALYSIS of the border effect and its consequences. In this discussion, I would like to provide some comments on the contributions of his study and add some thoughts of my own on the implications of the border and trade literature.

That literature is derived from McCallum's (1995) surprising result that, after controlling for both the size of provinces and states and the distance between them, interprovincial trade was some twenty-fold larger than cross-border trade. This finding is at once interesting and perplexing. Interesting because it suggests that borders act as a much stronger barrier to trade than anyone had realized. Perplexing because it is very difficult to envisage how trade policy-related barriers (i.e. tariff and non-tariff barriers) and/or 'natural' barriers to trade (such as differences in tastes and institutions) could account for such a strong effect.

McCallum's finding has inspired a growing literature that tries both to explain the puzzle and to evaluate the robustness of his basic result. Coulombe points out that a series of recent studies (Anderson and van Wincoop, 2001; Brown, 2003; and Brown and Anderson, 2002) should shift the orientation of this literature. Specifically, these studies find that the border effect is much smaller in magnitude when different data and methods are used. They also explain why McCallum's initial finding is misleading (on this point, see especially Anderson and van Wincoop, 2001).

One of the contributions of Coulombe's study is its extensive discussion of the Anderson and van Wincoop theoretical model and its potential limitations. In my mind, Anderson and van Wincoop provide the best theoretically-derived gravity model of trade to date and solve many of the issues associated with using the gravity equation to measure the border effect. Nonetheless, Coulombe's argument that their model does not fully take into account economic density and topology is intriguing and reflects concerns I have regarding my own estimates (Brown, 2003). At the very least, this suggests that future attempts to measure the border effect should test for the influence of economic density and topology. This issue aside, it is my view that recent estimates showing that the border dampens Canada-U.S. trade by a half provide a relatively accurate measure of the border effect, at least as it stood in 1993.

A limitation of previous studies of the border effect is that they cover a relatively short period of time, usually a brief period before and after the implementation of the Canada-U.S. Free Trade Agreement (FTA). The second contribution of Coulombe's study is the estimation of the border effect over a much longer period (1981-2000). Coulombe shows that the decline in the border effect documented elsewhere (e.g. Helliwell, 1998) started well before the introduction of the FTA and continued past 1993, when other estimates indicate that there was at least a pause in its decline.

This is a surprising finding for two reasons. First, exports as a percentage of GDP grew at a fairly slow pace prior to the implementation of the FTA. Consequently, we would expect to see very little decline in the border effect over this period. Second, exports' share of GDP rose rapidly after the implementation of the FTA. With this rise, we would expect to see the decline in the border effect accelerate. To explain this finding, the author uses his 'L' curve to show that the border effect declined prior to 1991 because interprovincial trade's share of GDP fell. After 1989, the border effect declined because international trade increased as a share of GDP. This provides a partial explanation of his surprising result that, in turn, raises two questions.

First, why should the share of interprovincial trade in GDP decline so rapidly over the 1981 to 1991 period? There are probably many reasons for this result, but two seem plausible to me. First, the non-trade portion of GDP grew more rapidly during this period. Second, prices of traded goods declined relative to those of non-traded goods over the period. At any rate, I would be more comfortable with this result if there was some intuitive story to explain it.

Almost equally perplexing is the fact that, as the international trade share of GDP rose, the interprovincial trade share remained constant. The author speculates that this is possible if, with increased trade, regions are becoming more specialized, allowing the international trade share to increase while the interprovincial trade share remains constant. Surprisingly, recent evidence suggests that the opposite was occurring over roughly the same time frame. That is, within Canada's manufacturing sector, regional economies are generally becoming more industrially diversified over time (Baldwin and Brown, 2003). Therefore, specialization across regions cannot explain this result. What may explain it, however, is specialization within plants.

In a recent paper, Baldwin, Beckstead and Caves (2001) show that Canadian plants have reduced the diversity of their products over time and that this process accelerated after the implementation of the FTA. This means that there may be increased product specialization across provinces rather then industry specialization and this may underlie the post-1991 shape of the 'L' curve. Still, without further investigation, this explanation remains speculative.

Finally, I would like to conclude this discussion with two additional points. First, it remains to be seen whether we are approaching a point where the border no longer matters. Certainly, the evidence provided in Coulombe's paper suggests that the border effect has declined since 1993. Given that the border effect is positively related to tariff and non-tariff barriers (Brown and Anderson, 2002), their elimination over the past decade probably means that we are approaching a level of trade that reflects 'natural' barriers to trade and the extra transaction costs associated with having a separate Canadian currency. Still, we need more direct estimates of the border effect using interstate trade as a frame of reference to arrive at strong conclusions on this issue.

Second, it has been shown that the spatial organization of production can have a significant impact on the intensity of trade across space, and consequently on estimates of the border effect. The opposite may also be true. As barriers to trade have fallen, the markets available to firms across regions in Canada have changed. Locations that might have once been relatively central to the Canadian market may look peripheral in the context of a North American market. Similarly, locations once relatively remote from major Canadian markets may find themselves with large markets right across the border. Declining trade barriers have potentially changed the locational decisions of businesses, favouring locations in Canada where the North American market is most accessible. Increased trade may change the spatial structure of the Canadian economy.

BIBLIOGRAPHY

Anderson, J.E., and E. van Wincoop. *Gravity with Gravitas: A Solution to the Border Puzzle.* NBER Working Paper No. 8079. National Bureau of Economic Research, 2001.

Baldwin, J.R., D. Beckstead and R. Caves. *Changes in the Diversity of Canadian Manufacturing Firms and Plants (1973-1997): A Move to Specialization.* Research Paper Series No. 179. Ottawa: Statistics Canada, Analytical Studies Branch, 2001.

Baldwin, J.R., and W.M. Brown. *Regional Manufacturing Employment Volatility in Canada: The Effects of Specialization and Trade.* Economic Analysis Research Paper Series No. 5. Ottawa: Statistics Canada, Analytical Studies Branch, 2003.

Brown, W.M. *Overcoming Distance, Overcoming Borders: Comparing North American Regional Trade.* Economic Analysis Research Paper Series No. 8. Ottawa: Statistics Canada, Analytical Studies Branch, 2003.

Brown, W.M., and W.P. Anderson. "Spatial Markets and the Potential for Economic Integration Between Canadian and U.S. Regions." *Papers in Regional Science* 81, 1 (2002): 99-120.

Helliwell, J.F. *How Much Do National Borders Matter?* Washington (D.C.): Brookings Institution Press, 1998.

McCallum, J. "National Borders Matter: Canada-U.S. Regional Trade Patterns." *American Economic Review* 85,3 (1995): 615-623.

Part II
Labour Market Impacts of Canada-U.S. Economic Integration

Thomas Lemieux
University of British Columbia

F15

F13   F16   J31   J24

3

Trade Liberalization and the Labour Market

Canada USA   R23   J16

INTRODUCTION

THE IMPACT OF TRADE LIBERALIZATION on labour markets has long been a source of controversy in both policy and academic circles. For example, during the debate surrounding the Canada-U.S. Free Trade Agreement (CUSFTA) in the late 1980s, labour unions and other opponents of free trade argued that trade liberalization with the United States would have large adverse impacts on the wages and employment of workers in protected industries. The introduction of the CUSFTA tariff reductions was shortly followed by a major recession in 1990-92, and this fact was viewed by many opponents of free trade as evidence of the adverse labour market impacts of free trade.

On the research side, several studies have looked systematically at the impact of industry-specific tariff cuts on wages and employment. The basic idea is to determine whether industries where tariffs declined the most (because they were highest in the first place) also experienced larger relative declines in wages and employment. Using industry aggregates from establishment data, Gaston and Trefler (1997) find some negative effects of tariff cuts on employment but little impact on wages (see also Beaulieu, 2000). More recently, however, Townsend (2002) found some significant negative effects of tariff cuts on wages using household data that allowed controlling for workers' characteristics like education, experience, gender, etc.

In this study, I take a broader look at the implications of trade liberalization on wages in Canada. Under a set of specific assumptions, the well-known factor price equalization (FPE) theorem predicts that trade liberalization between Canada and the United States should eventually lead to an equalization of the wages of different skill groups in the two countries. The broad question asked is whether Canada's wage structure and that of the United States have converged over the last two decades. By wage structure I mean the average wages for different classes of workers defined on the basis of their skills (education and experience) and other characteristics (gender in particular).

However, I also argue that the hypothesis that wage structures have become similar in Canada and the United States is too extreme. One reason is that FPE is only expected to hold under a relatively restrictive set of conditions (see Blackorby, Schworm and Venables, 1993). For example, FPE requires technology to be the same and the two economies to be on the "cone of diversification" (produce all goods).

On a more practical level, it does not seem reasonable to expect national wages to be identical in Canada and the United States if wages differ among regions of the same country. In the second section, I explain that in addition to trade, other factors like the mobility of workers and capital can help equalize factor prices across countries or regions. In all of these cases, it is reasonable to expect that the forces of FPE will be much stronger within a country than across countries, even in the presence of CUSFTA and North American Free Trade Agreement (NAFTA). This is confirmed by the work of McCallum (1995) and Helliwell (1998) that show large "border effects" in trade and worker mobility. Presumably, capital markets are also much more integrated across provinces than across international borders.

My empirical strategy is thus to use regional wage dispersion in Canada and the United States as a benchmark for assessing "how different" the wage structures are between the two countries. In particular, I compare average wages and the wage differential between more- and less-educated workers across regions of the two countries in 1984 and 2001. This is done using comparable data for both countries that make it possible to control for national and regional differences in workers' characteristics. The main finding is that, if anything, there has been a divergence between the Canadian and U.S. wage structures over the last 20 years. In many cases, however, the wage structure differences between the two countries are not large relative to differences in regional wage structures.

The study is organized as follows. In the section entitled *Theory and Existing Evidence*, I discuss the theoretical implications of trade liberalization on wages and review the existing empirical evidence for Canada, the United States and Mexico. The data used is discussed in the *Data* section, while the section entitled *National Level Evidence* presents some descriptive evidence on the evolution of the (national) wage structures in Canada and United States from 1984 to 2001. Then, in the section entitled *Regional Differences in Wage Structure*, I contrast Canada-U.S. differences to regional differences. Finally, some conclusions are presented in the last section.

THEORY AND EXISTING EVIDENCE

IN THIS SECTION, I DISCUSS SEVERAL PREDICTIONS of standard trade theory regarding the impact of trade liberalization on wages. I then turn to the empirical evidence for Canada, the United States and Mexico. Two reasons explain the study's focus on the three North American countries. First, it is only natural to examine these three economies given the focus of this conference on North American linkages. More importantly, however, the empirical literature on the three countries is complementary, as it tends to focus on different impacts of trade liberalization in each case.

THEORY

THE STANDARD HECKSCHER-OHLIN MODEL of international trade can be used to derive a set of interesting predictions on the effects of trade liberalization on wages. Important assumptions of the model include perfect competition, and similar preferences and production technologies in the different countries. As they move from autarky to free trade, the model predicts that countries that are more endowed in some factors will tend to specialize in the production of goods that use these factors more intensively. For example, relative to Canada and the United States, Mexico is well endowed with less-skilled labour. Under NAFTA, it should increasingly specialize in the production of goods that require an intensive use of this production factor.

The most direct impact of trade liberalization (the removal of trade barriers such as tariffs) is to equalize the price of tradable goods across countries. The famous factor price equalization (FPE) theorem states that the equalization of the price of goods should lead to an equalization of the price of production factors (capital and different skill levels of labour) provided that each trading country produces all of the traded goods. The latter condition means that all countries are on the "cone of diversification" in the sense that they do not strictly specialize in the production of a specific subset of goods.

Canada and the United States are both large countries with highly diversified economies that may well be on the cone of diversification. This is clearly not the case, however, at the regional level. For example, Ontario has no oil and gas extraction industry, while Alberta has no automobile industry. So even within the same country, free trade may not be enough to equalize wages across regions. For example, if male high school graduates and high school dropouts are in strong demand in Alberta's oil industry or in British Columbia's forest industry, they may command higher wages than in other parts of the country even if there is free trade among provinces. This will then create an incentive for other male high school graduates and dropouts to migrate from other provinces to Alberta or British Columbia.

Mexico and the United States provide another example where migration is clearly a major source of wage adjustment. In this case, the assumption that the two countries have the same production technologies is clearly unrealistic. As a result, factor prices will not be equalized even in the presence of free trade. Indeed, wages for given skill levels remain several times higher in the United States than in Mexico almost ten years after NAFTA was enacted.

An additional important assumption in the Heckscher-Ohlin model is that production factors (capital and labour) are perfectly mobile across industries. While this may be true in the long run, this assumption is clearly unrealistic in the short run. For example, it is well known that workers displaced as a result of mass layoffs experience large and sustained declines in their earnings (see, for example, Jacobson, Lalonde and Sullivan, 1993). So, if the textile and apparel industries were protected by large tariffs prior to CUSFTA and NAFTA, tariff cuts should have a negative impact on workers in these industries, at least in the short run. Once labour adjustments across industries have taken place (as in the Heckscher-Ohlin model), then wage impacts should only depend on changes in output prices induced by free trade.

These long-run effects may be quite different from short-term effects in specific industries. For instance, Canada has relatively less university-educated workers than the United States. In the absence of trade, the price of goods that require university-educated labour more intensively should be higher in Canada than in the United States. With free trade, the Canadian price of these goods will fall, which will have an adverse impact on the wages of university-educated workers in Canada. So, even if the wages of less-educated workers in the textile, apparel and other highly protected industries fall in the short run, less-educated workers as a whole may gain in the long run as Canada liberalizes trade with the United States.

EMPIRICAL EVIDENCE

THERE IS A LARGE BODY OF EMPIRICAL RESEARCH on the effect of trade liberalization on labour markets in the North American context. Interestingly, however, the focus of studies on Canada, the United States and Mexico tend to be quite different. In Canada, most studies have focused on the impact of trade and trade barriers on wages and employment at the industry level. For instance, Gaston and Trefler (1997) and Beaulieu (2000) have looked at the impact of CUSFTA tariff reductions on wages and employment at the industry level. As discussed earlier, these studies show some negative impact of tariff cuts on employment but little impact on wages. More recently, however, Townsend (2002) has found significant negative effects of tariff cuts on wages using household data that make it possible to control for workers' characteristics like education, experience, gender, etc.

In the United States, research has instead been centered on the potential role of trade liberalization with less-developed countries (LDCs) in the growing wage inequality since the early 1980s. By contrast, the potential impact of CUSFTA on U.S. labour markets has attracted very little interest in either policy or academic circles in the United States. The potential impact of NAFTA has not attracted much attention either, except perhaps during the 1992 presidential campaign.[1]

The focus on trade liberalization with LDCs has much to do with the well-known fact that, starting in the late 1970s, wage inequality increased steeply in the United States (Katz and Autor, 1999). In particular, after declining during the 1970s, the wage gap between college- and high school-educated workers widened sharply in the 1980s and again, but more slowly, in the 1990s. Since trade as a fraction of GDP also increased throughout this period, it is tempting to try to link these two phenomena. The argument goes as follows. Since the United States has a much more educated (skilled) labour force than LDCs, opening up trade between the United States and LDCs should decrease the relative demand for less-skilled workers in the former. This basic prediction comes from the standard Heckscher-Ohlin model. Since the United States is relatively more endowed with highly skilled labour, trade liberalization should induce U.S. firms to specialize in the production of goods that use highly skilled labour more intensively, while LDCs should specialize in the production of goods that use more intensively less-skilled labour.

As discussed earlier, one testable implication of the Heckscher-Ohlin model is that international trade should affect labour markets through the price of goods. In particular, the relative price of U.S. goods that use highly skilled labour more intensively should increase as trade is liberalized. However, there is little evidence in the data of an increase in the relative price of these "highly skilled" goods since the late 1970s.[2] As a result, trade has generally been dismissed as a major source of explanation of the growing wage inequality in the United States, though this issue continues to generate some debate in the literature.[3] Recent surveys of research, such as that of Katz and Autor (1999) and that of Acemoglu (2002), emphasize rather the role of skilled-biased technological change in the growing wage inequality.

It is beyond the scope of this study to assess the extent to which trade liberalization has contributed to the increase in wage inequality in the United States. The focus of the U.S. literature on trade and overall wage inequality is nonetheless interesting from a Canadian point of view. It highlights one important gap in Canadian research — it has not generally focused on the overall effects of trade liberalization on the wage structure and wage inequality. One contribution of this paper is to start to fill this gap.

The literature on trade liberalization and wages in Mexico offers yet another angle on this issue. As in the case of Canada, the Mexican literature has focused on the impact of trade with the United States, particularly the impact of NAFTA. However, the parallel with the Canadian situation stops there. While wage levels in Canada are roughly comparable to those in the United States, Mexican wages remain several times smaller than in that country. But although it would have been unrealistic to see Mexican wages equalized with those in the United States as a result of NAFTA, one reasonable conjecture is that NAFTA should have helped Mexican wages get closer to the U.S. level. Furthermore, since Mexico is well endowed with less-skilled labour, the Heckscher-Ohlin model predicts that opening up trade with the United States should benefit less-skilled workers and reduce wage inequality.

Neither prediction is consistent with the data, however. After some progress just after NAFTA was enacted, Mexican wages collapsed relative to U.S. wages during the peso crisis of the mid-1990s (Hanson, 2003). Furthermore, wage inequality increased during the same period, which is inconsistent with what the Heckscher-Ohlin model predicts. However, this prediction should probably be taken with some caution since many of the model assumptions are clearly violated in the case of the United States and Mexico. In particular, the assumption of similar production technologies in the two countries is highly unrealistic.

One interesting contribution of the Mexican literature, however, is that it also looked at the implications of trade liberalization for worker mobility and labour market impacts in different regions. For example, Hanson (2003) shows that employment and relative wages increased in the Maquiladora region (at the Northern border) where many U.S. manufacturers built assembly plants (*maquiladoras*) under NAFTA. Hanson (2003) also documents that many workers moved from the South to that region in order to take advantage of the employment opportunities. The predictions of trade theory thus appear to be more consistent with that data once the focus is switched from all of Mexico to the region most likely to be affected by NAFTA (the border region). Robertson (2000) also concludes that some regional labour markets in Mexico have become more integrated to the United States during this period.

From a Canadian perspective, the Mexican experience suggests that it may be important to look at the potential impacts of trade liberalization in a context where regional labour markets are not perfectly integrated. The message from Mexico is that trade can have very different effects on different regions. When factor prices differ widely between regions of the same country, it seems unreasonable to expect that trade will equalize factor prices among countries.

As mentioned earlier, McCallum (1995) and Helliwell (1998) show that Canadian provinces trade more extensively with each other than with nearby U.S. states. Furthermore, migration flows across provinces are an order of magnitude larger than those between Canada and the United States. This suggests that much more powerful forces would tend to equalize factor prices among provinces than between Canada and the United States. In what follows, I will thus examine Canada-U.S. wage differences in light of the regional dispersion of wages within Canada and the United States.

DATA

THE EMPIRICAL ANALYSIS USES COMPARABLE DATA on hourly wages for Canada and the United States. The best source of detailed information on hourly wages by classes of workers in Canada is the Labour Force Survey (LFS). Since 1997, the LFS has collected information on wages for all wage and salary workers. Individual workers have the option of either reporting their wages on an hourly basis or for longer time periods (weekly, bi-weekly, etc.). In the latter case, the hourly wage can be computed by dividing earnings for the relevant time period by the usual number hours of work during the period. Since over 100,000 adults are surveyed each month in the LFS, large samples are available each year even at the provincial level.[4] In the analysis presented below, both the Maritime provinces and Manitoba and Saskatchewan are grouped together to get samples of more comparable size for all regions of Canada. The LFS data used covers 2001 only, the last year for which completed yearly data were available at the time this paper was written.

While several sources of wage data are available for years prior to 1997, the wage measures used in these surveys are generally not comparable to those of the LFS. One exception is the 1984 Survey of Union Membership (SUM). Like the LFS, the SUM asked about wages earned from the main job at the time of the survey.[5] Both surveys also contain information on the union status of workers, which could be used as an alternative explanation for some regional wage differences. In what follows, data from the 1984 SUM and the 2001 LFS are used to study the evolution of wages during the period when both CUSFTA and NAFTA were introduced.

For the United States, the outgoing rotation group (ORG) supplement of the Current Population Survey (CPS) is the data source most comparable to the LFS or SUM. In particular, since 1983 the ORG supplement of the CPS has asked questions about wages and union status that are very comparable to the questions used in the SUM or the LFS (see Card, Lemieux and Riddell, 2003, for a more detailed comparison). Here, only data for 1984 and 2001 are used for the sake of comparison with Canada. A regional analysis is also performed using the nine standard census regions.

When comparing the level and distribution of wages across Canada and the United States or across regions of the two countries, it is important to control for socio-economic characteristics like age, education and gender that are largely known to influence wages. For example, wages could be higher in the United States than in Canada simply because Americans have traditionally been more educated than Canadians. While the age structure is not very different between the two countries, the migration of workers across regions of the same country can induce important differences in the age structure that also need to be controlled for.

From a theoretical point of view, the main reason for controlling for characteristics like age and education is that the FPE theorem implies that wages should be the same (in Canada and the United States) for specific skill groups of workers. So, even if the prices of all factors (wages by skill group) are equalized across countries, average wages will generally differ unless these countries have workforces with the same skill distribution. The implication of FPE is that average wages should only be the same once these skill characteristics have been controlled for.

One drawback of the SUM and LFS is that only coarse measures of age and educational achievement are available in the public-use files of these data sets. For example, only five education-level groups (less than high school, high school attended or completed, some postsecondary schooling, postsecondary diploma, and university diploma) and nine age groups (15-16, 17-19, 20-24, 25-34, 35-44, 45-54, 55-64, 65-69, 70+) are available in the SUM. Here, only the six age groups between age 17 and 64 are used since most individuals under 17 and over 64 are not active participants in the labour market (because of school attendance and retirement, respectively). The education and age variables are more detailed in the LFS than in the SUM. In particular, in the LFS it is possible to divide the "high school" group into those who have completed and those who have not completed their high school diploma. It is also possible to split university graduates into those with a bachelor's degree and those with a post-graduate degree. Workers aged 17 to 64 can also be divided into ten groups instead of six.

Whenever possible, the most detailed definitions of age and education have been used to control for the age and education structure. The one exception is the case of university–high school wage differences (see below), where regression equations are estimated using the coarser measure from the 1984 SUM for the sake of comparability across years. The more detailed U.S. age and education variables are also systematically aggregated into the same categories as those available for Canada.

All the results reported in the tables and figures are computed using the sampling weights. Allocated wages are also included in the analysis since Statistics Canada (unlike the U.S. Census Bureau) does not provide allocation flags indicating whether wages have been allocated for individuals who failed to report a valid wage in the survey. Finally, only observations with real wages (in 2001 dollars) between 2.50 and 90 dollars were kept to minimize the impact of potential outliers.

NATIONAL LEVEL EVIDENCE

WAGE LEVELS

TABLE 1 REPORTS SEVERAL MEASURES of average wage rates for Canada and the United States in 1984 and 2001.[6] Given the different secular trends of wages for men and women, results for these two groups are reported separately.

The first two rows of each panel show the evolution of average wages expressed both in nominal and real terms. With the exception of Canadian men for whom real wages declined slightly, real wages grew for all other groups. Consistent with many other studies, the rate of growth of female wages strongly outpaced that of male wages in both Canada and the United States. As a result, the ratio of female to male wages grew from 74 percent to 81 percent in Canada, and from 71 percent to 81 percent in the United States.

TABLE 1

AVERAGE WAGES IN CANADA AND THE UNITED STATES

	CANADA		UNITED STATES		CANADA/ UNITED STATES	
	1984	2001	1984	2001	1984	2001
Men						
Nominal	10.49	16.79	8.32	14.67	1.26	1.14
Real (2001$)	16.93	16.79	14.18	14.67	1.19	1.14
Real $US (ER)	13.80	10.85	14.18	14.67	0.97	0.74
Real $US (PPP)	13.94	13.43	14.18	14.67	0.98	0.92
With Canadian Characteristics	13.94	13.43	13.62	14.26	1.02	0.94
Women						
Nominal	7.77	13.65	6.01	11.93	1.29	1.14
Real (2001$)	12.55	13.65	10.24	11.93	1.23	1.14
Real $US (ER)	10.23	8.82	10.24	11.93	1.00	0.74
Real $US (PPP)	10.34	10.92	10.24	11.93	1.01	0.92
With Canadian Characteristics	10.34	10.92	9.87	11.76	1.05	0.93

The next set of rows express Canadian real wages in U.S. dollars using the actual (ER) and the purchasing power parity (PPP) exchange rates.[7] When expressed in U.S. dollars using the actual exchange rate, real wages in Canada fall dramatically relative to the United States. For both men and women, Canadian wages declined from close to parity in 1984 to only 74 percent of U.S. wages in 2001. The relative decline of Canadian wages is not as dramatic when PPP exchange rates are used instead. For men, wages fall from 98 percent to 92 percent of U.S. wages. The decline is more pronounced for Canadian women whose wages drop from 101 percent to 92 percent of U.S. wages.

The last row of Table 1 shows that the decline of Canadian wages relative to U.S. wages is more pronounced when controlling for observed characteristics. The numbers reported in this row are computed by first regressing log wages over a full set of interactions between age and education dummies. The regression estimates for the United States are then used to predict the wages that would prevail if U.S. workers had the same age and education distribution as in Canada. For example, in 1984 U.S. men would have earned 4 percent less ($13.62 instead of $14.18) under this counterfactual scenario, while they would have earned 2.8 percent less in 2001. The gap narrows over time as Canadian workers tend to catch-up in terms of skills relative to U.S. workers.[8] Since these skill improvements should have helped raise the relative wages of Canadians, the results reported when holding constant the distribution of characteristics (at their Canadian level) show a more significant decline in Canadian wages relative to U.S. wages.

In summary, the evolution of average wages in Canada relative to the United States is clearly inconsistent with the view that further trade integration should have lead to a convergence in wage levels. In fact, Canadian and U.S. wages have actually diverged over the last two decades, going from about parity in 1984 to a significant Canadian disadvantage in 2001. However, several other factors not linked to trade integration may in part explain this evolution. For example, Figure 5 illustrates the poor labour market performance (measured by the employment/population ratio) of Canada relative to the United States during the 1990s. Whatever factors explain this weak labour market performance may also account partially for the slower wage growth in Canada relative to the United States over that period.

THE DISTRIBUTION OF WAGES

As mentioned in the section entitled THEORY AND EXISTING EVIDENCE, the FPE theorem has important implications for the distribution of wages. In the special case where two countries have access to the same technology (and are on the cone of diversification), FPE implies that they should also have the same wage distribution, as expressed by standard measures of wage dispersion. Several of these standard measures of wage dispersion are reported in Table 2. Then, the potential role played by skill distribution differences in the wage dispersion differences is examined in Table 3.

The first measure of wage dispersion reported in Table 2 is the standard deviation of log wages. Consistent with other studies (e.g. Card, Lemieux and Riddell, 2003), the standard deviation of log wages grew much less in Canada

TABLE 2

SUMMARY MEASURES OF (LOG) WAGE DISPERSION

	CANADA			UNITED STATES		
	1984	2001	CHANGE	1984	2001	CHANGE
Men						
Standard Deviation	0.498	0.503	0.005	0.541	0.579	0.038
90-10 Gap	1.318	1.372	0.054	1.439	1.520	0.081
50-10 Gap	0.817	0.772	−0.045	0.790	0.721	−0.069
90-50 Gap	0.507	0.600	0.093	0.649	0.799	0.150
University-HS Gap	0.284	0.394	0.110	0.332	0.545	0.213
Women						
Standard Deviation	0.477	0.484	0.007	0.480	0.536	0.056
90-10 Gap	1.280	1.326	0.046	1.216	1.375	0.159
50-10 Gap	0.692	0.679	−0.013	0.566	0.588	0.022
90-50 Gap	0.588	0.647	0.059	0.650	0.787	0.137
University-HS Gap	0.468	0.502	0.034	0.414	0.586	0.172

TABLE 3

EFFECT OF THE DISTRIBUTION OF CHARACTERISTICS (AGE AND EDUCATION) ON THE STANDARD DEVIATION OF (LOG) WAGES

	CANADA	UNITED STATES	DIFFERENCE	CANADA	UNITED STATES	DIFFERENCE
	1984			2001		
Men						
Actual Characteristics	0.498	0.541	0.043	0.503	0.579	0.076
Canadian Characteristics	0.498	0.533	0.035	0.503	0.561	0.058
U.S. Characteristics	0.510	0.541	0.031	0.515	0.579	0.064
Women						
Actual Characteristics	0.479	0.481	0.002	0.484	0.536	0.052
Canadian Characteristics	0.479	0.474	−0.004	0.484	0.522	0.038
U.S. Characteristics	0.492	0.481	−0.011	0.497	0.536	0.039

than in the United States between 1984 and 2001. Furthermore, since the U.S. standard deviation was either similar (for women) or already larger (for men) than the Canadian standard deviation in 1984, wage dispersion actually diverged between the two countries over the period. Similarly, the gap between the 90th and the 10th centiles of (log) wages also widened faster in the United States than in Canada during this period. Interestingly, in both Canada and the United States, the increase in the 90-10 gap was driven by a significant rise in inequality at the upper end of the distribution (90-50 gap).

The wage gap between university and high school (HS) education is also reported in the last row of both panels. This gap is estimated from a regression of log wages over a set of dummy variables for the age and education categories. For the sake of comparability over time, the coarser 1984 definitions of age and education are used in the regression models. The university–high school wage gap is simply the difference between the coefficient on the dummy variable for university education (bachelor's degree or more) and the coefficient on the dummy variable for high school education (some or completed).[9]

Consistent with the other measures of wage dispersion, the university–high school wage gap grows faster in the United States than in Canada. However, the increase in the wage gap is substantial for men in Canada, going from 0.28 to 0.39. Expressed in percentage terms, these measures represent a 33 percent wage advantage for university graduates in 1984. The gap had increased to 48 percent in 2001. On the one hand, such a result is surprising in light of the many studies that indicate very little change in the university–high school wage gap in Canada during the 1980s and 1990s (see, for example, Murphy, Riddell and Romer, 1998, and Burbidge, Magee and Robb, 2002). On the other hand, this finding is consistent with recently released estimates from the 2001 Canadian Census which show a substantial increase in the earnings of male university graduates relative to high school-educated workers between 1990 and 2000.[10] Interestingly, these recent results indicate little change in the university–high school wage gap for women, which is also consistent with the results reported in Table 2.

Table 3 explores the role of Canada-U.S. differences in the distribution of skills (age and education) in differences in the standard deviation of log wages. The results compare the actual standard deviation of log wages to the standard deviation that would prevail if one country had the same distribution of skills as the other. For example, the second row shows the standard deviation computed with the Canadian skill distribution. The results indicate that the U.S. standard deviation decreases — from 0.541 to 0.533 in 1984, and from 0.579 to 0.561 in 2001 — when the U.S. skill distribution is replaced by the Canadian skill distribution. The counterfactual standard deviations are obtained using the re-weighting technique described in Lemieux (2002).

Though some of the Canada-U.S. difference in wage inequality can be explained by differences in the distribution of skills, this does not affect the basic finding that inequality grew much more in the United States than in Canada between 1984 and 2001. It is nonetheless interesting to notice that about one quarter of the Canada-U.S. difference in the standard deviation of log wages can be attributed to differences in the skill distribution.

In summary, the analysis at the national level indicates that, if anything, the structure of wages has diverged between Canada and the United States over the 1984-2001 period. Both the level and the dispersion of wages in Canada declined relative to the United States. These findings are clearly inconsistent with the hypothesis that economic integration should have tended to equalize wages on both sides of the border.

REGIONAL DIFFERENCES IN WAGE STRUCTURE

AS MENTIONED EARLIER, IT IS UNREASONABLE TO EXPECT wages to be equalized between Canada and the United States when there are large differences in wages among regions of these countries. Since the forces of wage equalization across regions of the same country should be much stronger than across countries, differences in the regional wage structure are a good benchmark for assessing "how different" the wage structures could be in the two countries. In this section, average wages and the wage differential between more- and less-educated workers across regions of the two countries are compared for 1984 and 2001.

WAGES LEVELS

FIGURES 1 AND 2 AND TABLE 4 SHOW DIFFERENCES in wages by region in Canada and the United States (all figures are in 2001$US based on PPP exchange rates). Wages are adjusted for differences in characteristics among regions using regression methods (unadjusted wages are reported in Appendix Table A1). The regression models include a set of regional dummy variables and a full set of interactions between age and education dummies. The coarse set of age and education categories (six age and five education dummies) is used for 1984 while the finer set of age and education categories (ten age and seven education dummies) is used for 2001. The adjusted wage rates reported in Figures 1 and 2 and Table 4 are simply the predicted regional wages computed at the average values of the age and education dummy variables for Canada. Since the dependent variable used in the regression models is log wages, the predicted log wages are converted in wage levels using the exponential function.

FIGURE 1a

AVERAGE WAGES BY REGION, MEN, ADJUSTED FOR AGE AND EDUCATION, 1984 (IN 2001 US$)

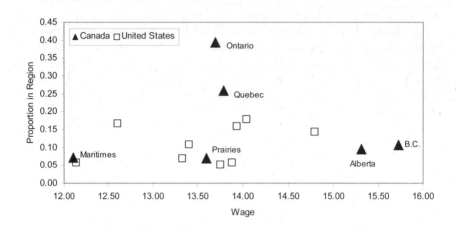

FIGURE 1b

AVERAGE WAGES BY REGION, MEN, ADJUSTED FOR AGE AND EDUCATION, 2001 (IN 2001 US$)

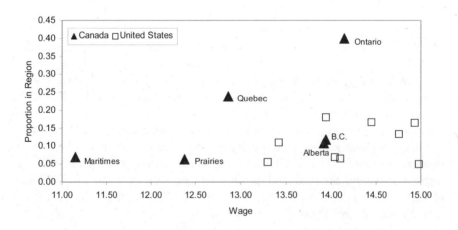

FIGURE 2a

AVERAGE WAGES BY REGION, WOMEN, ADJUSTED FOR AGE AND EDUCATION, 1984 (IN 2001 US$)

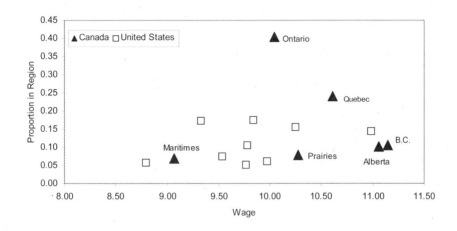

FIGURE 2b

AVERAGE WAGES BY REGION, WOMEN, ADJUSTED FOR AGE AND EDUCATION, 2001 (IN 2001 US$)

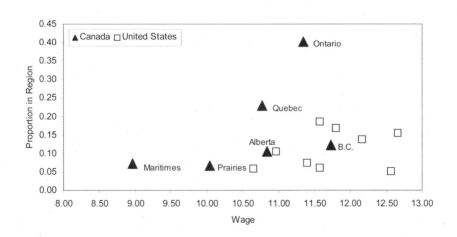

TABLE 4

AVERAGE REAL WAGES (IN 2001 $) BY REGION, ADJUSTED FOR AGE AND EDUCATION, 1984 AND 2001

	MEN				WOMEN		
1984		**2001**		**1984**		**2001**	
Maritimes	12.11	Maritimes	11.15	East South Central	8.80	Maritimes	8.97
East South Central	12.13	Prairies	12.38	Maritimes	9.07	Prairies	10.04
South Atlantic	12.60	Quebec	12.87	South Atlantic	9.33	East South Central	10.65
West North Central	13.32	East South Central	13.30	West North Central	9.53	Quebec	10.77
West South Central	13.40	West South Central	13.41	Mountain	9.77	Alberta	10.84
Prairies	13.60	Alberta	13.91	West South Central	9.78	West South Central	10.96
Ontario	13.69	British Columbia	13.94	East North Central	9.84	Ontario	11.35
Mountain	13.75	South Atlantic	13.94	New England	9.97	West North Central	11.39
Quebec	13.79	West North Central	14.04	Ontario	10.04	South Atlantic	11.57
New England	13.88	Mountain	14.10	Middle Atlantic	10.25	Mountain	11.57
Middle Atlantic	13.93	Ontario	14.14	Prairies	10.28	British Columbia	11.72
East North Central	14.04	East North Central	14.45	Quebec	10.61	East North Central	11.79
Pacific	14.79	Middle Atlantic	14.75	Pacific	10.98	Middle Atlantic	12.16
Alberta	15.31	Pacific	14.93	Alberta	11.06	New England	12.56
British Columbia	15.73	New England	14.98	British Columbia	11.14	Pacific	12.65
Canada	13.94	Canada	13.43	Canada	10.34	Canada	10.92
United States	13.62	United States	14.26	United States	9.87	United States	11.76

Table 4 reports the adjusted regional wages sorted in ascending order. Figures 1 and 2 display the same information graphically. Since the population is distributed unevenly across regions, the proportion on the national workforce in each region is plotted on the vertical axis. For example, Figure 1a indicates that close to 40 percent of the Canadian workforce is in Ontario, compared to less than 10 percent in the Maritimes or the Prairies.

One clear pattern emerging from the table and figures is that there are very large wage gaps between regions of the same country. The wage gap between the Maritimes and British Columbia ranges from $2.00 to $3.50 depending on year and gender. By contrast, the wage gap between Canada and the United States never exceeds $1.00 (Table 4). Another interesting pattern is that the average adjusted wage in Canada is always within the range of wage variations of the nine U.S. regions. For example, the average wage of men in Canada ($13.92) in 1984 exceeded the corresponding wage in all but two U.S. regions (East North Central and Pacific). By 2001, however, the average wage of men in Canada ($13.43) was below the corresponding wage in all but two U.S. regions (East South Central and West South Central).

Another interesting case is Ontario, the largest province, which also accounts for the bulk of Canada-U.S. trade. Wages in that province tend to be very close to average U.S. wages. For example, male wages in Ontario were $0.07 above the U.S. average in 1984, but $0.12 below in 2001. Female wages in Ontario are also very close to those in the United States.

By contrast, male wages in British Columbia and Alberta moved from about $2.00 above the U.S. average in 1984 to $0.30-$0.40 below in 2001. So, unlike Ontario wages which closely tracked U.S. wages, wages in these two Western provinces appear to have been affected by adverse labour market conditions between 1984 and 2001. One potential explanation for this pattern of regional wages is that labour markets in Alberta and British Columbia are disproportionately influenced by factors that do not play much of a role in either Ontario or the United States. Though a detailed investigation of these factors is beyond the scope of this study, it is tempting to look at the natural resources sector as a potential source of explanation for the poor performance of relative wages in Alberta and British Columbia.

As is well known, the oil and gas sector is relatively much larger in Alberta than in the rest of North America. Similarly, the B.C. economy disproportionately depends on the forest industry and related sectors. Figure 6 shows that real commodity prices declined throughout the 1984-2001 period. It is reasonable to think that these lower commodity prices had an adverse impact on wages in these two provinces.

In summary, the earlier conclusion that U.S. and Canadian wages have diverged between 1984 and 2001 is weakened when regional wage differences are used as a benchmark for assessing the extent of wage differences at the national level. In particular, part of the poor wage performance of Canada over this period could be attributed to a decline in commodity prices that disproportionately affected the Western provinces. By contrast, wages in Ontario remained very close to the U.S. average. Finally, Canada-U.S. wage differences are systematically smaller than the range of regional wage dispersion observed in each country.

UNIVERSITY–HIGH SCHOOL WAGE GAP

TABLE 5 AND FIGURES 3 AND 4 REPORT ESTIMATES of the university–high school wage gap across regions of Canada and the United States. These wage gaps are obtained by estimating separate log wage regressions for men and women in each region. The explanatory variables used are a set of age and education dummies. As before, the university–high school wage gap is defined as the difference between the coefficient on the dummy variable for a university degree and the coefficient on the dummy variable for a high school education (some or completed).

Table 5 and Figure 3 show that, with the remarkable exception of British Columbia, the regional distribution of the university–high school wage gap for men is very similar in Canada and the United States for 1984. By 2001, however, the university–high school wage gap in all nine U.S. regions exceeded the wage gap in all regions of Canada but the Maritimes. The average wage gap in Canada (0.391) is substantially below the range of wage gaps in the United States (from 0.457 in the West North Central region to 0.588 in the Pacific region). So, even when regional variation is used as a benchmark, it is obvious that there was a sharp divergence between the university–high school wage gap in Canada and in the United States over the 1984-2001 period.

The situation for women is quite different. In 1984, the university–high school wage gap was larger in all Canadian regions than in all U.S. regions, except for British Columbia. By 2001, however, the wage gap in all Canadian regions but Quebec and the Maritimes was either lower (Ontario and British Columbia) or at the lower end of the range of variation (Alberta and the Prairies) than the wage gap across U.S. regions. Leaving aside British Columbia, using regional variation as a benchmark indicates that the university–high school wage gap in Canada went from clearly above the corresponding measure in the United States in 1984 to similar or lower than in the United States in 2001. The evolution of the university–high school wage gap for women is thus the only case where there is evidence of a Canada-U.S. convergence in the wage structure over the 1984-2001 period.

TABLE 5

UNIVERSITY–HIGH SCHOOL WAGE GAP, 1984 AND 2001

MEN				WOMEN			
1984		**2001**		**1984**		**2001**	
British Columbia	0.110	**British Columbia**	0.291	**British Columbia**	0.309	**British Columbia**	0.407
East North Central	0.249	Ontario	0.376	West North Central	0.352	Ontario	0.466
West North Central	0.253	Prairies	0.379	Mountain	0.371	West North Central	0.485
Prairies	0.273	Alberta	0.388	East North Central	0.376	**Alberta**	0.487
Mountain	0.280	**Quebec**	0.445	New England	0.380	**Prairies**	0.492
Pacific	0.281	West North Central	0.457	Pacific	0.381	Mountain	0.493
Ontario	0.292	Mountain	0.461	Middle Atlantic	0.420	East South Central	0.557
Quebec	0.314	**Maritimes**	0.480	West South Central	0.425	New England	0.578
New England	0.337	East South Central	0.480	East South Central	0.445	East North Central	0.579
Alberta	0.345	East North Central	0.510	South Atlantic	0.461	South Atlantic	0.581
Middle Atlantic	0.349	New England	0.546	**Ontario**	0.475	**Quebec**	0.584
Maritimes	0.352	Middle Atlantic	0.548	**Alberta**	0.494	Pacific	0.588
West South Central	0.375	West South Central	0.571	**Quebec**	0.500	West South Central	0.626
East South Central	0.393	South Atlantic	0.572	**Prairies**	0.500	**Maritimes**	0.629
South Atlantic	0.417	Pacific	0.588	**Maritimes**	0.570	Middle Atlantic	0.635
Canada	0.286	**Canada**	0.391	**Canada**	0.474	**Canada**	0.502
United States	0.327	United States	0.539	United States	0.406	United States	0.578

FIGURE 3a

UNIVERSITY–HIGH SCHOOL WAGE GAP BY REGION, MEN, 1984

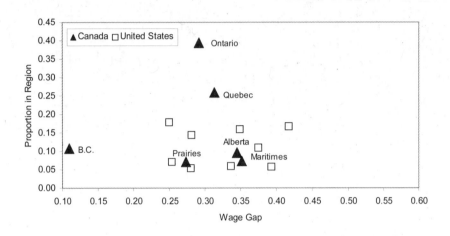

FIGURE 3b

UNIVERSITY–HIGH SCHOOL WAGE GAP BY REGION, MEN, 2001

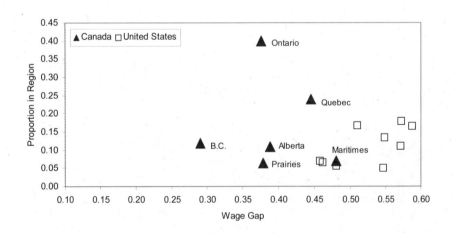

FIGURE 4a

UNIVERSITY–HIGH SCHOOL WAGE GAP BY REGION, WOMEN, 1984

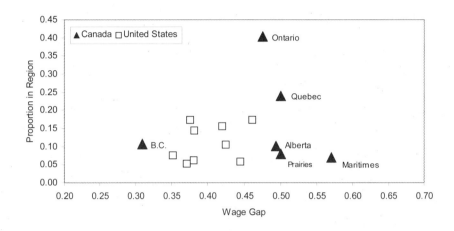

FIGURE 4b

UNIVERSITY–HIGH SCHOOL WAGE GAP BY REGION, WOMEN, 2001

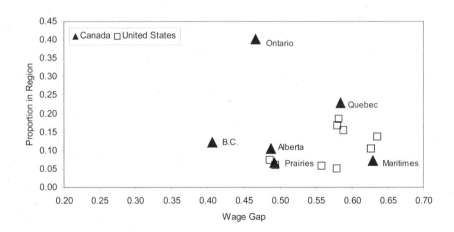

FIGURE 5

EMPLOYMENT RATE IN CANADA AND THE UNITED STATES

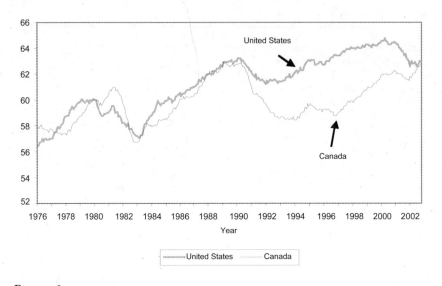

FIGURE 6

REAL COMMODITY PRICE INDEXES
(PRICES IN $US DEFLATED BY U.S. CPI)

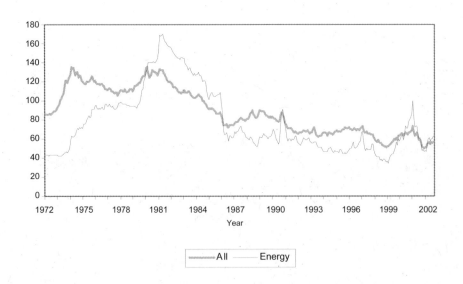

One striking feature of Table 5 and Figures 3 and 4 is the extent to which British Columbia has a lower university–high school wage gap than any other region in North America. The most striking example is men in 1984 where the university–high school wage gap is only 0.110, which is between 25 and 45 percent of the gap observed in other regions. Coupled with the fact that British Columbia had the highest wage level in 1984, this means that the wages of high school educated workers were extraordinarily high in British Columbia relative to the rest of North America in 1984. Perhaps the strong demand for men with a high school diploma or less in the forest industry and related sectors could partly explain this pattern. The very low wage gap between university and high school educated workers in British Columbia remains nonetheless a puzzle that would be worth examining in future research.

CONCLUSION

THIS STUDY LOOKS AT WHETHER TRADE LIBERALIZATION between Canada and the United States has induced a convergence of wages across the two countries. The empirical approach is to use regional variation in wages as a benchmark for assessing the extent of Canada-U.S. wage differences. The empirical evidence coming from comparable surveys conducted for 1984 and 2001 provides little support for the hypothesis that trade liberalization has induced a wage convergence between the two countries.

Wages levels were quite comparable in Canada and the United States in 1984. There was thus little scope for further equalization effects from trade liberalization. If anything, wage levels have diverged over this period because of a substantial decline in Canadian wages relative to U.S. wages.

In terms of the wage distribution, the results are more mixed. On the one hand, there is a clear divergence between the university–high school wage gap for Canadian and U.S. men. By any account, this wage gap is now clearly larger in the United States than in Canada, unlike the situation in 1984 where wage gaps were relatively comparable. On the other hand, there is some evidence that the university–high school wage gap became more similar for Canadian and U.S. women in 2001 than it was in 1984.

Thus, there is little evidence that trade liberalization with the United States has put much pressure on the Canadian wage structure. What appears more enigmatic is the extent of wage differences across regions of the same country. This topic deserves more attention in future research. Possible explanations for the observed regional wage differences, such as the industrial structure of employment (natural resources in the Western provinces, etc.) and the degree of unionization (see Table A2 in Appendix), are possible avenues to explore in the future.

ENDNOTES

1   One exception is presidential candidate Ross Perot who campaigned against NAFTA during the 1992 election.

2   See Slaughter (2000) for a survey of the "product-price" literature.

3   Authors such as Feenstra and Hanson (1999, 2003) have argued, for instance, that focusing on the role of trade in final goods may be misleading; once trade in intermediary inputs (offshore assembly) is taken into account, trade liberalization emerges as an important factor in the increasing wage inequality.

4   Over half a million wage observations are available each year in the LFS, though in many cases wage records are for the same individual over successive months. This happens because, in the LFS, individuals are normally followed during a six-month period. However, it is not possible to adjust statistical estimates (and standard errors) for group structure in the data since no individual identifiers are provided in the LFS public-use files.

5   Several other special surveys like the 1986-90 Labour Market Activity Survey (LMAS) are based on the work history of jobs in the previous year, which is not strictly comparable to a "point-in-time" survey like the SUM or the LFS.

6   For the sake of consistency with the rest of the analysis where log wages are used as the variable of interest, geometric averages of wages are reported in Table 1.

7   Statistics Canada's PPP exchange rates for household final consumption (Cansim II series V13930579) are used in the study. The PPP exchange rates are 0.78 and 0.80 for 1984 and 2001, respectively. The small appreciation in the Canadian dollar is consistent with the fact that CPI inflation was slightly lower in Canada than in the United States during this period. By contrast, the actual exchange rate plummeted from 0.77 to 0.65 over the same period.

8   For example, both Murphy, Riddell and Romer (1998) and Card and Lemieux (2001) show that educational achievement progressed faster in Canada than in the United States during the 1980s and 1990s.

9   The regression equations control for age instead of potential experience, which is more commonly used in Mincer-type earnings equations. It is not possible to construct an accurate measure of potential experience because age is reported in very broad categories (mostly 10-year intervals) in the SUM. One consequence of controlling for age instead of experience is to (typically) reduce the university–high school gap. Another consequence is that the university–high school wage gap will tend to increase as the average age of the population rises. This is due to the well-known fact that the university–high school gap typically increases as a function of age. See Card and Lemieux (2001) for more discussion on this point.

10   See the graphs for all full-time, full-year workers in Statistics Canada (2003).

ACKNOWLEDGMENTS

I WOULD LIKE TO THANK Craig Riddell and Daniel Trefler for comments on an earlier draft of the study.

BIBLIOGRAPHY

Acemoglu, Daron. "Technical Change, Inequality, and the Labor Market." *Journal of Economic Literature* 40 (2002): 7-72.

Beaulieu, Eugene. "The Canada-U.S. Free Trade Agreement and Labour Market Adjustment in Canada." *Canadian Journal of Economics* 33, 2 (May 2000): 540-563.

Blackorby, Charles, William Schworm and Anthony Venables. "Necessary and Sufficient Conditions for Factor Price Equalization." *Review of Economic Studies* 60 (1993): 413-434.

Burbidge J.B., L. Magee and A.L. Robb. "The Education Premium in Canada and the United States." *Canadian Public Policy* 28, 2 (June 2002): 203-217.

Card, David, and Thomas Lemieux. "Can Falling Supply Explain the Rising Return to College for Younger Men? A Cohort-Based Analysis." *Quarterly Journal of Economics* 116 (May 2001): 705-746.

Card, David, Thomas Lemieux and W. Craig Riddell. *Unionization and Wage Inequality: A Comparative Study of the U.S., the U.K. and Canada.* NBER Working Paper No. 9473. National Bureau of Economic Research, February 2003.

Feenstra, Robert C., and Gordon H. Hanson. "The Impact of Outsourcing and High-Technology Capital on Wages: Estimates for the United States, 1979-1990." *Quarterly Journal of Economics* 114, 3 (August 1999): 907-940.

——. "Global Production and Inequality: A Survey of Trade and Wages." In *Handbook of International Economics*. Edited by Kwan Choi and James Harrigan. Basil Blackwell, 2003, p. 146-187.

Gaston, Noel, and Daniel Trefler. "The Labour Market Consequences of the Canada-U.S. Free Trade Agreement." *Canadian Journal of Economics* 30, 1 (February 1997): 18-41.

Hanson, Gordon. *What Has Happened to Wages in Mexico since NAFTA.* NBER Working Paper No. 9563. National Bureau of Economic Research, March 2003.

Helliwell, John. *How Much Do National Borders Matter?* Washington, D.C.: Brookings Institution Press, 1998.

Jacobson, Louis, Robert Lalonde and Daniel Sullivan. "Earnings Losses of Displaced Workers." *American Economic Review* 83, 4 (September 1993): 685-709.

Katz, Lawrence, and David Autor. "Changes in the Wage Structure and Earnings Inequality." In *Handbook of Labor Economics*. Edited by O. Ashenfelter and D. Card. Amsterdam: Elsevier Science, 1999.

Lemieux, Thomas. "Decomposing Wage Distributions: A Unified Approach." *Canadian Journal of Economics* 35, 4 (November 2002): 646-688.

McCallum, John. "National Borders Matter: Canada-U.S. Regional Trade Patterns." *American Economic Review* 85 (June 1995): 615-623.

Murphy, Kevin M., W. Craig Riddell and Paul M. Romer. "Wages, Skills and Technology in the United States and Canada." In *General Purpose Technologies and Economic Growth*. Edited by Elhanan Helpman. Cambridge, Mass.: MIT Press, 1998, pp. 283-309.

Robertson, Raymond. "Wage Shocks and North American Labor Integration." *American Economic Review* 90 (September 2000): 742-764.

Slaughter, Matthew. "What Are the Results of Product-Price Studies and What Can We Learn from Their Differences?" In *The Impact of International Trade on Wages*, Edited by Robert C. Feenstra. Chicago: The University of Chicago Press, 2000, pp. 129-169.

Statistics Canada. *Earnings of Canadians: Making a Living in the New Economy, 2001 Census*. March 2003. Catalogue No. 96F0030XIE2001013.

Townsend, James. "Free Trade and the Canadian Wage Outcomes: A Micro Data Analysis." University of Winnipeg, 2002. Mimeo.

APPENDIX

TABLE A1

AVERAGE REAL WAGES ($2001, UNADJUSTED) BY REGION, 1984 AND 2001

MEN				WOMEN			
1984		**2001**		**1984**		**2001**	
Maritimes	12.05	**Maritimes**	11.15	East South Central	8.97	**Maritimes**	8.97
East South Central	12.23	**Prairies**	11.89	**Maritimes**	9.12	**Prairies**	9.83
South Atlantic	12.99	**Quebec**	12.91	South Atlantic	9.64	**Alberta**	10.64
Prairies	13.34	West South Central	13.20	West North Central	9.80	East South Central	10.70
West South Central	13.55	East South Central	13.40	West South Central	10.02	West South Central	10.73
Ontario	13.75	**Alberta**	13.58	**Ontario**	10.04	**Quebec**	10.79
West North Central	13.75	**British Columbia**	14.03	East North Central	10.13	**Ontario**	11.42
Quebec	13.82	Mountain	14.16	**Prairies**	10.19	Mountain	11.44
Mountain	14.26	**Ontario**	14.28	Mountain	10.21	West North Central	11.64
East North Central	14.61	South Atlantic	14.42	New England	10.41	**British Columbia**	11.76
New England	14.62	West North Central	14.59	**Quebec**	10.55	South Atlantic	11.81
Middle Atlantic	14.88	East North Central	14.88	Middle Atlantic	10.69	East North Central	11.89
Alberta	15.22	Pacific	15.28	**Alberta**	11.16	Middle Atlantic	12.65
British Columbia	15.76	Middle Atlantic	15.68	**British Columbia**	11.26	Pacific	12.76
Pacific	15.79	New England	16.02	Pacific	11.62	New England	13.32

TABLE A2

UNION COVERAGE RATE BY REGION, 1984 AND 2001

MEN				WOMEN			
1984		**2001**		**1984**		**2001**	
West South Central	0.130	West South Central	0.082	West South Central	0.089	West South Central	0.071
South Atlantic	0.164	South Atlantic	0.099	South Atlantic	0.111	South Atlantic	0.078
Mountain	0.186	Mountain	0.109	Mountain	0.125	East South Central	0.084
East South Central	0.208	East South Central	0.124	East South Central	0.127	Mountain	0.091
New England	0.257	New England	0.165	West North Central	0.152	West North Central	0.118
West North Central	0.269	West North Central	0.179	New England	0.180	New England	0.142
Pacific	0.296	Pacific	0.219	East North Central	0.195	East North Central	0.156
Alberta	**0.331**	**Alberta**	**0.232**	Pacific	0.221	Pacific	0.179
East North Central	0.342	East North Central	0.253	Middle Atlantic	0.258	Middle Atlantic	0.218
Middle Atlantic	0.364	Middle Atlantic	0.289	**Ontario**	**0.315**	**Ontario**	**0.266**
Ontario	**0.431**	**Ontario**	**0.315**	**Alberta**	**0.340**	**Alberta**	**0.269**
Prairies	**0.442**	**Maritimes**	**0.324**	**Maritimes**	**0.376**	**Maritimes**	**0.303**
Maritimes	**0.468**	**Prairies**	**0.348**	**British Columbia**	**0.389**	**British Columbia**	**0.340**
British Columbia	**0.530**	**British Columbia**	**0.415**	**Quebec**	**0.404**	**Quebec**	**0.377**
Quebec	**0.538**	**Quebec**		**Prairies**	**0.449**	**Prairies**	**0.381**
Canada	**0.463**	**Canada**	**0.323**	**Canada**	**0.369**	**Canada**	**0.311**
United States	0.260	United States	0.166	United States	0.171	United States	0.133

Comment

W. Craig Riddell
University of British Columbia

MOST OF THE CANADIAN RESEARCH on the labour market impacts of the North American Free Trade Agreement (NAFTA) and increased integration more generally has focused on the effects on wages and employment in specific industries. Related studies often take advantage of the facts that tariffs fell more in some industries than in others, and that those industries in which tariffs did not change (or changed very little) can be used as a comparison group to control for other influences on wages and employment. In these studies, the empirical strategy rests on the assumption that factors other than NAFTA influenced wages and employment to a similar degree in both high-tariff and low-tariff sectors. Stating this point somewhat differently, behaviours in low-tariff sectors provide a counterfactual estimate of what would have occurred in high-tariff sectors in the absence of NAFTA.

However, increased North American integration is expected to have broader effects on the wage structure that go beyond those that may affect specific industries. In particular, standard trade theory predicts pressures toward convergence in the wage structure, and examining the consequences of such pressures is the objective of Thomas Lemieux's study. This is a challenging task for at least two reasons. First, there are limitations in the data sources available for analyzing the Canadian wage structure during the relevant time period (before and after the introduction of NAFTA). Second, there is the usual but nonetheless challenging problem of taking into account other influences on the wage structure. A number of other developments over the past two decades are also likely to have impacted on the Canadian and U.S. wage structures, so some method of accounting for their influences is needed. A partial list of such developments would include:

- Overall productivity and economic growth performance;

- Two major recessions at the beginning of each decade, both more severe in Canada than in the United States;

- Changes in labour market institutions and policies, such as minimum wages and unionization;

- The magnitude and composition of immigrant flows;

- Differential changes in the educational attainment of new cohorts entering the labour force.

Developing an empirical framework that allows one to control for these other influences, and thus to identify the impact of increased integration, is a major challenge. Lemieux's approach is insightful and appealing. He uses the regional wage structure and its evolution as a benchmark against which to compare changes in the national wage structure. The argument is that the extent to which there has been convergence in wage structures across regions in a common labour market is a useful benchmark measure of how much convergence we can realistically expect from increased integration across countries.

There are three key findings:

1. In contrast to the predictions of standard trade theory, there has been no convergence of the Canadian and U.S. wage structures during the past two decades. Indeed, if anything the two wage structures have tended to diverge.

2. Canada-U.S. differences in the structure of wages are not large relative to regional differences within each country.

3. The magnitude of the divergence between the Canadian and U.S. wage structures is somewhat smaller when regional wage structures are used as a benchmark.

Before discussing these findings, it is worth pointing out some data limitations that place constraints on the analysis. A major reason why we know relatively little about the evolution of the Canadian wage structure is the lack of suitable data. Canada's monthly Labour Force Survey (LFS) added questions on wages only in 1997, whereas the U.S. Current Population Survey has provided data on wages and key related information such as union status on a monthly basis since the early 1980s, and on an annual basis since the early 1970s. In the absence of wage rate information in the monthly LFS, most Canadian researchers have turned to the Survey of Consumer Finances (SCF), an annual retrospective survey for which public use files are available since the early 1980s. However, this data source has several important limitations. There is no measure of the hourly wage rate. The 'wage' measure most frequently used is weekly earnings — annual earnings divided by the number of weeks worked in the previous year. This measure thus incorporates both the hourly wage rate and the number of hours worked per week. Beyond that, the SCF provides limited other information — for example, there is no measure of union status, a well-known influence on the wage structure. Finally, the SCF ended in 1997 so there is an historical break in the time-series information.

An alternative is to use the LFS for recent information and one of a small number of LFS supplements that were carried out prior to 1997. This was the choice made by Lemieux. He uses the 2001 LFS and the 1984 Survey of Union Membership (SUM). The advantages of the SUM is that it contains a good measure of the hourly wage rate and provides information on union status as well as other key factors such as gender, age and educational attainment. A potential disadvantage is that the years 1984 and 2001 were not points at which the economy was at a similar stage of the business cycle, so some of the comparison between the two time periods may reflect cyclical influences.

Most of what we believe about the evolution of the wage structure and wage inequality in Canada is based on studies using the SCF. It is therefore worth checking whether similar results are obtained from alternative data sources, which is a valuable side benefit of the present study based on the SUM and LFS.

Turning now to the main findings, the divergence between wage structures at the national level has two main elements. First, Canadian wages (in US$) were somewhat higher than U.S. wages in 1984, but substantially lower in 2001. Second, in 1984, wage dispersion was somewhat higher in the United States than in Canada and the gap increased substantially thereafter. These findings control for changes in the skills (age and education) of workers in the two countries.

A major source of increased wage dispersion in the United States was the rise in the wage premium associated with higher education (usually measured by the high school). For men, Lemieux finds that this wage differential increased in both countries, but much more so in the United States. For women, the high school–university wage differential rose only slightly in Canada but increased substantially in the United States.

These results suggest that pressures toward convergence are relatively weak compared with forces that operate in the opposite direction. Here are some developments that may have contributed to this divergence:

- The real minimum wage rose in Canada from the mid-1980s to the late 1990s, in contrast to the U.S. experience where the minimum wage remained approximately constant.

- The decline in natural resource prices over this period may have had a disproportionate effect on Canada, as is suggested by the drop in wages in Alberta and British Columbia relative to other Canadian regions.

Examination of the data for the two countries at the national level points to divergence rather than convergence. However, the divergence story is somewhat weakened when regional differences are taken into account. For example, wages in Ontario — the province that accounts for most of Canada-U.S. trade — were close to U.S. levels in both 1984 and 2001. At the regional level, there is also evidence of convergence in the high school–university wage differential for Canadian women relative to their U.S. counterparts. However, even taking into account the regional wage structure, there is clear divergence in the high school–university wage differential for Canadian men relative to U.S. men.

Overall, the absence of an increase in wage inequality in Canada over the past two decades — a time when there was a significant rise in wage inequality south of the border — is somewhat surprising. It suggests that pressures toward convergence with the U.S. wage structure were weak or offset by forces operating in the other direction. Sorting out the contributions of such factors as increased Canada-U.S. integration and changes in labour market institutions and policies like minimum wages and union coverage, and accounting for immigration and cyclical influences represent a major empirical challenge. Lemieux's study is a valuable contribution to our understanding, both because of its substantive findings and its insightful idea of using the regional wage structure as a benchmark against which to assess the extent of convergence that can realistically be expected in national wage structures.

Eugene Beaulieu   &   Christopher D. Joy
University of Calgary   Mount Royal College

4

The Political Economy of North American Integration, Labour Market Adjustments and Plant Closures in Canada *Canada*

F15   F13   L60
F16   D72   J24   L11

ABSTRACT

THIS STUDY EXAMINES THE POLITICAL ECONOMY of trade policy in Canada and links observed trade policy preferences to labour market outcomes and evidence on restructuring (or the rationalization of production) in the manufacturing sector. It contributes to our understanding of how economic integration plays out politically and how the politics are linked to the economic consequences of trade policy. It also identifies political cleavages that are likely to form in the current debate over economic integration. The study finds that skilled workers were more supportive of the Canada-U.S. Free Trade Agreement (FTA) than unskilled workers and links these preferences to the labour market effects of FTA. It presents evidence showing that plant closures and layoffs occurred in high-tariff industries, which industries are low-skill intensive. However, the link between the Heckscher-Ohlin-Vanek (HOV) model, trade policy preferences, and labour market outcomes is more tenuous.

INTRODUCTION

IN THE MID-1980S, ECONOMISTS IN CANADA offered theoretical arguments for and against (mostly for) further integration with the United States. At the time, there was relatively little empirical evidence on the *new* trade theories based on recent theoretical innovations. One of the conclusions of the

MacDonald Commission on the Economic Union and Development Prospects for Canada was:

> The most important advantage to Canadians of a free-trade agreement with the United States would be its effect on productivity and thus, in particular, on the competitiveness of our manufacturing sector. Improved and more stable access would create opportunities for Canadian business and increase the tendency toward specialization and rationalization of Canadian production.
> (MacDonald Commission, Volume 1, p. 325)

Economists did discuss the distributional aspects of the free trade agreement, but the main focus was on its net effect — which most economists concluded was positive. The economic prediction of gains to Canada from FTA was based on relatively small static welfare gains and large gains from the rationalization of production (and associated gains from scale economies) as well as a competitiveness effect.[1] As the above quote from the MacDonald Commission report illustrates, the economic case for deeper integration with the United States directly influenced policy makers at the highest level. Although the economic case for trade liberalization did recognize that the process involved adjustment and that there were distributional aspects to changes in trade policy, a net increase in welfare was predicted. However, the political debate over the agreement focused, in part, on these distributional aspects. Political cleavages were based on the impact that the agreement was expected to have on the labour market and on restructuring in the manufacturing sector (implying plant closures and openings). To date, these three intrinsically connected aspects of the political economy of economic integration (political cleavages, labour market adjustment, and restructuring of the manufacturing sector) have not been analyzed in a coherent and unified framework. It is important to understand the political economy of economic integration in a unified framework in order to assess the effects, and hence the salability and feasibility of future directions toward economic integration.

Twenty years after the national debate of the 1980s over trade policy, Canada today faces important decisions regarding the future course of its trade policy. Should it pursue deeper and closer integration within North America? Should it pursue increased integration within the broader region — the Americas? Should Canada focus instead on a multilateral approach? These approaches may not be mutually exclusive and this study will not address them directly. However, the study will empirically examine the politics and economics of North American integration in order to inform the current policy debate. In particular, the primary goal of the study is to provide a unified framework to analyze the political cleavages of trade policy in Canada, the impact of

North American integration on labour markets in Canada as well as its impact on restructuring in the manufacturing sector.

Our research has an important purpose in addition to informing the current debate over the direction of future trade policy. Evidence on the political support functions for trade policy provides direct evidence on who is more likely to support increased integration and indirect evidence on the nature of labour mobility in Canada. Linking revealed preferences to trade theory provides evidence regarding the underlying economic model (still an unsolved issue). Linking the preferences to labour market outcomes provides further evidence on the underlying economic model. Moreover, if preferences over trade policy are found to be consistent with labour market outcomes, this is an indication that the observed popular backlash against globalization reflects, at least in part, concerns about its economic consequences.

The study is primarily empirical in nature. But unlike some empirical examinations of the connection between trade policy and the labour market, the present study pays close attention to economic theory. It summarizes the underlying economic models that link trade policy to the labour market. The empirical analysis is informed by the theory and explores different theoretical hypotheses. The empirical section examines the underlying theory focusing on the three components of the political economy of economic integration spelled out above: political support for economic integration, labour market adjustment, and empirical evidence on manufacturing rationalization. The methodology and data used in the analysis are discussed separately for each.

The study sets first a theoretical background for the subsequent empirical analysis. The Heckscher-Ohlin-Vanek model, which is a version of the neoclassical Heckscher-Ohlin-Samuelson (HOS) model, is used in the study because it can make predictions about how changes in trade policy will impact different factors of production. It should be noted that the HOV model has performed poorly in empirical studies. In fact, it has performed so poorly that Trefler (1993) claims that "its predictions are always rejected empirically." Another important contribution in this field by Trefler (1995), entitled "The Case of the Missing Trade," has spawned an entire stream of literature and further illustrates the poor empirical performance of the HOV model.[2] More recently, however, Davis, Weinstein, Bradford and Shimpo (1997) show that the HOV framework is a valid underlying general equilibrium model for examining the impact on national economies of international disturbances (or trade policy changes). Moreover, Trefler and Zhu (2001) take another look at the evidence and concur with Davis et al. (1997). Trefler and Zhu conclude that "the model is most certainly useful for thinking about the impact of international trade on factor prices..." (2001, p. 148) Therefore, the HOV model is a reasonable approach for the purposes of this study. Moreover, work by Balistreri

(1997) shows that the HOV model does a reasonable job of explaining Canadian preferences over trade policy.

The HOV model provides an important link between the impact of trade policy on labour market outcomes and preferences over trade policy. Canadian preferences about the Canada-U.S. Free Trade Agreement are examined with individual-level survey data. Two aspects of these preferences are of particular importance. First, who was more likely to support FTA: skilled or unskilled workers? Second, were preferences determined by the industry in which the respondents were employed? If industry of employment is an important determinant of trade policy preferences, it suggests that workers are not mobile between industries, or that the short-run adjustment costs outweigh the long-run benefits of adjusting to a change in trade policy. Preferences over trade policy are also compared to the predictions of the HOV model.

After scrutinizing preferences over trade policy, the study looks at the impact of FTA on the labour market and on restructuring in the manufacturing sector. In particular, the study examines the structure of tariff reductions implemented through FTA and uses a *treatment-control* approach to probe the impact of FTA on earnings across occupations in the Canadian labour market. Micro-economic labour market data from the Survey of Consumer Finances for 1981, 1988, 1991 and 1997 are used to analyze the labour market. The study then considers the impact that a change in trade policy as dramatic as FTA could have on restructuring in the manufacturing sector. In the short run, this restructuring includes plant closures as the economy adjusts to the integrated market. The incidence and causes of plant closures in the Canadian manufacturing sector are explored and the link between FTA, preferences over FTA, plant closures and the impact on the labour market are then considered. This part of the analysis is based on a unique dataset compiled by the authors on all plant closures recorded in major Canadian newspapers between 1982 and 1997.

The study finds a consistent pattern between political coalitions and labour market outcomes in Canada. That is, the politics of trade policy in Canada and the labour market outcomes reveal that skilled workers were more likely to support economic integration and that they benefited from FTA. On the other hand, lower-skilled workers were more likely to oppose FTA and were adversely affected by North American integration. This highlights a connection between trade policy preferences and labour market outcomes. A corollary of these results is that workers are fairly mobile between industries. That is, if workers are mobile between sectors (industries), political cleavages and labour market consequences will be independent of the industry of employment. Finally, the pattern of plant closures in Canada is consistent with observed labour market outcomes and with political preferences. The connection between plant closures and labour market consequences helps explain the observed regionally-based political cleavages over trade policy.

The second section below provides an overview of the theory linking trade, labour market outcomes and preferences over trade policy. The third section examines the political economy of FTA and analyzes the pattern of political cleavages over FTA. The fourth section considers the impact of FTA on the labour market, while the fifth section looks at the impact of FTA on restructuring in the manufacturing sector. Finally, the last section draws some conclusions.

THEORY CONNECTING TRADE AND WAGES

TRADE POLICY CLEAVAGES

POLITICAL CLEAVAGES ARE DETERMINED by the distributional consequences of trade policy, which in turn depend on the underlying model of international trade. In the standard Heckscher-Ohlin-Samuelson model of international trade with perfect factor mobility, Stolper and Samuelson (1941) showed that an import tariff will increase or decrease the real return to each factor of production across all industries depending on the country's relative factor endowments. The Stolper-Samuelson theorem predicts, therefore, that the distributional effects of tariff changes depend entirely on the nature of factor ownership, not on the industry of employment. This result has become known as the *factor-industry detachment corollary* of the Stolper-Samuelson theorem.[3] In this case, political cleavages are formed along factor lines.

The polar opposite model is the all-factor-specific model, where factors are completely immobile between industries in the economy.[4] If factors are specific to the industry in which they are used, the real return to a factor increases (decreases) in industries that are positively (negatively) affected by trade policy. Here, the expected distributional consequences of tariff changes depend entirely on the industry of employment, not on the type of factor ownership. In this case, political cleavages are formed along industry lines.

The distinction between these polar cases is important for understanding the impact of trade policy on the distribution of income among domestic factors of production. Early empirical evidence suggests that preferences over trade policy are linked to industry. Magee (1980) examined the observed political alignments of business- and labour-lobby positions toward the 1973 comprehensive trade bill before the U.S. Congress. He concluded that political lobbying activity is organized along industry rather than factor lines. Irwin (1994, 1996) examined political cleavages over trade policy in the 1906 and 1923 British general elections, which were essentially referenda on free trade. He analyzed the county voting patterns from these elections to determine factor mobility and also concluded that cleavages are drawn along industry, not factor lines.

Hiscox (2002) considers the issue of coalitions over trade policies in six countries: the United States, Britain, France, Sweden, Canada, and Australia. He does not examine the empirical evidence for Canada, but argues that industry-group pressures dominated cleavages over trade policy. However, Pyne (2000) analyzes lobbying efforts surrounding FTA and finds strong evidence showing that industries do not matter. Using a methodology similar to that of Magee (1980), he examines representations made before the House of Commons committee studying the Canada-U.S. Free Trade Agreement. He finds strong support for the proposition that labour behaves as the Stolper-Samuelson theorem would predict, but qualified support for the notion that capital behaves according to that theorem. Other studies have looked at the relationship between stock market returns and import prices (Grossman and Levinsohn, 1989), or stock market returns and the Canada-U.S. Free Trade Agreement (Brander, 1991; Thompson, 1993, 1994). These studies find some evidence that capital is industry-specific.

Concerns with earlier studies make it difficult to draw conclusions about the correct model. The study by Magee (1980) is short-run in nature (based on U.S. trade policy over a four-year horizon), and therefore biased against finding factor mobility. Irwin's studies (1994, 1996) have some data limitations and their results refer to early 20th-century England when factors were less mobile than they are today. The stock market return studies focus exclusively on one factor, capital, which is generally considered industry-specific in the short run. In fact, there is some evidence that the all-factor-specific result is overturned in the long run. Beaulieu and Magee (2004) find that Political Action Committee contributions to congressional supporters of the North American Free Trade Agreement (NAFTA) were determined by the factor of production (capital or labour). They argue that political cleavages around NAFTA reflect long-run interests and find evidence supporting these long-run considerations. Pyne (2000) finds similar evidence for lobby positions on FTA in Canada. Rogowski (1987) examines historical episodes of global change in exposure to international trade and finds evidence that political cleavages are drawn along factor lines in the long run.

The first attempts to use micro-economic data to examine individual preferences over trade policy were independent studies by Balistreri (1997) and Beaulieu (1997). Both employ the same data as in the present study [from the Canadian National Election Study (CNES)] and examine preferences over trade policy, but they focus on different aspects of political cleavages. Beaulieu (1997, 2002b) looks directly at whether political cleavages are determined by factors of production or industry of employment. The evidence presented in his studies is that political cleavages reflect factor ownership and not industry of employment. Balistreri (1997) seeks to determine whether preferences of individual Canadians on FTA conform to the Heckscher-Ohlin-Vanek model. Balistreri treats occupations as factors of production and finds that Canadian preferences are consistent with the factor-content predictions of that model. However, he does not examine the validity of the factor-industry detachment corollary, but asserts that factors are mobile between sectors. Furthermore, he does not verify whether voting patterns reflect industry of employment.

More recently, additional evidence based on micro data has emerged in support of the factor-industry detachment corollary. Scheve and Slaughter (2001) analyze individual-level survey data on U.S. opinions about generic trade policy. They find that individual preferences on trade policy reflect factor, not industry interests. Beaulieu (2002a) examines U.S. congressional votes on FTA, NAFTA and GATT (General Agreement on Tariffs and Trade) and finds that the voting pattern on the floor of the U.S. Congress supports the factor-industry detachment corollary.

The present study provides additional evidence on political cleavages surrounding trade policy in Canada in the long run. It extends and builds on earlier work by Balistreri (1997) and Beaulieu (1997, 2002b) by analyzing individual preferences on a specific piece of trade policy legislation, FTA. The only major issue in the 1988 Canadian federal election was the ratification of FTA, and that election became a de facto referendum on the agreement. Therefore, the 1988 election provides an exceptional opportunity to study the distributional consequences of international trade and commercial policy in the long run. FTA is an international agreement and thus considered a long-run commitment, so there is no institutional bias toward short-run results as in Magee's study. Rather than testing the HOV model, as in Balistreri (1997), our study empirically examines whether the factor-industry detachment corollary held in Canada during the debates over free trade with the United States. It then considers whether voting patterns reflect HOV predictions and compares these predictions to labour market outcomes. Before analyzing the empirical evidence, a summary of the Heckscher-Ohlin-Vanek model is provided.

THE HECKSCHER-OHLIN-VANEK MODEL

THE HECKSCHER-OHLIN-VANEK VERSION of the Heckscher-Ohlin-Samuelson model is a simple way to incorporate factor content into trade. Essentially, the underlying theorem states that countries are net exporters of their abundant factors and importers of their scarce factors. The transmission mechanism is the fact that goods embody the services of factors used to produce them. This means that countries are able to trade at world prices, which allows them to specialize their resources along their factor-based comparative advantage. The HOV model has two appealing features that make it appropriate in the current context. First, factors can be distinguished in n-dimensions, which is an improvement over a simple two-factor (usually capital and labour) system. Second, factor abundance is measured against world endowments, not relative to other factors.

In order to establish the theoretical context, we must first make simplifying assumptions: (1) there are at least as many goods (n) as factors (m), therefore $n \geq m$; (2) preferences are homothetic and identical; (3) technologies are identical across countries; (4) economies are perfectly competitive; (5) there are no transportation costs; (6) goods trade freely at the international level, but factors do not; and (7) endowments are sufficiently similar to produce factor price equalization (FPE). Given these assumptions, we can describe the production of Country 1 as follows:

(1) $\qquad V = AX,$

where V is a vector of factor endowments ($m \times 1$); A is a matrix of positive technology constants; and X is a vector of outputs ($n \times 1$). This identity shows that a country's output, X, can be decomposed into its factor endowments, V, using the matrix of technology constants, A. Introducing trade and simplifying into a two-country world, we have:

(2) $\qquad AT = V - a(V + V^*) = V - aV^w,$

where T is a vector of net exports ($n \times 1$); V^* is Country 2's vector of factor endowments ($m \times 1$); a is Country 1's share in total world output; V is Country 1's vector of factor endowments; V^w is the world endowment vector ($V + V^*$ in a two-country world). The factors employed in the production of exports are the product of net exports and the technology coefficient (AT), and are equal to a country's *vector of excess factor supply*, $V - aV^w$. Equation (2) corresponds to the HOV theorem: a country exports (imports) the services of its relatively abundant (scarce) factors.

We are interested in what happens to factor prices, on average, after trade liberalization. Following Ethier (1984) and Balistreri (1997), let $p^0 = w^0 A(w^0)$ be the initial price (pre-FTA), and $p^1 = w^1 A(w^1)$ the terminal price (post-FTA). A is now a function of changes in w factor prices. Now let:

(3) $\qquad b(w) = wA(w)(p^1 - p^0)',$

where p and w are row vectors and $A(\ )$ is a function of discrete changes in w. Using the mean-value theorem to find the mean first derivative of $b(w)$, and using the inner-product rule to find the value of $b'(\bar{w})$, we get:

(4) $\qquad b(w^1) - b(w^0) = (w^1 - w^0)[A(\bar{w}) + (\bar{w})dA(\bar{w})](p^1 - p^0)'.$

From cost minimization, $(\overline{w})\, dA\,(\overline{w}) = 0$, and therefore:

$$b(w^1) - b(w^0) = (w^1 - w^0)[A\,(\overline{w})\,](p^1 - p^0)'.$$

From the zero-profit condition, $b(w^1) - b(w^0) = (p^1 - p^0)(p^1 - p^0)' > 0$ because the right-hand side is an inner product. Therefore:

(5) $\qquad (w^1 - w^0)[A\,(\overline{w})\,](p^1 - p^0)' > 0.$

This result implies that the elements of the vector of changes in factor prices $(w^1 - w^0)$ are positively correlated with the corresponding elements of $A\,(\overline{w})\,(p^1 - p^0)'$. In other words, large positive changes in w_i are, on average, associated with large a_{ij} and large positive changes in p_j. As Ethier explains: "There is a tendency for changes in relative commodity prices to be accompanied by increases in the rewards of factors employed most intensively by those goods whose prices have relatively risen the most and employed least intensively by those goods whose relative prices have fallen the most." (1984, p. 164)

In terms of FTA, this implies that if Canadian export prices rise relative to import prices, the returns to factors used relatively intensively in exports would be likely to increase relatively for Canada. As Balistreri (1997) points out, we can identify the group of factors by looking at the signs of factors in net exports from Equation (2), $AT = V - aV^w$. It is likely, therefore, that the income of factors whose services are exported will increase and those whose services are imported will decline. In the next section, we examine whether preferences over trade policies follow this pattern. In the subsequent section, we examine whether labour market outcomes are consistent with the factor content predictions and preferences over trade policy.

THE POLITICAL ECONOMY OF ECONOMIC INTEGRATION

THE FIRST PART OF THE EMPIRICAL ANALYSIS examines individual-level survey data to determine the political cleavages of trade policy in Canada. This section draws heavily on work by Beaulieu (1997, 2002b) and by Balistreri (1997). Three central issues are explored. First, did the industry of employment affect preferences over trade policy? Second, who was more likely to support FTA, and by implication what groups are more likely to support further trade liberalization? Third, are the patterns of political cleavages surrounding FTA consistent with the HOV model predictions? Survey data from the 1988 CNES are used because that event provides an exceptional opportunity to examine the political economy of trade legislation.[5]

THE VOTE ON FTA

THE EVENTS SURROUNDING THE SIGNING OF FTA and the 1988 general election in Canada are well documented elsewhere.[6] The following overview of those events serves to remind the reader that the 1988 vote in Canada was essentially a referendum on free trade.

The ratification process leading up to the election linked FTA to the election outcome. The Canadian and U.S. governments entered formal negotiations on September 26, 1985. After some setbacks at the negotiation table, the two sides reached an eleventh-hour agreement and signed FTA on October 3, 1987. Before the agreement could become law, both countries had to ratify it. By contrast with the United States, the ratification of the agreement gave rise to an enormous political battle in Canada.[7] The implementation of an international agreement is a federal responsibility and by constitutional convention, it must be tabled in the House of Commons. As the debate over FTA intensified, some opponents to the deal argued that the Government of Canada should let the people resolve the debate in a general election. In fact, John Turner, leader of the Liberal Party, then the Official Opposition, instructed the Liberal-dominated Senate to block passage of the FTA implementing legislation and demanded that the Prime Minister let Canadians decide![8] The Progressive Conservative government called a general election for November 21, 1988. The leaders of both opposition parties promised to abrogate FTA if elected, while the Senate leaders agreed to pass the agreement into legislation if the Conservative Party won a majority of seats in the lower house.[9]

Certainly, the historical-institutional account of the 1988 election suggests that it was an opportunity for Canadians to directly and effectively contribute to trade policy.[10] However, some observers see this interpretation as too simplistic. Pammett concludes that FTA was only one factor in the 1988 election, claiming that it was determined the same way most elections in Canada are — by a combination of decisions based on current rather than longer term considerations (1989, pp. 122-125). These considerations were often negative, with voters choosing the lesser-of-two-evils alternative. Le Duc argues that the 1988 election was just that, an election, not a referendum on free trade: "Canadian voters did not deliver a positive 'mandate' on free trade." (1991, p. 351)

Survey evidence presented in Table 1 contradicts Le Duc's interpretation of the 1988 election. Unlike any other policy issue raised in Canadian elections during the 1970s and 1980s, the electorate overwhelmingly considered FTA to be the single most important issue in 1988. In fact, FTA was perceived as the first or second most important issue of the campaign by 88 percent of those

TABLE 1

MOST IMPORTANT ELECTION ISSUES, 1974-88

	1974	1979	1980	1984	1988
Economic Issues					
Economy in General	5	11	9	17	2
Inflation, Cost of Living, Wage and					
Price Controls	46	14	14	2	0
Taxes	3	8	3	3	4
Government Spending, Deficit, Budget	3	4	17	12	7
Unemployment, Jobs	3	10	4	36	2
Free Trade	0	0	0	0	88
Other Economic Issues	3	1	1	3	0
Confederation Issues	6	28	13	5	8
Resources Issues	2	9	32	2	9
Social Issues					
Housing, Health, Medicare, Pensions, etc.	12	5	2	11	14
Other Issues					
Foreign Policy, Defence	2	2	3	3	1
Leaders, Leadership	6	14	15	8	5
Change, the Parties, Retrospective Evaluations	1	8	8	14	1
Trust, Patronage, Majority Government, the Pools	7	1	4	4	1
All Other Issues	3	2	2	4	3
None, No Important Issues, Don't Know	30	28	22	25	5
Number of Observations	2,445	2,668	1,786	3,377	1,202

Note: This table was adapted from Clarke, Jenson, Le Duc and Pammett (1991), Table 4.1, p. 70.
Percentages are rounded and do not add up to 100 percent because two responses were coded for
some respondents.

surveyed, against 5 percent for leadership. Moreover, only 5 percent considered the 1988 election as a *no issue* election, down from the 22 to 30 percent who did not identify an issue in previous elections. It is unusual for even 50 percent of respondents to identify a single issue as the most important in a general election. This sets the 1988 campaign apart from other recent general elections in Canada.[11]

Citing FTA as the most important issue is a necessary but not a sufficient condition for treating the 1988 election as a referendum on the matter. Some voters may have seen FTA as the most important issue in the election, but were simply not issue-driven voters. That is, their vote may have been determined by party affiliation, local candidates or leadership issues.[12] However, voting patterns were strongly associated with positions on FTA.

Approximately 71 percent of FTA supporters voted for the Conservative Party, while 81 percent of opponents to the agreement voted for one of the two parties opposed to FTA; voting patterns in the 1988 federal election were not statistically independent from positions on FTA.[13] This evidence supports the claim that Canadians' positions on FTA were highly correlated with their voting decisions.

Results indicating that a voter's position on FTA was highly correlated with his/her choice of party in the polling booth suggest that it is reasonable to treat the 1988 general election as a de facto referendum on FTA. They also corroborate the premise that voting coalitions were based on trade policy positions. It is thus reasonable to assume that voters were well informed about the consequences of FTA and had an incentive to vote *their pocketbooks*.

WHO SUPPORTED FTA?

AS ALREADY MENTIONED, the 1988 Canadian National Election Study is used to examine the preferences of the Canadian electorate toward FTA. The analysis is based on directly observed preferences over FTA, that is, an individual's 'Position on FTA' as expressed in the post-election survey. The type of factor ownership is defined by embodied human capital (skilled and unskilled labour), measured by the person's education level and by the implied skill level of the occupation. These measures are used because other measures of human capital are not reported in the survey data. Also, factor ownership is limited to human capital considerations primarily because ownership of physical capital and land is not captured in the data.

The empirical analysis encompasses factors of production and industries, as well as variables used to control for other potential determinants of revealed preferences on trade policy. The following comprehensive empirical model is estimated:

$$(6) \qquad \Pr(\text{support} = 1) = F\left((\beta_0) + \sum_{j=1}^{J} \beta_j skill_j + \sum_{i=1}^{I} \alpha_i ind_i + X\gamma \right),$$

where *support* is an indicator variable for supporting the agreement (*support*=1); $skill_j$ is an indicator variable for skill endowment; ind_i is an indicator variable for employment in industry i; and X is a matrix containing other variables that may affect the probability of supporting free trade. The β_j parameters are the j coefficients on the skill levels; α_i are the i coefficients on industry; and γ is a vector of coefficients on the control variables. The equation is estimated using a maximum-likelihood logit model. It is a comprehensive model because it includes both the factors of production and the industry of employment.

The econometric analysis employs control variables, X, for other potential determinants of preferences over trade policy. These other potential determinants include region, age, union membership and party affiliation. Although regional effects may reflect the regional concentration of industries, there may be historical and institutional reasons for regional effects that are independent of industry.[14] To the extent that unions provide rents to their members, the latter will likely oppose increased competition and, therefore, will be against FTA.

The Canada-U.S. Free Trade Agreement implied a great deal of transition in the labour market. Therefore, given an increased probability of facing job displacement, those with higher adjustment costs were less likely to support FTA. Persons with relatively high adjustment costs are typically older and married (if job displacement means relocating residence). However, the trade agreement would affect older workers not in the labour force most directly through consumption rather than through resource allocation effects. Therefore, retired voters (over 65 years) could be expected a priori to favour FTA to the extent that the agreement was supposed to benefit consumers, and to the extent that older persons would be affected more through consumption than through trade-induced resource allocation.

One potentially important determinant of preferences over trade policy is home ownership. House prices in locations with a heavy concentration of employment in industries heavily protected by tariffs may decline with the reduction or elimination of tariffs. Homeowners may oppose trade liberalization because of these effects, independent of the type of factor or industry in which they are employed. Home ownership effects may offset and obscure the predicted support for trade liberalization among retired voters as discussed above. Unfortunately, there is no information on home ownership in the CNES data. Scheve and Slaughter (2001) find evidence that home ownership affects preferences over trade policy in the United States.

Party affiliation may also have determined positions on FTA. The trade agreement was closely tied to the Progressive Conservative government and its re-election campaign in 1988. Affiliation with that party is expected to increase the probability of supporting FTA. Note that it would be a mistake to include current party affiliation on the right-hand side of the equation, because party support in 1988 is an endogenous variable. Therefore, the party for which a person voted in the previous general election (1984) was used to measure party affiliation in order to eliminate endogeneity problems associated with a contemporaneous measure of that variable. Using party affiliation in 1984 reduces the sample size to persons who were politically *active* both in 1984 and in 1988. However, our main focus is on whether factors or industries matter in positions taken over trade policy, and on whether skilled and unskilled workers supported FTA. The results reported below with respect to factor and industry preferences over trade policy are not significantly affected by the inclusion of a party affiliation variable, or by truncating the sample so as to include party affiliation in 1984.

The results from the estimation of Equation (6) are presented in Table 2. An important result that is robust across the different specifications of the comprehensive model is that skill endowment helps determine positions over FTA. That is, the type of factor ownership is a statistically significant and important determinant of preferences on trade policy, even when the industry of employment is included in the model. The sign of the estimated coefficients is robust to the different measures of human capital and to the different model specifications. Table 2 shows qualitatively similar results for high- and low-skilled occupations regardless of how skill is defined. Note that when skill is defined by occupation, the chi-squared statistic fails to reject the null hypothesis that the coefficient estimates on skill are statistically insignificant (see the second last row of Table 2 for Model 2). Note that even in this model, the coefficient estimate on high-skilled occupations is positive and statistically significant. The statistical insignificance of the joint hypothesis that occupations affect the probability of supporting FTA may reflect a more serious collinearity problem with the industry variables when skill is defined on the basis of occupation than when it is defined by education level.

Few of the industry dummy variables are statistically significant in the comprehensive model. Moreover, these variables are not jointly significant in either model shown in Table 2. This can be seen by considering the last row of Table 2, which presents the chi-squared statistics on the joint significance of industry variables. The result indicating that industry of employment does not determine preferences over trade policy is consistent with those of Thompson (1993, 1994), who found few significant effects of news about FTA on stock prices across industries.

These results reveal that factors of production are important determinants of preferences over trade policy and show support for the factor-industry detachment corollary of the Stolper-Samuelson theorem. Beaulieu (2002b) explores this issue through a number of different approaches and concludes that the evidence corroborates the factor-industry detachment corollary. This implies that labour is mobile across industries. Contrary to the evidence presented in Magee (1980) and Irwin (1994, 1996) and to the arguments of Hiscox (2002), factors of production are found to be an important determinant of individual preferences over FTA. This is supported by more recent evidence on long-term trade policy and/or evidence based on micro-economic data. The result found here for individual Canadians is consistent with the evidence on Canadian lobbying positions examined by Pyne (2000), with evidence from U.S. opinion

TABLE 2

COMPREHENSIVE MODEL OF SUPPORT FOR FTA[a]

	MODEL 1		MODEL 2	
	COEFFICIENT	STANDARD ERROR	COEFFICIENT	STANDARD ERROR
Factor Model [b,c]				
High School Completed	0.149	0.156		
Technical School/College	0.482***	0.185		
University	0.592***	0.175		
Semi-skilled Occupation			0.254	0.189
Highly Skilled Occupation			0.333*	0.191
Industry				
Forestry/Fishing	−0.014	0.470	−0.056	0.481
Mining	−0.611	0.526	−0.528	0.533
Construction	0.122	0.272	0.162	0.274
Food Manufacturing	−0.543	0.465	−0.454	0.477
Textiles	−0.706	0.503	−0.659	0.518
Wood, Furniture, Paper	0.253	0.449	0.282	0.448
Chemicals, Rubber	−0.743	0.812	−0.640	0.799
Clay/Metals	0.334	0.406	0.288	0.409
Machinery and Equipment Mfg.	−0.001	0.425	0.014	0.433
Transport, Public Utilities	−0.447*	0.271	−0.323	0.294
Retail	−0.081	0.245	0.013	0.270
Services	−0.236	0.222	−0.016	0.219
Public Service	0.132	0.382	0.294	0.390
Age				
18–29 years	−0.195	0.218	−0.024	0.212
30–49 years	0.087	0.186	0.234	0.180
50–64 years	0.070	0.201	0.111	0.201
Region				
Atlantic	−0.210	0.174	−0.264	0.172
Quebec	0.191	0.159	0.173	0.159
Ontario	−0.220	0.150	−0.217	0.150
Union Member	−0.258**	0.124	−0.267**	0.124
Party Affiliation	1.540***	0.116	1.520***	0.115
Constant	−0.884***	0.246	−1.078***	0.292

TABLE 2 (CONT'D)

COMPREHENSIVE MODEL OF SUPPORT FOR FTA

	MODEL 1	MODEL 2
Number of Observations	1,463	1,463
Log. Likelihood	−893.03	−898.40
Chi Squared	237.60***	226.86***
Pseudo R-squared	0.12	0.11
Joint Significance of Factors (Chi Squared)	13.66***	3.06
Joint Significance of Industries (Chi Squared)	13.76	9.58

Notes: a Omitted categories are: Agriculture, 65 years and over, West, Non-union, Voted other than PC (PC is the acronym for the Progressive Conservative Party, the governing party at the time).
      b When skill is defined by education the omitted category is Less than high school completion. The other three categories are Completed high school; Technical school or college; and University. University includes those with some university, those with a BA or MA, and those with professional school training or a PhD.
      c The omitted category when factors are defined by occupation is Low-skilled occupations. The low-skilled occupations are unskilled clerical and sales, unskilled manual labourers and farm labourers. Semi-skilled occupations are semi-professionals, technicians, middle-managers, supervisors, foreman, semi-skilled clerks, semi-skilled manual workers. Highly skilled occupations are self-employed professionals, employed professionals, high-level managers; skilled clerical and sales, skilled crafts and farmers (excluding farm labourers).
    *   Indicates significance at the 10-percent level.
   **   Indicates significance at the 5-percent level.
   *** Indicates significance at the 1-percent level.

polls examined by Scheve and Slaughter (2001), with congressional voting patterns examined by Beaulieu (2002a) and with U.S. lobby positions examined by Beaulieu and Magee (2004). It is also in line with evidence from Balistreri (1997) showing that Canadian preferences over FTA reflect factor proportions in a pattern consistent with the predictions from the HOV model. Moreover, it is supported by recent international evidence based on micro-level survey data from 24 developing and developed countries (including Canada).[15]

Another important result emerging from Table 2 is the compelling evidence that skilled workers were more likely to support FTA than unskilled workers. This finding is robust for different definitions of skill and different model specifications, though it is stronger when skill is defined by the highest education level attained. The result showing that skilled Canadians were more likely to support FTA than unskilled Canadians is also found in recent studies of Canadian preferences over trade policy and holds for more generic questions about trade policy. Mendelsohn, Wolfe and Parkin (2002) and Mendelsohn and Wolfe (2001) present evidence that skilled Canadians are more likely than unskilled Canadians to support trade liberalization in general. Beaulieu, Benarroch and Gaisford (2004b) examine survey data on 24 countries from the

1995 International Social Survey Programme (ISSP) and conclude that skilled workers in most sample countries, including Canada, are more likely than unskilled workers to support trade liberalization based on a generic question about trade policy.

Although the finding that industry of employment is not an important determinant of trade policy supports the factor-industry detachment corollary of the Stolper-Samuelson theorem, the fact that skilled workers in Canada favour free trade with the United States seems at odds with that framework. Given that skilled workers in the United States are more likely to support free trade, as found by Scheve and Slaughter (2001) and Beaulieu (2002a), support for FTA in Canada is inconsistent with the HOS model. However, when trade models include scale economies and imperfect competition along with comparative advantage, it is possible to anticipate gains for skilled workers in both countries. For example, Dinopoulos, Syropoulos and Xu (1999) develop a two-country model of monopolistic competition with quasi-homothetic preferences and non-homothetic production in which skilled workers in both countries gain from trade. Beaulieu, Benarroch and Gaisford (2004a) extend the HOS model to endogenize the decision to acquire skills and arrive at the same result: skilled workers in both skill-scarce and skill-abundant countries can gain from trade liberalization. Beaulieu, Benarroch and Gaisford (2004b) develop a simple model with intra-industry trade liberalization within a monopolistic-competitive skill-intensive (manufacturing) sector and a labour-intensive (primary) sector and show that skilled workers in both skill-abundant and skill-scarce countries support trade liberalization.

The issue now becomes whether support for FTA is consistent with the HOV model. The results from estimating a modified version of Equation (6) that excludes industry of employment but includes 21 occupations are presented in Table 3. The coefficients of the occupation dummy variables indicate which occupations were more, or less, likely to support FTA. The other control variables are the same as in Table 2. Dummy variables for the highest level of education attained are included in the first column and excluded in the second column. We are primarily interested in the coefficients on occupation and the pattern is similar in both columns. The five occupational categories most supportive of FTA were 1) scientists and engineers, 2) crafts and equipment operators, 3) sales, 4) forestry and logging, and 5) managerial. The least supportive were 1) religious occupations, 2) material handling, 3) mining and quarrying, 4) services, and 5) clerical.

TABLE 3

WHO SUPPORTED FTA: THE HOV MODEL

	COEFFICIENT ESTIMATE	STANDARD ERROR	COEFFICIENT ESTIMATE	STANDARD ERROR
Education				
High School Completed	0.127	0.130		
Some Post Secondary	0.279*	0.152		
University Degree	0.486***	0.153		
Occupation (HOV Factors)				
Managerial and Administrative	0.551**	0.219	0.678***	0.216
Natural Sciences, Engineering and Mathematics	0.964***	0.315	1.149***	0.311
Social Sciences	0.381	0.323	0.622**	0.316
Religion	−0.454	0.961	−0.177	0.944
Teaching	0.253	0.270	0.498*	0.260
Medicine and Health	0.323	0.267	0.462*	0.261
Art, Literature and Recreation	0.420	0.367	0.555	0.364
Clerical	0.085	0.221	0.093	0.218
Sales	0.596***	0.236	0.619***	0.234
Services	0.046	0.248	0.010	0.247
Farming, Horticultural and Animal Husbandry	0.453*	0.259	0.426*	0.258
Fishing, Hunting and Trapping	0.357	0.634	0.242	0.634
Forestry and Logging	0.565	0.607	0.444	0.605
Mining and Quarrying	−0.149	0.516	−0.188	0.513
Processing	0.226	0.330	0.142	0.328
Machining	0.522	0.391	0.436	0.389
Product Fabricating, Assembling and Repairing	0.251	0.264	0.190	0.263
Construction Trades	0.488*	0.265	0.443*	0.263
Transport Equipment Operating	0.396	0.297	0.302	0.295
Material Handling	−0.307	0.480	−0.431	0.478
Other Crafts and Equipment Operating	0.741**	0.370	0.673*	0.370
Age				
18-29 years	−0.103	0.177	0.028	0.172
30-49 years	0.175	0.151	0.293**	0.146
50-64 years	0.185	0.162	0.226	0.162
Region				
Atlantic	−0.317**	0.143	−0.353**	0.142
Quebec	0.233*	0.126	0.221*	0.126
Ontario	−0.182	0.119	−0.173	0.118

TABLE 3 (CONT'D)

WHO SUPPORTED FTA: THE HOV MODEL

	COEFFICIENT ESTIMATE	STANDARD ERROR	COEFFICIENT ESTIMATE	STANDARD ERROR
Union Member	−0.234**	0.103	−0.245**	0.102
Voted PC in 1984	1.466***	0.093	1.466***	0.092
Constant	−1.341***	0.228	−1.240***	0.220
Number of Observations	2,270		2,276	
Log Likelihood	−1,385.9		−1,394.48	
Chi Squared	373.9***		365.2***	
Pseudo R-squared	0.12		0.12	

Notes: The omitted categories are: No schooling, Agriculture, 65 years and over, West, Non-union, Voted other than PC (PC is the acronym for the Progressive Conservative Party, the governing party at the time).
   *   Indicates significance at the 10-percent level.
   **   Indicates significance at the 5-percent level.
   ***   Indicates significance at the 1-percent level.

How does this pattern compare with the predicted impact of FTA from measuring relative factor supply in Canada and the United States? Table 4 compares the coefficients on occupation from Table 3 to the probable impact on occupations measured by Balistreri (1997). The results are mixed. The HOV model predicts that four of the five most supportive occupations are likely to be positively affected by FTA. However, the HOV model predicts a negative impact for the most supportive occupational group, that of scientists and engineers. The model also predicts that three out of the five least supportive occupations would be adversely affected by FTA. Again, however, the HOV model predicts a positive effect for the least supportive occupational group, that of religious occupations. Balistreri (1997) takes a slightly different approach. Rather than including dummy variables for occupations, he uses a dummy variable indicating the direction of the probable effect of FTA. He finds this variable statistically significant and bearing the correct sign. That is, persons in occupations expected to benefit from FTA (based on the HOV model) were, on average, more likely to support the agreement.

We have found that cleavages about Canadian trade policy are formed along factor lines, not industry lines. We have also found that skilled workers were more likely to support FTA than unskilled workers. Finally, the pattern of support for the trade agreement across occupations is somewhat consistent with the predictions of the HOV model. The next question to address is whether labour market outcomes are consistent with the pattern of preferences and/or the HOV model.

TABLE 4

COMPARISON OF HOV FACTOR CONTENT AND DIFFERENCE IN PREFERENCES ACROSS OCCUPATIONS

OCCUPATION	CANADIAN EMPLOYMENT (000s)	U.S. EMPLOYMENT (000s)	1–s(VW/V) (x 100)	PROBABLE (w¹–w⁰)	COEFFICIENTS FROM PREFERENCES REGRESSION
Managerial and Administrative	1,545	12,451	14.92	+	0.551
Natural Sciences, Engineering and Mathematics	457	4,600	–3.93	–	0.964
Social Sciences	218	1,440	28.57	+	0.381
Religion	32	271	11.07	+	–0.454
Teaching	528	5,687	–10.55	–	0.253
Medicine and Health	628	4,993	15.94	+	0.323
Art, Literature and Recreation	233	1,542	28.45	+	0.420
Clerical	2,090	25,084	–22.11	–	0.085
Sales	1,192	11,240	2.05	+	0.596
Services	1,642	19,864	–23.01	–	0.046
Farming, Horticulture and Animal Husbandry	459	1,007	70.00	+	0.453
Fishing, Hunting and Trapping	40	61	76.29	+	0.357
Forestry and Logging	46	148	60.39	+	0.565
Mining and Quarrying	56	237	50.86	+	–0.149
Processing	341	8,885	–154.11	–	0.226
Machining	183	2,007	–12.40	–	0.522
Product Fabricating, Assembling and Repairing	930	6,520	24.76	+	0.251
Construction Trades	660	5,334	14.70	+	0.488
Transport Equipment Operating	450	3,987	7.40	+	0.396
Material Handling	254	3,724	–47.09	–	–0.307
Other Crafts and Equipment Operating	151	884	35.62	+	0.741
All Occupations	12,135	119,966			

Source: The first four columns are from Balistreri, 1997, Table 1, p. 10.

LABOUR MARKET EFFECTS OF THE FTA

THE RESULTS PRESENTED ABOVE provide strong evidence that skilled workers were more likely to support FTA than unskilled workers. This conclusion may come as a surprise if Canada is (presumed to be) skilled-labour scarce relative to the United States. Consequently, these results may not seem plausible. However, the HOV predictions were somewhat consistent with this pattern. Are trade policy preferences consistent with the labour market consequences of FTA?

This section of the study draws on Beaulieu (2000), who used industry-level data to examine the effects of FTA on employment and earnings in Canada's manufacturing sector. FTA was expected to initiate a rationalization of production in manufacturing industries in Canada and lead to a reallocation of workers from high- to low-cost producers. The predicted impact was specialization and trade creation, with a corresponding expansion of industries enjoying a comparative advantage vis-à-vis the United States and a contraction of industries having a comparative disadvantage. Gaston and Trefler (1997) show that employment decreased across all manufacturing industries between 1989 and 1993 and that FTA tariff reductions account for only 15 percent of the observed employment decline. But these authors do not consider the distributional consequences of the trade agreement. Beaulieu (2000) finds that FTA contributed to a decline in manufacturing employment in Canada and that lower-skilled workers were more adversely affected than skilled workers.

It is important to emphasize that the previous section examined Canadian views on a specific trade policy, FTA. As Table 5 illustrates, FTA lowered trade barriers for low-skill-intensive manufacturing industries in Canada. The ratio of non-production to production workers was 0.28 for high-tariff industries and 0.48 for low-tariff industries in Canada prior to FTA.[16] Therefore, the finding that skilled workers supported the agreement is consistent with the standard HOS predictions with respect to FTA tariff reductions.[17] In other words, FTA lowered or removed tariffs in relatively low-skill-intensive industries.

Figure 1 shows that the real earnings of non-production workers increased while the real earnings of production workers was stagnant or declined slightly from 1983 to 1989. Therefore, FTA was ratified during an extended period of declining real earnings for production workers relative to non-production workers. From 1990 to 1992, this trend reversed as production workers' earnings increased faster than those of non-production workers. But the trend reversal was short lived and non-production workers' earnings increased faster than those of production workers between 1992 and 1996. As for employment, the number of production jobs grew while non-production jobs were stagnant or declined from 1983 to 1989. As mentioned above, manufacturing employment fell after 1989 but the decline was faster among production workers from 1989 to 1992. Beaulieu (2000) applies an econometric analysis to industry-level data and finds that FTA had a larger impact on production employment than on non-production employment. However, FTA was found to have had no effect on real earnings in the manufacturing sector.

We are interested in understanding how FTA affected the labour market, and whether the observed impact is consistent with the preferences over trade policy examined in the previous section. Individual-level data from the Survey of Consumer Finances (SCF) are used to analyze how earnings were affected across the occupational groups identified above. Standard *Mincerian* wage regressions are estimated for 1981, 1988, 1991 and 1996. The dependent variable is the natural log of real earnings while the right-hand side variables include gender, province, education, marital status and age. Dummy variables for occupations are included and the coefficients on these variables are interpreted as the premium paid for a given occupation. The estimation results from this standard wage regression reported in Table 6 are the coefficients on occupation dummy variables. Other regression results are not shown in order to save space — and because we are primarily interested in how different occupations performed during the post-FTA period.

Table 6 displays the occupation coefficient estimates for 1981, 1988, 1991 and 1996. It shows the changes in coefficient estimates over this period and, in column 8 (Support), the estimated coefficients from the preferences regression (from Table 4) as well as the HOV predictions (also from Table 4). There is one modification from the earlier table: the CNES (survey) data cover 22 occupational categories, against 20 categories in the SCF data. 'Religion' and 'Other Occupations Not Elsewhere Classified (NEC)' have been dropped because they are not included in the SCF. This modification should not affect the overall results since the two categories are relatively small.

The first four columns of Table 6 report the occupational returns estimated in the regressions. Again, the estimated returns to occupations are reported in order to isolate the fraction of total wages dependent on the occupation. If the HOV theorem and the regression specifications were both perfect predictors of changes in relative returns, there should be a close correspondence in the sign and magnitude of the vector of excess supply and the relative magnitude and sign of changes in returns to occupations.

TABLE 5

CANADIAN AND U.S. TARIFF STRUCTURES AND THE CANADIAN MANUFACTURING LABOUR MARKET

INDUSTRY	TARIFF RATES, 1987		PERCENTAGE POINT CHANGE IN TARIFF RATE, 1987-90		RATIO OF NON-PRODUCTION/ PRODUCTION EMPLOYMENT[a]	SHARE OF TOTAL MANUFACTURING EMPLOYMENT[b]
	CANADA	UNITED STATES	CANADA	UNITED STATES		
Highest Tariff Industries						
Apparel	17.2	10.7	-3.4	-2.1	0.15	0.06
Tobacco Products	16.0	10.1	-3.2	-2.0	0.79	0.00
Leather	12.0	7.9	-8.1	-6.8	0.14	0.01
Furniture and Fixtures	11.0	3.0	-2.8	-2.8	0.14	0.03
Textiles	9.9	7.3	-2.0	-1.5	0.23	0.03
Rubber and Plastics	8.9	8.4	-1.9	-1.8	0.26	0.04
Highest Tariff Industries Overall	12.5	7.9	-3.6	-2.8	0.28	0.17
Medium Tariff Industries						
Fabricated Metals	6.8	3.2	-1.7	-1.0	0.17	0.09
Other Manufacturing	6.2	3.5	-1.4	-2.1	0.26	0.04
Electrical Appliances	6.1	3.7	-1.7	-1.2	0.48	0.08
Chemicals	5.6	2.2	-2.0	-0.4	0.84	0.05
Machinery	4.7	2.5	-2.2	-1.1	0.31	0.05
Food and Beverages	4.2	3.5	-0.9	-0.7	0.42	0.12
Paper	4.0	0.9	-1.6	-0.8	0.32	0.06
Medium Tariff Industries Overall	5.1	2.7	-1.6	-1.1	0.44	0.39

TABLE 5 (CONT'D)

CANADIAN AND U.S. TARIFF STRUCTURES AND THE CANADIAN MANUFACTURING LABOUR MARKET

INDUSTRY	TARIFF RATES, 1987		PERCENTAGE POINT CHANGE IN TARIFF RATE, 1987-90		RATIO OF NON-PRODUCTION/ PRODUCTION EMPLOYMENT[a]	SHARE OF TOTAL MANUFACTURING EMPLOYMENT[b]
	CANADA	UNITED STATES	CANADA	UNITED STATES		
Lowest Tariff Industries						
Primary Metals	4.0	2.2	-0.9	-0.6	0.30	0.05
Non-metallic Minerals	3.4	2.9	-1.3	-0.9	0.25	0.03
Lumber	2.7	1.4	-0.6	-0.5	0.16	0.06
Transportation Equipment	2.3	0.5	-0.6	-0.2	0.28	0.12
Printing and Publishing	1.4	0.5	-0.6	-0.1	0.62	0.07
Petroleum Products	0.5	0.4	-0.1	-0.4	1.30	0.01
Lowest Tariff Industries Overall	2.4	1.3	-0.7	-0.5	0.48	0.35
Total, Manufacturing	6.7	3.9	-1.9	-1.4	0.32	1.00

Notes: The source for the tariff data is Magun, Rao, Lodh, Lavallée and Pierce, 1988.
    a The non-production/production employment ratio by sector is for 1989.
    b Share of industry total employment in total manufacturing employment for 1989.

FIGURE 1

EVOLUTION OF NON-PRODUCTION AND PRODUCTION EMPLOYMENT AND
REAL AVERAGE ANNUAL EARNINGS* IN THE MANUFACTURING SECTOR, 1983-96

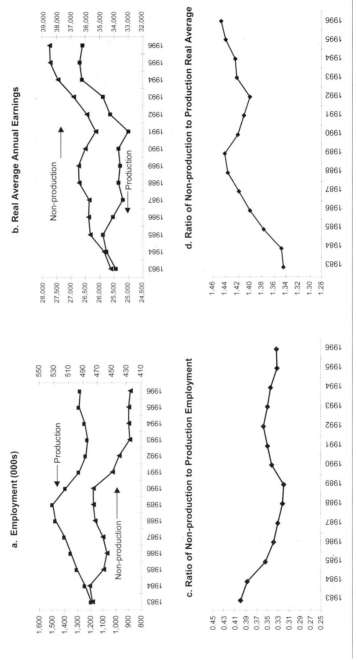

Note : * The Consumer Price Index (1987 = 100) was used to compute real earnings.

TABLE 6

LABOUR MARKET OUTCOMES, PREFERENCES AND PROBABLE HOV EFFECTS

OCCUPATION	1981	1988	1991	1997	1988-97	1981-97	1991-97	SUPPORT	PROBABLE $(w^1 - w^0)$
Managerial and Administrative	2.05	1.83	1.91	1.80	-0.03	-0.25	-0.12	0.55	+
Natural Sciences, Engineering and Mathematics	2.08	1.90	1.99	1.80	-0.10	-0.28	-0.19	0.96	–
Social Sciences	1.79	1.72	1.77	1.66	-0.06	-0.13	-0.11	0.38	+
Teaching	2.06	1.89	1.93	1.80	-0.09	-0.26	-0.13	0.25	–
Medicine and Health	1.98	1.83	1.93	1.73	-0.10	-0.25	-0.20	0.32	+
Art, Literature and Recreation	1.77	1.69	1.71	1.63	-0.06	-0.14	-0.08	0.42	+
Clerical	1.89	1.76	1.81	1.67	-0.10	-0.23	-0.14	0.08	–
Sales	1.71	1.59	1.65	1.57	-0.01	-0.14	-0.08	0.60	+
Services	1.67	1.57	1.63	1.46	-0.11	-0.21	-0.17	0.05	–
Farming, Horticulture and Animal Husbandry	0.70	0.69	0.85	0.96	0.27	0.26	0.12	0.45	+
Fishing, Hunting and Trapping	1.25	1.41	1.34	1.50	0.09	0.25	0.16	0.36	+
Forestry and Logging	1.83	1.76	1.84	1.62	-0.14	-0.22	-0.22	0.57	+
Mining and Quarrying	2.05	2.00	2.13	2.00	0.01	-0.05	-0.13	-0.15	+
Processing	1.88	1.79	1.85	1.71	-0.08	-0.17	-0.14	0.23	–
Machining	1.94	1.83	1.85	1.74	-0.09	-0.20	-0.12	0.52	–
Product Fabricating, Assembling and Repairing	1.86	1.74	1.79	1.66	-0.09	-0.21	-0.13	0.25	+
Construction Trades	1.94	1.80	1.87	1.64	-0.16	-0.29	-0.23	0.49	+
Transport Equipment Operating	1.84	1.70	1.78	1.62	-0.07	-0.21	-0.16	0.40	+
Material Handling	1.90	1.74	1.79	1.62	-0.12	-0.29	-0.18	-0.31	–
Other Crafts and Equipment Operating	1.99	1.88	1.93	1.75	-0.12	-0.23	-0.18	0.74	+

Note: The first four columns report the coefficient estimates on the occupation dummy variables from a standard log wage regression that includes age, sex, province, education, and marital status in addition to the occupation dummy variables.

Table 6 shows that the occupational categories making the largest contributions to predicted wages are natural sciences and engineering, teaching, managerial and administrative, and mining and quarrying. The lowest contributions come from farming, and fishing, hunting and trapping occupations. The next lowest returns are from services, sales and social sciences occupations. We are primarily interested in the evolution of these occupation premiums over time, and particularly in comparing pre- and post-FTA outcomes. The largest increases in occupation premiums are observed in farming and in fishing, hunting and trapping occupations. The HOV model predicted that these occupations would benefit from FTA and were more likely to support FTA. The largest declines in occupation premiums are seen in construction trades, forestry and logging, material handling, crafts and equipment operating, services, clerical, medicine and health, and natural sciences and engineering occupations. Are these labour market patterns consistent with the HOV predictions about FTA and the preferences discussed above? The results are mixed. The occupation showing the largest decline in premium, forestry and logging, was expected to benefit from FTA and was generally supportive of the agreement. Similarly, the premium on construction occupations declined but these occupations, on average, supported the agreement and were expected to benefit from it. On the other hand, material handling, services, and clerical occupations experienced declining wage premiums; the HOV model predicted that they would be adversely affected by FTA and they were among the least supportive of the agreement. The HOV analysis predicted that natural sciences and engineering occupations would be adversely affected by FTA and they experienced declines in occupation premiums; nonetheless, they were strong supporters of the agreement.

The results comparing labour market outcomes to trade policy preferences and HOV predictions provide mixed evidence on whether preferences over trade policy reflect labour market outcomes. However, there is strong evidence that unskilled workers were more opposed to FTA and that they were adversely affected in the labour market. These findings are consistent with the nature of tariff reductions that lower protection among low-skill-intensive industries. Next, we turn to the evidence on plant closures.

RESTRUCTURING IN THE MANUFACTURING SECTOR

KEITH HEAD AND JOHN RIES have made important contributions in examining whether theoretical predictions about rationalization are observed empirically and in trying to determine what would be the appropriate model.[18] At a previous North American Linkages conference, they presented an overview of recent evidence on the subject.[19] Their study assesses the impact of free trade on three aspects of Canadian manufacturing performance: 1) trade creation, trade diversion and increased dependence on a single trading partner; 2) inter-sectoral resource allocation among manufacturing sectors and greater speciali-zation within an economy; and 3) whether free trade enhanced productivity through better access to foreign markets, allowing firms to capitalize on plant-level economies of scale and increased competition.

One expected consequence of FTA was the closure of small inefficient plants in Canada's manufacturing industries. Proponents of FTA argued that plant closures were part of a rationalization process that would yield large bene-fits to Canada. Opponents of FTA agreed that plants would close, but claimed that these would be branch plants operating in Canada that would pull out in the wake of FTA and destroy thousands of jobs in the process. The impact of FTA on plant closures in Canada is not well understood and data on plant closures are not available from Statistics Canada. This section of the study expands and extends previous work by Beaulieu (2001) and examines the effect of FTA on plant closures by analyzing an original dataset collected from media reports of plant closures between 1982 and 1997.[20] Beaulieu (2001) shows that the information on plant closures in Ontario garnered from media reports is con-sistent with information about actual plant closures reported by the Ontario government. We therefore examine the reasons for plant closures and their dis-tribution across industries and provinces, and attempt to link plant closure data, labour market data and the personal preferences data analyzed above.

FREE TRADE AND PLANT CLOSURES IN CANADA

PLANT CLOSURES ARE USUALLY ATTRIBUTED to the ongoing quest for effi-ciency, a change in the overall structure of the manufacturing sector, or to an economic decline.[21] However, these reasons reflect a macroeconomic perspec-tive. Often, the general public is not concerned with the macro-economy when a specific plant shuts down. Its employees and the surrounding community are often interested in hearing the explanation or rationale behind the decision to close the plant. This interest inevitably leads the media to answer the public's call for information by investigating individual plant closures. As a result, the public gets an essentially micro-economic perspective on the reasons why a firm is closing a particular plant.

The reasons for plant closures reported in the media are classified in nine broad categories, defined on the basis of all plant closures reported in major Canadian newspapers between 1982 and 1997. These reasons are often taken from direct quotes attributed to plant managers or other sources. Table 7 presents a list of these nine categories, as well as a brief explanation of the context in which they were typically chosen: 1) poor market conditions; 2) consolidation; 3) costs; 4) relocation; 5) free trade; 6) labour problems; 7) macroeconomic cli-mate; 8) obsolescence; and 9) other.

TABLE 7

REASONS CITED FOR PLANT CLOSURES

Poor Market Conditions	If a reduction in demand was cited for the plant closure; if the plant was closed because of a long-term reduction in the price of the product which the plant produced; if the product the plant produced was facing a market where excess production was a problem. However, this excess capacity did not have to be in the market as a whole, it could be just among one firm's plants that produced the same product.
Consolidation	If the plant was closed and production picked up at another plant or if an increase in competition was cited as the reason for the plant closure.
Costs	If firms were trying to cut costs due to poor performance throughout the firm or if the plant had recently undergone a significant increase in its cost of operation and was shut down for this reason.
Relocation	If the firm cited an economic reason for relocation. These "economic reasons" covered a broad spectrum of specific motives. Cheaper labour costs were often cited in a relocation. Another popular explanation for relocation was that the firm decided to move closer to its main market.
Free Trade	This reason was recorded if the plant closure was attributed either to FTA or NAFTA in the media.
Labour Problems	If a firm and its workers could not agree to the terms of a new contract. There were a number of cases where workers cited a preference for plant closure rather than accepting the terms of the contract offered by the firm. If there was an inability to attract the number of skilled production workers needed at the plant.
Macroeconomic Climate	If the plant closure was blamed on the economy as a whole rather than on a specific aspect of the plant, firm, or market.
Obsolescence	If the plant was performing poorly compared to other plants producing the same product or because it had become obsolete either because of a major technological change or old age.
Other	A variety of reasons that did not fit into the eight categories mentioned above.

Figure 2 shows the number of plants that closed for each reason given in media reports. The primary reason for a plant closure was the consolidation or rationalization of production. Poor market conditions was the second most frequent reason cited for a plant closure. The consolidation and rationalization of plants during the period following the implementation of FTA can be interpretted as an indication that free trade is working along the lines modelled by Cox and Harris. This would provide evidence that free trade forced firms located in Canada to cut their *fat* and become more efficient. Frequently, there were cases where a firm's management was quoted as saying that it was consolidating operations because it had three or four plants working at only 50 percent of capacity. Given the fixed costs of operating each plant, it is more efficient from a resource allocation point of view to have three plants operating at 100 percent of capacity than five plants operating at 50 percent of capacity. Tariff protection may have allowed firms to operate with excess capacity but the elimination of tariffs may have made this practice untenable.

An alternative interpretation of the finding that most plant closures were attributed to consolidation is that this rationalization process was part of a larger trend in all industrialized countries and had very little to do with the implementation of FTA. One way to find out which is the correct interpretation is to examine the number of plant closures by industry and over time. The number of plant closures by industry is compared for high-, medium-, and low-tariff industries over periods both preceding and following the implementation of FTA. This allows us to apply a controlled-experiment approach to analyzing the role played by FTA in plant closures. It will also help us distinguish the effect of FTA from those of macroeconomic factors that influenced the behaviour of firms in the early 1990s.

Figure 3 shows the number of plant closures reported in the media between 1982 and 1997 by industry. A large portion of plant closures occurred in the food sector. Food industries make up about 18 percent of total plant closures. The transportation, electrical, and chemical industries also experienced more plant closures than other industries.

Table 8 gives the number of plant closures in Canada in high-, medium- and low-tariff industries over two periods: 1982-88 and 1989-95. It also shows tariff rate changes ratified in FTA and the percentage change in the number of establishments over the two periods.[22] High-tariff industries can be thought of as the *treated* group, while low-tariff industries form the *control* group. Is the pattern of plant closures different for the two groups?

The number of plant closures increased after 1988 in both groups. However, the number of closures increased proportionately more among high-tariff industries than among low-tariff industries. This can be seen by comparing the change in the share of closures in the manufacturing sector between high- and low-tariff industries, before and after FTA. Closures among high-tariff industries increased from 5 percent of total manufacturing closures prior to FTA to 10 percent of total manufacturing closures after. By contrast, closures among low-tariff industries remained about the same, increasing slightly from 26 percent of manufacturing plant closures prior to FTA to 27 percent after FTA. This difference suggests that FTA played a role in plant closures in Canada.

This pattern of plant closures is consistent with the pattern of labour market outcomes described above. Plant closures occurred in high-tariff industries. These are the low-skill-intensive industries. And low-skilled workers were more likely to oppose FTA.

FIGURE 2

REASONS FOR PLANT CLOSURES REPORTED IN THE MEDIA

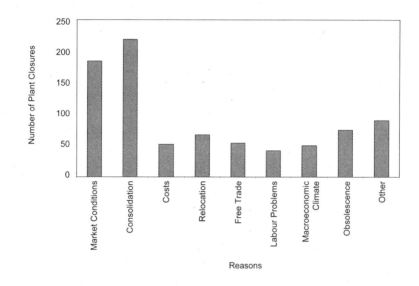

FIGURE 3

NUMBER OF PLANT CLOSURES IN CANADA BY INDUSTRY, 1982-97

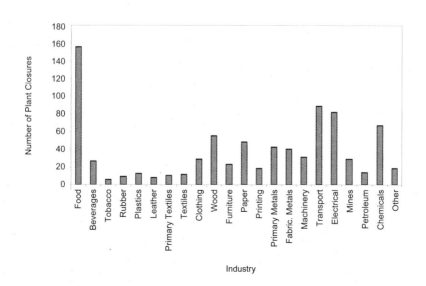

TABLE 8

TARIFF CHANGES, PLANT CLOSURES AND ESTABLISHMENTS BY INDUSTRY, 1982-95

SIC CODE	INDUSTRY	TARIFF CHANGES (PERCENTAGE POINTS)		NUMBER OF PLANT CLOSURES[1]		NUMBER OF ESTABLISHMENTS[2] (PERCENTAGE)	
		CANADA	UNITED STATES	1982-88	1989-95	1983-88	1989-95
High-tariff Industries							
24	Clothing	13.0	7.1	4	17	19	-36
18	Primary Textiles	10.3	5.7	1	7	-2	-19
17	Leather	9.9	6.3	1	7	-8	-35
26	Furniture and Fixtures	9.8	1.6	0	21	17	-28
12	Tobacco	8.6	12.4	1	5	-24	-16
High-tariff Industries Overall		**10.3**	**6.6**	**7 (5%)**	**57 (10%)**	**0**	**-27**
Moderate-tariff Industries							
15	Rubber	6.7	2.6	2	5	25	4
19	Textiles	6.6	5.5	2	8	18	-16
16	Plastics	5.6	2.6	1	9	24	1
27	Paper and Allied	5.6	2.0	10	36	7	-8
33	Electrical	5.4	3.3	16	55	32	-13
30	Fabricated Metals	5.0	1.9	8	29	15	-15
37	Chemicals	5.0	3.2	15	52	16	-13

TABLE 8 (CONT'D)

TARIFF CHANGES, PLANT CLOSURES AND ESTABLISHMENTS BY INDUSTRY, 1982-95

SIC Code	Industry	Tariff Changes (percentage points)		Number of Plant Closures[1]		Number of Establishments[2] (percentage)	
		Canada	United States	1982-88	1989-95	1983-88	1989-95
31	Machinery	4.9	2.4	7	22	33	-14
35	Non-metallic Minerals	4.8	2.0	6	19	5	-9
39	Other Manufacturing	4.7	2.7	1	17	22	-21
11	Beverages	4.1	2.6	3	18	-2	-18
10	Food	3.7	2.8	26	105	4	-12
	Moderate-tariff Industries Overall	**4.4**	**2.5**	**97(69%)**	**375(64%)**	**16**	**-11**
	Low-tariff Industries						
29	Primary Metals	3.1	2.5	6	33	17	-21
32	Transportation Equipment	3.0	0.7	18	57	24	-16
25	Wood	2.6	1.5	7	43	5	-15
28	Printing and Publishing	1.5	0.3	2	15	9	-15
36	Refined Petroleum and Coal	0.6	0.6	3	9	n.a.	n.a.
	Low-tariff Industries Overall	**2.2**	**1.1**	**36(27%)**	**157(27%)**	**14**	**-17**
	Total, Manufacturing	**5.8**	**3.4**	**140**	**589**	**14**	**-17**

Notes: 1 Figures in brackets are the percentages of total manufacturing plant closures.
2 Head and Ries kindly provided the data on the number of establishments by industry.

CONCLUSION

T HIS STUDY LOOKS AT THE POLITICAL ECONOMY of trade policy in Canada and links observed trade policy preferences to labour market outcomes and evidence on rationalization in the manufacturing sector. It contributes to our understanding of how economic integration plays out politically and how the politics are linked to economic consequences. The study provides information for assessing the underlying economic model of trade liberalization and helps inform public policies aimed at adjusting to economic integration. It also identifies political cleavages that are likely to form in the debate over further North American economic integration.

We find that cleavages in Canadian trade policy are drawn along factor lines, not industry lines. This implies that workers are mobile between industries. We also find that skilled workers were more likely to support FTA than unskilled workers. This finding has also been made in more recent studies of Canadian preferences toward trade policy. That skilled workers in both the United States and Canada support trade liberalization is inconsistent with the Heckscher-Ohlin-Samuelson trade model — but not with extended versions of the model that incorporate imperfect competition and economies of scale. Finally, the pattern of support for the agreement among occupations is somewhat consistent with the predictions of the HOV model.

The study then turns to the important question of whether preferences over trade policy reflect the economic impact of the free trade agreement. To establish a more direct link between policy preferences and the economic consequences of trade liberalization, we show that the observed cleavages in trade policy preferences reflect, at least in part, labour market pressures facing workers in Canada. The formal comparison of trade policy preferences and labour market outcomes for various occupations within the HOV framework did not reveal a strong link. However, the HOV model has notoriously performed poorly in empirical studies. Our study does show that less-skilled workers were adversely affected in the labour market following FTA, which is consistent with the preferences over trade policy observed in the CNES data. Moreover, plant closures occurred disproportionately among high-tariff industries, which were low-skill-intensive industries. Labour market contraction and plant closures adversely affected unskilled workers as the Canadian economy adjusted to FTA. This is consistent with observed trade policy preferences.

The study provides evidence that concerns about, and political opposition to, future trade liberalization will likely be grounded in the economic consequences of the pursued trade policy. However, voters do not behave as though their preferences are tied to a specific industry. People are mobile between industries. Therefore, adjustment policies should be targeted toward skill training for individuals, and not at specific industries.

ENDNOTES

1   See Hazledine (1990) for an overview and critique of the various Computable General Equilibrium (CGE) approaches to examining the welfare effects of trade liberalization in North America.

2   The complete title is "The Case of the Missing Trade and Other Mysteries", and the reference is provided in the Bibliography.

3   Leamer and Levinsohn, 1995.

4   Bhagwati, Panagariya and Srinivasan (1998, Ch. 7) provide an excellent summary of the literature on factor mobility and coin the term "all-factor-specific."

5   See the Data Appendix for more details.

6   Johnston, Blais, Brady and Crête (1992), and Clarke, Jenson, Le Duc and Pammett (1991) provide excellent accounts of the 1988 election. Johnston et al. use data from the 1988 Canadian National Election Study (the same data used here) to examine the dynamics of the 1988 campaign and provide an historical account of trade policy and politics in Canada.

7   Contrast this to the *non-issue* in Canada of Mexico's inclusion in the agreement (NAFTA) and the enormous political battle in the United States over the inclusion of that country into an integrated North American market. Beaulieu (2002a) examines congressional voting patterns on FTA, NAFTA, and GATT implementing legislation.

8   See Johnston et al. (1992) and Pammett (1989).

9   Recall that prior to the 1993 election, the three major political parties at the federal level in Canada were the Progressive Conservative Party, the Liberal Party, and the New Democratic Party.

10 Clarke and Kornberg (1992, p. 39) argue that, even in the historical context outlined above, it was not obvious at the beginning of the election that the FTA issue would dominate the agenda. The Conservatives initially planned to run on their own record. It was only through the dynamics of the campaign that the contending parties pushed FTA to the top of the agenda; this supports the view that the political parties *primed* the electorate or *controlled* the agenda.

11 In the CNES data used in this study, 64 percent of respondents said that FTA was the most important issue, while 12 percent thought that there were no important issues. These figures are not directly comparable with those of Table 1 because the latter reports on the first two most important issues, while the data used in this study reports on the single most important issue. Nonetheless, it confirms the idea that voters overwhelmingly considered FTA to be the most important issue affecting their voting decision.

12 This point is stressed in Clarke et al. (1991, pp. 146-147).

13 See Beaulieu (1997) for more details. Beaulieu reports that the Pearson χ^2 coefficient rejects the null hypothesis of statistical independence between voting patterns and positions on FTA. These results are based on data from the CNES described in the Data Appendix.

14 Harris (1985) finds that both winning and losing industries are concentrated in Ontario and Quebec.

15 See Mayda and Rodrik, 2001.

16 The ratio of non-production to production workers is a good proxy for the skilled-unskilled ratio. See Beaulieu, 2000, Table 1, p. 544.

17 Robertson (2000) finds a similar result when he examines the presumed puzzle of an increasing wage differential between skilled and unskilled labour in Mexico after the signing of NAFTA. He finds that when one examines the change in protection implied by NAFTA — rather than the factor content of trade — there is no puzzle.

18 See Head and Ries, 1999.

19 See Head and Ries, 2001.

20 See the Data Appendix for more details.

21 See Perucci and Targ (1988) for an example of this explanation.

22 Head and Ries provided the data on the change in the number of establishments by industry.

ACKNOWLEDGMENTS

THIS STUDY BENEFITED FROM COMMENTS on an earlier draft by Rick Harris and participants at the HRDC/IC Conference on North American Linkages, held in Montreal on November 20-22, 2002. The study also benefited from comments by Andrea Laroiya, Laura Jolles, Glenn MacIntyre, Andrew Royal, Hanako Saito, Natalia Sershun, Sinead Sinnott, Kostyantyn Stepankevych, Melissa Tan, Maria Tinajero, Mahmood Zarrabi, and Lipin Zhang. Any errors remain our own.

BIBLIOGRAPHY

Balistreri, Edward. "The Performance of the Heckscher-Ohlin-Vanek Model in Predicting Endogenous Policy Forces at the Individual Level." *Canadian Journal of Economics* 30, 1 (February 1997): 1-18.

Beaulieu, Eugene. "The Political Economy of Trade Policy in the United States and Canada: Political Cleavages and the Labor Market." Ph.D. Thesis, Columbia University, May 15, 1997.

——. "The Canada-U.S. Free Trade Agreement and Labour Market Adjustment in Canada." *Canadian Journal of Economics* 33, 2 (May 2000): 540-563.

——. "North American Integration and Plant Closures in Ontario." *Canadian Foreign Policy* 8, 2 (Winter 2001): 23-38.

———. "The Stolper-Samuelson Theorem Faces Congress." *Review of International Economics* 10, 2 (May 2002a): 337-354.

———. "Factor or Industry Cleavages in Trade Policy: An Empirical Analysis of the Stolper-Samuelson Theorem." *Economics and Politics* 14, 2 (July 2002b): 99-131.

Beaulieu, Eugene, Michael Benarroch and Jim Gaisford. "Trade Barriers and Wage Inequality in a North-South Model with Technology-driven Intra-industry Trade." 2004a. Forthcoming in *Journal of Development Economics*.

———. "Intra-industry Trade Liberalization, Wage Inequality and Trade Policy Preferences." University of Calgary, Discussion Paper No. 2004-06, 2004b.

Beaulieu, Eugene, and Chris Magee. "Four Simple Tests of Campaign Contributions and Trade Policy Preferences." *Economics and Politics* 16, 2 (July 2004): 163-187.

Bhagwati, J., A. Panagariya and T.N. Srinivasan. *Lectures on International Trade,* 2nd ed. Cambridge (MA): The MIT Press, 1998.

Brander, James. "Election Polls, Free Trade, and the Stock Market: Evidence from the Canadian General Election." *Canadian Journal of Economics* 24 (1991): 827-843.

Clarke, Harold D., and Allan Kornberg. "Support for the Canadian Federal Progressive Conservative Party since 1988: The Impact of Economic Evaluations and Economic Issues." *Canadian Journal of Political Science* 25, 1 (March 1992): 29-53.

Clarke, Harold D., Jane Jenson, Lawrence Le Duc and Jon H. Pammett. *Absent Mandate: Interpreting Change in Canadian Elections.* 2nd ed. Toronto: Gage Educational Publishing Company, 1991.

Davis, Donald R., David E. Weinstein, Scott C. Bradford and Kazushige Shimpo. "Using International and Japanese Regional Data to Determine When the Factor Abundance Theory of Trade Works." *American Economic Review* 87, 3 (June 1997): 421-446.

Dinopoulos, Elias, Constantinos Syropoulos and Bin Xu. "Intra-industry Trade and Wage Inequality." 1999. Mimeo.

Ethier, Wilfred J. "Higher Dimensional Issues in Trade Theory." In *Handbook of International Economics, Volume 1.* Edited by R.W. Jones and P.B. Kenen. Amsterdam: North Holland, 1984.

Gaston, Noel, and Daniel Trefler. "The Labour Market Consequences of the Canada-U.S. Free Trade Agreement." *Canadian Journal of Economics* 30,1 (February 1997): 18-42.

Grossman, Gene M., and James A. Levinsohn. "Import Competition and the Stock Market Return to Capital." *American Economic Review* 79 (1989): 1065-1087.

Harris, Richard G. "Summary of a Project on the General Equilibrium Evaluation of Canadian Trade Policy." In *Canada-United States Free Trade, Volume 11.* Chapter 8. Edited by John Whalley. Series of studies commissioned as part of the research program of *The Royal Commission on the Economic Union and Development Prospects for Canada* (MacDonald Commission). Toronto: University of Toronto Press, 1985.

Hazledine, Tim. "Why Do the Free Trade Gain Numbers Differ So Much? The Role of Industrial Organization in General Equilibrium." *Canadian Journal of Economics* 23, 4 (November 1990).

Head, Keith, and John Ries. "Rationalization Effects of Tariff Reductions." *Journal of International Economics* 47, 2 (April 1999): 295-320.

——. "Free Trade and Canadian Economic Performance: Which Theories Does the Evidence Support?" Paper presented at the conference entitled *North American Linkages: Opportunities and Challenges for Canada* sponsored by Industry Canada and the Centre for the Study of Living Standards, held in Calgary, June 20-22, 2001. Published in *North American Linkages: Opportunities and Challenges for Canada*. Edited by Richard G. Harris. The Industry Canada Research Series. Calgary: University of Calgary Press, 2003, pp. 181-206.

Hiscox, Michael J. *International Trade and Political Conflict: Commerce, Coalitions, and Mobility.* Princeton (NJ): Princeton University Press, 2002.

Irwin, Douglas A. "The Political Economy of Free Trade." *Journal of Law and Economics* 37 (1994): 75-108.

——. "Industry or Class Cleavages over Trade Policy? Evidence from the British General Election of 1923." In *The Political Economy of Trade Policy: Papers in Honor of Jagdish Bhagwati.* Edited by Robert C. Feenstra, Gene M. Grossman and Douglas A. Irwin. Cambridge (MA): The MIT Press, 1996.

Johnston, Richard, André Blais, Henry E. Brady and Jean Crête. *Letting the People Decide: Dynamics of a Canadian Election.* Stanford (CA): Stanford University Press, 1992.

Le Duc, Lawrence. "Voting for Free Trade?: The Canadian Voter and the 1988 Federal Election." In *Politics Canada: Seventh Edition.* Edited by Paul W. Fox and Graham White. Toronto: McGraw-Hill Ryerson, 1991, pp. 350-366.

Leamer, Edward E., and James Levinsohn. "International Trade Theory: The Evidence." In *Handbook of International Economics: Volume III.* Edited by Gene M. Grossman and Kenneth Rogoff. Amsterdam: Elsevier, 1995, pp. 1339-1390.

MacDonald Commission. *The Royal Commission on the Economic Union and Development Prospects for Canada.* Toronto: University of Toronto Press, 1985.

Magee, Stephen P. "Three Simple Tests of the Stolper-Samuelson Theorem." In *Issues in International Economics.* Edited by Peter Oppenheimer. Stockfield (UK): Oriel Press, 1980. Re-printed in *The Stolper-Samuelson Theorem: A Golden Jubilee.* Edited by Alan V. Deardorff and Robert M. Stern. Ann Arbor (MI): The University of Michigan Press, 1994, pp. 185-204.

Magun, Sunder, Someshwar Rao, Bimal Lodh, Laval Lavallée and Jonathan Pierce. "Open Borders: An Assessment of the Canada-U.S. Free Trade Agreement." Discussion Paper No. 344. Ottawa: Economic Council of Canada, 1988.

Mayda, A.M., and D. Rodrik. "Why Are Some People (and Countries) More Protectionist than Others? A Cross-country Analysis." Harvard University, 2001. Mimeo.

Mendelsohn, M., and R. Wolfe. "Probing the Aftermyth of Seattle: Canadian Public Opinion on International Trade, 1980-2000." *International Journal* 56, 2 (2001): 234-260.

Mendelsohn, M., R. Wolfe and A. Parkin. "Globalization, Trade Policy and the Permissive Consensus in Canada." *Canadian Public Policy* 28, 3 (September 2002): 351-371.

Pammett, Jon H. "The 1988 Vote." In *The Canadian General Election of 1988.* Edited by Alan Frizzell, Jon H. Pammett and Anthony Westell. Ottawa: Carleton University Press, 1989, pp. 115-130.

Perucci, C., and D. Targ. *Plant Closings: International Context & Social Costs*. New York: Aldine De Gruyer, 1988.

Porter, J., P. Pineo and H. McRoberts. *Revisions of the Pineo-Porter-McRoberts Socio-economic Classificatioin of Occupations for the 1981 Census*. Program for Quantitative Studies in Economies and Population Report No. 125. Hamilton, Canada: McMaster University, 1985.

Pyne, Derek. "Revealed Preference Tests of the Stolper-Samuelson Theorem." *International Trade Journal* 14, 4 (Winter 2000): 355-375.

Robertson, Raymond. "Trade Liberalisation and Wage Inequality: Lessons from the Mexican Experience." *World Economy* 23 (2000): 827-851.

Rogowski, Ronald. "Political Cleavages and Changing Exposure to Trade." *American Political Science Review* 81 (1987): 1122-1137.

Scheve, Kenneth F., and Matthew J. Slaughter. "What Determines Individual Trade Policy Preferences?" *Journal of International Economics* 54 (2001): 267-292.

Stolper, Wolfgang F., and Paul A. Samuelson. "Protection and Real Wages." *Review of Economic Studies* 9 (1941): 58-73.

Thompson, Aileen J. "The Anticipated Sectoral Adjustment to the Canada-United States Free Trade Agreement: An Event Study Analysis." *Canadian Journal of Economics* 26 (1993): 253-272.

——. "Trade Liberalization, Comparative Advantage, and Scale Economies: Stock Market Evidence from Canada." *Journal of International Economics* 37 (1994): 1-27.

Trefler, Daniel. "International Factor Prices: Leontief Was Right!" *Journal of Political Economy* 101 (December 1993): 961-987.

——. "The Case of the Missing Trade and Other Mysteries." *American Economic Review* 85 5 (December 1995): 1029-1046.

Trefler, Daniel, and Susan Chun Zhu. "Beyond the Algebra of Explanation: HOV for the Technology Age." *American Economic Review* 90, 2 (May 2001): 145-149.

DATA APPENDIX

THE PREFERENCES DATA

THE CANADIAN NATIONAL ELECTION STUDY contains socio-economic data as well as information on the voting behaviour and political attitudes of Canadians from surveys conducted before and after the 1988 election. Factor ownership in this analysis is based on the skill level. Two different measures of skill are used: one based on the highest level of education attained and the other based on the implied skill level of the occupation. The education variable in the raw CNES data is a categorical variable comprising 11 categories. Some categories have very few observations. For example, only 4 observations report 'no schooling'. Therefore, we aggregated to four education categories: less than high school, high school completed, some technical or college education, and some university education. Another reason for aggregating to four education categories is that education categories are interpreted as different factors of production: i.e. unskilled, low-skilled, semi-skilled, high-skilled labour. Those with less than high school completion are in a similar unskilled labour market, as are those with some university. Since the aggregation is somewhat arbitrary, it is important to examine whether the aggregation is affecting the results. This issue is explored in detail in Beaulieu (2002b). The results from aggregating to four education categories are shown to be robust to different specifications of the education dummy variables.

Factors are also measured by type of occupation. There are three factors of production based on three different types of occupations: high-skilled, semi-skilled and low-skilled. This classification is based on the socio-economic and skill-level characteristics of the occupations developed by Porter, Pineo and McRoberts (1985). High-skilled occupations are defined by employment in the following types of occupations: self-employed professionals, employed professionals, high-level managers, skilled clerical and sales persons, skilled crafts persons, and farmers (excluding farm labourers). Semi-skilled occupations are those of semi-professional employees, technicians, middle managers, supervisors, foreman, semi-skilled clerks, and semi-skilled manual workers. Low-skilled occupations are those of unskilled clerical and sales employees, unskilled manual labourers, and farm labourers. This classification of occupations allows us to differentiate between *skilled* and *unskilled* workers and treat them as different factors of production similar to the approach used when factors are defined in relation to educational levels.

THE LABOUR MARKET DATA

THE SURVEY OF CONSUMER FINANCES (SCF) is a supplement to Statistics Canada's Labour Force Survey (LFS). Currently, the SCF is available on a yearly basis from 1981 to 1996, excluding 1983. Prior to 1981, public use micro-data files do not encompass all workers and are only available every two years. The SCF is aggregated to an annual level, while the LFS is monthly. The survey consists of micro-level data and includes such variables as geographic area, income, family characteristics, marital status, age, education, immigration status, language, labour force status, class of worker, occupational classification, number of weeks worked, unemployment, previous and current job characteristics. Depending on the year of the survey, the number of respondents varies approximately between 67,000 and 95,000 individuals.

Although the SCF contains various measures of income, the one selected for use in this study is 'wages and salaries' which reports the value of wage and salary income for the reference year. From this, an hourly wage variable is calculated by dividing the 'wages and salaries' variable by the product of 'usual hours worked per week' and 'weeks worked'. Also, in both data sets, 'wages and salaries' have been deflated by the Consumer Price Index (CPI) in order to create a real hourly wage variable (expressed in $1986).[1]

THE PLANT CLOSURE DATA

THE PLANT CLOSURE DATA WERE COLLECTED by searching two main newspaper indexes, the Canadian Business & Current Affairs (CBCA) Index and the Canadian Newsdisc. These two indexes include major Canadian newspapers as well as several business periodicals and other media publications.[2] The goal was to find an index covering publications representative of various geographic locations across Canada. With these two indexes, virtually every major Canadian city is represented by at least one newspaper in the index. However, there are no newspapers in the indexes from the North, from Saskatchewan, nor from regions outside of major cities. In addition, the only Maritime province represented is Nova Scotia. To the extent that plant closures in the omitted regions are not covered by the major dailies in the cities covered, plant closure data will under-report the actual number of closures. But this is not a major problem since the focus of the study is on larger plants (those with more than 50 workers) operating in manufacturing industries, and larger plants attract more media attention.

All search results which were relevant to plant closures were located, read, and recorded if they were both conformant with our criteria and not already covered. Relevant articles documented permanent plant closures in Canada. The search turned up 3,909 matches in the index, of which 878 were recorded in the dataset because they were relevant. There were 3,031 newspaper articles discarded for several different reasons. First, the majority of articles were discarded because they were repetitions of stories about plant closures already present in the dataset. Second, many of the matches were articles of general interest on plant closures, or discussed the general problem of plant closures. Since these articles did not report any specific plant closure they were not recorded in the dataset. Some of the matches were discarded because the plant closures were outside Canada. Matching search results were also discarded if the plant was not a manufacturing plant. For example, if a grocery store closure came up as a match, it was discarded. This was done because the study is only concerned with the manufacturing sector, which is where free trade produces the most radical changes. Additionally, a few matches in the index were simply unrelated to manufacturing plant closures.

ENDNOTES

1   Statistics Canada, *Consumer Price Index*, Cansim Matrix 2450, Series E305030 (1986 = 100).

2   The CBCA covers eight major daily English-language newspapers: The *Calgary Herald*, the *Montreal Gazette*, *The Financial Post*, *The Toronto Star*, *The Globe & Mail*, *The Vancouver Sun*, the *Halifax Chronicle Herald*, and the *Winnipeg Free Press*.

P 151: 192-94

Comment

Canada

Richard G. Harris
Simon Fraser University

F16 L11

D72 F15 J24 F13

I ENJOYED READING THIS STUDY. It is a useful mix of international trade and political economy theory applied to some interesting data using sophisticated methods. The question is of considerable importance within the broader debate on globalization in Canada — who supports trade liberalization and why? In a world of rational choice and income maximization, individuals will support free trade if it increases their own real income. Economic theory does not provide a simple answer to the foregoing question. It depends on the structure of the economy and the pattern of liberalization. In this study, two interesting questions are addressed using data on the 1988 federal election.

First, what motivated voters to support (or not) Canada-U.S. free trade? In particular, does the industry of employment or, alternatively, individual skill endowment better explain voting behaviour? The results give some insight on whether voters were predicting the impact of the Free Trade Agreement (FTA) using a Heckscher-Ohlin (HO) view of trade and factor markets, or alternatively an industry specific-based view of trade impacts. Somewhat surprisingly given the existing literature, Beaulieu and Joy find that the industry of employment does not predict voter behaviour well, while skill level does. As the HO theory requires mobility of factors between industries, this finding is consistent with a model in which rational voters take the long view in assessing their own position on trade liberalization, and thus correctly predict their incomes after all adjustments to free trade have occurred.

The second part of the study investigates the ex-post consequences of the FTA. In light of the first exercise, this can be viewed as asking whether the voters got it right or not. The problem here is controlling for factors other than the impact of trade liberalization on the economy. Canada experienced a significant macro-recession in the early 1990s, and throughout the Organisation for Economic Co-operation and Development (OECD) the wages of unskilled workers stagnated. Using a Mincer wage regression framework, the authors check whether the predictions of the HO model of voter behaviour were consistent with the changes in wages observed after the FTA. Their results are quite mixed and, in some cases, dramatically contrary to the Heckscher-Ohlin-Vanek (HOV) model. Lastly, they review the evidence on the effect of the FTA on plant closures. They find that high-tariff industries had higher rates of closure relative to low-tariff industries.

While this is an interesting contribution to the literature on the political economy of trade policy, it is not clear that the results are sufficiently tight to warrant any strong conclusions. One standard problem is that even slight amendments to the HO model produce quite different predictions. Adding economies of scale, for example, can reverse many of the industry predictions. An HO interpretation is that skilled labour is abundant in Canada and that it is mobile between industries. Free trade would then raise the real return to this relatively abundant factor. However, it is also possible that the advent of free trade first and foremost induced a wave of long overdue structural adjustments and technological upgrading in Canadian industry. Skilled workers, even if relatively immobile, would have supported free trade because the alternative was even worse — a status quo based on old products and obsolescent technology. The authors suggest that the analysis is consistent with regional support for the FTA both before and after. This is far from clear. The West was a strong supporter of free trade, yet it is now fairly clear that the really big increases in exports to the United States occurred in Central Canada. While unskilled labour-intensive industries were heavily protected and located in Central Canada, it is also true that skill-intensive industries were also located in Central Canada. The support for free trade in the West may have been due in part to the belief that the FTA would lead to superior trade dispute resolution, and therefore lower anticipated protectionism in U.S. commodity importing markets. However, this channel of causation is quite different than the suggestion stemming from this study, which is that labour mobility is the major link between different sectors of the Canadian economy. Even if Canada's regional labour markets were completely segmented, it would not be difficult to rationalize the results of the study under those conditions.

Looking forward to possible greater economic integration within North America, does it matter or not what the state of factor mobility between industries and regions is? Given that most trade has already been liberalized between Canada and the United States, the next stage of integration is more likely to be a move towards a customs union with greater formal cross-border mobility of investment, business and skilled labour. Analytically, we can think of this as a reduction in trade costs for both factors and goods. It would increase trade volumes and business integration. But it is very unclear what might happen to specific industries if such integration goes forward — unlike the FTA case. The reason is simply that technological change and business re-organization are occurring at such a fast pace that the outcomes of economic integration at the firm and sector levels become increasingly uncertain. Under these circumstances, voters — particularly workers who are aging boomers — will be very wary of changes that could have unpredictable effects on their incomes and jobs. If this assessment is correct, the view that industries matter may prove to be a more powerful predictor of future voter behaviour than was the case in 1988.

Part III

Adjustments by Firms and Workers to Canada-U.S. Economic Integration

Ross Finnie
Queen's University and
Statistics Canada

J11
F22
J16
Canada

5

Leaving and Coming Back to Canada: Evidence from Longitudinal Data

INTRODUCTION

THERE IS NOW — AS IN CERTAIN OTHER PERIODS in the country's history — considerable interest in the out-migration of Canadians to other countries. How many leave the country in a given year? What are their characteristics? How many come back — and who are *they*? *When* do they return? What are the trends over time?

These questions are interesting not only for academic reasons, but also for their implications regarding a number of important policy issues. The *brain drain* issue, in particular, has attracted a good deal of debate in terms of what it implies for Canadian tax policy; what it might tell us about Canada's economic performance in comparison to its major competitors; what it suggests about our major social programs — which could make Canada a better place to live or, alternatively, push tax rates so high as to drive out its best and brightest elements; and so on.[1] However, previous research has been hampered by the unavailability of the type of general and extended longitudinal databases that are best suited to the study of emigration of Canadians and their return — or not — to this country. The purpose of this study is to exploit the unique strengths of Statistics Canada's Longitudinal Administrative Database (LAD), constructed from individuals' tax records, to shed new light on the extent and nature of the migration flows of Canadians to other countries and their patterns of return over the period 1982-99.

After describing the data, models and variables employed, the empirical results are presented in two main sections. The first section focuses on the patterns of Canadian emigration. It begins with a few simple graphs that summarize the overall rates of leaving over time, and follows with the presentation of estimation results derived from a model that essentially addresses the question: 'Who moves?'.

In our approach, the probability that a person leaves Canada in a given year is specified as a logit function of the individual's demographic characteristics (age, family type, language), economic situation [income level, receipt of Unemployment/Employment-Insurance (U/E-I) benefits], and locational attributes (province, size of area of residence). The models also include the provincial unemployment rate as a measure of current economic conditions, and a series of year variables to capture time trends, about which there is so much debate. Separate models are estimated for men and women.

In a variant of the model, a set of terms is added to allow for the relationship between the probability of leaving and the individual's income level to differ from the 1980s to the 1990s. This specification is used to verify if the rate of leaving has risen for people at the higher end of the economic ladder relative to those at lower income levels — as one would expect if there had been a worsening of the brain drain phenomenon.

Following presentation of the evidence on the annual rates of emigration from Canada over the last two decades, a similar analysis is performed for the rates of return of those who left. As far as the author is aware, this is the first such study on the return phenomenon (covering the general population, over an extended period of time, etc.) Again, the dearth of evidence stems principally from the associated data requirements: to be able to follow given individuals over time so as to identify leavers and — perhaps most challenging of all — those who return to the country, sometimes after an extended absence. Furthermore, because emigration is a rare event, the underlying sample must also be very large in order to have enough leavers to follow in the years subsequent to their departure. Finally, the data must be sufficiently detailed so as to allow for a useful and interesting examination of the characteristics of persons who leave and return.

The LAD database meets these requirements and makes it possible to estimate a hazard model of the probability that people first identified as having left will return to Canada. A discrete logit model approach is used. The dependent variable is whether an individual already observed as having left the country returns to Canada in a given year. The explanatory variables encompass those mentioned above in the context of the exit models, including a series of calendar-year variables to capture the time trends. The model also includes dummy variable indicators of the number of years elapsed since the person left the country (one, two, three...) to capture the relevant duration effects: holding other factors constant, what is the probability of returning as the time spent out of the country lengthens? Specifying these duration effects without imposing any functional form in this manner turns out to be important, because the duration terms wind up taking a slightly unusual form — although one that is not so surprising given the particular dynamic process in play.

The final section of the study summarizes and discusses the major findings and identifies avenues for further work.

DATA AND MODELS

THE LONGITUDINAL ADMINISTRATIVE DATABASE

THE LONGITUDINAL ADMINISTRATIVE DATABASE is a 20-percent represen- tative sample of all Canadian tax filers (and non-filing spouses identified by filers) selected from Revenue Canada (now Canada Revenue Agency) tax files using a random number generator based on Social Insurance Numbers (SINs).

The LAD is thus representative, and large (roughly four million individu- als per year), fulfilling two of the key data requirements. But it also meets the critical longitudinal condition in that individuals are followed over time, based on the SIN identifier. Individuals drop out of the LAD if they become non- filers, the principal reasons being that they have a low income and are, there- fore, not required to file (and choose not to do so — see below), have died, or — of greatest pertinence to this study — have left the country. New filers (young people, immigrants, etc.) automatically refresh the database in the gen- eral 20-percent ratio.

Finally, the LAD contains a sufficient range of variables to permit an in- teresting analysis of how leaving and returning to the country vary according to individuals' situational and personal attributes, with individuals matched into their appropriate family units on an annual basis, thereby providing individual and family-level information on income, taxes, and basic demographic charac- teristics, including place of residence, in a dynamic framework. The first year of the LAD is 1982 and the file ran through 1999, when this project was under- taken, thus determining the period covered by the analysis.

The LAD's coverage of the adult population is very good since, compared to some other countries (such as the United States) the rate of tax filing in Canada is very high: higher income Canadians are required to do so, while lower income individuals have an incentive to file in order to recover income tax and other payroll deductions made throughout the year and to receive various tax credits. The full set of annual tax files from which the LAD is con- structed is estimated to cover upwards of 95 percent of the target adult popula- tion (based on official population estimates), thus comparing very favourably with other survey-generated databases and even rivalling (or surpassing) the Census in this regard.

Furthermore, given that most individuals file a tax return every year, attrition from the LAD is quite low, which means that it remains representative on a longitudinal as well as on a cross-sectional basis. This compares to longitudinal databases assembled from surveys, which typically have greater difficulty following individuals, especially those who move, potentially resulting in serious sampling problems in the context of a mobility study like this one. In short, the LAD is a good performer in terms of representativeness, both from a cross-sectional and from a longitudinal standpoint.[2]

Individuals were included in the analysis if they were Canadian citizens (in order to separate out immigrants who are basically just passing through the country), were over the age of 18, and had no missing data for the variables used in the analysis (which resulted in a very small number of deletions). Individuals could be included in the analysis for certain years but not others, depending on their inclusion in the LAD and the years for which they met the sample selection criteria.

SPECIFICATION OF THE LEAVING MODEL

TWO DIFFERENT LOGIT MODELS ARE EMPLOYED, one for departures, the other for returns. In the first model, the endogenous variable is whether or not an individual leaves the country from one year to the next for any pair of years. More specifically, individuals are defined to have left Canada over the course of a given year if they are observed to reside in Canada at the end of year t, but then declare their departure from the country, or are otherwise observed to leave (see below), in year $t+1$. Each pair of years meeting the sample selection criteria listed above provides an observation for the model estimation. The regressors are meant to capture the various costs and benefits of emigrating, or other related influences, and are entered at the values of the first year (the *pre-move* year) for each pair of years that comprises an observation, and are thus *pre-determined* for any move.

The model is an ad hoc empirical specification, since it reduces the relevant dynamic processes to what happens from one year to the next at any point in time. This approach is used because trying to specify a proper hazard model, in particular, would require including individuals from the point at which they become at risk of moving — however that is defined (from age 18) — which would greatly restrict the analysis.

It is also a purely descriptive model as it does not employ a proper utility maximization framework, such as specifying the income streams an individual would likely face in Canada and abroad and assuming that a person would choose the higher one. There is simply not enough information in the LAD database to support such an approach, although future work may try to use proxies of the relevant measures in order to begin to get at these processes.

In any event, the model employed is quite intuitive, makes good use of the available data, should do a reasonable job at identifying the relationships between emigrating and the explanatory variables included, and should be sufficient for the purposes of identifying the time trends that attract such attention in both the technical literature and the public debate. In short, the simple logit model used here should prove satisfactory in making the best of the data available in order to improve our understanding of the emigration phenomenon.

THE RETURN MODEL

BY CONTRAST, THE RETURN MODEL REPRESENTS a proper hazard specification. It resembles the exit model turned on its head, where the dependent variable is the probability of returning to Canada from any given year to the next. But it differs in that individuals are tracked from the year they are observed to leave the country in a precise year-by-year fashion, and the model includes a set of dummy variables representing the number of years the person has been out of the country in order to capture duration effects. This type of hazard (or duration) model is used by Huff-Stevens (1994, 1999) to analyze poverty dynamics, by Gunderson and Melino (1990) to model strike duration, by Ham and Rae (1987) to analyze jobless duration, and by Finnie and Gray (2002) with LAD data to look at earnings dynamics, and similarly by Finnie and Sweetman (2003) to study low-income dynamics. The likelihood function of the hazard model is equivalent to the likelihood function of the logit approach (Keifer, 1990).

One special feature of this model is that it effectively tracks individuals during the period where they are outside the sample, i.e. when they are out of the country. However, these individuals *are* observed if and when they return — the event in question. The individuals' characteristics at the point of departure are included as regressors in the model. We are thus able to observe the rate of return based on those attributes — which, in many ways, are the most relevant for understanding the return phenomenon from a Canadian perspective. For example, how do return rates vary by age at departure, the province from which the individual left, the income level in the year prior to leaving, and so on?[3]

THE DEPENDENT VARIABLES: LEAVING AND RETURNING

LEAVING IS DEFINED IN ONE OF THREE WAYS, returning in two. Leaving definition 'A' is where an individual essentially declares the departure on his or her tax return, thus cleanly severing ties with the country. Definition 'B' adds to these declared departures individuals who have filed a declaration of non-residence in Canada (for tax purposes). Definition 'C' is broader still and includes those observed to have a foreign mailing address, even though they still have a legitimate tax province and have not declared their departure from the country on their tax return.

No single definition is perfect — it is, in fact, somewhat challenging to think of an appropriate definition even at the conceptual level; after all, what does *leaving Canada* mean? Fortunately, most of the findings are robust across all three definitions — except, that is, for the general levels and some of the basic time trends. Rather than attempting to identify which definition is *best*, the approach adopted here is to report the results for all three definitions in order to tell a fuller story of emigration patterns and trends.

Return definition 'A' is the obverse of the first leaving definition: it depends on an individual returning to the country and declaring it on his or her tax return. Definition 'B' expands the first definition by including those who had a Canadian address and were assigned a Canadian tax province. In each case, the individual had to meet the definition of having departed to be at risk of returning. These definitions result in six categories of exit and return — the combinations of the three exit types and two return types. Models have been run for all combinations, but the discussion focuses on the AA and CB combinations — i.e. the narrowest and widest definitions on each side. The trend/year variables are, however, shown for all six combinations.

THE EXPLANATORY VARIABLES

THE EXPLANATORY VARIABLES INCLUDE age, family status, province/region, a minority language indicator (English in Quebec, French outside Quebec — thus leaving the province/region variable to represent the majority language group in each jurisdiction), size of residence area, provincial unemployment rate, market income for the last full year in Canada, and an indicator of the receipt of U/E-I benefits in that same year.

At least one important variable is not on this list: the level of educational attainment. The reason for this omission is that there is no such measure on the LAD. This is unfortunate, especially with regards to any desired focus on the brain drain. However, there is an income indicator, and it will have to stand in for the omitted *brain* indicator.[4]

LEAVING

SIMPLE LEAVING RATES

FIGURE 1 SHOWS THE ANNUAL RATES of leaving Canada for the three definitions — i) a declared departure, ii) a declared departure or becoming a non-resident, iii) either of the above two conditions or moving to a foreign address — for all individuals and by sex.[5] Overall, the rates are generally very low, ranging from 0.04 percent (i.e. under one-half of one-tenth of 1 percent) to 0.14 percent (somewhat over one-tenth of 1 percent). In absolute terms, these represent 14,900 leavers in 1982 to 24,825 leavers in 1999 by definition A, 16,375 leavers in 1983 to 26,425 leavers in 1998 by definition B, and 20,075 leavers in 1983 to 26,725 leavers in 1998 by definition C.[6]

These rates and absolute numbers generally correspond to other estimates in the literature for the years other figures are available, as reviewed in Finnie (2001). However, the LAD data represent an annual series spanning an extended period of time with a consistent definition(s) of leaving that cannot be found elsewhere.

The departure rates naturally tend to be lowest for the narrowest definition of leaving (definition A) and rise with the broadening of the definition (B, C). Declared departures (definition A) increase slightly from the beginning of the period to the end, that is from around 0.10 percent in 1982 to 0.12 percent in 1999 — an increase of around 20 percent. In contrast, the broadest definition (C) actually declines slightly, from around 0.14 percent in 1983 to about 0.13 percent in 1998. The B definition rates and trends tend to lie between the other two, although the B and C definitions converge after about 1990, presumably due to a tightening of the treatment of tax filers with respect to province and residency.[7]

The leaving rates follow the economic cycle fairly closely, but not perfectly. The substantial decline in rates through the mid-to-late 1980s correspond to the strong growth of the Canadian economy during that period, but the rates bottomed out in 1987, whereas the economy continued to grow through 1988 before beginning to stall at the end of 1989. Rates subsequently rose through the early part of the 1990s, when the economy was in a lingering recession, and continued to do so until 1997, after which they declined, corresponding to the period when the Canadian economy finally displayed strong growth.

Overall, then, leaving rates are generally very low, they tend to be inversely related to prevailing economic conditions, and they have been either slightly higher or lower in the most recent years than at the beginning of the period, depending on the definition employed.

Perhaps of special interest is the reversal, toward the end of the decade, of the steady upward trend that characterized the first part of the 1990s. The data

FIGURE 1

LEAVING RATES

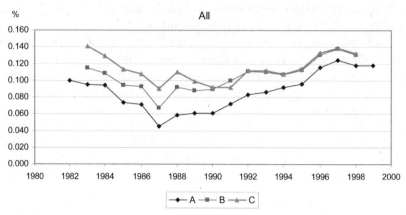

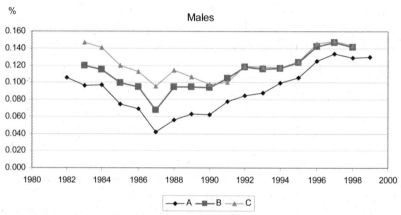

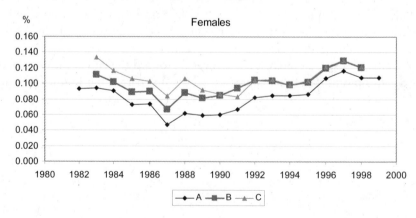

suggest that the initial rise was cyclically driven to a significant degree, and was reversed as the economy recovered, rather than representing some inexorable secular increase that would continue to rob the country of ever greater numbers of its most talented workers. That being said, rates were clearly higher at the end of the 1990s than at the end of the 1980s, although it is not clear what level they will reach if the economy remains strong — greater than before or not. Obviously, there are cyclical and trend effects at work and it is probably too soon to say exactly how important each of these is.

All these patterns are fairly similar for males and females, although the rates are slightly higher for men than women throughout.

THE LEAVING MODELS

THE LEAVING MODEL RESULTS are shown in Tables 1a, 1b and 1c, which correspond to the three leaving definitions employed. The findings are presented in terms of probabilities deriving from the models. That is, the model estimates were used to first estimate a baseline probability of leaving with each category variable set to zero, thus corresponding to the omitted categories for each set, and setting the only continuous variable — the unemployment rate — at its mean (8.7 percent). Each categorical variable was then 'turned on' one at a time, and the coefficient estimates were used to calculate a new predicted probability. These are the numbers shown in the tables. (The omitted category variables are shaded; all have, by construction, the same base-level probability.) The statistical significance of the associated coefficient estimates is also shown in the usual fashion (0.05 and 0.01 confidence levels).[8] The results are qualitatively very similar for the three sets of models, except for the year effects.

Holding other factors constant, the rates of leaving the country are fairly low for the youngest individuals (18-24), then rise (age 25-34), and decline thereafter. This would be consistent with a life-cycle model where the costs and benefits of moving, both economic and psychological, would point toward doing so earlier in life, but — it would appear — only after finishing school and getting a start in one's career.

Family status effects might be expected to reflect a similar set of cost and benefit factors, but the results are not entirely in line with what might have been anticipated. Couples with children tend to be more likely to leave, followed by singles, then couples with no children. These results differ from those found for inter-provincial mobility, where being married and having children are related to lower mobility rates, not higher ones.[9] Evidently, leaving the country is different than moving across provincial lines in this respect; individuals seem less likely to do it when they live on their own. Single parents actually have among the highest rates of leaving, but this could represent individuals not identified as married in the LAD data joining partners abroad.[10]

TABLE 1a

LEAVING MODELS: PREDICTED PROBABILITIES, LEAVING DEFINITION A

	MALES		FEMALES	
	I	II	I	II
BASE LEVEL	0.125**	0.135**	0.173**	0.165**
Age				
18-24	0.098**	0.105**	0.196**	0.187**
25-34	0.197**	0.211**	0.285**	0.272**
35-44	0.125	0.135	0.173	0.165
45-54	0.089**	0.095**	0.125**	0.119**
55-64	0.062**	0.067**	0.078**	0.074**
65+	0.033**	0.035**	0.041**	0.039**
Family Status				
Couple with Children	0.125	0.135	0.173	0.165
Couple, no Children	0.037**	0.040**	0.060**	0.058**
Single with Children	0.159**	0.170**	0.166**	0.159**
Single, no Children	0.102**	0.110**	0.162*	0.155*
Province/Region				
Ontario	0.125	0.135	0.173	0.165
Atlantic	0.065**	0.070**	0.094**	0.090**
British Columbia	0.150**	0.161**	0.216**	0.206**
North and Other	0.144*	0.154*	0.249**	0.237**
Prairies	0.122	0.131	0.169	0.162
Quebec	0.039**	0.042**	0.051**	0.048**
Minority Language				
English in Quebec	0.640**	0.687**	0.885**	0.845**
French Outside Quebec	0.138	0.148	0.178	0.170
Majority Language	0.125	0.135	0.173	0.165
Size of Area of Residence				
0-15,000	0.066**	0.071**	0.095**	0.091**
15,000-100,000	0.078**	0.084**	0.104**	0.099**
100,000+	0.125	0.135	0.173	0.165
Provincial Unemployment Rate				
8.7	0.125	0.135	0.173	0.165
9.7	0.125	0.134	0.172	0.164
Unemployment Insurance				
None	0.125	0.135	0.173	0.165
Some	0.074**	0.079**	0.136**	0.130**

TABLE 1a (CONT'D)

LEAVING MODELS: PREDICTED PROBABILITIES, LEAVING DEFINITION A

	MALES		FEMALES	
	I	II	I	II
BASE LEVEL	0.125**	0.135**	0.173**	0.165**
Market Income				
< 10,000	0.121	0.137	0.111**	0.100**
10,000-30,000	0.128	0.144*	0.136**	0.126**
30,000-60,000	0.125	0.135	0.173	0.165
60,000-100,000	0.296**	0.303**	0.281**	0.231**
100,000+	0.761**	0.781**	0.472**	0.301**
Market Income Interaction with post-1990 Dummy				
< 10,000		0.126		0.180*
10,000-30,000		0.125*		0.174
30,000-60,000		0.135		0.165
60,000-100,000		0.145*		0.202**
100,000+		0.143		0.277**
Calendar Year				
1983	0.125	0.135	0.173	0.165
1984	0.132	0.141	0.168	0.160
1985	0.098**	0.105**	0.135**	0.129**
1986	0.090**	0.096**	0.136**	0.130**
1987	0.054**	0.058**	0.089**	0.085**
1988	0.070**	0.075**	0.115**	0.110**
1989	0.079**	0.084**	0.111**	0.106**
1990	0.077**	0.083**	0.115**	0.109**
1991	0.098**	0.098**	0.128**	0.125**
1992	0.114*	0.115**	0.161	0.158
1993	0.116*	0.116**	0.158*	0.155
1994	0.137*	0.137	0.171	0.168
1995	0.144**	0.144	0.176	0.172
1996	0.168**	0.168**	0.217**	0.213**
1997	0.181**	0.181**	0.240**	0.235**
1998	0.172**	0.172**	0.223**	0.218**
1999	0.169**	0.169**	0.223**	0.218**

Notes: * Indicates significance at the 5-percent level.
** Indicates significance at the 1-percent level.
The shaded rows represent the categories associated with the base-level probabilities.

TABLE 1b

LEAVING MODELS: PREDICTED PROBABILITIES, LEAVING DEFINITION B

	MALES		FEMALES	
	I	II	I	II
BASE LEVEL	**0.158****	**0.166****	**0.199****	**0.191****
Age				
18-24	0.130**	0.135**	0.206	0.198
25-34	0.246**	0.258**	0.315**	0.302**
35-44	0.158	0.166	0.199	0.191
45-54	0.120**	0.125**	0.148**	0.142**
55-64	0.082**	0.086**	0.091**	0.088**
65+	0.043**	0.045**	0.048**	0.046**
Family Status				
Couple with Children	0.158	0.166	0.199	0.191
Couple, no Children	0.053**	0.056**	0.071**	0.068**
Single with Children	0.194**	0.203**	0.185**	0.178**
Single, no Children	0.130**	0.136**	0.192	0.184
Province/Region				
Ontario	0.158	0.166	0.199	0.191
Atlantic	0.098**	0.103**	0.119**	0.115**
British Columbia	0.184**	0.194**	0.245**	0.235**
North and Other	0.978**	1.023**	1.953**	1.869**
Prairies	0.154*	0.161	0.194	0.186
Quebec	0.053**	0.056**	0.061**	0.059**
Minority Language				
English in Quebec	0.713**	0.749**	0.910**	0.874**
French Outside Quebec	0.279	0.292	0.387	0.372
Majority Language	0.158	0.166	0.199	0.191
Size of Area of Residence				
0-15,000	0.087**	0.091**	0.106**	0.102**
15,000-100,000	0.099**	0.104**	0.115**	0.110**
100,000+	0.158	0.166	0.199	0.191
Provincial Unemployment Rate				
8.7	0.158	0.166	0.199	0.191
9.7	0.157	0.165	0.198	0.190
Unemployment Insurance				
None	0.158	0.166	0.199	0.191
Some	0.083**	0.087**	0.151**	0.145**

TABLE 1b (CONT'D)

LEAVING MODELS: PREDICTED PROBABILITIES, LEAVING DEFINITION B

	MALES		FEMALES	
	I	II	I	II
BASE LEVEL	**0.158****	**0.166****	**0.199****	**0.191****
Market Income				
< 10,000	0.149**	0.160	0.142**	0.130**
10,000-30,000	0.154	0.166	0.164**	0.154**
30,000-60,000	0.158	0.166	0.199	0.191
60,000-100,000	0.348**	0.344**	0.302**	0.267**
100,000+	0.757**	0.700**	0.459**	0.299**
Market Income Interaction with post-1990 Dummy				
< 10,000		0.162		0.204*
10,000-30,000		0.160		0.196
30,000-60,000		0.166		0.191
60,000-100,000		0.183*		0.215
100,000+		0.201**		0.314**
Calendar Year				
1983	0.158	0.166	0.199	0.191
1984	0.157	0.164	0.184*	0.177*
1985	0.131**	0.137**	0.159**	0.153**
1986	0.121**	0.126**	0.158**	0.152**
1987	0.088**	0.092**	0.119**	0.114**
1988	0.122**	0.127**	0.159**	0.152**
1989	0.120**	0.125**	0.144**	0.139**
1990	0.117**	0.123**	0.152**	0.146**
1991	0.135**	0.133**	0.173**	0.170**
1992	0.159	0.158	0.196	0.193
1993	0.159	0.158	0.197	0.194
1994	0.161	0.159	0.190	0.187
1995	0.167	0.166	0.195	0.192
1996	0.192**	0.190**	0.232**	0.228**
1997	0.200**	0.198**	0.252**	0.248**
1998	0.190**	0.187**	0.237**	0.233**
1999	0.172*	0.170	0.211	0.208*

Notes: * Indicates significance at the 5-percent level.
** Indicates significance at the 1-percent level.
The shaded rows represent the categories associated with the base-level probabilities.

TABLE 1c

LEAVING MODELS: PREDICTED PROBABILITIES, LEAVING DEFINITION C

	MALES		FEMALES	
	I	II	I	II
BASE LEVEL	0.194**	0.180**	0.243**	0.253**
Age				
18-24	0.202*	0.186	0.270*	0.281**
25-34	0.310**	0.287**	0.381**	0.397**
35-44	0.194	0.18C	0.243	0.253
45-54	0.145**	0.134**	0.176**	0.183**
55-64	0.095**	0.089**	0.106**	0.111**
65+	0.051**	0.047**	0.056**	0.059**
Family Status				
Couple with Children	0.194	0.18C	0.243	0.253
Couple, no Children	0.068**	0.064**	0.089**	0.093**
Single with Children	0.238**	0.222**	0.223**	0.233**
Single, no Children	0.145**	0.136**	0.224**	0.234**
Province/Region				
Ontario	0.194	0.18C	0.243	0.253
Atlantic	0.143**	0.134**	0.170**	0.178**
British Columbia	0.219**	0.204**	0.291**	0.303**
North and Other	0.745**	0.688**	1.181**	1.226**
Prairies	0.188*	0.175	0.234*	0.244*
Quebec	0.071**	0.066**	0.080**	0.083**
Minority Language				
English in Quebec	0.787**	0.735**	1.049**	1.095**
French Outside Quebec	0.335	0.310	0.412	0.429
Majority Language	0.194	0.18C	0.243	0.253
Size of Area of Residence				
0-15,000	0.118**	0.110**	0.139**	0.145**
15,000-99,000	0.129**	0.120**	0.151**	0.158**
100,000+	0.194	0.18C	0.243	0.253
Provincial Unemployment Rate				
8.7	0.194	0.18C	0.243	0.253 *
9.7	0.193	0.179	0.240	0.250
Unemployment Insurance				
None	0.194	0.18C	0.243	0.253
Some	0.094**	0.088**	0.193**	0.201**

TABLE 1c (CONT'D)

LEAVING MODELS: PREDICTED PROBABILITIES, LEAVING DEFINITION C

	MALES		FEMALES	
	I	II	I	II
BASE LEVEL	0.194**	0.180**	0.243**	0.253**
Market Income				
< 10,000	0.162**	0.139**	0.171**	0.183**
10,000-30,000	0.178**	0.163**	0.194**	0.203**
30,000-60,000	0.194	0.18C	0.243	0.253
60,000-100,000	0.406**	0.321**	0.387**	0.354**
100,000+	0.896**	0.640**	0.578**	0.370*
Market Income Interaction with post-1990 Dummy				
< 10,000		0.209**		0.242
10,000-30,000		0.187		0.252
30,000-60,000		0.18C		0.253
60,000-100,000		0.241**		0.303*
100,000+		0.277**		0.476**
Calendar Year				
1983	0.194	0.18C	0.243	0.253
1984	0.192	0.179	0.214**	0.223**
1985	0.157**	0.146**	0.190**	0.198**
1986	0.145**	0.135**	0.184**	0.192**
1987	0.125**	0.116**	0.152**	0.158**
1988	0.147**	0.137**	0.191**	0.199**
1989	0.136**	0.127**	0.165**	0.172**
1990	0.124**	0.115**	0.157**	0.164**
1991	0.131**	0.123**	0.153**	0.153**
1992	0.163**	0.154**	0.202**	0.202**
1993	0.165**	0.156**	0.205**	0.205**
1994	0.165**	0.156**	0.194**	0.194**
1995	0.172**	0.162**	0.203**	0.204**
1996	0.199	0.188	0.238	0.239
1997	0.204	0.192	0.258*	0.258
1998	0.195	0.183	0.243	0.243
1999	0.175*	0.164*	0.211**	0.211**

Notes: * Indicates significance at the 5-percent level.
       ** Indicates significance at the 1-percent level.
       The shaded rows represent the categories associated with the base-level probabilities.

The probability of leaving the country varies considerably by province. People living in Atlantic Canada are considerably less likely to leave than most others, those in British Columbia and the North are most likely to leave, and people living in Ontario and the Prairies (including Alberta) are in the middle. Most remarkable, however, are the extremely low rates for Quebec residents — with the indicated probabilities reflecting the majority Francophone speakers in that province, while the English-Quebec minority language indicator suggests that Anglophones have a much higher rate of leaving than do Francophones. By contrast, French speakers outside Quebec do not have statistically different leaving rates than others in the province/region where they live. Not surprisingly, individuals living in larger cities are, *ceteris paribus*, about twice as likely to leave as those in small cities and towns and rural dwellers.

The provincial unemployment rate appears to be statistically non significant, but given that there are sets of variables for both the calendar year and province/region — the dimensions along which this measure varies — this result is not surprising.

The market income variables are very interesting and indicate that the higher the individual's income, the greater the probability of leaving, especially at the highest levels ($60,000-$100,000 and $100,000+).[11] This tendency is particularly pronounced among men. To the extent that income levels capture the brain drain, rates of leaving are clearly greater for our best workers. That being said, their numbers are small, since relatively few individuals earn such high incomes, and the vast majority of leavers are found in the lower income categories.[12]

Those receiving unemployment/employment insurance benefits in a given year are less likely to leave. This could reflect a lack of employability (in other countries as well as in Canada), a dependency on this income support program, an absence of funds to finance a move, or some combination of these and/or other factors.

The raw time trends in leaving rates are depicted above. What do they look like after taking into account factors represented by the variables included in our models? These are captured by the calendar-year variables. The associated predicted probabilities are shown in the tables and plotted for all three leaving definitions in Figure 2. In fact, the raw and adjusted trends are very similar. The leaving rates decline significantly through most of the 1980s, but turn around after bottoming out in 1987 and increase through 1997, after which they decline. Therefore, the story would again seem to be one of strong cyclical effects and probably at least some sort of secular upward trend, but it is difficult to say, at this time, how strong that trend effect will turn out to be, or how long it will last.

FIGURE 2

CALENDAR-YEAR EFFECTS FOR THE LEAVING MODELS

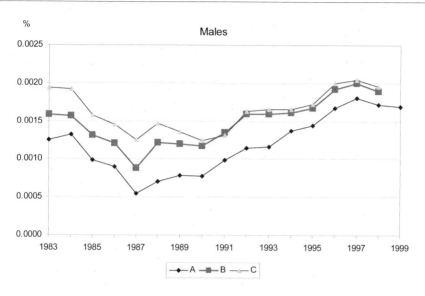

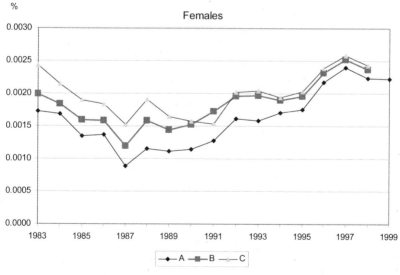

Finally, Model II (see Tables 1a, 1b and 1c) includes the interaction of the income variables with a dummy variable representing the 1990s. If more individuals at higher income levels were relatively more likely to leave in recent years, this would show up as positive coefficients on the interactions with higher income terms relative to lower income ones. The results suggest that there has been a strengthening over time of the relationship between income level and leaving, but the effect is not significant in all specifications and the magnitudes are not very large.

RETURNING

EMPIRICAL HAZARD RATES

FIGURE 3 SHOWS THE EMPIRICAL HAZARD RATES of returning to Canada for individuals who were observed as leaving over the study period. All six possible combinations of departure and return definitions are plotted (AA, AB, ... CB). The patterns are relatively robust in terms of the general shape, the only exception being for females when using the second, more expansive (B) definition of return (i.e. a declared return or observed Canadian tax province and Canadian address after leaving the country by any one of the three departure definitions).

Save for this exception, individuals are more likely to return after being away for two years rather than just one, but beyond this the rate of return declines, taking the classic negatively sloped form of most empirical hazards. Using the stricter AA definitions (declared departure and return) as an illustrative example, the rates are 3.27, 4.28, 3.50, 2.37 and 1.80 percent over the first five years. These numbers imply survivor rates (i.e. still out of the country) of 96.7, 92.6, 89.3, 87.2 and 85.5 percent. Thus, after five years, 14.5 percent of those who left have come back. However, these rates are averaged over the whole study period and do not control for any of the factors accounted for in the models. We now turn to the return models to take a closer look at this process.

THE RETURN MODELS

THE RESULTS FOR THE RETURN MODELS ARE SHOWN in Table 2. In order to conserve space, only those for the AA and CB combinations of departure and return are presented, but the results obtained for the other four combinations are quite similar for all variables except the year effects, as will be discussed further below. It is important to keep in mind that these results are for individuals already identified as leavers, so these are mobile persons to start with. Keeping this condition in mind helps make better sense of some of the findings.

FIGURE 3

EMPIRICAL RETURN RATES

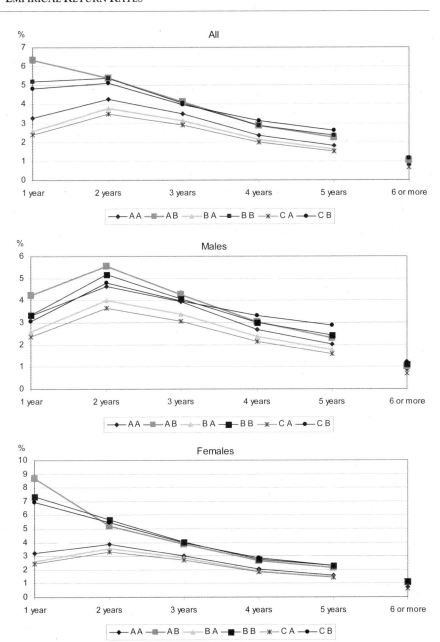

TABLE 2

PREDICTED PROBABILITY OF RETURN

	MALES		FEMALES	
LEAVE TYPE	A	C	A	C
RETURN TYPE	A	B	A	B
BASE LEVEL	**2.95****	**2.04****	**3.64****	**4.64****
Age				
18-24	4.13**	2.47**	5.22**	3.63**
25-34	3.78**	2.47**	4.44**	3.97**
35-44	2.95	2.04	3.64	4.64
45-54	2.89	1.92	3.49	3.35**
55-64	3.09	1.99	3.71	2.31**
65+	1.95**	1.42**	2.51**	1.65**
Family Status				
Couple with Children	2.95	2.04	3.64	4.64
Couple, no Children	3.32	1.87	4.21	2.88**
Single with Children	2.54**	1.83**	3.41	3.57**
Single, no Children	3.16	2.03	4.51**	3.48**
Province/Region				
Ontario	2.95	2.04	3.64	4.64
Atlantic	3.45	2.29	4.01	4.01*
British Columbia	3.34*	2.30**	4.01	3.97**
North and Other	3.66	1.72	4.16	3.81
Prairies	4.11**	2.68**	4.93**	4.98*
Quebec	4.15**	2.56**	5.04**	4.82
Minority Language				
English in Quebec	2.09**	1.61**	2.29**	3.73**
French Outside Quebec	4.51**	2.17	4.95	4.27
Majority Language	2.95	2.04	3.64	4.64
Size of Area of Residence				
0-15,000	3.26*	2.22*	4.08*	4.55
15,000-100,000	3.27	2.18	3.83	4.84
100,000+	2.95	2.04	3.64	4.64
Unemployment Insurance				
None	2.95	2.04	3.64	4.64
Some	3.08	2.29*	3.85	5.39**
Market Income in Year Prior to Departure				
< 10,000	1.85**	1.55**	2.61**	3.71**
10,000-30,000	2.00**	1.63**	2.99**	3.68**
30,000-60,000	2.95	2.04	3.64	4.64
60,000-100,000	4.03**	2.84**	4.38	5.46
100,000+	4.14**	3.36**	3.31	3.78

TABLE 2 (CONT'D)

PREDICTED PROBABILITY OF RETURN

	MALES		FEMALES	
LEAVE TYPE	A	C	A	C
RETURN TYPE	A	B	A	B
BASE LEVEL	2.95**	2.04**	3.64**	4.64**
Market Income Interaction with post-1990 Dummy				
< 10,000	3.02	2.00	4.60**	5.81**
10,000-30,000	3.94**	2.43*	3.90	5.84**
30,000-60,000	2.95	2.04	3.64	4.64
60,000-100,000	2.95	1.97	3.15	4.13
100.000+	2.89	1.78	4.48	5.20
Duration				
1 year	2.95	2.04	3.64	4.64
2 years	4.29**	3.19**	4.77**	3.59**
3 years	3.66**	2.56**	3.69	2.49**
4 years	2.53*	2.39**	2.48**	1.79**
5 years	2.01**	2.05	1.89**	1.36**
6 years	1.65**	1.61**	1.72**	0.97**
7 years	1.36**	1.15**	1.14**	0.74**
8 years	1.02**	0.79**	0.87**	0.62**
9 years	0.85**	0.55**	0.72**	0.53**
More than 9 years	0.50**	0.43**	0.46**	0.32**
Calendar Year				
1984	2.95	2.04	3.64	4.64
1985	3.10	2.34	2.43*	5.10
1986	3.54	6.04**	2.98	10.10**
1987	2.56	1.97	2.10**	4.87
1988	3.56	2.21	2.39**	5.67
1989	2.44	1.55	2.62*	5.24
1990	2.27	1.50*	1.99**	4.39
1991	2.27	1.69	2.09**	5.40
1992	1.92**	5.24**	1.25**	4.72
1993	2.19	1.87	2.29**	20.08**
1994	2.61	2.08	2.18**	11.14**
1995	2.52	2.17	2.39**	15.51**
1996	2.32	2.10	2.39**	15.01**
1997	2.60	2.25	2.51*	9.49**
1998	2.60	3.10**	3.11	13.00**
1999	2.99	3.77**	3.28	13.43**

Notes: * Indicates significance at the 5-percent level.
** Indicates significance at the 1-percent level.
The shaded rows represent the categories associated with the base-level probabilities.

Age, for example, displays an interesting pattern. People 65 and older are by far the least likely to return, but the patterns for other age groups are less easy to generalize across the different sets of findings. Generally, younger individuals are more likely to return, but this tendency is not uniform and, perhaps, less strong than might have been expected.

No clear pattern emerges for family status, except that unattached individuals have the highest rates of return. Singles are, perhaps, more willing and able to make risky moves and then move back if things don't work out than individuals with spouses and children.

There are no strong overall patterns by province or region, except that Francophone Quebecers tend to be among the high-probability returnees — on top of their very low leaving rates. In contrast, Quebec Anglophones are significantly less likely to return than their Francophone compatriots, showing the lowest rates of return of any province-language group in every case.

There is little of significance for the size of the area of residence. The same can be said for whether or not an individual received U/E-I benefits during the year prior to leaving.

Of considerably more interest is the pattern related to the individual's income level before leaving Canada. As high-income individuals ($60,000-$100,000) were several times more likely to leave than those at lower income levels, their return rates are also significantly higher, at least in the case of men. The differences are not as strong as for leaving, but they still point to those at higher income levels as being generally more mobile — here seen as being more likely to return as well as leave. Tests for shifts in the relationship between income level and the probability of return in the 1990s vs. the 1980s, similar to those performed for the leave models, revealed no clear pattern in this respect.

The duration terms are plotted in Figure 4 for the three A (declared) return definition results (i.e. using each of the departure definitions). They show the same general tendency as the raw rates presented earlier: a rise in the second year relative to the first, and a decline afterwards. Here, the terms are extended further, and are seen to continue to decline throughout, with no sign of flattening. The associated survivor rates implied by these rates, which represent the duration effects applied to the baseline person (all category variables set to 0), are 85.5 percent after 5 years and 81.1 percent after 10 years. Thus, most people who leave stay away, even if small numbers continue to trickle back home over time.

FIGURE 4

DURATION EFFECTS FOR THE RETURN MODELS

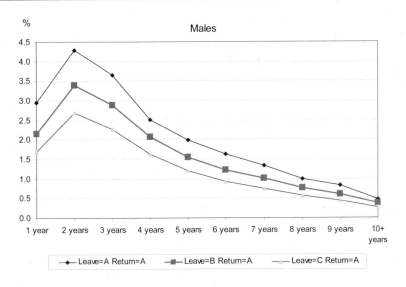

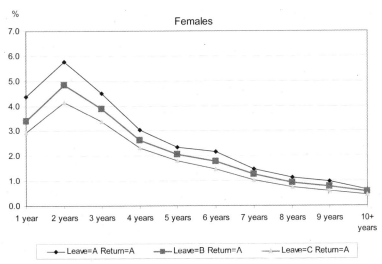

FIGURE 5

CANADA-YEAR EFFECTS FOR THE RETURN MODELS

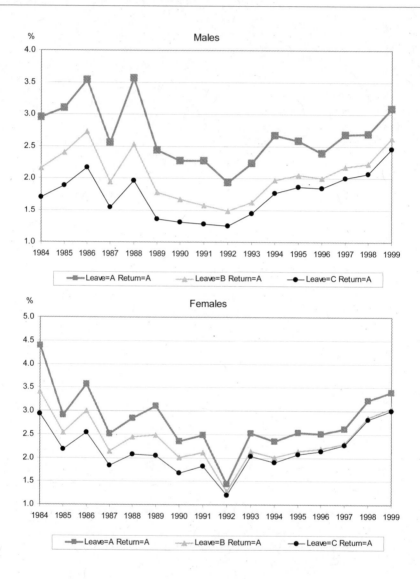

The return models also include calendar-year variables; these are plotted for the A return models (Figure 5).[13] There is a bit of noise in the patterns, but the overall trends are interesting. Most importantly, rates declined through 1992, then rose over the rest of the decade. Using the narrowest AA definition, return rates went from a low of 1.93 in 1992 to 3.08 in 1999 and were still trending upward. Using the other definitions of leaving (B, C) and the same definition of return (A), the graphs show an even steeper slope.

Thus, while rates of departure from the country generally rose in the 1990s (until they reversed toward the end of the decade), so did the rates of returning. Generally, these patterns point to a more mobile population, presumably driven by a more global labour market, more flexible institutional arrangements, a breakdown of legal barriers, and other factors that facilitate labour movements in both directions. Previously, we had evidence only on leavers, not knowing who returned. These data provide a fuller view of what has been occurring, and the rough matching of the outflow trends with the return movements is an interesting and important finding.

Furthermore, if annual rates of return have in fact doubled or so in the last decade (as these calendar-year effects suggest), and are perhaps continuing to rise, this would lead to very different overall rates of return as probabilities accumulated in more recent periods compared to earlier ones. If, in the past, overall rates were in the range of 15 percent after five years (as mentioned above), they would be much higher with the rising rates that seem to be emerging in recent years.

CONCLUSION

THIS STUDY HAS PROVIDED NEW EMPIRICAL EVIDENCE on the rates at which Canadians leave the country and return. The major findings may be summarized as follows:

- Overall, somewhere in the range of 0.1 percent — that is, about one tenth of one percent — of the adult population leaves the country in any given year.

- Raw departure rates have largely followed the business cycle: declining in the 1980s, reversing toward the end of the decade, rising through most of the 1990s, then turning back again as the Canadian economy gained strength in the last years of the decade.

- Departure rates decline with age (except for the very youngest), are higher for those in bigger cities and for couples with children and singles relative to childless couples, are much lower for Francophone

Quebecers, and are much higher for those at greater income levels, thus supporting the brain drain hypothesis to at least some degree.

- Only a small minority of people who leave ever return, with estimated hazard rates indicating that about 14-15 percent of leavers return after 5 years, and about 19 percent after 10 years.

- That being said, there was a substantial upward trend in return rates from 1992 onward, continuing right through the last data point in 1999, with the values indicating something like a doubling of return rates in recent years.

- Generally, other explanatory variables are not very significant in the return models, although — notably — return rates (like departure rates) are significantly higher for people at higher income levels.

Strong cyclical factors, but also important underlying trends, are thus at play in both leaving and return rates. There seems to be a general upward trend in departures, but the declines observed in the most recent years along with earlier declines during most of the 1980s suggest that the numbers will not necessarily continue to increase in the future, especially if the Canadian economy continues to perform well. Furthermore, although return rates have historically been relatively low, the strong increases observed through the 1990s suggest mobility is more and more a two-way street. Not only does Canada attract large numbers of immigrants from other countries, but also a growing number of its own expatriates, including a disproportionate number of those with higher incomes.

In short, the data support the notion that Canada is in a global labour market, and while a small, yet perhaps important, proportion of the population leaves every year, the trend does not appear to be an ever-increasing upwards spiral. And, some — increasingly — return.

There is surely much that can, and should, be done to stem some aspects of these outflows, especially among the best and brightest, as discussed in Finnie (2001) and accompanying studies in that publication. It is hoped that the work reported here will contribute to the debate that will unfold on these issues.

ENDNOTES

1   See Finnie (2001) for a review of the recent empirical evidence and discussion of the related policy issues. That review includes CMA (1999), Conference Board of Canada (1999), DeVoretz (1999), DeVoretz and Laryea (1998), Emery (1999), Frank and Bélair (1999, 2000), Globerman (1999), Helliwell (1999, 2000), Hoefer,

Norris and Ruddick (2000), IRPP (1998, 1999), Iqbal (1999), McKendry et al. (1996), Mintz (2001), Schwanen (2000), Simpson (2000), Wagner (2000), and Zhao, Drew and Murray (2000).

2 Atkinson, Bourguignon and Morrison (1992) and OECD (1996) discuss the typically better coverage and lower attrition of administrative databases over survey databases. See Finnie (1998) for evidence on attrition from the LAD and the relationship of this attrition to migration behaviour over selected intervals.

3 Return rates need to be adjusted for the fact that individuals who die while out of the country would no longer be at risk of returning and should be censored at that point. This is done by applying age-specific mortality rates and censoring individuals' records at the time they are deemed to die by this probabilistic assignment. In fact, this treatment does not change the key results of the model.

4 The notion of *brain* is not always well defined in the brain drain debate. For example, it sometimes includes entrepreneurs, whether or not they have/are brains. The income indicator included in the models would normally capture those income-related definitions better than an education measure, but both types of measures would clearly be desirable.

5 In each case, the state of being at risk is adjusted appropriately. In short, if the person has already been identified to leave by one of the conditions of the relevant definition, he or she can no longer be at risk of leaving.

6 The B and C definitions have no exits for 1982 because they are based on a change in tax province or address from one year to the next, thus requiring the individual to first be observed in Canada. As the data start in 1982, the first exit can only be observed in 1983. Similarly, by the B and C definitions, an exit is identified as occurring in the year *before* any observed change in tax province or residency, because in the year the individual actually leaves, he or she is identified as having Canadian residency and a tax province. This is why there are no exits in 1999 for definitions B and C.

7 The difference between definitions B and C is with respect to those who have a Canadian address but foreign residency. In later years, those with foreign addresses were more likely to be assigned a foreign residency, and vice versa, thus forcing a convergence of the definitions.

8 The full logit model results are available from the author.

9 Finnie (forthcoming).

10 Although individuals are supposed to declare their marital status on their tax returns and the LAD attempts to match common-law partners into couples (including the use of address matches), if a person does not declare him- or herself to be married and a match is otherwise missed, the individual may be erroneously identified as unmarried — in this case, as a single parent (where the spouse is out of the country).

11 Market income captures wages and salaries, net self-employment and professional income, dividend and interest income, and all other private (non-government) sources except capital gains (omitted partly due to adjustments related to tax rules in certain years).

12 See Finnie (2001).

13   The B models have some odd patterns that may be related to how the Canada Revenue Agency treats individuals who file tax returns indicating Canadian addresses without actually having declared their return to the country. This could be the reason why the duration terms have a slightly different shape for the B return definition as well — at least for women.

ACKNOWLEDGMENTS

THIS STUDY WAS MADE POSSIBLE by the financial support received from Industry Canada. The author is also very grateful to Eric Olsen, who carried out the data analysis; to the Small Area and Administrative Data Division of Statistics Canada, who provided access to the LAD database and some related background file development; to the Social Sciences and Humanities Research Council for a research grant that was critical in the earlier stages of the author's work with the LAD database; to Scott Murray for his participation and support in this and related work; to Jennifer Hunt, Richard Roy and other participants at the North American Linkages workshop held in Montreal, in November 2002, for their comments; and to Joanne Fleming for her careful copy editing.

BIBLIOGRAPHY

Atkinson, A.B., F. Bourguignon and C. Morrison. *Empirical Studies of Earnings Mobility*. Switzerland: Harwood Academic Publishers, 1992.

CMA. *Investing in Health Futures: No Time Like the Present*. Report prepared for the 132nd Annual Meeting. Ottawa: Canadian Medical Association, 1999, 39 p.

Conference Board of Canada. *Are We Losing Our Minds? Trends, Determinants and the Role of Taxation in the Brain Drain to the United States*. Ottawa, 1999, 35 p.

DeVoretz, Don. "The Brain Drain Is Real and It Costs Us." *Policy Options* 20, 7. Montreal: Institute for Research on Public Policy, 1999, pp. 18-24.

DeVoretz, Don, and Samuel A. Laryea. "Canadian Human Capital Transfers: The United States and Beyond." *Commentary*, No. 115. Toronto: C.D. Howe Institute 1998, 40 p.

Emery, Herb. "The Evidence vs. the Tax-Cutters." *Policy Options* 20, 7. Montreal: Institute for Research on Public Policy, 1999, pp. 25-29.

Finnie, Ross. "Who Moves? – A Panel Logit Model Analysis of Inter-Provincial Migration in Canada." *Applied Economics*. Forthcoming.

——. "The Brain Drain: Myth and Reality – What It Is and What Should Be Done." (With accompanying comments by Peter Kuhn, John Helliwell, Daniel Schwanen, Peter Barrett and David Stewart-Patterson.) *Choices* 7, 6. Montreal: Institute for Research on Public Policy, November 2001, 68 p.

——. "Inter-Provincial Mobility in Canada: A Longitudinal Analysis". Working Paper. Ottawa: Human Resources Development Canada (Applied Research Branch), 1998.

Finnie, Ross, and David Gray. "The Dynamics of the Earnings Distribution in Canada: An Econometric Analysis." *Labour Economics* 9, 6 (2002): 763-800.

Finnie, Ross, and Arthur Sweetman. "Poverty Dynamics: New Empirical Evidence for Canada." *Canadian Journal of Economics* 36, 2 (May 2003).

Frank, Jeffrey, and Éric Bélair. *South of the Border: Graduates from the Class of '95 Who Moved to the United States*. Statistics Canada, 1999.

——. "Pathways to the United States: Graduates from the Class of '95." Ottawa: Statistics Canada, *Education Quarterly Review* 6, 3 (2000): 36-44. Cat. No. 81-003-XIE.

Globerman, Steven. *Trade Liberalisation and the Migration of Skilled Workers*. Perspectives on North American Free Trade Series, No. 3. Ottawa: Industry Canada, 1999, 35 p.

Gunderson, M., and A. Melino. "The Effects of Public Policy on Strike Duration." *Journal of Labor Economics* 8 (1990): 295-316.

Ham, J., and S. Rae. "Unemployment Insurance and Male Unemployment in Canada." *Journal of Labor Economics* 5 (1987): 325-353.

Helliwell, John. "Checking the Brain Drain: Evidence and Implications." *Policy Options* 20, 7. Montreal: Institute for Research on Public Policy, 1999, pp. 6-17.

——. "Globalization: Myths, Facts and Consequences." C.D. Howe Benefactors' Lecture. Toronto: C.D. Howe Institute, 2000, 55 p.

Hoefer, Mike, Doug Norris and Elizabeth Ruddick. "Canadians Authorized to Work in the United States Under NAFTA Provisions." Paper presented at the November Metropolis Conference in Vancouver, 2000.

Huff-Stevens, Ann. "The Dynamics of Poverty Spells: Updating Bane and Ellwood." *American Economic Review* 84, 2 (May 1994): 34-37.

——. "Climbing Out of Poverty, Falling Back In: Measuring the Persistence of Poverty over Multiple Spells." *Journal of Human Resources* 34 (1999): 557-588.

IRPP. "A Tax Cutting Strategy for Canada." Symposium. *Policy Options* 19, 10. Montreal: Institute for Research on Public Policy, December 1998, 48 p.

——. "The Brain Drain." Symposium. *Policy Options*, 20, 7. Montreal: Institute for Research on Public Policy, September 1999, pp. 3-33.

Iqbal, Mahmood. "Are We Losing Our Minds?" *Policy Options* 20, 7. Montreal: Institute for Research on Public Policy, 1999, pp. 34-38.

Keifer, N. "Econometric Methods for Grouped Duration Data." In *Panel Data and Labour Market Studies*. Edited by J. Hartog, G. Ridder and J. Theeuwes, Elsevier Science Publishers, 1990, pp. 97-117.

McKendry, Robert J.R., George A. Wells, Paula Dale, Owen Adams, Lynde Buske, Jill Strachan and Lourdes Flor (1996), "Factors Influencing the Emigration of Physicians, from Canada to the United States." *Canadian Medical Association Journal* 4, 2 (January 1996): 171-181.

Mintz, Jack. *Most Favoured Nation.* Policy Study, No. 36. Toronto: C.D. Howe Institute, 2001.

OECD. "Earnings Inequality, Low-Paid Employment and Earnings Mobility." *Employment Outlook.* Paris: Organisation for Economic Co-operation and Development, 1996, Chapter 3, pp. 59-108.

Schwanen, Daniel. "Putting the Brain Drain in Context." *Commentary*, No. 140. C.D. Howe Institute, 2000.

Simpson, Jeffrey. *Star-Spangled Canadians: Canadians Living the American Dream.* Toronto: Harper-Collins, 2000.

Wagner, Don. "Do Tax Differences Contribute Toward the Brain Drain from Canada to the U.S.?" Paper presented at the 34th Annual Meeting of the Canadian Economics Association, Vancouver, 2000.

Zhao, John, Doug Drew and T. Scott Murray. "Brain Drain and Brain Gain: The Migration of Knowledge Workers from and to Canada." Ottawa: Statistics Canada, *Education Quarterly Review* 6, 3 (2000): 8-44. Cat. No. 81-003-XIE.

Comment

Jennifer Hunt
McGill University

I LEARNED A LOT FROM READING THIS STUDY. Ross Finnie has a wonderful data set: it is unusual to have one so well suited to the study of emigration, and I have never seen a dataset that also permitted the study of potential return migration. Therefore, the data provide a rare opportunity whose importance and interest are obvious. Canada fears reduced growth owing to the brain drain to the United States, while paradoxically many in the United States fear the arrival of these brains. This study gives us key insights into who moves out of Canada, for how long, and why.

There are two aspects to the study. One is the characteristics of individuals moving in and out of Canada, while the other is the determinants of the time-series variation in outflows (and returns). The data are better suited for the former, although one of its drawbacks is that, currently, the destination country is unknown. It would be interesting to know, if necessary from another source, what proportion of emigrants go to the United States. However, much can also be learned about the latter. Finnie discusses the role of the business cycle in Canada, observing that Canadians appear more likely to leave when the Canadian economy is doing badly. Although this seems obvious at first, more theoretical reflection and empirical evidence could be useful. For example, if the United States were the dominant destination and if its business cycle were perfectly synchronized with that of Canada, one might expect fewer Canadians to emigrate during downturns. This would be true if emigrants typically first find a job, then move, since at a given level of unemployment an individual is more likely to find a job at home — where his or her connections are — than abroad. The finding in several studies that within-country migration falls when the national unemployment rate rises lends credence to this possibility (see, for example, Decressin, 1994).

If, indeed, Canadians are more likely to emigrate when the economy is doing badly, it is odd that the provincial unemployment rate is insignificant in the emigration regressions and that the year dummies pick up the cyclical pattern. I would be interested in seeing different specifications to explore further this aspect. I would be curious to find out whether the coefficient on the unemployment variable is significant when the year dummies are dropped, or when the individual-level information on employment insurance is dropped. The unemployment rate in the U.S. census region or state nearest to the individual's residence could be included, as well as the Canadian provincial unemployment rate, or the ratio of the two, to capture the idea outlined above that it is the difference between source and destination that is important. Information about wages in the home province could also be included.

This study allows interesting comparisons with my own study of migration from Eastern Germany to Western Germany since the transition (Burda and Hunt, 2001; Hunt, 2002). Finnie can measure return migration better than I could with my small sample, but it appears nonetheless that return migration is higher in the German case. Speculation about the reasons that may explain this difference could be the subject of fruitful future research. I find that individuals who have recently been laid off or who have recently completed college are particularly likely to move, suggesting some further avenues for exploration in the Canadian data. I also find that those living near the border are likely to commute rather than move, which suggests that it could be useful to control for the square of the distance to the American border in the emigration regressions: those very close might commute rather than move, but those very far might be less well-informed about existing possibilities abroad. It would also be very interesting to interact this variable with unemployment and wage information. I also find some evidence that the employment situation of the spouse is a factor in the moving decision, so if the Canadian data permit, this aspect could also be explored. Finally, I find that younger individuals are much more sensitive than older individuals to wage gaps, while the reverse is true for unemployment gaps, suggesting that many determinants of emigration should be interacted with age.

Some final points that could usefully be addressed in the study are the importance of facilitated entrance to the United States following the free trade agreement, the role of non-citizens in emigration, comparison of the determinants of emigration with the determinants of interprovincial migration, and the joint study of departure and return information.

BIBLIOGRAPHY

Burda, Michael, and Jennifer Hunt. "From Reunification to Economic Integration: Productivity and the Labor Market in Eastern Germany." *Brookings Papers on Economic Activity* 1 (2001): 1-72.

Decressin, Joerg. "International Migration in West Germany and Implications for East-West Salary Convergence." *Weltwirtschaftliches Archiv* (1994): 231-257.

Hunt, Jennifer. "Why Do People Still Live in East Germany?" University of Montreal Working Paper, 2002.

Richard P. Chaykowski   &   George A. Slotsve
Queen's University   Northern Illinois University

6

Innovation and Response in Industrial Relations and Workplace Practices Under Increased Canada-U.S. Economic Integration

INTRODUCTION

Canada USA NAFTA F15 F16 J53 031 033 M52 M54

IN NORTH AMERICA, the Free Trade Agreement (FTA) and North American Free Trade Agreement (NAFTA) have significantly increased the exposure of Canadian firms to (primarily) U.S. competition. One aspect of concern about the overall competitive capability of the Canadian economy is productivity growth and, at the firm level, this concern centers on labour productivity. Not surprisingly, then, the transformation of production systems has coincided in both countries with dramatic changes in workplace practices and work systems. Some of the emergent work systems comprise innovative or advanced industrial relations and human resources management practices that represent a significant departure from those developed under the *industrial model* that prevailed throughout most of the latter half of the 20th century.

There is mounting evidence that some of these innovations, including problem-solving teams, self-directed work groups, quality circles, total quality management approaches, and so forth, are associated with higher productivity.[1] In some cases, firms have adopted these workplace innovations as *bundles* of practices that are referred to as "high performance work practices" (HPWP). Under increased competitive pressures, they have been utilized, together with investments in training and more highly skilled workforces, to achieve greater productivity within firms.

Yet, we know surprisingly little about the extent to which firms adopt such practices as an identifiable *strategic* business decision to increase their productivity or competitiveness. More specifically, we do not know whether firms adopt innovative workplace practices (or increase training investments) when faced with mounting national or international competition. Alternatively, management may adopt such work practices as a consequence of changes in the engineering technologies of production systems that render traditional forms of work organization inefficient. While it is likely that the observed adoption of innovative practices by firms results from strategic decisions to alter their organizational technology or is a response to changes in engineering technology, we have little systematic empirical evidence on the factors that affect the diffusion and adoption of these high performance work practices.

Another aspect of the increased exposure of Canadian firms to international competition, especially from the United States, is the mobility of labour. Recent evidence suggests an increase in the international mobility of high-skilled labour.[2] This has raised some concern given the high marginal (economic) impact of the loss of high-skilled workers (especially in the context of the development of a knowledge-based economy), and the potential loss associated with public investment in skilled labour. Concern in Canada has been focused on migration levels to the United States, especially in light of some evidence of a rise in permanent and temporary emigration to that country and of a net loss of workers in knowledge-based occupations.

Economic integration under NAFTA has increased the flow of capital and intensified competition in product markets — it may also be raising competition in the labour market for higher skilled workers. This could affect, for example, the compensation packages or types of employment arrangements offered to employees. This could be the result of demand-side effects arising from technological change or could reflect an attempt by workers to capture rents, made possible by the mobility regime introduced under NAFTA.

However, the employment arrangements and work practices that comprise a firm's work system may also be a factor influencing workers' decisions to change firm or industry, or to migrate internationally. While they may create work environments (conditions) that are desirable in their own right, they could influence more generally the future prospects for training or wage levels. The latter is particularly important in rapidly expanding or innovative industries. In view of these developments and of the growing body of research evidence linking innovative industrial relations and work practices to productivity, we examine two general issues in this study. The first and primary one is the issue, from a firm-level industrial relations and human resources practices standpoint, of the impact of increased foreign competition on the adoption of HPWP in Canadian firms. The second issue, which is more exploratory, is how increased competition, and its associated effects on the adoption of HPWP, might affect the mobility of labour between the two countries.

In the second section, we begin by providing some context on how innovative industrial relations and workplace practices have evolved over the past two decades in Canada and the United States, including key areas where they are similar or distinct. In so doing, we consider how trade liberalization between the two countries has impacted the conduct and practice of industrial relations in Canada. We focus, in particular, on innovative industrial relations and human resources practices — industrial relations, compensation and work practices/arrangements associated with *high performance* work systems (HPWS).

As we conclude from our assessment of the extant research literature on the adoption of HPWP and their effects on productivity, to date there has been no attempt to more formally model the adoption process and the impact of HPWP on firm productivity. Since the major focus of our analysis is whether the use of innovative or *best practices* in industrial relations and work organization in Canadian firms is associated with the international competition faced by firms, we present a formal model of the adoption of HPWP under free trade and derive basic implications regarding the effects of changes in key variables on the adoption of HPWP, including skill-biased technological change and changes in various factor input prices.

This model allows us to extend the analysis to consider whether or not, under freer trade, there are possible linkages and associations between labour mobility, on the one hand, and the organization of production and the characteristics of employment systems (e.g. work arrangements, job attributes, employment provisions such as compensation), on the other hand. Existing (empirical) research evidence on labour mobility between Canada and the United States under NAFTA, especially among higher skilled employees, is quite limited. Consequently, this segment of the analysis will be instrumental in suggesting research strategies for addressing labour mobility issues and in identifying knowledge and data gaps for further research.

We then proceed to empirically examine the relationship between foreign ownership and the degree of competition from U.S.-owned firms, and the use of industrial relations and work practices that are considered new or innovative or that otherwise yield higher productivity,[3] in the areas of organizational change,[4] work organization,[5] employee involvement,[6] flexible compensation,[7] and extent of training (formal and on-the-job). This segment of the analysis makes use of Statistics Canada's *Workplace and Employee Survey* (WES). We first provide a description of the adoption of these practices across Canadian establishments. Our main analysis uses a regression framework to examine whether the scope of competition and business strategies affect the utilization of these practices, while controlling for a variety of establishment-level characteristics that may affect the usage intensity of work practices.

We conclude the study with a look at some of the major conclusions and implications of the analysis. We also consider several aspects of industrial relations and work practices that would benefit from a closer examination, including the development of a better taxonomy for high performance work practices, the link between the types of work practices used in an organization and its skill mix, the possible link between the types of work practices used in an organization and worker mobility, the relationship between alternative business strategies (quality leader) and the use of alternative work practices, the relationship between the characteristics of the institutional (i.e. legal and policy) context and the provision and mix of work practices used by firms. Finally, we suggest directions for further research on these issues.

FIRM-LEVEL ADOPTION AND IMPACTS OF INNOVATIVE AND HIGH PERFORMANCE WORK PRACTICES IN CANADA AND THE UNITED STATES

ONE OF THE MORE SIGNIFICANT CHANGES in Canadian labour markets over the past several decades has been the transformation of institutional structures and arrangements, especially at the firm or workplace level.[8] In the industrial era, efficiency was typically associated with large scale, the standardization of product quality and the standardization of production systems.[9] While technological change occurred, it was typically incremental and directed at engineering improvements to the production process that tended to increase productivity, mostly at the margin. Not surprisingly, firms developed rule-oriented internal labour markets; workers would be hired at the lower levels (*ports of entry*) of the organization and would subsequently advance through the ranks as they received training (often within the firm), accrued seniority and revealed their abilities to the organization's senior management.

These characteristics, in turn, defined the work systems and rules, the employment contracts, the subject matter of collective bargaining and the relative contribution of labour inputs to productivity. Highly delineated job responsibilities, standardized pay systems, hierarchical organizational structures and arms-length employee-management relations that minimized employee involvement characterized these work systems. This production model was also associated with a relatively high degree of employment security (aside from cyclical economic impacts) and long-term employment contracting.[10]

By the 1970s, a number of factors combined to transform this once-dominant mass production system. While the mix of forces at work, their relative importance, and their impact over time varied across countries, the major factors included extensive advances in engineering technology, increased competition arising internally (from deregulation) and externally (from free trade and globalization) and significant shifts in consumer demand in favour of more specialized and often higher quality products. The implications for industrial relations and human resources management have been crucial because these forces have fundamentally transformed organizations, employment relationships, work systems and various aspects of labour markets:[11] organizations and their workforces are typically smaller; workforces often require higher skilled workers who are utilized with greater flexibility; in some cases, we have witnessed the emergence of a *core* of permanent, full-time employees who are supplemented by a *periphery* of non-standard workers (including part-time or contract workers); finally, work arrangements have been radically altered. These changes have been occurring across industries and internationally, especially throughout the industrialized world.

There are two important aspects of these developments that relate to industrial relations and human resources management. First, there is a growing recognition of the strategic business importance of organizational technology as somewhat independent of production technology. As noted above, the production model of the industrial era, driven by advances in engineering technology, essentially *determined* work organization and methods. In the current era, management has sought to develop and exploit innovative forms of work organization independently of the new work system requirements implied by emerging production technologies. Second, the drive to develop and implement innovative work practices has been motivated by a desire to make gains in operational efficiency (productivity).[12] These developments have supported and given rise to what has been coined "high performance work practices," or a "high performance work system."

While there is no generally accepted set of organizational practices that, taken together, constitute a high performance work system, various categories of workplace practices tend to fall under this rubric, including flexible work systems (flexible work organization, job rotation, multiskilling and teams), employee involvement and communication, emphasis on skills development and training, and variable compensation systems (for Canada, see Betcherman, McMullen, Leckie and Caron, 1994; and Betcherman and Chaykowski, 1996). The two key aspects of HPWP adoption of concern to us are whether they have an impact on firm productivity and whether or not the implementation of these practices, individually or in bundles, matters with respect to their effectiveness.

There is a large and burgeoning research literature on these two issues. Both the methodology employed to investigate them and the particular workplace practices examined tend to vary considerably across studies.[13] Empirical investigations of these two issues, and recent reviews of the relevant literature, tend to reveal that the adoption of HPWP does have a positive effect on productivity, but it appears that such effects occur when workplace practices are adopted as bundles that are, presumably, somewhat complementary and match the broader management practices within the organization (see Gunderson, 2002; Becker and Huselid, 1998; Guest, 1997; Becker and Gerhart, 1996; Ichniowski, Kochan, Levine, Olson and Strauss, 1996; Ehrenberg, 1990).[14]

A major element missing from the research on the decision to adopt innovative work practices, or the link between the adoption of workplace practices associated with HPWS and productivity, is a formal conceptual framework for thinking about the underlying mechanisms by which the adoption of these practices affects productivity. For example, empirical studies of the adoption decisions of organizations tend to view these as analogous to investment decisions about production technologies, or innovations (Ichniowski and Shaw, 1995). In this framework, the adoption decision is a function of the expected net returns. This type of decision model is consistent with our depiction of workplace innovations as "organizational technology."

Studies of the impacts of high performance work practices on firm performance tend to implicitly or explicitly begin by specifying a production function although, typically, the model is not formally developed (e.g. Black and Lynch, 2001, 1996; Freeman and Kleiner, 2000). In such cases, workplace practices are viewed as a factor input and modeled in a similar way to other factor inputs such as labour and capital. They then examine how these HPWP affect performance, where performance is usually measured in terms of productivity or profitability. Early studies tended to view HPWP as increasing the productivity of a firm's factor inputs. More recent studies examine the relationship between HPWP and profitability (or some other overall measure of the firm's performance) since it is possible for productivity to rise without increasing profitability (due to the higher costs resulting from the introduction of HPWP). In the following section, we build on previous work based on a production function approach by formally modelling the adoption of HPWP under free trade and deriving basic predictions about the effects of changes in key variables on the adoption of HPWP.

Adoption of High Performance Work Practices, Competition and Worker Mobility

Firm Competition and Workplace Practices

OUR MAIN FOCUS IS TO DETERMINE whether increased competition affects the use of high performance work practices within firms. Freer trade (globalization) is believed to have increased the interdependence of national economies over the last couple of decades. In particular, the FTA and NAFTA have been thought to further the interdependence between Canada and the

United States. As a result, firms exposed to growing competition seek new sources of competitive advantage. Possible traditional strategies include raising productivity or lowering (unit) costs by adopting advanced production technologies, or seeking out absolute advantages in access to key inputs (e.g. natural resources), or by using technology to achieve product differentiation (e.g. in design or quality). Another (complementary) strategy is to seek to improve productivity or quality by adopting some or many of the workplace and organizational practices associated with high performance work systems.

What is the effect of freer trade on the emergence of advanced workplace human resources practices? The basic framework for thinking about the connection between increased competition and the use of high performance work practices is presented in Figure 1. In this model, firms' response to increased competition (e.g. on price or quality) is to attempt to raise productivity. The traditional approach to achieve this is to focus on developing innovations and efficiencies in production technologies (paths A2 and B2); innovations in production technologies may also induce the firm to develop new forms of work practices (path C). But innovative work practices may also have an independent

FIGURE 1

COMPETITION, PRODUCTIVITY AND HIGH-PERFORMANCE WORK PRACTICES LINKAGES

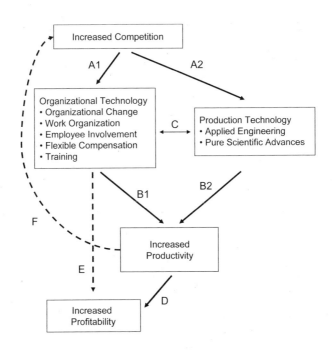

235

effect on firm productivity (paths A1 and B1), in which case the firm will pursue the adoption of these high performance work practices as a separate, but likely complementary, management strategy.[15] In what follows, we develop a more formal model of the process by which HPWP affect firm productivity.

MODEL OF THE FIRM'S PRODUCTION FUNCTION AND PROFIT MAXIMIZATION WITH THE ADOPTION OF HPWP AND COMPETITION

WE ASSUME THAT THERE ARE TWO COUNTRIES (Canada and the United States) that sign trade agreements resulting in freer trade and, therefore, greater bilateral competition. We further assume that the two countries experiencing tighter economic integration have an integrated capital market and access to similar technologies. Therefore, firms faced with increased competition will adopt as many HPWP as is profitable. HPWP can be thought of as being embedded in the production function in the sense that they can affect inputs or the production technology. The object, then, is to consider a production function that parameterizes work practices or, more specifically, the set of practices that characterize a high performance work system:

- HPWP that increase work or job flexibility (e.g. job rotation, multi-skilling, flexible job design) may make it easier for the firm to substitute between K and L or between different types of labour (skilled and unskilled). In turn, this will affect the elasticities of demand for labour.

- High investment in training or investment in training that increases skills will increase the productivity of labour, L.

- Flexible compensation systems (e.g. incentive pay, profit sharing) are expected to create work incentives and thereby increase worker effort and, hence, labour productivity.

- Industrial relations (IR) and human resources (HR) systems that emphasize employee involvement (e.g. information sharing, problem-solving groups, joint committees, self-directed work groups, employee involvement programs) may improve efficiency in three respects:

  a) First, they may raise directly the productivity of capital. This effect results from the improved utilization of a given stock and type of capital, K (e.g. maintenance or process improvements).

  b) Second, they may facilitate a more efficient utilization of capital by, for example, allowing the firm to combine K, L or different types of L more effectively,[16] thereby increasing productivity.

c) Third, they may promote a more efficient utilization of L through better work organization, or increase employee morale, thereby increasing the productivity of L.

We begin by thinking of the firm as maximizing profits subject to a production technology where the production process is viewed as occurring in two stages. In the first stage, the firm combines HPWP with other factor inputs (such as skilled labour, unskilled labour, and capital) to produce *effective units* of these factor inputs. The solution to this first-stage problem yields factor demand functions for skilled labour, unskilled labour, capital and HPWP. The per-unit total cost of producing each of these effective factor inputs is their relevant factor price in the second stage.

In the second stage, the firm produces output by combining effective units of skilled labour, effective units of unskilled labour and effective units of capital in such a way as to maximize profits. The solution to the second-stage problem yields the profit-maximizing level of output and the factor demand function in terms of effective units of skilled labour, effective units of unskilled labour and effective units of capital.

We begin by specifying the stage-two (profit maximization) problem where we assume that the firm has a (generalized) constant elasticity of substitution (CES) production function,[17] given by:[18]

(1) $Y = A[\beta(S_e)^\rho + (1-\beta)(U_e)^\rho + (K_e)^\rho]^{\frac{\gamma}{\rho}}$.

S_e $[= f_1(b,S)]$ denotes effective units of skilled labour, where b are HPWP inputs such as advanced training, or multiskilling, that increase the productivity of skilled labour; U_e $[= f_2(a,U)]$ denotes effective units of unskilled labour, where a are HPWP inputs such as employee involvement or variable compensation schemes that increase the productivity of unskilled labour; and K_e $[= f_3(c,K)]$ denotes effective units of capital, where c are HPWP inputs that increase the productivity of capital by raising the efficiency of its utilization.

We use the term "effective units" to distinguish a basic input (i.e. skilled labour, S) into the technical production process from a final productive input (i.e. S_e) which is produced by combining the raw input with HPWP inputs. Following Johnson and Stafford (1999), the parameter β (where $0< \beta <1$) captures skill-biased technological change, the parameter A captures factor-neutral technological change, and γ $(\gamma \leq 1)$ denotes returns to scale.[19]

The profit function is given by:

(2) $\Pi = pY - w_e^s S_e - w_e^u U_e - w_e^k K_e$,

where w_e^s, w_e^u, and w_e^k denote the effective factor input prices (unit cost) of skilled labour, unskilled labour and capital, respectively, and where p denotes the output price.

The conditional effective factor demand functions are obtained by maximizing profits [Equation (2)] subject to the production function [Equation (1)]. The conditional effective factor demand functions are:

(3a) $\qquad U_e = (\dfrac{Y}{A})^{\frac{1}{\gamma}} \{M\}^{\frac{-1}{\rho}} [\beta w_e^u]^{\frac{1}{\rho-1}}$

(3b) $\qquad S_e = (\dfrac{Y}{A})^{\frac{1}{\gamma}} \{M\}^{\frac{-1}{\rho}} [(1-\beta)w_e^s]^{\frac{1}{\rho-1}}$

(3c) $\qquad K_e = (\dfrac{Y}{A})^{\frac{1}{\gamma}} \{M\}^{\frac{-1}{\rho}} [\beta(1-\beta)w_e^k]^{\frac{1}{\rho-1}}$,

where, to simplify the expressions, we have defined:

(4) $\qquad M = \beta[(1-\beta)w_e^s]^{\frac{\rho}{\rho-1}} + (1-\beta)[\beta w_e^u]^{\frac{\rho}{\rho-1}} + [(1-\beta)\beta w_e^k]^{\frac{\rho}{\rho-1}}$.

Substituting the conditional effective factor demand functions [Equations (3a)-(3c)] into the production function [Equation (1)] yields the following supply function:[20]

(5) $\qquad Y = [\gamma p \beta(1-\beta)]^{\frac{-\gamma}{\gamma-1}} A^{\frac{-1}{\gamma-1}} \{M\}^{\frac{\gamma(\rho-1)}{\rho(\gamma-1)}}$.

The effective factor demand functions are obtained by substituting the solution for the supply function [Equation (5)] into the conditional effective factor demand functions [Equations (3a)-(3c)], and are given by:

(6a) $\qquad U_e = [\gamma p \beta(1-\beta)A]^{\frac{-1}{\gamma-1}} \{M\}^{\frac{\rho-\gamma}{\rho(\gamma-1)}} [\beta w_e^u]^{\frac{1}{\rho-1}}$

(6b) $\qquad S_e = [\gamma p \beta(1-\beta)A]^{\frac{-1}{\gamma-1}} \{M\}^{\frac{\rho-\gamma}{\rho(\gamma-1)}} [(1-\beta)w_e^s]^{\frac{1}{\rho-1}}$

(6c) $\qquad K_e = [\gamma p \beta(1-\beta)A]^{\frac{-1}{\gamma-1}} \{M\}^{\frac{\rho-\gamma}{\rho(\gamma-1)}} [\beta(1-\beta)w_e^k]^{\frac{1}{\rho-1}}$.

To obtain the profit function, we substitute the effective factor demand functions [Equations (6a)-(6c)] into Equation (2). This yields:

$$\Pi = [pA]^{\frac{-1}{\gamma-1}} [\beta(1-\beta)]^{\frac{-\gamma}{\gamma-1}} \{M\}^{\frac{\gamma(\rho-1)}{\rho(\gamma-1)}} \gamma^{\frac{-\gamma}{\gamma-1}} (1-\gamma) .$$

We next turn to the firm's stage-one production problem. In stage one, the firm produces the stage-two effective factor inputs by combining raw factor inputs with HPWP inputs. The profit-maximizing level of effective factor inputs to produce in stage one is given by the effective factor demand functions [Equations (6a)-(6c)] solved for the stage-two profit maximization problem. The firm produces the effective factor inputs by minimizing costs. In producing effective units of skilled labour, the firm minimizes the cost function:

(7) $C_e^s = w_b b + w_s S ,$

subject to the CES production function for effective units of skilled labour:

(8) $S_e = [\lambda(b)^v + (1-\lambda)(S)^v]^{\frac{1}{v}} .$

In Equation (7), b denotes the HPWP inputs defined above, S denotes skilled labour, w_b denotes the price of b, and w_s denotes the price of S. The parameter λ ($0 < \lambda < 1$) captures HPWP-biased technological change (i.e. technology that is biased in favour of utilizing HPWP in the production of S_e) and $0 \neq v < 1$. S_e is the profit-maximizing level of effective units of skilled labour determined in the firm's stage-two problem [Equation (6b)]. Consequently, inputs b and S are combined such that $MP_s/w_s = MP_b/w_b$ that is, the marginal product per dollar spent must be the same for inputs b and S. The cost-minimization problem yields the conditional factor demand functions:

(9a) $b = S_e [M_b]^{\frac{-1}{v}} [(1-\lambda)w_b]^{\frac{1}{v-1}}$

(9b) $S = S_e [M_b]^{\frac{-1}{v}} [\lambda w_s]^{\frac{1}{v-1}} ,$

where, to simplify the expressions, we have defined:

$$M_b = \lambda[(1-\lambda)w_b]^{\frac{v}{v-1}} + (1-\lambda)[\lambda w_s]^{\frac{v}{v-1}} .$$

Substituting the conditional factor demand functions [Equations (9a)-(9b)] into Equation (7) yields the cost function:

$$C_e^s = S_e [M_b]^{\frac{\upsilon-1}{\upsilon}} \left(\frac{1}{\lambda(1-\lambda)} \right).$$

The unit cost of producing an effective unit of skilled labour is given by:

(9c) $w_e^s = \dfrac{C_e^s}{S_e} = [M_b]^{\frac{\upsilon-1}{\upsilon}} \left(\dfrac{1}{\lambda(1-\lambda)} \right).$

Similarly, the firm produces effective units of unskilled labour with the CES production function $U_e = [\alpha(a)^\psi + (1-\alpha)(U)^\psi]^{1/\psi}$ using HPWP inputs a and unskilled labour inputs U, and effective units of capital with the CES production function $K_e = [\delta(c)^\omega + (1-\delta)(K)^\omega]^{1/\omega}$ using HPWP inputs c and capital inputs K. Consequently, a and U are combined such that $Mp_u/w_u = Mp_a/w_a$, and c and K are combined such that $Mp_k/w_k = Mp_c/w_c$. The conditional factor demand functions for a, U, c and K are defined in an analogous way to the conditional factor demand functions for b and S. That is,

(10a) $a = U_e [M_a]^{\frac{-1}{\psi}} [(1-\alpha)w_a]^{\frac{1}{\psi-1}}$

(10b) $U = U_e [M_a]^{\frac{-1}{\psi}} [\alpha w_u]^{\frac{1}{\psi-1}}$

(10c) $w_e^u = \dfrac{C_e^u}{U_e} = [M_a]^{\frac{\psi-1}{\psi}} \left(\dfrac{1}{\alpha(1-\alpha)} \right),$

and

(11a) $c = K_e [M_c]^{\frac{-1}{\omega}} [(1-\delta)w_c]^{\frac{1}{\omega-1}}$

(11b) $K = K_e [M_c]^{\frac{-1}{\omega}} [\delta w_k]^{\frac{1}{\omega-1}}$

(11c) $w_e^k = \dfrac{C_e^k}{K_e} = [M_c]^{\frac{\omega-1}{\omega}} \left(\dfrac{1}{\delta(1-\delta)} \right),$

where

$$M_a = \alpha[(1-\alpha)w_a]^{\frac{\psi}{\psi-1}} + (1-\alpha)[\alpha w_u]^{\frac{\psi}{\psi-1}}$$

$$M_c = \delta[(1-\delta)w_c]^{\frac{\omega}{\omega-1}} + (1-\delta)[\delta w_k]^{\frac{\omega}{\omega-1}}.$$

240

To obtain the final solutions to the maximization problem, we substitute Equations (9c), (10c) and (11c) into Equations (3)-(6).[21]

Based on this model, we can undertake comparative statics analyses of changes in the price of skilled labour, changes in the price of implementing high performance work practices, and skill-biased technological change on the demand for labour and capital. These analyses are presented in Appendix A. The basic theoretical predictions are:

1. A rise in the price of HPWP that augment skilled labour decreases the demand for those HPWP (relative to the demand for S and relative to HPWP inputs that augment either unskilled labour or capital).[22] In addition, if the input price of HPWP that augment skilled labour increases, then there is a decline in the demand for *effective* units of skilled labour (relative to effective units of unskilled labour and effective units of capital).

2. An increase in the price of skilled labour increases the demand for HPWP inputs that augment skilled labour in the production process relative to raw labour input itself, while decreasing the demand for skilled labour relative to either unskilled labour or capital.[23] In addition, if the input price of skilled labour increases, then there will be a decline in the demand for *effective* units of skilled labour (relative to effective units of unskilled labour and of effective units of capital).

3. If technological change biased in favour of the usage of effective units of skilled labour (i.e. the labour units produced by the employment of skilled labour in combination with HPWP) occurs, then:

   - The demand for effective units of skilled labour rises (relative to the demand for effective units of unskilled labour and for effective units of capital).

   - The demand for effective units of unskilled labour declines relative to the demand for effective units of capital.

   - Firm demand for HPWP inputs that augment skilled labour increases relative to the demand for HPWP inputs that augment unskilled labour and relative to those that augment capital.

   - The demand for raw skilled labour rises relative to the demand for unskilled labour or capital; as well, the demand for unskilled labour declines relative to the demand for capital.

4. If technological change that is biased in favour of the usage of HPWP occurs, then the demand for HPWP that augment skilled labour rises

relative to the demand for raw inputs of skilled labour in the production of effective units of skilled labour.

IMPLICATIONS OF FREE(R) TRADE OR GLOBALIZATION

WE NOW CONSIDER TWO FIRMS located in different countries.[24] Let 1 denote Canada and 2 denote the United States. We assume, first, that both types of labour are perfectly mobile between countries; second, that firms have access to an integrated capital market; and third, that the S, U, and K are fully employed. Consequently, after globalization, firms face the same factor input world prices[25] w_s^*, w_u^* and w_k^*. Empirical studies of the Canadian and U.S. wage distributions suggest that the top and bottom ends of the U.S. wage distribution have longer tails than the Canadian wage distribution; consequently, we assume that, prior to globalization, $w_s^1 < w_s^* < w_s^2$, $w_u^1 > w_u^* > w_u^2$, and $w_k^1 \cong w_k^* \cong w_k^2$.

We also assume that the institutional differences that affect the range of workplace and organizational practices (associated with HPWS) which a country's firms have access to, or are able to adopt, still exist after globalization. That is, we assume that one country has a comparative advantage in the development, adoption and utilization of these HPWS practices.[26] If firms seeking a competitive advantage adopt more innovative work practices then this will, in turn, attract certain types of workers who are better qualified to make the most of these practices (self-selection), thereby increasing firm productivity (profitability). Therefore, due to differences in the labour market institutional and regulatory environments, firms face different parameter values for β, λ, α and δ, and face different HPWP input factor prices, w_a, w_b and w_c.

During the process of globalization, the wage of skilled labour in Canada will rise to the world level. This implies that, from a Canadian perspective:

- The demand for HPWP inputs used to produce effective units of skilled labour will rise relative to the demand for units of skilled labour and to the demand for effective units of skilled labour.

- The unit cost of producing effective units of skilled labour will increase.

- The demand for effective units of skilled labour will fall relative to the demand for effective units of unskilled labour and to the demand for effective units of capital.

- The demand for (raw) units of skilled labour will fall relative to the demand for (raw) units of unskilled labour and to the demand for (raw) units of capital.

- The demand for (raw) units of skilled labour will fall relative to the demand for effective units of skilled labour.

Consequently, Canada will use relatively more HPWP (b) in the production of effective units of skilled labour (S_e); it will use fewer units of skilled labour (S) relative to unskilled labour (U) and relative to capital (K); and it will use fewer effective units of skilled labour (S_e) relative to effective units of unskilled labour (U_e) and relative to effective units of capital (K_e).

In addition, during the globalization process, the price of unskilled labour tends to fall. Consequently, from a Canadian perspective, we expect:

- The demand for HPWP inputs used to produce effective units of unskilled labour to fall relative to the demand for units of unskilled labour and relative to the demand for effective units of unskilled labour.

- The unit cost of producing effective units of unskilled labour to decrease.

- The demand for effective units of unskilled labour to rise relative to the demand for effective units of skilled labour and to the demand for effective units of capital.

- The demand for (raw) units of unskilled labour to rise relative to the demand for (raw) units of skilled labour and to the demand for (raw) units of capital.

- The demand for (raw) units of unskilled labour to rise relative to the demand for effective units of skilled labour.

Consequently, Canada will use relatively less HPWP (a) in the production of effective units of unskilled labour (U_e); it will use more units of unskilled labour (U) relative to skilled labour (S) and capital (K); and it will use more effective units of unskilled labour (U_e) relative to effective units of skilled labour (S_e) and to effective units of capital (K_e).

We might also expect w_b to fall in Canada as a result of globalization due to increased information sharing about best practices leading to a lower cost of implementing HPWP with fewer mistakes. In this case, from a Canadian perspective, we expect:

- The demand for HPWP used in the production of effective units of skilled labour to rise relative to the demand for (raw) skilled labour and to the demand for effective units of skilled labour.

- The demand for HPWP (b) used in the production of effective units of skilled labour to rise relative to the demand for HPWP used in the production of effective units of unskilled labour (a) and to the demand for HPWP used in the production of effective units of capital (c).

- The demand for effective units of skilled labour to rise relative to the demand for effective units of unskilled labour and to the demand for effective units of capital.

- The demand for (raw) skilled labour to fall relative to the demand for effective units of skilled labour.

- The unit cost of producing effective units of skilled labour to fall.

In addition to these consequences, what will happen in the labour market also depends upon what happens to consumer tastes for goods produced in each country.[27] Suppose that consumer tastes shift toward goods produced in the United States (a fall in ξ). Given $\beta_1 > \beta_2$, the result of this shift (in aggregate between the two countries) is similar to a decrease in β. Consequently, from a Canadian perspective, we expect:

- The demand for effective units of skilled labour to fall relative to the demand for effective units of unskilled labour and to the demand for effective units of capital.

- The demand for HPWP used in the production of effective units of skilled labour to fall relative to the demand for (raw) skilled labour.

- The demand for HPWP (b) used in the production of effective units of skilled labour to fall relative to the demand for HPWP used in the production of effective units of unskilled labour (a) and to the demand for HPWP used in the production of effective units of capital (c).

- The demand for (raw) units of skilled labour to fall relative to the demand for (raw) unskilled units of labour and to the demand for capital.

- The demand for effective units of unskilled labour to rise relative to the demand for effective units of capital.

- The demand for (raw) units of unskilled labour to rise relative to the demand for (raw) units of capital.

IMPLICATIONS OF THE MODEL FOR MOBILITY

LET US ASSUME THAT, prior to free trade (globalization), the wages of skilled labour are lower, and those of unskilled labour higher, in Canada than in the United States (i.e. $w_s^1 < w_s^* < w_s^2$, $w_u^1 > w_u^* > w_u^2$, and $w_k^1 \cong w_k^* \cong w_k^2$). Under these initial conditions, we expect skilled workers to emigrate from Canada (since they are paid a higher wage in the United States) and unskilled workers to immigrate to Canada (since they are paid a higher wage in Canada).

However, workers may have preferences over the various HPWP; that is, they care about the type of work organization, compensation systems or training practices to which they will be subject in their workplace.

Alternative HPWP Bundles

We envision workers as choosing amongst the offered HPWP bundles such that they maximize their utility. A HPWP bundle consists of a wage offer and a set of HPWP. We denote the HPWP bundle offered to skilled workers as (w_s, a, b, c) and the bundle offered to unskilled workers as (w_u, a, b, c). Due to differences in the institutional and legal environments of the two countries, either Canada or the United States will have a comparative advantage in the provision of various *combinations* of HPWP a, b, and c that affect workers' utility. Consequently, while skilled (unskilled) workers will tend to migrate between Canada and the United States since the wages of skilled workers (w_s) are higher and those of unskilled workers (w_u) lower than in the United States, self-selection based on a, b, and c will occur among migrants.

Changes in Prices of HPWP Inputs

In addition, if w_b falls and w_s rises as a result of globalization, then we would expect firms in Canada to increase HPWP inputs (b) relative to skilled labour (S) in the production of effective units of skilled labour (S_e). On the other hand, since both w_a and w_u fall, the factor input ratio a/U used by the firm depends upon whether the factor price ratio w_a/w_u rises or falls. Consequently, changes in the relative prices w_b and w_s will cause b to rise in Canada and changes in the relative prices w_a and w_u may cause a to rise or fall in Canada. These changes will also affect the compensation packages offered in Canada, which will also affect mobility (via self-selection).

EMPIRICAL ANALYSIS OF THE ADOPTION OF HIGH PERFORMANCE WORK PRACTICES AND FOREIGN COMPETITION

THE PREVALENCE OF INNOVATIVE HPWP

WHILE IT IS GENERALLY ACKNOWLEDGED that innovative and high performance types of work practices have become more prevalent across establishments in the past two to three decades, there is little in the way of systematic evidence on the prevalence of these work practices over time. There is more evidence on a variety of work practices for various cross-sections in time. In Canada, the Human Resources Practices Survey of 1993 and the

Workplace Training Survey of 1995 provide some insights into changes across points in time.[28] In the United States, one of the more focused set of surveys has been conducted by Osterman (2000, 1994). These Canadian and U.S. results are presented in Table 1.

Data from these surveys suggest that while approximately one-half of establishments have sets of work practices that are traditional, the use of innovative and high performance practices is probably on the rise. Obviously, the practices surveyed are a limited set of the full range of human resources and industrial relations practices being developed, and there is considerable variation

---

TABLE 1

INCIDENCE OF SELECTED HRM PRACTICES IN PROMINENT CANADIAN AND U.S. ESTABLISHMENT SURVEYS, 1990S (PERCENTAGE)

Canada: Human Resources Practices Survey[a]

	HRM* CLUSTERS, 1993	
Traditional	Compensation	Participation
70	12	18

Canada: Workplace Training Survey[b]

HRM PRACTICES, 1995			
Formal Communications	Team-based Systems	Employee Involvement	Variable Compensation
66.8	55.5	46.7	28

United States: Osterman Establishment Survey[c]

INNOVATIVE WORK PRACTICES, 1992			
Quality Circles	Job Rotation	Teams	TQM**
27.4	26.6	40.5	24.5

United States: Osterman Establishment Survey[d]

INNOVATIVE WORK PRACTICES, 1997			
Quality Circles	Job Rotation	Employee Involvement	Variable Compensation
57.7	55.5	38.4	57.2

Notes: *   HRM: Human resources management.
     ** TQM: Total quality management.
Sources: a   Betcherman, McMullen, Leckie and Caron (1994) Figure 18, *Human Resources Practices Survey* conducted in 1992 by Canadian Facts. The survey includes 714 establishments in four industries (wood products, fabricated metals, electrical and electronic products, and business services) and covers the period 1988-1993.
     b   Betcherman (1999), Figure 3, based on 1995 *Workplace Training Survey* by Ekos Research.
     c   Osterman (2000; 1994). Telephone survey including 694 establishments of 50 or more employees in for-profit firms drawn from Dun and Bradstreet.
     d   Osterman (2000; 1994). Follow-up survey to 1992 survey, including 683 establishments.

in incidence across types of work practices; but a conservative conclusion is that many of these practices are now in use and they are diffusing (albeit slowly) across firms.

THE ANALYSIS AND ESTIMATION APPROACH

OUR ANALYSIS CONCENTRATES on the relationship between foreign ownership and the degree of competition (especially from U.S.-owned firms), and its effect on the use of industrial relations and work practices that are considered new, innovative or productivity-enhancing. We focus on the type and intensity of usage of a number of various work practices typically associated with HPWP.

The five workplace practices dimensions that we consider are:

- organizational change (organizational integration, reliance on temporary workers, reliance on part-time workers, re-engineering, and reduction of managerial levels);

- work organization (flexible hours, job rotation and multiskilling, total quality management, flexible job design, problem-solving teams, self-directed work groups);

- employee involvement (suggestion programs, information sharing, labour-management committees);

- flexible compensation (individual incentives, gain sharing, profit sharing, merit pay); and

- extent of training (formal and on-the-job training).

Refer to Table 2 for a list of the specific variables used to depict these work practices.

In order to examine the factors affecting the intensity of use of work practices by establishments, we construct an aggregate index of high performance workplace practices designed to capture the overall intensity of usage. For each establishment, the aggregate index is defined as the average number of HPWP utilized across the five dimensions (where, within each dimension, we normalize by the total number of possible practices in the dimension).[29]

Our analysis also focuses on the factors that determine whether an establishment is ranked higher or lower relative to other establishments in the use of HPWP. We construct this dependent variable (HPWP1) by ordering establishments from the lowest to the highest values in the aggregate index of HPWP usage. We then assign to each establishment the quintile ranking where their aggregate index value falls.

TABLE 2

WORKPLACE PRACTICE DIMENSIONS AND DEPENDENT VARIABLES

VARIABLE	DEFINITION
Organization Change	
Orgchg	Value of 0-5 including presence/absence of the following organizational changes: Greater Integration; More Reliance on Temporary Workers; More Reliance on Part-time Staff; Re-engineering; Reduced Managerial Levels.
Work Organization	
Wrkorg	Value of 0-6 including presence/absence of the following forms of work organization: Flexible Hours; More Reliance Job Rotation or Multiskilling; Implement Total Quality Management; Flexible Job Design; Problem-solving Teams; Self-directed Work Groups.
Employee Involvement	
Empin	Value of 0-3 including presence/absence of the following forms of employee involvement: Employee Suggestion Program; Information Sharing; Labour-Management Committee.
Flexible Compensation	
Fcomp	Value of 0-4 including presence/absence of the following forms of flexible compensation: Individual Incentive; Gain Sharing; Profit Sharing; Merit Pay.
Training Extent	
Trning	Value of 0-2 including whether formal and On-the-Job Training (OJT) is above average: Formal Training Extent greater than average; On-the-Job Training Extent greater than average.
High-performance Work Practices Intensity	
hpwp	(fcomp/4 + empin/3 + orgchg/5 + wrkorg/6 + ptrning/2) / 5
Hpwp1	1 if hpwp $\leq$ 25% 2 if hpwp > 25% and hpwp $\leq$ 50% 3 if hpwp > 50% and hpwp $\leq$ 75% 4 if hpwp > 75%

From the theoretical model, we expect the number of such practices adopted by an establishment to be determined from the profit maximization problem, where profits are a function of: the level of competition (from locally-owned, Canadian-owned, U.S.-owned and rest-of-world-owned firms); the price level; the productivity performance relative to the competition; the geographic location and industry; the business strategy (new geographical markets, improved product, improved performance); the introduction of a new or improved process or product; the occupational composition of the establishment; the presence of a human resources unit; and the proportion of employees covered by a collective bargaining agreement.

The estimation framework adopted is a basic reduced-form regression model of the type:

$$N_{i,j} = f[C_i, R_i, H_i, IND_i, OCC_i, B_i, Revamp_i, e_i].$$

Here, $N_{i,j}$ equals the number of work practices adopted by the ith establishment (or the quintile ranking of the establishment) for the jth workplace practices category or dimension. The key variables of the analysis are included in the vector C_i that includes competition characteristics (including the percentage of assets that are foreign held).

Other control variables include: R_i, a vector of regional variables; H_i, a vector of industrial relations controls (presence of a human resources unit, proportion of employees covered by a collective bargaining agreement); IND_i, a vector of industry controls; OCC_i, a vector of occupation controls (including proportion of the workforce employed full-time); B_i, a vector of business strategy controls (including the introduction of a new or improved process or product); and $Revamp_i$, the operating revenue per employee. Finally, e_i is an error term. Refer to Table 3 for a complete definition of each variable. Since the dependent variable is ordered and given that the error term in the above equation is normally distributed, we estimated that equation as an ordered probit. In the remainder of this section, we outline our expectations for the signs of the key explanatory variables, including the level of competition, the relative price, productivity and profitability, respectively.

We expect the importance of competition variables to vary depending upon the geographical locus of competition. At the local level, competing establishments face the same institutional, legal and regulatory environment. However, as the geographical scope of competition becomes broader, there is greater variation in institutional, legal and regulatory environments among competing establishments. We conjecture that establishments will have greater incentives to exploit differences in the costs of providing HPWP the broader the geographical dispersion of its competitors since establishments can exploit variations in the institutional, legal and regulatory environment. In addition, we expect that, the greater the competition faced by a firm, the stronger the incentive to exploit variations in the institutional, legal and regulatory environment, and to innovate. The exception is the local level, where competing establishments face the same institutional, legal and regulatory environment and have thus little or no room to compete based on variation in the cost of providing HPWP. We include several variables to capture the level of competition faced by establishments (including from local, Canadian, U.S. and rest-of-the-world firms); the variables used in the analysis are listed in Table 3.

TABLE 3

VARIABLE DEFINITIONS

VARIABLE	DEFINITION
f_assets	Percentage of Assets Foreign Held
cmp_dom	Compete Domestic-owned Firms (0 = No; 1 = Local or Canada; 2 = Local and Canada)
cmp_int	Compete International-owned Firms (0 = No; 1 = US or Rest of World; 2 = US and Rest of World)
lev_loc	Level Comp'n Local-owned (1 = Not Applicable; 2 = Not Important; 3 = Slightly Important; 4 = Important; 5 = Very Important; 6 = Crucial)
lev_can	Level Comp'n Canada-owned (1 = Not Applicable; 2 = Not Important; 3 = Slightly Important; 4 = Important; 5 = Very Important; 6 = Crucial)
lev_usa	Level Comp'n USA-owned (1 = Not Applicable; 2 = Not Important; 3 = Slightly Important; 4 = Important; 5 = Very Important; 6 = Crucial)
lev_oth	Level Comp'n Rest of World-owned (1 = Not Applicable; 2 = Not Important; 3 = Slightly Important; 4 = Important; 5 = Very Important; 6 = Crucial)
prc_lev	Price Level Relative to Competition (1 = Higher; 2 = Similar; 3 = Lower)
prf39_a	Productivity Performance Relative to Main Competitors (1 = Much Worse; 2 = Worse; 3 = Similar; 4 = Better; 5 = Much Better)
prf39_c	Profitability Performance Relative to Main Competitors (1 = Much Worse; 2 = Worse; 3 = Similar; 4 = Better; 5 = Much Better)
FMining	= 1 if Forestry or Mining; 0 otherwise
Manu	= 1 if Manufacturing; 0 otherwise (Omitted Category)
Const	= 1 if Construction; 0 otherwise
TSW	= 1 if Transport/Storage/Wholesale; 0 otherwise
CUtil	= 1 if Communications/Utilities; 0 otherwise
RComm	= 1 if Retail/Commercial; 0 otherwise
FIns	= 1 if Finance/Insurance; 0 otherwise
REstate	= 1 if Real Estate; 0 otherwise
BService	= 1 if Business Services; 0 otherwise
EducHC	= 1 if Education/Health Care; 0 otherwise
ICulture	= 1 if Information/Cultural; 0 otherwise
Atlantic	= 1 if Atlantic; 0 otherwise
Quebec	= 1 if Quebec; 0 otherwise
Ontario	= 1 if Ontario; 0 otherwise (omitted Category)
Prairie	= 1 if Prairies; 0 otherwise
Alberta	= 1 if Alberta; 0 otherwise
BC	= 1 if British Columbia; 0 otherwise
pft	Proportion of Workforce employed Full-time
pmnpr	Proportion of Workforce that is Managers and Professional (Omitted Category)
pslad	Proportion of Workforce that is Sales and Administrative
ptcun	Proportion of Workforce that is Technical and Production

TABLE 3 (CONT'D)

VARIABLE DEFINITIONS

VARIABLE	DEFINITION
hrunit	= 1 if Human Resource Unit; 0 otherwise
cba_prop	Proportion Employees Covered by CBA
revamp	Operating Revenue per Employee
new_prd	= 1 if New Product Introduced; 0 otherwise
impv_prd	= 1 if Improved Product Introduced; 0 otherwise
new_prc	= 1 if New Process Introduced; 0 otherwise
impv_prc	= 1 if Improved Process Introduced; 0 otherwise
techres	= 1 if Internal Resistance to Technical Change; 0 otherwise
mktinfo	= 1 if used Government Market Information; 0 otherwise
strtgy4	Business Strategy New Geographical Markets (1 = Not Applicable; 2 = Not Important; 3 = Slightly Important; 4 = Important; 5 = Very Important; 6 = Crucial)
strtgy6	Business Strategy Improve Product (1 = Not Applicable; 2 = Not Important; 3 = Slightly Important; 4 = Important; 5 = Very Important; 6 = Crucial)
strtgy15	Business Strategy Improve Performance Measures (1 = Not Applicable; 2 = Not Important; 3 = Slightly Important; 4 = Important; 5 = Very Important; 6 = Crucial)

Although the theoretical model is one of perfect competition (therefore predicting an equilibrium with one world price for an establishment's output), the actual degree of competition can vary widely due, for example, to institutional constraints, resulting in at least some degree of price variation across establishments. We expect that the higher the price that an establishment can charge (relative to its competitors), the larger the number HPWP this establishment can afford to provide.

Empirically, the effect of an establishment's productivity relative to that of its competitors is ambiguous. On the one hand, the more productive is an establishment (relative to its competitors), the less pressure there is on it to adopt HPWP as a means of improving productivity. On the other hand, a possible reason for the establishment's higher relative productivity may be that it has already adopted a number of HPWP. We thus include this variable but without prior expectations.

Finally, the effect of an establishment's profitability (relative to its competitors) is ambiguous. From the theoretical model, establishments will choose the optimal level and mix of HPWP in order to maximize their profits, but establishments in Canada and the United States (or across provinces) face different institutional and regulatory environments resulting in variation in the price of providing HPWP. Consequently, whether profits (relative to competitors) are positively or negatively associated with the number of HPWP is an empirical question.

THE DATA AND SAMPLE

THE EMPIRICAL ANALYSIS USES data from Statistics Canada's *Workplace and Employee Survey* (WES), which is a matched employer-employee data set based on a national survey of establishments and employees of these establishments. While the data permit identification of both individual employees and characteristics of the establishment where they work, we focus on the employer or establishment survey for 1999. That survey includes detailed information on the characteristics of the workforce, human resources management practices and changes (e.g. job and work organization, training; compensation systems); industrial relations practices and collective bargaining in unionized organizations; and changes in organizational practices and technology over time.

We confine our analysis to private and public sector firms (including what is considered the quasi-public sector) and firms that compete. The analysis also focuses on high performance work and organizational practices, so we further refined the establishment survey sample by excluding not-for-profit establishments from the analysis, by excluding establishments with 10 or fewer employees (because the work organization variables — employee suggestions programs, flexible job design, information sharing, problem-solving teams, labour-management committees, and self-directed work groups — are defined only for firms with more than 10 employees), and by excluding firms that had not competed recently or that had no competitors.[30] The usable (unweighted) sample size for our analysis is 3,174 observations.

In addition, the data include information about the characteristics of each establishment: industry; region; employment; proportion of employees covered by a collective agreement; level of competition faced by each establishment originating from locally-owned, Canadian-owned, U.S.-owned or rest-of-the-world-owned firms; price level; productivity performance and profitability performance relative to the establishment's competitors; information on business strategies (e.g. new geographical markets, improved product, improved performance measures); and presence of a human resources unit.

EMPIRICAL ANALYSIS AND RESULTS

STATISTICS CANADA'S WORKPLACE AND EMPLOYEE SURVEY provides comprehensive data on the incidence of a broad range of innovative high performance practices. Using the establishment survey data of the WES, we calculated the incidence of a range of work practices for 1999, grouped as compensation practices (Figure 2), employee involvement (Figure 3), organizational change (Figure 4), work organization (Figure 5) and training (Figure 6). The data support the conclusions, based on earlier surveys (see Table 1), that a sizeable proportion of Canadian establishments tend to have adopted these work practices (although not, as yet, a majority) and that the incidence of these practices varies considerably.

Summary statistics on the characteristics of the establishments surveyed are presented in Table 4. The proportion of assets that are foreign held is, on average, small (6.2 percent). Across establishments, the proportion of the workforce employed full-time is 75.7 percent, while 44.4 percent of employees are either technical or production workers. Approximately 17 percent of establishments are in the manufacturing sector, 16 percent in transportation, storage and wholesale, and 26 percent in services. For each category of workplace practices (e.g. organizational change, work organization, employee involvement, flexible compensation, extent of training) and the aggregate index of high performance work practices, we calculated the proportion of establishments that had each number of component practices within a category (Table 4, Panel C). The category with the largest proportion of establishments having none of the practices was organizational change (51 percent), with the other four categories ranging from 39 to 44 percent (establishments with none of the practices).

FIGURE 2

PERCENTAGE OF ESTABLISHMENTS WITH FLEXIBLE COMPENSATION PRACTICES, 1999

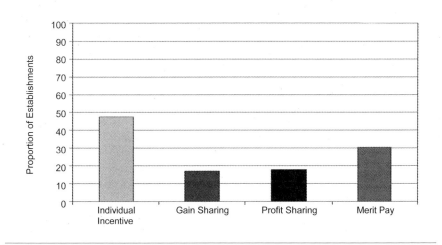

Source: Authors' calculations based on Statistics Canada, *Workplace and Employee Survey.*

FIGURE 3

PERCENTAGE OF ESTABLISHMENTS WITH EMPLOYEE INVOLVMENT PRACTICES, 1999

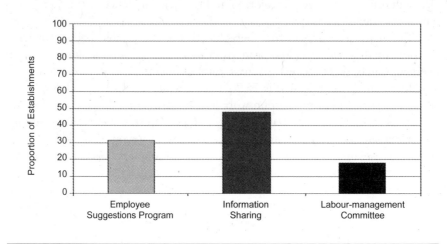

Source: Authors' calculations based on Statistics Canada, *Workplace and Employee Survey*.

FIGURE 4

PERCENTAGE OF ESTABLISHMENTS UNDERTAKING ORGANIZATIONAL CHANGE, 1999

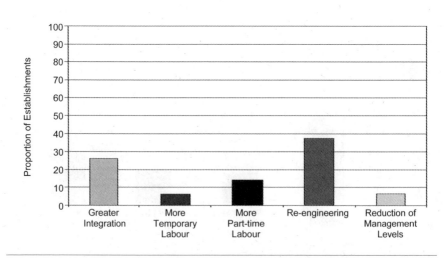

Source: Authors' calculations based on Statistics Canada, *Workplace and Employee Survey*.

FIGURE 5

PERCENTAGE OF ESTABLISHMENTS WITH INNOVATIVE WORK ORGANIZATION PRACTICES, 1999

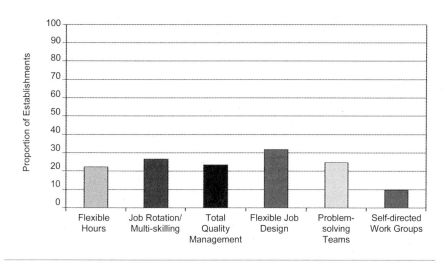

Source: Authors' calculations based on Statistics Canada, *Workplace and Employee Survey*.

FIGURE 6

PERCENTAGE OF ESTABLISHMENTS WITH ABOVE-AVERAGE TRAINING INVESTMENTS, 1999

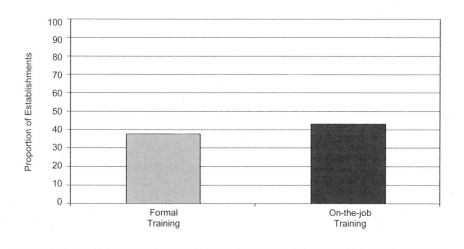

Source: Authors' calculations based on Statistics Canada, *Workplace and Employee Survey*.

The pattern of usage intensity across categories is similar, with a large proportion of establishments having at least one practice within a category, and a slightly smaller percentage of establishments having two; relatively few establishments have three or more practices within a category (where possible). The highest correlations (see Table 5) among work practices indexes for usage intensity were between employee involvement and organizational change and work organization, respectively; and between training and employee involvement.

TABLE 4	
DESCRIPTIVE STATISTICS	
PANEL A FOREIGN ASSETS AND OPERATING REVENUE	
VARIABLE	**MEANS**
Percentage of Assets Foreign Held	6.22
Operating Revenue per Employee	152,633
PANEL B EXPLANATORY VARIABLES	
VARIABLE	**AVERAGE PERCENTAGE ACROSS ESTABLISHMENTS**
% FT	75.70
% Man & Prof	22.49
% Sales & Adm	33.12
% Prod & Tech	44.37
% Empl. CBA	12.20
FMining	1.58
Manu	16.54
Const	5.75
TSW	15.68
CUtil	1.62
RComm	32.45
FIns	8.01
REstate	1.52
BService	12.67
EducHC	1.88
ICulture	2.30
Atlantic	6.42
Quebec	21.64
Ontario	40.18
Prairie	6.34
Alberta	11.59
BC	12.71

TABLE 4 (CONT'D)

DESCRIPTIVE STATISTICS

PANEL C
ORGANIZATIONAL AND WORK PRACTICES ASSOCIATED WITH
HIGH PERFORMANCE WORK SYSTEMS

VARIABLE	FREQUENCY	PERCENTAGE OF ESTABLISHMENTS WITHIN CATEGORY
Organization Change		
0	70,531	50.84
1	28,652	20.65
2	24,209	17.45
3	12,048	8.68
4	3,149	2.27
5	140	0.10
Work Organization		
0	55,478	39.99
1	29,744	21.44
2	25,052	18.06
3	11,801	8.51
4	6,177	4.45
5	9,701	6.99
6	775	0.56
Employee Involvement		
0	58,532	42.19
1	36,201	26.09
2	32,082	23.13
3	11,914	8.59
Flexible Compensation		
0	53,803	38.78
1	37,746	27.21
2	27,612	19.90
3	15,011	10.82
4	4,557	3.29
Training Extent		
0	61,057	44.01
1	43,254	31.18
2	34,419	24.81
High Performance Work Practices		
1	66,846	48.18
2	49,424	35.63
3	21,544	15.53
4	915	0.66

TABLE 5

CORRELATION MATRIX FOR ORGANIZATIONAL AND WORK PRACTICES ASSOCIATED WITH HIGH-PERFORMANCE WORK SYSTEMS

	HPWP1	ORGANIZA- TIONAL CHANGE	WORK ORGANIZA- TION	EMPLOYEE INVOLVE- MENT	FLEXIBLE COMPENSA- TION	TRAINING
Hpwp1	1.0000					
Organizational Change	0.5696	1.0000				
Work Organization	0.6855	0.5019	1.0000			
Employee Involvement	0.7109	0.3599	0.5170	1.0000		
Flexible Compensation	0.4032	0.1004	0.1995	0.1601	1.0000	
Training	0.6193	0.2213	0.2552	0.3472	0.1107	1.0000

The regression results are presented in Table 6 for each of the five work practices dimensions and the aggregate index.[31] In what follows, we summarize some of the key results. While the specific variables that explain usage intensity vary across work practices dimensions, there are some interesting regularities in the results.

Province

The province in which the establishment operates tends to affect usage intensity. Location in the Atlantic provinces is associated with a lower usage intensity of Organizational Change, Work Organization and Employee Involvement practices, while location in Quebec is associated with a lower usage intensity of Work Organization and Employee Involvement practices. In contrast, location in British Columbia is associated with a higher usage intensity of Organizational Change practices, while location in Alberta is associated with a higher usage intensity of Flexible Compensation and Training practices.

Industry

The industry of the establishment is only significant for Organizational Change (positively related to forestry and mining; communications and utilities; and information and culture); for Flexible Compensation (positively related to information and culture); and for Training (positively related to forestry and mining; transportation, storage and wholesale; communications and utilities; retail and commercial; finance and insurance; education and health care; and information and culture).

TABLE 6

ORDERED PROBIT RESULTS FOR ORGANIZATIONAL AND WORK PRACTICES ASSOCIATED WITH HIGH PERFORMANCE WORK SYSTEMS

INDEPENDENT VARIABLES	DEPENDENT VARIABLES					
	Hpwp1	Organ'l Change	Work Org'n	Empl. Invol.	Flex. Comp.	Training
% Assets	0.0003	–0.0009	–0.0024	0.0005	0.0045*	0.0010
for Held	(0.002)	(0.002)	(0.001)	(0.002)	(0.001)	(0.002)
Local Comp'n	–0.0829*	–0.0938*	–0.0639**	–0.0346	–0.0558	–0.0401
	(0.032)	(0.038)	(0.033)	(0.034)	(0.036)	(0.037)
Can. Comp'n	0.0454	0.1132*	0.0777*	0.0750*	0.0960*	–0.0340
	(0.044)	(0.039)	(0.031)	(0.032)	(0.039)	(0.037)
US Comp'n	0.0152	–0.0425	–0.0216	0.0028	0.0086	0.0693**
	(0.044)	(0.040)	(0.039)	(0.040)	(0.046)	(0.041)
ROW Comp	0.0248	0.0338	0.0142	–0.0175	–0.0429	–0.0372
	(0.051)	(0.042)	(0.043)	(0.046)	(0.043)	(0.041)
Rel P	–0.2136	–0.1745	–0.1246	–0.1261	–0.2994*	–0.0913
	(0.137)	(0.152)	(0.109)	(0.109)	(0.113)	(0.139)
Rel Prod'y	0.0118	–0.0828	0.0043	–0.1292**	0.1237	0.0452
	(0.088)	(0.079)	(0.077)	(0.073)	(0.085)	(0.078)
Rel Prof'y	–0.0034	–0.0868	–0.0567	0.0424	–0.0560	0.0152
	(0.092)	(0.101)	(0.065)	(0.064)	(0.086)	(0.088)
FMining	0.5506**	0.7315*	0.3448	0.2050	–0.1321	0.6284**
	(0.309)	(0.302)	(0.240)	(0.196)	(0.229)	(0.338)
Const	0.3736	0.2256	–0.0719	–0.0671	0.2362	0.4122
	(0.318)	(0.323)	(0.295)	(0.286)	(0.255)	(0.271)
TSW	0.4125	0.1447	–0.0392	–0.0460	–0.1106	0.4492*
	(0.253)	(0.221)	(0.179)	(0.187)	(0.193)	(0.200)
CUtil	0.4150*	0.4665*	–0.0835	–0.0636	–0.0857	0.4933*
	(0.198)	(0.216)	(0.219)	(0.239)	(0.176)	(0.232)
RComm	0.5799*	0.1235	0.1639	0.1628	0.0262	0.6105*
	(0.225)	(0.192)	(0.198)	(0.242)	(0.203)	(0.216)
Fins	0.5451	0.4206	0.0586	–0.0009	–0.0047	0.5456**
	(0.363)	(0.288)	(0.323)	(0.355)	(0.302)	(0.303)
Restate	0.5286	0.2352	–0.0947	–0.1625	0.1004	0.4424
	(0.348)	(0.245)	(0.281)	(0.372)	(0.296)	(0.307)
BService	0.2688	0.2828	0.2038	0.1243	0.0391	0.3156
	(0.230)	(0.221)	(0.246)	(0.270)	(0.244)	(0.211)
EducHC	0.2780	–0.1447	–0.2188	0.0709	–0.6124	0.7461**
	(0.344)	(0.342)	(0.496)	(0.428)	(0.488)	(0.425)

TABLE 6 (CONT'D)

ORDERED PROBIT RESULTS FOR ORGANIZATIONAL AND WORK PRACTICES ASSOCIATED WITH HIGH PERFORMANCE WORK SYSTEMS

INDEPENDENT VARIABLES	DEPENDENT VARIABLES					
	Hpwp1	Organ'l Change	Work Org'n	Empl. Invol.	Flex. Comp.	Training
ICulture	0.6955*	0.7141*	−0.0765	0.0160	0.5984*	0.6212*
	(0.272)	(0.240)	(0.197)	(0.181)	(0.254)	(0.292)
Atlantic	−0.4192**	−0.3728**	−0.5078*	−0.3112**	0.1629	0.1679
	(0.232)	(0.194)	(0.196)	(0.188)	(0.205)	(0.208)
Quebec	−0.2666**	−0.2918	−0.3962*	−0.3695*	−0.1535	0.1849
	(0.161)	(0.183)	(0.153)	(0.145)	(0.186)	(0.198)
Prairie	0.0601	−0.2550	−0.5297*	−0.2645	0.2786	0.3509
	(0.268)	(0.215)	(0.211)	(0.209)	(0.253)	(0.287)
Alberta	0.1550	−0.1507	0.0143	0.0834	0.6064*	0.4495**
	(0.294)	(0.222)	(0.235)	(0.238)	(0.266)	(0.254)
BC	0.0974	0.4304*	−0.0344	0.0342	−0.0163	−0.0279
	(0.236)	(0.207)	(0.193)	(0.165)	(0.191)	(0.208)
Pft	0.0431	−0.5050**	0.0447	−0.2383	0.3189	0.2308
	(0.292)	(0.303)	(0.315)	(0.282)	(0.344)	(0.306)
Pslad	0.1087	0.4176	0.0732	−0.1719	−0.0040	0.0970
	(0.402)	(0.353)	(0.455)	(0.380)	(0.421)	(0.474)
ptcun	−0.2331	0.6246*	0.2213	−0.3175	−0.5894**	−0.3081
	(0.321)	(0.306)	(0.341)	(0.309)	(0.301)	(0.382)
hrunit	0.1257	0.1609	−0.1359	0.0477	0.4027*	0.2887
	(0.191)	(0.168)	(0.190)	(0.196)	(0.162)	(0.204)
cba_prop	0.6221*	−0.3710	0.0158	0.8794*	−0.2991	0.6552*
	(0.180)	(0.234)	(0.201)	(0.188)	(0.198)	(0.193)
Oper. Rev. per Emp.	−6.40e−8	1.13e−7	−3.5e−7**	−1.51e−7	2.41e−7	1.48e−8
	(1.62e−7)	(2.03e−7)	(1.93e−7)	(2.09e−7)	(1.61e−7)	(1.40e−7)
new_prd	0.1485	0.2921**	0.0823	0.1185	−0.0391	−0.1123
	(0.146)	(0.161)	(0.141)	(0.147)	(0.128)	(0.179)
impv_prd	−0.0621	−0.0533	0.1434	0.0231	0.0535	0.0269
	(0.150)	(0.151)	(0.152)	(0.150)	(0.189)	(0.199)
new_prc	0.4185*	0.4327*	0.3624*	0.1517	−0.0932	0.3289
	(0.185)	(0.194)	(0.166)	(0.165)	(0.246)	(0.209)
impv_prc	0.6366*	0.4214*	0.3969*	0.5691*	0.1827	0.2700
	(0.173)	(0.199)	(0.171)	(0.139)	(0.219)	(0.192)
techres	0.1637	0.1755	−0.0005	−0.0729	0.3834*	−0.1734
	(0.171)	(0.148)	(0.171)	(0.177)	(0.171)	(0.171)

TABLE 6 (CONT'D)

ORDERED PROBIT RESULTS FOR ORGANIZATIONAL AND WORK PRACTICES ASSOCIATED WITH HIGH PERFORMANCE WORK SYSTEMS

INDEPENDENT VARIABLES	DEPENDENT VARIABLES					
	Hpwp1	Organ'l Change	Work Org'n	Empl. Invol.	Flex. Comp.	Training
mktinfo	0.1284	0.3653**	0.2533	0.1365	0.3226	0.0822
	(0.242)	(0.186)	(0.215)	(0.278)	(0.240)	(0.213)
strtgy4	0.1072*	0.0786*	0.0447	0.0814**	0.0293	0.0542
	(0.043)	(0.036)	(0.051)	(0.042)	(0.051)	(0.050)
strtgy6	0.2551*	0.2208*	0.2164*	0.1619*	0.1346**	0.2183*
	(0.073)	(0.076)	(0.065)	(0.069)	(0.072)	(0.071)
strtgy15	0.0407	0.0254	0.0872	–0.0163	0.0336	–0.0856
	(0.062)	(0.082)	(0.067)	(0.073)	(0.076)	(0.070)
cut_1	2.0214	1.1358	1.2175	0.2714	0.0109	1.4482
cut_2	3.3989	1.8049	1.8477	1.0699	0.8708	2.3493
cut_3	5.2051	2.5973	2.4990	2.0855	1.7051	
cut_4		3.4937	2.8808		2.5473	
cut_5		4.6982	3.2331			
cut_6			4.5244			
N	120,374	120,374	120,374	120,374	120,374	120,374
Log-L	–99,747	–126,625	–168,249	–134,692	–153,449	–116,141
Pseudo-R^2	0.2021	0.1503	0.1014	0.1066	0.0949	0.0954

Note: Bootstrapped standard errors are reported in parenthesis. * (**) denotes statistically different from zero using a 95% (90%) confidence interval.

Unionization

The proportion of employees in the establishment covered by a collective agreement is positively related to usage intensity of both Employee Involvement and Training Practices. These results are consistent with unions' general emphasis on representation and training investments in the workplace.

Business Strategies

Some form of business strategy is relevant in four of the five dimensions of work practices. In the case of Organizational Change, usage intensity is positively associated with the business strategy for new geographical markets. However, the most important business strategy is product improvement. That strategy is associated with higher usage intensity for the following dimensions: Organizational Change, Work Organization, Flexible Compensation and Training.

Relative Price and Productivity/Profitability Performance

The relative price and performance variables matter for two dimensions. First, productivity performance relative to competitors is negatively associated with usage intensity of Employee Involvement practices. Second, the higher a firm's price relative to its competitors, the higher the usage intensity of Flexible Compensation schemes.

Competition

The level of competition matters for the intensity of usage of practices in each of the five dimensions, but to varying degrees:

- First, the level of local competition for an establishment is negatively associated with the usage intensity of both Organizational Change and Work Organization practices. This suggests that establishments that compete locally are less inclined to undertake the more extensive structural organizational changes associated with innovations along these two dimensions.

- Second, the level of Canadian competition is positively associated with the usage intensity of Organizational Change, Work Organization, Employee Involvement and Flexible Compensation practices. Since most firms compete nationally to at least some degree, these results suggest that they undertake innovation across the full spectrum of organizational structures, human resources practices and industrial relations practices — with the interesting exception of Training.

- Third, the level of competition from the United States is positively associated with the usage intensity of Training. Recall that the Training dimension captures an establishment's training intensity relative to others; this result suggests that establishments with an above-average training intensity are associated with greater competition from the United States.

These results are also reflected in the regression for the aggregate index of overall intensity of usage of high performance (and related) workplace practices (see Table 6). Each of the variables representing industry, province and extent of unionization affects usage intensity. Business strategies aimed at extending markets or improving products are associated with lower overall usage intensity;

finally, the importance of local competition is negatively associated with usage intensity.

CONCLUSIONS AND FUTURE RESEARCH DIRECTIONS

A KEY ASPECT OF THE TRANSFORMATION of production systems and organizations has been the increase in experimentation and innovation in work, human resources management and industrial relations practices. There has also been a shift in management toward viewing innovative practices as organizational technology that can increase productivity and, hence, profitability. In this context, the decision to adopt these work practices becomes a strategic business decision.

Although a wide variety of innovative human resources and industrial relations practices has emerged, there are sets of practices that are thought to contribute to the productivity of the organization and that, taken together as a system, are referred to as "high performance work practices." Survey evidence from Canada and the United States suggests that, while more traditional forms of work practices tend to predominate in many sectors of the economy, the use of innovative practices is likely increasing and that a sizeable minority of establishments use one or more of them. Empirical evidence is also mounting on the potential positive effects of these practices on firm productivity.

We extended the previous analysis by developing a formal model of the adoption of HPWP under free trade. The model implies that more costly HPWP will dampen the relative demand for those practices, while an increase in the cost of skilled labour would increase the demand for HPWP that augment the efficiency of skilled labour, thus mitigating the effect of rising labour costs. This suggests that institutional factors in a country that affect the cost of adoption (e.g. information, learning best practices, etc.,) will have a direct impact on the degree of workplace innovation.

The model also predicts that technological change biased in favour of using HPWP would increase the relative demand for HPWP that augment the use of skilled labour. This result also underscores the importance of the linkages between production technologies and organizational technologies.

The model predicts that technological change biased in favour of using labour units produced by the employment of skilled labour in combination with HPWP will increase the demand for both skilled labour inputs and HPWP that augment their output efficiency. In practice, this type of technological change is likely associated with advanced, or *cutting-edge*, engineering technologies among Canadian competitors. This suggests that Canadian firms pursuing advanced production technologies will ultimately pursue some types of high performance work practices in order to remain competitive.

The model predicts that differences in the provision of HPWP could affect the migration of workers, both skilled and unskilled. This is a consequence of the fact that countries such as Canada and the United States will have different institutional arrangements that result in differing comparative advantages in the provision of various bundles of HPWP, and that workers have different preferences among the organizational practices under which they work.

The empirical results suggest that a wide variety of innovative and high performance types of practices are utilized in Canadian establishments. While a minority of firms utilizes more than one practice, the results suggest that utilization levels are substantial. Whether it is increasing will require future longitudinal analysis, which the WES is designed to facilitate.

The results also suggest that, among establishments, usage intensity over the five dimensions of practices (Organizational Change, Work Organization, Employee Involvement, Flexible Compensation and extent of Training) varies across provinces, industry, and unionization, as one might expect. Interestingly, active business strategies typically found in competitive firms, such as improving products or expanding their geographic reach, are associated with higher usage intensity in each of the Organizational Change, Work Organization, Flexible Compensation and Training dimensions. The level of competition that the establishment faces also matters. While higher local competition is associated with less organizational and work organization innovation, facing Canadian competition is associated with higher usage intensity in each dimension except Training. A key result is that U.S. competition is linked with higher Training intensity. This is a potentially important area for future research.

Several extensions along this line of research follow. One theoretical avenue would be to extend the model to formally introduce trade considerations in order to examine the implications of globalization. In the realm of empirical extensions, we would suggest the following five research areas.

First, while a number of human resources practices are considered high performance, there is currently no consistent definition of HPWP in the literature. More research is needed to determine what practices ought to be considered high performance practices. For example, what bundles of practices constitute a HPWP system? Can different types of HPWP systems be identified? Finally, are some practices contributing more to the performance of organizations than others?

Second, while HPWP and the workforce skill mix (within establishments) are expected to be related, we need to know more about how. For example, certain HPWP may tend to be associated with the employment of skilled workers while other HPWP may be associated with unskilled workers. It would be useful to better understand which worker characteristics systematically differ across firms with different systems or mixes of HPWP. To address this issue, information is needed on both the worker side (skills or characteristics) and the firm side (HPWP); that is, an employee-employer linked (cross-sectional) data set would be required. A potential problem with using WES data, though, is that a maximum of 12 employees were surveyed per firm; this may not be a sufficiently large sample to fully characterize the workforce skill mix at each firm. There may be some other types of variables that could be used to capture skill mix in establishment-level workforces.

Third, we need to better understand the relationship, if any, between the types of work systems that firms adopt (e.g. HPWP) and whether or not it affects mobility. We expect the mobility of workers among firms to be related to the characteristics of workers, on the one hand, and the various HPWP offered by the firms, on the other. In this case, a longitudinal employee-employer linked data set would be needed to follow workers across firms. The nature of mobility could, however, be very different in the short run versus the long run due to demand-side fluctuations. This points to the need to analyze both shorter and longer term panels. At present, WES data could be used to examine mobility in the short run. However, in considering long-run issues, it would be useful, for example, if the WES contained more detailed information on the reason for leaving (or quitting) the last job. Specifically, if the individual left the last job to pursue "better career opportunities," it would be useful to know what these opportunities were (e.g. types of improved training opportunities, improved HPWP provided by the employer, and improved work arrangements).

It would also be of interest to examine the migration decisions of workers between firms located in Canada and the United States. This would, ideally, require a longitudinal employee-employer linked data set with information collected on employees and employers in both countries.

Fourth, it would be useful to carefully consider the linkages between firms' business strategies and work systems. The use of HPWP is expected to be a function of firms' overall business strategy. Consequently, it would be useful to explore the relationship between aspects of business strategy and the use of specific human resources or industrial relations practices (e.g. flexible compensation schemes, human capital investments, etc.). Relevant strategic dimensions might include whether firms wish to be high- or low-wage producers, or whether the adoption of production methods or systems is linked to a technology strategy, or whether there is a human resources strategy to attract skilled workers.

Finally, we need more research aimed at improving our understanding of how the institutional, legal and regulatory environments can impact the provision and mix of HPWP in firms. Are there aspects of the institutional context that influence the types of HPWP adopted or their usage intensity? Does the institutional context influence the diffusion of effective human resources practices?

The WES will only allow a limited analysis of this issue because we do not expect a large amount of variation in the institutional and, especially, the legal and regulatory environments in Canada. In this case, analysis of WES data would need to be supplemented by an analysis of data for other countries (e.g. the United States, Australia and the United Kingdom).

ENDNOTES

1 Most of the evidence from empirical research relates to the United States; see the reviews by Becker and Huselid (1998), Guest (1997) and Ichniowski et al. (1996). For recent evidence, see Black and Lynch (2001), Cappelli and Neumark (2001) and Huselid (1995).

2 See Zhao (2000) and Zhao, Drew and Murray (2000).

3 Innovative practices are considered non-traditional or innovative from the standpoint of the extant industrial relations research literature and are often, but not exclusively, associated with high performance work systems.

4 Including organizational integration, reliance on temporary workers, reliance on part-time workers, re-engineering, and reduction of managerial levels.

5 Including flexible hours, job rotation and multiskilling, total quality management, flexible job design, problem-solving teams, and self-directed work groups.

6 Including suggestion programs, information sharing, and labour-management committees.

7 As examples, individual incentives, gain sharing, profit sharing, and merit pay.

8 See, for example, Verma and Chaykowski (1999) and Betcherman et al. (1994).

9 See, for example, the discussion by Cappelli, Bassi, Katz, Knoke, Osterman and Useem, 1997.

10 Doeringer and Piore (1971) provide the classic description of internal labour markets, and Piore and Sabel (1984) offer an assessment of the pressures transforming the mass production system.

11 For reviews and analyses of these developments, see Katz and Darbishire (2000), Betcherman and Lowe (1997), Cappelli et al. (1997) and Bélanger, Edwards and Haiven (1994). See Verma and Chaykowski (1999) and Cappelli et al. (1997) for assessments of the emerging workplace and employment models, and Appelbaum, Bailey, Berg and Kalleberg (2000) and Appelbaum and Batt (1994) on the transformation of production systems.

12 For recent evidence on, and discussion of, the incidence of HPWP, see Betcherman (1999) and Osterman (1994, 2000).

13 For example, see Addison, Siebert, Wagner and Wei (2000), Bartel (1994), Bhargava (1994), Black and Lynch (2001), Ichniowski, Shaw and Prennushi (1997), Huselid (1995), Kruse (1993), Lanoie, Raymond and Shearer (1996), MacDuffie (1995), Shepard, Clifton and Kruse (1996), Cooke (1994) and Conte and Kruse (1991).

14 Gunderson (2002) provides a comprehensive review of individual empirical studies of the impacts of the wide range of workplace practices adopted by firms.

15 In what follows, we are concerned solely with innovative organizational practices that may reasonably be classified as high performance work practices (HPWP).

16 That is, without regard to the substitutability of labour and capital.

17 The CES production function is defined for $0 \neq \rho < 1$. Assuming $\gamma = 1$, the elasticity of substitution is given by $\sigma = 1 / 1 - \rho$. In this case, as $\rho \to 1$, $\sigma \to \infty$ and the production function is linear (perfect substitutability between inputs); as $\rho \to -\infty$, $\sigma \to 0$, which yields a Leontief production function (no substitutability between inputs); and, as $\rho \to 0$, $\sigma \to 1$, which yields a Cobb-Douglas production function. When $-\infty < \rho < 1$, then $0 < \sigma < \infty$, and the production function exhibits less than perfect substitutability between inputs.

18 To distinguish between firms, we could subscript all variables by i. We suppress these subscripts until later in the study.

19 The production function exhibits constant returns to scale when $\gamma = 1$ and decreasing returns to scale when $\gamma < 1$.

20 The supply function and the profit function are only defined for $\gamma < 1$.

21 We have assumed a long-run horizon, in which a, b, c, S, U and K are variable. Alternatively, in the medium-run a, b, c, S and U are variable and K is fixed; that is, we define the medium-run as a period of time over which at least one factor is fixed (K) but HPWP are variable. In the short-run, S and U are variable and a, b, c and K are fixed; that is, we define short-run as a period of time over which not only capital but also HPWP are fixed.

22 Specifically, an increase in w_b decreases the demand for b relative to the demand for S; as w_b increases, the firm demand for HPWP inputs b declines relative to the demand for HPWP inputs a; as w_b increases, the firm demand for HPWP inputs b declines relative to the demand for HPWP inputs c.

23 Specifically, an increase in w_s increases the demand for b relative to the demand for S; an increase in w_s decreases the demand for input factor S relative to the demands for input factor U; an increase in w_s decreases the demand for input factor S relative to the demands for input factor K.

24 Although we refer to the supply agents as firms they could equally well be thought of as representing aggregate economies. That is, the firm problem specified earlier in the study could be viewed as an aggregate production and profit function.

25 All wages and prices are denominated in a common currency (e.g. the U.S. dollar).

26 The same approach applies if we examine one industry in country 1 and one industry in country 2.

27 See Appendix B for the consumer model.

28 The *Survey of Work Arrangements* provides what is probably a more comprehensive look at work practices but with the limitation of a cross-section.

29 These dimensions include: organizational change, work organization, employee involvement, flexible compensation and extent of training. See Table 3.

30 Specifically, we excluded establishments that had not completed one fiscal year in order for operating revenue to be defined, and excluded firms with no competitors (since the focus of the study is competition and in order for price, productivity and profitability relative to competitors to be defined).

31 The standard errors in the regression results have been boot-strapped in *Stata*, as recommended by Statistics Canada.

BIBLIOGRAPHY

Addison, J.T., W.S. Siebert, J. Wagner and X. Wei. "Worker Participation and Firm Performance: Evidence from Germany and Britain." *British Journal of Industrial Relations* 38 (2000): 7-48.

Appelbaum, E., T. Bailey, P. Berg and A. Kalleberg. *Manufacturing Advantage: Why High-Performance Work Systems Pay Off.* Ithaca, N.Y.: Cornell University Press, 2000.

Appelbaum, E., and R. Batt. *The New American Workplace: Transforming Work Systems in the United States.* Ithaca, N.Y.: Cornell ILR Press, 1994.

Bartel, A. "Productivity Gains From the Implementation of Employee Training Programs." *Industrial Relations* 33 (1994): 441-425.

Becker, B.E., and B. Gerhart. "The Impact of Human Resource Management on Organizational Performance: Progress and Prospects." *Academy of Management Journal* 39 (1996): 799-801.

Becker, B., and M.A. Huselid. "High Performance Work Systems and Firm Performance: A Synthesis of Research and Managerial Implications." *Research in Personnel and Human Resources* 16 (1998): 53-101.

Bélanger, J., P. Edwards and L. Haiven, (eds). *Workplace Industrial Relations and the Global Challenge.* Ithaca, N.Y.: Cornell ILR Press, 1994.

Betcherman, G. "Workplace Change in Canada: The Broad Context." In *Contract and Commitment: Employment Relations in the New Economy.* Edited by A. Verma and R.P. Chaykowski. Kingston, Ont.: IRC Press, Industrial Relations Centre, Queen's University, 1999, pp. 21-40.

Betcherman, G., and R.P. Chaykowski. *The Changing Workplace: Challenges for Public Policy*, Research Paper R-96-13E. Ottawa: Human Resources Development Canada, Strategic Policy Applied Research Branch, September 1996.

Betcherman, G., and G. Lowe. *The Future of Work in Canada. A Synthesis Report.* Ottawa: Canadian Policy Research Networks, 1997.

Betcherman, G., K. McMullen, N. Leckie and C. Caron. *The Canadian Workplace in Transition.* Kingston, Ont.: IRC Press, Industrial Relations Centre, Queen's University, 1994.

Bhargava, S. "Profit Sharing and the Financial Performance of Companies: Evidence From the U.K. Panel Data." *Economic Journal* 104 (1994): 1044-1056.

Black, S., and L. Lynch. "Human Capital Investments and Productivity." *American Economic Review* 86 (1996): 263-267.

——. "How to Compete: The Impact of Workplace Practices and Information Technology on Productivity." *Review of Economics and Statistics* 83, 3 (2001): 434-445.

Cappelli, P., L. Bassi, H. Katz, D. Knoke, P. Osterman and M. Useem. *Change at Work.* New York: Oxford University Press, 1997.

Cappelli, P., and D. Neumark. "Do High-Performance Work Practices Improve Establishment Level Outcomes?" *Industrial and Labor Relations Review* 54 (July 2001): 737-775.

Conte, M., and D.L. Kruse. "Esops and Profit-sharing Plans: Do They Link Employee Pay to Company Performance?" *Financial Management* 20 (1991): 91-100.

Cooke, W. "Employee Participation Programs, Group-based Incentives, and Company Performance: A Union–Nonunion Comparison." *Industrial and Labor Relations Review* 47 (1994): 594-609.

Doeringer, P., and M. Piore. *Internal Labor Markets and Manpower Analysis*. Lexington, Mass.: Heath, 1971.

Ehrenberg, R. (ed.). *Do Compensation Policies Matter?* Ithaca, N.Y.: Cornell University Press, 1990.

Freeman, R.B., and M.M. Kleiner. "Who Benefits Most from Employee Involvement: Firms or Workers?" *American Economic Review* 90 (2000): 219-223.

Guest, D. "Human Resource Management and Performance: A Review and Research Agenda." *International Journal of Human Resource Management* 8 (1997): 263-276.

Gunderson, M. *Rethinking Productivity from a Workplace Perspective*. Discussion Paper No. W/17. Ottawa: Canadian Policy Research Networks, 2002.

Huselid, M.A. "The Impact of Human Resource Management Practices on Turnover, Productivity, and Corporate Financial Performance." *Academy of Management Journal* 38 (1995): 635-672.

Ichniowski, C., and K. Shaw. "Old Dogs and New Tricks: Determinants of the Adoption of Productivity-Enhancing Work Practices." *Brookings Papers on Economic Activity* (1995): 1-55.

Ichniowski, C., K. Shaw and G. Prennushi. The Effects of Human Resource Management Practices on Productivity: A Study of Steel Finishing Lines." *American Economic Review* 87, 3 (1997): 291-313.

Ichniowski, C., T.A. Kochan, D. Levine, C. Olson and G. Strauss. "What Works at Work: Overview and Assessment." *Industrial Relations* 35 (1996): 299-333.

Johnson, G., and F. Stafford. "The Labor Market Implications of International Trade." In *Handbook of Labor Economics*, Vol. 3b. Edited by O. Ashenfelter and D. Card, Elsevier Science, 1999, pp. 2215-2288.

Katz, H., and O. Darbishire. *Converging Divergences: Worldwide Changes in Employment Systems*. Ithaca and London: Cornell University Press, 2000.

Kruse, D. *Profit Sharing: Does It Make A Difference?* Kalamazoo, MI: Upjohn Institute for Employment Research, 1993.

Lanoie, P., F. Raymond and B. Shearer. *Work Sharing and Productivity: Evidence from a Natural Experiment*. Scientific Series No. 96s-06. Montreal, Qc.: CIRANO, 1996.

MacDuffie, J.P. "Human Resource Bundles and Manufacturing Performance: Organizational Logic and Flexible Production Systems in the World Auto Industry." *Industrial and Labor Relations Review* 48 (1995): 197-221.

Osterman, P. "How Common Is Workplace Transformation and Who Adopts It?" *Industrial and Labor Relations Review* 47, 2 (January 1994): 173-188.

——. "Work Reorganization in an Era of Restructuring: Trends in Diffusion and Effects on Employee Welfare." *Industrial and Labor Relations Review* 53, 2 (January 2000): 179-196.

Piore, M., and C. Sabel. *The Second Industrial Divide*. New York: Basic Books, 1984.

Shepard, E., T. Clifton and D. Kruse. "Flexible Work Hours and Productivity." *Industrial Relations* 35 (1996): 123-139.

Verma, A., and R.P. Chaykowski (eds). *Contract and Commitment: Employment Relations in the New Economy*. Kingston, Ont.: IRC Press, Industrial Relations Centre, Queen's University, 1999.

Zhao, J. "Brain Drain and Brain Gain: The Migration of Knowledge Workers from and to Canada." *Education Quarterly Review* 6, 3 (2000).

Zhao, J., D. Drew and T.S. Murray. "Knowledge Workers on the Move." *Perspectives on Labour and Income* 12, 2 (2000): 32-46.

APPENDIX A

COMPARATIVE STATICS ANALYSIS OF CHANGES IN THE PRICES OF SKILLED LABOUR AND HPWP, AND IN SKILL-BIASED TECHNOLOGICAL CHANGE

CHANGES IN THE PRICES OF SKILLED LABOUR AND HPWP

To begin, we consider an increase in w_b and w_s.[1] The solution to the cost-minimization problem states that the optimal mix of HPWP inputs b and skilled labour, given S_e, is determined by equating the factor input price ratio with the ratio of the marginal products of the factors. Consequently, the *substitution effect* of an increase in w_b (w_s) implies that the firm will use relatively more (less) S in the production of a given level of S_e. In terms of relative factor demands:

$$(12\text{a}) \quad \frac{\partial \frac{b}{S}}{\partial w_b} = \left(\frac{1}{\upsilon - 1}\right)\left[\frac{(1-\lambda)w_b}{\lambda w_s}\right]^{\frac{-\upsilon}{\upsilon-1}}\left(\frac{(1-\lambda)}{\lambda w_s}\right) < 0$$

$$(12\text{b}) \quad \frac{\partial \frac{b}{S}}{\partial w_s} = \left(\frac{1}{\upsilon - 1}\right)\left[\frac{(1-\lambda)w_b}{\lambda w_s}\right]^{\frac{-\upsilon}{\upsilon-1}}\left(\frac{(1-\lambda)w_b}{(\lambda w_s)^2}\right)(-\lambda) > 0,$$

given $\upsilon < 1$. That is, an increase in w_b decreases the demand for b relative to the demand for S and, given an increase in w_s, increases the demand for b relative to the demand for S.

However, an increase in w_b (w_s) will also change the optimal amount of effective units of skilled labour, S_e^*, employed (scale effect) because an increase in w_b (w_s) increases the unit cost of effective units of skilled labour, w_e^s:

(13) $\quad \dfrac{\partial w_e^s}{\partial w_b} = [M_b]^{\frac{-1}{v}}[(1-\lambda)w_b]^{\frac{1}{v-1}} = \dfrac{b}{S_e} > 0$ and

$\quad\quad \dfrac{\partial w_e^s}{\partial w_s} = [M_b]^{\frac{-1}{v}}[\lambda w_s]^{\frac{1}{v-1}} = \dfrac{S}{S_e} > 0$.

We next consider the effect of an increase in w_b and w_s on the effective factor input ratios:[2]

(14) $\quad \dfrac{S_e}{U_e} = \left[\dfrac{(1-\beta)w_e^s}{\beta w_e^u}\right]^{\frac{1}{\rho-1}}$

(15) $\quad \dfrac{S_e}{K_e} = \left[\dfrac{w_e^s}{\beta w_e^k}\right]^{\frac{1}{\rho-1}}$

(16) $\quad \dfrac{U_e}{K_e} = \left[\dfrac{w_e^u}{(1-\beta)w_e^k}\right]^{\frac{1}{\rho-1}}$.

Differentiating Equations (14) and (15) with respect to w_b yields:

(17a) $\quad \dfrac{\partial \dfrac{S_e}{U_e}}{\partial w_b} = \left(\dfrac{1}{\rho-1}\right)\left[\dfrac{(1-\beta)w_e^s}{\beta w_e^u}\right]^{\frac{-\rho}{\rho-1}}\left(\dfrac{1-\beta}{\beta w_e^u}\right)\dfrac{\partial w_e^s}{\partial w_b} < 0$

(17b) $\quad \dfrac{\partial \dfrac{S_e}{K_e}}{\partial w_b} = \left(\dfrac{1}{\rho-1}\right)\left[\dfrac{w_e^s}{\beta w_e^k}\right]^{\frac{-\rho}{\rho-1}}\left(\dfrac{1}{\beta w_e^k}\right)\dfrac{\partial w_e^s}{\partial w_b} < 0$

$\quad \dfrac{\partial \dfrac{U_e}{K_e}}{\partial w_b} = 0$, given $\rho < 1$. That is, if the input price of HPWP b increases, then there is a decline in the demand for effective units of skilled labour relative to effective units of unskilled labour and a decline in the demand for effective units of skilled labour relative to effective units of capital.

Similarly, differentiating Equations (14) and (15) with respect to w_s yields:

(17a')
$$\frac{\partial \dfrac{S_e}{U_e}}{\partial w_s} = \left(\frac{1}{\rho-1}\right)\left[\frac{(1-\beta)w_e^s}{\beta w_e^u}\right]^{\frac{-\rho}{\rho-1}}\left(\frac{1-\beta}{\beta w_e^u}\right)\frac{\partial w_e^s}{\partial w_s} < 0$$

(17b')
$$\frac{\partial \dfrac{S_e}{K_e}}{\partial w_s} = \left(\frac{1}{\rho-1}\right)\left[\frac{w_e^s}{\beta w_e^k}\right]^{\frac{-\rho}{\rho-1}}\left(\frac{1}{\beta w_e^k}\right)\frac{\partial w_e^s}{\partial w_s} < 0$$

$$\frac{\partial \dfrac{U_e}{K_e}}{\partial w_s} = 0\,,$$

given $\rho < 1$. That is, if the input price of skilled labour increases, then there is a decline in the demand for effective units of skilled labour relative to effective units of unskilled labour and a decline in the demand for effective units of skilled labour relative to effective units of capital.

We also need to consider how the firm's demand for b relative to a and c will change when w_b or w_s increases. However, it is useful to note (after simplifying) that:

$$\frac{\partial \dfrac{b}{S_e}}{\partial w_b} = \left(\frac{1}{\upsilon-1}\right)[M_b]^{\frac{-1-\upsilon}{\upsilon}}(1-\lambda)^2[(1-\lambda)w_b]^{\frac{2-\upsilon}{\upsilon-1}}[\lambda w_s]^{\frac{\upsilon}{\upsilon-1}} < 0$$

$$\frac{\partial \dfrac{S}{S_e}}{\partial w_b} = \left(\frac{-\lambda(1-\lambda)}{\upsilon-1}\right)[M_b]^{\frac{-1-\upsilon}{\upsilon}}[(1-\lambda)w_b]^{\frac{1}{\upsilon-1}}[\lambda w_s]^{\frac{1}{\upsilon-1}} > 0$$

$$\frac{\partial \dfrac{b}{S_e}}{\partial w_s} = \left(\frac{-\lambda(1-\lambda)}{\upsilon-1}\right)[M_b]^{\frac{-1-\upsilon}{\upsilon}}[(1-\lambda)w_b]^{\frac{1}{\upsilon-1}}[\lambda w_s]^{\frac{1}{\upsilon-1}} > 0$$

$$\dfrac{\partial \dfrac{S}{S_e}}{\partial w_s} = \left(\dfrac{1}{\upsilon-1}\right)[M_b]^{\frac{-1-\upsilon}{\upsilon}}(\lambda)^2[(1-\lambda)w_b]^{\frac{\upsilon}{\upsilon-1}}[\lambda w_s]^{\frac{2-\upsilon}{\upsilon-1}} < 0,$$

given $\upsilon < 1$. Consequently, differentiating the ratio of Equation (9a) to Equation (10a), we obtain:

(18a)
$$\dfrac{\partial \dfrac{b}{a}}{\partial w_b} = \left[\dfrac{[M_b]^{\frac{-1}{\upsilon}}[(1-\lambda)w_b]^{\frac{1}{\upsilon-1}}}{[M_a]^{\frac{-1}{\psi}}[(1-\alpha)w_a]^{\frac{1}{\psi-1}}}\right]\left(\dfrac{\partial \dfrac{S_e}{U_e}}{\partial w_b}\right) + \left[\dfrac{S_e}{a}\right]\dfrac{\partial \dfrac{b}{S_e}}{\partial w_b} < 0$$

(18a')
$$\dfrac{\partial \dfrac{b}{a}}{\partial w_s} = \left[\dfrac{[M_b]^{\frac{-1}{\upsilon}}[(1-\lambda)w_b]^{\frac{1}{\upsilon-1}}}{[M_a]^{\frac{-1}{\psi}}[(1-\alpha)w_a]^{\frac{1}{\psi-1}}}\right]\left(\dfrac{\partial \dfrac{S_e}{U_e}}{\partial w_s}\right) + \left[\dfrac{S_e}{a}\right]\dfrac{\partial \dfrac{b}{S_e}}{\partial w_s}?0,$$

given $\rho < 1$ and $\upsilon < 1$. That is, as w_b increases, the firm demand for HPWP inputs b declines relative to the demand for HPWP inputs a. Differentiating the ratio of Equation (9a) to Equation (11a), we obtain:

(18b)
$$\dfrac{\partial \dfrac{b}{c}}{\partial w_b} = \left[\dfrac{[M_b]^{\frac{-1}{\upsilon}}[(1-\lambda)w_b]^{\frac{1}{\upsilon-1}}}{[M_c]^{\frac{-1}{\omega}}[(1-\delta)w_c]^{\frac{1}{\omega-1}}}\right]\left(\dfrac{\partial \dfrac{S_e}{K_e}}{\partial w_b}\right) + \left[\dfrac{S_e}{c}\right]\dfrac{\partial \dfrac{b}{S_e}}{\partial w_b} < 0$$

(18b')
$$\dfrac{\partial \dfrac{b}{c}}{\partial w_s} = \left[\dfrac{[M_b]^{\frac{-1}{\upsilon}}[(1-\lambda)w_b]^{\frac{1}{\upsilon-1}}}{[M_c]^{\frac{-1}{\omega}}[(1-\delta)w_c]^{\frac{1}{\omega-1}}}\right]\left(\dfrac{\partial \dfrac{S_e}{K_e}}{\partial w_s}\right) + \left[\dfrac{S_e}{c}\right]\dfrac{\partial \dfrac{b}{S_e}}{\partial w_s}?0,$$

given $\rho < 1$ and $\upsilon < 1$. That is, as w_b increases, the firm demand for HPWP inputs b declines relative to the demand for HPWP inputs c.

273

Finally, we consider the effect of an increase in w_b and w_s on the raw factor ratios. From Equations (9b), (10b) and (11b), we obtain the following factor ratios:

(19)
$$\frac{S}{U} = \left(\frac{S_e}{U_e}\right) \left[\frac{[M_b]^{\frac{-1}{\upsilon}}}{[M_a]^{\frac{-1}{\psi}}}\right] \left(\frac{[\lambda w_s]^{\frac{1}{\upsilon-1}}}{[\alpha w_u]^{\frac{1}{\psi-1}}}\right)$$

(20)
$$\frac{S}{K} = \left(\frac{S_e}{K_e}\right) \left[\frac{[M_b]^{\frac{-1}{\upsilon}}}{[M_c]^{\frac{-1}{\omega}}}\right] \left(\frac{[\lambda w_e]^{\frac{1}{\upsilon-1}}}{[\delta w_k]^{\frac{1}{\omega-1}}}\right)$$

(21)
$$\frac{U'}{K} = \left(\frac{U_e}{K_e}\right) \left[\frac{[M_a]^{\frac{-1}{\psi}}}{[M_c]^{\frac{-1}{\omega}}}\right] \left(\frac{[\alpha w_u]^{\frac{1}{\psi-1}}}{[\delta w_k]^{\frac{1}{\omega-1}}}\right).$$

Now, differentiating Equations (19)-(21) with respect to w_b and w_s yields:

(22a)
$$\frac{\partial \frac{S}{U}}{\partial w_b} = \left[\frac{[M_b]^{\frac{-1}{\upsilon}}}{[M_a]^{\frac{-1}{\psi}}}\right]\left(\frac{[\lambda w_s]^{\frac{1}{\upsilon-1}}}{[\alpha w_u]^{\frac{1}{\psi-1}}}\right)\left[\frac{\partial \frac{S_e}{U_e}}{\partial w_b}\right] + \left(\frac{S_e}{U}\right)\left[\frac{\partial \frac{S}{S_e}}{\partial w_b}\right] ? 0$$

(22b)
$$\frac{\partial \frac{S}{K}}{\partial w_b} = \left[\frac{[M_b]^{\frac{-1}{\upsilon}}}{[M_c]^{\frac{-1}{\omega}}}\right]\left(\frac{[\lambda w_s]^{\frac{1}{\upsilon-1}}}{[\delta w_k]^{\frac{1}{\omega-1}}}\right)\left[\frac{\partial \frac{S_e}{K_e}}{\partial w_b}\right] + \left(\frac{S_e}{K}\right)\left[\frac{\partial \frac{S}{S_e}}{\partial w_b}\right] ? 0$$

(22c)
$$\frac{\partial \frac{U}{K}}{\partial w_b} = 0$$

(22a')
$$\frac{\partial \frac{S}{U}}{\partial w_s} = \left[\frac{[M_b]^{\frac{-1}{\upsilon}}}{[M_a]^{\frac{-1}{\psi}}}\right]\left(\frac{[\lambda w_s]^{\frac{1}{\upsilon-1}}}{[\alpha w_u]^{\frac{1}{\psi-1}}}\right)\left[\frac{\partial \frac{S_e}{U_e}}{\partial w_s}\right] + \left(\frac{S_e}{U}\right)\left[\frac{\partial \frac{S}{S_e}}{\partial w_s}\right] < 0$$

$$(22b') \quad \frac{\partial \frac{S}{K}}{\partial w_s} = \begin{bmatrix} [M_b]^{\frac{-1}{\upsilon}} \\ [M_c]^{\frac{-1}{\omega}} \end{bmatrix} \left(\frac{[\lambda w_s]^{\frac{1}{\upsilon-1}}}{[\delta w_k]^{\frac{1}{\omega-1}}} \right) \begin{bmatrix} \frac{\partial \frac{S_e}{K_e}}{\partial w_s} \end{bmatrix} + \left(\frac{S_e}{K} \right) \begin{bmatrix} \frac{\partial \frac{S}{S_e}}{\partial w_s} \end{bmatrix} < 0$$

$$(22c') \quad \frac{\partial \frac{U}{K}}{\partial w_s} = 0.$$

That is, an increase in w_s decreases the demand for input factor S relative to the demands for input factors U and K.

CHANGES IN SKILL-BIASED TECHNOLOGICAL CHANGE

NEXT, CONSIDER THE EFFECT OF A CHANGE IN β (effective skill-biased technological change) on the effective factor input ratios. From Equations (14)-(16), we obtain:

$$(23a) \quad \frac{\partial \frac{S_e}{U_e}}{\partial \beta} = \left(\frac{1}{\rho - 1} \right) \left[\frac{(1 - \beta)w_e^s}{\beta w_e^u} \right]^{\frac{-\rho}{\rho-1}} \left[\frac{w_e^s}{w_e^u} \right] \left[\frac{-1}{\beta^2} \right] > 0$$

$$(23b) \quad \frac{\partial \frac{S_e}{K_e}}{\partial \beta} = \left(\frac{1}{\rho - 1} \right) \left[\frac{w_e^s}{\beta w_e^k} \right]^{\frac{-\rho}{\rho-1}} \left[\frac{w_e^s}{w_e^k} \right] \left[\frac{-1}{\beta^2} \right] > 0$$

$$(23c) \quad \frac{\partial \frac{U_e}{K_e}}{\partial \beta} = \left(\frac{1}{\rho - 1} \right) \left[\frac{w_e^u}{(1 - \beta)w_e^k} \right]^{\frac{-\rho}{\rho-1}} \left[\frac{w_e^u}{w_e^k} \right] \left[\frac{1}{(1 - \beta)^2} \right] < 0,$$

given $\rho < 1$. That is, if effective skill-biased technological change occurs (β increases), then the demand for effective units of skilled labour rises relative to the demand for effective units of unskilled labour and effective units of capital; as well, the demand for effective units of unskilled labour declines relative to the demand for effective units of capital.

We also need to consider how the firm's demand for b (HPWP used in the production of effective units of skilled labour) relative to a (HPWP used in the production of effective units of unskilled labour) and c (HPWP used in the production of effective units of capital) will change when β increases. Differentiating the ratio of Equation (9a) to Equation (10a), we obtain:

$$(24a) \quad \frac{\partial \dfrac{b}{a}}{\partial \beta} = \left[\frac{[M_b]^{\frac{-1}{\upsilon}}[(1-\lambda)w_b]^{\frac{1}{\upsilon-1}}}{[M_a]^{\frac{-1}{\psi}}[(1-\alpha)w_a]^{\frac{1}{\psi-1}}} \right]\left(\frac{\partial \dfrac{S_e}{U_e}}{\partial \beta} \right) > 0,$$

given $\rho < 1$. That is, as β increases the firm demand for HPWP inputs b increases relative to the demand for HPWP inputs a. Differentiating the ratio of Equation (9a) to Equation (11a), we obtain:

$$(24b) \quad \frac{\partial \dfrac{b}{c}}{\partial \beta} = \left| \frac{[M_b]^{\frac{-1}{\upsilon}}[(1-\lambda)w_b]^{\frac{1}{\upsilon-1}}}{[M_c]^{\frac{-1}{\omega}}[(1-\delta)w_c]^{\frac{1}{\omega-1}}} \right| \left(\frac{\partial \dfrac{S_e}{K_e}}{\partial \beta} \right) > 0,$$

given $\rho < 1$. That is, as β increases the firm demand for HPWP inputs b increases relative to the demand for HPWP inputs c.[3]

The effects of an effective skill-biased technological change on the raw factor input ratios are given by differentiating Equations (19)-(21) with respect to β:

$$(25a) \quad \frac{\partial \dfrac{S}{U}}{\partial \beta} = \left[\frac{[M_b]^{\frac{-1}{\upsilon}}}{[M_a]^{\frac{-1}{\psi}}} \right]\left(\frac{[\lambda w_s]^{\frac{1}{\upsilon-1}}}{[\alpha w_u]^{\frac{1}{\psi-1}}} \right)\left[\frac{\partial \dfrac{S_e}{U_e}}{\partial \beta} \right] > 0$$

$$(25b) \quad \frac{\partial \dfrac{S}{K}}{\partial \beta} = \left[\frac{[M_b]^{\frac{-1}{\upsilon}}}{[M_c]^{\frac{-1}{\omega}}} \right]\left(\frac{[\lambda w_s]^{\frac{1}{\upsilon-1}}}{[\delta w_u]^{\frac{1}{\omega-1}}} \right)\left[\frac{\partial \dfrac{S_e}{K_e}}{\partial \beta} \right] > 0$$

$$(25c) \quad \frac{\partial \dfrac{U}{K}}{\partial \beta} = \left[\frac{[M_a]^{\frac{-1}{\psi}}}{[M_c]^{\frac{-1}{\omega}}} \right]\left(\frac{[\lambda w_u]^{\frac{1}{\psi-1}}}{[\delta w_k]^{\frac{1}{\omega-1}}} \right)\left[\frac{\partial \dfrac{U_e}{K_e}}{\partial \beta} \right] < 0.$$

That is, if effective skill-biased technological change occurs (β increases), then the demand for skilled labour rises relative to the demands for unskilled labour and capital; as well, the demand for unskilled labour declines relative to the demand for capital.

The effect of a change in technology that is biased in favour of utilizing HPWP in the production of S_e (i.e. λ) on the relative demands of b and S in the production of S_e is found by differentiating the ratio of Equation (9a) to Equation (9b), which yields:

$$(26) \qquad \frac{\partial \dfrac{b}{S}}{\partial \lambda} = \left(\frac{-1}{\upsilon - 1} \right) \left[\frac{(1 - \lambda) w_b}{\lambda w_s} \right]^{\frac{-\upsilon}{\upsilon - 1}} \left(\frac{w_b}{\lambda^2 w_s} \right) > 0 ,$$

given $\upsilon < 1$. That is, if HPWP-biased technological change occurs (λ increases), then the demand for inputs b rises relative to the demand for inputs S in the production of S_e.

The effect of a change in λ on w_e^s (the unit cost of producing effective units of skilled labour) is ambiguous. However, we can state the following sufficient conditions:

$$(27a) \qquad \frac{\partial w_e^s}{\partial \lambda} < 0 \text{ if } \lambda < \frac{1}{2} \text{ and } \upsilon < \frac{-\lambda}{1 - 2\lambda}$$

$$(27b) \qquad \frac{\partial w_e^s}{\partial \lambda} > 0 \text{ if } \lambda > \frac{1}{2} \text{ and } -\upsilon > \frac{1 - \lambda}{2\lambda - 1} .$$

Consequently,

$$(28a) \qquad \frac{\partial \dfrac{S_e}{U_e}}{\partial \lambda} = \left(\frac{1}{\rho - 1} \right) \left[\frac{(1 - \beta) w_e^s}{\beta w_e^u} \right]^{\frac{-\rho}{\rho - 1}} \left(\frac{1 - \beta}{\beta w_e^u} \right) \frac{\partial w_e^s}{\partial \lambda}$$

$$(28b) \qquad \frac{\partial \dfrac{S_e}{K_e}}{\partial \lambda} = \left(\frac{1}{\rho - 1} \right) \left[\frac{w_e^s}{\beta w_e^k} \right]^{\frac{-\rho}{\rho - 1}} \left(\frac{1}{\beta w_e^k} \right) \frac{\partial w_e^s}{\partial \lambda} ,$$

where the sign of the derivatives in Equation (28) is the opposite of the sign of $\dfrac{\partial w_e^s}{\partial \lambda}$.

Finally,

(29) $\dfrac{\partial \dfrac{b}{a}}{\partial \lambda} > 0$ and $\dfrac{\partial \dfrac{b}{c}}{\partial \lambda} > 0$ if $\lambda < \dfrac{1}{2}$, $\upsilon < \dfrac{-\lambda}{1-2\lambda}$ and $\dfrac{1-\lambda}{\lambda} > \dfrac{\upsilon-1}{\upsilon} > \dfrac{\lambda}{1-\lambda}$

(30) $\dfrac{\partial \dfrac{S}{U}}{\partial \lambda} < 0$ and $\dfrac{\partial \dfrac{S}{K}}{\partial \lambda} < 0$ if $\lambda > \dfrac{1}{2}$, $-\upsilon > \dfrac{1-\lambda}{2\lambda-1}$ and $\dfrac{1-\lambda}{\lambda} < \dfrac{\upsilon-1}{\upsilon} < \dfrac{\lambda}{1-\lambda}$.

It should be noted that when the derivative of a/b with respect to λ can be signed, the sign of the derivative of S/U with respect to λ is ambiguous, and vice versa.[4]

ENDNOTES

1   An increase in w_a, w_c, w_u and w_k yields an analogous set of conditions as those we provided for w_b and w_s.

2   These ratios can be obtained from either Equation (3) or Equation (6).

3   A factor-neutral technological change (A) does not affect the relative effective factor demand functions. That is, $\dfrac{\partial \dfrac{S_e}{U_e}}{\partial A} = 0$, $\dfrac{\partial \dfrac{S_e}{K_e}}{\partial A} = 0$, and $\dfrac{\partial \dfrac{U_e}{K_e}}{\partial A} = 0$.

4   Actually, one of the above conditions is redundant since $\dfrac{1-\lambda}{\lambda} > \dfrac{\lambda}{1-\lambda}$ implies $\lambda < \dfrac{1}{2}$ and $\dfrac{1-\lambda}{\lambda} < \dfrac{\lambda}{1-\lambda}$ implies $\lambda > \dfrac{1}{2}$.

APPENDIX B

EFFECTS OF CHANGES IN CONSUMER DEMAND

WE BEGIN BY SPECIFYING a CES economy utility function (V) given by:

(31) $V = [\xi(X_1)^r + (1-\xi)(X_2)^r]^{\frac{1}{r}}$,

where X_i denotes good i ($i = 1,2$), $0 \neq r < 1$, and the parameter ξ ($\xi < 1$) captures consumer tastes (demand shifter).

The economy-wide budget constraint is given by:

$$(32) \qquad I = p_1 X_1 + p_2 X_2,$$

where p_i denotes the price of good i and I denotes income.

Maximizing Equation (31) subject to Equation (32) yields the Marshallian demand functions:

$$(33) \qquad X_1 = I \left[p_1 [(1-\xi)p_1]^{\frac{1}{r-1}} + p_2 [\xi p_2]^{\frac{1}{r-1}} \right]^{-1} [(1-\xi)p_1]^{\frac{1}{r-1}}$$

$$(34) \qquad X_2 = I \left[p_1 [(1-\xi)p_1]^{\frac{1}{r-1}} + p_2 [\xi p_2]^{\frac{1}{r-1}} \right]^{-1} [\xi p_2]^{\frac{1}{r-1}}.$$

For convenience, we will define the relative Marshallian demand as:

$$(35) \qquad \frac{X_1}{X_2} = \left[\frac{1-\xi}{\xi} \right]^{\frac{1}{r-1}} \left[\frac{p_1}{p_2} \right]^{\frac{1}{r-1}}.$$

A shift in consumer tastes toward 1 (an increase in ξ) leads to an increase in the demand for good 1 relative to the demand for good 2. That is, differentiating Equation (35) with respect to ξ yields:

$$(36) \qquad \frac{\partial \frac{X_1}{X_2}}{\partial \xi} = \left(\frac{1}{r-1} \right) \left(\frac{-1}{\xi^2} \right) \left[\frac{1-\xi}{\xi} \right]^{\frac{-r}{r-1}} \left[\frac{p_1}{p_2} \right]^{\frac{1}{r-1}} > 0.$$

In equilibrium, the demand for each good is equal to the supply of each good. That is, $X_i = Y_i$.

279

APPENDIX C

TABLE C1

SUMMARY STATISTICS FOR COMPETITION VARIABLES (PERCENTAGE)

	COMPETE DOMESTICALLY	COMPETE INTERNATIONALLY
0	2.12	53.21
1	41.12	24.70
2	56.76	22.09

LEVEL OF COMPETITION	LOCAL	CANADA	UNITED STATES	ROW
Not Applicable	10.44	34.92	57.45	73.67
Not Important	5.23	1.95	4.08	5.57
Slightly Important	10.10	8.90	5.18	4.57
Important	23.57	19.89	12.01	5.05
Very Important	29.23	22.63	13.11	5.97
Crucial	21.43	11.70	8.18	5.16

PRICE RELATIVE TO COMPETITION	HIGHER	SIMILAR	LOWER
	13.81	72.05	14.14

PERFORMANCE RELATIVE TO COMPETITION	PRODUCTIVITY	PROFITABILITY
Much Worse	0.66	0.76
Worse	5.24	15.15
Similar	39.25	43.47
Better	35.78	28.88
Much Better	19.07	11.75

	HR UNIT	NEW PRODUCT	IMPROVED PRODUCT	NEW PROCESS	IMPROVED PROCESS	RESIST TO CHANGE	GOVERN. MARKET INFORMA- TION
No	92.98	51.02	44.17	60.22	52.89	85.24	94.99
Yes	7.02	48.98	55.83	39.78	47.11	14.76	5.01

IMPORTANCE OF STRATEGY	NEW GEOGRAPHICAL MARKETS	IMPROVE PRODUCT	IMPROVE PERFORMANCE
Not Applicable	29.64	4.49	5.16
Not Important	11.94	1.21	2.58
Slightly Important	11.56	4.20	9.10
Important	26.86	29.01	42.78
Very Important	15.67	41.04	31.75
Critical	4.33	20.05	8.64

TABLE C2

SUMMARY STATISTICS FOR ORGANIZATIONAL AND WORK PRACTICES, (PERCENTAGE)

AVAILABILITY	INDIVIDUAL INCENTIVE	GAINS SHARING	PROFIT SHARING	MERIT PAY
No	52.63	82.97	82.29	69.49
Yes	47.37	17.03	17.71	30.51

AVAILABILITY	EMPLOYEE SUGGESTION PROGRAM	INFORMATION SHARING	LABOUR-MANAGEMENT COMMITTEE
No	68.59	51.71	81.59
Yes	31.41	48.29	18.41

AVAILABILITY	GREATER INTEGRATION	MORE RELIANCE ON TEMPORARY WORKERS	MORE RELIANCE ON PART-TIME STAFF	RE-ENGINEERING	REDUCE MANAGERIAL LEVELS
No	73.72	93.19	85.86	62.53	93.50
Yes	26.28	6.81	14.14	37.47	6.50

AVAILABILITY	ADOPT FLEXIBLE HOURS	INCREASED JOB ROTATION	IMPLEMENT TOTAL QUALITY MANAGE-MENT	FLEXIBLE JOB DESIGN	PROBLEM SOLVING TEAMS	SELF-DIRECTED WORK GROUPS
No	77.77	73.27	76.55	68.14	75.02	90.04
Yes	22.23	26.73	23.45	31.86	24.98	9.96

	FORMAL TRAINING EXTENT	ON-THE-JOB TRAINING EXTENT
Below Mean	62.35	56.85
Above Mean	37.65	43.15

TABLE C3

CORRELATION MATRIX WITHIN SPECIFIC ORGANIZATIONAL AND WORK
PRACTICES ASSOCIATED WITH HIGH-PERFORMANCE WORK SYSTEMS

	Orgchg	Orgchg1	Orgchg5	Orgchg6	Orgchg7	Orgchg10
Orgchg	1.0000					
Orgcgh1	0.7444	1.0000				
Orgchg5	0.4289	0.1064	1.0000			
Orgchg6	0.6122	0.3065	0.2679	1.0000		
Orgchg7	0.7735	0.4724	0.1526	0.2480	1.0000	
Orgchg10	0.3714	0.1119	0.0495	0.0472	0.1847	1.0000

	Wrkorg	Orgchg9	Orgchg11	Orgchg12	Wrk_org2	Wrk_org4	Wrk_org6
Wrkorg	1.0000						
Orgchg9	0.6251	1.0000					
Orgchg11	0.6751	0.3188	1.0000				
Orgchg12	0.6281	0.2537	0.4499	1.0000			
Wrk_org2	0.6813	0.3358	0.2862	0.2093	1.0000		
Wrk_org4	0.6532	0.2736	0.2515	0.2757	0.3659	1.0000	
Wrk_org6	0.4432	0.1147	0.1453	0.1108	0.2739	0.2413	1.0000

	Empin	Wrk_org1	Wrk_org3	Wrk_org5
Empin	1.0000			
Wrk_org1	0.7470	1.0000		
Wrk_org3	0.8081	0.4033	1.0000	
Wrk_org5	0.6389	0.2062	0.3090	1.0000

	Fcomp	Incen	Gains	Proft	Merit
Fcomp	1.0000				
Incen	0.7285	1.0000			
Gains	0.6565	0.2833	1.0000		
Proft	0.5475	0.1808	0.2418	1.0000	
Merit	0.6958	0.3380	0.3013	0.1329	1.0000

	Trning	Fmltrn_e1	Ojttrn_e1
Trning	1.0000		
Fmltrn_e1	0.8194	1.0000	
Ojttrn_e1	0.8280	0.3569	1.0000

TABLE C4

ORDERED PROBIT RESULTS FOR ORGANIZATIONAL AND WORK PRACTICES ASSOCIATED WITH HIGH-PERFORMANCE WORK SYSTEMS

INDEPENDENT VARIABLES	DEPENDENT VARIABLES					
	Hpwp1	Orgchg	Wrkorg	Empin	Fcomp	Trning
f_assets	0.0009	−0.0008	−0.0024	0.0010	0.0053*	0.0008
	(0.002)	(0.002)	(0.002)	(0.002)	(0.001)	(0.002)
cmp_dom	0.1794**	0.3053*	0.1533	0.2995*	0.2585*	−0.0192
	(0.098)	(0.116)	(0.114)	(0.116)	(0.109)	(0.107)
cmp_int	0.1174	0.1565**	0.1086	0.0005	−0.0981	0.0889
	(0.094)	(0.091)	(0.099)	(0.094)	(0.100)	(0.087)
prc_lev	−0.2138**	−0.1883	−0.1304	−0.1245	−0.2839*	−0.0913
	(0.109)	(0.140)	(0.115)	(0.126)	(0.118)	(0.147)
prf39_a	0.0041	−0.0980	−0.0065	−0.1287	0.1243	0.0427
	(0.076)	(0.079)	(0.067)	(0.093)	(0.090)	(0.087)
prf39_c	0.0056	−0.0568	−0.0375	0.0482	−0.0593	0.0122
	(0.093)	(0.069)	(0.068)	(0.076)	(0.077)	(0.097)
FMining	0.5162	0.7198*	0.3504	0.1662	−0.1932	0.6005**
	(0.377)	(0.293)	(0.243)	(0.230)	(0.246)	(0.307)
Const	0.2913	0.1871	−0.0981	−0.1383	0.1217	0.3594
	(0.301)	(0.275)	(0.285)	(0.276)	(0.229)	(0.267)
TSW	0.3647	0.1471	−0.0430	−0.0751	−0.1694	0.4289*
	(0.242)	(0.209)	(0.166)	(0.182)	(0.189)	(0.215)
CUtil	0.3944**	0.5083*	−0.0634	−0.0714	−0.1082	0.4686*
	(0.199)	(0.198)	(0.229)	(0.242)	(0.182)	(0.213)
RComm	0.4994*	0.0602	0.1211	0.1041	−0.1061	0.5953*
	(0.189)	(0.187)	(0.172)	(0.260)	(0.191)	(0.220)
FIns	0.5469**	0.4988**	0.1029	0.0225	−0.0051	0.4965
	(0.307)	(0.293)	(0.254)	(0.306)	(0.287)	(0.300)
REstate	0.5669**	0.3627	−0.0284	−0.1285	0.0918	0.4526
	(0.307)	(0.242)	(0.288)	(0.313)	(0.301)	(0.279)
BService	0.2224	0.2527	0.1889	0.0966	−0.0271	0.2815
	(0.216)	(0.182)	(0.217)	(0.261)	(0.255)	(0.221)
EducHC	0.2823	−0.0266	−0.1515	0.0702	−0.7109	0.7467
	(0.343)	(0.322)	(0.544)	(0.475)	(0.489)	(0.584)
ICulture	0.6500*	0.7057*	−0.0599	−0.0003	0.5681*	0.5914*
	(0.248)	(0.241)	(0.206)	(0.215)	(0.256)	(0.281)

TABLE C4 (CONT'D)

ORDERED PROBIT RESULTS FOR ORGANIZATIONAL AND WORK PRACTICES
ASSOCIATED WITH HIGH-PERFORMANCE WORK SYSTEMS

INDEPENDENT VARIABLES	DEPENDENT VARIABLES					
	Hpwp1	Orgchg	Wrkorg	Empin	Fcomp	Trning
Atlantic	0.3939**	0.2986**	–0.4763*	–0.2871	0.1457	0.1401
	(0.222)	(0.181)	(0.190)	(0.198)	(0.222)	(0.196)
Quebec	–0.2488	–0.2458	–0.3788*	–0.3609*	–0.2108	0.1817
	(0.157)	(0.167)	(0.143)	(0.166)	(0.190)	(0.186)
Prairie	0.0915	–0.2046	–0.5016*	–0.2489	0.2604	0.3606
	(0.254)	(0.199)	(0.214)	(0.240)	(0.262)	(0.247)
Alberta	0.1883	–0.1028	0.0367**	0.1019	0.5761*	0.4585*
	(0.273)	(0.214)	(0.222)	(0.247)	(0.251)	(0.210)
BC	0.1215	0.4783*	–0.0083	0.0328	–0.0362	–0.0296
	(0.223)	(0.180)	(0.191	(0.192	(0.227)	(0.198)
pft	0.0628	–0.4940*	0.0670	–0.2208	0.3376	0.2068
	(0.302)	(0.238)	(0.334)	(0.316)	(0.333)	(0.314)
pslad	0.1204	0.3416	0.0518	–0.1524	0.0663	0.1039
	(0.426)	(0.384)	(0.456)	(0.407)	(0.451)	(0.477)
ptcun	–0.2205	0.6045	0.2178	–0.2957	–0.5600**	–0.2847
	(0.333)	(0.310)	(0.374)	(0.327)	(0.325)	(0.376)
hrunit	0.2562	0.2750**	–0.0739	0.1617	0.5517*	0.3536*
	(0.185)	(0.153)	(0.174)	(0.192)	(0.175)	(0.159)
cba_prop	0.6009*	–0.3728	0.0159	0.8741*	–0.2951	0.6267*
	(0.225)	(0.247)	(0.175)	(0.193)	(0.192)	(0.219)
revamp	–6.74e–8	1.31e–7	–3.27e–7	–1.57e–7	2.40e–7	–5.73e–9
	(1.65e–7)	(1.80e–7)	(2.21e–7)	(1.89e–7)	(1.58e–7)	(1.53e–7)
new_prd	0.1780	0.3630*	0.1347	0.1422	–0.0031	–0.1167
	(0.150)	(0.140)	(0.127)	(0.135)	(0.146)	(0.138)
impv_prd	–0.058	–0.0617	0.1157	0.0254	0.0304	0.0234
	(0.167)	(0.167)	(0.153)	(0.141)	(0.187)	(0.174)
new_prc	0.3672*	0.3689*	0.3304	0.1225	–0.0845	0.3041
	(0.176)	(0.180)	(0.169)	(0.156)	(0.210)	(0.202)
impv_prc	0.6155*	0.3737*	0.3707*	0.5558*	0.1724	0.2665
	(0.183)	(0.177)	(0.158)	(0.154)	(0.232)	(0.216)
techres	0.1197	0.1025	–0.0419	–0.1038	0.3406**	–0.1774
	(0.153)	(0.138)	(0.151)	(0.162)	(0.196)	(0.181)
mktinfo	0.1546	0.4078*	0.2812	0.1424	0.3301	0.0765
	(0.263)	(0.170)	(0.218)	(0.271)	(0.209)	(0.242)

TABLE C4 (CONT'D)

ORDERED PROBIT RESULTS FOR ORGANIZATIONAL AND WORK PRACTICES ASSOCIATED WITH HIGH-PERFORMANCE WORK SYSTEMS

INDEPENDENT VARIABLES	DEPENDENT VARIABLES					
	Hpwp1	Orgchg	Wrkorg	Empin	Fcomp	Trning
strtgy4	0.1078*	0.0774**	0.0450	0.0832**	0.0415	0.0482
	(0.040)	(0.041)	(0.040)	(0.042)	(0.045)	(0.044)
strtgy6	0.2500*	0.2074*	0.2102*	0.1622*	0.1491**	0.2208*
	(0.076)	(0.068)	(0.066)	(0.057)	(0.076)	(0.066)
strtgy15	0.0304	0.0086	0.0739	–0.0184	0.0304	–0.0897
	(0.065)	(0.083)	(0.066)	(0.075)	(0.072)	(0.067)
cut_1	2.4100	1.6268	1.4928	0.6841	0.3866	1.5678
cut_2	3.7878	2.2930	2.1198	1.4841	1.2387	2.4645
cut_3	5.6028	3.0894	2.7696	2.5023	2.0616	
cut_4		3.9967	3.1524		2.9006	
cut_5		5.1676	3.5069			
cut_6			4.8027			
N	120,374	120,374	120,374	120,374	120,374	120,374
Log-L	–99,917	–126,559	–168,525	–134,442	–154,194	–116,549
Pseudo-R^2	0.2007	0.1507	0.1000	0.1082	0.0905	0.0922

Notes: Bootstrapped standard errors are reported in parenthesis.
* (**) denotes statistically different from zero using a 95 percent (90 percent) confidence interval.

286-93

p229.

Comment

Canada
USA

F15
F16
F22
M54

D83

Peter Kuhn
University of California

THIS STUDY CONSIDERS TWO QUESTIONS. First, what is the likely impact of increased foreign competition on the adoption of "high-performance work practices" (HPWP) in Canadian firms? Second, what are the likely effects of both HPWP and economic integration on labour mobility between Canada and the United States? In addressing these two issues, the study uses two methods. One is a formal, theoretical model of HPWP adoption. The purpose of this model is, in part, to suggest possible effects of economic integration that we may not have thought of otherwise. The second method is an empirical investigation of the incidence of HPWP in a recent cross-section of Canadian firms.

In my discussion, I will first consider the theoretical and empirical sections of Chaykowski and Slotsve's study. I will then provide some background to their study by speculating on the fundamental reasons behind all the trends considered in their study: why is there such a strong trend towards HPWP (including greater performance pay and wage inequality) and economic integration in many countries, including both Canada and the United States?

THEORY

CHAYKOWSKI AND SLOTSVE'S MODEL of HPWP ADOPTION asks us to think of a representative, price-taking firm. This firm is located either in a country where the wage differential between skilled and unskilled labour is high (the United States) or low (Canada). Economic integration between the two countries is modelled as an increase in the wage differential between skilled and unskilled workers in Canada and a (presumably much smaller) narrowing of the wage gap in the United States. The precise mechanism via which economic integration causes these changes in wages is not modelled, but this seems like a plausible way to start thinking about these issues.[1]

Within the representative firm, three types of HPWP are modelled, one corresponding to each "raw" factor of production: capital, skilled labour and unskilled labour. Further, HPWP are modelled in what, to industrial relations researchers, must appear to be a curious way: HPWP of each type are "purchased" at a fixed price per unit, then combined with the raw factor in question

286

to produce more "effective" units of that factor. Clearly, this procedure makes use of a modelling technology that is familiar to economists. But it would be helpful if the authors could give us some guidance regarding how their "capital-augmenting", "skilled-labour-augmenting" and "unskilled-labour augmenting" HPWP correspond to the more familiar categories of HPWP, such as team production, incentive pay, employee involvement, etc. that are used by industrial relations researchers, as well as by the authors themselves in their empirical work. Relatedly, how should we think about the 'prices' of these HPWP? For example, should we think of, say, a bonus system as a skilled-labour-intensive HPWP, allowing the firm to get more work effort from its skilled workers? If so, what is the 'price' of this bonus system? Is it measurable and what does this price depend on? Similar questions can be asked of the other two types of HPWP; in general more detail about what, precisely, are the real-world counterparts to the authors' theoretical constructs would be helpful.

The above comments do make one wonder whether an approach based on agency theory or personnel economics would be more useful than the current approach, which is based more on the traditional economic theory of the firm. [For excellent recent examples of the agency-based approach to real-world compensation issues, see Carmichael and MacLeod's analyses of multiskilling (1993) or of incentive pay (2000)]. An agency-based approach would explicitly model issues of moral hazard, job design, team production, and firm commitment that play important roles in the design of current HPWP systems.

The above reservations aside, what does Chaykowski/Slotsve's model suggest about the likely effects of economic integration on HPWP adoption in Canada? By assumption, economic integration makes skilled labour more expensive in Canada. As a result, firms will use fewer units of skilled labour (measured both in raw and effective units, though presumably the empirically relevant concept is raw units). In contrast, however, the authors also claim that the use of skilled-labour-intensive HPWP (b in the authors' notation) should rise in Canada relative to the use of certain other inputs (among them the number of skilled workers employed). In short, the authors claim that, when wages of skilled workers rise in Canada due to economic integration with the United States, Canadian firms' profit-maximizing response will be to use fewer skilled workers but also to apply more HPWP to these workers. The application of this costly HPWP 'ointment' to skilled workers will extract more effective units of labour from them. Maybe. But perhaps the greater scarcity of skilled workers in Canada will make these workers more resistant to firms' attempts to extract more effort from them via HPWP-related incentive schemes. Again, one is tempted to think that an agency-theory-based model might address the core issues here more effectively.

Finally, what are the implications of economic integration for labour mobility in the authors' model? First, they claim that before integration, skilled workers have an incentive to leave Canada (because their wages are lower there) and unskilled workers have an incentive to leave the United States (though it is unclear that they would be admitted to Canada). This is certainly true if workers do not care about HPWP. However, if (as the authors themselves argue) HPWP do enter — either positively or negatively — into workers' utility functions, this is not necessarily the case. Skilled workers may be quite happy to stay in Canada despite lower wages if the pace of work is more relaxed. This is a useful point about Canada-U.S. emigration that is not often made; perhaps it can help explain Canada's poor productivity performance in recent decades.

Supposing, now, that there is still some net incentive for skilled Canadian workers to emigrate before economic integration, how will integration affect that incentive? Integration (which, importantly, might itself consist of previous emigration) will reduce incentives for further skilled emigration from Canada by raising skilled workers' wages. But according to the authors' model, it may raise HPWP in Canada. If this reduces workers' utility (say, by increasing work intensity), it will give rise to a counteracting effect, making it less attractive to stay in Canada. The resulting positive feedback loop suggests the possibility of an unstable outcome as previous emigration raises incentives for further emigration. However, when workers care about HPWP, the correct way to model firms is not as price-takers (as the current model does) but as utility-takers (as in the compensating-differential literature; e.g. Rosen, 1974). Once firms are modelled this way, I suspect that this intriguing possibility will disappear.

EMPIRICAL ANALYSIS

THE AUTHORS' EMPIRICAL ANALYSIS uses Statistics Canada's recent Worker and Employee Survey (WES) to examine the incidence of HPWP in a cross-section of Canadian firms. Given the theoretical analysis above, the authors are particularly interested in the association between measures of foreign competition faced by the firm and the use of HPWP. Certainly, this is an interesting question which speaks to at least three related but distinct intuitive notions. First, it may be the case that the 'shock' of foreign competition requires Canadian firms to work their workers harder — effort intensification may result from exposure to greater competition. Second, foreign competition may spur the adoption of best-practice human resource management technologies that would otherwise diffuse more slowly. In this second view, HPWP are a technological innovation that raises output without necessarily raising effort. Third, it may simply be the case that Canadian firms with innovative work practices are the only ones who choose, or are able, to compete in export markets. In this latter view, HPWP 'cause' foreign competition rather than the other way around.

A positive cross-sectional association between foreign (or, for that matter, domestic) competition and HPWP is consistent with all three hypotheses sketched above. Importantly, however, it is not implied by the authors' own theoretical model. In that model, economic integration works via international convergence in the relative wages of skilled and unskilled workers. Normally, because workers are mobile between industries within a country, we think of these factor prices as being set at the economy-wide level, not at the level of industries or firms. For the mechanism sketched by the authors to affect cross-sectional differences in Canadian firms' use of HPWP, labour markets would have to be highly segmented across industries in Canada, yet quite responsive to Canada-U.S. integration on an industry-by-industry basis. This seems unlikely. Thus, while I am very interested in the authors' empirical analysis, I do not see it as directly relevant to their theoretical model.

The authors' empirical analysis is, for the most part, straightforward; as a result I will not comment extensively on the methodology. However, it is worth pointing out that their results are both interesting and unexpected: HPWP, in general, are associated with greater product-market competition. But it is primarily domestic, not foreign, competition that is associated with HPWP. This is not necessarily surprising as the bulk of competition faced by domestic firms still comes from other domestic firms; international competitors are important but not the main consideration for most Canadian firms. The one element of HPWP that is associated with greater foreign competition is training.

I conclude this section with one observation about methods, and one about interpretation of the results. The authors' main regressions for HPWP incidence in Table 6 contain control variables for the firm productivity (*Rel. Prod'y*: relative productivity compared to main competitors). The authors' discussion of this variable indicates that they realize it is endogenous — presumably, HPWP are adopted in order to increase the firm's productivity. If so, the rationale for holding productivity constant in analyzing which firms adopt HPWP is dubious at best. Thus, I would like to know how much the authors' main results would change if this variable was removed from the regression.

Regarding interpretation, it will be tempting for some to interpret the authors' results as implying that foreign competition induces firms to provide more training to their workers. This is not the case. It could simply be that only firms with well-trained workers choose to compete in export markets. In attempting to distinguish these two hypotheses, the authors would do well to consider various approaches that have been taken in the substantial recent literature on the connection between firms' export propensities and their productivity: Does competition in export markets force firms to become more productive, or is it just that productive firms choose to export? Useful recent examples of such writings include Bernard and Jensen (1999) and Hallward-Driemeier, Iarossi and Sokoloff (2002).

WHAT'S DRIVING IT ALL?

IN THIS STUDY AS WELL AS IN THE RELATED WORKSHOP, the authors have examined the relationships among changes in work organization, compensation policy, wage inequality, international linkages of product and labour markets, and the intensification of work effort. All these things seem to be changing together, with many of the changes reinforcing each other. But what is driving the whole process? In part to delve behind the analysis of the current study, and in part to pull together a number of ideas from the workshop, I engage in this section in some pure speculation regarding a possible underlying cause.

Information Production vs. Goods Production

It is by now commonplace that advanced nations like Canada and the United States are entering into an 'information economy', one in which the bulk of GDP is generated not by the production of physical goods or in-person services[2] but by the production of information. There is a crucial sense that the information's production technology differs from that of goods, which might explain many of the trends noted above.

The distinguishing feature of information production is simply that, in many cases, the marginal cost of providing a given piece of information to an additional customer is so low that a firm's or worker's output is essentially a public good. Writing a piece of software that calculates income taxes is costly. Once the software has been produced, however, distributing it to an additional customer on CD or via the Internet costs almost nothing. In contrast, while there may be some economies of scale in shoe or haircut production, the costs of providing an extra customer with shoes or a haircut are, by comparison, much higher.

To illustrate some of the implications of goods- vs. information production for firms and workers, consider the following simple example of a shoe-producing firm. Net of non-labour costs, worker A at this firm produces 15 dollars worth of shoes per hour, while worker B produces 30 dollars worth of shoes per hour. Clearly, the firm can afford to pay worker A up to 15 dollars per hour, and B up to 30 dollars per hour. A 100-percent productivity difference between the two workers translates into a 100-percent difference in the revenues those workers produce for the firm, and at most into a 100-percent wage differential between them.

Now imagine a firm producing a specialized kind of tax software, distributed on CD or over the Internet. Worker A in that firm is capable of writing the second-best software program in the market. Worker B can write a program that is, in some fundamental sense, only 15 percent better than A's, but this would make it the best software program in the market. Because the software can be reproduced essentially for free, all the customers in the market can be served, and will want to be served, by the best software program (in contrast, we cannot all have the same barber or shoemaker). Thus, by using worker B, the firm can generate millions of dollars in revenue; worker A generates zero revenue because the entire market will be served by a different firm with a better program. Because the worker's output (information) is a public good, small differences in worker productivity (15 percent in our example) can translate into astronomical differences in the firm's revenues. As a consequence, the firm can now afford to pay worker B millions more than worker A, even though B is only marginally more able at writing software than A.

The phenomena of 'publicness', and of high-wage 'superstars' serving extremely large markets have existed for some time in the arts, media and sports. Formal models of the phenomenon are well developed and well known (Rosen, 1981; Shapiro and Varian, 1999). What is newer is the increasing importance of this phenomenon throughout the economy, as easily-reproducible information becomes the main commodity we produce. Taking as given that information production is increasingly important, I describe in the following section some of the likely consequences of this trend.

Implications of Information Production

One obvious implication of information's production technology is an improvement in overall economic efficiency. As Sherwin Rosen noted, before music was recordable or broadcastable, only a select few people in the world's major cities could ever hear the world's best opera singer. Now everyone can. There is an important sense in which we are all better off if the information goods that the average person can consume are the best in the world.

Some other implications of information production have already been noted. One is increasing wage inequality, especially at the top of the wage distribution: small differences in productivity can translate into much larger wage differences than before. Another is a sense that business has become more 'competitive': even in the face of significant product quality differences, two shoemakers can easily coexist in a town because each can only serve a limited number of customers. In contrast, markets for software tend to be 'winner-take-all' competitions; thus, the marginal reward for being the best in the industry has become much greater, while second prize has become less desirable. Relatedly, one would expect to see a trend towards effort intensification: put loosely, in winner-take-all markets, it is 'better to be the best' in your industry or profession just once, than to be merely good for your entire lifetime. So why not 'go all out' to achieve your 15 minutes of fame, then relax? Evidence that an increasing fraction of U.S. men and women are working very long work weeks, and that this increase in hours is highly concentrated among highly skilled, high-wage workers whose real wages are also rising rapidly (Kuhn and Lozano, 2002), is consistent with this notion. The business community's rhetoric about the increased importance of 'excellence' and of being the best in the industry may not be just rhetoric: it may reflect the stark realities of competing in a world where one's main product is a public good that is reproducible at negligible cost.

A final implication of information production that is particularly relevant to this conference is that, when one's product is information, market size and market access matter much more. This is a simple consequence of the extreme economies of scale that characterize information production: by gaining access to the U.S. market, a Canadian software company can increase its revenues tenfold with a negligible rise in costs.

Perhaps the fact that the goods we are selling, more and more, are information goods with huge scale economies, explains why the pressure for market integration has increased so dramatically across the world over the past few decades.

Of course, as both Anderson and Helliwell have argued in this workshop, market access means much more than a reduction in trade barriers. For Canadian firms serving a U.S. market, market access involves understanding the needs and wants of their potential U.S. customers as well as, or better than, U.S. companies do. This kind of understanding is promoted by familiarity with American (business and popular) culture and by frequent travel and cultural exchange with Americans. Although it is unlikely to be popular with Canadian nationalists, encouraging this sort of exchange is something that Canadian governments might do more in order to foster competitive success in an information world.

Summary

The shift from goods production to information production may have profound implications for the structure of both product and labour markets. These include increased wage inequality (at least at the top of the wage distribution), a sense of greater competitiveness in product markets, effort intensification among highly skilled workers, and mounting pressures for the international integration of product markets. If this shift towards information production is as important as I suspect it is, then there are at least two key policy implications for Canada. One, already noted, is the much greater importance of access to (and understanding of) world markets as a key to continued prosperity. Another may be the need to recognize that the winner-take-all markets which can characterize information production may generate extremely high rents for a small number of highly skilled people: Canadians who succeed in serving a world market with the information it wants can do very well indeed, and may create desirable jobs for others in the process. As a society, Canadians need to decide how to react to this. A national penchant for equality argues for taxing these exceptional gains away. On the other hand, high taxation of these gains risks discouraging this kind of success in the first place, or even encouraging emigration to jurisdictions where the producer of information is closer to his/her main market, and thus better able to understand its needs. Some trade-off between these objectives will have to be made.

ENDNOTES

1   Note that these assumed wage changes *cannot* be generated by a reduction in trade barriers in the current model because there is only one consumption good; they *could* be generated by increased labour mobility between the two countries.

2   In-person services, like haircuts and massages, must be produced separately for each customer to whom they are supplied.

BIBLIOGRAPHY

Bernard, A., and J.B. Jensen. *Exporting and Productivity*. NBER Working Paper No. 7135, May 1999.

Carmichael, L., and W.B. MacLeod. "Multiskilling and the Japanese Firm." *Economic Journal* 103, 416 (January 1993): 142-160.

——. "Worker Cooperation and the Ratchet Effect." *Journal of Labor Economics* 18 (January 2000): 1-19.

Hallward-Driemeier, M., G. Iarossi, and K. Sokoloff. *Exports and Manufacturing Productivity in East Asia: A Comparative Analysis with Firm-Level Data*. NBER Working Paper No. 8894, April 2002.

Kuhn, P., and F. Lozano. "The Expanding Workweek: Understanding the Increase in Long Work Hours among U.S. Men." Santa Barbara: University of California, November 2002. Unpublished paper.

Rosen, S. "Hedonic Prices and Implicit Markets: Product Differentiation in Pure Competition." *Journal of Political Economy* (January/February 1974): 34-55.

——. "The Economics of Superstars." *American Economic Review* (December 1981).

Shapiro, C., and H. Varian. *Information Rules: A Strategic Guide to the Network Economy*. Boston: Harvard Business School Press, 1999.

Panel II

Assessing the Extent of Current Canada-U.S.
Economic Linkages and their Costs and Benefits

Canada, NAFTA
USA, F21
F15 E65
L14

The Free Trade Agreement and
Economic Transformation

Glen Hodgson
Export Development Canada

INTRODUCTION[1]

WITHIN THE CONTEXT OF ASSESSING THE ECONOMIC IMPACT of the Free
Trade Agreement (FTA) and the North American Free Trade Agreement (NAFTA), this study addresses four issues: (1) the new trade model that
is emerging globally; (2) the economic transformation that has occurred in
Canada (and the United States and Mexico) since the advent of the FTA with
the United States; (3) a 'thought experiment' on what Canadian and global
economic performance might have been without the FTA and the subsequent
NAFTA; and (4) where next for North American trade?

THE NEW TRADE MODEL – GLOBAL SUPPLY CHAINS

THE PROCESS OF GLOBALIZATION has brought considerable change to the international economic landscape. Trade liberalization, both at the regional and
multilateral level, is promoting increasing specialization of production through
more widespread and aggressive sourcing of inputs from abroad — what is now
called the global supply chain of production. The products we use today are

usually the result of investment and production in several countries, with only the location of the final assembly explicitly indicated on the package.

The Free Trade Agreement between Canada and the United States played a pivotal role in the globalization process. It was not the first major regional free trade agreement, and arguably it had as much to do with market access and dispute settlement as with lowering tariffs between Canada and the United States, since most manufactured goods already passed freely between the two countries. Nevertheless, the FTA committed the United States and its political institutions to freer trade, and therefore helped create the conditions for expanded regional free trade (through NAFTA) and freer multilateral trade through the creation of the World Trade Organization (WTO). The FTA and NAFTA also provided added motivation for other countries and regions to adopt more open trade and investment policies.

Prior to the implementation of the FTA in 1989, Canadian trade patterns reflected the remnants of a very different approach to trade policy, one that resulted in a 'branch plant' Canadian manufacturing economy. The branch plant economy was principally the result of a trade policy implemented in the early 20th century and intended to give preference to Canadian-made manufactured goods over imported goods in order to build Canada's industrial base. A cornerstone of that policy was a tariff system that increased the cost of imported finished goods, making them less competitive in the Canadian market. However, the unintended result of the high-tariff policy was to encourage foreign direct investment to leap over the tariff barrier and set up manufacturing branch plants in Canada to serve the small Canadian market.

The consequences of this protectionist approach were numerous and mostly negative. By the mid-1960s, nearly 60 percent of Canada's manufacturing base was both foreign-owned and relatively inefficient. Since branch plants were designed to serve a domestic market of less than 25 million consumers, they seldom achieved optimum scale. Canada's research and development (R&D) activity and productivity growth rates significantly lagged international trends. Canadian exports remained highly resource intensive, and our imports were generally capital-goods intensive. There was also very limited international expansion by Canadian firms, since few possessed the critical mass of capital, skills and products or services needed to go global. Finally, Canada's external current account was in chronic deficit, due in part to the net outflows of dividends, remittances and profits related to investments by foreigners in Canada. The creation of the General Agreement on Tariffs and Trade (GATT) in the post-World War II period and the gradual multilateral liberalization of trade progressively lowered the Canadian tariff wall, but the economic structural legacy changed only slowly.

CANADA'S ECONOMIC TRANSFORMATION UNDER THE FTA

WITH THE FTA'S CLEAR MESSAGE AND INITIATIVES in support of freer bilateral trade, Canadian firms were increasingly able to extend their supply chains globally, working with partners in foreign countries in order to optimize their competitive position on world markets. The purpose of such rationalization and specialization is to earn more profit by focusing on what one does best; behind that change is a combination of increased productivity, lower cost and quality control. Under a more open trading regime, investment abroad by Canadian business and foreign direct investment (FDI) flowing into Canada are complements rather than substitutes to international trade. They are fundamental tools used in building a global supply chain.

How much have things changed under the FTA and NAFTA? A few data points help to paint the picture. For Canada, total trade (imports plus exports) now exceeds 80 percent of its gross domestic product (GDP), up from 52 percent in 1990. This means that the Canadian economy is now over 50 percent more open than it was a decade ago, with the efficiency benefits of greater trade flowing through the entire economy. The share of Canadian exports to the United States has risen to about 85 percent, up from 75 percent in the mid-1980s. Another development is the falling share of domestic content in Canadian exports. It fell to about 63 percent in 2002 from 71 percent in 1989. These are all signs of transformation, and indeed of growing North American economic integration.

Canadian businesses have also become increasingly reliant on FDI in both directions to expedite that transformation. As shown in Figure 1, building a global supply chain where all the parts fit logically together induced Canadian firms to invest abroad in record amounts during the 1990s, and also induced foreigners to invest in Canada in record amounts. The United States represented the majority share of Canadian FDI in both directions, though these shares are below the high U.S. trade shares.

While FDI flows have declined globally since 2000 as a result of a slower world economy and increased uncertainty, they should resume modest growth in 2004 once the global recovery is more firmly established.

In addition, after nearly a century of relying heavily on inflows of foreign direct investment, Canada shifted in the late 1990s into the position of a net outward investor (see Figure 2). Inbound FDI — the traditional Canadian orientation — boosts domestic investment levels, creates jobs and generates more trade with the rest of the world. Inbound FDI also raises the profits of the foreign firms making the investment and creates an expectation that those profits will be repatriated at some future date. The benefits to Canada of outbound FDI are not as well understood, but may potentially be very significant. Outbound FDI generates investment and jobs in the foreign economy and profits for the Canadian firm and, most importantly, it increases export flows from Canada far into the future. The combined effect of stronger FDI in and out of Canada, and the resulting supply chains, makes Canadian firms more efficient

FIGURE 1

CANADIAN FOREIGN DIRECT INVESTMENT FLOWS
(FOUR-QUARTER MOVING AVERAGE)

Sources: EDC Economics, and Statistics Canada.

FIGURE 2

RATIO OF CANADIAN OUTWARD FDI STOCK TO INWARD FDI STOCK

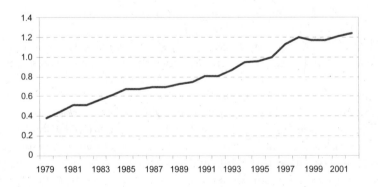

Sources: EDC Economics, and Statistics Canada.

and better able to compete in international markets. And becoming a net outward investor nation and earning related investment income is icing on the cake.

Changes have also taken place in U.S. and Mexican trade under the FTA and NAFTA. U.S. trade has risen modestly from 20 percent of GDP in 1990 to 24 percent in 2001. The Canadian share of U.S. imports actually fell by 1 percent during the 1990s, to 18.5 percent, while the U.S. share of Canadian exports fell back to 64 percent after initially rising under the FTA. These results seem counter-intuitive but they reflect the fact that nominal U.S. trade is nearly three times larger than Canadian trade.

The real beneficiaries of expanded U.S. trade, driven by the free trade philosophy of FTA and NAFTA and based on global supply chains, were developing countries — Mexico and China in particular — which were able to raise their economic potential through trade. Mexican trade as a share of GDP rose from 32 to 58 percent during the 1990s, while China's trade-to-GDP ratio similarly grew from 27 to 49 percent. Their combined share of the U.S. import market grew from 1 to 4 percent over the decade. During the same period, Mexico has successfully transformed itself from a crisis country into an investment grade performer, and China has been able to sustain growth rates in the 7-8 percent range, in part by supplanting the United States as the most popular destination for FDI. Thus, the bigger story of the FTA and NAFTA is a global one: these agreements have been drivers in the transition to a more open, efficient and productive global economy, contributing to an upward shift in global growth potential that benefits some developing countries in particular — contrary to what some critics of globalization would have us believe.

WHAT IF THERE HAD BEEN NO FTA AND NAFTA?

SINCE THERE IS NO COUNTERFACTUAL CASE against which to assess the impact of the FTA, let us next conduct a simple 'thought experiment' on what economic performance might have been in Canada and globally without the FTA and NAFTA. The underlying assumptions are: (1) the Soviet bloc still collapses under the weight of its own inefficiency; (2) the integration and expansion of the European Union continues; (3) the WTO is created; and (4) Canada-U.S. trade continues on a pre-FTA growth path. The key question that cannot be answered is whether the United States would have remained similarly committed to freer trade, or would bilateral protectionist sentiments have heightened during the economic slowdown of the early 1990s?

Under the above assumptions and using some simple arithmetic, Canada's trade would have risen to about 63 percent of GDP in 2001, not 81 percent. U.S. trade may have grown slightly, and global FDI growth — a key component for allowing developing markets to share in the benefits of globalization —

would have been slower throughout the 1990s. The dynamic benefits of the FTA and NAFTA for the Canadian economy would have been lost, resulting in less building of global supply chains by Canadian business, slower growth and downward pressure on the Canadian dollar.

The outcome of this simple experiment is that Canada's national wealth today would be lower. Without the FTA, we would probably look more like Australia, which has not had the benefit of increased economic integration with a strong trading partner. That would translate into greater reliance on commodity exports, a more fragile currency and more uneven growth prospects. Now this is admittedly a rather simple experiment, and others have done much more detailed economic modelling and analysis; but based on the realistic assumptions above, it is hard to imagine a scenario with no FTA where the economic outcomes for Canada would be markedly better.

WHAT NEXT FOR NORTH AMERICAN TRADE?

WHAT DOES THE FUTURE HOLD for Canada's economic integration within North America? Keeping the U.S. border open has become a constant priority in the aftermath of September 11, and indeed will need to remain a priority if the benefits of the FTA and NAFTA are to be preserved. There are areas of further potential growth within NAFTA, such as greater liberalization of finacial services and investment. And NAFTA itself could be expanded by opening up new frontiers in Latin America under a free trade area of the Americas, currently under active negotiation.

Canada and Mexico have each pursued new avenues of bilateral free trade within the Americas, and the day is fast approaching where these individual strands should be knitted together into a more integral and coherent whole. At that point, new and perhaps even greater challenges will have to be confronted — like common security and improved (and fairer) mobility of labour within the American Hemisphere. Canada will have a choice between letting things happen and playing an active role in shaping that agenda — an active approach at least gives us the opportunity to try and influence the outcome.

CONCLUSION

CANADA HAS BENEFITTED FROM THE FTA through an acceleration of its economic transformation toward a global supply chain model of international trade, with foreign direct investment acting as a complement, not a substitute, to increased trade. There have also been global benefits — a boost to global growth potential resulting from the opening of the U.S. economy, reinforcing the U.S. commitment to freer trade and creating opportunities through enhanced trade for other economies, especially in the developing world.

The policy challenge ahead for Canadians is how to position themselves to shape the future trade agenda for North America and influence their destiny.

ENDNOTE

1 The views expressed here are those of the author, and not necessarily of Export Development Canada.

Why the 'Big Idea' is a Bad Idea

Andrew Jackson
Canadian Labour Congress

IN RECENT MONTHS, the same people who championed the FTA and NAFTA have been promoting the 'big idea' of still closer economic integration with the United States. What Tom D'Aquino of the Canadian Council of Chief Executives, former Prime Minister Mulroney and Wendy Dobson of the C.D. Howe Institute have in mind is a grand 'strategic bargain' in which Canada would give the United States a strong North American security perimeter (including close co-ordination of immigration and defence policies) and even greater access to Canadian energy resources. In return, we would (yet again!) supposedly obtain secure access to the U.S. market.

The 'big idea' seeks to strike down U.S. trade and border measures through negotiation of a customs union. As noted by the recent House of Commons Committee report on North American relations, a customs union features common external tariffs and border measures which involve a loss of national autonomy over international trade and investment policy. The European Union, for example, speaks with just one voice at the WTO. While the precise shape of any future North American deal is hard to predict, not least because of the distinct lack of interest in Washington, it is clear that Canadian business is prepared to surrender a lot of policy levers in return for the holy grail of Canadian trade policy — 'protection from U.S. protectionism.'

The 'big idea' is a bad idea for many reasons, not least the explicit threat it poses to the expression of distinctive Canadian values on defence, international affairs, and immigration and refugee issues. It is also a very bad idea in terms of its implications for economic and social policy. Specifically, the 'big idea' challenges our necessary ability to shape industrial development; to control our energy sector and move towards a more environmentally sustainable economy; to levy taxes at the level needed to maintain a distinctive Canadian social model; and to limit the impacts of international trade and investment agreements on our social and cultural policies.

Canadians are commonly told that 'free trade' has been a huge success in terms of boosting exports to the United States. In truth, almost all of our export growth has been due to the expansion of the U.S. market in the 1990s, the low level of the Canadian dollar, soaring energy exports and the historical strength of the auto sector. The trade deals have dramatically failed to do what they were supposed to do: close the long-standing Canada-U.S. gap in manufacturing productivity. Between 1992 and 2000, manufacturing output per hour worked rose by just 16 percent in Canada compared to 43 percent in the United States, and the gap grew wider as the decade wore on. This carries a significant price in terms of foregone wage growth and prospects for our future prosperity.

Ironically, the large and growing productivity gap is constantly lamented by the same people who argued that free trade would give a major boost to industrial efficiency. But NAFTA has done little to solve the underlying structural problem: an industrial sector which is still too heavily tilted to the production of crude resource-based and basic industrial goods (45 percent of exports) and far too weak when it comes to the production of sophisticated finished products. To be sure, we have some strong non-resource sectors like auto, steel, and telecommunication equipment. But less than one-sixth of Canada's manufacturing production is machinery and equipment, well under half the U.S. level, and it is this key discrepancy that explains our weak productivity growth. Canada does as well as, or better than, the United States in the resource, steel and auto industries, but the greatest productivity gains have taken place in advanced capital-goods industries where we are still very weak.

One problem with the 'big idea' is that it distracts attention from our real problem, a collective failure by corporate Canada to innovate and invest adequately in R&D, in workers' skills and in new plants and equipment. Worse, a new deal would almost certainly limit our ability to pursue national industrial policies to help build 'knowledge-intensive' industries. Would we retain our (regrettably, largely unused) right to screen foreign takeovers of Canada's industrial leaders? (Would we really want Nortel or Bombardier to be taken over, given that Canadian taxpayers have sunk huge amounts of R&D subsidies into these firms to build our innovation base?) Could Canada and the United States really speak with one voice at the WTO when it comes to the negotiation of future rules on industrial subsidies? Our interest lies in building up capacity in sectors where we lack a historical advantage, while the United States wants to challenge threats to its dominance in advanced industries.

When it comes to industrial policy, a much more sensible approach would be to retain and expand our room for manoeuvre under current WTO rules, while exploring opportunities for closer North American co-operation in the few very closely integrated sectors where we have joint interests. For example, it is possible to think of common trade policies to expand North American content and jobs in auto, steel, aerospace and lumber.

Proponents of the 'big idea' favour closer continental energy integration, even though, under NAFTA, Canada surrendered most tools of control, such as differential export pricing and quantitative export controls. Canadians should be deeply concerned about their fast-rising natural gas exports and high levels of oil exports given the rapid depletion of the cheapest, most accessible conventional resources and the prospect of rising real prices as the United States rapidly exhausts its own resource base. While it is far from clear that we would want to return to a Trudeau-era regulatory regime, it is surely reasonable to make use of our right under WTO rules to ensure that exports of non-renewable resources do not hinder our ability to meet future Canadian needs. Rather than closer integration in the oil and gas sector and joint development of environmentally-fragile Arctic resources, we need to restore export regulation by the National Energy Board for conservation purposes. And tight integration of electricity grids is a very bad idea, indeed. Today, cheap hydro electric power gives most Canadians much lower prices than U.S. consumers and industries. In the wake of the Enron and California power deregulation fiascos, the case for publicly owned and regulated power utilities is much more compelling than that for deregulated continental markets.

Moreover, deeper energy integration would undermine our ability to build a more sustainable economy and deal with the very serious challenge of global warming. Ratification of the Kyoto Protocol and its first-stage targets prompted a storm of criticism from Alberta and most of the oil and gas industry, on the grounds that charges for carbon emissions would undercut the development of tar sands and frontier resources. The primary oil and gas sector is a major producer of greenhouse gas emissions, and the carbon intensity of non-conventional resource development which will dominate the future of the industry is very high. Initially, the Kyoto Protocol will have a very limited impact. But the fact remains that there is a fundamental longer-term contradiction between completely integrated continental energy markets and rapid primary energy sector development on the one hand, and energy conservation measures, slower resource development and the fostering of 'green industries' and soft energy paths on the other. We should retain control of our own energy future.

When it comes to preserving the Canadian social model, proponents of the 'big idea' like to talk of a purely economic arrangement. That is hardly surprising since the great majority of Canadians remain deeply committed to a more egalitarian and secure society than that found south of the border. But there is no such thing as a purely economic deal. As soon as the ink was dry on the FTA, business began to complain vociferously that the Canadian model was a barrier to competitiveness.

Canada is a significantly more equal society than the United States because of a higher level of tax-funded social programs and public services, and a higher floor of labour rights and standards. The 15-percent U.S. per capita income advantage over Canadians is enjoyed only by the top one-third or so of the U.S. income distribution. Canadian poverty rates, by a common definition of less than half of median income, are much lower than those of the United States (10 percent vs. 17 percent) and the minimum gap between the top and bottom deciles of the family, after-tax income distribution is 4 to 1 in Canada compared to 6.5 to 1 in the United States. The unionization rate in Canada's private sector is more than double that of the United States.

In many respects, Canada's more social democratic model is a positive factor in economic terms. It gives us a more highly-skilled workforce and more cost-effective and accessible social protections (with health care being the key example). But the same organizations promoting the 'big idea' have consistently lobbied in favour of cutting income taxes for corporations and high earners to U.S. levels, not to mention more privatized delivery of social services. The 'tax cuts for competitiveness' argument has clearly had an impact on public policy. After the elimination of the federal deficit through deep cuts to social programs in the early to mid-1990s, the lion's share of the growing federal surplus went to the Martin tax cuts. As a share of GDP, federal taxes have fallen by about two percentage points since 1997, notwithstanding the consistently strong support of most Canadians for re-investment in social programs and public services. Public opinion research shows that only the very affluent have strongly supported the tax cut agenda, not least because the U.S. model of low taxes and low social service provision would leave them better off. At a cultural level, it is only corporate elites who routinely compare their level of after-tax income to that of Americans.

The 'tax cuts for competitiveness' economic argument was hugely exaggerated. But it had credibility because of the threatened shift of investment and jobs to the United States. Extending deep economic integration from the goods sector to the many parts of the services sector still not greatly impacted by NAFTA would lead to much higher levels of cross-border movement of professionals and managers, and would surely strengthen downward competitive pressures on the tax base.

The Canadian social model has been strained rather than undercut by NAFTA. It would not automatically disappear because of closer economic integration. But the equalizing impact of progressive taxes would be further diminished and there would be strong pressures not to increase general tax levels to finance better social programs and public services.

The Canadian social model would also be directly threatened by a customs union with its implied common (read U.S.) voice in international trade and investment negotiations. The current formal position of the Canadian government is that social and public services should not be 'on the table' for the WTO negotiations on services, and that our ability to maintain not-for-profit delivery of public services should be maintained. As argued in the Romanow Commission report, clear threats already exist under NAFTA. If a province privatized hospital or home care services, for example, it would be difficult for a future government to return to not-for-profit delivery without paying compensation to U.S. corporate interests, which are a growing presence in the health care system. It is in Canada's interests to defend measures to 'carve out' social services and culture from WTO negotiations in order to preserve the space for choice and to shut out a U.S. commercial presence. But the United States is promoting further liberalization in both areas at the WTO. The direct implication of a common trade policy for sovereignty in 'non-economic areas' is a time-bomb hidden in the 'big idea' of a customs union.

To conclude, on a wide range of policy fronts, the 'big idea' is a bad idea that would undercut the necessary space for defending distinctive Canadian values and interests. That does not mean that the status quo of NAFTA is ideal. On some fronts, we should seek to reverse NAFTA constraints, such as the Chapter 11 investment provisions that threaten legitimate government regulation, and the one-sided commitment to unimpeded energy exports. On other fronts, we might want to deepen the relationship through new arrangements. Simplifying a lot of border procedures clearly makes sense. And sectoral trade deals could work in closely integrated sectors. Also on the agenda should be the replacement of the largely toothless NAFTA side deals with more effective means to create a high floor of labour rights and environmental standards. Pressures toward tax harmonization in a world of mobile capital and transnationals could be countered by an explicit agreement to create a North American tax floor.

The future of North America is open, but it does not reside in further reinforcing the neo-liberal economic and social model that lies at the heart of the 'big idea.' Canadians have no desire to abandon their distinctive social model, and every reason to doubt that 'free markets' are the path to prosperity. They want sensible working arrangements to manage economic linkages, measures to stop destructive competition that serves only transnational corporate interests, and preservation of sovereignty in areas where it is most important.

Export Market Asymmetry and Canadian Policy

Jayson Myers
Canadian Manufacturers & Exporters

HERE IS A SUMMARY OF THE COMMENTS made by Jayson Myers during the panel discussions at the conference.

Myers pointed out that integration in North America is very asymmetric. The U.S. market is extremely important for Canadian exporters, but the Canadian market is not nearly as important for U.S. exporters. In addition, Canadian operations are often only a small component of a U.S. multinational's global or even North American operations. However, there is a high degree of interdependence between the two countries. For example, even if the Canadian automobile market is only a modest part of the global market, a shutdown or delay at a Canadian manufacturing facility may cause a costly delay to operations in the United States or in other parts of the world.

The implication of this is that Canadian policies are very important for the location of foreign investment. The benefits of actually locating in Canada — to gain access to markets, for example — are very small, while the risks of interrupting global production could be quite large. Therefore, Canada faces the challenge of not just being competitive in order to attract foreign investment, but of offering a clear Canadian advantage. Another issue raised by Myers is that the development of public policy must be guided by a clear methodology in order to determine when that policy should take a North American perspective, and when it should have a global outlook.

Part IV

Implications of Canada-U.S. Integration for Social Policy: Is There a Race to the Bottom?

Rafael Gomez & *Morley Gunderson* **7**
London School of Economics *University of Toronto*

Does Economic Integration Lead to Social Policy Convergence? An Analysis of North American Linkages and Social Policy

INTRODUCTION

THE CONCEPT OF LINKAGES ACROSS COUNTRIES brings to mind a vision of trade, capital flows, culture, and the movement of people. These are obviously important, involving integration across different markets — for goods, capital, ideas (pertaining to intellectual property rights) and human capital (pertaining to the mobility of labour and the brain drain). However, linkages across various elements of social policy are equally important, though more often neglected.

The purpose of this study is to relate economic integration in these other markets to the linkages in social policy observed across North America. Put simply, we are interested in whether economic integration can (both in theory and in practice) lead to social policy convergence across countries. The study does not focus on alternative routes to policy convergence, such as those recently advanced by Mukand and Rodrik (2002) and discussed subsequently. To the extent that factors such as *best practice emulation* are considered, they enter our analysis only as indirect effects — operating first through the channel of economic efficiency and the instrumental need to adopt a singular and recognizable global policy optimum. We feel justified in this approach, primarily because the number of convergence mechanisms present in the economic literature could fill several volumes, let alone a single review such as this.

The study begins by outlining how linkages are enhanced through economic integration. Then, it outlines how linkages in social policy can be usefully analyzed in the context of a market which is affected by the interaction of the demand for social policy interventions on the part of various stakeholders such as workers, and the supply of such initiatives as provided by governments, multinational enterprises (MNEs) and other suppliers, including non-governmental organizations (NGOs), families, communities and the voluntary sector. The various elements of social policy are outlined, followed by a discussion of how both the demand for, and supply of, social policy are influenced by growing integration and linkages in more traditional markets (e.g. markets for goods, capital, ideas and human capital). Alternative theoretical perspectives are then outlined, with particular emphasis on their implications for convergence or divergence in social policy. Special attention is also given to the various linkages necessary for harmonization of social policy initiatives to the lowest common denominator. To illustrate the issues, empirical evidence on convergence or divergence of social policy is then examined. The study concludes with a summary and policy discussion.

CONVERGENCE THROUGH BROADER AND DEEPER ECONOMIC INTEGRATION

CONVERGENCE ARGUMENTS ARE WELL INGRAINED in social scientific thought, and tests of convergence theory abound. This study attempts to evaluate a number of the most recent studies (both theoretical and empirical) pertaining to convergence in the social policy realm. At the heart of the debate over economic integration and its impact on domestic social policies is the notion that economic outcomes are related to institutions in what Freeman (2000) has recently termed "a single-peaked social maximand." Convergence, in this instance, implies that there is a particular (singular) set of social policies, denoted N*, that produces the highest aggregate output for an economy, Y*. Every move in the direction of N* therefore raises economic well-being. As is illustrated in Figure 1a, convergence in the area of social policy occurs because there are increasing gains from moves in the direction of N* such that it behoves all economies to adopt the optimal policy mix. Countries to the left and right of the optimal social policy mix, N*, are therefore penalized with lower levels of economic performance.

The problem with the single-peaked approach is that there is nothing in theory that rules out multiple social policy mixes. It could well be the case that different institutions produce very similar levels of economic well-being.

FIGURE 1a

SOCIAL POLICY AND ECONOMIC OUTCOMES UNDER CONVERGENCE

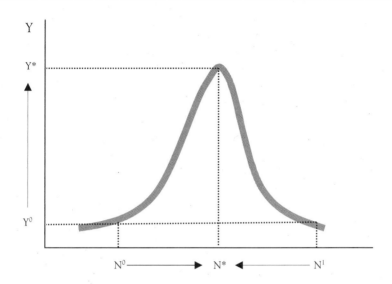

Source: Adapted from Freeman, 2000.

Notes: N^1: New Zealand-style social policy mix.
          N^0: Canada-style social policy mix.
          N^*: United States-style social policy mix.
          Y: Aggregate output; Y^*: Highest aggregate output.

Moreover, local peaks may be separated by *valleys*, indicating that there may be substantial transition costs (T) involved in moving from one policy mix to another. As depicted in Figure 1b, even if an optimum exists, it may not be worthwhile for countries with only a slightly lower output, $Y < Y^*$, to undergo the costly process of policy change, especially if the windfall, $Y^* - Y = \Delta Y$, is smaller than the transition cost: $T > \Delta Y$.

The bottom line is that there are equally compelling cases to be made *for* and *against* convergence in social policy arrangements in a context of economic integration. In what follows, the two cases are presented more formally, and the theory and evidence assessed in a more concrete manner. First, however, we must define what economic integration actually means.

FIGURE 1b

SOCIAL POLICY AND ECONOMIC OUTCOMES UNDER CONVERGENCE (WITH POSITIVE TRANSITION COSTS)

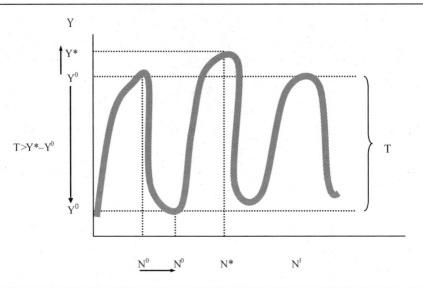

Source: Adapted from Freeman, 2000.

Notes: T: Transition costs.
  N^1: New Zealand-style social policy mix.
  N^0: Canada-style social policy mix.
  N^*: United States-style social policy mix.
  Y: Aggregate output; Y^*: Highest aggregate output.

DEFINITIONS OF ECONOMIC INTEGRATION

ECONOMIC INTEGRATION INVOLVES DIMENSIONS of both *deepening* and *broadening*.[1] The *deepening* dimension refers to the expansion across trade, capital, labour, technology and MNE activities. These five market and functional areas and their links with integration are summarized in Table 1.

The *broadening* dimension of integration refers to the expansion across different countries and regions as involved, for example, through the Auto Pact of 1965, to the Canada-United States Free Trade Agreement (FTA) of 1989, to the North American Free Trade Agreement (NAFTA) of 1992, and to possible further Western Hemisphere extensions to a Free Trade Agreement of the Americas. Broadening is also occurring through the general forces of globalization as the world becomes increasingly integrated through reductions in transportation costs and increased ease of communication and coordination.

312

TABLE 1

FIVE AREAS OF DEEPENING INTEGRATION

AREA	DEFINITION
1. Trade	Integration of trade in goods and services largely attained through reductions in tariffs and non-tariff barriers. Can act as a substitute for labour mobility.
2. Capital Flows	Integration enhances capital flows, both short-term financial capital (*hot* money) and long-term investments and plant location.
3. Labour and Human Capital Mobility	Integration enhances mobility often through immigration (brain *gain*) and emigration (brain *drain*), temporary work permits, visas for managerial, professional and technical personnel, and intra-firm transfers.
4. Technology and Knowledge Transfers	Integration enhances knowledge and technology transfers. Often associated with new information technology (IT) and involving transfer of intellectual property rights.
5. Multinational Enterprises	MNE operations lead to integration, with outsourcing, internal trade and a wide range of functions, including head office placement, research and development, production, assembly and warehousing, often performed in different countries.

In theory, different aspects of the deepening of integration can be substitutes or complements for one another. Freer trade, for example, could be a substitute for labour mobility as traded goods embody labour that otherwise may move.[2] As well, increased direct foreign investment by the United States in Canadian branch plants was a common way of *jumping the tariff wall* when tariff and non-tariff barriers restricted trade flows. However, the different flows involved in deeper integration can also be complements, for example when increased immigration leads to increased trade with the country of origin, as new communities establish backward linkages with suppliers and forward linkages with customers in the host country, or when capital flows are enhanced through remittances from the host country.

While the deepening and broadening of integration are generally thought of as expanded economic exchange, it can also involve social policy integration. The linkages whereby this can occur are both *direct* (pressures may exist towards a standardization of social policies across countries or across jurisdictions within a country) and *indirect* (the ability of a country to follow its own policy path may be affected by the larger flows of trade, capital and people). In essence, the various flows involved in deeper integration are inextricably linked, not only with each other, but also with social policy.

The Market for Social Policy

L ABOUR AND SOCIAL POLICIES are generally designed to affect outcomes pertaining to such factors as unionization, strikes, inequality, poverty, income, job loss, health, crime, safety and discrimination. This is done through a range of legislations and regulations, including:[3]

- *Labour relations legislation* that governs the establishment and conduct of collective bargaining;
- *Labour standards legislation* that pertains to such factors as minimum wages, regulations of hours of work and overtime, termination and notice requirements, and leave policies;
- Unemployment insurance (UI);
- Workers' compensation legislation;
- Health and safety regulations;
- Human rights and anti-discrimination requirements, including pay and employment equity;
- Pension policy;
- Welfare and family benefits; and
- Taxes.

These policy initiatives and the social outcomes they affect are the focus of our analysis.[4]

The Demand for Social Policy and the Process of Economic Development

THE DEMAND FOR SOCIAL POLICY INITIATIVES is affected by a wide range of factors including our wealth, the changing needs of society for such initiatives, the availability of private or other alternatives, and the power of interest groups that can influence such initiatives. Many aspects of this demand are also linked to deeper and broader integration, as outlined previously. As our general standard of living and wealth improves, we should be able to afford more social policy initiatives in such areas as health and safety, human rights, accommodation for disabled persons, pensions and old age security, health care, child care, and assistance to otherwise disadvantaged persons. In essence, the income elasticity of demand for such elements of social policy is positive. To the extent that the integration discussed previously is wealth-enhancing (e.g. gains from trade liberalization and increased capital flows), then the demand for such social policy initiatives will grow as integration progresses.

The demand for such social policy initiatives should also increase because of the adjustment required by greater integration and globalization. Even if there are efficiency gains from trade liberalization, the process clearly creates winners and losers, and unfortunately the losers are the less skilled and more disadvantaged workers displaced by low-wage import competition.[5] The need for adjustment assistance can thus emanate from both *downside* effects (e.g. job losses, plant closures) and *upside* consequences (e.g. job vacancies, skill shortages, training requirements), putting a premium on assistance that can facilitate the reallocation of labour from declining to expanding sectors and regions.

THE DEMAND FOR SOCIAL POLICY AND INTEREST GROUP POLITICS

THE DEMAND FOR SOCIAL POLICY INITIATIVES is also affected by the power and influence of various interest groups in society. The aging of the workforce in Canada and the United States, for example, will exert pressure for more pensions and old age security as well as health care for a longer living population (Cheal, 2000), but not in countries with a relatively younger population like Mexico. The increased labour force participation of women in North America during the 1960s and 1970s increased the demand for pay and employment equity in the 1980s and 1990s. The growing number of two-earner families is creating demands for childcare and *family-friendly* labour standards in areas like family leave. The growing heterogeneity and diversity of the workforce is generating greater demands for human rights and anti-discrimination policies.

As will be discussed in more detail subsequently, the importance of multinationals in a context of increasing economic integration can have complex effects on the demand for social policy initiatives. As an interest group, multinationals can resist costly legislation and regulations, but they may also support such initiatives if they already provide them (e.g. health and safety and labour standards). As well, multinationals (and other firms) may regard some legislative initiatives as substitutes for unions (e.g. if the state guarantees minimal labour standards and health and safety, there may be less demand for unions to provide them). Especially in developing countries, multinationals may also value the social cohesion that is obtained through state policies that can mitigate against instability, crime and general disorder.

In general, the demand for many types of social policy initiatives is increasing due to the consequences of deeper and broader integration. This is especially the case since change inevitably brings *new* demands, but *old* demands tend not to dissipate because of the asymmetry involved in vested interests and bureaucratic structures. While many of our labour and social policy initiatives were established in earlier periods, when needs were very different (Gunderson and Riddell, 1995, 2001), it is extremely difficult to reallocate public resources from these initiatives to make room for emerging changes. Policy initiatives seem to continually ratchet upward rather than to reallocate from declining to expanding sources of demand.

THE SUPPLY OF POLICY INITIATIVES

AT THE SAME TIME as integration is increasing demand for social policy initiatives, many of the same pressures are circumscribing the role of governments to supply such initiatives. This is so because with freer trade and higher capital mobility, businesses are increasingly able to locate in the jurisdiction offering the lowest regulatory costs, and export back to countries or jurisdictions with higher regulatory costs. This applies whether social policy initiatives involve the regulation of business or programs financed through taxes. In either case, governments are under pressure to compete for business investment and jobs associated with such investment.

One obvious way of competing is to appear *open for business* in the sense of reducing regulatory or tax costs. This gives rise to the concern (elaborated upon below) that there will be a *race to the bottom* — towards the jurisdiction with the fewest regulatory burdens and social standards. In essence, at the political bargaining table where policy is determined, the *threat* of exit through capital mobility and outsourcing gives business the upper hand. The same applies to skilled labour, which is also now more mobile and can escape high progressive taxes. The only immobile factor of production that cannot escape the tax is less skilled, low-wage labour, which is already burdened by the adverse effects of trade liberalization and technological change, as well as institutional pressures from declining unionization and minimum wages.[6] Even payroll taxes initially imposed on employers can be shifted back in the form of lower wages in return for the social policies financed by payroll taxes (e.g. public pensions, workers' compensation, and employment insurance).[7] In such an environment, governments find it more difficult to supply the policy initiatives that are increasingly demanded (although there are counter forces and these are discussed subsequently).

REASONS FOR SOCIAL POLICY CONVERGENCE UNDER INTEGRATION

THE PREVIOUS DISCUSSION alluded to a number of mechanisms that should lead to a convergence of social policy initiatives within and across different countries. As expanded upon in this section, the theoretical mechanisms include: i) political competition for business investment and jobs; ii) pressure from consumer groups and NGOs; iii) multinational activity; iv) social clauses and side accords in trade agreements; v) threats of countervail and trade sanctions; vi) emulation of best practices in the policy arena; and vii) growth convergence fostering policy convergence. The strength of each of these theoretical rationales is assessed below.

POLITICAL COMPETITION FOR INVESTMENT AND JOBS FOSTERING DOWNWARD HARMONIZATION

AS ALREADY INDICATED, the threat of capital mobility and plant relocation may induce governments to limit their social policy initiatives so as to attract investment and associated jobs. This can be true across countries and across different jurisdictions (e.g. at the provincial and even at the municipal level) within countries. Some fear that this will lead to "harmonization to the lowest common denominator" — governments will not be able to develop more generous social systems — and that the *rule of law* will give way to the *rule of the market* especially as determined by multinationals that will outsource to the lowest cost environment.

For others, of course, this is simply good old-fashioned competition applied to the political marketplace. Governments simply have to pay more attention to the financial consequences of their decisions, and that is as it should be. If jurisdictions bid to attract investment and associated jobs, then presumably this reflects the social opportunity cost of their public infrastructure as well as the preferences of their constituencies, at least in democratic societies. If it reflects the preferences of elites and interest groups that control governments, then this is a problem affecting the political system — a problem that would prevail and be less transparent under a closed rather than a more open, market-oriented, integrated system.

Many of the forces working against the convergence of social policy initiatives will be discussed in the next section. At this stage, it is important to emphasize that for harmonization to take place towards the lowest common denominator, five conditions must prevail and four links (see Figure 2) must remain unbroken (Gunderson, 1998a, 1999).

First, the policy initiatives must be enforced — otherwise they do not impose costs on employers. Policies that impose extreme regulatory burdens are often not extensively enforced in part because of the severity of those burdens. This appears to have been the case, for example, with Ontario's maximum hours of work regulations, where a complicated set of permits were required to exceed the maximum number of hours. These permits appear to have been ignored as evidenced by the fact that, for every *legal* hour of work beyond the maximum, approximately 24 *illegal* hours were worked without a permit (Donner, 1987, p. 49). It is therefore the case that a government failing to devote resources to the enforcement of legislation can be an effective way of *killing* the legislation in practice, even if it remains *on the books*.

Second, social policy initiatives may yield benefits to employers that offset, in part, their costs.[8] Workers' compensation imposes a payroll tax, but that system was historically accepted by both employees *and* employers since employees gave up the right to sue their employer in return for no-fault indemnity benefits if injured. Presumably, abandoning workers' compensation would mean a return to the tort liability system with all of its associated costs, and especially the cost of expensive litigation (as occurs now, for example, in non-work related personal injury cases through the court system). It would also mean that employers would have to pay higher compensating wage premiums in return for uninsured workplace risks.

Benefits to employers from legislation and social policies are evident in a wide range of other areas. Advance layoff notice legislation may enable employees to engage in job search and thereby fill the possible shortages of other employers. Employment insurance may allow employees to search longer for a better job match that can be beneficial to both employers and employees. Health and safety regulations reduce absences from work due to injury, and also reduce the compensating wage premium that employers would otherwise pay for workplace risks. Labour market information provided by governments reduces skill shortages. More generally, social safety nets may soften worker resistance to technological change, and so-called "costly" social programs may be less costly than prisons, crime or health expenditures that could arise if social programs were not in place. Put simply, an ounce of prevention may be worth a pound of cure.

Social programs can thus be an important component of a public infrastructure that can sustain private investment.[9] Such programs do yield benefits, even to the *bottom line* of businesses, and the *net* cost to business of the tax and regulatory burdens imposed is not as great as first appears.

Third, some of the cost of social policy initiatives is shifted backward onto workers or forward onto consumers — again reducing the net cost to business. As indicated previously, in the case of the payroll tax component imposed on employers (e.g. for public pensions, workers' compensation, employment insurance and health benefits), most of the tax burden is shifted to workers in the form of lower compensating wages. Employers can get away with paying lower risk premiums because of the benefits workers receive from social programs. Much of the cost of legislated overtime premiums is also shifted back to workers in the form of lower wages for the straight-time component (Trejo, 1991). Finally, the cost that employers initially bear by having to *reasonably accommodate* the return to work of injured workers is partially shifted back, at least if workers go back to work for another employer (Gunderson and Hyatt, 1996).

Fourth, for social policies to deter business investment and capital flows, employers must respond to *any net cost* arising from these policies by altering their investment and plant location decisions. While this can certainly occur if costs are substantial, the evidence appears mixed on the importance of net marginal social policy costs from such decisions.[10] It is certainly not the case that investments flood into countries that impose the lowest regulatory burdens, in part because these countries are not perceived as providing a legal and social environment conducive to doing business.[11] Social policies often *buy* social stability, and such stability is conducive to doing business.

Fifth, for downward harmonization to take place, governments must respond to any threat of capital flight and plant relocation by curtailing their social policy initiatives. This need not occur in a democratic country, as governments — reflecting the preferences of their constituencies — may not want to compete on that basis. They may well be willing to pay the price of lost investment, if such investment were dependent upon unacceptable social standards.

In summary, for harmonization of social policy initiatives to occur and be to the lowest common denominator, *all* of the contextual conditions mentioned above must prevail. Figure 2 illustrates how a break in any one of the four links will prevent a race to the bottom in terms of social policies.

While it is unlikely that all of these conditions will prevail, it is true that they increasingly prevail to some degree under greater economic integration. Most policies are enforced to a degree; the benefits to employers do not fully offset the costs; the costs cannot be fully shifted back to workers; employers will alter their investment and plant location decisions in response to costly policies; and governments are under pressure to compete for business investment and associated jobs. Therefore, in such circumstances, there will probably be a tendency towards harmonization, and that tendency will aim at the lowest common denominator.

FIGURE 2

NECESSARY LINKS IN A DOWNWARD SOCIAL POLICY SPIRAL

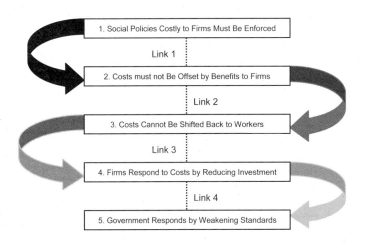

PRESSURES FROM CONSUMER GROUPS AND NGOS

WHILE GOVERNMENT COMPETITION for investment and associated jobs will foster harmonization towards the lowest common denominator, there are pressures that may offset much of this factor and, in fact, lead to upward harmonization towards the highest common denominator.

In a world of deeper and broader economic integration, consumer groups, activists and NGOs can apply considerable pressure on firms to improve their labour standards and practices (Kech and Sikkink, 1998). This is especially true of firms that produce global brand-name products. The fact that they *live by their image* means that they may *die by their image* and this sensitivity makes them vulnerable to public pressure. This was evident in one of the earliest modern campaigns against Kathy Lee Gifford's line of clothing produced under sweatshop conditions in Honduras and sold through Wal-Mart outlets, and more recently in Naomi Klein's (1999) book, *No Logo: Taking Aim at the Brand Bullies,* that targets multinationals like Nike and Reebok.

Tactics range from consumer boycotts to Internet *outings* and to *social labels* that inform consumers of the working conditions under which a product is made (Freeman, 1994; International Labour Organization, 1997). The latter is particularly appealing to economists since it simply informs consumers about the attributes of the products they are consuming, but follows the principle of consumer sovereignty. Although survey evidence suggests that consumers are willing to pay a positive price for the social content of the goods they consume (Elliott and Freeman, 2001), the effectiveness of this approach may be questioned since consumers could verbally support the cause while often still buying the cheapest product.

MULTINATIONAL ACTIVITY AND UPWARD HARMONIZATION

HARMONIZATION UNDER ECONOMIC INTEGRATION can also be fostered by the practices of multinationals. While multinationals obviously follow the laws of the host countries where they do business, they tend to operate under a higher standard than do domestic employers in those countries. As such, they foster upward harmonization towards the standards and norms of their home country. This upward harmonization occurs through five mechanisms:

1. Multinationals are influenced by the practices of their home country, effectively "exporting" those practices to the host country.

2. They often apply a more uniform set of corporate practices across their different operations.

3. Multinationals are extremely sensitive to their public image in part because they often produce brand-name goods whose sales depend on that image.

4. They generally want to appear as good corporate citizens in countries where they operate in part because foreign ownership regulations are influenced by public opinion about multinationals.

5. Multinationals often operate under voluntary corporate codes of conduct[12] and adhere to guidelines such as those suggested for multinationals by the Organisation for Economic Co-operation and Development (OECD) in 1976 and by the International Labour Organization (ILO) in 1977, emphasizing the provision of standards at least as good as those provided in the host country.[13]

Since they foster upward harmonization in generally lower-standard host countries, but downward harmonization in the higher-standard countries that are trying to compete for their investment and associated jobs (as discussed previously), multinationals facilitate convergence of policies and practices in both ways. The pressure they exert to lower standards in countries with high standards and to raise them in countries with low standards should therefore lead to a convergence towards some "internal policy" mean.

SOCIAL CLAUSES AND SIDE ACCORDS IN TRADE AGREEMENTS

THE CONVERGENCE OF SOCIAL POLICIES may also be fostered by social clauses or side accords in trade agreements (Gunderson, 2001). For example, the North American Agreement on Labour Cooperation (NAALC), which is part of NAFTA,[14] requires each of the three trading partners to enforce its own internal labour policies, with the sanctions being mainly the adverse publicity for not doing so. For supporters of free trade, such initiatives are often regarded as thinly disguised protectionism designed to artificially raise costs in the low-cost countries (in this case Mexico), although they are also often regarded as a small price worth paying to reduce resistance to trade liberalization. The perspective of labour advocates ranges from such initiatives being toothless and designed to deflect pressure away from co-ordinated policies with real sanctions, to being a small step forward to attract public attention and to provide a base for more co-ordinated policy initiatives.

Stronger initiatives are involved when social clauses are negotiated as part of trade agreements, as is the case of the European Union (EU).[15] Social clauses are enforced through the courts (ultimately the European Court of Justice), with decisions binding on member countries. In the EU case, these provisions were specifically designed to lead to an upward harmonization, with lower standard countries (e.g. Greece, Spain and Portugal) required to harmonize upward their policies with those of countries that have higher standards (e.g. Sweden, Germany and France). However, social funds were provided to assist the relatively poorer countries in implementing such upward harmoniza-tion. Social clauses guaranteeing labour standards have also been discussed as part of the negotiations on the World Trade Organization (WTO) rules (De Wet, 1995; Maskus, 1997; Gomez, 2002).

THREATS OF COUNTERVAIL AND TRADE SANCTIONS

POLICY HARMONIZATION MAY ALSO OCCUR through the threat of countervail-ing duties or trade sanctions against domestic policies that involve export sub-sidies. This is obviously more likely when free trade agreements are already in place since they generally prohibit the subsidization of exports (or permit the imposition of countervailing duties to offset the effect of such subsidies).

To the extent that domestic social policies can be interpreted as involving a subsidy to exports, there may be pressure to lower them so as not to attract a countervailing duty. When NAFTA was first instituted, there were complaints in the United States that Canada was subsidizing its exports by providing free health insurance while U.S. producers generally provided such insurance through employer-sponsored plans that implied costly premiums for them. This ignores the fact that health insurance in Canada is paid out of general tax revenues or payroll taxes, which impose similar costs on employers. If health insurance is less costly in Canada (a difficult proposition to establish since the quality of health care and costly queues can differ), then it must reflect more cost-effective public delivery by comparison with a private system.

Social policies like employment insurance could involve subsidies to sea-sonal industries like fishing and forestry since payroll taxes do not cover benefit payouts in these industries, although the precise level of any subsidy would be difficult to establish. These examples highlight the fact that the pressure for harmonization of social policies through the threat of countervailing duties is probably more a theoretical than a practical possibility.

EMULATION OF BEST PRACTICES IN THE POLICY ARENA

WHILE WE TEND TO THINK of the emulation of best practices as a phenomenon where private sector employers are emulating the best practices of other private sector employers,[16] such emulation also occurs in the policy arena (Gunderson, 1998a, p. 32). With stronger economic linkages in other areas, governments in different trading regimes interact more and are increasingly exposed to each other's policy practices. In such circumstances, they are more likely to adopt the best practices of other countries, just as private sector employers that trade with each other are more likely to adopt the best practices of their competitors. Recently, Mukand and Rodrik (2002) have added a wrinkle to this familiar phenomenon that involves non-linear benefits from policy mimicking. In their model, not every country benefits from best practices emulation, owing to the unsuitability of such reforms based on "distance" from the country of origin. The idea is that neighbours either very close or very far from the best practices of a successful country are the ones looking at the largest potential benefits. This is because close neighbours often share highly similar characteristics that make adoption appropriate, while distant neighbours can pick and choose the policy mechanism most suitable to their own situation, without the pressure of having to adopt the entire best practices mix. However, close neighbours face big potential losses from policy emulation because they are exposed to the dual problem of being close enough to the practices of the successful neighbour to influence policy makers, but too distant in terms of initial conditions to warrant wholesale adoption.

As noted by Mukand and Rodrik (2002), while the emulation of best practices fosters harmonization, it could be upwards or downwards, depending upon the extent to which the best practices involve more or fewer social policy initiatives. For example, with greater exposure to Canada and the United States, Latin American countries have paid considerably more attention to unemployment insurance as an alternative to their existing system of termination costs imposed on employers. After NAFTA, the health care reform initiatives of the mid-1990s in the United States examined carefully Canada's public health care system, while Canadians looked extensively at the welfare reforms implemented in the United States around the same period. And perhaps the best example of policy emulation in a context of increased integration (actual policy change did occur in this instance), is given by the Unemployment Insurance/Employment Insurance reforms undertaken in Canada in the mid-1990s. These reforms, which brought Canada's system in line with U.S. provisions, were informed by a body of social science research that was influenced, to a large degree, by the experience of our southern neighbour.

The effect of economic integration on policy in these instances is clearly of an indirect nature, since examinations of other countries' practices can occur whether or not there is deeper or broader integration on other dimensions.[17] But, as noted in Gunderson (1998a) and Mukand and Rodrik (2002), emulation is likely to be more prominent when countries are exposed to foreign practices in other areas.

GROWTH CONVERGENCE FOSTERING POLICY CONVERGENCE

CONVERGENCE OF ECONOMIC GROWTH fostered by economic integration can also lead to a convergence of social policies. Growth rate convergence occurs as less developed countries (or regions within a country) grow more rapidly since they are at a stage of increasing returns in their growth potential, while more developed countries expand at a slower pace since they are at a stage of decreasing returns in their potential growth.[18]

To the extent that there is positive income elasticity of demand for social policies, this implies that demand for such policies will grow more rapidly in lower-income countries than in higher-income countries.[19] In essence, lower-income countries tend to adapt to the standards of higher-income countries to which their growth rates are converging. As they develop, lower-income countries are better able to afford the more extensive social policies of their wealthier counterparts and they can *cherry pick* by adopting successful social policies while avoiding those that failed. In other words, they do not have to go through the same costly process of innovation and experimentation and can therefore *free-ride* on the experience of higher-income countries. This is, of course, the same as the ability of less developed countries to adopt the winning technologies of the more developed countries.

REASONS FOR DIVERGENCE OF SOCIAL POLICY UNDER INTEGRATION

THE PREVIOUS DISCUSSION focused on theoretical reasons for harmonization of social policy initiatives under increased economic integration, with some convergence pressures leading to downward harmonization and others leading to upward harmonization. In this section, seven key forces of integration leading to sustained policy divergence (or at least slow diffusion) will be analyzed.

ENDOGENOUS GROWTH AND POSITIVE SPILLOVERS

THE PREVIOUS ANALYSIS SUGGESTED a possible convergence of social policy initiatives following from the convergence of economic growth rates, which in turn is based on the logic of diminishing returns. However, the endogenous growth literature[20] suggests that higher-income countries (or regions within a country) need not be subject to diminishing returns — in fact, they may enjoy increasing returns to the extent that there are infinite ways to combine inputs and continue to grow. The theory of increasing returns hinges on so-called positive *spillover* and *agglomeration* effects that arise from knowledge and human capital clusters. Clusters characterize many important new industries such as pharmacology and information technology. In essence, growth begets further growth in these industries.

In contrast, lower-income countries may be caught in low-equilibrium traps, unable to muster the resources to initiate a take-off of sustained growth. There are few knowledge spillovers if the stock of human capital is limited to start with. The situation is exacerbated if the *best and brightest* elements migrate to growth centres, thereby depriving low-wage regions of the very individuals who could assist in the growth process.

In such circumstances, it is difficult to engage in activities that facilitate increasing returns, such as: taxing private income to provide the basic public infrastructure of broad-based education; properly enforcing private contracts; and providing social stability that is generally regarded as a pre-condition for private investment and sustained economic growth. Low-income/low-tax paying regions can be caught in a real dilemma — unable to afford needed social policies because they cannot grow fast enough to provide the basic social policies that are generally considered essential to sustained growth. In this scenario, poverty begets further poverty, including a paucity of basic social policies. Following from the endogenous growth literature, a divergence of social policies may therefore be sustained for an extended period of time, just as divergent growth rates may be sustained.

PATH DEPENDENCE AND IMPORTANCE OF INITIAL CONDITIONS

ANOTHER FINDING THAT EMERGES from the endogenous growth literature is that economic growth rates may indeed converge, but the convergence rate will be path dependent and specific to each individual country. That is, steady-state growth is determined by initial conditions, which can be established by historical accident or by any other means.[21] Applied to social policies, this logic implies that social systems may also be path dependent (i.e. based on the initial conditions prevailing when those policies were established). In the social policy arena, this can occur through a variety of mechanisms.

Bureaucracies, which are created around policy initiatives, may be reluctant to change those policies because they develop an expertise in them that may not be transferable to other initiatives. Bureaucracies may also develop vested interests around particular policies. For example, if workers' compensation in Canada were privatized (as is the case in many U.S. states), issues would arise about the transferability of employees from public systems to private carriers. The same logic would apply to private sector carriers in the United States if that country moved to an entirely public system. Thus, private actors may also develop vested interests around particular policies as, for example, when employment insurance supports firms in seasonal industries by keeping workers in these industries tied to their firm even when unemployed. A whole way of life may develop around social programs, with difficult adjustment problems if these programs are altered. Firms that adjust to the tax costs of particular social policies are reluctant to assume the tax costs of new and different programs, thereby creating a bias towards the maintenance of old programs.

In such circumstances, countries (or regions within countries) are able to stay on the path they initially started on, resulting in a sustained divergence of social policies which was highlighted earlier in Figure 1b. As Banting, Hoberg and Simeon (1997, p. 15) aptly note, this can explain why there may be more sustained divergence in older programs like health care given their historical legacy, as compared to newer programs (e.g. environmental protection and child care) which exhibit greater policy convergence.

DIFFERENCES IN EMBEDDED CULTURE, VALUES AND INSTITUTIONS

DIFFERENCES IN SOCIAL POLICIES can also be sustained by differences in culture, values and institutions since social policies reflect (in large part) differences in electoral outcomes, which in turn are related to value systems and related institutions. Perhaps the strongest statement in this regard is from Lipset: "Canada has been and is a more class-aware, elitist, law-abiding, statist, collectively-oriented and particularistic (group-oriented) society than the United States. These fundamental distinctions stem in large part from the American Revolution and the diverse social and environmental ecologies flowing from the division of British North America. The social effects of this separation were then reinforced by variations in literature, religious tradition, political and legal institutions, and socio-economic structures." (1989, p. 8) Lipset argues that, despite their outward similarities, the United States and Canada began with fundamentally different initial conditions in that the American revolution started the United States off on a state-dependent path involving individualism and distrust of the state, while Canada started off in a climate of loyalty to Britain and respect for large institutions, and hence less distrust of collective action through the state. Such initial circumstances should foster a greater acceptance of collectivist and social policies in Canada than in the United States.

Similar perspectives are inherent to embeddedness theories,[22] which claim that the behaviour of individuals and institutions (including social policies) are embedded in the broader system of social relations and networks in society. In this framework, pressures from market forces that could foster convergence of social policies must confront resistance from the broader social relations that sustain diversity.

TIEBOUT-TYPE EQUILIBRIUM INVOLVING HETEROGENEOUS TAX-EXPENDITURE PACKAGES

COUNTRIES, OR JURISDICTIONS WITHIN COUNTRIES, can have different combinations of social policies, and of taxes required to sustain those policies, simply because of varying taxpayer *preferences*. Divergent preferences could emanate from distinct national starting points (as seen above), or simply because taxpayers are conditioned by factors other than historical dependence. For example, some individuals may prefer high social spending and be willing to pay the taxes required for such spending, while others may prefer low-tax and low-expenditure packages. In theory, individuals will sort themselves into jurisdictions offering the optimal package for their preferences. Multiple equilibriums can therefore be sustained by the homogeneity of preferences within each jurisdiction (Tiebout, 1956). This could even apply to companies, some of which may want to avoid all regulatory costs, while others may be willing to pay higher taxes for public infrastructures that serve their needs.

In practice, of course, so-called *Tiebout equilibriums* are made difficult by the thinness of markets for such packages. It may be possible to move to a low-tax, low social services province, but this becomes more difficult if, for example, firms also want low social services generally, but are unwilling to pay higher taxes for public infrastructures like education. The problem is further compounded if individuals also want the province or state to be near the ocean, or to be prominently Francophone. Social services and public expenditures are not separate, divisible components that can be *priced out* and then packaged and sold in Lego-type bundles. As well, mobility is generally restricted across countries and it certainly imposes other costs even when legally permitted.[23]

Nevertheless, broad bundles of tax-expenditure packages can prevail across jurisdictions and such divergent policy packages can be sustained by divergent taxpayers' preferences and needs. While a variety of other factors are at work, Quebecers appear more willing to accept a higher tax package for social services than are Albertans. Europeans appear more willing to accept a stronger role for the state in providing social services than are Americans, while Canadians seem to be positioned — as always — somewhere in the middle (i.e. in a convex combination of European and American preferences).

Divergent social policies can also be sustained in equilibrium because social policy objectives can be attained through different types of social policy (as seen in Figure 1b). That is, there are different policy avenues to reach the same objective. Some can involve state expenditures on social policies (e.g. social assistance for disabled persons), whereas others can involve regulations requiring employers to provide assistance (e.g. reasonable accommodation for disabled workers). Firms can be required to make costly workers' compensation payments for industrial accidents, or they can be required to provide costly health and safety training that can lower the incidence of such accidents. Streets can be made safer by building prisons or by providing social services that reduce criminal activity. In all of these situations, the tax costs could be the same — they simply involve different social policy initiatives that are equally sustainable given the same tax costs. Different paths towards the same objectives thus involve a sustained divergence of social policy packages (although their costs may not diverge).

HETEROGENEOUS POLICY DEMANDS FROM HETEROGENEOUS POPULATIONS

DIFFERENT DEMANDS FOR SOCIAL POLICY may also emanate from the fact that populations differ in various ways, such as ethnicity and age structure. A population with a large youth cohort, for example, will require more social expenditures for education but less for health. However, a population with a large component of older persons will have extensive pension and health care obligations, especially as the aging population influences the voting systems that serves to establish those social priorities. A population with a small cohort of working-age individuals will find it difficult to have a tax base to pay for any social program. The fact that there is a significant and growing discrepancy in age structure across OECD countries only serves to highlight the divergence in social policies that is likely to be sustained as a result (Gomez, Gunderson and Luchak, 2002).

In addition, if the current generation of taxpayers finds it difficult to pay for social services, it may try to pass along their cost to future generations of taxpayers, as can be done through pay-as-you-go systems. This is the case, for example, in public pension schemes where the current generation of taxpayers supports the benefits paid out to the retired cohort, in the expectation that future generations will pay for their retirement benefits when they leave the labour force. Such systems are sustainable when there is normal growth in the population and in productivity, and hence in incomes. But, as is currently the case, when growth rates of older cohorts are higher than those of younger ones, large intergenerational burdens can be placed on future cohorts of taxpayers. However, members of the next generation may well refuse to honour the implicit social contract imposed on them, especially since these are easily forecasted events that could have been funded by the current generation of taxpayers. In essence, diversity of social policy initiatives may arise from diversity in willingness and ability to pay for such intergenerational transfers.

BORDER EFFECTS

BORDER EFFECTS — differences prevailing across borders that do not seem explainable by basic economic forces — can also sustain divergent social policies. Helliwell (1998, 2001) and others have applied gravity models to show that trade between cities of similar size and distance is approximately 18 times greater *within* Canada than it is *between* Canada and the United States. That is, *borders matter* in the sense that we prefer to trade within our country even when it does not seem profitable to do so. Indeed, even the most determined convergence theorists have been unable to discount the effect of the Canada-U.S. border. No less an authority and convergence theorist par excellence, Frederick Engels was perplexed at the differences he observed between Canada and the United States. While writing more than a century ago, Engels — convinced that such an anachronism (Canada) would soon disappear — was clearly bothered by the fact that his system of materialistic determinism was somehow being called into question by a marked Canada-U.S. difference:

> It is a strange transition from the States to Canada. First one imagines that one is in Europe again, and then one thinks one is in a positively retrogressing and decaying country. Here one sees how necessary the feverish speculative spirit of the Americans is for the rapid development of a new country (if capitalist production is taken as a basis); and in ten years this sleepy Canada will be ripe for annexation — the farmers in Manitoba, etc., will demand it themselves.... And they [Canadians] may tug and resist as much as they like; the economic necessity of an infusion of Yankee blood will have its way and abolish this ridiculous boundary line — and when the time comes, John Bull will say "Amen" to the matter. (Engels, 1888)

To the extent that borders matter for trade, it is not surprising that they should also matter with respect to social policies, sustaining programs inside the border and inhibiting convergence across national boundaries. If internal trade is sustained within a country, internal social policies should also be sustainable.

However, the mechanisms that give rise to a preference for internal trade over external trade (i.e. familiarity and networks, as well as similarities of culture, laws, regulations and institutions) may not be as easily applicable to sustaining social policies as they are to sustaining trade. Furthermore, the evidence suggests that border effects dissipated dramatically following the implementation of NAFTA: from 18:1 in favour of internal trade in 1990 (just before NAFTA) to 12:1 in 1993 (just after NAFTA) — a reduction of one-third in the importance of the border over a brief three-year period. This suggests that the deeper and wider economic integration that followed NAFTA led to a substantial re-orientation of trade from within Canada (east-west) to between Canada and the United States (north-south). To the extent that border effects that favour internal trade also sustain internal social policies, this would imply that unique domestic policies are becoming more difficult to maintain and that they would also increasingly evolve along a north-south axis.

SOCIAL CAPITAL

SOCIAL CAPITAL INVOLVES INVESTMENT of time and resources in the informal networks of social relations and reciprocal support within a community.[24] It can take various forms: volunteering, peer group effects, community networks, trust, mutual assistance, and community norms. As a form of capital, it can provide services through various means including information networks, insurance, security, and reduced transaction costs.

To the extent that broader and deeper economic integration involves a re-orientation from local communities towards the broader international community, internal social capital within a community may dissipate somewhat. As stated in Lin, Cook and Burt: "Social capital not only serves as an exogenous force, leading to certain outcomes, but more importantly, is itself the consequences of other exogenous and dynamic forces." (2001, p. viii) This is also consistent with the decline of border effects resulting from increased integration, as discussed previously.

Social capital is often considered a substitute for social services provided through the state, which means that any decline in the use of social capital due to integration could increase the need for more formal state policies. Social policies provided through the formal mechanism of the state are therefore expected to fill the void left by the social capital that otherwise may have served a similar function.

OTHER BARRIERS TO THE DIFFUSION OF SOCIAL POLICIES

A DIVERSITY OF SOCIAL POLICIES can also be sustained by barriers that inhibit the adoption and diffusion of best practices in the area of social policy development. In that regard, parallels exist with many of the barriers that inhibit the adoption and diffusion of best workplace and human resource practices.[25]

While we have some information on what works and does not work in the area of social policy, there is certainly not a sufficient degree of consensus on the best policies that should be uniformly adopted in all contexts. Witness, for example, the current debate around minimum wage policies — an area where there once was a consensus, but where that consensus has now been literally shattered (Benjamin, Gunderson and Riddell, 2002, p. 217). Even if there is consensus over efficient policy initiatives, there is little agreement as to whether they will work in every environment. There is reasonable agreement that the German apprenticeship system functions well in providing a skilled workforce to that country. However, there is no agreement on whether it could be transplanted in countries like Canada or the United States given the requirement for early (and largely irreversible) streaming into vocational and academic disciplines.

Resistance from groups who have a vested interest in the status quo can be a barrier to the adoption and diffusion of best practices policy initiatives. Such groups can include bureaucrats who administer existing policies and even employers and employees who have already adapted to these policies.

Politicians who are responsible for social policy change often have a short time horizon — perhaps four years to the next election. In such circumstances, they are reluctant to engage in massive social policy reform based on best practices given that the costs may be immediate but the benefits accruing only in the distant future — and possibly reaped by parties now in opposition.

Just as social barriers to labour-management cooperation inhibit the adoption and diffusion of best practices in the workplace, barriers such as mistrust are likely to hinder the cooperation that may be necessary to adopt best practices in the policy arena. Social policy initiatives sometimes require the cooperation of labour and management or of different interest groups whose very existence could be threatened by cooperation. In the international arena, such cooperation is invariably impeded when it involves giving up any real degree of sovereignty to international organizations.

For these various reasons, many of the barriers to the adoption and diffusion of best practices in technology or human resource policies at the workplace may also limit social policy initiatives in the political arena. Divergence in social policies is therefore sustained and convergence towards best practices may never occur.

IS THERE EVIDENCE OF POLICY AND SOCIAL OUTCOME CONVERGENCE?

THE PREVIOUS DISCUSSION NOTED THAT, under increased economic integration, convergence of social policies could proceed downward to the lowest common denominator or upward to countries that provide more extensive social policies. Working in the other direction are equally compelling reasons as to why social policy diversity can be sustained and may even be expanded under the pressures of deeper and broader integration. Because of conflicting theoretical claims, an appeal to the empirical evidence must be made in order to see if there has been policy convergence (and if so, downwards or upwards), or sustained (expanded) diversity following recent moves (FTA and NAFTA) that have both broadened and deepened economic integration in North America.

EXAMINING THE NORTH AMERICAN EVIDENCE: CONVERGENCE OR DIVERGENCE OF SOCIAL POLICIES?

THERE IS A PERCEPTION THAT CANADA has stricter labour laws, employment standards and social policies than the United States, and systematic analysis bears this out. Based on a comprehensive assessment of legislation pertaining to collective bargaining, equal opportunity, unjust dismissal, occupational health and safety, workers' compensation, advance notice of layoffs, and unemployment insurance, Block and Roberts conclude that "A broad-based overview of labour standards [the term they use to describe all of these policies] in the two countries suggests that the conventional wisdom is correct — Canadian labour standards are, indeed, higher than U.S. labour standards." (1997, p. 39) That analysis provided a snapshot of the situation around 1997 with no analysis of changes over time so that it is not possible to infer whether there has been convergence in the aggregate.

Convergence between Canada and the United States in a number of areas outside of labour and social policy has been documented in various studies published in Banting, Hoberg and Simeon (1997). This is the case for: macroeconomic policy with its emphasis on debt reduction and inflation control (Boothe and Purvis, 1997); more market-oriented industrial policies pertaining to trade liberalization, industrial subsidies, regional development, research and development, education and training (Howse and Chandler, 1997); environmental policies with Canada harmonizing upward to the United States (Hoberg, 1997, 2000); and individual political rights and judicial protection from the state, largely through the adoption of the Charter of Rights in Canada (Manfredi, 1997). We focus on whether there has also been a tendency towards convergence in labour and social policies and their outcomes.

A comprehensive statistical analysis of the evidence on the full array of social policies is beyond the scope of this study, especially in light of the fact that there are no systematic, comprehensive reviews from which to draw. As well, there is little systematic evidence on the topic and certainly no consensus has emerged. As such, the evidence discussed here (though extensive) is illustrative rather than exhaustive. We do, however, provide a qualitative meta-analysis of the existing empirical literature. The empirical methodology is in the time-honoured tradition of *vulturemetrics* — soaring over the remains of others, and scooping down to pick the choicest parts. Our focus tends to be on issues of convergence between Canada and the United States, although broader comparisons across other countries (especially within the OECD) are sometimes made. A summary of the findings is provided in Table 2. We begin with labour policies and outcomes and end with a comparison of tax rates.

UNIONIZATION AND LABOUR LAWS

ALTHOUGH IT IS NOT A SOCIAL POLICY PER SE, unionization is an institutional force that has an important impact on other elements of social policy and is influenced by legislative policy initiatives. It is also an element often discussed in the convergence-divergence debate.

Union density has declined since the 1970s in most developed countries except for Scandinavian countries, which tend to have a centralized bargaining structure, and for Canada (Lipsig-Mummé, 2001, p. 534; Benjamin, Gunderson

TABLE 2

SUMMARY OF CONVERGENCE OR DIVERGENCE ACROSS VARIOUS LABOUR AND SOCIAL POLICIES

LABOUR / SOCIAL POLICY OR OUTCOME	DIVERGENCE OR CONVERGENCE	DIRECTION
1. Unionization and Labour Laws	Convergence to lower levels of unionization and labour laws in countries with decentralized bargaining (Canada is the exception, although with some recent convergence to the United States).	↓
2. Strikes	Convergence to fewer strikes, especially in the private sector, and downward convergence to more restrictions on strikes in the public sector.	↓
3. Minimum Wages	Convergence to lower real minimum wages.	↓
4. Unemployment Insurance	Convergence to more restrictive access.	↓
5. Workers' Compensation	Sustained divergence.	↔
6. Occupational Health and Safety	Sustained divergence.	↔
7. Pay Equity	Convergence to no mandatory requirements.	↓
8. Employment Equity	Uncertain.	—
9. Age Discrimination and Mandatory Retirement	Sustained divergence but pressure for upward convergence to the United States.	↑
10. Pensions	Convergence on funding side. Increased divergence on benefit side.	↓ ↔
11. Welfare / Family Benefits	Convergence for working families. Divergence for families with no earned income.	↓ ↔
12. Overall Social Expenditures	Sustained divergence with some convergence to mean (i.e. downward in high-spending countries and upward in low-spending ones).	↔
13. Labour Standards in General	Convergence often to the mean (i.e. downward in countries with high standards and upward in countries with low standards).	↔
14. Taxes	Mixed interpretation with political scientists suggesting no convergence but most economists suggesting downward convergence to lower taxes.	↔
Overall Conclusion	General convergence, usually downward to the lower common denominator, but considerable sustained divergence.	↓

Source: Authors' interpretation of various studies, as outlined in the text.

and Riddell, 2002, p. 421). In that regard, Canada is somewhat of an anomaly, having a decentralized bargaining structure without substantial union decline. The contrast is especially prominent with our major trading partner, the United States. In the mid-1960s, unionization rates were largely the same in both countries at around 30 percent of the paid non-agricultural workforce. Since then, union density has plummeted continuously in the United States to less than half that level, while it has risen slightly in Canada until around the mid-1980s; however, it currently stands at around its 1965 rate of 30 percent (Gomez and Gunderson, 2002).

The international decline of unionization in most developed countries is attributed in large part to global economic pressures (Lipsig-Mummé, 2001, p. 535) — somewhat supporting the convergence hypothesis to the lowest common denominator — but also to differing institutional arrangements such as the presence of work councils and closed-shop restrictions (Visser, 2002). The continued divergence of countries with more centralized bargaining structures is attributed in part to unions' ability to influence political factors that can sustain their existence (Jacoby, 1995) — somewhat supporting the divergence perspective highlighting that nation states still have a substantial degree of freedom to determine their policy initiatives in the face of globalization.

As indicated, Canada is somewhat of an anomaly and reasons for the sustained divergence between Canada and the United States have raised considerable debate (Benjamin, Gunderson and Riddell, 2002, pp. 420-434). Moreover, if we factor in collective bargaining coverage rates (which, in countries like France, differ enormously from membership rolls), a more resilient picture of union presence in the context of economic integration begins to emerge.

One hypothesis as to why the United States and Canada have diverged in this policy-outcome realm, is that changes in the structure of the economy and of the labour force (e.g. from manufacturing to services, from blue-collar to white-collar jobs, from male to female employment, from full-time to part-time work, from large firms to small firms) have been unfavourable to unions since these shifts focus on non-union workers. However, most of these changes occurred in both Canada and the United States. Riddell (1993) attributes only about 15 percent of the difference in union coverage between the two countries to differences in these structural factors, with the larger (highly unionized) public sector in Canada accounting for about half of that small difference.

A second hypothesis is that there has been a decline in public attitudes towards unions and in the desire for collective representation. This has occurred, but it has occurred in a similar fashion in both Canada and the United States (Riddell, 1993).

According to a third hypothesis, there has been an increase in *union substitutes* in such forms as legislative protections and social services from governments and progressive human resource management practices on the part of employers. While the exact contribution of these factors has not been extensively researched, they are unlikely to account for the divergence since governments in Canada have tended to provide more social and employment security (Riddell, 1993; Benjamin, Gunderson and Riddell, 2002, pp. 429-430).

The fourth hypothesis, and the one that seems to receive the most support, is that unions in Canada have been sustained by labour laws and their enforcement. Aspects of those laws include: certification through the signing of cards rather than the requirement to vote; stricter enforcement of unfair labour practices during certification campaigns or decertification attempts; first-contract arbitration in some Canadian jurisdictions; bankruptcy and succession procedures; stronger union security provisions such as the dues check-off; and stronger prohibitions on the use of replacement workers during strikes (Betcherman and Gunderson, 1990; Kumar, 1993; Riddell, 1993). In essence, the legislative environment in Canada was more conducive to offsetting the pressures from globalization that would otherwise foster a decline in unionization. This tends to support the divergence perspective that governments have a substantial degree of freedom in spite of economic integration.

Other possible reasons for the sustained unionization rates in Canada have not been investigated as systematically. They include the possibility that Canadian employers who are at a competitive disadvantage because of higher union costs are shielded from competition somewhat by the exchange rate, as well as the possibility that unions are imposing fewer costs because of a declining union wage premium (Gunderson and Hyatt, 2001, p. 393).

Some recent developments, however, suggest that unionization in Canada may be converging towards rates observed elsewhere, and especially in the United States. Specifically, since 1984, collective agreement coverage in Canada has declined by seven percentage points, the same decline that has occurred in the United States over that period. Riddell and Riddell (2001) attribute much of this decline to a convergence towards U.S.-style labour laws, and in particular a change in many jurisdictions from certification through card signing to a requirement to vote.

Compelling evidence that economic integration inhibits union organizing is found in the comprehensive analysis of Bronfenbrenner (2000), which is based on surveys, interviews, documentary evidence and electronic data bases. The data on certification attempts in the United States in 1998 and 1999 show that: "... the recent acceleration in capital mobility has had a devastating impact on the extent and nature of union organizing campaigns. Where employers can credibly threaten to shut down and/or move their operations in response to union activity, they do so in large numbers" (p. v).

In the same vein, Bronfenbrenner finds that this threat is almost twice as high in mobile industries such as manufacturing, communication and wholesale distribution, compared to immobile industries such as construction, health care, education, retail and other services. Likely reflecting the perceived effect of Canadian laws as assisting certification, she recommends (p. vii) the adoption of Canadian-style laws such as first-contract arbitration and card signing instead of voting requirements, and stricter enforcement of unfair labour practices, to offset what she regards as an undesirable trend in the United States.

Overall, the evidence is mixed on the convergence-divergence perspective with respect to unionization and labour legislation. Globally, there appears to be convergence to the lowest common denominator with respect to unionization rates; however, countries with centralized bargaining structures have been able to use the influence of the state to sustain unionization. The same seems to apply to Canada's decentralized bargaining system (an outlier in this respect), although recent evidence indicates some convergence towards lower unionization rates and weaker labour laws. More direct evidence from the United States strongly suggests that the threat of capital mobility and plant relocation is a strong deterrent to establishing and sustaining unions.

STRIKES AND INDUSTRIAL CONFLICTS

STRIKES ARE THE MOST VISIBLE MANIFESTATION of employee (union) power. The forces of economic integration should lead to a downward convergence of strike activity because the cost of strikes are higher for both employers and employees when customers can shift to alternative sources of supply, possibly on a permanent basis even after the strike has ended. Strikes can also deter new investment (and jobs associated with that investment) in strike-prone countries. Obviously, these effects are likely to be more prominent in the private sector compared to the public sector since loss of market share to international competitors is not an extensive risk in the latter. Similarly, public sector employers in areas like administration, education, health and social services are not likely to move their operations to another country in response to a strike!

While other factors may be at work, the empirical evidence is consistent with the notion that globalization is leading to a downward convergence of strike activity on an international scale (Aligisakis, 1997), and also in Canada (Gunderson, Hyatt and Ponak, 2001). As well, that decline has been much more substantial in the private sector than in the public sector (Gunderson, 2002b).

While bargaining parties in the public sector do not operate under the same *hard* budget constraint of private sector employers under globalization, they do operate under a series of legislative regulations governing strikes. In Canada, these legislative restrictions have become much more stringent in recent years.

These tighter restrictions include: public sector wage controls over much of the 1980s and into the 1990s; suspension of collective bargaining and even mid-contract wage rollbacks (e.g. the federal government freezing wages and sus-pending collective bargaining from 1991 to 1997; social contracts in various provinces where unpaid leave days were mandated); more frequent use of back-to-work legislation; increasing the portion of designated employees who do not have the right to strike; and requiring arbitrators to take into consideration the ability to pay of a public sector employer (Gunderson, 2002b). In the United States, since the mid-1980s, legislation and court interpretations have also led to more stringent restrictions on the strike weapon in the public sector (Lund and Maranto, 1996).

Overall, the evidence pertaining to strikes suggests a downward harmoni-zation (both globally and in Canada and the United States), especially in the private sector where global competitive pressures are greatest. As well, there has been downward harmonization in public sector legislation towards in-creased restrictions on the strike weapon in the public sector, both in Canada and the United States.

MINIMUM WAGES

DESPITE NOMINAL INCREASES in the United States and Canada during the 1990s, the real value of minimum wages (i.e. minimum wages relative to the consumer price index or a measure of the average industrial wage) has tended to decline in both countries since the mid-1970s (Benjamin, 2001, pp. 191-194). While this does not imply convergence, it does suggest that both have followed a similar path towards the lowest common denominator of a lower minimum wage. This common path suggests a concern for employment in low-wage in-dustries increasingly subjected to international competition from developing countries. Although the evidence on this is anecdotal, Canadian jurisdictions that are contemplating an increase in their minimum wage increasingly look south to competitive states in the United States for comparison purposes, as opposed to looking east or west across different Canadian jurisdictions.

UNEMPLOYMENT INSURANCE

ESPECIALLY SINCE THE *LIBERALIZATION* of unemployment insurance (UI) in Canada in 1971, this program has been substantially more generous in Canada than in the United States. For example, even though the U.S. population is ten times that of Canada, *total* expenditures on UI in the United States were only slightly higher than in Canada during the 1980s (Green and Riddell, 1993). While some of this is due to the higher unemployment rate in Canada, most is attributed to greater generosity on such dimensions as coverage, qualifying period, benefit rates and duration. Over time, however, reforms affecting most of these dimensions (especially in 1989 and 1994) have been strongly in the direction of convergence to the lower common denominator of the U.S. model (Banting, 1997; Boychuk and Banting, 2003; Gunderson and Riddell, 2001). Boychuk and Banting (2003, p. 538) further note that this cross-border downward convergence has been strong between contiguous regions (e.g. Ontario and the Great Lakes; British Columbia and Washington), although they appropriately regard this apparent response to competitive pressures with contiguous regions as somewhat of a puzzle since UI is essentially a federal program.

WORKERS' COMPENSATION

WORKERS' COMPENSATION SYSTEMS are notoriously difficult to compare across jurisdictions *within* Canada and the United States since they vary by province and state, and they can vary on so many different aspects such as coverage, eligibility, benefit replacement, benefit duration, survivor benefits, return-to-work requirements, waiting periods, vocational rehabilitation provisions, appeal procedures, and access to the health care system. Based on a comparison of many of these provisions, Block and Roberts (1997, p. 33) indicate that Canadian provinces tend to be slightly more generous than U.S. states in the area of workers' compensation.

The delivery systems are also vastly different between the two countries. Workers' compensation in Canada is provided through a single monopoly board in each province/territory. This is in marked contrast to the United States where monopoly boards exist only in 5 states, while 24 have exclusively private insurance carriers and 19 have a combination of state and private carriers (Gunderson and Hyatt, 1999, p. 548).

In spite of the fact that virtually every province in Canada has reviewed its workers' compensation system during the 1990s, in part because of escalating costs (Gunderson and Hyatt, 2000a, p. 3), the suggested reforms are not obviously in the direction of the U.S. model. There appears to be little pressure to shift to a private or mixed system, partly because the U.S. evidence is mixed on the cost effectiveness of such systems (Gunderson and Hyatt, 1999, pp. 561-563), because some evidence suggests that costs are substantially lower in Canada compared to the United States (Thomason and Burton, 2000), and because most of the expenditures are in the form of transfer benefits to recipients so that any *saving* would largely be at the expense of recipients (Dewees, 2000). Boychuk and Banting (2003) also conclude that workers' compensation comparisons between Canada and the United States exhibit sustained divergence over the past 20 years. While there appears to be few signs of convergence, pressures have been felt in Canada to pay more attention to the incentive effects of workers' compensation in return-to-work decisions, with those pressures

generally being in the direction of market incentives on such aspects as experience rating.

HEALTH AND SAFETY LEGISLATION

HEALTH AND SAFETY LEGISLATION IN THE UNITED STATES is generally characterized as following a more *regulatory* model that emphasizes detailed regulations at the workplace. In Canada, such regulations prevail but there is more
emphasis on what is labelled the "internal responsibility system," with labour
and management being jointly responsible (Kralj, 2000), a system that is facilitated by the higher degree of unionization in Canada. The internal responsibility system is fostered by the three rights: the right to know or to be informed of
workplace hazards; the right to representation through legislative requirements
for joint health and safety committees; and the right to refuse unsafe work.
While these systems appear to be quite different on paper, the extent to which
they are different in practice is less well known.

Overall, these systems do not seem to have undergone dramatic changes
in recent years. As such, the health and safety systems are characterized by sustained diversity more than convergence. This may reflect reduced cost pressures on these systems as a result of substantial reductions in workplace accidents, in part due to industrial restructuring towards sectors with fewer accident rates (Gunderson and Hyatt, 2000b). There is also considerable political
support for health and safety at the workplace. As with workers' compensation,
however, there is increased emphasis in Canada on using market incentives
(e.g. experience rating) to reduce workplace accidents (Kralj, 2000).

PAY EQUITY LEGISLATION

CANADA HAS ONE OF THE MOST STRINGENT PAY EQUITY LEGISLATIONS in the
world (Gunderson, 1994) applying in all jurisdictions except Alberta. It is also
proactively applied to the private sector and to the public sector in Ontario
and, more recently, in Quebec (Gunderson, 1994; Benjamin, Gunderson and
Riddell, 2002, p. 370).

Most pay equity initiatives in Canada were adopted in the 1980s, with
more recent ones being *milder* initiatives where governments voluntarily com-
mit themselves to the principle as part of the collective bargaining process.
There has been no replication of the stringent model adopted in Ontario in
1987, involving proactive application to *both* the public and private sectors.
Furthermore, Ontario appears to be more in a *maintenance* mode, with limited
activity in this area (Gunderson, 2002c). An exception is Quebec, which
adopted a proactive system for both the public and private sectors in 1996;
however, its implementation has been slow. Furthermore, the federal government

was compelled (by the Human Rights Commission and upheld by the Federal Court) to settle a $3.6 billion pay equity complaint with the Public Service Alliance of Canada — a case that took 15 years to resolve. As discussed previously, the federal government is not under the same competitive international pressures as private sector employers.

Although pay equity exists in Europe (where it is termed *equal pay for work of equal value*), it is essentially complaints-based and weakly enforced. Similarly, it is not widespread in the United States (where it is termed *comparable worth*), existing in a small number of state governments and local public sector employers. Whether the retrenchment of pay equity activity in Canada towards European and U.S. levels reflects global competitive pressures is an open question, but it does appear that this legislative initiative in Canada is indeed converging towards a lower standard.

EMPLOYMENT EQUITY

EMPLOYMENT EQUITY REQUIRES employers to have an internal representation of target groups (women, visible minorities, Aboriginal peoples and disabled persons) that is equal to their representation in the external workforce. In Canada, such legislation exists in the federal jurisdiction and for public servants in British Columbia, Saskatchewan and Manitoba. In Ontario, legislation was adopted in 1993 by the New Democratic government, but it was immediately repealed (before it could be implemented) by the Progressive Conservative government when it came to power. Enforcement of such initiatives in Canada is generally regarded as weak.

Such initiatives are more prominent in the United States (where they are termed *affirmative action*), under the impetus of the civil rights movement for blacks in the 1960s, and were subsequently extended to women in the 1970s. However, there has generally been a retrenchment in these initiatives since the 1980s. Whether this retrenchment and the weaker enforcement in Canada are in response to global competitive pressures is also an open question.

AGE DISCRIMINATION AND MANDATORY RETIREMENT

WHILE CANADA AND THE UNITED STATES both have legislation prohibiting age discrimination, they have followed divergent paths with respect to mandatory retirement (Gomez, Gunderson and Luchak, 2002). Mandatory retirement was banned in the United States in 1986, but it has been largely sustained in Canada even though it was extensively debated around that time, and upheld largely through Supreme Court decisions.

Reasons for the divergent policy responses are not obvious since both countries have similar age structures, concerns with public pensions and expenses associated with an aging population, pressures to facilitate transition into retirement, and increased emphasis on fighting discrimination. The divergent responses may reflect other differences such as stronger unions (which tend to favour mandatory retirement as a form of work sharing and in return for pensions) and more redistributive public pensions in Canada guaranteeing a minimum level of income for the elderly.

Whatever the explanation, a divergent policy response is observed in the area of mandatory retirement. However, changes appear to be in the direction of upward harmonization to the United States as evidenced by the fact that Manitoba and Quebec have effectively banned mandatory retirement, while the federal government has voluntarily eliminated it for its civil servants. As well, a number of other jurisdictions are investigating the possibility of banning mandatory retirement (Gomez, Gunderson and Luchak, 2002) and the idea is gaining increasing attention internationally (Hornstein, 2001).[26]

While these patterns do not support the hypothesis of convergence to the lowest common denominator in response to competitive international pressures, there is a caveat. Mandatory retirement is under provincial jurisdiction in Canada; hence, each province may have been reluctant to ban mandatory retirement for fear of costs this measure may impose on employers. In essence, while there is no convergence to U.S. regulations, there has been considerable sustained convergence to the lowest common denominator (i.e. no regulation) in Canada.

PENSIONS

PENSION SYSTEMS IN BOTH CANADA AND THE UNITED STATES are subjected to similar demographic pressures associated with an aging workforce and a longer-lived population. In Canada, the pension system is often described as comprising three tiers:

1. A universal, non-contributory Old Age Security (OAS) flat-rate demogrant given to all Canadians age 65 and over irrespective of their earnings and work history, possibly supplemented by a means-tested Guaranteed Income Supplement (GIS), both financed out of general tax revenues.

2. The contributory earnings-related Canada/Quebec Pension Plan (C/QPP), financed out of a payroll tax, with benefit payouts related to earnings and work history.

3. Private, work-related pensions in the form of employer-sponsored, occupational Registered Pension Plans (RPPs), financed by employers usually with employee contributions; and private savings in the form of tax-deferred Registered Retirement Savings Plans, with public support for these plans coming largely in the form of favourable tax treatment and hence foregone tax revenues.

In Canada, public spending (or revenues foregone through favourable tax treatment) is roughly equally divided one third for each of the three tiers. By contrast, in the United States, spending on the first tier (a universal demogrant possibly with an income-tested supplement) is close to zero, with two thirds of public spending concentrated on the second tier of contributory, earnings-related pensions, termed Social Security (Boychuk and Banting, 2003, p. 539). The third tier of private tax-supported pension and private savings plans gets one third of public spending, as in Canada. Therefore, the main difference in pension arrangements between Canada and the United States comes from a much greater emphasis on Social Security in the United States compared to the comparable C/QPP in Canada (two thirds *vs.* one third of public spending on pensions, respectively) and a much greater emphasis on the universal demogrant (and conditional supplement) in Canada (one third *vs.* almost no public spending, respectively). As a result of the universal OAS and conditional GIS, the Canadian pension system is more progressive than the U.S. system (Boychuk and Banting, 2003; Gunderson, Hyatt and Pesando, 2000).

Boychuk and Banting (2003, p. 539) note that there has been some convergence in the two systems in that the lower contribution rates of the C/QPP in Canada have been moving upward to the higher contribution rates of Social Security in the United States. However, on the benefit side, there has been increased divergence since benefit reductions have been more pronounced in the United States, mainly following the increase in the age of entitlement — from 65 to 67 years — that is slowly phased-in, beginning in 2000 and ending in 2021. They also argue that the greater redistributive nature of pensions in Canada will likely continue into the future, and they conclude generally that "... the overall pattern in the retirement income field over the last 20 years is one of divergence. ... and the changes already in place are not likely to alter these patterns significantly over time." (p. 543)

WELFARE AND FAMILY BENEFITS

THE PATTERN OF MIXED CONVERGENCE AND DIVERGENCE that prevails between welfare and family benefits in Canada and the United States is very difficult to untangle (Boychuk and Banting, 2003). Welfare payments have generally diverged between 1980 and 1990 (falling in the United States but rising in

Canada), but they have converged somewhat in recent years (falling more rapidly in Canada than in the United States) although Canada is still more *generous* overall. Both countries have increasingly emphasized incentives to get potentially employable individuals off welfare and into the workforce. In contrast, family benefits have significantly converged as Canada moved away from its universal family allowance to a system of income-tested refundable tax credits similar to the Earned Income Tax Credit of the United States.

Overall, the combined impact of both welfare and family benefits has led to a sustained divergence for families with no earned income (with a slight decline in benefits in both countries), but a marked convergence for families with earned income.

OVERALL SOCIAL EXPENDITURES

THE PREVIOUS DISCUSSION focused on particular laws and programs as they may be affected by the forces of globalization and broader and deeper economic integration. Overall, on the public spending side, there does not appear to be convergence of expenditures on social programs as a proportion of gross domestic product (GDP), at least for OECD countries. In fact, social expenditures have generally increased slightly in those countries (Boychuk and Banting, 2003, p. 534). This interpretation is shared by the United Nation's *World Public Sector Report*: "... the assumption that globalization reduces the size of government is not supported by evidence." (2001, p. 5) The fact is that open (globalized) economies have larger, not smaller, government expenditures. These studies tend to emphasize the importance of public sector infrastructures and social safety nets in promoting competitiveness and openness. They recognize, however, that causality may work in the other direction; that is, economic growth may facilitate increased social expenditures. Boychuk and Banting (2003, p. 535) also point out that there has been considerable convergence in social policy within the European Union, even though it is not the case across the OECD in general. This convergence is a combination of downward changes amongst the wealthier countries of northern Europe and upward convergence amongst the poorer southern countries.

LABOUR STANDARDS IN GENERAL

AN EARLY STUDY BY THE OECD (1994) looked at the issue of convergence of labour standards in general across OECD countries. For different dimensions of labour standards, it found:

1. *Work time regulations*: Convergence downward towards fewer regulations and more flexibility.

2. *Fixed term contracts*: Convergence downward towards more flexibility.

3. *Employment protection*: Convergence downward towards fewer regulations.

4. *Minimum wages*: Convergence downward (i.e. lower real value and less binding rules).

5. *Employee representation rights*: Mixed (i.e. convergence towards average — upward in countries where autocratic regimes became more democratic and downward in other countries).

6. *Social protection* (health, pensions, unemployment insurance and income support): Convergence towards average — upward in poorer countries and downward in wealthier countries.

Overall, the pattern tended to be one of convergence, usually downward but often towards the mean (i.e. upward in countries with low standards and downward in countries with high standards). As the OECD report concluded, "The general pattern that emerges is that some convergence towards more flexible rules and arrangements governing labour standards have occurred during the 1980s ... with some exceptions ... and with considerable cross-country differences remaining." (1994, p. 152)

The OECD study also showed that increased trade, integration and growth tend to improve, not weaken, labour standards in general (p. 155). An index of labour standards was also developed and related to trade and investment. The conclusion at the time was that stricter labour standards do not impose costs that deter trade (p. 157), although there is some evidence that countries with less costly standards attract greater foreign investment (p. 160).

More recently, McBride and Williams (2001) examined the OECD Jobs Strategy set out in 1994, which they labelled a neo-liberal ideal of labour market policy because of its emphasis on market incentives and market-oriented reform, and especially because it encourages active labour market policies that facilitate adjustment in the direction of market forces and away from passive income maintenance programs which can discourage such adjustments. They reviewed a number of subsequent OECD evaluation studies and concluded that "... the OECD's reports on implementation reveal significant policy divergence: national frameworks continue to vary substantially." (p. 292) The conclusion that convergence has not occurred, however, does not speak directly to whether there has been a *tendency towards* convergence in labour policies. Their own analysis of subsequent implementation reports suggests that there has been such a tendency and that it has been towards the lower common denominator (i.e. less regulations) in such areas as unemployment insurance, payroll taxes, decentralized collective bargaining, employment protection, work time flexibility and active labour market policies in general (p. 293). Perhaps a reasonable overall conclusion is that there has been a tendency towards convergence in a wide array of labour market policies across OECD countries, and that convergence has been downward to the lower common denominator, but substantial differences in labour market policies still prevail.

TAXES

TAXES CAN PROVIDE A GOOD BOTTOM-LINE summary measure for testing convergence since taxes are used to finance a wide range of public programs, and mobile capital can respond to tax costs that are *excessive* relative to public services financed through taxes. However, using the tax measure raises some difficulties. There is a variety of taxes (corporate, payroll, personal, and consumption) that can affect investment decisions, and focusing on one may miss others. While the focus tends to be on corporate tax rates, even personal income taxes that can influence labour costs, especially for professionals and executives, can have an impact on investment decisions. As well, focusing on tax *rates* may miss variations in tax *bases* in terms of what income is taxed (subject to depreciation and inventory allowances, credits, deductibles and tax holidays) with both affecting the *effective* tax (OECD, 1991). Taxes can also be shifted from where they are initially applied. As indicated previously, almost all the payroll tax portion initially imposed on business is ultimately shifted to labour in the form of lower compensating wages in return for the benefits derived from programs (e.g. employment insurance, workers' compensation, pensions) financed by the payroll tax.

The empirical evidence on the effect of globalization on tax convergence tends to be mixed. Poddar, Neubig and English (2000) find that tax rates differ widely. Moreover, in nearly all OECD countries, tax revenue as a percent of GDP was higher in 1997 than in 1965. Nevertheless, the authors conclude (by citing anecdotal evidence) that tax rates are subject to increased downward pressure. Olewiler (1999) also finds substantial divergence in tax rates among OECD countries, but notes a shift (in the aggregate) of taxes towards less mobile factors of production in the form of property and payroll taxes.

In reviewing much of that evidence, Slemrod concludes "Thus, there is no consensus in the political science literature that openness, liberalization, or globalization have led to reduced taxation of capital income, including use of the corporate income tax, although lower corporate taxes were sometimes pursued as a policy package with financial liberalization." (2001, p. 9) He further arrives at the intriguing conclusion that "It is not unfair to summarize the literature by saying that the political scientists who have studied this question find no evidence that globalization has led to corporate tax decreases, while the (two) economists have found such evidence."[27] Slemrod's own evidence (consistent with the findings of other economists) is that there has been downward convergence in both the statutory corporate tax rates and the effective rates that encompass the tax base. Both the standard deviation and the average of these rates fell over the 1980s, and especially in the 1990s, suggesting both convergence (declining standard deviation) and convergence towards the lower common denominator (declining average).

After reviewing ten quantitative studies of the impact of taxes on U.S. outward foreign direct investment and ten studies focusing on inward foreign investment in the United States, Hines concludes that "… taxation exerts a significant effect on the magnitude and location of FDI." (1997, p. 414) Based on a large number of interviews with firm managers who make locational decisions, Wilson concludes that for administration and distribution activities: "… tax considerations largely *dictate* [emphasis added] location decisions for business activities." (1993, p. 195) In a comprehensive analysis of these and other studies, Avi-Yonah concludes that "… taxation has a major influence on multinationals' decisions to locate their investment capital." (2000, p. 1608) As an example, he mentions that the abolishment by the United States in 1984 of the withholding tax of 30 percent on interest earned by foreign residents "… resulted in a classic 'race to the bottom' …. One after another, all the major economies have abolished their withholding taxes on interest for fear of losing mobile capital flows to the United States." (p. 1581) He also notes that "Tax competition has led to the proliferation of production tax havens. Currently, at least 103 countries offer special tax concessions to foreign corporations that set up production or administrative facilities within their borders." (p. 1588)

Overall, our reading is that integration and the threat of capital mobility may have shifted the incidence of taxation onto less mobile factors of production (such as land and less-skilled labour), but the evidence is not conclusive on whether integration has fostered a downward convergence of taxes.

SUMMARY AND CONCLUDING OBSERVATIONS

IN THE INTRODUCTION TO OUR EMPIRICAL SECTION, we highlighted evidence from various studies published in Banting, Hoberg and Simeon (1997) indicating that there has been a tendency towards convergence of Canadian policies to those of the United States in a number of areas, including macroeconomic policy, industrial policy, environmental policy, as well as individual political rights and judicial protection from the state. With respect to social policy, however, Simeon, Hoberg and Banting conclude that "If economic policies reveal a general convergence between the two countries, *social policy* offers some reassurance to those Canadians who are fearful of harmonization pressures as a consequence of free trade." (1997, p. 393) This perspective appears to be common amongst political scientists. Cameron and Stein conclude that

"Globalization ... offers more degrees of freedom than is conventionally thought." (2000, p. S30) For their part, McBride and Williams conclude that "Despite clear evidence of international political pressures aimed at producing policy convergence in the labour market area, and the assumptions of the 'economistic' reading of globalization, that states face tangible repercussions from the failure to embrace neo-liberal strategies, convergence has not occurred." (2001, p. 302) They also cite Garrett: "... no pervasive policy race to the neo-liberal bottom" (1998a, p. 823) has emerged amongst OECD countries.

Our interpretation of the limited available evidence (summarized in Table 2) is somewhat along these lines, although it differs considerably in degree. More specifically, our interpretation is fourfold:

1. The forces of integration are fostering a *tendency* towards convergence of policies, *including* labour and social policies, and that convergence tends to be *towards* the lower common denominator.

2. Such downward harmonization is not always undesirable (as would be implied by phrases like: "race to the bottom," "social dumping," "harmonization to the lowest common denominator," and "regulatory meltdown"). Much of it may be desirable since it should eliminate inefficient and rent-seeking policies, with policies that have positive feedback effects on efficiency (and many do) not only surviving but thriving in the more integrated environment. In essence, governments are now more compelled to pay attention to the cost consequences of their policies, but this is generally a desirable and not an undesirable source of pressure. Our interpretation is that the state does have fewer degrees of freedom in developing social policy initiatives, but this is generally a desirable constraining influence. The state faces a *harder* rather than a *softer* budget constraint in deciding its policies, but this simply compels it to confront the reality that we cannot simply solve social problems by *throwing money* at them.

3. In such circumstances, a considerable diversity of policies can and does still prevail, reflecting a diversity of preferences and ability and willingness to pay, as well as the different positive roles played by various policy initiatives.

4. The area of concern — and this applies to many social policies — is that the set of social policies that have pure equity-oriented purposes to assist vulnerable disadvantaged groups, and that do not have positive feedback effects on efficiency and competitiveness, will be most difficult to sustain. Yet, they are likely to be the most important policies given the number of vulnerable groups being bypassed by the benefits of globalization.

If either of us could carry a tune, we would end with the following rendition: ♬ ... while you see divergence, we see convergence ♬. We would not end, however, with the refrain: ♪ ... let's call the whole thing off. ♪ Instead, we would conclude with a call for more evidence in this important area, and fortunately there seems to be a convergence of views from all sides on this point. Such additional evidence is likely to foster a convergence of views, although the direction of that convergence remains an open and interesting question.

ENDNOTES

1   See Castro-Rea (1996), Gomez and Gunderson (2002), Gunderson (2001), Hoberg (2000) and Weintraub (1994).

2   This is exemplified by Mexico's former President Salinas' statement that "You can take our goods or our people." — implying that if the United States did not open its doors to free trade with Mexico then illegal immigration would increase.

3   We decided to exclude health and education policies on the basis that they seem more appropriate to a discussion of the state's basic role in fostering economic development.

4   While the focus of this analysis is on the impact of economic integration and linkages on social policies and programs, Gomez and Gunderson (2002) also discuss the impact on various labour market *outcomes* such as wages, wage inequality, wage structures, employment and mobility, as well as on the internal workplace practices of firms. The latter are also emphasized in Chaykowski and Gunderson, 2001, 2002.

5   Evidence that wage inequality had been exacerbated by trade liberalization (albeit less so than by technological change) is summarized in Cline (1997), Collins (1996), Richardson (1995) and Wood (1996). Feenstra and Hanson (1997) also indicate that foreign direct investment by the United States in Mexico has increased wage inequality in both countries, by increasing the demand for skilled labour in Mexico and reducing the demand for skilled labour in the United States.

6   The importance of minimum wages and unions is emphasized in DiNardo, Fortin and Lemieux (1996), DiNardo and Lemieux (1997), Lee (1999), Lemieux (1993) and Fortin and Lemieux (1997).

7   Dahlby (1993) and Kesselman (1996) mention how almost all of the cost of payroll taxes initially imposed on employers is ultimately shifted back to labour.

8   Examples of benefits to employers from such policy initiatives are discussed in Gunderson (1998a, 1999) and Chaykowski and Gunderson (2001).

9   As aptly stated by Cameron and Stein (2000, p. S27): "Crime, social disorder, disease and poverty all reduce a country's competitiveness; other things being equal, people and firms will prefer to locate in areas where the quality of life is good."

10   Evidence on the effect of labour and social policies and regulations on plant location decisions is discussed in Gunderson (1998a, p. 41) and Gunderson (1999, p. 92).

11 International evidence that a viable-size public sector is conducive to attracting investment is provided in the United Nation's *World Public Sector Report*, 2001.

12 For a discussion of corporate codes of conduct, see Compa and Darricarrère (1996), Erickson and Mitchell (1996) and Liubicic (1998).

13 For a discussion of the OECD and ILO guidelines, see Gunther (1992) and Blanpain (2000).

14 The NAALC is discussed in Diamond (1996) and Robinson (1994).

15 Social clauses in the EU are discussed in Addison and Siebert (1992, 1994), Due, Madsen and Stroby-Jensen (1991) and Sapir (1996).

16 For a discussion of the emulation of best practices fostering convergence of human resource and workplace practices within the internal labour markets of firms, see Chaykowski and Gunderson (2001) and Katz and Darbishire (2000). Divergence can also occur, however, in many areas as when pattern bargaining breaks down and wages and employment terms reflect different abilities to pay.

17 We would like to thank Michael Smith for reminding us of this extremely pertinent case, and reminding us also that policy emulation is not strictly a direct effect of economic integration but rather a second-order effect that can occur even in the absence of such integration.

18 As summarized in Gunderson (1996), evidence on convergence of growth rates across countries is provided in Barro (1991), across states in the United States in Barro and Sala-I-Martin (1991), and across provinces in Canada in Helliwell (1996), Lee and Coulombe (1995) and Milne and Tucker (1992).

19 Evidence that enhanced growth in low-income countries fosters upward harmonization in their labour standards and social policies is provided in Fields (1995), Freeman (1994) and Krueger (1996). Casella (1996) provides a formal model of the process.

20 See Lucas (1988) and Romer (1986, 1990) for early studies on endogenous growth.

21 See Arthurs (1989) and David (1986) for early work on path dependence, with numerous examples discussed in Krugman (1991) and a subsequent discussion in Gunderson (1998b), and within the realm of social policy in Banting, Hoberg and Simeon (1997).

22 Embeddedness perspectives are outlined in Granovetter (1985), building upon earlier work by Karl Polanyi as outlined in Granovetter (1993).

23 The experience of the EU in this regard is illustrative. Despite adopting a common passport for over a decade, Europe still displays low mobility rates across countries.

24 See Coleman (1988) and Putnam (2000).

25 The discussion in this section follows from the analysis in Gunderson (2002a), which outlines the barriers that inhibit the adoption and diffusion of best practices in the area of workplace initiatives and human resource practices.

26 The Economist recently ran a cover page story entitled "The Retirement Age: Bin it", *The Economist*, November 14-20, 2002, p. 14.

27 Studies by political scientists include Garrett (1996, 1998a, 1998b), Hallerberg and Basinger (1998), Steinmo and Swank (2001), Swank (1998) and Quinn (1997). The studies by economists were Grubert (2001) and Rodrik (1997).

ACKNOWLEDGMENTS

WE ARE GRATEFUL for the comments received at the November 20-22, 2002, meeting of the North American Linkages project, held in Montreal. In particular we are grateful to Michael Smith for his helpful and detailed comments.

BIBLIOGRAPHY

Addison, J., and W. Siebert. "The Social Charter: Whatever Next?" *British Journal of Industrial Relations* 30 (1992): 495-513.

———. "Recent Developments in Social Policy in the New European Union." *Industrial and Labor Relations Review* 48 (October 1994): 5-27.

Aligisakis, M. "Labour Disputes in Western Europe: Typology and Tendencies." *International Labour Review* 136 (1997): 73-94.

Arthurs, B. "Competing Technologies and Lock-In by Historical Events." *Economic Journal* 99 (March 1989): 116-131.

Avi-Yonah, R. "Globalization, Tax Competition, and the Fiscal Crises of the Welfare State." *Harvard Law Review* 113 (May 2000): 1573-1674.

Banting, K. "The Social Policy Divide: The Welfare State in Canada and the United States." In *Degrees of Freedom: Canada and the United States in a Changing World*. Edited by K. Banting, G. Hoberg and R. Simeon. Montreal and Kingston: McGill-Queen's University Press, 1997.

Banting, K., G. Hoberg and R. Simeon. "Introduction." In *Degrees of Freedom: Canada and the United States in a Changing World*. Edited by K. Banting, G. Hoberg and R. Simeon. Montreal and Kingston: McGill-Queen's University Press, 1997.

Barro, R. "Economic Growth in a Cross Section of Countries." *Quarterly Journal of Economics* 105 (1991): 407-443.

Barro, R., and X. Sala-I-Martin. "Convergence Across States and Regions." *Brookings Papers on Economic Activity* 1 (1991): 107-158.

Benjamin, D. "Minimum Wages in Canada." In *Labor Market Policies in Canada and Latin America*. Edited by A. Berry. Boston: Kluwer Academic Publishers, 2001.

Benjamin, D., M. Gunderson and C. Riddell. *Labour Market Economics: Theory, Evidence and Policy in Canada*. Toronto: McGraw-Hill, 2002.

Betcherman, G., and M. Gunderson. "Canada-U.S. Free Trade and Labour Relations." *Labor Law Journal* 41 (August 1990): 444-460.

Blanpain, R. (ed.) "Multinational Enterprises and the Social Challenges of the XXIst Century: The ILO Declaration on Fundamental Principles at Work — Public and Private Corporate Codes of Conduct." *Bulletin of Comparative Labour Relations* 37 (2000), special issue.

Block, R., and K. Roberts. *An Analysis of Labor Standards in the United States and Canada*. East Lansing: Michigan State University, 1997.

Boothe, P., and D. Purvis. "Macroeconomic Policy in Canada and the United States." In *Degrees of Freedom: Canada and the United States in a Changing World*. Edited by

K. Banting, G. Hoberg and R. Simeon. Montreal and Kingston: McGill-Queen's University Press, 1997.

Boychuk, G., and K. Banting. "The Paradox of Convergence: National Versus Subnational Patterns of Convergence in Canadian and U.S. Income Maintenance Policy." In *North American Linkages: Opportunities and Challenges for Canada*. Edited by Richard G. Harris. The Industry Canada Research Series. Calgary: University of Calgary Press, 2003, pp. 533-572.

Bronfenbrenner, K. *Uneasy Terrain: The Impact of Capital Mobility on Workers, Wages and Union Organizing*. Washington (DC): U.S. Trade Deficit Review Commission, 2000.

Cameron, D., and J. Gross Stein. "Globalization, Culture and Society: The State as a Place Amidst Shifting Spaces." *Canadian Public Policy* 26, Supplement (August 2000): S15-S34.

Casella, A. "Free Trade and Evolving Standards." In *Fair Trade and Harmonization, Vol. 1: Economic Analysis*. Edited by J. Bhagwati and R. Hudec. Cambridge (MA): MIT Press, 1996.

Castro-Rea, J. "Towards a Single North American Policy? The Effects of NAFTA on Mexican and Canadian Domestic Politics." In *Economic Integration in the Americas*. Edited by C. Paraskevopoulos, R. Grinspun and G. Eaton. Brookfield: Edward Elgar, 1996.

Chaykowski, R., and M. Gunderson. "The Implication of Globalization for Labour and Labour Markets." In *Globalization and the Canadian Economy: Implications for Labour Markets, Society and the State*. Edited by R. Chaykowski. Kingston: Queen's University School of Policy Studies, 2001.

——. "North American Labour Policy Under a Transformed Economic and Workplace Environment." In *Work and Employment Relations in the High-Performance Workplace*. Edited by G. Murray, J. Bélanger, A. Gilles and P.-A. Lapointe. New York: Continuum, 2002.

Cheal, D. "Aging and Demographic Change." *Canadian Public Policy* 26, Supplement (August 2000), pp. S109-S123.

Cline, W. *Trade and Wage Inequality*. Washington (DC): Institute for International Economics, 1997.

Coleman, J. "Social Capital in the Creation of Human Capital." *American Journal of Sociology* 94 (1988): S95-S121.

Collins, S. (ed.) *Imports, Exports and the American Worker*. Washington (DC): The Brookings Institution, 1996.

Compa, L., and T. Darricarrère. "Private Labor Rights Enforcement Through Corporate Codes of Conduct." In *Human Rights, Labor Rights, and International Trade*. Edited by L. Compa and S. Diamond. Philadelphia: University of Pennsylvania Press, 1996.

Dahlby, B. "Payroll Taxes." In *Business Taxation in Ontario*. Edited by A. Maslove. Toronto: University of Toronto Press, 1993.

David, P. "Understanding the Economics of QWERTY." In *Economic History and the Modern Economist*. Edited by W. Parker. London: Basil Blackwell, 1986.

Dewees, D. "Private Participation in Workers' Compensation." In *Workers' Compensation: Foundation for Reform*. Edited by M. Gunderson and D. Hyatt. Toronto: University of Toronto Press, 2000.

De Wet, E. "Labour Standards in the Globalized Economy: The Inclusion of a Social Clause in the General Agreement on Tariffs and Trade / World Trade Organization." *Human Rights Quarterly* 17 (1995).

Diamond, S. "Labor Rights in the Global Economy: A Case Study of the North American Free Trade Agreement." In *Human Rights, Labor Rights, and International Trade*. Edited by L. Compa and S. Diamond. Philadelphia: University of Pennsylvania Press, 1996.

DiNardo, J., N. Fortin and T. Lemieux. "Labor Market Institutions and the Distribution of Wages, 1973-1992: A Semi-Parametric Approach." *Econometrica* (1996): 1001-1044.

DiNardo, J., and T. Lemieux. "Diverging Male Wage Inequality in the United States and Canada, 1981-88: Do Institutions Explain the Difference?" *Industrial and Labor Relations Review* 50 (1997): 629-651.

Donner, A. (chair). *Working Time: the Report of the Task Force on Hours of Work and Overtime*. Toronto: Ontario Ministry of Labour, 1987.

Due, J., D. Madsen and C. Stroby-Jensen. "The Social Dimension: Convergence or Divergence of IR in the Single European Market." *Industrial Relations Journal* (Summer 1991): 85-102.

Elliott, K., and R. Freeman. *White Hats or Don Quixotes? Human Rights Vigilantes in the Global Economy*. NBER Working Paper No. 8102. National Bureau of Economic Research, January 2001.

Erickson, C., and D. Mitchell. "Labour Standards in International Trade Agreements." *Labour Law Journal* 47 (December 1996): 763-773.

Fields, G. *Trade and Labour Standards: A Review of the Issues*. Paris: OECD, 1995.

Feenstra, R., and G. Hanson. "Foreign Direct Investment and Relative Wages: Evidence from Mexico's Maquilladoras." *Journal of International Economics* 42 (1997):371-393.

Freeman, R. "A Hard-Headed Look at Labour Standards." In *Creating Economic Opportunities: The Role of Labour Standards in Economic Restructuring*. Edited by W. Sengenberger and D. Campbell. Geneva: International Labour Office, 1994.

——. "Is the U.S. Labor Market the Model for Advanced Countries?" *Canadian Public Policy* 26, Supplement (2000): 187-200.

Fortin, N., and T. Lemieux. "Institutional Changes and Rising Wage Inequality: Is There a Linkage?" *Journal of Economic Perspectives* 11 (Spring 1997): 75-96.

Garrett, G. "Capital Mobility, Trade and the Domestic Politics of Economic Policy." In *Internationalization and Domestic Politics*. Edited by R. Keohane and H. Milner. Cambridge: Cambridge University Press, 1996.

——. *Partisan Politics in a Global Economy*. Cambridge: Cambridge University Press, 1998a.

——. "Global Markets and National Politics: Collision Course or Virtuous Circle?" *International Organisation* 52 (1998b): 787-824.

Gomez, R. "Multilateral Worker Protection in an Era of Footloose Capital." In *Human Resource Development and Workplace Governance in the Caribbean*. Edited by N. Cowell and C. Branche. Kingston: Ian Randle Publishers Ltd., 2002.

Gomez, R., and M. Gunderson. "The Integration of Labour Markets in North America." In *Capacity for Choice: Canada in a New North America*. Edited by G. Hoberg. Toronto: University of Toronto Press, 2002.

Gomez, R., M. Gunderson and A. Luchak. "Mandatory Retirement: Lessons from Canada." *Employee Relations: An International Journal* (September 2002).

Granovetter, M. "Economic Action and Social Structure: The Problem of Embeddedness." *American Journal of Sociology* 91 (November 1985): 481-510.

——. "The Nature of Economic Relationships." In *Explorations in Economic Sociology.* Edited by R. Swedberg. New York: Russel Sage Foundation, 1993.

Green, D., and W.C. Riddell. "The Economic Effects of Unemployment Insurance in Canada." *Journal of Labor Economics* 11, 1, Part II (January 1993): S96-S147.

Grubert, H. "Tax Planning by Companies and Tax Competition by Governments." *International Taxation and Multinational Activity.* Edited by J. Hines Jr. Chicago: University of Chicago Press, 2001.

Gunderson, M. *Comparable Worth and Gender Discrimination: An International Perspective.* Geneva: International Labour Office, 1994.

——. "Regional Productivity and Income Convergence in Canada Under Increasing Economic Integration." *Canadian Journal of Regional Science* 19 (Spring 1996): 1-24.

——. "Harmonization of Labour Policies Under Trade Liberalization." *Industrial Relations* 53, 1 (1998a): 24-52.

——. "Regional Impacts of Trade and Investment on Labour." *Canadian Journal of Regional Science* 21 (Summer 1998b): 197-226.

——. "Labour Standards, Income Distribution and Trade." *Integration and Trade* 3 (January 1999): 82-104.

——. "North American Economic Integration and Globalization." In *The State of Economics: Festschrift in Honour of David Slater.* Edited by P. Grady and A. Sharpe. Montreal and Kingston: McGill-Queen's University Press, 2001.

——. *Rethinking Productivity from a Workplace Perspective.* Ottawa: Canadian Policy Research Networks, 2002a.

——. "Collective Bargaining and Dispute Resolution in the Public Sector." *Handbook on Public Administration.* Edited by C. Dunn. Oxford University Press, 2002b.

——. "The Evolution and Mechanics of Pay Equity in Ontario." *Canadian Public Policy* 28 (May 2002c): S117-S131.

Gunderson, M., and D. Hyatt. "Do Injured Workers Pay for Reasonable Accommodation?" *Industrial and Labor Relations Review* 50 (October 1996): 92-104.

——. "Privatization of Workers' Compensation: Will the Cure Kill the Patient?" *International Journal of Law and Psychiatry* 22 (1999): 547-565.

——. "Foundation for Worker's Compensation Reform." In *Workers' Compensation: Foundation for Reform.* Edited by M. Gunderson and D. Hyatt. Toronto: University of Toronto Press, 2000a.

——. "Workforce and Workplace Change: Implications for Injuries and Compensation." In *Injury and the New World of Work.* Edited by T. Sullivan. Vancouver: UBC Press, 2000b.

——. "Union Impact on Compensation, Productivity and Management of the Organization." In *Union-Management Relations in Canada,* 4th ed. Edited by M. Gunderson, A. Ponak and D. Taras. Toronto: Addison-Wesley, 2001.

Gunderson, M., D. Hyatt and J. Pesando. "Public Pension Plans in the United States and Canada." In *Employee Benefits and Labor Markets in Canada and the United States.*

Edited by W. Alpert and S. Woodbury. Kalamazoo (MI): Upjohn Institute for Employment Research, 2000.

Gunderson, M., D. Hyatt and A. Ponak. "Strikes and Dispute Resolution." In *Union-Management Relations in Canada*. 4th ed. Edited by M. Gunderson, A. Ponak and D. Taras. Toronto: Addison-Wesley, 2001.

Gunderson, M., and C. Riddell. "Jobs, Labour Standards and Promoting Competitive Advantage: Canada's Policy Challenge." *Labour* (1995): S125-S148.

——. "Unemployment Insurance: Lessons from Canada." In *Labor Market Policies in Canada and Latin America*. Edited by A. Berry. Boston: Kluwer Academic Publishers, 2001.

Gunther, H. "The Tripartite Declaration of Principles Concerning Multinational Enterprises and Social Policy." *International Encyclopedia for Labour Law and Industrial Relations*. Vol. 1. Edited by R. Blanpain. London: Kluwer, 1992.

Hallerberg, M., and S. Basinger. "Internationalization and Changes in Tax Policy in OECD Countries." *Comparative Political Studies* 31 (1998): 321-353.

Helliwell, J. "Convergence and Migration Amongst Provinces." *Canadian Journal of Economics* 29 (1996): 324-330.

——. *How Much Do National Borders Matter?* Washington (DC): Brookings Institution Press, 1998.

——. "Canada: Life Beyond the Looking Glass." *Journal of Economic Perspectives* 15 (Winter 2001): 107-134.

Hines, J. "Tax Policies and the Activities of Multinational Corporations." *Fiscal Policy: Lessons from Economic Research*. Edited by A. Auerbach. Cambridge: MIT Press, 1997.

Hoberg, G. "Governing the Environment: Comparing Canada and the United States." In *Degrees of Freedom: Canada and the United States in a Changing World*. Edited by K. Banting, G. Hoberg and R. Simeon. Montreal and Kingston: McGill-Queen's University Press, 1997.

——. "Canada and North America Integration." *Canadian Public Policy* 26, Supplement (August 2000): S35-S50.

Hornstein, Z. (ed.) *Outlawing Age Discrimination: Foreign Lessons, UK Choices*. Bristol: Policy Press, 2001.

Howse, R., and M. Chandler. "Industrial Policy in Canada and the United States." In *Degrees of Freedom: Canada and the United States in a Changing World*. Edited by K. Banting, G. Hoberg and R. Simeon. Montreal and Kingston: McGill-Queen's University Press, 1997.

International Labour Organization. *The ILO, Standard Setting and Globalization: Report of the Director General*. Geneva: ILO, 1997.

Jacoby, S. (ed.) *The Workers of Nations: Industrial Relations in a Global Economy*. Cambridge: Oxford University Press, 1995.

Katz, H., and O. Darbishire. *Converging Divergences: Worldwide Changes in Employment Systems*. Ithaca (NY): ILR Press/Cornell University Press, 2000.

Kesselman, J. "Payroll Taxes in the Finance of Social Security." *Canadian Public Policy* 22 (June 1996): 162-179.

Kech, M., and K. Sikkink. *Activists Beyond Borders: Advocacy Networks in International Politics*. Ithaca (NY): Cornell University Press, 1998.

Klein, N. *No Logo: Taking Aim at the Brand Bullies*. New York: Picador, 1999.

Kralj, B. "Occupational Health and Safety: Effectiveness of Economic and Regulatory Mechanisms." In *Workers' Compensation: Foundation for Reform*. Edited by M. Gunderson and D. Hyatt. Toronto: University of Toronto Press, 2000.

Krueger, A. *Observations on International Labor Standards and Trade*. NBER Working Paper No. 5632. National Bureau of Economic Research, June 1996.

Krugman, P. *Geography and Trade*. Cambridge (MA): MIT Press, 1991.

Kumar, P. *From Uniformity to Divergence: Industrial Relations in Canada and the United States*. Kingston: Queen's University IRC Press, 1993.

Lee, D. "Wage Inequality in the U.S. During the 1980s: Rising Dispersion or Falling Minimum Wage?" *Quarterly Journal of Economics* 114 (August 1999): 977-1023.

Lee, F., and S. Coulombe. "Regional Productivity Convergence in Canada." *Canadian Journal of Economics* 18 (1995): 39-56.

Lemieux, T. "Unions and Wage Inequality in Canada and the United States." In *Small Differences that Matter: Labor Markets and Income Maintenance in Canada and the United States*. Edited by D. Card and R. Freeman. Chicago: University of Chicago Press, 1993.

Lin, N., K. Cook and R. Burt. *Social Capital: Theory and Research*. New York: Aldine de Gruyter, 2001.

Lipset, S.M. *Continental Divide: The Values and Institutions of the United States and Canada*. New York: Routledge, 1989.

Lipsig-Mummé, C. "Trade Unions and Labour Relations in a Comparative Perspective." In *Union-Management Relations in Canada*. 4th ed. Edited by M. Gunderson, A. Ponak and D. Taras. Toronto: Addison-Wesley, 2001.

Liubicic, R. "Corporate Codes of Conduct and Product Labelling Schemes: The Limits and Possibilities of Promoting International Labor Rights Through Private Initiatives." *Law and Policy in International Business* 30, 1 (1998): 112-158.

Lucas, R. "On the Mechanics of Economic Development." *Journal of Monetary Economics* 22 (1988): 3-42.

Lund, J., and C. Maranto. "Public Sector Law: An Update." In *Public Sector Employment in Transition*. Edited by D. Belman, M. Gunderson and D. Hyatt. Madison: Industrial Relations Research Association, 1996.

Manfredi, C. "The Judicialization of Politics: Rights and Public Policy in Canada and the United States." In *Degrees of Freedom: Canada and the United States in a Changing World*. Edited by K. Banting, G. Hoberg and R. Simeon. Montreal and Kingston: McGill-Queen's University Press, 1997.

Maskus, K. *Should Core Labor Standards Be Imposed Through International* Policy? Washington (DC): World Bank Working Paper No. 1817, 1997.

McBride, S., and R. Williams. "Globalisation and the Restructuring of Labor Markets and Policy Convergence: The OECD 'Jobs Strategy'" *Global Social Policy* 1, 3 (2001): 281-309.

Milne, W., and M. Tucker. "Income Convergence Across Canadian Provinces." *Atlantic Canada Economic Association Papers* 21 (1992): 170-182.

Mukand, S., and D. Rodrik. *In Search of the Holy Grail: Policy Convergence, Experimentation, and Economic Performance*. NBER Working Paper No. 9134. National Bureau of Economic Research, 2002.

Organisation for Economic Co-operation and Development. *Taxing Profits in a Global Economy*. Paris: OECD, 1991.

——. *Labour Market Outlook*. Paris: OECD, 1994.

Olewiler, N. *National Tax Policy for an International Economy: Divergence in a Converging World?* Bell Canada Papers on Economic and Public Policy, McGill-Queen's University Press, 1999.

Poddar, S., T. Neubig and M. English. "Emerging Trends and Their Implications for the Tax Mix and the Taxation of Capital." *Canadian Tax Journal* 48, 1 (2000): 101-123.

Putnam, R. *Bowling Alone: The Collapse and Revival of American Community*. New York: Simon and Schuster, 2000.

Quinn, D. "The Correlates of Change in International Financial Regulation." *American Political Science Review* 91 (1997): 531-552.

Richardson, J.D. "Income Inequality and Trade." *Journal of Economic Perspectives* 9 (1995): 33-55.

Riddell, W.C. "Unionization in Canada and the United States." In *Small Differences that Matter: Labour Markets and Income Maintenance in Canada and the United States*. Edited by D. Card and R. Freeman. Chicago: University of Chicago Press, 1993.

Riddell, C., and W.C. Riddell. "Changing Patterns of Unionisation: the North American Experience 1984-1998." Discussion Paper. University of British Columbia, Department of Economics, June 2001.

Robinson, I. "NAFTA, Social Unionism and Labour Movement Power in Canada and the United States." *Relations industrielles/ Industrial Relations* 49 (1994).

Rodrik, D. *Has Globalization Gone Too Far?* Washington (DC): Institute for International Economics, 1997.

Romer, P. "Increasing Returns and Long-Run Growth." *Journal of Political Economy* 94 (1986): 1002-1037.

——. "Endogenous Technological Change." *Journal of Political Economy* 98 (1990): 71-101.

Sapir, A. "Trade Liberalization and the Harmonization of Social Policies: Lessons from European Integration." In *Fair Trade and Harmonization, Vol. 1: Economic Analysis*. Edited by J. Bhagwati and R. Hudec. Cambridge (MA): MIT Press, 1996.

Simeon, R., G. Hoberg and K. Banting. "Globalization, Fragmentation, and the Social Contract." In *Degrees of Freedom: Canada and the United States in a Changing World*. Edited by K. Banting, G. Hoberg and R. Simeon. Montreal and Kingston: McGill-Queen's University Press, 1997.

Slemrod, J. "Are Corporate Tax Rates, or Countries, Converging?" University of Michigan, 2001.

Steinmo, S., and D. Swank. "The New Political Economy of Taxation in Advanced Capitalist Democracies." *American Journal of Political Science*, 2001.

Swank, D. "Funding the Welfare State: Globalization and the Taxation of Business in Advanced Market Economies." *Political Studies* 46 (1998): 671-692.

Thomason, R., and J. Burton. "The Costs of Workers' Compensation in Ontario and British Columbia." In *Workers' Compensation: Foundation for Reform*. Edited by M. Gunderson and D. Hyatt. Toronto: University of Toronto Press, 2000.

Tiebout, C. "A Pure Theory of Local Expenditure." *Journal of Political Economy* 64 (1956): 416-424.

Trejo, S. "Compensating Differentials and Overtime Pay Regulation." *American Economic Review* 81 (September 1991): 719-740.

United Nations. *World Public Sector Report.* Geneva: UN, 2001.

Visser, J. "Why Fewer Workers Join Unions in Europe." *British Journal of Economics* 49 (2002): 403-430.

Weintraub, S. *NAFTA: What Comes Next?* Washington (DC): Centre for Strategic and International Studies, 1994.

Wilson, P. "The Role of Taxes in Location and Sourcing Decisions." In *Studies in International Taxation.* Edited by A. Giovannini, R.G. Hubbard and J. Slemrod. 1993.

Wood, A. "How Trade Hurt Unskilled Workers." *Journal of Economic Perspectives* 9 (1996): 57-80.

Comment

Michael R. Smith
McGill University

GOMEZ AND GUNDERSON HAVE PRODUCED a characteristically thorough review of the possible and apparent effects on social policy of North American economic integration. Their study is so thorough that reading it was, at times, somewhat irritating. Each time I thought I might have detected a gap in their treatment, a couple of pages later they promptly filled it. My interpretation of their general conclusion is that there are substantial forces pushing towards convergence of social policies but that a great deal of policy diversity remains, largely because of varying preferences across political units.[1] I think that they are right. So, all I can offer are some suggestions with respect to the overall structure of their argument.

This structure is presented in Box 1. The list demonstrates the thoroughness of their review of the evidence. Nonetheless, it seems to me that two important areas are missing — education and training, and health, which have as much to do with social policy, I would have thought, as, say, policies on successor rights in unionized establishments. It may be true, as they note, that health and education have effects on economic growth. But so do the other factors they list. Still, confining myself for the moment to the factors they consider, I suggest, in Box 2, a somewhat different way of arranging the issues. The main

---

BOX 1

THE STRUCTURE OF THE GOMEZ/GUNDERSON STUDY

Reasons for convergence

Reasons for divergence

Evidence of convergence / divergence under 14 headings:

- Union density and labour laws
- Strikes and industrial conflicts
- Minimum wages
- Unemployment insurance
- Workers' compensation
- Health and safety legislation
- Pay equity legislation
- Employment equity
- Age discrimination and mandatory retirement
- Pensions
- Welfare and family benefits
- Overall social expenditures
- Labour standards in general
- Taxes

---

point of it is to say that in the outcomes they focus on, there are two main mechanisms that might lead *governments* onto a path of policy convergence. One involves the effects of economic linkages on taxation. The other involves their effects on the extent to which the regulations they impose increase the costs, and reduce the international competitiveness, of domestic employers.

At the same time, the economic linkages may have direct effects on employer options. Suppose that, at some point in time, employers are able to offer some range of benefits because they are sheltered from competition — that is, suppose that they share *rents* with their employees. Then, suppose that, at a later point in time — after, say, the FTA and NAFTA — the environment becomes more competitive. The rents formerly shared would disappear and employers would be forced to strip away the benefits that constituted the employee share of the rents. This is not, strictly speaking, a question of social policy. But it may have effects on employers' willingness to accept costly social policies with little protest. It may also lead to a more aggressive search for means of evasion. Gomez and Gunderson rightly raise the issue of enforcement (p. 317). Insofar as employers move out of a particular benefit area it may, besides, put increased pressure on the government to move into that area.[2]

Consider the issues raised by Gomez and Gunderson with Box 2 in mind.

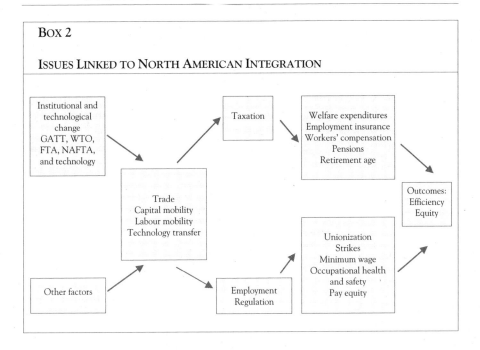

BOX 2

ISSUES LINKED TO NORTH AMERICAN INTEGRATION

TAXATION

A CENTRAL POINT THAT I WANT TO MAKE with Box 2 is that taxation is *not just* one potential effect of North American integration along with many others. A range of other potential effects is contingent on what happens to the taxing capacity of governments. In the context of whatever legislation exists, people's retirement choices will be influenced by their post-retirement income, which means their pension to some significant degree. But government-provided pensions are often funded on a pay-as-you-go basis — out of tax revenues, that is. Supporting a particular pension level would be a more wrenching decision where a tax base is being squeezed. The same thing is true of health, education, welfare, unemployment insurance, and (possibly) worker compensation programs. All this is to suggest that a discussion of taxation probably ought to feature more prominently in the study.

The conclusion to this section of their study is fairly inconclusive. One might paraphrase it as follows: it all depends on who you believe. Broadly speaking, if you believe political scientists, there is no tax convergence. If you believe economists, there is tax convergence. Let me elaborate a bit on two of the studies of tax trends cited by Gomez and Gunderson. Olewiler (1999) is an economist. Poddar, Neubig and English (2000) are or were employees of the

Ernst & Young accounting firm. The results of the two studies are summarized in Box 3.

What do the findings from these two studies suggest? First, there is no evidence of convergence in tax rates over the period when the General Agreement on Tariffs and Trade (GATT) and the WTO were integrating the markets of rich countries across the world. Second, there is no evidence of convergence in the tax rates of Canada and the United States during the period when the effects of the FTA and NAFTA were added to those of the GATT and WTO. Third, the differentials in tax rates between countries have been, and remain, large.

BOX 3

TAX TRENDS ACCORDING TO OLEWILER (1999)

Broadly speaking, from the late 1970s to the mid-1990s:
- Across a subset of OECD countries, there was no overall change in the marginal tax rate for high-income earners.
- Marginal tax rates rose for young, single people in 12 of 15 OECD countries — though, in principle, these should be among the most mobile employees.
- On average, the tax burden on middle-income employees in G7 countries rose.
- Corporate tax rates have fluctuated but were, on average, about as high in 1997 as they had been in 1983.
- The standard deviation of corporate tax rates across countries rose over the period.
- In 1995, there was quite a wide variation (ranging from about 32 percent in Japan to below 20 percent in the United Kingdom) in effective tax rates — that is, rates adjusted for various allowances including, for example, research and development expenditures.
- By industry, effective tax rates on business in Canada are substantially different from tax rates in the United States.
- From 1975 to 1996, taxes as a percentage of GDP rose in Canada, the United States, a sample of European countries, and in the OECD as a whole.
- In aggregate, there is some evidence of a displacement of taxes to less mobile factors.

TAX TRENDS ACCORDING TO PODDAR, NEUBIG AND ENGLISH (2000)

- Government revenue as a percentage of GDP was higher in 1997 than in 1965 in all of the G7 countries. In five of those countries, the 1997 percentage was the highest of the eight points in time for which a percentage was reported.
- Corporate taxes as a percentage of GDP in Canada were about as high in 1997 as in 1965, but in the United States there has been a fall of slightly more than a one percentage point. Note, however, that corporate taxes count for a small percentage of total tax receipts — 3.8 percent in Canada and 2.8 percent in the United States in 1997.
- In 1997, large variations remained across the G7 countries in the rates of taxation of individuals and corporations.

Poddar, Neubig and English (2000) make it clear that, in their view, tax rates are now subject to strong downward pressures. One of those pressures, they observe, is 'more perfect markets', by which they mean, in part, international economic integration. However, they also identify other important factors producing downward pressures on taxes. I will return to one of those shortly. The point I want to make is that these two studies, at least, suggest astonishing resilience of tax rates despite a secular tendency towards economic integration over the postwar period. But if tax rates *can* remain high within the context of economic integration — and in a number of countries they seem to have done so — so can spending on social programs.

This does leave open the question of how it is possible for tax rates to remain so divergent. Gomez and Gunderson deal with this issue. Taxes may be used to pay for things that attract investment. Education might be an example of this. The authors plausibly suggest that safe streets would also tend to attract investors. Alternatively, taxes may be driving away investors, but the weight of political preferences (however aggregated) may favour the programs that taxes support. Obviously, for purposes of policy, it is very important that we know which of theses accounts is correct — recognizing that both may be correct but relevant to different policy and institutional areas.

OTHER FACTORS

I THINK THAT GOMEZ AND GUNDERSON'S METHOD can be summarized as follows: show that, when all relevant forces are considered together, *either* convergence or divergence is possible; conclude, therefore, that this is an empirical question; then, review the relevant evidence on convergence in general and on a race to the bottom in particular. This procedure might lead one to forget that factors other than economic integration *might* lead to convergence or to outcomes that could indicate a race to the bottom.[3] I will illustrate this with two issues discussed in their study — taxation and unemployment insurance.

Consider, first, trends in taxation. As noted above, Poddar, Neubig and English do conclude that tax rates are currently subject to considerable downward pressure. And we know that Canadian governments have recently taken some timid steps towards tax reduction. Why? One factor they identify is economic integration — though not primarily integration with the United States. Thus: "International tax issues will continue to grow in importance as the barriers to international trade, capital flows, and labour mobility are reduced. International tax competition will increase rather than abating, especially as emerging countries, such as India and China, provide major investment opportunities, in which little or no tax on income from capital exists." (2000, p. 113) It is interesting that they cite pressure from India and China rather than the United States or Mexico. From the standpoint of *North American economic integration,* this is important because there is at least some possibility that further integration might be accompanied by treaties on tax rates imposed on capital.

However, whatever the pressures from economic integration, several other factors are likely to lead to tax cuts, or have already done so. I will only consider one. Taxes had to rise — more or less across the OECD, including the United States — to eliminate the deficits created during the 1970s and 1980s by "activist governments" that "optimistically undertook new expenditure programs" (Poddar, Neubig and English, 2004, p. 104). Once those deficits had been brought under control, it was possible to cut taxes. Something like this has happened in Canada. As far as I can see, a decision to reduce taxes that had been increased to pay down a deficit need have little or nothing to do with economic integration.[4]

Now consider the case of unemployment insurance. Gomez and Gunderson observe (briefly) that, after 1971, Canada had a more generous UI program than the United States, but that a series of reforms in and after 1989 "have been strongly in the direction of convergence to the lower common denominator of the U.S. model" (p. 338). They seem to regard this as evidence of an economic integration effect.

There is a long history of attempts to appraise the efficiency consequences of unemployment insurance programs in general, and of the Canadian program in particular. In 1981, the state of the evidence allowed Hum (1981) to conclude reasonably that UI contributed to the efficiency of labour markets.[5] He thought that it probably did so because it made possible longer job searches which, in turn, increased the likelihood of a good match between job and applicant. As a result of what I consider to be one of the larger accomplishments of Canadian social sciences, we know that this is a naive view. The following findings are pertinent.

- Repeat usage has been a fundamental aspect of the UI system, raising the possibility that the job matches sought have included potential future UI qualification as one consideration (Corak, 1993a).

- Further evidence in support of this interpretation is the fact that the probability of an additional UI claim increased with consecutive claims (Corak, 1993a; Lemieux and MacLeod, 1995, pp. 26-27).[6]

- Still further evidence that some potential employees were seeking packages that included some combination of employment and UI eligibility is the fact that the duration of a claim tended to increase with consecutive claims (Corak, 1993b).

- Further evidence that qualification for UI also became a target for some job-seekers is the fact that employment duration tended to coincide with the average provincial variable employment requirements to qualify for UI (Christofides and McKenna, 1995). And, in the 1988-89 period, the probability of moving out of employment was predicted by the average provincial variable employment requirements (Christofides and McKenna, 1996).

- Seasonal workers tend to terminate their jobs at, or shortly after, the point at which benefits will fill the rest of the 52 week year.[7] The source of this clustering of terminations was layoffs rather than quits. Green and Sargent (1995, p. 46) conclude that this "may suggest a somewhat sophisticated use of the UI system in selecting the termination dates of some jobs ... seasonal layoffs and quits do not occur just when an individual qualifies for UI, but rather at later points where relevant maximum entitlement points are reached."

- The development of job search/UI eligibility matches in particular industries is further suggested by the fact that, among high-frequency UI claimants, residents of Atlantic Canada and Quebec are disproportionately present, as are employees in logging, fishing, forestry, quarrying, construction and some manufacturing industries — in particular wood, food preparation and tobacco (Wesa, 1995; Corak and Pyper, 1995).

- In 1990, a legislative deadlock between the House of Commons and the Senate had the effect of suspending the 10-week UI qualifying requirement, and extending it to 14 weeks in regions where it had formerly been 10 weeks. During the period of the inadvertent change in the qualifying period, the likelihood of shifting out of employment at 10 weeks fell, and the likelihood of shifting out at 14 weeks, and a bit beyond 14 weeks, rose (Green and Riddell, 1995). Note that the shift occurred for layoffs rather than quits.

- Receiving UI did not increase the likelihood of enrolling in a government training program or of interprovincial migration to take a job (Lin, 1995).

- Using a panel study of unemployed Canadians, Crémieux, Fortin, Storer and Van Audenrode (1995a, 1995b) found that recipients of UI spent no more hours in job search than did non-recipients. Repeat users of UI seemed to deploy less effort to find a job.

- In 1993, the UI program was modified. The replacement rate was reduced from 60 percent to 57 percent and (with limited exceptions) benefits for those who quit their job were eliminated (Bill C-113). This, however, had no effect on the total number of people qualifying for UI. What seems to have happened is that quits were reclassified as dismissals (Kuhn, 1995, p. 26).

I think that all of this shows that, by the beginning of the 1990s, it was becoming clear to policy-makers that the more optimistic interpretations of the Canadian UI system were probably wrong. The net effect of the UI system in Canada was not an increase in labour market efficiency. Rather, it led to adaptive behaviour that increased the likelihood of further unemployment. It was also rather expensive, in a context of rising budget deficits. My (perhaps optimistic) interpretation of reductions in the generosity of the Canadian UI system is that it constituted a sensible policy choice, informed by evidence from a body of unusually high quality social research. It had little to do with whatever North American economic integration was going on. I do not, then, interpret those changes as an effect of that integration.

THE REGULATION OF EMPLOYERS

WELFARE, UNEMPLOYMENT INSURANCE AND PENSIONS, all covered in Gomez and Gunderson's study, cost a lot. So do health and education, which are not covered in their study but probably ought to be. We know that the main source of growth in government expenditures has been, in fact, transfer programs (Ruggeri and Hermanutz, 1997). Cost, and therefore, taxing capacity, are central in determining the services provided in these areas, though there may be effects on competitiveness other than cost (say, for example, the tendency for the pre-1991 UI program to freeze people into less productive jobs).

This is not the case for labour relations, the minimum wage, occupational health and safety, and pay equity policies. The only cost to government in these cases is enforcement — and much of that cost can be transferred to private parties — courts or tribunals can be or are empowered to assign costs in disputes.

As was the case with respect to the effects of UI, in each of these areas there are more or less forceful arguments to the effect that efficiency is either increased or unaffected by regulations. There is the endlessly cited example of Freeman and Medoff (1984) who claimed that unions may increase efficiency by providing a vehicle for expressing employee concerns (so that problems get solved and turnover falls) and by encouraging the displacement of incompetent managers. There is Card and Krueger's (1995) argument that a higher minimum wage simply forced employers to raise what they paid to the level required to deter excessive turnover. And it is not hard to come up with an argument that says that work accidents are costly and that there are gains to ensuring that suitable numbers of women are induced to participate in the workforce by non-discriminatory wages.

I remain a bit sceptical with respect to all of these arguments (though less so for work accidents and gender differences in pay).[8] But that does not change the fact that Canada can, if it chooses, maintain a markedly different approach to regulations than the United States. Gomez and Gunderson, appropriately, emphasise this. Canadian governments have clearly maintained a markedly different approach in their labour relations legislation. However, the critical question here is: does it have a cost? It seems to me that the next step is to examine seriously a set of areas of regulations and weigh the evidence for and against arguments — like those of Freeman and Medoff on unionization — that claim some improvement in efficiency from regulations. If there are net improvements in efficiency from, say, labour relations regulations, then there is no need to worry about competitive pressures from North American economic integration. But there may not be efficiency gains. There may be net costs. My guess is that this will prove to be the case for Canada's labour relations legislation.

Of course, even if there are net efficiency costs, regulations might be retained on equity grounds. But an intelligent discussion requires that we know whether there is a loss of efficiency to equity in some regulatory areas, and some estimate of the magnitude of the related costs.

In the meantime, there is some pertinent background information that provides food for thought.[9]

- From 1981 to 1999, multifactor productivity grew in Canada at an annual rate of 0.2 percent as compared to a 0.9 percent rate in the United States.

- From 1981 to 1999, GDP grew at an annual rate of 2.9 percent in Canada and at a 3.6 percent rate in the United States.

- Even though the performance of both countries improved after 1995, the U.S. performance remained superior to Canada's on both indicators (U.S. economic growth of 4.9 percent versus 4.8 percent in Canada; U.S. productivity growth of 1.3 percent versus 1.0 percent in Canada).

Economic growth is not a straightforward concept. Multifactor productivity is even less straightforward, and its measurement problems are huge. Still, the broad trend is clear and is surely reflected in the sustained depreciation of the Canadian dollar, by about 35 percent from the mid-1970s. As Baumol, Blackman, and Wolff (1989) argue, *sustained* currency depreciations are pretty good evidence of poor productivity growth. For most of the last 20 years, Canada has been getting poorer relative to the United States. A reasonable working hypothesis is that this had something to do with our institutions and the social policies that maintain them. Their net effect on growth is probably negative. But growth does seem to be good for the poor in Canada (Zyblock and Lin, 2000). So this is a reason for close scrutiny of policies and institutions, of which Gomez and Gunderson's study can only be regarded as the beginning.

ENDNOTES

1   In the same paragraph where they cite the role of preferences in supporting diversity, they also refer to "the different positive roles played by various policy initiatives." (p. 347) That is to say, sometimes greater social policy generosity may be preferred by investors to less social policy generosity. But it should be clear that this is an argument against the 'race to the bottom' rather than convergence. If economic integration increases the pressures on governments to adopt social policies favourable to investors and if greater social policy generosity is preferred by those investors, then we should observe convergence — either Canada converging upwards to higher standards in the United States or the United States converging upwards to higher standards in Canada.

2   In fact, Gomez and Gunderson discuss an example of a change in employment relations that might originate in a direct effect of competition on employers, unmediated by social policy. I have in mind the discussion of workplace practices (pp. 340-341).

3   Gomez and Gunderson are certainly aware that other factors might be at work in producing convergence or a race to the bottom. But, in its current form, their text seems not to systematically incorporate that possibility.

4   This might be considered to be a variant on Banting's (1997, p. 304) 'convergence as a result of parallel domestic factors'.

5   Tests to that point — and for some time afterwards — typically involved the introduction of a UI dummy variable into a time-series regression where the unemployment rate was endogenous. The methodological difficulties raised by this procedure are well known (Myatt, 1996).

6   Another way of presenting the same result is through the construction of a Lorenz curve of UI spells. On the basis of such an analysis, Lemieux and MacLeod (1995, p. 21) report that "31 percent of claimants who had only one spell of UI over the 21-year period accounted for only 8 percent of total spells, 7 percent of claimants with 11 spells or more accounted for 22 percent of total spells". Their analysis applies to the 1972-92 period. Note that women were excluded from this analysis because of the complication of maternity leave.

7   They do not, it should be clear, cluster at the point where there is qualification for benefits. The clustering is "at the point at which individuals qualify for just enough benefits to fill up the rest of the year" (Green and Sargent, 1995, p. 45). Note that these authors also found a similar effect for non-seasonal jobs, but the magnitude of the effect for these jobs was rather small.

8   I should make it clear that, in aggregate, I am sceptical of these claims. Particular unions in particular circumstances may contribute to more efficient outcomes. For example, there is some evidence that, as compared to the United States, teacher quality is superior

in Canada because teachers unions prevented the decline in relative teachers' earnings that took place in the United States during the 1970s (Economic Council of Canada, 1992, pp. 156-157). Of course, union protection need not be the only method for preserving teacher quality. In any case, Canada does seem to do better than the United States in comparisons of literacy, broadly defined (Tuijnman, 2001).

9 The productivity and growth percentages are taken from Armstrong, Harchaoui, Jackson and Tarkhani (2002). Also relevant are Harris (1999) and Coulombe (2000).

BIBLIOGRAPHY

Armstrong, P., T.M. Harchaoui, C. Jackson and F. Tarkhani. *A Comparison of Canada-U.S. Economic Growth in the Information Age, 1981-2000: The Importance of Investment in Information and Communication Technologies.* No. 11F0027MIE. Ottawa: Statistics Canada, 2002.

Banting, K. "The Social Policy Divide: The Welfare State in Canada and the United States." In *Degrees of Freedom: Canada and the United States in a Changing World.* Edited by K. Banting, G. Hoberg and R. Simeon. Montreal and Kingston: McGill-Queen's University Press, 1997, pp. 267-309.

Baumol, W.J., S.A.B. Blackman and E.N. Wolff. *Productivity and American Leadership: The Long View.* Cambridge (MA): MIT Press, 1989.

Card, D.B., and A.E. Krueger. *Myth and Measurement: The New Economics of the Minimum Wage.* Princeton (NJ): Princeton University Press, 1995.

Christofides, L.N., and C.J. McKenna. *Employment Patterns and Unemployment Insurance.* Ottawa: Human Resources Development Canada, 1995.

———. "Unemployment Insurance and Employment Patterns in Canada." *Canadian Journal of Economics* (1996): S8-S11, special issue.

Corak, M. "Unemployment Insurance Once Again: The Incidence of Repeat Participation in the Canadian UI Program." *Canadian Public Policy* 19 (1993a): 162-176.

———. "Is Unemployment Insurance Addictive? Evidence from the Benefit Durations of Repeat Users." *Industrial and Labor Relations Review* 47 (1993b): 62-72.

Corak, M., and W. Pyper. *Firms, Industries and Cross-Subsidies: Patterns in the Distribution of UI Benefits and Taxes.* Ottawa: Human Resources Development Canada, 1995.

Coulombe, S. *The Canada-U.S. Productivity Growth Paradox.* Working Paper No. 32. Ottawa: Industry Canada, 2000.

Crémieux, P.-Y., P. Fortin, P. Storer and M. Van Audenrode. *Unemployment Insurance and Job Search Productivity.* Ottawa: Human Resources Development Canada, 1995a.

———. *The Impact of Unemployment Insurance on Wages, Search Intensity and the Probability of Re-Employment.* Ottawa: Human Resources Development Canada, 1995b.

Economic Council of Canada. *Education and Training in Canada.* Ottawa, 1992.

Freeman, R.B., and J.L. Medoff. *What Do Unions Do?* New York: Basic Books, 1984.

Green, D.A., and W.C. Riddell. *Qualifying for Unemployment Insurance: An Empirical Analysis of Canada.* Ottawa: Human Resources Development Canada, 1995.

Green, D.A., and T.C. Sargent. *Unemployment Insurance and Employment Durations: Seasonal and Non-Seasonal Jobs.* Ottawa: Human Resources Development Canada, 1995.

Harris, R.G. *Determinants of Canadian Productivity Growth: Issues and Prospects.* Discussion Paper No. 8. Ottawa: Industry Canada, 1999.

Hum, D. *Unemployment Insurance and Work Effort: Issues, Evidence, and Policy Directions.* Toronto: Ontario Economic Council, 1981.

Kuhn, P. *Effects of Bill-113 on UI Take-Up Rates.* Ottawa: Human Resources Development Canada, 1995.

Lemieux, T., and W.B. MacLeod. *State Dependence and Unemployment Insurance.* Ottawa: Human Resources Development Canada, 1995.

Lin, Z. *Interprovincial Labour Mobility in Canada: The Role of Unemployment Insurance, Social Assistance and Training.* Ottawa: Human Resources Development Canada, 1995.

Myatt, T. "Why Do We Know so Little About Unemployment Determination and the Effects of Unemployment Insurance?" In *The Unemployment Crisis: All for Nought?* Edited by B.K. MacLean and L. Osberg. Montreal and Kingston: McGill-Queen's University Press, 1996, pp. 107-128.

Olewiler, N. "National Tax Policy for an International Economy: Divergence in a Converging World?" In *Room to Manoeuvre? Globalization and Policy Convergence.* Edited by T.J. Courchene. Montreal and Kingston: McGill-Queen's University Press, 1999, pp. 345-382.

Poddar, S., T. Neubig and M. English. "Emerging Trends and their Implications for the Tax Mix and the Taxation of Capital." *Canadian Tax Journal* 48 (2000): 101-123.

Ruggeri, G.C., and D. Hermanutz. *Leviathan Revisited: The Growth of Government in Canada since 1961.* Aldershot: Avebury, 1997.

Tuijnman, A. *Benchmarking Adult Literacy in North America: An International Study.* Ottawa: Statistics Canada, 2001.

Wesa, L. *Seasonal Employment and the Repeat Use of Unemployment Insurance.* Ottawa: Human Resources Development Canada, 1995.

Zyblock, M., and Z. Lin. "Trickling Down or Fizzling Out? Economic Performance, Transfers, Inequality, and Low Income in Canada." *Journal of Income Distribution* 9 (2000): 137-154.

Gerard W. Boychuk
University of Waterloo

8

Redistribution, Social Protection and North American Linkages: The Prospects for Distinctive Canadian Social Policy Under Increased North American Labour Mobility

Canada
USA   *I38 P16   J61   H75*
        F22   R12   J11

INTRODUCTION

> Understanding the political economy of labour mobility will be critical to
> anticipating the future of distinctive social policies in Canada.
> Hoberg, Banting and Simeon, 2002, p. 272.

THE PROSPECT OF DEEPENING NORTH AMERICAN LINKAGES raises the issue of whether the limits of *feasible egalitarianism* are coming to be drawn ever more tightly and the ability of Canadian governments to maintain distinctive social policies increasingly constrained.[1] Increased labour market integration is a key element in the debate over possible future scenarios of deepening North American linkages and is likely to become even more important in this debate. (Hakim and Litan, 2002, p. 7; Harris and Schmitt, 2001, p. 1) At the same time, labour mobility is also seen to be key in determining the ability of Canadian governments to maintain distinctive policies of redistribution and social protection:[2] "The durability of the [Canada-U.S.] social policy divide will depend on a variety of forces, including labour mobility and pressures for harmonization of tax levels. The mobility of labour is crucial to Canada's capacity to maintain its distinctive welfare state." (Hoberg, Banting and Simeon, 2002, p. 272)

Labour market integration raises questions analogous to those pertaining to the effects of economic integration on policy latitude more generally: To what extent could different institutional arrangements governing labour market integration impact on Canada's capacity to use income redistribution to meet its social objectives? The answer to this question rests on two related, yet distinct, questions. First, is there evidence within common labour markets of a dynamic of downward harmonization across jurisdictions in redistribution and social protection? Second, to the degree that such evidence exists, to what extent does the operation of a similar dynamic seem likely to shape Canadian policy under various scenarios of increased labour mobility between Canada and the United States? Inextricably linked to this latter question is the issue of the magnitude of existing differences in levels of redistribution and social protection and whether these are sufficiently low in the United States to pull Canadian levels downward.

To answer these questions, the study empirically assesses patterns of convergence and divergence in broad indicators of social protection and redistribution[3] over the 1975-2000 period within a common labour market area (the U.S. states), as well as patterns emerging across neighbouring U.S. states and Canadian provinces. This approach helps to identify the extent to which distinctive redistributive and social protection policies can be maintained across jurisdictions sharing a common labour market even when access to social benefits is relatively unrestricted across jurisdictions. In turn, this level of feasible distinctiveness provides a framework to assess whether existing differences in redistribution and social protection between Canada and the United States could be feasibly maintained in a context of labour market integration.

Evidence from the U.S. states, even closely-linked states, suggests that there is considerable room to maintain distinctive social policies within a common labour market. In addition, while cross-border comparisons are plagued by significant methodological and empirical weaknesses, differences in levels of redistribution and social protection between neighbouring states and provinces do not appear greater, on average, than differences between tightly-linked U.S. states. Thus, there is no a priori reason to assume that existing levels of distinctiveness could not feasibly be maintained under increased labour market integration. In contrast, a more striking cross-border difference is that taxes and government transfers in Canada significantly contribute to making income distributions more uniform across provinces while, in the United States, they exacerbate interstate differences. More pressing than whether existing levels of redistribution and social protection can be maintained within individual provinces is the question of whether the regionally levelling role of Canadian policies can be maintained under increased continental labour market integration.

The first section of the study outlines the conceptual framework for an empirical examination of the linkage between labour market integration, redistribution and social protection. The second section specifies the methodology of the study. The third section outlines the empirical findings. Finally, the fourth section considers the broad implications of these findings and outlines possible avenues for further research.

CONCEPTUAL FRAMEWORK – THE LINK BETWEEN LABOUR MARKET INTEGRATION, REDISTRIBUTION AND SOCIAL PROTECTION

CLEARLY, THERE ARE COMPELLING REASONS to expect that labour market integration will exert pressures on distinctive approaches to redistribution and social protection. However, a consideration of such pressures must be balanced against a consideration of factors that allow or actually encourage policy distinctiveness. How the balance between convergent and non-convergent forces plays out will depend in part on the specific arrangements governing an integrated labour market — especially the framework for access to social benefits. Perceptions of convergence or divergence may also depend on whether the main focus is individual programs and specific levels of taxation or the overall pattern of redistribution.

CONVERGENT DYNAMICS RESULTING FROM LABOUR MARKET INTEGRATION

A STANDARD INTERPRETATION of the harmonizing effects of labour market integration is that the "reduction of impediments to international flows of goods and factors of production ... raise[s] the economic costs of programs by the national state to redistribute income to the poor and to provide economic security for their populations." (Bowles, 2000, p. 2)[4] The overall result is that "trade liberalization and other aspects of globalization are thus thought to restrict the range of redistributive policy which is politically sustainable in democratic nation states." (Bowles, 2000, p. 2)

A central element of the logic for convergence in redistributive and social protection policy resulting from labour mobility is the *push effect*: "a nation-specific tax on a mobile factor induces ... relocation of these factors." Thus, "cross-border mobility of citizens allows the lucky to escape the tax costs of supporting the unlucky." (Bowles, 2000, p. 2) A second convergent dynamic is the *pull effect*: the migration of low-income individuals to jurisdictions with the most favourable redistribution and social protection policies. If they do not harmonize their levels of redistribution and social protection, these jurisdictions run the risk of becoming *welfare magnets*. This is the logic underpinning the *race to the bottom* argument in U.S. social policy literature.[5]

There is probably not much doubt about the existence of such dynamics. The issue is the causal weight of these convergent forces relative both to each other and to forces favourable to policy distinctiveness. Moreover, how forcefully will these dynamics operate under different scenarios for the extension of social benefits within an integrated labour market? Finally, are such dynamics likely to cause convergence only in certain programs or specific types of taxation, or are these effects likely to filter through to cause a more fundamental shift in the overall role of governments in redistribution and social protection?

CONVERGENCE IN WHAT? – MEASURING CONVERGENCE

EXAMINATIONS OF CONVERGENCE typically focus on a single specific element of the redistributive equation — either the program side or the taxation side. However, there is a serious risk of misinterpreting the results of these disaggregated analyses. For example, as Helliwell notes, "… detailed analysis of the tax effects show that while taxes do significantly influence migration decisions, the total effects of even quite large tax differences are surprisingly small." (2002, p. 38) The most obvious potential explanation of this limited impact is that higher taxes may simply be offset by higher transfers, leaving individual actors indifferent across jurisdictions. Similarly, findings of convergence or divergence in either taxes or transfers may mask broader patterns of similarity and difference in the overall redistributive role of the state. In order to avoid mistaking convergence or divergence in either tax burden or program benefits for an overall convergence or divergence in the redistributive role of the state, our study focuses on the *net* impact of *both* taxes and transfers on the income distribution. As Hoberg, Banting and Simeon note, the "… most comprehensive indicator of the distinctiveness of Canada's social policy regime is the overall redistributive impact of the state in the two countries." (2002, p. 266) Framed most broadly, the issue is whether governments are less able to maintain a distinctive overall role in net redistribution and social protection (the combined effects of taxes and transfers) under conditions of labour market integration.

An examination centered on income redistribution through taxes and government transfers has at least four serious shortcomings. The first is that available measures focus primarily on vertical redistribution between different income categories and ignore horizontal redistribution between individuals within the same income category. Being essentially static, neither do such comparisons capture redistribution over time in which the roles of individuals as net contributors or net beneficiaries may change over their life-cycle. Second, the focus on cash income (or cash-equivalent in-kind benefits) and income and payroll taxes may overlook important factors affecting redistribution such as the provision of public goods (which may be consumed disproportionately or valued differently by different income categories), or the differential redistributive effects of other forms of taxation such as user fees for various government services or consumption taxes, both of which are not captured in statistics on after-tax/transfer income. Third, the distribution of market income is treated as exogenously determined even though taxes and government expenditures may have important impacts on it through improved human capital or through incentive and disincentive effects. These effects may differ widely across jurisdictions, but are not captured when focusing on income redistribution. Fourth, a focus on income redistribution ignores the broader issue of wealth redistribution. All four problems reflect the possibility that jurisdictions may be converging on important aspects of policy that are not captured by the specific policy dimension being considered — in this case, the effect of government taxation and spending on the overall distribution of income. However, keeping these caveats in mind, the study considers the possible effects of labour market integration on the latter.

SCENARIOS FOR CANADA-U.S. LABOUR MARKET INTEGRATION: ACCESS TO SOCIAL BENEFITS

THE EFFECTS OF LABOUR MARKET INTEGRATION on governments' ability to maintain a distinctive approach to redistribution and social protection will depend heavily on the institutional arrangements governing labour market integration. Of specific importance with regard to the issue of redistribution and social protection is the basis of social benefit entitlement. There are three alternatives for access to social benefits in an integrated Canada-U.S. labour market, with entitlement being determined by citizenship, residence, or both. As Harris and Schmitt argue, labour market integration does not necessarily imply any one specific model: "Within a true common market there is labor mobility but not necessarily citizenship mobility. That is an individual's rights to social and transfer programs can be defined by citizenship and not available unless one resides in one's home country. [...] Increasing labor mobility therefore may or may not imply increasing access to local social programs and public goods for non-citizen workers." (2001, p. 3) While, access to social benefits may continue to be based on residence and citizenship much as they are now, entitlement could, alternatively, be based primarily on residence with benefits made available to workers from the partner country. Finally, access to social benefits could be extended on the basis of citizenship independent of residence, such that Canadian citizens working in the United States would still qualify for certain Canadian benefits such as health care or employment insurance.

The situation in the European Union (EU) highlights the complexity of the issues raised by the question of access to social benefits in a context of labour mobility. Labour market integration in the European Union has affected the domestic social policy-making of member states through a complex mix of access to social benefits based on citizenship, residence or a combination of both. Regarding the exclusion of non-citizens from benefits, "[a] member state may no longer limit most social benefits to its citizens. As regards 'foreigners' from within the European Union, the state no longer has any power to determine whether foreign people have a right to benefits or not. Benefits must be granted to all or withheld from all. This development is remarkable since 'citizen-making' through social benefits — demarcating the outsider — was a watershed in the history of state-building on the continent ..." (Liebfried and Pierson, 2000, p. 279) Regarding the restriction of social benefit access by residence, "[a] member state may no longer insist that its benefits apply only to its territory and thus may be consumed only there. As a result, today's state can exercise its power to determine the territory of consumption only to a limited extent — basically when providing in-kind or universal means-tested benefits, and still in unemployment insurance." (p. 292) As for the state's ability to maintain a relative monopoly over social policy within its own jurisdictional boundaries, "[a] member state is no longer entirely (though still largely) free to prevent other social policy regimes from directly competing on its own territory with the regime it has built. In Germany, for instance, there are many 'posted' construction workers from other EU countries, who work for extended periods at their national wage level, while covered by many of their home country's social regulations. Thus, the state has lost some of its exclusive power to determine how the people living within its borders are protected ..." (p. 292) Regarding social policy in the European Union, Liebfried and Pierson conclude that "[i]f complete national *de jure* authority in these respects is what sovereignty in social policy is all about, it has already ceased to exist in the EU." (p. 292)

Without debating the likelihood of the adoption of any of these various models under a scenario of Canada-U.S. labour market integration, each has significantly different implications for the dynamics governing redistribution and social protection in an integrated Canada-U.S. labour market. Clearly, extension of access to social benefits on the basis of residence alone is likely to generate pressures on social programs: "Mobility of low-income labour could lead jurisdictions to tighten eligibility criteria to avoid becoming 'welfare magnets'." (Hoberg, Banting and Simeon, 2002, p. 272)[6] Such convergent pressures would not exist under a scenario where social benefits continue to be provided on the basis of both citizenship and residence. However, even in this latter scenario, the push factor by which mobile labour might exit high-tax jurisdictions would still be in operation and may be significant.

The implications of these different scenarios for labour mobility are also likely to differ considerably as a result of asymmetries in current and potential patterns of migration across various ranges of the income distribution. At the upper end of the income distribution, mobility might not be all that affected regardless of social benefit entitlements: "There is a general view that skilled labour is already very mobile across the Canada-U.S. border and thus any further changes in labour mobility provision are likely to have little effect." (Harris and Schmitt, 2001, p. 26)[7] In any case, social benefits make up a significantly lower proportion of total income for high-income earners and, thus, differences in social benefits are much less likely to induce migration. A considerably different picture likely exists for individuals at the bottom of the income distribution, whose access to public benefits acts as a crucial safety net. If public benefits (extended either by the home country or by the host country) are not available to individuals working in the partner country, cross-border labour mobility is likely to be significantly attenuated relative to mobility within countries where social benefits are, generally, reasonably portable. Under this scenario, cross-border labour markets seem more likely to remain significantly segmented in practice for the middle and lower ranges of the income distribution. Finally, those at the very bottom of the income distribution may simply lack the financial wherewithal to pursue more generous benefit arrangements in other jurisdictions regardless of the basis of entitlement.

The study examines the U.S. states, across which access to social benefits is, for the most part, unrestricted. Thus, the discussion is centered primarily on the likely effects of moving towards labour market integration that includes the unrestricted extension of social benefits. In this sense, the U.S. states provide a *hard case*. Some of the aspects of labour market integration among U.S. states — especially the relatively unrestricted access to social benefits across the U.S. labour market — may not obtain in the case of Canada-U.S. labour market integration, and it is very unlikely that Canada-U.S. labour market integration would adopt a more extreme form of integration than currently exists among U.S. states.

THE SCOPE FOR POLICY DISTINCTIVENESS WITHIN A COMMON LABOUR MARKET

THERE ARE TWO BROAD CLASSES OF ARGUMENTS by which levels of redistribution and social protection may differ across jurisdictions even under conditions of factor (capital and labour) mobility. First, while increasing mobility of goods and factors of production "may limit the effectiveness of some conventional strategies of redistribution," it does not "rule out all egalitarian interventions" if these do not contribute to a deadweight economic loss. As such, "[t]here remains a large class of governmental and other collective interventions leading to substantial improvements in the wages, employment prospects, and economic security of the less well off." (Bowles, 2000, p. 4) According to Bowles, there are three ways by which egalitarian redistribution in open economies may succeed: increasing productivity, improving labour discipline, or simply redistributing labour income without eroding effort incentives. (pp. 24-25) These three possibilities provide the explanation for the pattern he observed, by which "some of the more politically and economically successful redistributive policies ... have been implemented in small open economies, which would ... seem to provide a prohibitive environment for egalitarian interventions." (p. 3) He concludes that "unless the cases are entirely idiosyncratic they suggest that the commonplace opposition between globalization and egalitarianism may be overdrawn." (p. 3)

Second, even where redistribution constitutes a deadweight economic loss, differences in social policies within a common labour market may persist, and social policy differences have long been observed within nationally integrated labour markets. To help explain such differences, the Tiebout hypothesis "was originally formulated to explain differing local levels of taxation and public services within a national economy." (Kesselman, 2001, p. 79) Tiebout hypothesized that jurisdictions can co-exist with differing institutions and policy choices in equilibrium under circumstances of complete labour mobility: "Differences in the tastes, preferences, cultures, histories, geographies, and natural resources of nations can lead to differing public policies that are competitive with respect to retaining and attracting diverse groups of individuals." (p. 80) First, redistribution and social protection may generate public goods providing indirect benefits to net contributors including, for example, lower crime rates and greater liveability of urban areas. Second, living in a society with greater levels of social cohesion and social inclusion may be considered by some to be a good in and of itself with differences in such preferences being reflected in differences in redistributive and social protection policies.

Thus, convergence is not a logical necessity but, rather, an empirical possibility that may result from the interplay of distinct and sometimes contradictory dynamics. The issue of the likely effects of labour market integration between Canada and the United States for distinct approaches to redistribution and social protection remains an open empirical question.

METHODOLOGY – EXAMINING U.S. STATES AND U.S. STATES VS. CANADIAN PROVINCES

ASSESSING THE LIKELY MAGNITUDE of constraining effects on redistribution and social protection arising from labour market integration raises two sets of empirical questions. First, what is the evidence regarding the force of convergent factors generated under conditions of labour market integration and relatively unrestricted access to social benefits? Second, do the existing differences in redistribution and social protection in the jurisdictions in which labour market integration is to take place lie outside the range of difference that may be feasibly maintained given the evidence on the first question?

The U.S. states provide the best example for considering the likely effects of Canada-U.S. labour market integration on redistribution and social protection, for three reasons: the high level of labour market integration and relatively unrestricted access to social benefits across jurisdictions, the relative freedom of states to pursue distinct policies of redistribution and social protection and, finally, the geographical proximity of individual states and the high level of mobility among them. First, the United States is a good example of an integrated labour market. While the cross-national comparative literature provides an excellent reference point for examining the possible effects of trade liberalization and capital mobility, for the most part cross-national labour mobility is generally relatively restricted. There are, of course, notable exceptions where barriers to labour mobility have been significantly lowered such as the European Union. However, this example is not necessarily applicable in the North American context. Cultural differences between various EU members are much more robust than cultural differences between Canada and the United States, and thus more likely to act as informal barriers to labour mobility; in contrast, cultural and linguistic barriers to labour mobility among U.S. states are considerably more limited. While the cultural differences between Canada and the United States probably lie somewhere between the magnitude of differences found between European countries and those existing among U.S. states, a focus on the former is likely to provide too conservative an estimate of the likely mobility between Canada and the United States in the context of an integrated labour market.[8] Second, social benefit access across U.S. states is relatively unrestricted in comparison with the much more complex set of arrangements existing in the European Union.

Examining the indirect effects of labour market mobility on redistribution and social protection requires that the jurisdictions in question have the requisite policy independence to adopt distinct approaches to redistribution and social protection. In the United States, there are, of course, important national policies (Social Security pensions for the aged, Supplemental Security Income for the aged and disabled, Medicare, Earned Income Credit) and federal-state programs (Aid to Families with Dependent Children/Temporary Assistance to Needy Families, unemployment insurance, Medicaid) which provide some basic national uniformity in social protection programs while limiting the latitude of individual states to shape distinct approaches to redistribution and social protection. However, as confirmed by evidence on differences in net redistribution among states presented below, states have retained considerable latitude to shape distinct approaches to redistribution and social protection.[9] The situation in Canada is comparable for many of these programs, with two notable exceptions — Employment Insurance, which is fully a federal responsibility, and the federal role in equalization, which does not exist in the United States.[10]

Latitude for distinctive state policy approaches has also been increasing over the past twenty years in the face of significant devolution of the U.S. federal system — often referred to as the "devolution revolution". (Hanson, 1999, pp. 32-33) This reduction in the role of the federal government "... began with President Ronald Reagan, accelerated with the Republican takeover of Congress in 1995, and was aided and abetted by President Bill Clinton's keen desire to balance the federal budget and 'end welfare as we know it'." (Gray, 1999, p. 1) To the degree that federal involvement sheltered individual states from the convergent dynamics generated by a common labour market, the increasing policy responsibility of the states should, over the course of the past twenty years, provide an even clearer indication of the scope for feasible policy distinctiveness in the context of a common labour market with relatively unrestricted access to social benefits.[11]

The U.S. states also seem to provide a reasonable basis of comparison for labour market integration between Canada and the United States due to the high level of mobility and relatively limited distance between states.[12] For example, labour market mobility between relatively far-flung provinces may not be a very good indicator of the likely effects of labour mobility between Canadian provinces and U.S. states because of the relatively small distance between the latter in some notable cases. Harris and Schmitt note, for many provinces, the "[t]he closer proximity of northern U.S. states than distant Canadian provinces ...." (2001, p. 32) This situation was most aptly captured in Krugman's now famous statement that "... Canada is essentially closer to the United States than it is to itself." (1991, p. 2) At the same time, interstate mobility rates in the United States are relatively high — in comparison with cross-national mobility among EU countries and interprovincial mobility in Canada.[13] If interstate mobility rates were lower (or lower than one would hypothetically expect between potentially integrating jurisdictions), it would not be clear that the U.S. example would reveal the full effects of the convergent pressures resulting from labour mobility.

The comparability of U.S. states to the hypothetical situation of a common labour market between Canada and the United States can be further enhanced by examining those states forming the northernmost boundary of the continental United States.[14] Such focus helps to provide greater comparability between U.S. states and Canadian provinces by reducing the diversity found across the 50 U.S. states, which "constitute a much more diversified set of regional economies than the Canadian provinces from the point of view of industrial structure, geography, and climate." (Coulombe and Day, 1999, p. 156) As these authors note, "[t]he border states are fairly similar in both geography and in most cases economic structure to the Canadian provinces" (p. 157) and, as such, provide a similar range of diversity in economic structure as the Canadian provinces. Thus, the study also examines dispersion in redistribution and social protection among this specific sub-set of U.S. states.

This discussion points toward an assumption that, while open to debate, seems reasonable in speculating about the effects of Canada-U.S. labour market integration on distinctive Canadian approaches to redistribution and social protection: *Whatever level of policy distinctiveness tightly-linked U.S. states (such as pairs of contiguous U.S. states, states with high intermigration, and pairs of neighbouring states along the northern U.S. border) have been able to maintain among themselves under conditions of labour market integration and relatively unrestricted access to social benefits should be feasibly attainable between Canada and the United States under similar conditions.*

Ironically, the benefit that the U.S. states provide as an example of relatively independent policy jurisdictions within the framework of a common labour market raises significant problems in assessing the existing degree of difference between Canadian and U.S. levels of redistribution and social protection. Examinations of Canada's ability to maintain policy distinctiveness in a context of increasing labour market integration need to consider the fact that Canadian regions will be integrating — not with some amorphous mass called the United States — but, rather, with particular U.S. regions and states which themselves differ widely in their approaches to redistribution and social protection. Assumptions regarding the magnitude and direction of differences in redistribution and social protection between Canadian provinces and the U.S. states with which they are integrating cannot be drawn simply from national aggregates. Thus, a second element of the study's empirical methodology is to undertake comparisons of levels of redistribution and social protection for specific pairs of neighbouring U.S. states and Canadian provinces.

The study turns to two specific empirical issues: establishing the extent of differences in redistribution and social protection that have existed over time between U.S. states, and (which is more challenging) attempting to assess whether existing differences between Canada and the United States (and Canadian provinces and neighbouring U.S. states more specifically) lie outside this range of feasible policy distinctiveness.

In order to probe these questions, the study compares share gains for the bottom half of the income distribution as well as for the lowest and highest quintiles.[15] (See Appendix B for data sources and methodology.) A significant problem in examining divergence among states in redistribution and social protection is the significance of in-kind benefits in the United States — which are, in many cases, heavily geared towards redistribution (Medicaid, Food Stamps, housing benefits). As these in-kind benefit transfers are a central pillar of the U.S. welfare system, the study compares U.S. states using data that estimate the value of these benefits (including the value of medical benefits) in order to capture their redistributive effects.[16]

However, medical benefits raise more serious difficulties for cross-border comparisons. While, in the United States, medical benefits for the non-elderly are targeted and comprise the single largest income-tested program of social protection for the poor, health benefits are provided on a universal basis in Canada. Quantitative work on the redistributive impact of public health care expenditures in Canada is relatively limited. A recent study has examined the redistributive impact of public health care by assigning the total dollar value of health care consumed. Unfortunately, the approach used in U.S. data is to assign the *fungible* value of medical benefits.[17] Such an approach significantly understates the redistributive impact of medical benefits in the United States relative to the Canadian methodology, and the resulting data are not comparable. Thus, in all direct comparisons of redistribution and social protection between U.S. and Canadian jurisdictions, our study presents two sets of comparisons based on different definitions of government transfer income in the United States: cash transfers only, and in-kind benefit transfers excluding public medical benefits.

EMPIRICAL FINDINGS

THE EMPIRICAL SEGMENT OF THE STUDY is divided into two sections. The first section examines similarities and differences in redistribution and social protection across U.S. states. The second section integrates comparisons across U.S. states with an examination of redistribution and social protection in Canadian provinces.

SHARE GAINS IN U.S. STATES – EVIDENCE OF A RACE TO THE BOTTOM?

THIS SECTION LOOKS AT PATTERNS in the average share gains of the various income categories across all states as well as the dispersion among states. It argues that there is little evidence of a race to the bottom in redistribution, although there is a non-convergent pattern of erosion in social protection. The study then examines specific pairs of states matched on the basis of geographical contiguity and high intermobility in order to determine whether aggregating states masks a convergence among specific pairs of states. However, this exercise reconfirms the picture drawn by aggregate measures and does not yield evidence of a race to the bottom among these subsets of U.S. states.

Aggregate Cross-state Average Share Gains and Dispersion in Share Gains

To the extent that there has been a shift in the share gains of various income categories in the United States over the 1980-2000 period, evidence of a race to the bottom in redistribution and social protection is slight. While there has been an erosion of the share gain of the lowest quintile, there has been a concomitant increase in the share reduction of the highest quintile, with the share gain of the bottom half remaining unchanged over the period. Thus, the evidence seems to suggest a shift in share gains towards the middle of the income distribution both away from the bottom and the top of the income distribution, with the mix of government taxes and transfers appearing to increasingly benefit the middle class. Social protection (defined here specifically as redistribution in favour of the lowest quintile) has eroded although there does not appear to be cross-state convergence. Finally, there is no evidence that redistribution as measured by the Gini coefficient[18] has been weakened in some overall sense but, rather, that there has been a pattern of upward convergence.

Evidence of a non-convergent downward trend — though not a race to the bottom — is clear in the share gains of the lowest quintile. The average share gain of the lowest quintile declined gradually but consistently from 4.7 percent in 1980 to 4.1 percent in 2000 — a drop of 13 percent over the 20-year period (Figure 1). However, dispersion among states fluctuated upwards over the same period and never declined below the levels of 1980 (0.31) (Figure 2). It is possible that this increased dispersion may be indicative of the early stages of a race to the bottom with some states reducing the share gain of the bottom quintile more quickly than others. However, no convergent race to the bottom is apparent.

FIGURE 1

SHARE GAINS, BOTTOM HALF, QUINTILE 1 AND QUINTILE 5,
ALL STATES AND BORDER STATES, 1980-2000

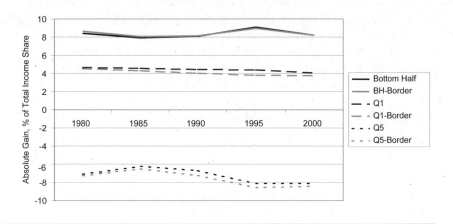

Notes: All share gain calculations made by author. For sources, see Appendix A. Unless otherwise noted,
all figures use Census Bureau Definition 14 (which includes the estimated fungible value of public
medical benefits in final income) to calculate share gains.

FIGURE 2

DISPERSION IN SHARE GAINS, BOTTOM HALF, QUINTILE 1
AND QUINTILE 5, ALL STATES, 1980-2000

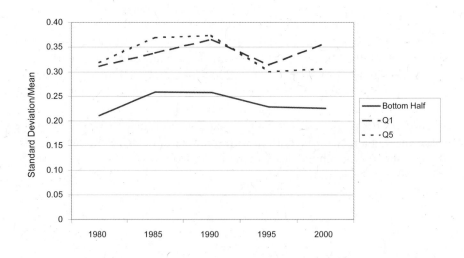

Nor is any downward convergence evident in changes in the share gains of the bottom half of the income distribution over this period. The average share gain of the bottom half of the income distribution dipped somewhat throughout the 1980s (from 8.4 percent in 1980 to around 7.9 percent in 1990), but then increased in the mid-1990s (to over 9 percent) before dipping back in 2000 to the same level as in the late 1980s (Figure 1). Dispersion among states was higher in 1985 and 1990 than in 1980 (0.21), but ended the period at roughly the same level at which it started (0.23) (Figure 2).

The patterns in the share reductions of the highest quintile run against the downward convergence hypothesis. While the share reduction of the top quintile initially decreased from 1980 (–7.1 percent) to 1985 (–6.2 percent), by 2000 it had increased (–8.2 percent) by over 30 percent relative to its 1985 level (Figure 1). Dispersion among states in the share reduction of the top quintile increased over the 1980s (from 0.32 in 1980 to 0.37 in 1990), but decreased again over the 1990s. By 1995, dispersion was lower (0.30) than in 1980 although there is no clear pattern of convergence (Figure 2).

Patterns in border states follow national patterns quite closely, although they are somewhat more pronounced in some instances. While the average share gains of the bottom half of the income distribution followed national patterns very closely (Figure 1), dispersion in share gains for this income category dropped by just under 30 percent over the period (Figure 3). While the share gain of the lowest quintile in border states fell by 17 percent over the period, dispersion among states in the share gain of the lowest quintile (while fluctuating considerably) was consistently higher over the period than it was in 1980 (0.20); in 2000 (at 0.30), it was 50 percent higher than in 1980. Again, while the average share reduction of the top quintile in border states followed national patterns very closely, dispersion among these states fell by 25 percent between 1985 (0.38) and 2000 (0.28). Similar to the pattern of all states, there is limited evidence of a downward (though non-convergent) trend in the share gain of the lowest quintile, no evidence of a downward trend in the share gain of the bottom half, and an upward convergence in the share reduction of the highest quintile.

Similarly, there is no evidence of a race to the bottom from data on the effects of cash transfers in reducing Gini coefficients (Figure 4) or in the dispersion of Gini coefficient reductions resulting from cash transfers (Figure 5).[19] The impact of cash transfers in reducing Gini coefficients in the United States has grown over the 1974-97 period, while the dispersion among states in this regard has declined by just under 25 percent. Thus, the pattern here is one of upward (rather than downward) harmonization.[20]

FIGURE 3

DISPERSION IN SHARE GAINS, BOTTOM HALF, QUINTILE 1
AND QUINTILE 5, BORDER STATES, 1980-2000

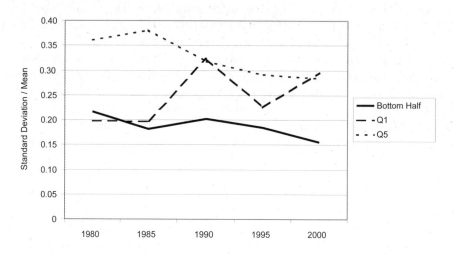

FIGURE 4

GINI COEFFICIENT REDUCTION, CASH TRANSFERS ONLY,
UNITED STATES, 1974-97

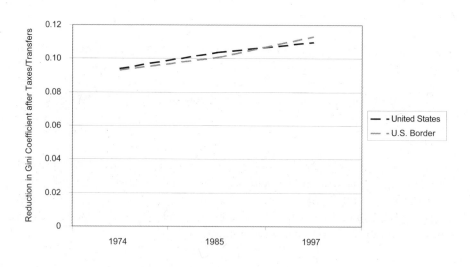

Notes: Values for the United States are for the total U.S. population (i.e. weighted to state populations).
Values for U.S. border states are simply the arithmetic mean of all 15 border states.

FIGURE 5

DISPERSION IN GINI COEFFICIENT REDUCTION,
CASH TRANSFERS ONLY, 1974-97

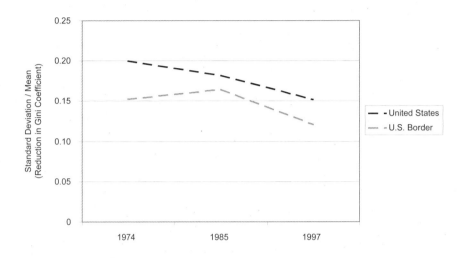

Differences in Share Gains in Matched State Pairs

Aggregate measures of dispersion may mask convergent patterns among specific jurisdictions. This is particularly problematic because, in most arguments hypothesizing convergence, the dynamics of convergence are likely to operate most powerfully between specific pairs or subsets of jurisdictions. Even if the ultimate result over time is a generalized process of convergence, such convergence is likely to emerge earliest and most forcefully among some matched pairs of jurisdictions. Thus, it is important to consider the possibility of convergence among them.

Convergence in redistribution and social protection resulting from increased labour market integration is most likely to emerge between two specific pairings of states: those that are geographically contiguous and those having the highest levels of intermigration.[21] Consequently, this section examines dispersion in the share gains of various income categories between matching pairs of states based on geographical contiguity and, alternatively, high migration flows.[22] This can help determine whether states that are contiguous or have high intermigration (and are thus likely to have more highly integrated labour markets) are also more similar on average to each other in terms of redistribution and social protection than states in general and whether they have been converging.

385

The patterns emerging from aggregate indicators of dispersion are not significantly altered by shifting the focus to state pairs matched either by geographical contiguity or high intermobility (see Figures 6, 7 and 8, which show the average differences between matched pairs of states). Differences among pairs of contiguous states and high intermigration states are somewhat lower in general than differences among all pairs of states. However, these differences are both small and inconsistent for the share gains of the bottom half and the top quintile, while they are somewhat more notable for the lowest quintile. More pronounced are the lower levels of difference among contiguous border states relative to other pairings. On balance, however, even at this more highly specified level of examination, there is little evidence of a downward convergence dynamic.

SHARE GAINS IN CANADA AND THE UNITED STATES

THE FOLLOWING SECTION COMPARES share gains and dispersion in share gains in Canada and the United States. The first subsection examines aggregate share gains in Canada and the United States as well as aggregate indicators of dispersion in share gains across U.S. states and Canadian provinces. The second subsection examines whether patterns of convergence or divergence not evident in these aggregate comparisons are noticeable in comparisons of neighbouring cross-border pairs of states and provinces.

FIGURE 6

SHARE GAIN DIFFERENCES, BOTTOM HALF,
VARIOUS PAIRINGS, 1980-2000

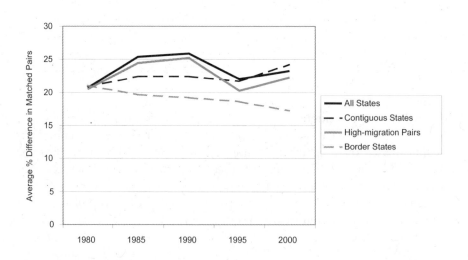

FIGURE 7

SHARE GAIN DIFFERENCES, QUINTILE 1,
VARIOUS PAIRINGS, 1980-2000

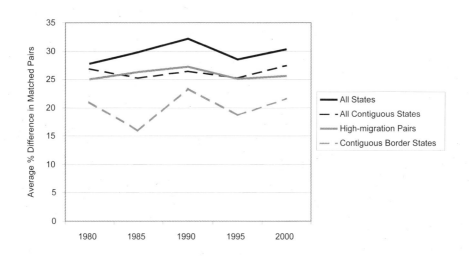

FIGURE 8

SHARE GAIN DIFFERENCES, QUINTILE 5,
VARIOUS PAIRINGS, 1980-2000

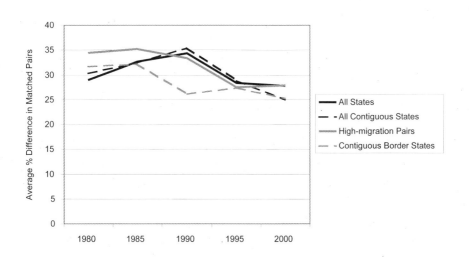

Canada and the United States – Aggregate Indicators of Difference

Share Gains in Canada and the United States

The overall picture that emerges from national aggregate comparisons of share gains in Canada and the United States is one of divergence.[23] The share gain of the bottom half of the income distribution in Canada was considerably more similar to that of the United States in the early 1980s than in 2000 (Figures 9 and 9a). Share gains in Canada increased significantly over the 1980s by comparison with the United States. The same broad pattern holds for the share gains of the bottom quintile (Figures 10 and 10a). A similar (albeit reversed-image) trend is observed in the share reductions of the top quintile in Canada and the United States (Figures 11 and 11a). This general pattern of divergence is also evident in comparisons of Gini coefficients, as presented in Figure 12.

Two crucial caveats should be made here. First, while convergence between Canada and the United States is evident across all three income categories from 1995 to 2000, the overall pattern has been one of divergence over the course of the 1990s — continuing a pattern of divergence throughout the entire period. Whether the slight convergence observed since the 1990s marks the beginning of a more significant convergent trend remains to be seen. Second, whether similar patterns hold for individual pairs of Canadian provinces and their cross-border neighbouring U.S. states also remains to be determined.

Dispersion in Share Gains Across Canadian Provinces and U.S. States

Comparing levels of dispersion in share gains across U.S. states and across Canadian provinces reveals an interesting trend. Not surprisingly in light of the more significant role played by the federal government in redistributive transfers in Canada, dispersion is lower among Canadian provinces than among U.S. states (Figures 13, 14 and 15). The exception is the share gains of the bottom half, where dispersion is actually lower among border states than among Canadian provinces (Figure 13).

A more interesting pattern lies in the fit between dispersion in share gains and dispersion in market income across the U.S. states and across Canadian provinces. In the latter, there is a very strong inverse relationship between the share of market income of various income categories and the associated share gain through taxes and government transfers (Table 1). In provinces where market income is less evenly distributed, the share gains of the bottom half of the income distribution are higher.[24] In the United States, however, the relationship between share of market income and share gain from taxes and transfers is somewhat weaker but, more notably, the direction is reversed. In states where the bottom half's share of market income is low, the share gains from taxes and transfers also tend to be low.[25]

FIGURE 9

AVERAGE SHARE GAINS, BOTTOM HALF, CANADA AND UNITED STATES, 1980-2000

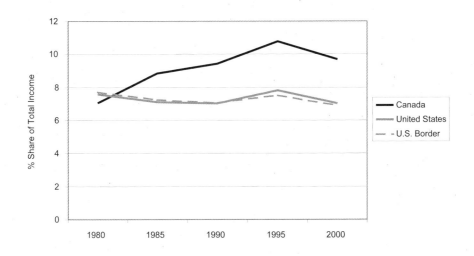

FIGURE 9a

SHARE GAINS, BOTTOM HALF, WEIGHTED NATIONAL AVERAGE, CASH TRANSFERS ONLY, 1974-97

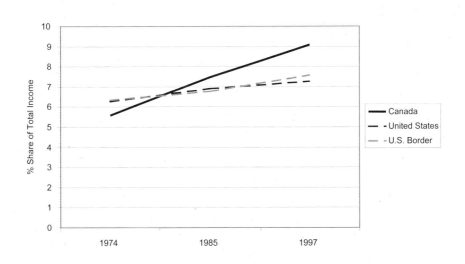

FIGURE 10

AVERAGE SHARE GAINS, QUINTILE 1,
CANADA AND UNITED STATES, 1980-2000

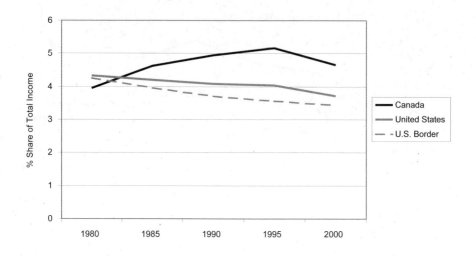

FIGURE 10a

SHARE GAINS, QUINTILE 1, WEIGHTED NATIONAL AVERAGE,
CASH TRANSFERS ONLY, 1974-97

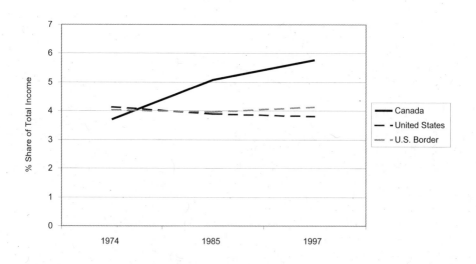

FIGURE 11

AVERAGE SHARE GAINS, QUINTILE 5,
CANADA AND UNITED STATES, 1980-2000

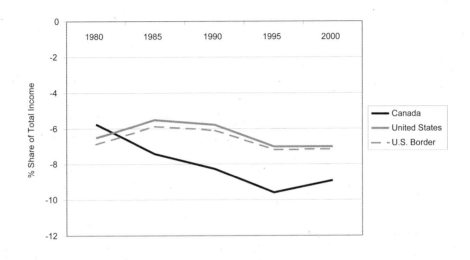

FIGURE 11a

SHARE GAINS, QUINTILE 5, WEIGHTED NATIONAL AVERAGE,
CASH TRANSFERS ONLY, 1974-97

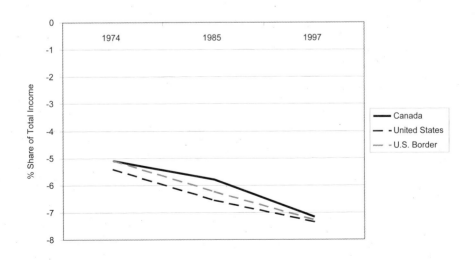

FIGURE 12

GINI COEFFICIENT REDUCTION, WEIGHTED NATIONAL AVERAGE,
CASH TRANSFERS ONLY, 1974-97

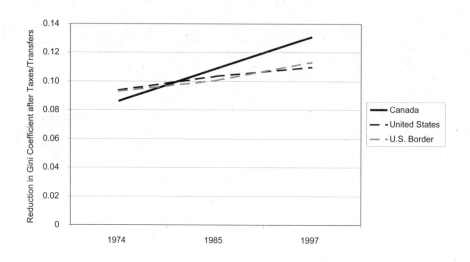

FIGURE 13

DISPERSION IN SHARE GAINS, BOTTOM HALF,
CANADA AND UNITED STATES, 1980-2000

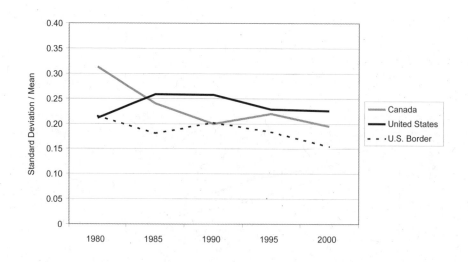

FIGURE 14

DISPERSION IN SHARE GAINS, QUINTILE 1,
CANADA AND UNITED STATES, 1980-2000

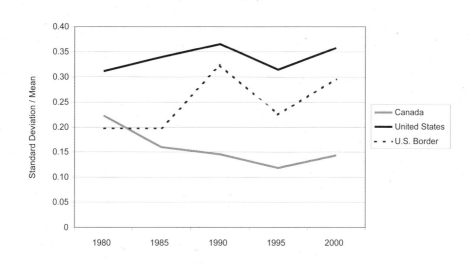

FIGURE 15

DISPERSION IN SHARE GAINS, QUINTILE 5,
CANADA AND UNITED STATES, 1980-2000

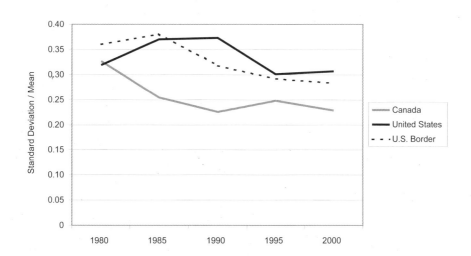

TABLE 1

CORRELATION OF MARKET INCOME SHARE AND SHARE GAIN, BOTTOM HALF
OF INCOME DISTRIBUTION, CANADA AND UNITED STATES, 1980-2000
(PEARSON'S R)

	1980	1985	1990	1995	2000
Canadian Provinces	–0.92	–0.92	–0.94	–0.96	–0.94
U.S. States	+0.54	+0.58	+0.73	+0.69	+0.62

As revealed by the strong inverse relationship in Canadian provinces between the share of market income and the share gains of the bottom half of the
income distribution, taxes and government transfers reduce the dispersion in
final income (i.e. after taxes and transfers) across provinces relative to the initial dispersion in market income. The dispersion in the market income shares of
the bottom half is much lower among Canadian provinces than among U.S.
states, and the dispersion in final income (after taxes and transfers) among
provinces is remarkably low (Figure 16). Because low market income shares
and low share gains are positively correlated in the United States, the dispersion among U.S. states is actually higher *after* taxes and government transfers.[26]
This constitutes a *crucial* difference in the effects of taxes and government
transfers in Canadian provinces by comparison with U.S. states.

FIGURE 16

PROVINCE/STATE DISPERSION IN INCOME, BOTTOM HALF,
CANADA AND UNITED STATES, 1980-2000

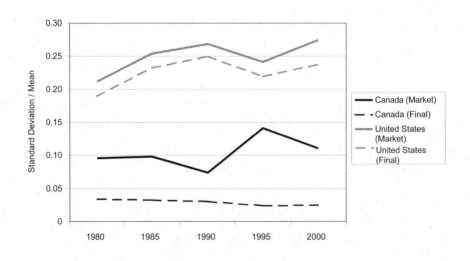

Differences in Share Gain in Neighbouring U.S. States and Canadian Provinces

The final section of the study examines differences in the share gains of various income categories both in matching pairs of Canadian provinces and contiguous U.S. states and in matching pairs of neighbouring border states. These comparisons are used to probe two basic questions: first, whether the patterns arising from comparisons of all provinces and states (as discussed in the preceding section) mask important trends of convergence or divergence between specific pairs of provinces and neighbouring states; second, whether the differences among contiguous U.S. states and Canadian provinces are significantly greater than those existing between variously paired U.S. states (based on contiguity and high intermobility), with the latter providing a benchmark for the level of distinctiveness that might be feasibly maintained among jurisdictions sharing a common labour market.

Patterns of Convergence/Divergence in Neighbouring States and Provinces

An examination of specific matching pairs of provinces and contiguous states reveals certain patterns not evident in the broader comparisons of Canadian provinces and U.S. states, which emphasized fairly uniform divergence across income categories. The evidence for the bottom half of the income distribution is mixed, but there is an overall pattern of divergence between provinces and contiguous states in the share gains of the bottom quintile. At the same time, there is a clear pattern of upward convergence in the share reductions of the top quintile. Thus, while different from the patterns shown by the aggregate comparisons, these patterns run contrary to expectations generated by the race to the bottom hypothesis.

Average differences in the share gains of the bottom quintile in neighbouring provinces and states are consistent with the pattern of divergence emerging from an overall comparison of border states and Canadian provinces. In comparisons of the share gains of the bottom quintile that include in-kind benefits, the pattern of differences over time is more variable than for the other two income categories, as can be seen in Figure 17. However, there is a slight pattern of divergence over the entire period. This pattern of divergence is much more pronounced in comparisons based on cash transfers only (Figure 17a). Here, average differences increased by almost 60 percent from 1974 to 1997. The picture provided by the share gains of the bottom half of the income distribution is more ambiguous. The average difference in the share gains of the bottom half dropped by 35 percent from 1980 to 1985 (Figure 17). This initial cross-border convergence was followed by a period of relatively stable difference levels from 1985 to 2000, with differences continuing to decrease slightly and then increasing slightly. Conversely, the results for cash transfers only

(Figure 17a) reveal a pattern of moderate divergence over the period 1974-97. In contrast, the share reductions of the top quintile in neighbouring provinces and states show a clearer pattern of convergence. For this income category, the average difference in share gains between contiguous state-province pairs fell by 43 percent over the 1980s (Figure 17). This was followed by a brief period of divergence, but by 2000 average differences had returned to their 1990 levels. Over the entire period, average differences fell by 36 percent. A similarly clear pattern of convergence emerges from share reductions based on cash transfers only (Figure 17a). Average differences between neighbouring provinces and states fell by almost half over the 1974-97 period. Finally, average differences in Gini coefficient reductions, though dipping in the middle of the period, were roughly the same in 1997 as they were in 1974 (Figure 17a).

Cross-border Differences in an Interstate Perspective

Differences between neighbouring state and province pairs can be compared to differences among various sets of matched pairs of states in order to assess whether the former lie within a range that seems feasible in an open labour market characterized by relatively unrestricted access to social benefits.

Differences in share gains among contiguous state-province pairs are, for the most part, comparable to or smaller than differences among pairings of all states, all contiguous states, high-migration states, and contiguous border states (Figures 18, 19 and 20).[27] Table 2 presents data on the average differences between variously paired sets of U.S. states (contiguous border states, top migration states, and contiguous states) both at the most recent point in time for which data are available and averaged over the 1980-2000 period. The average differences among neighbouring states and provinces over the most recent periods (for which data are available) are comparable to, or lower than, average differences among various pairings of U.S. states, with only two exceptions. The first is the share gains of the bottom half of the income distribution where neighbouring states and provinces have notably higher average differences than contiguous border states (although contiguous states as a group and the top migration pairs both have average differences higher than, or comparable to, differences between neighbouring state-province pairs). The second exception is evident in cross-border comparisons based on cash transfers only, in which differences in the share gains of the bottom quintile are notably higher for state-province pairs than for any other pairs of states. With these exceptions, current differences in share gains between provinces and their neighbouring states do not notably depart from the differences observed for the various types of state pairs and, in some cases (such as the share reductions for the highest quintile), they are notably lower.

FIGURE 17

AVERAGE DIFFERENCE IN MATCHED PAIRS, CONTIGUOUS PROVINCE-STATE PAIRS, INCLUDING U.S. NON-MEDICAL IN-KIND BENEFITS, 1980-2000

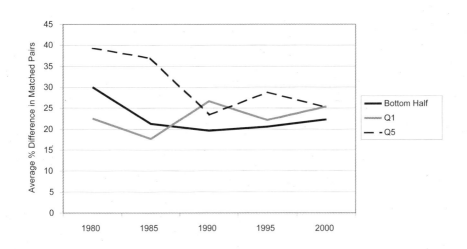

FIGURE 17a

AVERAGE DIFFERENCE IN MATCHED PAIRS, CONTIGUOUS PROVINCE-STATE PAIRS, CASH TRANSFERS ONLY, 1974-97

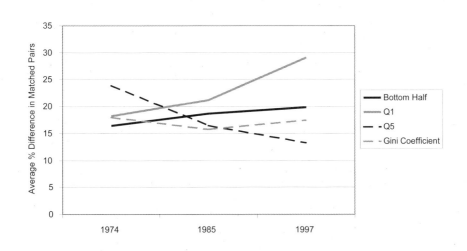

FIGURE 18

SHARE GAIN DIFFERENCES, BOTTOM HALF, INCLUDING U.S. NON-MEDICAL IN-KIND BENEFITS, 1980-2000

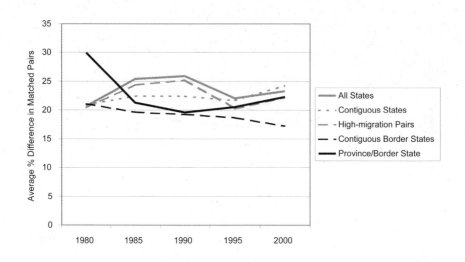

FIGURE 19

SHARE GAIN DIFFERENCES, QUINTILE 1, INCLUDING U.S. NON-MEDICAL IN-KIND BENEFITS, 1980-2000

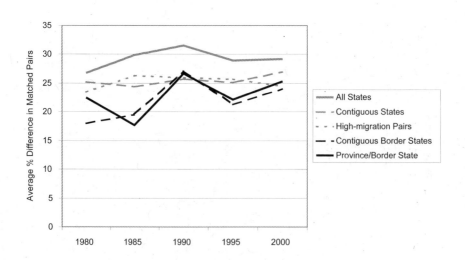

TABLE 2

AVERAGE DIFFERENCES BETWEEN MATCHED STATES (CONTIGUOUS, TOP MIGRATION, BORDER STATES) AND CONTIGUOUS STATES AND PROVINCES, 1974-2000 (PERCENTAGE)

INCOME CLASS	U.S. TRANSFER GAIN DEFINITION	CONTIGUOUS PROVINCE-STATE DIFFERENCES (2000/1997)*	CONTIGUOUS BORDER STATES DIFFERENCES (2000)	CONTIGUOUS BORDER STATES DIFFERENCES (AVERAGE 1980-2000)	CONTIGUOUS STATES (ALL) DIFFERENCES (2000)	CONTIGUOUS STATES (ALL) DIFFERENCES (AVERAGE 1980-2000)	TOP MIGRATION PAIRS DIFFERENCES (2000)	TOP MIGRATION PAIRS DIFFERENCES (AVERAGE 1980-2000)
Bottom Half	Including Non-medical In-kind Benefits (U.S. only)	22.3	16.6	16.6	24.3	22.4	22.2	22.5
	Cash Transfers Only	19.8						
Q1	Including Non-medical In-kind Benefits (U.S. only)	25.4	24.9	22.2	27.0	25.5	24.5	25.2
	Cash Transfers Only	29.1						
Q5	Including Non-medical In-kind Benefits (U.S. only)	25.3	28.6	29.8	29.4	33.7	32.9	35.2
	Cash Transfers Only	13.3						

Note: * Data for "cash transfers only" are for 1997.

FIGURE 20

SHARE GAIN DIFFERENCES, QUINTILE 5, INCLUDING
U.S. NON-MEDICAL IN-KIND BENEFITS, 1980-2000

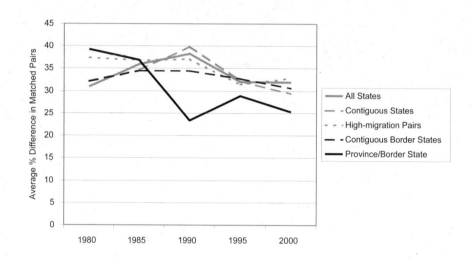

Differences in share gains between U.S. states can provide a benchmark
for speculating about the magnitude of differences that can be maintained between jurisdictions in the context of a common labour market and relatively
unrestricted access to social benefits. Differences in redistribution and social
protection currently existing between Canadian provinces and their neighbouring U.S. states do not lie outside this range.[28] This suggests that these differences may well lie inside the range of differences that can be feasibly maintained by jurisdictions sharing a common labour market.

CONCLUSION

WHILE FAR FROM CONCLUSIVE, the evidence presented here suggests that
Canada-U.S. labour market integration would not necessarily result in a
downward convergence of redistribution and social protection. In the United
States, many observers similarly predicted a downward harmonization in taxation, redistribution, and social protection following the decentralization of the
U.S. federal system that began with Reagan's *New Federalism* in the early 1980s
and accelerated throughout the 1990s. While there has been some erosion in
social protection, there is no overall indication of a broader pattern of downward harmonization in redistribution over this period; there are some notable

trends to the contrary and aggregate patterns do not appear to mask convergence among more closely linked pairs of states. Overall, the evidence suggests that individual states continue to retain considerable latitude to maintain distinctive approaches to redistribution and social protection relative to the states with which they are most closely linked, even in the context of a common labour market characterized by relatively unrestricted access to social benefits across jurisdictions.

Existing differences in redistribution and social protection between Canadian provinces and the nearest U.S. states do not seem to lie outside this range of feasible distinctiveness. Aggregate differences between Canada and the United States fade to a significant degree as individual Canadian provinces are compared with neighbouring U.S. states. Thus, differences in levels of redistribution and social protection between Canadian provinces and neighbouring U.S. states might also be more feasibly maintained than seem to be the case on the basis of aggregate cross-national comparisons. However, there are important differences between the two countries. Taxes and transfers significantly reduce the interprovincial dispersion in shares of market income for the various income categories, while they exacerbate such differences across U.S. states. Rather than asking if a given level of redistribution and social protection can be maintained in Canada or in specific Canadian provinces in a context of cross-border labour market integration, a more crucial question may be whether such integration would undermine the sustainability of this interregional pattern.

SUGGESTIONS FOR FUTURE RESEARCH

THIS STUDY ONLY SCRATCHES THE SURFACE of a much broader research agenda stemming from the issue of the likely effects of Canada-U.S. labour market integration on redistribution and social protection. The study points to a number of avenues for further research and the following section discusses three broad suggestions.

Conceptualizing Access to Social Benefits in an Integrated Labour Market

Perhaps the most crucial task in considering the potential implications of labour market integration on redistribution and social protection is to clearly conceptualize the various possible models for access to social benefits in an integrated labour market. It appears difficult to proceed with a realistic assessment of the likely outcomes in terms of redistribution and social protection without first undertaking this step. As outlined above, consideration of the potential effects of labour market integration on redistribution and social protection requires some crucial assumptions regarding the basis for access to social benefits.

A comparative examination of the various existing arrangements for access to different types of social benefits in the European Union would make an important contribution to understanding the likely effects of different benefit arrangements in a scenario of Canada-U.S. labour market integration. First, such an examination would help identify the various possible models of access to benefits and the dynamics which might foster or hinder the adoption of a given model. Second, it could help to identify the likely effects of a specific model of access to benefits on the level and nature of social benefits across member countries and, indirectly, on the level of redistribution and social protection.[29]

Better Comparisons

The most obvious avenue for future research identified by the study is the need to design better methodologies and empirical measures for comparing redistribution and social protection that can be applied not only to overall comparisons between Canada and the United States, but also to comparisons between specific Canadian provinces and U.S. states. In terms of empirical indicators, we would need comparable measures that include the redistributive effects of non-cash benefits (especially for health care) across states and provinces, income redistribution within income categories over time, and wealth redistribution over time.

Not only do comparisons of redistribution and social protection need to be more encompassing both in terms of a wide range of social benefits and dynamic effects over time, but redistribution and social protection need to be disaggregated. For example, research is required to isolate the redistributive effects of federal and provincial programs. Studies of the convergent effects of economic integration have generally focused on national programs. There are several reasons to suspect, however, that cross-border convergence would emerge earlier and more forcefully at the provincial level than at the federal level. (Boychuk and Banting, 2003) First, provinces control some of the most important policy levers for adjusting to increasing economic integration and competitive pressures. Second, provinces have distinct economic structures and trading patterns requiring unique policy adjustment; thus, provincial governments are arguably more sensitive than the federal government to the competitive pressures generated by cross-border economic integration and competition. According to Courchene and Telmer, provinces will increasingly tailor their policies to those prevailing in the U.S. states with which they are increasingly integrating and/or competing. (1998, pp. 289-291) In order to examine such convergence, it is necessary to isolate provincial contributions to redistribution and social protection relative to the effects of federal initiatives.[30]

Integration of Research Findings

The discussion above points to the need for further work to draw together the findings of disaggregated analyses (such as discrete studies of social programs or taxation policies) with the broad type of aggregate analysis of redistribution and social protection undertaken here. If there is convergence in overall redistribution and social protection, it will be the result of changes in specific programs and policies. Changes at the program level might have important long-term implications for the broad redistributive role of government that may take considerable time to emerge from an aggregate analysis. Conversely, convergence in particular program areas must be judged in a broader framework that considers whether other elements of the redistribution and social protection system are simultaneously adjusting, such that the overall redistributive impact remains largely unchanged. It is only through an examination of policy convergence and divergence from these various perspectives that an adequate appreciation of cross-border patterns of policy development, which are central to assessing the likely effects of deeper economic integration, will emerge.

ENDNOTES

1   The term "feasible egalitarianism" is drawn from Bowles, 2000.

2   The study makes a distinction between *redistribution* (shifting income downward at any point of the income distribution) and *social protection* (which refers here to redistribution to those at the bottom of the income distribution).

3   This broad aggregated approach to redistribution draws upon the methodology developed in Arjona, Ladaique and Pearson, 2001. Aggregate indicators may, however, obscure important patterns of convergence and divergence at more disaggregated levels. For an example of a more disaggregated approach, see Boychuk and Banting, 2003.

4   The study does not examine direct constraints on redistribution and social protection policy (of the type that might emerge under a social charter, for example) but, rather, the effects emerging indirectly as a result of increased labour mobility.

5   While this proposition was widely accepted in the U.S. social policy literature in the early and mid-1990s, evidence to support it has been weak at best and, over time, the claim has lost much of its credence in the public policy literature. However, the logic of the race to the bottom may remain an important policy dynamic to the degree that policymakers believe it is at work. For a discussion, see Boychuk, 2003; and Noël, 1999.

6   Regarding such extension of benefits, Hoberg, Banting and Simeon note that "[i]n the absence of fundamental change in Canadian-U.S. relations, this is unlikely to happen." (2002, p. 272)

7   Harris and Schmitt note that this perception "has emerged out of a decade-long economic boom in the United States coupled with some critical skilled labour shortages in the United States" and that "[s]hould a prolonged slump or oversupply of labour in these areas emerge, cross-border mobility may quickly dissipate." (2001, p. 26)

8   The most striking and important exception to this is the province of Quebec.

9   For an overview of differences in the federal structures of the Canadian and U.S. tax systems, see Alpert, Shoven and Whalley, 1992.

10   As such, the Canadian example is not particularly instructive regarding the effects of labour market integration on policy distinctiveness as differences in redistribution and social protection between Canadian provinces are heavily conditioned by the effects of federal policy, including Employment Insurance and federal equalization, in ways that may both exacerbate and reduce regional differences.

11   For example, Rom provides a good overview of the ways in which "[s]tate governments are increasingly taking responsibility for health and welfare programs." (1999, p. 349)

12   This is not meant to refer to the actual average distance between all U.S. states (which is comparable to the average distance between all Canadian provinces) but rather to the average proximity of the next closest state or states.

13   Finnie has estimated out-migration rates for the provinces at 1.5 percent over the 1982-89 period, dropping to 1.2 percent in 1994. Interstate mobility rates have held constant since the early 1970s at roughly 3 percent per year.

14   This subset includes 15 states: Idaho, Indiana, Illinois, Maine, Michigan, Minnesota, Montana, New Hampshire, New York, North Dakota, Ohio, Pennsylvania, Vermont, Washington and Wisconsin.

15   Arjona, Ladaique and Pearson report that "[t]he OECD work on income distribution has developed a measure of how much net redistribution is performed by tax/transfer systems ...: the increase in the share of total income received by the bottom half of the income distribution due to taxes and transfers." (2001, p. 24) They describe the concept of *share gain* as follows: "the share gain for a given decile is defined as the increase in the income share of that decile as transfers take place. These variables capture how the income shares of the bottom half and of the bottom quintile of the distribution of market income ... increase as redistribution takes place, i.e. as tax/transfers have effect." (p. 25) I also present data on the difference between the share of market income and the share of final income (i.e. after government taxes and transfers) for the highest or fifth quintile. Since the value of this difference in the cases to which I am referring is always negative, the study refers to them as *share reductions*.

16   This data is not publicly available on a state-by-state basis and was obtained directly from the U.S. Census Bureau through a special tabulation request.

17   The U.S. Census Bureau methodology for calculating the value of public health benefits is as follows: "The fungible approach for valuing medical coverage assigns income to the extent that having [public] insurance would free up resources that would have been spent on medical care. The estimated fungible value depends on family income, the cost of food and housing needs, and the market value of the medical benefits. If family income is not sufficient to cover the family's basic food

and housing requirements, the fungible methodology treats medicare and Medicaid as having no income value. If family income exceeds the cost of food and housing requirements, the fungible value of medicare and Medicaid is equal to the amount which exceeds the value assigned for food and housing requirements." (U.S. Census Bureau, *Alternative Measures of Income* [www.census.gov/hhes/income/histinc/redefs.html]).

18   The Gini coefficient is "a statistical measure which has a value of '0' if every person in the economy had the same amount of income and a value of '1' if one person had all the income, and everybody else had no income at all. An increase in the Gini coefficient represents an increase in inequality." (Arjona, Ladaique and Pearson, 2001, p. 17) This study measures the Gini coefficient reduction, or absolute reduction in this coefficient resulting from taxes and government transfers.

19   Gini coefficients were available for data on cash transfers only, but not for data including the value of in-kind benefits.

20   Gini coefficients "are particularly sensitive to changes in the middle of the income distribution." (Arjona, Ladaique and Pearson, 2001, p. 16) This explains why the results based on the reduction in Gini coefficients may vary from those using the share gain of the bottom half.

21   While the two sometimes overlap, intermigration is heavily determined by both the size and proximity of other states. This is similar to the gravity effects of size and distance in the context of interjurisdictional trade. See Helliwell, 2002.

22   Each state was paired both with the state that contributed the highest proportion of in-migrants and the recipient state to which the state sent the greatest proportion of out-migrants. Migration data are based on the state of residence in 1990 *vs.* the state of residence in 1985 [www.census.gov/population/sociodemo/migration/90mig.txt].

23   The following section compares share gains for various income classes using measures of government transfer income that include in-kind benefits exclusive of medical benefits (U.S. Census Bureau, Definition 14a). For these comparisons, data on Canada include *cash transfers only*. A second set of comparisons is based on share gains calculated using cash transfers only.

24   A similar correlation exists between the share of market income and the share gain from taxes and transfers for the lowest quintile.

25   While it is relatively clear that federal programs explain the strong negative correlation between the share of market income and the share gain from taxes and transfers in Canadian provinces, it is not clear what explains the positive correlation between these two factors in U.S. states. It is not a natural result of market income being distributed more evenly in high-income states, which are also more able to afford redistribution. Rather, high income states tend to have a more unequal distribution of market income. (The market share of the bottom half is negatively correlated with aggregate measures of state wealth such as personal per capita income.)

26   This pattern is only evident through examining standard deviation as opposed to standard deviation as a percent of the mean. When measuring dispersion as standard deviation divided by the mean, the share gain from taxes and transfers raises

the denominator (mean share of income) enough that standard deviation divided by the mean appears lower, as in Figure 16.

27 This holds whether differences between states and provinces are calculated including non-medical in-kind benefits or cash transfers only. For a rough indication, compare Figure 17a with Figures 18, 19 and 20. See Appendix A for a discussion of the statistical significance of variation between Canadian provinces and U.S. states and of variation in the differences between state-province pairs and contiguous state pairs.

28 A crucial caveat here is that these comparisons do not include the redistributive impact of public health care in the two countries.

29 Similarly, research might be undertaken to plumb the dynamics of these different types of benefit arrangements where they exist among sub-national jurisdictions (e.g. Swiss cantons).

30 Initial work by Boychuk and Banting (2003) suggests that it is not the case that provincial program convergence is offset by continued distinctiveness in federal programs but, rather, that it is federal programs which demonstrate the greatest degree of convergence with U.S. social programs.

ACKNOWLEDGMENTS

I WOULD LIKE TO THANK RICHARD ROY for his important input at the design stage of this research project, Kevin Wipf for his research assistance, and Alain Noël and Debora Vannijnatten for their comments on an earlier draft of the study. In addition, I would like to thank Brian Murphy of Statistics Canada as well as Caroline Carbaugh and Kirk Davis of the U.S. Census Bureau for their help in providing the special data tabulations on which the study is based. Any errors in fact or interpretation remain mine.

BIBLIOGRAPHY

Alpert, William T., John B. Shoven and John Whalley. "Introduction." In *Canada-U.S. Tax Comparisons*. Edited by John B. Shove and John Whalley. Chicago: University of Chicago Press, 1992, pp. 1-23.

Arjona, Roman, Maxime Ladaique and Mark Pearson. "Growth, Inequality and Social Protection." Labour Market and Social Policy Occasional Paper No. 51. Paris: Organisation for Economic Co-operation and Development, June 2001.

Boychuk, Gerard W. "Social Assistance and Canadian Federalism." In *New Trends in Canadian Federalism*. 2nd ed. Edited by François Rocher and Miriam Smith. Peterborough (Ont.): Broadview, 2003, pp. 269-294.

Boychuk, Gerard W., and Keith G. Banting. "The Paradox of Convergence: National Versus Subnational Patterns of Convergence in Canadian and U.S. Income Maintenance Policy." In *North American Linkages: Opportunities and Challenges for Canada*. Edited by Richard G. Harris. The Industry Canada Research Series. Calgary: University of Calgary Press, 2003, pp. 533-572.

Bowles, Samuel. *Globalization and Redistribution: Feasible Egalitarianism in a Competitive World*. NBER Working Paper. September 2000.

Coulombe, Serge, and Kathleen M. Day. "Economic Growth and Regional Income Disparities in Canada and the Northern United States." *Canadian Public Policy 25*, 2 (1999): 155-178.

Courchene, Thomas J., and Colin R. Telmer. *From Heartland to North American Region State: The Social, Fiscal, and Federal Evolution of Ontario*. Toronto: University of Toronto, Faculty of Management, 1998.

Gray, Virginia. "The Socioeconomic and Political Context of States." In *Politics in the American States: A Comparative Analysis*. 7th ed. Edited by Virginia Gray, Russell L. Hanson and Herbert Jacob. Washington (D.C.): CQ Press, 1999, pp. 1-31.

Hakim, Peter, and Robert Litan. "The Future of North America: Beyond Free Trade." Inter-American Dialogue Project, Brookings Institution, February 2002. Unpublished research note.

Hanson, Russell L. "Intergovernmental Relations." In *Politics in the American States: A Comparative Analysis*. 7th ed. Edited by Virginia Gray, Russell L. Hanson and Herbert Jacob. Washington (D.C.): CQ Press, 1999, pp. 32-65.

Harris, Richard, and Nicholas Schmitt. "The Consequences of Increased Labour Mobility within an Integrating North America." Paper presented to the Industry Canada Conference on North American Integration. Calgary, Alberta, June 2001.

Helliwell, John F. *Globalization and Well-Being.* Vancouver: University of British Columbia Press, 2002.

Hoberg, George, Keith G. Banting and Richard Simeon. "The Scope for Domestic Choice: Policy Autonomy in a Globalizing World." In *Capacity for Choice: Canada in a New North America*. Edited by George Hoberg. Toronto: University of Toronto Press, 2002, pp. 252-298.

Kesselman, Jonathan. "Policies to Stem the Brain Drain — Without Americanizing Canada." *Canadian Public Policy 27*, 1 (March 2001): 77-93.

Krugman, Paul. *Geography and Trade*. Cambridge (MA): Leuven University Press and MIT Press, 1991.

Liebfried, Stephan, and Paul Pierson. "Social Policy." In *Policy-Making in the European Union*. 4th ed. Edited by Helen Wallace and William Wallace. Oxford: Oxford University Press, 2000, pp. 267-292.

Noël, Alain. "Is Decentralization Conservative? Federalism and the Contemporary Debate on the Canadian Welfare State." In *Stretching the Federation: The Art of the State in Canada*. Edited by Robert Young. Kingston (Ont.): Institute of Intergovernmental Relations, 1999, pp. 195-219.

Rom, Mark Carl. "Transforming State Health and Welfare Programs." In *Politics in the American States: A Comparative Analysis*. 7th ed. Edited by Virginia Gray, Russell L. Hanson and Herbert Jacob. Washington (DC): CQ Press, 1999, pp. 349-392.

APPENDIX A

STATISTICAL SIGNIFICANCE OF DIFFERENCES IN SHARE GAINS

IN TABLES A-1 AND A-2, T-RATIOS are used to determine the statistical significance of variation in the average share gain between all Canadian provinces and U.S. border states for various income categories.[1] In Tables A-3 and A-4, t-ratios are used to determine the statistical significance of variation in the average difference in share gains between contiguous border states pairs and contiguous state-province pairs.

TABLE A-1

SHARE GAINS, ALL CANADIAN PROVINCES AND U.S. BORDER STATES, CASH TRANSFERS ONLY, T-RATIOS, 1974-97

	1974	1985	1997
Bottom Half	0.90	2.69*	4.06**
Q1	0.71	3.95**	6.43**
Q5	−1.66	−1.23	−1.62
Reduction in Gini Coefficient	1.67	2.57**	4.05**

Notes: *   Significant at the 5% confidence level.
      ** Significant at the 1% confidence level.

TABLE A-2

SHARE GAINS, ALL CANADIAN PROVINCES AND U.S. BORDER STATES, INCLUDING U.S. NON-MEDICAL IN-KIND BENEFITS, T-RATIOS, 1980-2000

	1980	1985	1990	1995	2000
Bottom Half	0.92	1.76	2.71*	2.98**	3.44**
Q1	−1.37	1.48	2.69*	4.28**	2.70*
Q5	1.36	−1.20	−1.85	−1.90	−1.33

Notes: *   Significant at the 5% confidence level.
      ** Significant at the 1% confidence level.

TABLE A-3

SHARE GAIN DIFFERENCES, CONTIGUOUS BORDER STATES PAIRS AND
CONTIGUOUS STATE-PROVINCE PAIRS, CASH TRANSFERS ONLY, T-RATIOS,
1974-97

	1974	1985	1997
Bottom Half	−1.10	−0.81	−3.65**
Q1	−0.44	−1.51	−6.51**
Q5	−0.37	0.62	0.27
Reduction in Gini Coefficient	−0.64	−0.34	−2.73**

Notes: * Significant at the 5% confidence level.
     ** Significant at the 1% confidence level.

TABLE A-4

SHARE GAIN DIFFERENCES, CONTIGUOUS BORDER STATES PAIRS AND
CONTIGUOUS STATE-PROVINCE PAIRS, INCLUDING U.S. NON-MEDICAL
IN-KIND BENEFITS, 1980-2000

	1980	1985	1990	1995	2000
Bottom Half	−1.51	−0.23	−0.49	−1.03	−1.12
Q1	−0.62	−0.16	−0.63	−0.58	−0.09
Q5	−1.00	0.11	0.62	0.34	0.39

Notes: * Significant at the 5% confidence level.
     ** Significant at the 1% confidence level.

There were no statistically significant differences between the share gains of the various income categories in Canadian provinces and U.S. border states in the mid-1970s (Tables A-1 and A-2). Over time, however, the differences between border states and Canadian provinces have grown so that, with the exception of the 5th quintile, by the late 1990s, these differences were statistically significant. Share reductions of the top quintile provide a marked exception and, regardless of whether in-kind benefits are included in comparisons, differences between Canadian provinces and U.S. border states are not statistically significant, even in the most recent periods.

The same pattern holds when comparing contiguous border states pairs and contiguous state-province pairs (Table A-3). While, for the most part, differences among contiguous border states have been lower than differences among contiguous province-state pairs, these differences were not statistically significant until the 1990s. To the extent that they are significant, it is largely because much of the variation across U.S. states stems from differences in in-kind benefits rather than cash transfers only. However, when in-kind benefits are included in the calculations of U.S. share gains, differences between contiguous border states pairs and contiguous state-province pairs are no longer statistically significant (Table A-4).

ENDNOTE

1 Higher t-ratios indicate a greater degree of difference between the designated group (Canadian provinces) and the other group (U.S. border states). Positive t-ratios mean that the scores of Canadian provinces on this indicator are higher than those of U.S. border states. Negative t-ratios mean that the scores of Canadian provinces on this indicator are lower those of U.S. border states.

APPENDIX B

DATA SOURCES

CANADIAN DATA

THE CANADIAN DATA are drawn from the *Income in Canada* database:

- *market income*;
- *total income* is market income plus total government transfers;
- *final income* is the equivalent of total after-tax income.

U.S. DATA INCLUDING THE VALUE OF IN-KIND BENEFITS

DATA FOR U.S. STATES that include the imputed value of in-kind benefits are drawn from the "experimental poverty data" section of the Current Population Survey, March Supplement, and were obtained directly through the U.S. Bureau of Statistics, Special Tabulations Unit. (They are available upon request from the author at gboychuk@watarts.uwaterloo.ca.)

The U.S. Census Bureau supplied data on income share by quintile for four income definitions that are provided in *Alternative Measures of Income* [www.census.gov/hhes/income/histinc/redefs.html]:

- *market income* (inclusive of the effects of in-kind benefits) in this study refers to values for the U.S. Census Bureau *Alternative Measure of Income* Definition 4, which includes money income (before taxes and government transfers) plus capital gains and imputed health insurance supplements to wage or salary income;

- *income after tax* (Definition 8) refers to market income (Definition 4) less payroll taxes and income taxes, plus the earned income credit, less state income taxes;

- *final income* (Definition 14) refers to income after tax (Definition 8) plus the estimated fungible value of Medicare, plus the value of regular-price school lunches, plus means-tested government cash transfers (including Aid to Families with Dependent Children, Temporary Assistance to Needy Families, Social Insurance, other public assistance programs, and means-tested veterans' payments), plus the estimated fungible value of Medicaid, plus the value of other means-tested government non-cash transfers including food stamps, rent subsidies, and free and reduced-price school lunches);

- Definition 14a in the paper refers to final income (Definition 14) less the estimated fungible values of Medicaid and Medicare.

CANADA-U.S. COMPARISONS OF CASH-INCOME ONLY DATA

COMPARATIVE DATA ON CASH-INCOME SHARES by quintile and Gini coefficients for Canadian provinces and all U.S. states were prepared as a special tabulation by Statistics Canada for 1974, 1985, 1995 and 1997 using the methodology developed in Wolfson and Murphy, 2000. Special thanks to Brian Murphy.

BIBLIOGRAPHY

Wolfson, Michael, and Brian Murphy. "Income Inequality in North America: Does the 49th Parallel Still Matter?" *Canadian Economic Observer* (August 2000): 3.1-3.22.

p 369 :

Comment

Alain Noël
University of Montreal

THIS STUDY IS REMARKABLE IN MANY WAYS. It raises an important but difficult question, and proposes a credible and original answer, one that truly breaks new ground and allows us to move beyond purely formal, speculative, or ideological arguments.

As is suggested in the study just presented by Rafael Gomez and Morley Gunderson, there is an abundance of theoretical arguments on economic integration and social policy, but little reliable empirical evidence. Gomez and Gunderson do us a great service by surveying, sector by sector, the patterns of convergence and divergence in North America. They find mixed evidence, pointing — in their opinion — toward some downward divergence. Boychuk goes a step further: he looks not at policy instruments, but rather directly at outcomes for citizens. This is a very important theoretical and empirical move. As noted by American political scientist Jacob Hacker in a recent paper, social scientists interested in the welfare state have tended to pay too much attention to "formal policy rules" and not enough to "their real-world effects." (Hacker, 2002, p. 2) Indeed, even stable programs may have new consequences if the economic and social context is changing the nature of social risks.

I have comments and suggestions for the author, but they are intended to encourage him to go a few steps further, so that he can get the best out of an analysis that is already very impressive and, possibly, pursue this line of research beyond this study.

Theoretically, the study is very well anchored and coherent. Boychuk uses Samuel Bowles' notion of 'feasible egalitarianism' in a competitive world, and considers the states' and provinces' capacity to redistribute income through transfers and taxes, in the context of open labour markets. Share gains — the difference between market income and post-transfers/post-taxes income for a given proportion of the population — are used as indicators of a state's capacity to redistribute income, and comparisons are made among U.S. states and among various sets of U.S. states and Canadian provinces. The empirical findings come out clearly: in the United States, there is no 'race to the bottom' between the states and no convergence toward a less egalitarian equilibrium; between Canada and the United States, the pattern is more one of divergence, with

Canadian provinces' increasing share gains over time, in comparison to U.S. states in particular. Boychuk concludes, appropriately, that there is little evidence of a North American 'race to the bottom' that would be induced by open labour markets, although one may ask whether inter-regional redistribution as it exists is sustainable in the long run.

These results are consistent with those of earlier studies indicating that, overall, major social programs have not been redefined in a less generous way in the wake of North American integration (see Simeon, Hoberg and Banting, 1997, p. 393). They are consistent, as well, with the broader literature on the welfare state, which stresses continuity rather than change, even in an era of retrenchment (Pierson, 2001). To my satisfaction, Boychuk's findings also support the view that decentralized political arrangements do not necessarily foster 'races to the bottom' (Noël, 1999).

Potentially, however, there is even more to these results. Although the author does not refer to this argument, his findings can also be read as a complement to the more specific and well-documented story of an increasingly egalitarian Canada in a less and less egalitarian North America (see Hanratty and Blank, 1992; Myles, 1996; Banting, 1997, p. 309). The evolution of share gains in the two countries is indeed consistent with this account, which suggests not so much a deterioration of social policy in the United States as a failure to respond to a labour market increasingly disadvantageous for low-skilled workers. In Canada, the labour market would also be producing more inequalities than twenty years ago, but more responsive policies would more or less preserve the income distribution of earlier years, and in fact probably yield an even more egalitarian outcome than before.

Share gains cannot show these evolutions directly because they incorporate into a single indicator both market and policy outcomes. But some additions to the study could easily correct this problem. Boychuk already has relevant data on market and policy outcomes since he constructed the share gains data himself. It would be extremely helpful if the study could show these data in a few tables and discuss their significance. The idea would be to clarify the respective roles of market outcomes, transfers and taxes in the evolution of share gains for different segments of the population in U.S. states and Canadian provinces. I assume the Hanratty and Blank story is still correct for the lower paid (as is suggested for the United States in Hacker, 2002), but I may be wrong. The issue is certainly worth investigating, at least in a preliminary way.

The story for share reductions may be different, and it would also benefit from an analysis of the data that would disentangle the roles of the market, of transfers and of taxes. Many policy analysts and governments assume income taxes for the higher paid are bound to decrease due to competitive pressures.

Is this already happening? Share reductions data are not sufficient to tell, because they also incorporate labour market changes.

Again, this is a remarkable study that offers much-needed empirical evidence on a critical question. The argument is well constructed, the evidence original and compelling, and the interpretation nuanced and convincing. My only suggestion would be to take the study a step further with a discussion of the respective evolutions and contributions of the three components of share gains (market outcomes, transfers and taxes) and with a closer look, in the same perspective, at share reductions.

BIBLIOGRAPHY

Banting, Keith. "The Social Policy Divide: The Welfare State in Canada and the United States." In *Degrees of Freedom: Canada and the United States in a Changing World.* Edited by Keith Banting, George Hoberg and Richard Simeon. Montreal and Kingston: McGill-Queen's University Press, 1997.

Hacker, Jacob S. "Privatizing Risk without Privatizing Benefits: U.S. Welfare State Reform in Comparative Perspective." Paper presented at the 2002 Annual Meeting of the American Political Science Association, Boston, September 1, 2002. (www.apsanet.org).

Hanratty, Maria J., and Rebecca M. Blank. "Down and Out in North America: Recent Trends in Poverty Rates in the United States and Canada." *Quarterly Journal of Economics* 107, 1 (February 1992).

Myles, John. "When Markets Fail: Social Welfare in Canada and the United States." In *Welfare States in Transition: National Adaptations in Global Economies.* Edited by Gøsta Esping-Andersen. Thousand Oaks: Sage, 1996.

Noël, Alain. "Is Decentralization Conservative? Federalism and the Contemporary Debate on the Canadian Welfare State." In *Stretching the Federation: The Art of the State in Canada.* Edited by Robert Young. Kingston: Institute of Intergovernmental Relations, 1999.

Pierson, Paul, ed. *The New Politics of the Welfare State.* Oxford: Oxford University Press, 2001.

Simeon, Richard, George Hoberg and Keith Banting. "Globalization, Fragmentation, and the Social Contract." In *Degrees of Freedom: Canada and the United States in a Changing World.* Edited by Keith Banting, George Hoberg and Richard Simeon. Montreal and Kingston: McGill-Queen's University Press, 1997.

Part V

Assessing the Extent and Consequences of Canada-U.S. Labour Mobility

Don J. DeVoretz   &   Diane Coulombe
RIIM   RIIM

9

Labour Mobility Between Canada and the United States: Quo Vadis 2004?

While highly skilled professionals can now move back and forth under NAFTA that is not the case for most workers. So if one is thinking through the logical progression one would want to open that.
(D. Dodge, *National Post*, October 23, 2002, p. A-11)

INTRODUCTION

THE CENTRAL GOAL OF THIS ESSAY is to explain why Canadian mobility to the United States, as reported by many observers, appears moderate even with the special mobility provisions under Chapter 16 of the North American Free Trade Agreement (NAFTA) for Canadians and large pecuniary incentives for them to move. In particular, we attempt to identify, both through econometric evidence and an analysis of the literature, the legislative and non-legislative barriers that produce this outcome.[1] In order to address the broader question of North American labour market integration, we pose a counterfactual question to measure the *home bias* in factor mobility between Canada and the United States. In short, this question is: Would Canadians (Americans) be more mobile within their own economy than between their nation states when faced with the same economic incentives? In effect, we measure the home-country bias inherent in migration by removing the border and comparing this simulated movement within Canada to the actual Canada-U.S. movement. The difference in magnitude of these within-Canada and .between-countries flows is our measure of the home-country bias or mobility without any legislative barriers. Finally, given the post-September 11 U.S. border regulations with respect to both Canadian citizens and Canadian landed immigrants, we analyze and forecast the consequences of these regulations on future NAFTA mobility.

The rest of the study is organized as follows. First, we review the legal and economic literature on Canada-U.S. mobility-border issues. We then turn to our previously estimated econometric model in order to formulate a counter-factual question to test for the existence of a home-country bias on mobility. Finally, we ask if any of this prior information is relevant to future labour mobility conditions given the new U.S. policy of increased scrutiny of Canadians at the border.

LITERATURE REVIEW

THE RECENT LITERATURE ON THE MOVEMENT of highly skilled Canadians to the United States has grown in size and scope over the last decade.[2] The debate that arose over the *brain exchange* issue was fuelled by bad data, differing political views on nationalism, and varying political agendas (DeVoretz and Iturralde, 1999). The estimated size and significance of the post-1990 net flow of highly skilled immigrants between Canada and the United States varied by data sources, definitions — including or excluding temporary flows — as well as confusion over such basic concepts as the size of the stocks and flows of skilled movers. We will avoid all this controversy by focusing on the border issue. In short, given any number of movers, we ask: Does the border represent in 2004 a significant impediment to further North American labour market integration, regardless of the size of the current number of movers? Thus, while covering both permanent and temporary movement between NAFTA members (Canada, the United States and Mexico), our analysis will primarily focus on temporary movements under the NAFTA-created TN visa, with some consideration of other temporary entry visas. The reason for this focus on one form of temporary visas, namely the TN visa, is that its existence is owing to NAFTA (Section 16). Moreover, the TN visa was seen within the context of the treaty as a primary instrument to facilitate trade while insuring that neither the Canadian nor the U.S. labour markets would be injured.[3]

Given this focus on the TN visa, we summarize the extensive legal literature in this area by reviewing two overviews written before and after September 11, 2001. Vazquez-Azpiri (2000) assesses the TN visa instrument by looking at whether it was providing a simple, rapid and predictable mechanism for the entry of Canadian information technology (IT) professionals to the United States prior to September 11. He sees the IT occupational category as a litmus test for the administration of the TN visa since the definitions of IT workers and the associated degree requirements are ambiguous and subject to administrative whim. In other words, if problems with the TN visa should arise, they should first appear in the IT group, given its evolving occupational definitions. In addition, focusing on IT professionals allows the author to compare the efficacy of the TN visa to the other significant temporary U.S. visa for foreign IT workers, the H-1B visa.[4] Chapter 16, in Part 5 of NAFTA, imposes upon each state party an obligation to apply the labour mobility provisions of Chapter 16 "… so as to avoid unduly impairing or delaying the trade in goods or services".[5] Vazquez-Azpiri concludes from his U.S. legal practice that:

> The TN category of the NAFTA is not functioning as effectively as it could or should. The unqualified boon to cross-border labour mobility between the United States and Canada … has never materialized, and what we have today (2000) is a needlessly complicated admission system fraught with pitfalls and often arbitrarily implemented … (which) produces an unacceptably high number of denials.
> (Vazquez-Azpiri, 2000, p. 15)

Specifically, he argues that the TN category is deficient in three basic respects. First, the stated U.S. policy of ensuring safe borders (before September 11, 2001) and the protection of domestic labour are in conflict with the NAFTA stated desire to facilitate temporary entry. Second, unlike the H-1B visa instrument, the TN visa provides a rigid definition of an IT worker which does not change over time.[6] Third, the TN officers who adjudicate the applications require strict compliance to an outdated occupation list. In sum, the single biggest virtue of the TN visa — port of entry adjudication — has become its single biggest hazard since it is the source of an uneven application of the entry rules.

This evaluation of the TN visa is, of course, limited to the pre-2001 experience of Canadian IT workers attempting to gain entry to the United States through this one firm. What about other entry categories under the TN? What has been the experience of a sample of all Canadians using a Canadian firm to obtain a TN visa after September 11, 2001?

Figure 1 dramatically portrays the historical experience of a non-random group of Canadian TN applicants as of October 2001.[7] The NAFTA ports of entry in Canada appear on the vertical axis, while the net number of admissions (positive minus negative) for each port of entry appears on the horizontal axis. Several features of Figure 1 are important to note. First, for all Canadian entry ports to the United States, the number of rejections equals the number of admissions, in itself a revealing finding. Next, there appears to be no geographic pattern of rejection/acceptance rates across entry port cities. However, the Detroit and Vancouver (Vancouver-Blaine) entry points have an astonishing net rejection rate of over 50 percent, indicating that heavily utilized ports of entry have high rejection rates.[8] Finally, the large variation in experiences shows that the degree of individual discretion at various ports of entry influences an individual applicant's chances of admission under a TN visa.

Richardson (2002) argues that in the post-September 11 era, these high rates of rejection of Canadian TN applicants and differential acceptance rates

FIGURE 1

NET ADMISSIONS UNDER NAFTA (ACCEPTANCES – REJECTIONS), BY PORT OF ENTRY, OCTOBER 2001

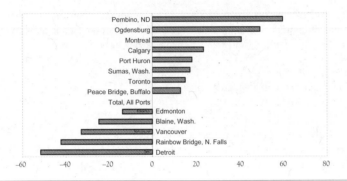

Source: www.grasmick.com/peacepoe.htm

across ports of entry are owing to two factors. First, in late 2001, the position of NAFTA issuing officer at ports of entry to the United States was eliminated. Thus, those who were expert in interpreting the available guidelines for TN visa issuance to the United States are no longer available and have been replaced by line officers. Richardson notes that the latter lack a specialized knowledge of NAFTA Section 16 provisions and are primarily concerned with security matters. Richardson also argues that these problems are magnified for Canadian IT workers who often have exotic job descriptions, which do not match the outdated 1995 occupation list. Given the inflexibility displayed by assessing officers, this leads to narrower interpretations and high rejection rates for Canadians in new IT occupations applying for a TN visa.

In sum, this review of two legal-based overviews —— one from a U.S.-based author and the other from a Canadian — provides a negative picture of the TN visa as a mechanism for further Canadian integration to the U.S. labour market. However, there are many other occupations beyond the above-mentioned IT worker, and other temporary visas which Canadians can use aside from the TN visa. We review the larger context below.

The remaining group of U.S. temporary visas available to Canadians (and others) is an eclectic mixture with an *alphabet soup* of designations.[9] The H-1B visa predates the TN visa and is the principal substitute visa for highly skilled Canadians wishing to enter the United States. The key features of the H-1B visa include the following: it applies to a degree-holding professional who plans to stay for six years of less, and the applicant's employer must prove that the hiring of this professional will have no impact on U.S. workers. The L visa is issued to intra-company executive transferees and is valid for up to seven years. The E visa is issued for one year to investors and traders who want to manage a substantial personal investment in the United States or work with a firm that conducts its principal business with the visa holder's country of origin (i.e. Canada).[10]

The central question that begs an answer is: If the TN visa applicant suffers from such arbitrary adjudication, have Canadians switched to another visa to ensure an integrated labour market adjustment?[11]

Figure 2 provides an answer to that question and puts the lid on the concept of a substitutable U.S. temporary visa. The TN visa is, in fact, the predominant visa issued to Canadians and it has grown in spectacular fashion: from 9,148 in 1991-92 to 85,704 in 1999-2000. The remaining visas issued to Canadians, including the nearest substitute (the H-1B visa), remain near constant and represent a minor fraction (less than 4 percent) of the total number of temporary visas issued to Canadians.[12] Hence, there is no substitution across visa entry gates and the total number of temporary visas issued to Canadians has grown 600 percent in eight fiscal years.[13]

All of the literature reported above has assessed the available temporary visa instruments in terms of legal criteria. Globerman and DeVoretz (1998) provide a

FIGURE 2

MOVEMENTS OF CANADIAN TEMPORARY WORKERS TO THE UNITED STATES (FISCAL YEARS)

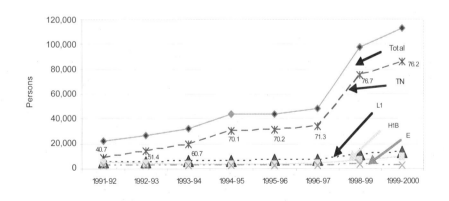

Source: Immigration and Naturalization Services (INS).

unique economic viewpoint to assess the efficacy of any of these temporary visas. They argue that the motivation to apply for any of these temporary visas arises only if there is a labour market disequilibrium from which a rent can be captured by either the firm or the individual through cross-border movement. Further, whether the individual or the firm receives the greater share of the rent depends on which party bears the greatest cost burden in acquiring the visa and any human capital gain resulting from the move. Thus, they predict that the differential use of any of these visas will be based on a cost-benefit analysis by the particular applicant given his/her motivation to move. However, their analysis leads to one major conclusion: that the transaction cost of the TN visa is extremely low, and hence prior to September 11, 2001 a professional would have chosen a TN visa over the high-cost H-1B visa.[14] An inspection of Figure 2 bears this out, since over 76 percent of all temporary visas issued between 1991 and 2000 fall in the TN category. Thus, they would concur with Richardson that the post-September 11 difficulties (cited above) in the implementation of the TN visa may prove a serious development in constraining the TN as a vehicle for labour market integration between Canada and the United States.[15] Globerman and DeVoretz (1998, p. 27) also note that:

> It seems unlikely that most temporary immigrants undertake short-run migration for direct gains in income ... Rather, it seems more reasonable to view short-run immigration as a form of investment in human capital.

To the extent that this investment analysis is correct, the following interpretation emerges. An applicant with a short-term investment horizon will choose a visa that has a minimum transaction cost while allowing him or her to self-invest through on-the-job training. Still following the investment view of visa acquisition, the individual would apply for a temporary visa given its low cost and the fact that it may later allow conversion to a more permanent U.S. visa. In the financial sector, for example, a Canadian bank could initiate an employee transfer to the United States with either a TN visa or L visa since the length of time allowed in the United States under either visa is sufficient for training purposes, when no conversion to a permanent status is planned (at least by the employer). The choice between the TN visa and L visa thus depends solely on the transaction cost of obtaining a visa, and at least prior to September 11, 2001 the TN visa would be the visa of choice. On the other hand, if a firm (or individual) is motivated to move to the United States to exploit firm-specific advantages, then the move is not an investment and it has a medium- to long-term horizon in order to capture income gains. If it takes more than six years to capture these income benefits, the TN entry permit would again be the preferred temporary visa because there is no limit on its tenure.

In sum, the main conclusion stemming from the Globerman and DeVoretz analysis is that the degree of labour market integration initiated by either an individual of through an employee transfer within a multinational corporation ultimately depends on the availability of a set of low-cost temporary visas with different tenures.

In 1997, the OECD organized a conference, entitled *Migration: Free Trade and Regional Integration in North America*, to explore the same question as in this study, again exclusively from an economic perspective. To answer this question from a Canadian vantage point, DeVoretz and Laryea (1998) tested Dales' (1964) thesis that there is a labour mobility triangle between Canada, the United States and the rest of the world (ROW), and that this triangle has grown in importance under NAFTA. This modern day interpretation of Dales' thesis states that under conditions of free(r) labour mobility between Canada and the United States (with, for example, a TN visa) and an elastic supply of highly skilled immigrants from the rest of the world to Canada, several labour market outcomes in Canada can be predicted. First, a combination of wage compression and/or labour displacement should occur in Canada as large numbers of highly skilled individuals enter Canada from the ROW and produce a substantial emigration of highly skilled Canadian citizens to the United States. This latter prediction is of particular interest in 2003 since only Canadian citizens (mostly native-born) can emigrate to the United States under the low-cost TN visa. Thus, the required conditions for Dales' dire predictions appear to have been in place in the post-Free Trade Agreement (FTA) and post-NAFTA eras.[16] What did the DeVoretz-Laryea review of the econometric evidence on this triangular model in 1998 reveal? The authors found that:

> For limited sectors and types of human capital, a portion of each aspect of Dales' thesis holds. In 59 industries ... labour displacement was significant, while in a smaller set of industries wage compression appeared. Finally, emigration to the United States ... reappeared....
> (DeVoretz and Laryea, 1998, p. 143)

The implication of these findings for Canada-U.S. labour migration is that integration in selected occupations extends beyond North America. Canadian emigration to the United States coupled with replacement immigration to Canada from the rest of the world form a conscious Canadian immigration policy with profound labour market outcomes for Canada including what Dales termed extensive economic growth. In other words, Canada's gross national product rises while Canadian income per capita declines.[17] Under this process of simultaneous Canadian emigration to the United States and immigration to Canada, and given an elastic supply curve, wage rates (and income per capita) must fall unless complementary capital enters the labour market with a rise in final product price.[18]

It remains to be seen if the evidence reported by DeVoretz and Laryea is still valid in 2004 for at least the 63 occupations with NAFTA TN mobility provisions. Moreover, the dire consequences forecasted by Dales (1964) and documented by DeVoretz and Laryea (1998) require basically a static labour market. Whether offsetting capital, productivity or product price changes have occurred between 1997 and 2002 is yet to be determined. We return to this question in our concluding section.

Iqbal (2001) takes a more contemporary but narrower economic view and focuses only on the North American forces that contribute to highly skilled labour market integration in North America. The advent of the low-cost TN visa coupled with higher post-tax income in the United States and a warmer climate are argued by Iqbal (based on a very limited data set) to influence the number of highly skilled Canadians going to the United States. Perhaps more importantly, Iqbal asserts (2001, p. 320) that:

> The emotional and psychological barriers that used to keep Canadians at home are much less relevant. The health care and welfare services do not carry much weight ... (since they) can afford to buy these services (as) they need with the new wealth they are acquiring.

Much has changed since September 11, 2001. The U.S. economy has gone into a recession, the spectre of terrorism has permeated the daily lives of urban Americans and, most importantly, the TN visa is perhaps no longer the frictionless entry point that Iqbal implies with his sanguine psychological analysis. In fact, the only way to assess the psychological and perhaps economic barriers that limit the movement of Canadians to the United States is to estimate a *stayer* function. We will turn to this aspect when reviewing the work of DeVoretz and Iturralde (2001) below.

With a much more sophisticated approach and a larger data set, Wagner (2002) retests the Iqbal proposition that Canadian and U.S. post-tax income differences affect Canadian labour market mobility for highly skilled individuals. Through the use of an imaginative counterfactual technique, Wagner infers that Canadians who recently emigrated to the United States stood to reap the largest tax gains owing to the existing differential tax regimes. He further concludes from his counterfactual experiments (2002, p. 24) that:

> ... if both taxes and income opportunities had been equal in Canada and the United States the number of university graduate households migrating south would have declined by 41 percent, (and) that income and tax differences may fully account for the net outflow of people from Canada to the United States.

If Wagner's conclusions are to be taken literally, then there are no non-economic barriers to further North American market integration for highly skilled labour. However, like Iqbal, Wagner only focuses on the motivations of Canadian migrants in 2000. Clearly, in this self-selection process, existing Canadian stayers must have the same estimated reactions as the earlier movers for Wagner's bold conclusion to hold.

McHale (2002) reviews the existing TN visa evidence of Finnie (2001) and Helliwell (1999) and strongly disagrees with their conclusions that the overall number of Canadians leaving for the United States on a TN visa is small (Finnie) or declining (Helliwell). McHale updates the data reported by Helliwell from the U.S. Current Population Survey (CPS) and his startling findings are reproduced below.

McHale's evidence from the CPS data both reverses the Finnie-Helliwell contention that the movement of Canadians to the United States was small and declining. On the contrary, McHale finds that the number of Canadians resident in the United States approached 950,000 in 2002, which represented an increase of 400,000 (80 percent) in five years (1996-2002). Moreover, this spectacular absolute increase could only have occurred through the use of a temporary (TN) visa since 400,000 permanent entry visas were not issued to Canadians during this period. More importantly, it is possible to decompose the CPS data on this resident Canadian cohort into the economically active, with and without university education. The decomposed data reveal that the economically active group represented 280,000 Canadians aged 25 to 64 with at least a bachelor's degree who were resident in the United States in 2002. This group of economically active Canadians living in the United States totalled only

FIGURE 3

ESTIMATED CANADIAN-BORN ECONOMICALLY ACTIVE POPULATION RESIDING IN THE UNITED STATES, 1994-2002

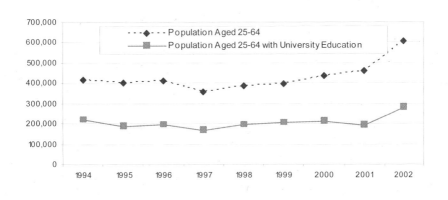

Source: U.S. Census Bureau, *Current Population Survey*, March Supplements, 1994-2002.

164,555 in 1997. Thus, between 1997 and 2002, 116,000 or more university trained Canadians aged 25 to 64 moved to the United States. This represents an average brain drain of 23,000 individuals annually over this period. McHale wryly concludes from this evidence that "... something dramatic may have been happening in recent years." (2002, p. 29) He further states that "... the size of the increase and its consistency with the surge in NAFTA-related visas is a warning that Canada might be losing substantial skills." (2002, p. 29) In sum, McHale's analysis of the brain exchange data indicates that the integration of the North American labour market made substantial progress during the *bubble* period in the United States.

Future North American labour market integration will depend on a host of evolving economic and psychological conditions and on how the current cohort of Canadian (American) stayers react to these potentially motivating forces. DeVoretz and Iturralde address this situation by asking why, in the face of lower mobility costs (TN visa) and large potential income gains, have so many Canadian professionals stayed in Canada? Before we report their findings, it is necessary to place the stayer model in a wider theoretical context to understand why further labour market integration may be difficult despite the presence of favourable prior conditions — a low-cost visa and potentially high income gains from migration.

Figure 4 allows us to define more precisely the concept of North American labour market integration in the absence of any barriers. In a static world (with a fixed demand curve, D_c), the degree of labour market integration is determined by the elasticity of supply imbedded in the supply curve of immigrants from the sending member country (S'_c or S''_c) relative to the elasticity of supply implied by the home member country labour supply curve, S_c.[19] At one extreme, when the elasticity of supply of immigrants is infinite (S''_c) and the wage rate in the sending country is W_w, the implied degree of integration is d-0, that is when 100 percent of the labour force in the receiving NAFTA country is foreign born. At the other extreme, when the supply curves in both member countries are identical (at S_c), and given a wage rate of W_c, the equilibrium level of integration corresponds to zero foreign-born labour in the NAFTA receiving member country.[20] Now, what would be a reasonable depiction of the equilibrium level of labour force integration given the conditions that existed between Canada and the United States in 2002? If we argue that there are minimal legal or institutional barriers (i.e. an efficient TN visa) and given a modest real wage difference and some home-country bias, the level of integration would be measured as $(a-b)/0b$, or one-third of the labour force. Thus, even in the absence of institutional and legal barriers, the integration of the North American labour market is a theoretically precise concept whose equilibrium level ranges from 0 to 100 percent.[21] Moreover, the equilibrium levels of North American

FIGURE 4

A THEORETICAL DEFINITION OF NORTH AMERICAN INTEGRATION

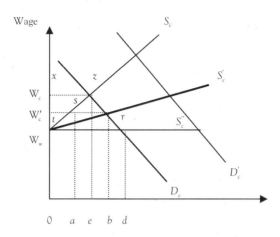

integration will differ across occupations, if these have varying labour supply elasticities between NAFTA member states. In other words, aggregate data on the percentage of Canadians (Americans) in the U.S. (Canadian) labour market is a misleading measure of integration. Integration must be measured for individual occupations given some wage differential between NAFTA member states.[22] Finally, the theory suggests that countries should specialize with respect to the level of labour market integration by occupation. For example, Country A should exhibit non-zero integration in a subset of industries whose supply elasticities lie below Country B's elasticities, and of course Country B will exhibit no integration.[23]

Moreover, given these supply elasticity differences, the degree of integration should be greater, the higher the intercept of the labour demand curve for this occupation.

In sum, this model in its reduced form allows for the possibility of a significant number of stayers (low integration) in a frictionless world at equilibrium.

Figure 5 depicts an extreme case in which the U.S. employer offers a substantially higher wage ($W_{US} > W_{CAN}$) but no labour movement occurs for wage offers above the wage rate, W. This occurs because no U.S. employer will offer a wage rate to induce movement when he/she could hire at home at a lower wage rate. For example, if A–B workers are to be hired to fill the demand arising in the United States from a shift in the demand curve from L_D to $L"_D$, the U.S. employer will hire exclusively in the United States at a wage rate $W"_{US}$ since this wage

FIGURE 5

THEORETICAL EXTREMES, NORTH AMERICAN LABOUR MARKET INTEGRATION

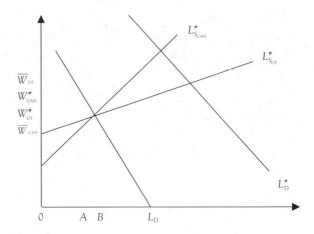

rate is less than the Canadian wage rate, W''_{CAN}.[24] Hence, there should be a large number of Canadian stayers under these conditions.

In fact, Figure 5 is the theoretical paradigm underlying the DeVoretz and Iturralde (2000) estimates of a staying function for highly skilled Canadians in a merged North American labour market. Given this theoretical view, these authors estimate a logit model which measures the log odds of a Canadian professional staying in Canada given several conditioning factors including income differences, marital status, age, education, family size and mobility history. Armed with their logit results, DeVoretz and Iturralde conduct a series of simulations to depict the life-cycle staying function of Canadian professionals. Their results are reproduced in Figure 6, which allows us to summarize their findings on the economic and social forces that limit cross-border labour movements, and hence integration in the pre-2000 NAFTA period.

From Figure 6 we can infer that, given the average economic conditions that prevailed in the mid-1990s, the log odds that a highly skilled Canadian married male would stay in Canada exceeded 90 percent after the age of 30 for a person who had not previously moved within Canada. Past the age of 33, none of the groups of highly skilled Canadians considered has log odds of leaving higher than 25 percent. Finally, changes in the household status, at any age, altered the probability of a highly skilled Canadian staying at home. For example, for 27-year-old males who have moved previously, the probability of staying is 75 percent for those who are married, but it rises above 95 percent for those who are unmarried.

428

FIGURE 6

EFFECTS OF GENDER, MARITAL STATUS AND MOBILITY ON PREDICTED PROBABILITIES OF SKILLED LABOUR FORCE MEMBERS STAYING IN CANADA, BY AGE CATEGORY, 1995 AND 1996*

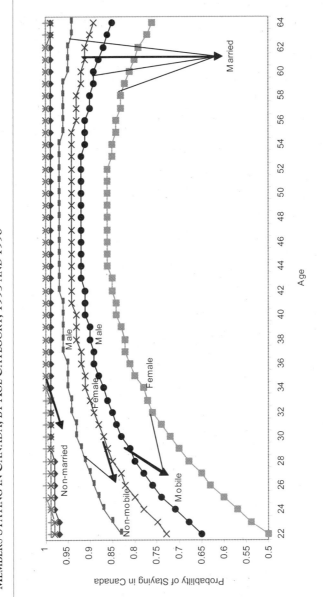

Note: * Probability as a function of age at the sample means of total income and family.

Sources: 1996 Canadian Census, Public Use Microdata Individual Files, and 1995 *Current Population Survey,* Person and Family Data Files, U.S. Census Bureau.

In a second experiment, DeVoretz and Iturralde estimate the income required to keep a highly skilled worker in Canada. How large must be the annual income gain between Canada and the United States for all NAFTA-defined professions to induce a substantial change in the probability of staying (leaving)?

Figure 7 shows the simulation results which indicate that, in 1991, the annual income gain required to induce a collapse in the probability of staying was $99,000, but this number had declined to $46,000 in 1996. Two points emerge from this simulation. First, there is a substantial reservation income before Canadian professionals can be induced to move and, secondly, this reservation income (gain) has declined in magnitude over time, at least prior to 2001.[25]

In sum, this diverse literature review from both a legal and economic perspective suggests that an efficient instrument — the TN visa — existed between 1995 and 2001 to allow a moderate but growing level of North American labour market integration.

FIGURE 7

EFFECTS OF MOBILITY ON PREDICTED PROBABILITIES OF STAYING FOR SKILLED CANADIAN MALES BY CHANGE IN TOTAL INCOME CATEGORY, 1991 AND 1996*

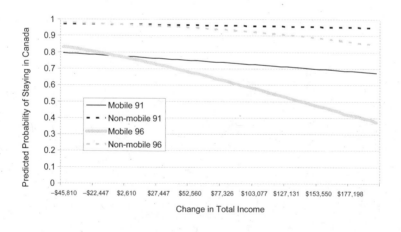

Note: * Probabilities as a function of change in total income at the sample means of family size and age.

Sources: 1991 and 1996 Canadian Census, Public Use Microdata Individual File; 1990 Decennial Public Use Persons and Household, and 1995 *Current Population Survey*, Person and Family Data Files, U.S. Census Bureau.

COUNTERFACTUAL EXPERIMENTS

THE READER WILL RECALL THAT THE DEGREE OF HOME BIAS in the North American context was to be determined with a counterfactual methodology. In short, we ask: If there were no border between Canada and the United States, would this alter the stayer-mover function estimated by DeVoretz and Iturralde? The precise technique behind this counterfactual analysis is to use the mean values reported by DeVoretz and Iturralde (2000) and replace their estimated coefficients with similar coefficients derived from estimated mobility functions for within-Canada movers. Fortunately, Gaetz (1998) provides estimates for a near identical mover-stayer model of internal Canadian migrants based on a similar data set.[27] We report in Table 1 the key ingredients of this simulation process, which are the mean values of the variables, and the corresponding coefficients.

Table 1 reveals significant differences in mean values between the DeVoretz-Iturralde foreign-based mover-stayer population and Gaetz's results for internal Canadian movers.[28] Because the DeVoretz and Iturralde Canadian population sample consisted only of B.A. or higher degree holders, their population is older (by 6-7 years) and more likely to be married. The remaining variables for Gaetz and for DeVoretz and Iturralde are similar in value except for the crucial mean income gain derived from a Canada-U.S. move (C$12,666) — against a C$2,580 gain for a move within Canada. This mean value difference and the associated differences in the income gain coefficients (−0.000012 *vs.* −0.0013) will prove crucial in our simulations. However, the essential age variable in the life-cycle simulation is similar in both studies, with all the remaining variables (family size, gender and marital status) yielding opposite signs in the two models. In sum, given the differences in magnitude and signs of all the coefficients between the Gaetz and DeVoretz-Iturralde estimates, the evidence of a home-country bias is not clear. Thus, we proceed to perform a stylized simulation to detect any bias.

We turn to Figure 8 to illustrate if a home-country bias exists in one stylized case. In this example, we have a married male head of household with no previous mobility experience and a bachelor's degree who assumes all the remaining mean values of the DeVoretz-Iturralde case and the Gaetz coefficients. What is immediately obvious is that no appreciable home bias appears in this case. This minimal home-bias effect arises from the offsetting differences reported above in the sign or magnitude of the coefficients for all non-age variables between the DeVoretz-Iturralde and Gaetz studies. This does imply some caution in accepting such comparison.[29]

TABLE 1

VALUES FROM GAETZ AND FROM DEVORETZ AND ITURRALDE

VARIABLE	MOVER (DEVORETZ-ITURRALDE)	STAYER (DEVORETZ-ITURRALDE)	MOVER (GAETZ)	STAYER (GAETZ)	COEFFICIENTS (DEVORETZ-ITURRALDE)	COEFFICIENTS (GAETZ)
Age	43.1	42.1	35.6	36.3	0.23	0.19
Age^2	n.a.	n.a.	n.a.	n.a.	−0.002	−0.0001
Family Size	2.2	3.0	2.61	2.7	1.76	−0.16
Male	0.61	0.65	0.57	0.55	0.6	−10.0
Married	0.78	0.67	0.58	0.6	1.54	−0.19
B.A. Degree	n.a.	n.a.	0.09	0.1	n.a.	0.05
Income Gain	12,666 $CAN	n.a.	2,580 $CAN	n.a.	−0.000012	−0.0013

Source: DeVoretz and Iturralde (2000), and Gaetz (1998).

FIGURE 8

COUNTERFACTUAL EXPERIMENT, EXTERNAL AND INTERNAL MIGRATION

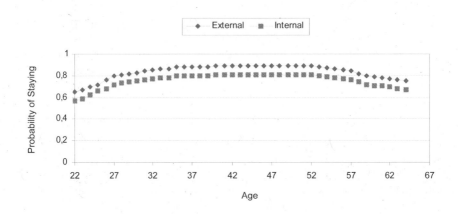

RECENT BORDER RESTRICTIONS AND LABOUR MARKET INTEGRATION

THE LITERATURE REVIEW, the reported econometric evidence and the associated counterfactual experiments all predate the October 2002 actions of the United States to increase security at the Canada-U.S. border. This omission in our analysis could be seriously misleading since the series of new regulations put into place will greatly increase the transaction costs of a movement for some Canadian residents, both citizens and non-citizens. We describe these regulations below and present an analysis to portray the new complexities that selected Canadian residents attempting to obtain a TN visa will face at the border. First, we argue that it is no longer the visa instrument you choose (TN, B or L) but how the United States defines your degree of Canadian citizenship that will affect your ability to integrate into the North American labour market. In a sense, these new border events have undermined all of our foregoing analysis and will raise the transaction costs for some Canadians regardless of the visa instrument they decide to use. We expand on this point below.

In the book he published with Meyers, entitled *Caught in the Middle: Border Communities in the Era of Globalization*, Papademetriou argued, just before September 11, 2001, that all borders are local. In fact, he optimistically suggested that a stationary, well-defined border was a relic of the past, especially in the Canada-U.S. case. The practice of pre-clearance of U.S. visitors at inland Canadian airports was seen as a precursor of a more flexible inland clearance system for the North American auto industry, as well as advent of fast-tracking for selected and screened frequent U.S.-Canada travelers. In fact, he argued, as we do, that the NAFTA or TN visas had become the fast track for 100,000 Canadian professionals in 2000 to enter the United States and vice-versa for U.S. citizens. The economic benefits to selected parties in both countries appeared to Papademetriou to be so large that these alternative methods of border clearance would be the norm in the future.

Then came September 11, 2001. In the intervening 14 months, Canada and the United States have moved back from this amorphous conception of a floating border to notions of a common secure North American *cordon sanitaire* with additional prickly expressions of national sovereignty at each country's check points.

In 2003, we must now ask what would be the future conceptions in Canada and the United States of a common and unfortified border? We would argue that these conceptions are very far apart, with the likelihood that further strains and frictions will appear to create more barriers to mobility for North (Canada) to South (United States) flows.

The latest set of strains has emerged both within the Canadian government and between Canada and the United States over the necessity of requiring visas for some Canadian residents prior to entry into the United States. This has led to confusion on the Canadian side of the border. Canada's then Immigration Minister, Denis Coderre, argued vehemently against visa requirements for non-citizen Canadian immigrants. However, Canada's Foreign Minister stated that the United States has the right to circumscribe entry based on a nation's right to ensure secure borders. In fact, Prime Minister Chrétien took an extreme position on the visa issue, noting that:

> If they do not have a Canadian passport, it's no longer my problem. Let them become Canadian citizens and we will protect them.
> (Prime Minister Chrétien, November 6, 2002)

In effect, over six million Canadians who are either resident non-citizens (landed) or foreign-born citizens will no longer automatically consider themselves candidates for swift clearance at the U.S. border.

To better understand the possible long-term implications of this new development on North American labour market integration, we will outline what we feel are the fundamental sources of tension at the border to illustrate the depth of future border frictions. A common place to start the intellectual search for the sources of current and future border tensions is, oddly, each country's census questionnaire. In particular, we must scrutinize the rationale behind each country's need to administer an identical set of questions to its residents once every ten years. These questions are, in short: Where were you born? What is your citizenship? Where did you live five years ago? They seek to define, from each country's national perspective, who is considered an insider and who is an outsider. You are presumably a complete insider if you were born and hold citizenship in the country where the census is taken and if you have not moved in the last five years. The issue of entitlement and treatment at the border becomes more complicated for those whose answer is a less certain match and the prospect of an outsider appears. The most common case of a quasi-insider is a person who has ascended to citizenship in the country of the census but was not born there and was not resident in the country of citizenship five years ago (or less). How Canada and the United States react to their individual constituents' answers to these questions, especially at the border, reflects the fundamental differences in the two countries' definitions of outsider, and this will ultimately determine the nature of the future political debate over a common continental border.

Let us look at the Canadian perspective on citizenship first. Given that immigration is a cornerstone of Canada's economic development policy, it has a very inclusive definition of citizenship. In fact, from a Canadian perspective, there are several definitions of Canadian citizenship which extend across the spectrum of insider-outsider. The Canadian passport holder may be a dual or tri-citizen. Moreover, Canada recognizes that holding another citizenship is compatible with being a Canadian and constitutes an equally valid definition of citizenship as that of a Canadian-born citizen who holds only one citizenship.

Here lies the first of several wedges in the Canadian *vs.* U.S. perceptions of the border since the United States does not recognize this Canadian view.

The United States currently discourages joint allegiances of its naturalized citizens. In fact, it is merely transferring its narrower definition of foreign-born citizenship to its border scrutiny of other nationals, including foreign-born Canadian residents.

We argue that the existence of dual (or multiple) citizenship(s) in Canada increases the transaction costs for any Canadian who wants to move across the Canada-U.S. border since it raises a series of unanswered questions. For example, who decides the primary citizenship of a Canadian dual citizen? Is it the individual or the state? Moreover, if it is the individual who decides on the primacy of one citizenship, can he/she choose a flag of convenience? In other words, can a Canadian passport holder declare one citizenship while resident in Country A and a second citizenship while in Canada or the United States? These are not easily answered questions, but our point is that Canada and the United States have fundamentally different answers to these key questions, which ultimately increase the transaction costs at the border for Canadian movers.

In the future, these transaction costs will increase given that Canada is currently experiencing a globalization of both its citizenship population and its passport holders. This prediction comes from two sources. First, Canada will have a growing number of dual citizens given its cohort of landed immigrant residents. Second, Canada is also increasingly exporting its new citizens to third countries. Currently, one third of all recent immigrants to Canada return to their country of origin, often with a Canadian passport. This raises a new concept of insider/outsider when a foreign-born Canadian arrives at the U.S. border for scrutiny. In fact, one must ask how will a U.S. border official assess the degree of taste for peace, order and good government of a foreign-born Canadian citizen who, for the last five years, has resided in Shanghai or Dacca?

In short, the differential answers to the three central census questions of birth, citizenship and residence will lead to increased transaction costs for some if not all Canada's foreign-born citizens travelling to the United States. Moreover, the Canadian foreign-born population will simply self-select out of the process of North American labour market integration given these rising costs. In addition, several Canadian lawyers have predicted that Canadian firms with operations in the United States will stop hiring some Canadian foreign nationals in Canada. However, the most damaging scenario for halt in North American labour market integration would unfold based on the advice of one Canadian observer.

> If the United States refuses to budge, Ottawa should require green card holders to have visas to enter Canada. This will show the Americans they need to treat Canada with more respect.
> (S. Adebayo, *Toronto Star*, November 6, 2002)

SUMMARY AND CONCLUSIONS

THE MANDATE FOR THIS STUDY was to evaluate the degree of North American labour market integration in the past and prospects for the future. The evidence suggests that a high degree of labour market integration exists in selected occupations. The post-1989 instrument — the TN visa — has thus lowered transaction costs in terms of time and money for a Canadian (or American or Mexican) with a *bona fide* job offer and citizenship to move within North America. Despite the pleas of reviewed lawyers about idiosyncratic behaviour, their overall conclusion is that the institutional barriers between member states have been reduced with the introduction of the TN visa.

The economic literature reviewed reinforces this interpretation when it provides a theoretical rationale for a firm (individual) to exploit the short-term gains inherent in the TN visa and theoretically defines the limits of North American labour market integration. This theoretical analysis clearly indicates that each of the NAFTA-covered occupations will have a different level of equilibrium integration based upon each country's reservation wage and occupational supply and demand elasticities. In other words, equilibrium labour market integration for a particular occupation can be defined over a wide range (0 to 100 percent) of either country's labour force.

What of the empirical economic evidence on North American labour market integration? The decade of confusion over the size of the movement of highly skilled Canadians to the United States has been set to rest by McHale's reported flows for 2000. Clearly, the number of highly skilled Canadians resident in the United States has vastly increased between 1995 and 2000, and this movement was due to the TN visa.

This evidence, coupled with the results of counterfactual experiments, indicates that, *circa* 2001, the Canada-U.S. highly skilled labour market was integrated, with no home-country bias exhibited by highly skilled Canadian movers between internal or external movement under similar economic conditions.

All of the evidence leading to this conclusion is historical and omits the post-September 11, 2001 border events. Measures taken by the U.S. government until now have raised the transaction costs of obtaining a TN visa. Moreover, future actions will further raise these transaction costs for potential movers, firms and individual border agents, and will lead to a segmented highly skilled labour market in Canada. There is already evidence of an emerging segmented market. Many foreign-born (Commonwealth) Canadian citizens are now subject to an added visa requirement (requiring six months of processing) prior to entering the United States with a TN visa. Still, Canadians born in Middle Eastern countries will generally be registered and finger-printed before admission to the United States. These higher transaction costs at the border will raise the reservation wage of all Canadians and increase the already high probability of staying in Canada for those who were resident in 2003 and beyond. Finally, Canadian firms will react to this differential U.S. border treatment of Canadian-born citizens and all other Canadian citizens in both their cross-border hiring and promotion practices. In short, U.S. border regulations since 2002 have the potential to create a segmented Canadian labour market consisting of Canadian-born citizens and other Canadians. This will affect the equilibrium levels of North American labour market integration and lead to a two-tiered wage rate — one for insiders and one for outsiders.

In sum, the integration of the North American labour market has halted and is in a process of reversal.

ENDNOTES

1   In the context of the European labour market, Straubhaar (1988) asked this question in the 1980s. He concluded that language barriers and social welfare systems reduced the already limited mobility on the European labour market. More recently, the persistent labour-market immobility between East and West Germany in spite of large real income differences could not be rationalized by language or welfare benefit differences (Hunt, 2000).

2   It is interesting to note that there is no literature on Americans moving to Canada although the flow is not insubstantial. This lack of analysis is due to the fact that most U.S. movement to Canada is perceived as temporary.

3   We briefly note here that the TN visa under NAFTA Chapter 16 allows the movement of Canadian or American traders, investors, professionals, business people and their dependents by seeking admission at any port of entry with a letter of employment and evidence of professional or appropriate status.

4   The H-1B visa is open to workers worldwide including, of course, Canadians. It is more restrictive than the TN visa since it requires a labour market test that the prospective worker is needed and is only valid for 6 years. The H-1B had an annual cap of 115,000 in 2002, while there is no limit on the number of TN visas.

5   NAFTA Article 1602.

6   Canadians can use either the TN or H-1B visa to enter the United States as professionals. The H-1B visa has a more flexible definition of eligible occupations but many more restrictions on tenure and convertibility. See the appendix for a detailed comparison of TN to H-1B visas.

7   This is a continuing poll conducted by the law firm of Joseph Grasmick and definitely not random.

8   This implies an astonishing rejection rate of 75 percent.

9   The appendix contains an evaluation of alternative visas vis-à-vis the TN entry permit.

10 The B visa is granted to Canadians (or others) who are conducting temporary and intermittent business in the United States. The main benefit of this visa is that no

work permit or formal application is required. This visa is valid for up to one year but each business trip must not exceed six months. The main disadvantage of this visa is that you cannot work for a U.S. employer. This visa is typically used by its holders for conferences and training in the United States.

11 More to the point, Helliwell (1999) has argued that any growth in the number of TN visas was at the expense of other visa applications and thus the total Canadian demand for U.S. temporary visas is fixed.

12 Care must be exercised in interpreting the numbers in Figure 2 since these are TN visa issuances. No one knows how many Canadians live in the United States with these visas. Based on educated guesses, 33 percent of the total number of TN visas issued are still in use. If this is true, it would imply that, in 2002, over 100,000 Canadians lived quasi-permanently in the United States with TN visas.

13 Note that fiscal year 1997-98 is missing.

14 We define transaction costs as a combination of the pecuniary costs (legal, fees) and time-waiting costs.

15 Obviously, for Americans coming to Canada the TN may still be an efficacious entry device, depending on Canadian security concerns.

16 FTA (the free trade agreement between Canada and the United States) predated NAFTA (1989) and essentially contained the same mobility provisions with a near equivalent version of the TN visa.

17 DeVoretz and Laryea (1998) use the Harberger triangle to illustrate this point. Under static conditions, an increase in the supply of highly skilled labour through ROW immigration implies a low wage rate as Canada moves down the labour demand curve. This result is only reversed if capital enters the occupation to shift the labour demand curve to the right to offset the downward movement along the labour demand curve.

18 The Hicksian conditions of price elasticity of demand for the final product coupled with labour supply elasticity can help determine the exact conditions under which Dales' prediction of declining wage rates would hold.

19 Clearly, if the demand elasticity changes, so does the degree of substitution between foreign and domestic labour. In our case, we posit a reasonably elastic demand curve. For a Wayne Gretzky and similar individuals, the demand curve is completely vertical and no substitution would occur regardless of the immigrants supply elasticity.

20 Full integration with zero immigration to Country A would also occur if the supply curve in Country B lays anywhere above the supply function in Country A. In that case, Country A would send immigrants to Country B and we would have a situation of equilibrium integration with a zero level of foreigners in Country A and a non-zero level in Country B.

21 Formally, equilibrium integration would occur when the employer will not hire a NAFTA immigrant given the prevailing wage difference between the potential immigrants supply price and the prevailing supply price in the home country.

22 Theoretically, one could aggregate across occupations of similar demand and supply elasticities to determine the degree of integration in a more broadly classified group with common elasticities. For example, if hockey and all other sports had

similar supply and demand elasticities, we could think of an equilibrium level of sports integration.

23   This proposition only holds if Country A and Country B have identical labour demand curves or if Country A's demand curve lies above that of Country B.

24   If, given the opportunity, the first 0A workers hired in the United States would have been Canadian since the opposite supply-elasticity conditions hold — indicating the possible existence of a realistic mixed mover-stayer case in which few move and most stay.

25   This decline in the reservation income gain corresponds to the reported rise in the mid 1990s of the number of TN visa holders in the United States.

26   Gaetz (1998) uses the 1996 Canadian census as do DeVoretz and Iturralde. There are minor differences in their model specifications: Gaetz adds years of schooling, and DeVoretz and Iturralde have a variable to measure a previous internal move. We can add the dummy value for Gaetz B.A.-level to our simulation and we assume no prior movement to gain comparability in the two models.

27   They both filtered their populations for the post-25-year-old males and females.

28   This is complicated by the fact that there is no a priori on the signs for marital status, gender and family size in the migration literature. Hence, either study could have the correct sign for these variables in their respective populations.

BIBLIOGRAPHY

Dales, J. "The Cost of Protectionism with High International Mobility of Factors." *Canadian Journal of Economics and Political Science* 30 (1964): 512-525.

DeVoretz, D.J., and C. Iturralde. "The Brain Drain is Real and It Costs Us." Institute for Research on Public Policy. *Policy Options* (1999): 16-24.

——. "Probability of Staying in Canada." RIIM Working Paper Series. Vancouver: Vancouver Centre of Excellence on Immigration and Integration, August 2000.

——. "Why Do Highly Skilled Canadians Stay in Canada?" Institute for Research on Public Policy. *Policy Options* (March 2001): 59-63.

DeVoretz, D.J., and S. Laryea. "Migration and the Labour Market: Sector and Regional Effects in Canada." In *Migration, Free Trade and Regional Integration in North America.* Paris: OECD, 1998.

Finnie, R. "The Brain Drain: Myth and Reality, What it is and What Should be Done." Institute for Research on Public Policy. *Choices* 7, 6 (2001): 3-29.

Gaetz, C.E. "Interprovincial Migration in Canada, 1986-1991. A Multinomial Logit Approach." Unpublished Master's thesis project. Simon Fraser University, 1998, p. 54.

Globerman, S., and D.J. DeVoretz. "Trade Liberalisation and the Migration of Skilled Workers." Manuscript prepared for Industry Canada. 1998.

Helliwell, J. "Checking the Brain Drain: Evidence and Implications." Institute for Research on Public Policy. *Policy Options* (September 1999): 6-17.

Hunt, J. "Why Do People Still Live in East Germany?" IZA Paper No. 123, Bonn: Forschungsinstitut zur zukunft der Arbeit, March 2000.

Iqbal, M. "The Migration of High-skilled Workers from Canada to the U.S.: The Economic Basis of the Brain Drain." In *The International Migration of the Highly Skilled*. Edited by W.A. Cornelius, Thomas J. Espenshade and Idean Salehyan, San Diego, California: CCIS Anthologies, 2001.

McHale, J. "Canadian Immigration Policy in Comparative Perspective." Presented at the John Deutsch Conference on Canadian Immigration Policy for the 21st Century, October 2002.

Papademetriou, D., and D. Meyers (ed.). *Caught in the Middle: Border Communities in the Era of Globalization.* Washington, D.C.: Carnegie Endowment for International Peace, October 2001.

Richardson, K. "Sieve or Shield: NAFTA and its influence within Canada, RIIM Working Paper 02-16, Vancouver Centre of Excellence on Immigration and Integration, Vancouver (B.C.), 2002.

Straubhaar, T. "International Labour Migration Within a Common Market: Some Aspects of the EC Experience." *Journal of Common Market Studies* 27 (1988): 45-61.

Vazquez-Azpiri, J. "Through the Eye of a Needle: Canadian Information Technology Professionals and the TN Category of the NAFTA." *Interpreter Releases* 77, 24 (2000).

Wagner, D. "Do Tax Differences Contribute Toward the Brain Drain from Canada to the US?" Manuscript. 2002.

APPENDIX

U.S. TEMPORARY ENTRY VISAS: A COMPARISON

NOTES ON THE DIFFERENCES between admission standards for professionals under NAFTA's H-1B visa and TN visa.

H-1B

- Canadians who qualify for TN status usually also qualify for H-1B status. However, there are cases where some people qualify for one but not for the other. In general, TN professionals without a bachelor's degree cannot easily make the transition to H-1B status.

- Requires intent by the employer and employee that the placement be temporary. If either side fails this requirement, status will be denied. (Note: It is not necessary that the actual position be temporary; only that the placement of the non-U.S. citizen be temporary.)

- "Dual Intent" is a very interesting concept that means that you can simultaneously intend to do temporary work now, but at some later date work permanently.

- Professional: both the beneficiary and the position must be professional in nature. The law defines a profession as a specialty occupation that requires critical and practical application of a body of highly specialized knowledge.

- Professional with bachelor's degree is the minimum requirement. Diploma must be presented to the INS as proof.

- A professional without a bachelor's degree, but with considerable professional experience, must carefully document his or her special qualifications. This is an intensive process. (Note: Nurses do not qualify for H-1 status but can appeal for TN status.)

- Must acquire a U.S. licence if one is required by the state in which employment is located.

- Must demonstrate a need for a high-level employee. This requires that the potential employer submit an application package giving description of the business, product or service's complexity, evidence of the U.S. premises, and selected company brochures.

- Petition must contain a Labor Condition Application approved by the Department of Labor. This requirement seeks to insure that, by hiring an H-1B applicant, the employer will not be hurting U.S. workers.

- Length of time to obtain H-1B status: Processing time for this status is relatively short; assembling the documentation is the most time-consuming part. A response will arrive 6-10 weeks after submission. There is currently a limit on the number of H-1B visas granted per year.

- Ease of obtaining H-1B status: With a bachelor's degree and a carefully prepared petition there is a high probability of success.

- Duration of H-1B status: Initially granted for a three-year period with a three-year extension available. After this period, one must remain outside of the country for at least one year before re-applying for H status.

TN-1 STATUS

THIS NEW PROVISION OF NAFTA pertains to Canadian and Mexican citizens who are temporary visitors, treaty traders, investors, temporary workers, and professionals. The immigration-related provisions of NAFTA are very similar to those contained in the prior FTA. The new NAFTA provisions cover the same non-immigrant classifications as the FTA: B-1, E, L-1, and professionals.

Major Advantages of TN-1 Over H-1B Status

- Although only granted for one year at a time, the number of renewals permitted is currently unlimited, whereas H-1B status has a time limit.

- No forms are required for TN-1 status.

- TN-1 status can be obtained in person at the border.

- TN-1 status is available to some people who do not qualify for H-1B status. The reverse is also true.

Requirements for TN-1 Status

- The applicant must be a Canadian or Mexican citizen.

- Documents required: Letter from U.S. or Canadian employer specifying the nature of the applicant's U.S. business activity; copy of diploma or degree; proof of possession of a license to practice profession in the United States; documentation of remuneration arrangements with U.S. employer; letter from U.S. employer stating that U.S. employment is to be temporary.

- Length of time to obtain TN-1 status: For a well documented case 20-minutes to one hour.

- Ease of obtaining TN-1 status: Quite simple if a well-proven case is presented.

- Duration of stay: live and work for one year; can be renewed for additional years. Renewal can be obtained at the border with an updated company-supporting letter.

Pros and Cons of the TN-1 Status

- The flexibility of this status gives a U.S. employer the opportunity to assess a Canadian employee's performance and adaptability to the organization and then, if both parties are satisfied and want the arrangement to be permanent, a permanent residence visa can be applied for.

- The main advantage is that a labour certification is not required. This means that no one has to prove that the Canadian is or is not taking a job away from a U.S. worker.

- The fast turnaround time in obtaining the TN-1 status.

OTHER U.S. TEMPORARY VISAS

THE L VISA IS ISSUED TO INTRA-COMPANY TRANSFEREES who are executives, managers and workers with specialized knowledge, and who are transferred to the United States to work for their company, a subsidiary or affiliate. This visa is valid for up to seven years for managers and for up to five years for other employees.

The E visa is issued to investors and traders — investors wanting to manage a substantial personal investment in the United States and traders who go to the United States to work for a company that conducts its principal business with the visa holder's country of origin (i.e. Canada). The duration of this visa is one year, with one-year extensions available.

The B visa is granted to individuals conducting temporary and intermittent business activities in the United States. The main benefit of this visa is that no work permit or formal application is required. This visa is valid for up to one year, but each business trip must not exceed six months. The main disadvantage of this visa is that it does not allow the holder to work for a U.S. employer. This visa is typically used for conferences and training in the United States.

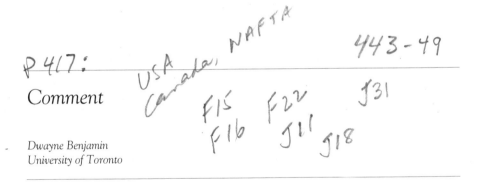

Comment

Dwayne Benjamin
University of Toronto

SUMMARY

DEVORETZ AND COULOMBE explore the possible extent of increased labour market integration between Canada and the United States. Their evidence is drawn from a wider than usual variety of sources:

- *Surveys of immigration lawyers*: The responses of immigration lawyers underline the heterogeneous interpretation of immigration rules, especially across different, understaffed U.S. ports of entry.

- *Evidence of Canadian immigration to the United States over the 1990s*: The results presented in Figures 2 and 3 show striking evidence of significant Canadian immigration to the United States during the 1990s, especially in the TN (NAFTA) visa category. These increases in migration existed despite the problems cited by the lawyers.

- *'Counterfactual' analysis*: What if the United States was a potential Canadian migration destination no different from another Canadian province? If we could construct such a counterfactual argument, it would be possible to simulate the level of migration Canadians would make to the United States if the border between Canada and the United States was erased. DeVoretz and Coulombe find that the border (apparently) plays only a small role in migration decisions, which they interpret as showing that there is no 'home bias' in Canadians' migration decisions.

The authors thus come to the conclusion that as many migrants who so wanted left for the United States during the 1990s, and that this movement was largely facilitated by the TN visa. However, they conclude by noting that the post 9-11 border is essentially closed and that labour market integration has halted.

COMMENTS

GIVEN THE EVIDENCE PRESENTED IN FIGURES 2 AND 3, it is hard to dispute their main contention that the 1990s saw a significant increase in Canadian immigration to the United States and that this was facilitated in large part by the relative ease of obtaining a TN visa. Also, given the 9-11 events and the subsequent tightening of the U.S. border, I cannot argue with their other main claim that all bets are off as to whether trends reflected in Figures 2 and 3 will continue for the next ten years. I found the speculations on U.S. distinctions about the degree of Canadian citizenship especially intriguing. On a personal note, I agree with their implication that I should resist all attempts to have information on my place of birth (Orillia, Ontario) removed from my passport. This information might save me considerable future hassles at the border.

My primary criticism of the study is methodological, and focuses in particular on the authors' claim that there is no evidence of a 'home bias' in Canadians' migration decisions. The implication of their claim is that, if the border was erased, we would observe no more migration to the United States than we see now. If true, this would be a surprising result indeed.

That claim rests on the foundation of the counterfactual exercise, associated with Table 1 and Figure 8. The basic idea is simple: imagine that migration decisions concerning the United States are made the same as those within Canada. For example, if Joe Bloggins considers moving to Toronto from Winnipeg, he can enter the income gain into his spreadsheet. If the net gain is positive, he moves. Under the counterfactual exercise, the only difference between moving to Toronto and moving to New York (assuming identical transport costs) is the expected income gain: if the expected income gain in both cities is the same, Joe would be indifferent to moving to either, and so his probability of migrating to both is the same. The authors describe any departure from this as a home bias, for example, if Joe required a higher income to induce him to go to New York (or any other U.S. city) rather than Toronto.

To conduct their counterfactual exercise, they use estimates (calculated elsewhere) of migration equations for (1) Canadian interprovincial migration, and (2) Canadian migration to the United States. They ask whether the probability of migrating to the United States would be significantly higher if the decision was made according to the Canadian internal migration equation, albeit with the U.S. income difference. In the end, the authors find that the probability would not change much, which they interpret as reflecting no home bias. The key numbers used in their calculations are the income coefficients (the response of migration to expected income gains), and the expected income gains. The income coefficient in the 'Stay in Canada vs. the United States' equation is –0.000012, as compared to –0.0013 in the 'Stay in home province vs. move somewhere else in Canada' equation. Without arguing about where these numbers come from and taking them at face value, they actually imply a huge degree of home bias, because the U.S. coefficient is 100 times larger than the within-Canada coefficient. This means that if it takes $10,000 of annual salary difference to get Joe Bloggins to move from Winnipeg to Toronto, it would take $1,000,000 to coax him to move to New York. While interpretation of 'big' and 'small' is in the eye of the beholder, in my eye I could be coaxed to go to New York from Winnipeg for considerably less than $1,000,000. So, these coefficients alone cast doubt (for me) on the conclusion that there is no home bias.

But why is there no difference when they substitute the within-Canada coefficients? To some extent, this reflects the small size of the coefficients: income plays only a modest role in the migration decision (more on this later). The remainder is driven by the relatively low returns to moving to the United States vs. staying in Canada. The authors estimate an expected increase in income of $2,580 for migrating within Canada, compared to $12,666 for moving to the United States. So the net gain is on the order of $10,000 of salary, which combined with low income sensitivity leads to very little extra migration to the United States, even if the migrant treats it like any other Canadian province.

The entire counterfactual exercise will be sensitive to estimates of both the income gain of moving to the United States and individual responsiveness to that gain. Both magnitudes are very difficult to estimate. Let's begin with the expected income gain: how much can an individual expect to earn if he or she moves to the United States? A reasonable estimate might be what similar Canadians earn in the United States compared to Canada. For concreteness, imagine that earnings in Canada (Y_C) and in the United States (Y_A) are determined by the following human capital equations:

$$Y_C = X\beta_C + u_C$$
$$Y_A = X\beta_A + u_A.$$

So, given his characteristics, X, that individual calculates his earnings in the two countries, which depend on the parameters β_C, β_A as well as on unobservables, u_C, u_A. The income gain from moving to the United States is given by:

$$[Y_A - Y_C] = X(\beta_A - \beta_C) + [u_A - u_C]$$
$$= X\delta + u.$$

The person will move if the expected gain exceeds the cost of moving, c, that is:

$$E[Y_A - Y_C] > c, \quad \text{i.e.,}$$
$$X\delta + u - c > 0$$
$$u > -X\delta + c, \quad \text{or}$$
$$u > \lambda(X, c).$$

Whatever the parameters, we expect individuals with higher differences in unobserved earnings in the United States than Canada ($u_A > u_C$) to move. This could arise either from an absolute earnings advantage in the United States (a superstar who would earn 'relatively' big dollars in both countries) or from a comparative advantage in the United States (a person who, while average in Canada, has a skill that is especially valuable in the United States). Of course, we can tell even more complicated stories. The main point is that there is no reason to expect Canadian migrant earnings in the United States to be a very good predictor of 'stayers' earnings in the United States should they decide to move. Canadian movers and stayers (systematically) differ in unobservable ways. This is a classic example of sample selection bias[1].

This selection problem makes the authors' exercise almost impossible — at least requiring significantly more empirical justification. It renders estimation of the sensitivity of migration to expected earnings quite difficult (ignoring the inherent data problems of pooling Canadians in the United States with those from Canadian data sets). If Canadian migrants are positively selected, then we may exaggerate the U.S. earnings levels required to induce migration. Perhaps U.S. earnings levels are unattainable in Canada (a comedian can earn only a modest income in Canada, but vast sums in Los Angeles). Basically, we can tell stories that render the counterfactual exercise meaningless.

Is there any evidence of selection? Consider the following exercise, which highlights the difficulties of precisely answering the question. I selected samples of Canadian-born men from both the 1990 U.S. census and 1991 Canadian census, and plotted a graph of the densities of annual earnings of these men in Canada and the United States. To maximize comparability, I restricted the sample to white men between the ages of 24 and 64. There is no obvious way to adjust for differences in exchange rate, prices, taxes, etc., which further underlines the difficulty of the entire exercise. However, for simplicity, I converted Canadian earnings into U.S. dollars using a 0.86 exchange rate, which (approximately) prevailed at the time. The results are shown in Figure C1. Most interestingly, the earnings of Canadians in the United States are positively skewed (compared to the earnings distribution of similar men in Canada), as there is a significantly greater proportion of earners in the upper tail than is the case in Canada, where the distribution is more equal.

How does this actually affect the authors' conclusions? On one hand, it is possible that we are observing an equilibrium level of migration to the

FIGURE C1

DISTRIBUTION OF EARNINGS IN CANADA AND THE UNITED STATES

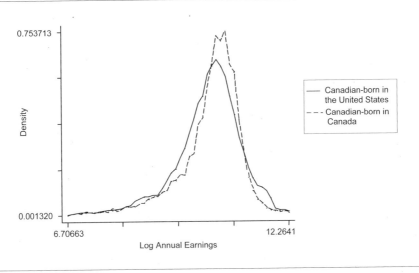

Note: Author calculations using the 1990 U.S. Census PUMS and the 1991 Canadian census public microdata. These plots show the kernel density estimates of the log earnings distribution for white men aged 25-64, for Canadians living in the United States and Canadians living in Canada. Canadian earnings are converted to U.S. dollars at an exchange rate of 0.86 (an approximation of the rate which prevailed at the time).

FIGURE C2

CORRELATION OF STATE OF RESIDENCE FOR CANADIAN-BORN AND U.S.-BORN MIGRANTS

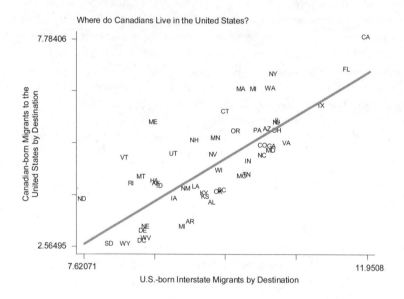

Note: Author calculations using the 1990 U.S. Census PUMS. This plot shows the log of the number of Canadian-born men aged between 16-64 living in a given state, versus the number of U.S.-born men living in the same state, but born outside of the state (i.e. U.S. interstate migrants). A regression line is added for reference.

United States and, therefore, as much labour market integration as we would expect if the border was eliminated. But that possibility exists independently of the evidence they provide. On the other hand, it suggests that there remain significant income gains for talented Canadians, but that these gains do not exceed the cost — including border and visa hassles — associated with moving to the United States. This implies a 'home bias' that could disappear with a more open border. Their methodology does not allow us to conclude either way.

Finally, I would like to turn the authors' counterfactual exercise on its head to illustrate another complexity of cross-border migration. Consider comparing Canadian immigrants to the United States with U.S. interstate migrants. This is easy to do using U.S. census data. In Figure C2, I plotted the log number of Canadian migrants in a U.S. state against the log number of U.S.-born migrants from other U.S. states (restricting the sample to white men between the ages of 16 and 64). Basically, this plot shows the correlation of Canadian immigrant destinations with U.S. internal migrants. This exercise shows that there is significant labour market 'integration' insofar as Canadian migrants to the United States closely resemble U.S. migrants within that country. While there is a slight preference by Canadians for U.S.-Canada border states (lying above the regression line), the overall correlation is quite high. This lends support to the 'half-full' interpretation that DeVoretz and Coulombe offer concerning Canada-U.S. labour market integration. It also shows that Canadians go where the returns are high, and that they are (apparently) drawn by similar economic forces as Americans. Rather than focusing exclusively on the 'Canada-U.S.' migration decision, it appears worthwhile to better understand the underlying forces encouraging mobility within the United States.

Finally — while there is no evidence to support this — I must agree with the authors that post 9-11, U.S. security concerns can be expected to reduce the process of integration that occurred during the 1990s and that non-native-born Canadians will be most affected.

ENDNOTE

1   See Borjas (1987).

BIBLIOGRAPHY

Borjas, George. "Self-Selection and the Earnings of Immigrants." *American Economic Review* 77, 4 (1987): 531-553.

Jean Mercenier   &   Nicolas Schmitt
Cergy-Pontoise University   University of Geneva and
                         Simon Fraser University

10

F13 F16

F22

J31 J24

L26   O33

A Simple General Equilibrium Model With International Labour Market Linkages

INTRODUCTION

AN IMPORTANT ASPECT OF GLOBALIZATION is the growing importance of international labour mobility. Although, in overall volumes, migrations remain largely traditional (i.e. non-skilled labour from non-OECD (Organisation of Economic Co-operation and Development) countries to OECD countries; see Gross and Schmitt, 2002), there is growing intra-OECD country labour mobility and there is a perception that a substantially higher level of international labour mobility may be just around the corner. Current intra-OECD labour mobility exhibits a relatively high mean and variance with respect to skill level as compared to worldwide international labour mobility. In this regard, Canada and the United States are probably at the forefront of that evolution due in large part to the relatively high degree of labour mobility at the national level and to the natural pressure thus created on cross-border mobility under current migration policies. In Europe, despite legally free mobility within the European Union, migration flows, though rising, remain modest. For instance, it is rumoured that well over 250,000 French citizens have recently moved to London and that a high share of these migrants are young, highly skilled and entrepreneurial individuals fleeing the French bureaucracy in favour of British laissez-faire. The number of cross-border commuters is growing steadily in border regions (for instance between Switzerland and neighbouring countries). With rapidly aging populations, Germany, Italy, Austria and Switzerland are adopting policies aimed at attracting and facilitating the migration of skilled individuals.[1]

However, even if mobility within the European Union were to increase dramatically, it is unlikely that it will ever be able to contain the impacts of a rapidly aging population. Hence, migration will have to come from outside the European Union (Fertig and Schmidt, 2002).

What are the economic costs and benefits of international labour mobility in a modern economy? Should it be encouraged? Should it be encouraged for some skills but not for others? Is international labour mobility of skilled workers an important factor for specialization? Although these questions are interesting, they require new tools. In particular, the existing literature largely treats skills as homogeneous and identical across countries. If international labour mobility with homogeneous skills is potentially important because of its scale effect, such treatment of international mobility and its impact on modern economies is obviously oversimplified. For high-value-added manufacturing and service sectors, we need to differentiate skills and, more importantly, assign a significant role to highly skilled individuals in the production of goods and services. The main purpose of this study is to suggest a modeling approach to highlight the potential economic effects of migration when differentiating labour by skills. One could imagine building an applied general equilibrium model with these features, and our study could be considered a tentative first step in this direction.

The study is organized as follows. In the section entitled *Trade Liberalization and International Labour Mobility*, we review the main channels through which international labour mobility affects the economy. In the next section, entitled *A Model of Trade, Wage Distribution and International Labour Mobility*, we focus on one particular mechanism based on trade and income inequality. We develop a model where individuals choose to migrate wherever their skills support the highest wage. In the following section, we conduct simulation exercises using fictitious data in order to highlight the basic mechanisms at work.

TRADE LIBERALIZATION AND INTERNATIONAL LABOUR MOBILITY

THE TRADITIONAL HECKSCHER-OHLIN APPROACH to international trade and factor mobility predicts that international factor mobility will not occur with free international trade of products since all efficiency gains can be realized by international trade alone. This classic result due to Mundell (1957) thus suggests that trade and international labour mobility are substitutes. Because the assumptions underlying the neoclassical approach are quite stringent, it is easy to find models where this substitution does not hold and, therefore, where the pressures to migrate increase with freer trade. Such complementarity between trade and labour mobility can be obtained in a variety of cases (for surveys and a discussion, see Faini, de Melo and Zimmermann, 1999; and Venables, 1999). In fact, many cases have now been identified and it is probably fair to say that, today, economists place a greater emphasis on such complementarity than on the more classic substitution between trade and factor mobility. This is important because complementarity between trade and factor flows implies that the economic effects of integration can be very different with or without international factor mobility, and thus with or without integration of different labour markets. We first review some of the main predictions about the relationship between trade and factor flows coming from the workhorse models used in the field.

MAIN TRADE MODELS

TODAY, THE MOST COMMONLY USED TRADE MODELS are without doubt the Heckscher-Ohlin model, the specific factor model, the intra-industry trade monopolistic competition model, and the "core-periphery" model of economic geography. In a world without distortion where the same factors of production are used to produce every good, the Heckscher-Ohlin model predicts substitution between trade and factor flows. Essentially, in this world, smaller international price differences for a product lead to smaller differences in factor prices. Thus, if there is no incentive to move factors across borders before trade liberalization, freer trade certainly does not create international factor mobility. And, if there is an incentive to move factors across borders before trade liberalization, this incentive necessarily decreases with freer trade. In other words, the Heckscher-Ohlin approach leads to the classical substitution between trade and factor mobility.

This result does not necessarily hold with the specific factor model. This point is important because factor specificity is probably a key element of modern economies. It is indeed fair to say that, with globalization, there is an overall increase in factor specificity (including labour specificity) through factor specialization. To see why factor specificity could lead to complementarity between trade and international labour mobility, suppose that capital or natural resources are specific and that trade liberalization decreases the price of the importable without increasing the price of the exportable. If labour is the intersectoral mobile factor in this economy, the nominal wage will fall. However, the real wage may rise (in terms of the importable) or fall (in terms of the exportable) with ambiguous effects on the incentive to migrate. Suppose now that labour is specific to an import-competing sector. By lowering its real return, trade liberalization increases the incentive to migrate to another country. The important point here is that trade liberalization does not necessarily lead to a lower incentive to migrate, as in Mundell's story, because factor specificity adds a rich set of possible interactions between factors. As a result, factor flows accompanying trade liberalization may make economies more different.[2]

Complementarity between trade and factor flows also arises in models of imperfect competition and increasing returns to scale. Suppose for example that one sector is characterized by Dixit-Stiglitz monopolistic competition, while the factors of production used in that sector conform to the Heckscher-Ohlin model (see Venables, 1999, for such a model). Consumers buy all the differentiated products from this sector, with constant elasticity of substitution (CES) between products. This approach adds several important elements. First, an absolute advantage now matters since a larger country implies a greater number of differentiated products and a more competitive environment. When the differentiated products are used as intermediate inputs in other sectors, then the more competitive environment amounts to a cost reduction in these sectors, translating into higher returns to other factors used in production. Second, firms tend to locate in the larger country because consumers spend more on the differentiated products. This means a higher demand for factors of production in the larger country, and thus higher factor prices. This combined with a lower cost of living (since there is more competition in the larger country) also contribute to raise factor prices in terms of the numeraire. Not surprisingly, factor mobility could be destabilizing in this model. Full agglomeration occurs only in the unlikely case of perfect mobility of all factors. Even if not every factor is mobile (say one of two are not mobile), trade liberalization may lead the smaller economy to become even 'smaller', resulting in a core-periphery type of structure (Krugman, 1991). Whether this occurs in a continuous or a discontinuous fashion depends on the specificity of the model. In particular, for this to occur, at least one factor of production must be perfectly mobile. Hence, there is complementarity between trade and labour mobility since 'free trade' does not eliminate the incentives to migrate. As can be easily imagined, the economic impact of relaxing international migration rules could be quite significant in such an environment,[3] with possible core-periphery type of outcomes.[4]

Other mechanisms leading to complementarity between trade and factor flows could be imagined, but they would not necessarily be relevant for developed economies like those of Canada, the United States or Western European countries. It should be clear, for instance, that mechanisms based on differences in technology among countries are probably not good candidates simply because it is unlikely that substantial technological differences exist among Western countries. Other avenues are not very promising either. They include migration as a response to adjustment lags (e.g. in investment) and complementarity due to the presence of migration networks. These networks imply a potential positive reinforcement effect between trade and migration. Although this explanation certainly has validity for countries like the United States or

Canada with respect to the rest of the world,[5] it is probably not very significant between two developed economies.

Factor specificity, imperfect competition, and geography and trade seem the most relevant building blocks to capture important elements of modern economies and the effects of labour mobility in a freer trade environment. However, two important problems must be addressed. First, the geography and trade approach is notoriously sensitive to assumptions and quite complex to apply. Integrating such a building block into an applied general equilibrium model is not an easy task. Second, although it is straightforward to consider skilled labour as the mobile factor and unskilled labour as the immobile factor, nothing in the trade and geography approach actually links these factors to labour. In other words, the main mechanisms at work are independent of the functioning of labour markets or of the role of workers. For these reasons, we turn our attention to trade models characterized by labour heterogeneity.

MODELS OF LABOUR HETEROGENEITY AND TRADE

AS SHOULD BE CLEAR FROM ABOVE, it is possible to re-interpret the monopolistic competition/geography and trade type of model as a model of international mobility of skilled labour (see Commander, Kangasniemi and Winters, 2002, for more details). We want to depart from this model by introducing more structure on the firm's production side to account for labour heterogeneity. The main advantage is to have differentiation at the input level, specifically among workers, introducing the possibility of international movements of workers with well-defined characteristics. By doing so, one can address specific concerns, such as: Would a country like Canada lose firms (or industries) using very highly skilled labour if international labour mobility was made easier? What would be the impact on other sectors and on wages? Could Canada become a peripheral region for activities where market size and skills are important features?

Models of this type work as follows. The production technology requires skilled individuals (let's call them entrepreneurs) along with labour and/or capital in order to produce goods. These models have two key aspects. First, skilled labour is a complementary input to other factors of production. Hence, there are non-convexities in the model, so that a given level of talent (skill) can have a very different impact depending on the size of the market. This is a Rosen "superstar" type of effect (Rosen, 1981). Second, the impact of talent is modeled in one of two ways, namely as an efficiency effect or as a demand effect. Consider an entrepreneur exercising his talent through a firm. When this talent translates into an efficiency effect or a production effect, the total production derived from a given set of inputs is higher the more the entrepreneur is talented. Whether it is due to organizational or marketing talent, a more able entrepreneur is simply able to produce more than a less able entrepreneur. This productivity effect is useful because it can be incorporated into a model with homogeneous products. Hence, in such a model, the efficiency effect translates into a firm-size effect and a profit effect (given a fixed supply of entrepreneurs). The set-up is particularly simple in a model where individuals choose the role they want to play, such as the choice between acting as an entrepreneur (hiring other workers and/or capital) or as a worker. In this case, the number and the size distribution of firms become endogenous. Not surprisingly, the most talented individuals act as entrepreneurs while less talented individuals act as workers. Consequently, if (workers') wages rise for any reason, it implies that, *ceteris paribus*, the number of firms (or entrepreneurs) will decrease. The basic model is due to Lucas (1978) and it has been used by Murphy, Shleifer and Vishny (1991), Rauch (1991) and Schmitt and Soubeyran (2002). For instance, Rauch (1991) investigates the connection between the pattern of trade and the pattern of migration in a Heckscher-Ohlin framework, while Schmitt and Soubeyran (2002) use this framework to investigate theoretical aspects of the international mobility of brains in a two-country environment.[6]

An alternative way to model the impact of talents is through a demand effect. In this case, the entrepreneur's ability is not associated with her production ability but with how she (or her product or service) is viewed by consumers. Hence, there is a demand-volume effect associated with higher skilled entrepreneurs (think about entertainers). Manasse and Turrini (2001) model this case by assuming a correspondence between the entrepreneur's skill and product quality. They then assume a correspondence between the quality of a product and its demand. This means that products are differentiated at least along the quality spectrum.[7] It also implies that imperfect competition is the more natural environment in which to set this demand effect of skilled entrepreneurs.

So, what are the economic effects of international labour mobility inferred by this approach? To illustrate why labour heterogeneity may imply significant economic effects compared to a more standard approach, consider the following case. A standard approach with homogeneous labour typically assumes that labour and capital are substitutes in production (as in the trade and geography approach; see Venables, 1999). Hence, international labour mobility essentially implies some substitution away from capital for the host country and scale effects in production. When skilled entrepreneurs and labour and/or capital are required to produce differentiated goods, the introduction of international labour mobility of skilled entrepreneurs has a direct impact on the number of products and, thus, the number of firms in an industry, as skilled entrepreneurs are required complementary inputs to other factors of production (whether the entrepreneurs' effect operates through efficiency or demand). When a country loses skilled entrepreneurs, there are non-trivial sectoral and general equilibrium consequences for it.[8]

This may suggest that the out-migration of skilled individuals has mainly negative economic effects. But it is not always the case. Several arguments suggest that out-migration can favour growth in the country losing skilled labour. Such is the case, for instance, when human capital formation is boosted by the prospects of emigration. Here, emigration provides more opportunities for skilled labour than the confines of the domestic market, thus offering a potentially higher return on human capital investment. The average level of human capital may be higher following an out-migration of skilled labour than in the absence of mobility (Wildasin, 2002; Stark, Helmenstein and Prskawetz, 1998).[9] In the same vein, arguments can be made about increased labour market integration as a mean to enhance the flexibility and functioning of national labour markets (Wildasin, 2000). These effects are dynamic in nature and will not be considered further here.

However, another potential positive effect of out-migration can be taken into account in the proposed approach. It is the effect linked to the possibility that individuals may not be able to exercise fully their talent in their country of origin but could do so in the country of immigration. Whether this is due to differences in market size or to the absence of complementary inputs in the country of origin does not matter. The important point is that new knowledge, products or services may emerge from migration, benefiting both the country of emigration and the country of immigration. Another way to put it is to recognize that it is efficient for the world that individuals can migrate to a country where market size or complementary inputs allow them to create new products, services or knowledge that they would not have created otherwise.[10]

An important question is, of course, whether incorporating labour heterogeneity and the role of entrepreneurs into an applied general equilibrium model is relevant to the Canada-U.S. case. First, it must be clear that such an approach makes more sense for high-value-added service and manufacturing sectors (like high technology, biotechnology and the like) than for more traditional manufacturing sectors. In other words, it is relevant for knowledge-based sectors more than for any other sector. Second, the fact that highly skilled individuals are (or could be) entrepreneurs in one country or another is clearly a static long-term effect. Consequently, like most applied general equilibrium analysis, this one has essentially a long-term horizon. Third, the fact that these individuals are entrepreneurs should not necessarily be taken literally. It simply means that highly skilled entrepreneurs are essential production inputs. Whether they are literally the residual claimant is not crucial to the story.

A MODEL OF TRADE, WAGE DISTRIBUTION AND INTERNATIONAL LABOUR MOBILITY

THE COMPARISON BETWEEN CANADA AND THE UNITED STATES over the last two decades or so generally leads to three key observations (Harris and Schmitt, 2003): (i) there is increased wage inequality across skill groups in both Canada and the United States; (ii) there is a productivity gap between the two countries; and (iii) there was significant growth in trade and foreign direct investment following trade liberalization in North America. The model proposed below can take into account the first two phenomena. By 'taking into account', we do not necessarily mean an endogenous determination of all the relevant effects, but a model that can endogenize the first element and that could be calibrated to account for the second.

The model developed in this section builds on Manasse and Turrini (2001). The main purpose of their study is to link labour heterogeneity in a country and international trade (or technological change). Their aim is not to investigate the economic impact of the international movement of skilled workers, but rather to explain income inequality through trade, technological change and globalization. We consider this link as one of the main causes of the international movement of skilled workers among developed countries. Simply put, if it is true that, everything else being equal, trade (or technological change) creates income inequality within a country and across countries, then it must also create incentives for individuals to move across borders in order to take advantage of these inequalities because it likely means that the return to a given skill level is becoming increasingly different among countries. An easy way to cast the complementarity between trade and international labour flows implied by this model is to say that trade tends to create income inequalities within and across countries (in the presence of positive transport costs) and that international labour mobility tends to mitigate these inequalities.

The principle here is essentially the same as in more traditional models of international labour mobility, except that it works not only at the country level but also at the individual level. In a standard model of international labour mobility with a homogeneous labour force, the necessary ingredient for international mobility is a difference in (uniform) country real wages. With labour heterogeneity, the average wage may differ not only across countries but across individual wages. This means that, for an individual's skill level, the wage difference between two countries can be positive, negative or nil, and that if international trade creates more inequalities in the absence of international labour mobility, then trade liberalization and international mobility may induce certain categories of workers to emigrate to a particular country and other categories to immigrate. It is the economic consequences of this particular link between trade liberalization, international mobility and the location of firms and entrepreneurs that we want to investigate.

Consider two countries indexed i, j with two sectors indexed x, y. Sector y (called hereafter High Tech) produces differentiated goods (that are imperfect substitutes), while sector x (called hereafter Low Tech) produces a homogeneous good. Each country has two factors of production: entrepreneurs and raw labour. Unskilled labour is homogeneous, in fixed overall supply and competitively priced. In contrast, an entrepreneur is a specific factor used only in the High Tech sector. The domestic supply of entrepreneurs is also in fixed overall supply, but this factor is differentiated according to skills n such that $n \in [\underline{n}, \overline{n}]$. The entrepreneur is the residual claimant in the firm where she exercises her talent. The production of each differentiated good requires one unit of entrepreneur and a variable amount of raw labour proportional to the quantity produced. The entrepreneur's skill improves the quality of the product and thus the quantity demanded. Hence, producing differentiated goods has both a horizontal component in the Dixit-Stiglitz tradition and a vertical component since quality matters. In the absence of international mobility of entrepreneurs, and unlike the typical Dixit-Stiglitz model, there is a fixed number of firms determined by the supply of entrepreneurs.[11] However, each firm earns zero profit since the entrepreneur captures the entire quasi-rent generated by her talent. The production in the Low Tech sector is very standard: firms are price takers and the production function is Ricardian for raw labour. In the current version of the model, we assume this homogeneous product to be a purely non-traded good.

International trade of goods produced in High Tech involves two specific costs (both expressed in terms of raw labour): a variable cost, which can be interpreted as a transport cost (of the iceberg type), and a fixed cost interpreted as a cost to access a foreign market (for instance, to establish a sales network). This fixed cost of trade is critically important because it partitions firms into two subsets: those who are able to export and those who are confined to the domestic market.

The demand side comes from a standard Dixit-Stiglitz sub-utility function, except for the role of quality. Higher perceived product quality increases utility and thus the demand for the product. Manasse and Turrini adopt a relatively ad hoc specification since they simply assume the existence of a function T mapping technology and the entrepreneur's skill into a quality component as perceived by consumers. Hence, the representative consumer's utility function, over the set of products N available to him, takes the general CES form:

$$(1) \qquad U^{\sigma-1/\sigma} = \sum_{n \in N} T_n(a)^{1/\sigma} d_n^{(\sigma-1)/\sigma}, \ \sigma > 1,$$

where d_n is the quantity consumed of product n and $T_n(a)$ is the quality of the product as evaluated by the representative consumer and which depends on the entrepreneur's skill n used to produce good n and on the technology of production represented by the parameter a.

It is important to underline here two characteristics of the model. First, if raw labour is used in proportion of the quantity produced of one differentiated good, one unit of talent is used whether the market is small or large. Second, only talent (for a given technology) adds quality to a product. In other words, even if horizontal differentiation needs both the primary factors and one entrepreneur, vertical differentiation requires the skill of an entrepreneur only. It is these non-convexities in production and in consumption that give a superstar-Rosen-type flavour to the model.

Given (1), country i's demand for a variant takes the following form:

$$E_{i,i,n} = T_{i,n}(a_i) \left[\frac{p_i^y}{p_i} \right] c_i^y$$

$$E_{j,i,n} = T_{j,n}(a_j) \left[\frac{p_i^y}{p_j / \tau_{j,i}} \right] c_i^y .$$

Hence, the demand for one variant depends on its quality $T_{i,n}(a_i)$, $T_{j,n}(a_j)$, on income devoted to the consumption of differentiated products c_i^y, and on the price aggregator p_i^y over available differentiated products individually priced p_i and p_j adjusted for the (iceberg-type) barrier to trade $\tau_{j,i}$. These demands depend on the entrepreneur's skill through two channels: the quality perceived by consumers and the price of the product.

Because the utility function is CES, firms with the same technology have the same mark-up. Thus, higher product quality simply translates into a higher volume of sales and not into a higher price. Since the entrepreneur is the residual claimant, her wage is equal to the operating profit. This profit is different depending on whether the firm exports or not. If it does not trade, then the wage of the non-trader-entrepreneur $w_{i,n}^{low}$ is simply equal to:

(2) $w_{i,n}^{low} = \left[p_i - v_i \right] E_{i,i,n} ,$

where v_i is the variable unit cost as well as the price of raw labour (Ricardian technology). Of course, the profit of the entrepreneur depends on her skill. If the entrepreneur is trading, her wage is equal to:

$$(3) \qquad w_{i,n}^{high} = \left[p_i - v_i \right] \left(E_{i,i,n} + \frac{E_{i,j,n}}{\tau_{i,j}} \right) - v_i \gamma_i \phi_{i,n}^{\eta},$$

where the last term is the fixed cost of exporting.[12] This cost is assumed to decline ($\eta < 0$) with the number of type-n exporters (penetration of foreign markets is easier when many producers are willing to sell abroad). The main difference with the non-trader-entrepreneur is that the entrepreneur's skill allows for sales at home and abroad. In other words, talents gain from market size. In this case, the trader-entrepreneur's wage increases more than proportionately with skill. Because of the difference in market size, the general relationship between the entrepreneur's wage and skill is illustrated in Figure 1.

FIGURE 1

RELATIONSHIP BETWEEN ENTREPRENEUR'S WAGE AND SKILL

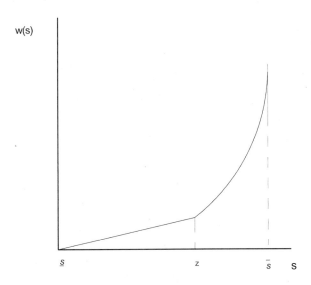

Entrepreneur n_i chooses to be a trader or a non-trader depending on whether exporting provides a higher operating profit or not. At low levels of n, the non-trader entrepreneur's wage increases with skill. As soon as the firm trades, her wage increases more than proportionately as a given level of entrepreneur's talent now reaches a much larger market. The exporting firm necessarily generates a higher gross profit than a non-exporting firm. However, because exporting involves a fixed cost, only the most talented entrepreneurs participate in the export market. Of course, the skill level z_i of the entrepreneur who is just indifferent between trading and not trading is endogenous. Therefore, at z_i, we have $w_{i,z_i}^{low} = w_{i,z_i}^{high}$. Trade liberalization, whether through a lower transport cost or a lower fixed access cost, boosts the wage of the trader-entrepreneur (since the foreign market can now be more easily accessed) and thus decreases the level of the critical skill necessary to participate in the export market. Trade liberalization creates wage inequality insofar as the relative earnings of a trader-entrepreneur rises compared to the earnings of a non-trader entrepreneur.

It is important to note that, in the absence of migration, the total number (and the range of product quality) of goods produced (and thus of entrepreneurs) in each country is exogenously fixed. This is not the case for consumption since the number of goods consumed depends on the number of products that are traded.[13]

Let's now introduce international labour mobility. Suppose first that only skilled entrepreneurs can move between the two countries. A skilled entrepreneur can move across the border and be either a trader- or a non-trader entrepreneur in the other country. In other words, being of one type in one country does not pre-determine the type of entrepreneur in the other country.[14] Since we have just established that, in one country, an individual with skill n_i chooses to be a trader or a non-trader according to

$$Max\left\{\frac{w_{i,n}^{low}}{p_i^{con}}, \frac{w_{i,n}^{high}}{p_i^{con}}\right\},$$

this entrepreneur will migrate from country i to country j if and only if

$$(4) \qquad Max\left\{\frac{w_{i,n}^{low}}{p_i^{con}}, \frac{w_{i,n}^{high}}{p_i^{con}}\right\} < Max\left\{\frac{w_{j,n}^{low}}{p_j^{con}}, \frac{w_{j,n}^{high}}{p_j^{con}}\right\} - \rho_{i,j},$$

where $\rho_{i,j}$ is the fixed cost of moving to country j and p_i^{con}, p_j^{con} are the consumer price indices in each country. Similarly, an entrepreneur migrates from country j to country i if and only if

$$(5) \qquad Max\left\{\frac{w_{j,n}^{low}}{p_j^{con}}, \frac{w_{j,n}^{high}}{p_j^{con}}\right\} < Max\left\{\frac{w_{i,n}^{low}}{p_i^{con}}, \frac{w_{i,n}^{high}}{p_i^{con}}\right\} - \rho_{j,i}.$$

It is of course quite possible that for some range of skills, skilled individuals will want to move from one country to another, while for other ranges, they will have no incentive to migrate or will have an incentive to migrate in the other direction. In other words, it is quite possible in this model that the pattern of migration of skilled individuals would be a two-way migration. Obviously, even within a single sector, the possible migration patterns are much richer than in more traditional models of international labour mobility.

Consider now the possibility that unskilled labour migrate across the border. Since v_i is the wage of unskilled labour, workers will move from country i to country j if

$$(6) \qquad \frac{v_i}{p_i^{con}} < \frac{v_j}{p_j^{con}} - \rho_{i,j},$$

where $\rho_{i,j}$ is the (static) cost of moving across the border for unskilled labour. Unskilled labour moves in the other direction if

$$(7) \qquad \frac{v_i}{p_i^{con}} - \rho_{j,i} > \frac{v_j}{p_j^{con}}.$$

Not surprisingly, only a one-way migration pattern is possible with international mobility of unskilled labour.

The main difficulty with having international migrations (of skilled or unskilled labour) is that it affects the demands for the products since workers and entrepreneurs are also consumers. In the case of entrepreneurs, we need to take into account the distribution of entrepreneurs and truncate it according to who is leaving and who is staying. Similarly, these migrants affect the distribution of entrepreneurs in the host country. In addition, we need to know which role (trader or non-trader) they play in each country. In the next section, we develop a simple general equilibrium model where, using artificial data, we investigate the sensitivity of trade and labour flows to exogenous shocks.

SIMULATION EXERCISES

W E NOW USE A TWO-COUNTRY VERSION OF THE ABOVE MODEL in order to investigate the model's sensitivity to international labour mobility. The equations used in this model are presented in the Appendix. We proceed in two steps. First, we set the model in a free-migration environment (migration costs are set to zero) and in a quasi free-trade environment (the per unit transport cost is equal to zero but the fixed export cost is positive), and we simply ask: Given a specific asymmetry between the two countries, what are the effects of introducing free international mobility of entrepreneurs?

Assume that the two countries are strictly identical. There is clearly no incentive to migrate (for any skill level, the wages are the same across countries). But there is nonetheless trade between the two countries (at least as long as the iceberg transport cost is not prohibitive) since products are differentiated both horizontally and vertically. Not surprisingly, the model boils down to a standard intra-industry trade model with two factors of production (skilled labour and raw labour). In order to investigate the effects of international labour mobility, we must introduce asymmetries between the two countries. We consider four different types of asymmetries: (i) Country 1 has a larger endowment of skilled individuals than Country 2 (but the same endowment of raw labour); (ii) Country 1 has a larger endowment of unskilled labour than Country 2; (iii) Firms exporting from Country 1 faces a higher fixed export cost than firms exporting from Country 2; and (iv) The technology in the Low Tech sector is more productive in Country 1 than in Country 2.

For each of these cases, we compare the equilibrium with and without international mobility of skilled labour (entrepreneurs). In Figure 2, we depict the results with two graphs: one representing the distribution of entrepreneur's wage per skill (Figure 2a, similar to Figure 1), the other the distribution of firms in each country per skill (and thus quality). We set the model in such a way that the initial distribution of firms without international mobility (and thus the initial distribution of skills) is the same and is uniform in both countries.

Consider the first case, where *Country 1 has 20 percent more skilled labour than Country 2* but both countries have the same endowment of raw labour. As Figure 2b illustrates, this difference is uniformly distributed over the range of entrepreneur's skills (Country 1 has a uniform density of entrepreneurs equal to 1.2, while Country 2 has a uniform density equal to 1). To understand how the model works, we start from the initial symmetric international equilibrium and implement a 20-percent increase in Country 1's endowment of entrepreneurs. We first assume no migration and an exogenous skill level z_i that separates exporting entrepreneurs from non-exporting entrepreneurs. At given prices, the resource constraint implies that the increase in $\phi_{in} \forall n$ induces a 20-percent

FIGURE 2a

SKILLED LABOUR ASYMMETRY

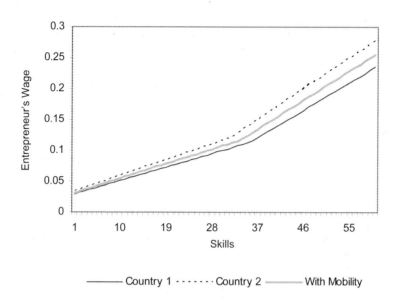

FIGURE 2b

SKILLED LABOUR ASYMMETRY

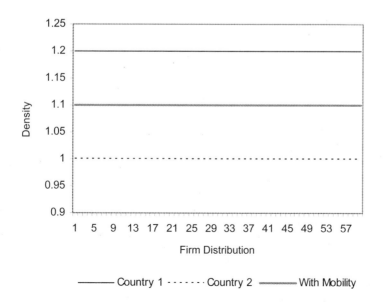

decrease in the individual firm's size for each type of good n; hence, both w_1^{low} and w_1^{high} fall. Because of the fixed export cost, the downward shift of the w_1^{high} curve is more important and the intersection between the two curves moves to the right. However, a higher ϕ_{in} implies more diversity for the Dixit-Stiglitz household, both domestic and foreign: substitution in consumption follows at the expense of the competitively produced good and c_j^y $\forall j$ rises. The individual domestic firm's sales increase both in the local ($\forall n$) and in the foreign ($\forall n > z_i$) market so that both w_1^{low} and w_1^{high} now increase. However, competition for raw resources induces v_i to rise, which hurts the exporters' profits relatively more (through the fixed cost) than other producers so that the upward shift of the w_1^{low} curve exceeds the other; the new intersection between the two curves is moved further to the right. Endogenizing z_1 thus results in an increase in the minimal talent level required for exporting. Not surprisingly, given the initial increase in ϕ_{1n}, at the resulting equilibrium an individual entrepreneur's real earning is lower in Country 1 than in Country 2, for all skill levels. Allowing for migration re-establishes international symmetry. The relative abundance of entrepreneurs now increases the lowest skill level required for profitable exports in both countries. Table 1, Experiment 1 summarizes some aggregate results of the two equilibria — with and without international mobility of talents.

With the introduction of international mobility of entrepreneurs, the welfare (of the representative consumer) decreases in Country 1 and increases in Country 2 by about 1 percent (Table 1). This is due, among other things, to the change in product variety for consumers in each country. Without mobility, consumers of Country 1 benefit from a larger offering of products than consumers in Country 2 since there are more entrepreneurs in Country 1 and some of the additional products are non-traded. The mobility of entrepreneurs re-equilibrates the number of products available to consumers irrespective of their location. The welfare effect is relatively small simply because two forces act in opposite directions. With mobility, some non-traded products are no longer available to consumers of Country 1, but Country 2 exports a larger fraction of the total number of its differentiated products than it did without international mobility.

Consider now the second case, where the asymmetry is with respect to the endowment of unskilled (or raw) labour: *Country 1 is endowed with a 20 percent larger number of unskilled workers than Country 2.* Again, we trace the effects of this asymmetry by using the initially symmetric international equilibrium with

TABLE 1

THE EFFECTS OF FOUR SIMPLE ASYMMETRIES

	COUNTRY 1		COUNTRY 2	
	NO MOBILITY	WITH MOBILITY	NO MOBILITY	WITH MOBILITY
EXPERIMENT 1: + 20% ENTREPRENEURS IN COUNTRY 1				
Welfare	1.018	1.009	0.998	1.008
$p_i^x = v_i$	1.026	1.000	1.000	1.000
p_i^y	0.340	0.338	0.345	0.338
c_i^x	343.100	343.300	343.400	343.300
c_i^y	1037.000	1017.000	995.700	1017.000
Pop	360.000	329.700	300.000	330.300
$PopExp$	153.600	151.100	149.000	151.600
EXPERIMENT 2: + 20% UNSKILLED LABOUR IN COUNTRY 1				
Welfare	1.199	1.222	1.008	0.987
$p_i^x = v_i$	0.969	1.004	1.000	1.000
p_i^y	0.335	0.334	0.336	0.351
c_i^x	413.000	412.900	342.400	342.400
c_i^y	1194.500	1242.100	1018.500	976.300
Pop	300.000	381.400	300.000	218.600
$PopExp$	166.000	168.300	162.000	162.700
EXPERIMENT 3: + 20% EXPORT FIXED COST IN COUNTRY 1				
Welfare	0.996	0.993	0.997	1.000
$p_i^x = v_i$	0.991	0.986	1.000	1.000
p_i^y	0.342	0.341	0.346	0.346
c_i^x	342.900	342.300	343.600	344.300
c_i^y	993.200	989.000	993.300	996.600
Pop	300.000	311.400	300.000	288.600
$PopExp$	130.000	138.000	147.000	136.300

TABLE 1 (CONT'D)				
THE EFFECTS OF FOUR SIMPLE ASYMMETRIES				
	COUNTRY 1		COUNTRY 2	
	NO MOBILITY	WITH MOBILITY	NO MOBILITY	WITH MOBILITY
EXPERIMENT 4: + 20% LABOUR PRODUCTIVITY IN COUNTRY 1'S LOW-TECH SECTOR				
Welfare	1.095	1.100	1.000	0.995
p_i^x	0.883	0.845	1.000	1.000
p_i^y	0.343	0.344	0.343	0.348
v_i	1.000	1.0130	1.000	1.000
c_i^x	411.900	411.300	343.200	343.900
c_i^y	1000.000	1010.600	1000.000	988.900
Pop	300.000	327.500	300.000	272.500
PopExp	151.000	158.900	151.000	142.100

no migration and z_i fixed as a starting point. Since the number of entrepreneurs is the same in both countries, so is the number of firms in the High Tech sector in the absence of international mobility of entrepreneurs. However, more abundant and, thus, cheaper raw labour implies that the scale of these firms is larger in Country 1 (compare, for instance, v_i between the two countries without mobility; see Table 1, Experiment 2). Though profits of both domestic exporters and non-exporters are boosted, the impact on the former is larger because of the fixed export cost. The intersection between the two wage profiles moves to the left, indicating that less-talented entrepreneurs are now able to undertake profitable export activities. Not surprisingly, entrepreneurs' real wages are higher in Country 1 for all skills (Figure 3a).

Costless migration induces entrepreneurs to move to Country 1 in order to take advantage of cheaper resources and a larger market. Interestingly, there is a strong composition effect in this migration since those who are massively moving to Country 1 are the *non-trader* entrepreneurs. As both panels of Figure 3 indicate, this migration of non-trader entrepreneurs increases with skill level in Country 1. This is simply due to the fact that the incentive to migrate increases with the skill level since it is directly related to the difference in real earnings between the two countries. However, the same is not true for trading firms as there is a two-way flow of medium/high skills: some intermediate skills are attracted into the home country, while there is an outflow of high talents.

FIGURE 3a

UNSKILLED LABOUR ASYMMETRY

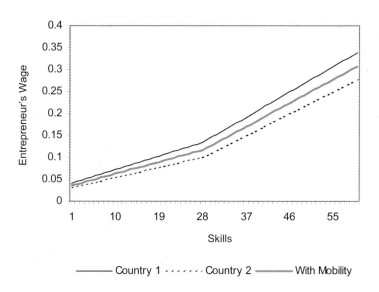

FIGURE 3b

UNSKILLED LABOUR ASYMMETRY

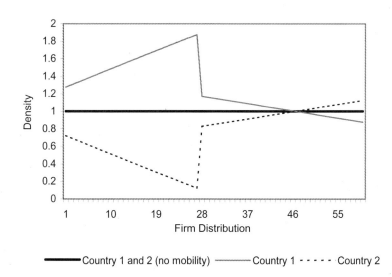

This is not surprising: because $z_1 < z_2$ at the no-migration equilibrium, moving into Country 1 makes it possible for some foreign intermediate-skill entrepreneurs to become exporters and increase their profits, everything else being equal. This motivation to migrate is obviously not shared by the most talented who are exporters independently of their geographic location. More importantly, the balance-of-trade equilibrium requires that if there is a net inflow of intermediate-skill exporters, there must be — due to terms-of-trade changes — a net outflow of (a smaller number of) high-skill exporters. There is also a second effect. The large inflow of entrepreneurs in Country 1 raises the cost of producing High Tech goods domestically. Indeed, v_i increases by 3.6 percent while remaining unchanged abroad (see Table 1, Experiment 2). Since the fixed cost of exporting is expressed in terms of raw labour, exporting from Country 1 would be more costly, everything else being equal, than it was without mobility. However, there are now more exporters in Country 1 than before, which makes penetration of foreign markets less costly from the home country, thanks to the export externality.[15] Hence, the fixed cost of exporting may actually be lower in Country 1 despite the difference in v_i. Obviously, this effect is particularly crucial for the marginal traders since the export cost is most significant in the decisions of these firms. Here too, intermediate-skill entrepreneurs have a specific incentive to move into Country 1 that the most talented ones do not share: for the latter, access is ensured to all markets, domestic and foreign. And again, the balance-of-trade equilibrium requires that if there is a net inflow of intermediate-skill exporters, there must be a net outflow of high-skill exporters.

In this case, allowing for entrepreneur mobility increases welfare by about 2 percent in Country 1 and decreases it by 2.1 percent in Country 2 (Table 1). This significant welfare effect is not surprising given the improvement in the terms of trade of Country 1 and the substantial net increase in the number of differentiated goods available to its consumers (especially non-traded goods).

We see from the two previous experiments that the size of the relative skilled- versus unskilled-labour endowments matters a lot in this model. Depending on where the asymmetry lies, the introduction of international entrepreneur mobility has very different qualitative and quantitative effects. When the endowment of skilled entrepreneurs in Country 1 is greater than in Country 2, entrepreneurs move to the latter, whereas when the unskilled labour endowment is larger in Country 1, the dominant flow is that of entrepreneurs moving to Country 1. These asymmetries also result in different production specialization and trading patterns. In the first two experiments, more High Tech products (traded and non-traded) are produced in Country 1 without labour mobility than with mobility. This means that fewer resources are being used in the High Tech sector, and Country 1 exports relatively less High Tech products with mobility than without mobility. In the second asymmetry, the opposite occurs. With mobility, there is a relative specialization in production toward the High Tech sector at the expense of the Low Tech sector in Country 1 but, quite interestingly, it leads to relative specialization along the quality dimension within the High Tech sector. Indeed, mobility leads Country 1 to specialize mainly in low and intermediate quality variants, while Country 2 tends to specialize in high quality export products.

The quantitative effects are also quite different. In the first experiment (+20 percent skilled labour in Country 1), the flow of skilled entrepreneurs moving from Country 1 to Country 2 is roughly equal to half the difference in endowment (representing 10 percent of the initial number of entrepreneurs in Country 2). In the second case (+20 percent raw labour in Country 1), the *total number* of skilled entrepreneurs migrating between the two countries represents about 34 percent of the initial endowment of entrepreneurs in each country (for a net change equal to 27 percent of the initial endowment). This is quite a significant effect.

Consider now the third case, where *the γ set-up cost of exporting High Tech products from Country 1 is 20 percent higher*. Non-trading firms are only indirectly affected by the cost of the primary factor. As is to be expected, in the absence of international labour mobility, the entrepreneurs' wages are very similar in the two countries (Figure 4a). Given such small differences in terms of operating profits, introducing international mobility of entrepreneurs cannot change the entrepreneur's wage much. Nonetheless, the effect on the migration of entrepreneurs is significant, especially for those working in trading firms, where some entrepreneurs migrate from Country 1 to Country 2, while others migrate from Country 2 to Country 1 (Figure 4b). The higher fixed cost of exporting leads to lower raw labour cost in Country 1 with or without labour mobility. Indeed, mobility reduces the price of labour even further, which induces a decrease in the fixed cost of exporting in Country 1. At the equilibrium with mobility, Country 1 ends up with more traders than Country 2 despite the 20 percent higher fixed cost of exporting. Hence, in equilibrium, given the number of exporters and the price of labour in Country 1, the fixed cost is lower in that country than in Country 2. It is apparent that, even if the two countries are similar except for the fixed cost of exporting, many "trading" entrepreneurs will migrate across the border. Mobility brings greater *specialization* along the quality dimension among High Tech products: Country 1 specializes relatively in low quality traded products, while Country 2 specializes relatively in high quality traded products. Indeed, at each end of the quality range of traded products, there is almost complete specialization in each country. At the very high end, nearly *all* trading firms produce in Country 2 and, at the other end (but still among the trading firms), nearly all trading firms produce in Country 1.

FIGURE 4a

EXPORT COST ASYMMETRY

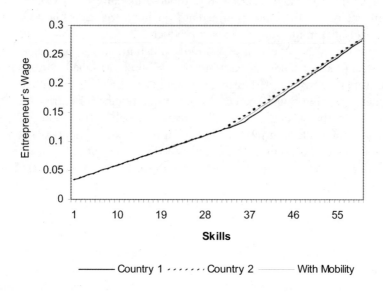

FIGURE 4b

EXPORT COST ASYMMETRY

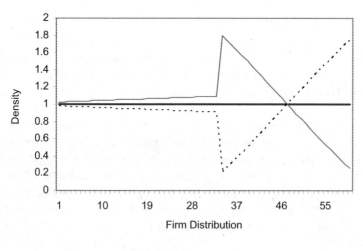

FIGURE 5a

TECHNOLOGICAL ASYMMETRY

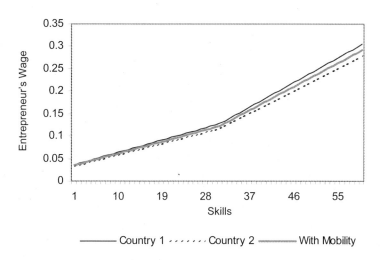

FIGURE 5b

TECHNOLOGICAL ASYMMETRY

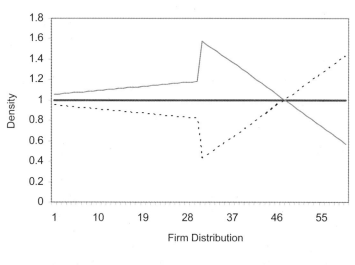

Despite the migration of a significant fraction of entrepreneurs, welfare only marginally changes in each country (with a slight decrease in Country 1 and a slight increase in Country 2; see Table 1).

In the last experiment, factors are more productive in Country 1 than in Country 2 in the Low Tech sector: *+20 percent total factor productivity in Country 1's Low Tech sector*. In the absence of international labour mobility, resources will be heavily used in the Low Tech sector as the price of the Low Tech product is low. Because the consumption function takes a Cobb-Douglas form over the Low Tech and High Tech products and because the Low Tech product is a non-traded good, the effect of this higher productivity shock is confined to the Low Tech sector. As Figure 5 shows, movements of entrepreneurs take place when mobility is allowed since the real value of the quasi rents in the High Tech sector is now higher in Country 1. Migration follows from Country 2 to the home country, with effects on non-trading as well as on trading firms. The number of trading firms increases in Country 1, with a similar externality effect and, through it, similar production specialization (at least for trading firms) and trade pattern effects, as in previous simulations. It should be noted that, in this case, mobility affects mainly trading firms because the difference in real quasi-rents between the two countries increases with skill level. Hence, there is a much stronger incentive to move for trading firms than for non-trading firms. Of course, the balance-of-trade condition prevents that these entrepreneurs from moving in one direction only.

CONCLUSION

WHAT TO MAKE OF THESE SIMULATIONS? Of course, we have used artificial data so that none of these simulations directly apply to the Canada-U.S. case. We have also completely disregarded how we might make the model operational with real data. However, the particular model used here raises a number of issues about the meaning of skills, the correspondence between skills and firms, not to mention the correspondence between skills and product quality. Though specific, we believe that this type of model has great potential for a number of reasons.

First, there is a link between trade, earning inequality and labour mobility. The link between trade and earning inequality comes from two sources. Since trade affects the wages of unskilled and skilled workers (entrepreneurs), and wages among entrepreneurs, trade-induced increases in inequality may mean here that the wages of skilled workers increase with respect to the wages of unskilled workers, and it can mean that the wages of highly skilled workers (in trading firms) increase with respect to the wages of less highly skilled workers (in non-trading firms). Since these inequalities occur not only within a country but across countries, they create incentives to migrate across the border in order to take advantage of earning differentials. Second, skills matter in this model and the returns to skills are positive, giving the model a Rosen "super-star" flavour.

Third, because individuals (at least skilled workers) are differentiated, migration decisions are potentially different among individuals. Introducing international labour mobility leads to changes in specialization at the production level across sectors and within sectors producing differentiated goods. In turn, this leads to changes in trade patterns. This is an interesting result because the changes in trade patterns across and within sectors are not due to trade liberalization per se but *are by-products of liberalizing international labour migration*.

In order to illustrate why this last point may make this model relevant for the Canada-U.S. case, consider the following. In a study commissioned by the EU Commission, Fontagné, Freudenberg and Péridy (1998) have uncovered interesting changes in trade patterns within the European Union between 1980 and 1994. They first divided trade between every pair of EU member countries into inter- and intra-industry trade, and further divided intra-industry trade into horizontal (Helpman-Krugman type) and vertical (Shaked and Sutton-quality type) trade. To this end, they simply compared the price of export with the price of import. If, at the level of the variants, the price of export is roughly similar to the price of import, then trade in this variant belongs to the horizontal intra-industry trade category. If there is a significant difference (positive or negative) between the two prices, then trade in this variant belongs to the vertical intra-industry trade category. Aggregating these trade shares, they discovered that if, as expected, the share of overall intra-industry in total trade increased over the period, it is not due to an increase in the share of horizontal intra-industry trade but to an increase in the share of vertical intra-industry trade. In other words, based on their methodology, some kind of specialization has taken place in Europe at the country level despite the presence of similar countries (say France and Germany) and of trade liberalization. Nobody has yet offered a good explanation for this phenomenon.

Applying a similar methodology to the Canada-U.S. case over the 1989-99 period, Andresen, Harris and Schmitt (2001) find similar changes but on a much smaller scale than in Europe. Why? We do not really have a good answer either. However, our simulations suggest that this may have a very simple explanation: the difference between the results obtained for Europe and for North America might simply be associated with differences in the degree of economic integration. The 1992 Unique Market (decided well before 1992) may well have triggered location decisions among firms (for instance) focused at serving Europe as a whole rather than at serving only a specific European country, whereas NAFTA did not have the same impact on firms' location decisions (or on individuals' location decisions) because of its more limited focus.[16] This suggests that, in evaluating the effects of a deeper integration between Canada and the United States and, in particular, measures of integration dealing with international labour mobility, an important aspect would be the consequences of these measures on international trade and on the patterns of trade.

The above advantages are purely static. Needless to say, in a dynamic environment, other elements could be added to a model of this type, for example human capital formation, the impact of an aging population, or quality-ladder/endogenous growth components.

ENDNOTES

1   For instance, Germany is adopting a Canadian-point-type system to evaluate immigrants. A bilateral agreement between Switzerland and the European Union has been in force since June 1, 2002. After a five-year transition period, it is supposed to free up labour mobility between Switzerland and the European Union. The main reason for these policies seems to be linked to labour shortages in specific highly skilled activities.

2   See Markusen (1988) for a model belonging to this category and specifically addressing positive and normative aspects of human capital formation, skilled labour and the brain drain.

3   The 2002 state-by-state statistics on the U.S. high-tech industry, published by the American Electronics Association, are revealing about growth and job concentration in an economy with free mobility: California had the highest number of high-tech jobs (nearly 8 percent of its workers), followed by Texas, New York and Massachusetts. The latter had roughly one quarter of the number of high-tech jobs that California had. South Dakota had the highest job loss rate in the high-tech industry (–15 percent), and Montana the highest job growth rate (+17 percent).

4   See Ludema and Wooton (1999) for a model of geography and trade with imperfect factor mobility. Their conclusion is that the de-industrialization just mentioned is not unavoidable, especially when a country can control trade liberalization, the degree of factor mobility and the sequence of implementation of these two policies. Tabuchi and Thisse (2001) also consider imperfect factor mobility through taste heterogeneity in workers' perceptions of the characteristics of regions.

5   See Gould (1994) concerning the United States and Head and Ries (1998) or Head, Ries and Wagner (1998) concerning Canada.

6   Grossman (2002) introduces imperfect labour contracts in a model with two-country trade and labour heterogeneity whose characteristics are similar to the one developed above. He shows that in the presence of two sectors (one with team production, the other with individual production), the most talented individuals have an incentive to flock to the sector with individual production in the presence of imperfect labour contracts, especially in the country with greater labour heterogeneity. Hence, imperfect labour contracts are a source of comparative advantage, and freer trade can exacerbate this polarization in the allocation of labour.

7   Manasse and Turrini (2001) also use horizontal differentiation through a standard Dixit-Stiglitz model of monopolistic competition.

8   The fact that skilled workers are intrinsically more mobile than unskilled workers is supported by empirical evidence (see, for example, Shields and Shields, 1989). See also Finnie (2001) who shows that Canada has been losing a significant fraction of its market elite as judged by individuals' income tax data.

9   See Beine, Docquier and Rapoport (2001) for an empirical investigation concerning developing countries. There is no reason why this argument would apply only to developing countries. See Faini (2002) for a paper doubting the positive effects of a brain drain on the home country, and Wildasin (2002) for a theoretical analysis of labour market integration and investment in human capital.

10 Coe and Helpman (1995) show that international R&D spillovers are not trivial for Canada. Eaton and Kortum (2002) suggest that a country like Canada benefits from technology improvements (whether created by Canadian out-migrating brains or not) in the United States because it is both close to the United States and its economy has the flexibility to downsize manufacturing.

11 See below the discussion on this point.

12 Recall that the mark-up is the same on domestic and foreign sales. This implies that p in (3) is also the producer price in foreign sales.

13 This exogenous feature of the number of goods produced (or of entrepreneurs) in the absence of international migration can be relaxed in one of two ways: one is to endogenize the number of products, the other is to endogenize the number of entrepreneurs. In the first case, this can be achieved by introducing a fixed cost of production; here, full employment of resources dictates that a product can be traded only if some other non-traded product exits the industry (see Schmitt and Yu, 2001, for such a model). Alternatively, one can endogenize the number of entrepreneurs. For instance, individuals can work as entrepreneurs or as workers depending on the comparison or earnings in each activity. If they are workers, they belong to the "unskilled" group (see Schmitt and Soubeyran, 2002, for such a model).

14 Hence, a non-trader entrepreneur in Canada could be a trader-entrepreneur in the United States. It is through this type of trade creation mechanism that the model captures the 'gains' from the brain drain.

15 The reason for the presence of such externality is twofold. First, realism suggests that it is more costly to pioneer than to follow. The second reason is more technical. As is easily seen, our assumptions imply that, without the externality, $w_{i,n}^{high}$ depends on n exclusively through the quality index $T_{i,n}$, so that a technological link ties together the rents earned by entrepreneurs of different skills. Introducing the externality breaks this unrealistic tie.

16 Given the low degree of intra-EU worker mobility, it is hard to believe that international labour mobility alone causes these differences between Europe and North America.

BIBLIOGRAPHY

Andresen, Martin, Richard Harris and Nicolas Schmitt. "Canada-U.S. Intra-Industry Trade Patterns." Prepared for Jim Melvin's Festschrift, 2001. Mimeo.

Beine, Michel, Frédéric Docquier and Hillel Rapoport. "Brain Drain and Economic Growth: Theory and Evidence." *Journal of Development Economics* 64, 1 (2001): 275-289.

Coe, David, and Elhanan Helpman. "International R&D Spillovers." *European Economic Review* 39, 5 (1995): 859-887.

Commander, Simon, Mari Kangasniemi and L. Alan Winters. "The Brain Drain: Curse or Boon? A Survey of the Literature." 2002. Mimeo.

Eaton, Jonathan, and Samuel Kortum. "Technology, Geography and Trade." *Econometrica* 70, 5 (2002): 1741-1779.

Faini, Riccardo. "Migration, Remittances and Growth." September 2002. Mimeo.

Faini, Riccardo, Jaime de Melo and Klaus Zimmermann. "Trade and Migration: An Introduction." In *Migration: The Controversies and the Evidence*. Edited by R. Faini, J. de Melo and K. Zimmermann. Cambridge: CEPR and Cambridge University Press, 1999, pp. 1-20.

Fertig, Michael, and Christoph Schmidt. *Mobility Within Europe – What Do We (still not) Know?* IZA Discussion Paper No. 447. Bonn: Institute for the Study of Labour, 2002.

Finnie, Ross. *The Brain Drain: Myth and Reality: What It Is and what Should Be Done?* Working Paper No. 13. Queen's University (School of Policy Studies), 2001.

Fontagné, Lionel, M. Freudenberg and Nicolas Péridy. *Intra-Industry Trade and the Single Market: Quality Matters*. CEPR Discussion Paper No. 1959. 1998.

Gould, David. "Immigration Links to the Home Country: Empirical Implications for U.S. Bilateral Trade Flows." *Review of Economics and Statistics* 76, 2 (1994): 302-316.

Gross, Dominique, and Nicolas Schmitt. "The Role of Cultural Clustering in Attracting New Immigrants." *Journal of Regional Science* 43, 2 (2002): 295-318.

Grossman, Gene. *The Distribution of Talent and the Pattern and Consequence of International Trade*. CESIfo Working Paper No. 745. June 2002.

Harris, Richard G., and Nicolas Schmitt. "The Consequences of Increased Labour Mobility Within an Integrating North America." In *North American Linkages: Opportunities and Challenges for Canada*. Edited by R.G. Harris. Industry Canada Research Series. Calgary: University of Calgary Press, 2003 pp. 313-354.

Head, Keith, and John Ries. "Immigration and Trade Creation: Econometric Evidence from Canada." *Canadian Journal of Economics* 31, 1 (1998): 47-62.

Head, Keith, John Ries and Don Wagner. *Immigrants and the Trade of Province*. RIIM Working Paper No. 98-21, Vancouver (B.C.), December 1998.

Krugman, Paul. "Increasing Returns and Economic Geography." *Journal of Political Economy* 99 (1991): 483-499.

Lucas, Robert. "On the Size Distribution of Business Firms." *Bell Journal of Economics* 9 (1978): 508-523.

Ludema, Rodney, and Ian Wooton. "Regional Integration, Trade and Migration: Are Demand Linkages Relevant for Europe?" In *Migration: The Controversies and the Evidence*. Edited by R. Faini, J. de Melo and K. Zimmermann. Cambridge: CEPR and Cambridge University Press, 1999, pp. 51-68.

Manasse, Paolo, and Alessandro Turrini. "Trade, Wages and 'Superstars'." *Journal of International Economics* 54 (2001): 97-117.

Markusen, Jim. "Production, Trade and Migration with Differentiated, Skilled Workers." *Canadian Journal of Economics* 21, 3 (1988): 492-506.

Mundell, Robert. "International Trade and Factor Mobility." *American Economic Review* 47 (1957): 321-335.

Murphy, K.M., Andrew Shleifer and Robert Vishny. "The Allocation of Talent: Implications for Growth." *Quarterly Journal of Economics* 106, 2 (1991): 503-530.

Rauch, James. "Reconciling the Pattern of Trade with the Pattern of Migration." *American Economic Review* 81, 4 (1991): 775-796.

Rosen, Sherwin. "The Economics of Superstars." *American Economic Review* 71 (1981): 845-858.

Schmitt, Nicolas, and Antoine Soubeyran. "International Labor Mobility, Brain Gain and Distribution of Firms." 2002. Mimeo.

Schmitt, Nicolas, and Zhihao Yu. "Economies of Scale and the Volume of Intra-Industry Trade." *Economics Letters* 74 (2001): 127-132.

Shields, G.M., and M.P. Shields. "The Emergence of Migration Theory and a Suggested New Direction." *Journal of Economic Surveys* 3 (1989): 277-304.

Stark, Oded, Christian Helmenstein and Alexia Prskawetz. "Human Capital Depletion, Human Capital Formation and Migration: A Blessing or a Curse?" *Economics Letters* 60, 3 (1998): 363-367.

Tabuchi, Takatoshi, and Jacques-François Thisse. "Labor Mobility and Economic Geography." January 2001. Mimeo.

Venables, Anthony. "Trade Liberalization and Factor Mobility: An Overview." In *Migration: The Controversies and the Evidence*. Edited by R. Faini, J. de Melo and K. Zimmermann. Cambridge: CEPR and Cambridge University Press, 1999, pp. 23-48.

Wildasin, David. "Economic Integration and Labour Market Institutions: Worker Mobility, Earning Risk and Contract Structure." 2000. Mimeo.

———. "Labor Market Integration, Investment in Risky Human Capital, and Fiscal Competition." *American Economic Review* 90, 1 (2002): 73-95.

APPENDIX

$$i,j \quad = \quad \text{country index}$$

PARAMETERS

$$
\begin{aligned}
n_i &= \text{variety index} \\
T_{i,n}(a_i)^1 &= \text{quality index of variety } n_i \\
\sigma &= \text{differentiation elasticity between goods of type } n \\
\tau_{i,j} &= \text{(iceberg) transportation cost on flows from } i \text{ to } j \\
\gamma_i &= \text{fixed costs of exports} \\
\eta &= \text{export-cost externality parameter}
\end{aligned}
$$

VARIABLES

$$
\begin{aligned}
z_i &= \text{index of lowest quality type exported} \\
Inc_i &= \text{income} \\
L_i^{sup} &= \text{raw labour supply} \\
v_i &= \text{price of raw labour} \\
\phi_{i,n} &= \text{number of entrepreneurs producing variety } n \\
w_{i,n}^{low} &= \text{low-skilled type } n \text{ entrepreneur's earnings} \\
w_{i,n}^{high} &= \text{high-skilled type } n \text{ entrepreneur's earnings} \\
p_i^x &= \text{price of competitive good } x \\
c_i^x &= \text{consumption of competitive good } x \\
p_i^y &= \text{price of (aggregate) good } y \\
c_i^y &= \text{consumption of (aggregate) good } y \\
\theta_i^x &= \text{consumption share of competitive good } x \\
p_i &= \text{price of good of variety } n \\
E_{i,j,n} &= \text{sales of goods of variety } n \text{ by a firm in } i \text{ to a household in } j.
\end{aligned}
$$

MODEL

Households

$$Inc_i = v_i L_i^{sup} + \sum_{n_i \leq z_i} \phi_{i,n} w_{i,n}^{low} + \sum_{n_i > z_i} \phi_{i,n} w_{i,n}^{high}$$

$$\log p_i^{con} + \phi_i^x \log c_i^x + (1 - \theta_i^x) \log c_i^y = Inc_i$$

$$p_i^x c_i^x = \theta_i^x Inc_i$$

$$p_i^y c_i^y = (1 - \theta_i^x) Inc_i$$

$$\left[p_i^y \right]^{1-\sigma} = \sum_{n_i} \phi_{i,n} T_{i,n} \left[p_i \right]^{1-\sigma} + \sum_{n_j \leq z_j} \phi_{j,n} T_{j,n} \left[\frac{p_j}{\tau_{j,i}} \right]^{1-\sigma}$$

$$E_{i,i,n} = T_{i,n} \left[\frac{p_i^y}{p_i} \right]^{\sigma} c_i^y$$

$$E_{j,i,n} = T_{j,n} \left[\frac{p_i^y}{p_j / \tau_{j,i}} \right]^{\sigma} c_i^y$$

Firms of Sector *x*

$$p_i^x = v_i$$

$$L_i^x = c_i^x$$

Firms of Sector *y*

$$p_i = v_i \left[\frac{\sigma}{\sigma - 1} \right]$$

$$w_{i,n}^{low} = \left[p_i - v_i \right] E_{i,i,n}$$

$$w_{i,n}^{high} = \left[p_i - v_i \right] \left(E_{i,i,n} + \frac{E_{i,j,n}}{\tau_{i,j}} \right) - v_i \gamma_i \phi_{i,n}{}^{\eta}, \qquad \eta < 0$$

$$L_i^y = \sum_{n_i \leq z_i} \phi_{i,n} E_{i,i,n} + \sum_{n_i > z_i} \phi_{i,n} \left(E_{i,i,n} + \frac{E_{i,j,n}}{\tau_{i,j}} \right) + \gamma_i \phi_{i,n}{}^{\eta}, \qquad \eta < 0$$

Raw Labour Market

$$L_i^x + L_i^y = L_i^{sup}$$

Migration of Entrepreneurs

$$\underset{\phi_{i,n}}{Max} \left\{ \frac{w_{i,n}^{low}}{p_i^{con}}, \frac{w_{i,n}^{high}}{p_i^{con}} \right\} = \underset{\phi_{j,n}}{Max} \left\{ \frac{w_{j,n}^{low}}{p_j^{con}}, \frac{w_{j,n}^{high}}{p_j^{con}} \right\}, \qquad \phi_{i,n} + \phi_{j,n} = \overline{\phi}_n$$

ENDNOTE

1 We use an identical linear function for the two countries: $T_{i,n}(a_i) \equiv c + an_i$, noted $T_{i,n}(a_i) \equiv T_{i,n}$ hereafter.

482-86

p451:

Comment

Alan V. Deardorff
University of Michigan

F22 J14
J61
Flb J24

LET ME SAY FIRST THAT THIS IS AN INTERESTING and thought-provoking study. It provides a novel model for examining an important issue that I had not seen addressed in this way before. That is the migration that may take place among industrialized countries such as Canada and the United States, specifically migration of the types of highly-skilled individuals who provide the entrepreneurial talent to advanced industries. The model here is particularly intriguing in that it allows for the possibility that such individuals, differing among themselves in the nature or degree of their abilities, may be induced to migrate in both directions between these countries. Such a possibility must surely be allowed for in considering labour movements among countries of comparable income levels, like OECD member countries.

Indeed, in some of the discussions of labour movements and the brain drain during yesterday's sessions, I was struck by the thought that one surely ought to look not just at migration from Canada to the United States, but also at migration in the other direction. These south-to-north flows across our common border may be, I suppose, much smaller than the reverse, but I know from having watched our University of Michigan students consider and take jobs in Canada that they are not zero. A model that yields such a two-way flow of migration as a possibility strikes me as inherently more credible than the sorts of model we are accustomed to see in traditional trade theory, where labour simply flows from poor countries to rich countries.

The authors set out to develop a model that will answer several questions. As they say: "What are the economic costs and benefits of international labour mobility in a modern economy? Should it be encouraged? Should it be encouraged for some skills but not for others?" I think these are difficult and important questions, and I applaud their efforts to answer them. However, they describe their study as providing only a start in this direction, and I have to agree. I'm not sure that the study in its current form provides answers to these questions, or even that it provides a framework that will generate such answers. And I am particularly doubtful of their larger objective of using the model as a basis for an applied general equilibrium model for this purpose.

I will explain these doubts below, but first let me say why conceptually I agree with the authors that these types of questions need to be addressed.

There are, I think, two common themes that come up again and again in discussions of migration among advanced countries. One is the brain drain — the belief that emigration of highly skilled workers is harmful to the country they leave. This is discussed somewhat in the study, and I don't have anything else to say about it.

The other theme, however, is that countries benefit from the inflow of such skilled workers. That seems to be accepted in many advanced countries to a degree that I frankly find somewhat surprising. Indeed, the authors express this view, in passing, when they mention that Germany, Italy, Austria and Switzerland "are adopting policies aimed at attracting and facilitating the migration of skilled individuals." I don't doubt that these countries are using such policies, but I have to wonder why. These are advanced countries that are surely characterized by a relative abundance of skilled labour. One would think that, if they need anything, it would not be what they already have so much of.

Now, I have no doubt that voluntary migration into a country, whether skilled labour or other, is likely to provide net benefits to the country as a whole — on the standard assumptions that migrants will contribute to national income somewhat more than they take for themselves and that there is a net gain to society as a whole. But this net gain is not large, and it is the difference between the much larger loss that is borne by the portion of the existing population that competes directly with immigrants and the still larger gain that accrues to everybody else — the owners of all other factors of production. Thus, if skilled workers enter a (any) country, we would expect the wage of other comparably skilled workers to fall and the returns to capital and the wages of unskilled workers to rise, the latter gains being somewhat larger than the former loss. That does not strike me as a bad thing in countries like Canada and the United States, especially since the benefits to unskilled labour act in the direction of improving the income distribution. But this would be a rather indirect way of improving the income distribution. And therefore I don't think this is what most countries have in mind when attempting to attract skilled labour.

The authors actually suggest a possible reason in the rest of the sentence that I quoted partially above. The policies are attributed to countries "with their rapidly aging populations," suggesting that the desired skilled immigration is expected to pay taxes that will fund the pensions of current workers, probably both skilled and unskilled, as they retire. That may well be part of the reason for favouring skilled immigration, though it strikes me that this motive should make the country eager for immigrant workers of any type, with a preference for skilled workers only because they earn more and therefore contribute more in taxes. In any case, I would point out that this motive for immigration is not present in the authors' model, so if they believe that it is an important part of the story, then their model misses its mark.

What does their model say about the types of immigration that a country ought to prefer? That depends on the reasons for the immigration, and although I like the way that they model heterogeneous labour, I cannot see that the answers they implicitly give to this question are all that compelling. Looking at their four "experiments" as reported in Table 1, I find the following:

Experiment 1 — Countries differ in their endowments of skilled labour. Result: The most-skilled labour migrates from where it is abundant to where it is scarce, lowering welfare in the former and raising it in the latter. This is plausible and may explain why a poor country would welcome more skilled labour, but it does not apply to the case at hand.

Experiment 2 — Countries differ in their endowments of unskilled labour. Result: Essentially the same, in that skilled labour migrates from the country where unskilled labour is scarce to where it is abundant, lowering welfare in the former and raising it in the latter. Again, this does not apply to the case at hand.

Experiment 3 — Countries differ in their costs of exporting. Result: because, in this model, skilled labour stands to gain from exporting, it flows to the country where exporting costs are low, making it better off. This story does seem to apply to rich countries, since it is not implausible that they may have lower fixed costs of exporting. And it is almost as plausible that skilled immigrants might be attracted by market opportunities that arise as a result. But is this the reason why these countries are so eager to attract skilled immigrants — to help them export? Perhaps so, but it would surely be a very novel explanation.

Experiment 4 — Countries differ in the productivity of their non-traded, low-tech sector. Result: skilled labour is attracted to the country with higher productivity, which gains (slightly) as a result. Frankly, I have trouble seeing why migration takes place in this case, since the higher productivity is not found in the sector where skilled labour can be used and it only raises the wage of unskilled labour that skilled labour must employ in order to produce. But the authors do explain this, saying that skilled labour is attracted by higher "quasi rents." If I understand correctly, this seems to be due to the fixed mark-up over marginal cost that the particular structure of the model implies, together with the particular structure of preferences and the fixity of aggregate supply of skilled labour, so that entrepreneurs earn more profits when their costs are higher.

I guess that is right, but if so, this explanation of a preference for migration seems even more tortuous than the previous one.

In short, although the model has some very interesting and certainly novel features, I don't feel that I have learned from it the reason why countries are so eager to attract skilled workers. Why, then, do I think they behave this way? There are several reasons that I can think of, most of which I have seen mentioned in popular discussions, but none of which seems to be part of the authors' model.

- *Fiscal implications*: The fact that countries confidently expect that skilled workers will pay a good deal more in taxes than they draw in public services.

- *Employer pressures*: Lobbying by firms that face temporary shortages of particular skills and would prefer immigration to paying wage premiums.

- *Labour shortages*: In countries with rigid labour markets, excess demand for particular skills creates bottlenecks that can be cured by immigration.

These reasons are neither as novel nor as interesting as the stories that the authors can tell with their model. But if the aim is to provide a tool for policy analysis that can be used to understand what is really going on, I suspect that a model that excludes all of these features may not be of much help.

Which brings me to my second question — whether applied general equilibrium (AGE) analysis is, in fact, a promising tool for addressing these issues. As some may know, I have spent part of my career building and using such models for the analysis of trade policy issues, so presumably I have reason to be predisposed in their favour. And I am, in the sense that for some problems I consider AGE modeling as better than any alternative tool available. But it is nonetheless a methodology that raises many problems. Perhaps the greatest of these is that the results of an AGE model are completely dependent on the theoretical model being used with little or no way for the data to tell us whether the model is right. An econometric model can fail to fit the data, and if so there is a good chance that standard statistical checks will alert us to the fact that it is a bad model. But an AGE model has no such check. Since the parameters of the model are selected to match a single set of observations of the model's variables, the only check is whether this is, in fact, possible. If the model is bad enough, then no such parameters will exist, but this is a very weak test. For the most part, our trust in an AGE model's so-called empirical results should be no greater than our trust in its theoretical structure.

For that reason, I have always thought it very important — at least in the AGE modeling that I have done with my colleagues — to rely as far as possible only on very familiar theoretical structures that enjoy wide understanding and some sort of consensus as to their validity. The last thing I want to do is use a new and novel model, even if I really like the story that such a model tells. For even if a familiar model is wrong, at least the ways that it may be wrong will be better understood, because of its familiarity, and users of the results will be able to interpret them and evaluate appropriate doubts in ways that they could not do with an unfamiliar model.

So that makes me doubtful, as I said at the outset, that this particular modeling exercise will achieve its stated aim of eventually providing an AGE model that will really help us to understand migration. In fact, I will be surprised if the authors can even find the mapping from the model's variables and parameters to the data that would be needed to turn this into a usable AGE model. But even if they can, the model is far too original, in my opinion, to be usable for that purpose.

My suggestion, then, would be that they forget about their AGE motivation, and concentrate instead on more conventional theorizing and testing. That is, use the model to explore and explain how the world may work, then do their best to estimate the model empirically so as to find out if it does indeed provide a useful approximation to reality.

Part VI

Analytical and Policy Implications of Cross-Border Labour Market Integration

David E. Wildasin
University of Kentucky

11

Fiscal Policy, Human Capital and Canada-U.S. Labour Market Integration

> [I]t is a little superfluous for any foreigner to come to Rotterdam to lecture about economics at all. I feel a bit like a 17th century New England smuggler lecturing on seamanship to Admiral Tromp... I suppose the logic of the situation is that I am not an import at all; I am to be processed and re-exported, like cocoa beans.
> (R.M. Solow, on presenting invited lectures in Rotterdam, 1963, p. 7)

INTRODUCTION

LIBERALIZATION OF TRADE IN NORTH AMERICA has potentially important consequences for the functioning of labour markets and the development of human resources in this region. What are the implications of greater economic integration for earnings, earnings inequality, labour mobility and human capital investment and financing? The objective of this study is to help to clarify these issues conceptually, to discuss some of their empirical dimensions and to suggest some possible implications for policy and for future research.

The integration of markets for (either, or both) goods and factors of production (defined, loosely, as a reduction in fundamental barriers to exchange due to broadly-defined technological change as well as reductions in barriers resulting from liberalization of policy) has complex effects because it changes the general equilibrium of the entire economy. Labour markets may be affected directly by technological changes that facilitate international migration, such as reductions in search and moving costs, or by policy changes such as those embodied in the North American Free Trade Agreement (NAFTA) that allow greater international mobility within North America for business or other purposes. They may also be affected indirectly by changes in trade policy, most obviously because of changes in the sectoral composition of demand, and hence through resulting changes in the demand for different productive inputs. Perhaps less obviously, changes in trade policy can lead to changes in the optimal organization of commercial activity, including changes in the size and scope of firms and the degree of vertical integration of the production process, in turn leading to changes in the deployment of managerial, technical, and scientific human resources across space and international boundaries. Because these effects are potentially highly interrelated, it is useful to consider the process of economic integration not only in terms of its immediate impacts on particular markets, for example by examining the extent to which international migration flows change in the short run or whether these flows affect or are immediately affected by wages or earnings, tax policy or other specific variables, but also from a general equilibrium perspective that recognizes the interrelationships among markets and among various spheres of policy. Furthermore, the effects of structural economic change do not occur instantaneously and short-run effects can differ markedly from long-run effects.

As one simple illustration of these remarks, note that policies that change the rewards to more- or less-skilled workers — as NAFTA may have done according to studies cited below — change the incentives for skill acquisition. But the supply response to these incentives is complex and may well vary over time. For example, in the short run, many members of the existing workforce are unlikely to upgrade their skills or change their occupational specializations. As a broad generalization, middle-aged and older workers lacking advanced training seldom have sufficiently strong incentives to divert the time and money needed to acquire a university education, and mid-career physicists or nuclear engineers are not likely to have powerful incentives to change careers in order to become lawyers or accountants. The strength of these incentives depends partly on real income differentials and whether other supply responses — for example, international migration — limit the incentives to alter the human capital of the existing workforce. Over time, the supply response will reflect the entry of new workers into the labour force, including young people who, like their predecessors, make choices about the level and type of investment (whether to attend college, whether to study law, medicine, mathematics, or history) based on current and prospective market conditions. The supply response also depends on public policy adjustments, including not only the overall funding of education at all levels, but adjustment, as required, in the types of instruction offered. In higher education, for example, employment regulations and traditions make it difficult to shrink the deployment of resources in some areas in order to expand the availability of resources in other areas. Similarly, capital flows — across sectors within countries and across international boundaries — also respond to, and influence, ongoing adjustments in the labour market. This adjustment process is not instantaneous and the dynamics of capital adjustment are likely to be highly interrelated with those of the labour market.

The full complexity of these interactions is obviously beyond the scope of a single analysis. The present discussion is intended to identify some significant elements of the process of economic integration with a view to understanding some of their implications for the formation and utilization of human capital.

The second section, entitled *Theoretical Considerations: Trade and Migration*, reviews some basic theory about linkages between trade and factor pricing. It is often suggested that trade liberalization can substitute for the geographic integration of factor markets. However, the conditions under which this is true are not always satisfied either within or among countries. It is important to understand the linkage between trade and migration because, as shown in the third section entitled *Internal Migration in Canada and the United States*, internal migration is a persistent feature of the Canadian and U.S. labour markets. This section presents a very simple analytical framework that is helpful in understanding some of the allocative and distributional effects of internal migration. It also discusses the significant gross migration flows among regions in Canada and the United States and the particular importance of mobility for highly-educated workers — suggesting that the spatial integration of labour markets is linked to the types of skill-specialization normally associated with higher education. The fourth section, entitled *Higher Education in Canada and the United States*, briefly reviews the Canadian and U.S. experience with higher-education financing, drawing attention to recent trends in the funding of higher-education institutions and to the changing roles of national and subnational governments and of the private and public sectors in general. The fifth section, entitled *Labour Market Integration and Fiscal Competition in North America*, discusses how the integration of factor markets affects the environment within which policy is made. Factor mobility means that regions must compete for human and other resources. Government fiscal policies affect the allocation of resources among regions, and, in particular, competition for highly-skilled workers can affect the structure of government revenue systems. Competition for mobile resources, along with several other factors, may help to explain some of the recent trends in higher-education finance and may contribute to further evolution of policy in this area and of tax policy generally. The discussion concludes by noting several major research questions awaiting investigation that are important to develop a more secure foundation for policy analysis.

THEORETICAL CONSIDERATIONS: TRADE AND MIGRATION

FACTOR PRICE EQUALIZATION: A BRIEF RECAPITULATION

A NALYSIS OF THE ECONOMIC IMPACT of international migration in the context of a broader process of economic integration must quickly come to grips with a powerful insight from traditional international trade theory: the factor-price equalization theorem. According to this theorem — one of the textbook results of international trade theory — opening up international trade in goods and services should lead a country to expand its production in industries that rely heavily on inputs — capital, labour and natural resources — that are relatively cheap there, and to contract out its production in industries that use intensively inputs which are relatively costly in that country. Because of their favourable cost structure, firms in the former industries will be able to compete advantageously against foreign producers, allowing the country to export those goods and services, whereas the reverse is true for the latter industries: in these industries, imports will penetrate the domestic market, resulting in reduced employment, investment and output. As this process unfolds, the expansion of domestic export industries and the contraction of domestic import-competing industries will result in increased demand for domestic inputs that are relatively cheap and reduced demand for inputs that are relatively expensive. So, for instance, a country with abundant and thus comparatively cheap high-skilled labour will expand production of goods and services that require such labour, relying on imports from abroad to meet the demand for goods and services that require low-skilled labour. As this happens, the earnings of high-skilled workers in the domestic market rise, while the earnings of low-skilled workers fall. The opposite occurs in other countries, driving up the earnings of low-skilled workers and reducing the earnings of high-skilled workers.

Under some assumptions, principally that countries have access to identical constant-returns-to-scale production technologies, that markets are perfectly competitive, and that factors of production can move freely from contracting to expanding industries, the process of trade should lead to complete international equality of relative factor prices — factor price equalization. Thus, for instance, the wage per unit of managerial services relative to the wage per unit of blue-collar services should be equalized. Similarly, the relative return per unit of capital services, the return per effective unit of land or natural resources, and other factor prices should tend to converge as trade expands. These are among the expected consequences of trade liberalization policies like NAFTA or of other political or technological changes that reduce existing trade barriers.

The factor-price equalization theorem suggests that international trade affects the distribution of income. Correctly understood, however, factor price equalization does not imply that the annual real income per manager or per blue-collar worker is equalized across countries. Managers or blue-collar workers in one country may embody more or fewer effective units of their respective skills than workers in another country. Factor price equalization implies (for example) that if low-skilled workers in one country are able to produce twice as many units of low-skilled services as workers in another country, their incomes will be twice as high. This presents a serious challenge for empirical research, since it is difficult to determine whether (for example) better-educated workers in one country have higher incomes because they embody more units of the same types of human resources as lower-skilled workers in the *same* country or whether the skills that they acquire through education are *different* and more highly rewarded than those of less-educated workers.[1]

To formulate this distinction more precisely, suppose that production in a particular industry in country (or region) j uses a combination of capital k_j, natural resources n_j, and several different types of labour l_{ij}, where $i = 1, ...m$ indexes the labour type (for instance, high-skilled labour might be of type 1 and low-skilled labour might be of type 2).[2] With marginal-productivity factor pricing, and letting p_j denote the price of the output of this industry, the wages of workers of type i in local labour markets are given by:

$$(1) \qquad w_{ij} = p_j \frac{\partial f_j(k_j, n_j, l_{1j}...l_{mj})}{\partial l_{ij}},$$

where $f_i(\cdot)$, the level of industry output, depends not only on labour inputs but also on other productive resources (capital, natural resources, etc.). In general, the degree of substitutability between different types of labour can range from none to complete. In the latter case, the wages of high- and low-skilled workers will differ only because they possess different quantities of skills that are effectively homogeneous — that is, they have different effective labour supplies.

It is worth noting that this special assumption of perfect substitutability — augmented with the further assumption that labour is the only factor of production so that the marginal productivity of labour is a technological constant — has been the basis of a large literature on optimal income taxation, beginning (in its modern form) with the seminal work of Mirrlees (1971). It also has been a maintained assumption in many traditional macro growth models where, for instance, capital and labour are treated as the only inputs in the aggregate production function. In this context, labour is not treated as the sole input and the degree of substitutability between labour and capital is one of the important parameters of the model; customarily, an elasticity of substitution of one (the Cobb-Douglas case) or less is thought to fit the data best. In this respect, growth models offer a richer framework for the analysis of income distribution because they distinguish between labour and non-labour income.

However, in models where all labour (and labour supply behaviour) is homogeneous, changes in *earnings* inequality must ultimately be traced to changes in the distribution of the amount of effective labour services within the working population. In this context, for instance, an increase in earnings inequality during the 1990s could be attributed to some combination of an increase in the skills of high-skilled workers (experience, or on-the-job training) and of a reduction in the skills of low-skilled workers (a depreciation of these workers' human capital). A more plausible explanation for changes in the distribution of earnings, however, is that workers of different types are *not* perfect substitutes for one another, at least in the short run, during which workers' skill levels are treated as exogenously fixed.

In any event, whether different types of labour are perfect substitutes, workers of the same type in different countries are perfect substitutes by definition. With free trade and given the other assumptions of the factor-price equalization theorem, the wage rates of these workers should be the same across countries. In this case, international differences in earnings per worker of a given type must be attributed to differences across countries in the effective number of units of labour supplied per worker. Once again, this raises thorny issues for the empirical analysis since it is difficult to determine whether workers with different earnings embody different amounts of the same type of labour or different types of labour.

While the factor-price equalization theorem is most commonly referenced in the context of international trade, it should be noted that it can be applied, as well, *within* countries. Indeed, trade within countries is often fundamentally less costly, and less impeded by restrictive policies, than trade among countries. In this context, the theorem implies that free trade among regions of a country should result in equalization of factor prices among these regions. Internal migration is discussed further below.

TRADE AND MIGRATION: SUBSTITUTES OR COMPLEMENTS?

THE FAMOUS ANALYSIS BY MUNDELL (1957), drawing on classical Heckscher-Ohlin-Samuelson trade theory, argues that trade and factor mobility can be substitutes for one another. The essence of the argument derives from the factor-price equalization theorem: if trade tends to drive factor prices in different countries or regions closer together, and if factor reallocation across space is driven by factor price differentials, then trade can reduce, or substitute entirely for, factor movements. The rationale for this argument should be apparent from the foregoing remarks. The economic theory of factor movements across space rests on the fundamental hypothesis that factor owners — workers, in the case of human resources — seek the highest attainable net returns for the resources they own.[3] Real differences in net rates of return across regions create incentives for arbitrage, with workers or capital flowing from places where net rates of return are low to places where they are high.[4]

The applicability of this analysis is limited, however, for several reasons. Perhaps most importantly, at least for our purposes, it neglects the spatial structure of factor markets *within* countries, which are effectively treated as single points in space.[5] With trade, factors of production are reallocated away from contracting industries in import sectors and toward expanding industries in export sectors. But in standard trade theory models, these factor reallocations do not occur among spatially separated regions since countries — the geographical unit of analysis in the standard model — have no spatial structure. In reality, of course, factor reallocations among industries within countries do involve spatial reallocations. The most obvious historical example is the process of urbanization, associated with the development of the modern manufacturing industry, and the movement of population from rural to urban areas. The *intersectoral* reallocation of productive resources that accompanies international trade is also, ordinarily, an *interregional* reallocation of resources.

These observations are worth bearing in mind when considering *intranational* movements of labour and capital. They can help to explain why countries like Canada and the United States are characterized both by liberal conditions of internal trade (there are no explicit tariffs on interprovincial or interstate commerce, nor are regulatory impediments allowed, generally, to interfere with free internal commerce) *and* by high levels of internal factor flows, as discussed further below.

Nevertheless, the basic insight that trade affects factor prices is crucial. When applied to human resources, it implies that the return to investment in human capital is affected by trade: countries that export human-capital intensive commodities and that import goods that can be produced with relatively small amounts of skilled labour, for example, should experience widening wage differentials between more-skilled and less-skilled workers. In recent years, a number of empirical analyses (see the discussion below) have attempted to find an explanation for the increased dispersion of wages in Canada and the United States, and it appears that a consensus has formed that trade, broadly speaking, helps to explain a significant portion, though not all, of the widening of wage differentials within these two countries.

INTERNAL MIGRATION IN CANADA AND THE UNITED STATES

THIS SECTION CONSIDERS THE ROLE OF INTERNAL MIGRATION in Canada and the United States. The economies of both countries span large geographical areas and are characterized by a high degree of integration of internal markets for goods and services. In view of the theoretical considerations discussed in the previous section, it is natural to ask whether free internal trade has obviated any important economic role for internal migration in these two countries.

As we shall see, labour migration has, on the contrary, played a large role historically in the economies of Canada and the United States, and this important role shows no signs of diminishing over time. Much internal migration takes the form of a *cross-hauling* of labour — two-way labour flows among regions. In order to understand the economic implications of labour mobility and labour market integration, it is important to develop theoretical explanations of why such migration flows might be observed. The discussion below emphasizes the potential role of migration as a mechanism for spatial matching of the supply of and demand for specialized, heterogeneous labour skills.

INTERSECTORAL AND SPATIAL REALLOCATION OF LABOUR

THE EXTENT TO WHICH TRADE AND MIGRATION are substitutes can be considered not only in the context of *international* trade, but in the context of trade within a country. Indeed, if trade in a country is free and if the other assumptions underlying the factor-price equalization theorem are satisfied, it would follow that internal migration or capital movements would be economically irrelevant, except insofar as workers have residential preferences that would motivate them to move from one region to another. In such an economy, a complete prohibition on interregional factor movements would affect neither the distribution of income nor the efficiency of resource allocation. In fact, this logic can be extended down to the lowest level of spatial analysis, leading to the conclusion that factor movements are always irrelevant so long as the assumptions of the factor-price equalization theorem are satisfied.

This *reductio ad absurdum* draws attention to an implicit assumption in most treatments of the factor-price equalization theorem. While it is explicitly acknowledged that factor price equalization requires free *intersectoral* mobility of factors of production, in practice this presupposes free spatial mobility of factors. As one classic illustration of practical importance, consider the gradual shift of production and of productive resources from agriculture to manufacturing (and more recently to services) in the Canadian and U.S. economies during the past century. Whereas 21.0 percent of employed members of the U.S. workforce were engaged in agriculture in 1939, that percentage had fallen to 2.3 percent by 2001. This employment shift has been accompanied by rural-urban migration and increased urbanization of the population. For example, 39.6 percent of the U.S. population lived in urban areas in 1900, with the remainder living in rural areas; by 1940, 56.1 percent were urbanized and, by 1990, 75.2 percent of the population lived in urban areas. Canadian statistics tell a similar story. In 1871, 25.6 percent of the Canadian population lived in urban areas; by 1901, this figure had risen to 37.4 percent; in 1941, 54.3 percent of the population was urbanized and, by 1996, the urban contingent had increased to 77.9 percent of the total population. As in the U.S. case, growing urbanization was accompanied by an intersectoral shift of labour away from agriculture. In 1881, 48.1 percent of the workforce was engaged in agriculture, a figure that had fallen to 40.2 percent in 1901, to 25.8 percent in 1941 and to 3.3 percent in 1996.

More generally, labour and capital mobility — spatial as well as, and as part of, intersectoral resource mobility — have been of critical importance in the economic development of both the Canadian and U.S. economies throughout their history. Of course, trade within these economies has been subject to some restrictions due to regulatory and other policies (as has been true also of the mobility of labour and capital), but both economies stand out, by world and historical standards, for their high degree of internal free trade over large geographical areas. Their experience provides strong evidence to suggest that trade and factor mobility are not highly substitutable but, in fact, can coexist for long periods of time.

Modeling Internal Migration

Why is internal migration a persistent feature of the Canadian and U.S. labour markets? Many factors are undoubtedly at work, but the natural starting point for the analysis — and a standard one in the literature (see, for example, Topel, 1986) — is to suppose that internal migration is driven by the desire of migrants to achieve higher levels of real income. The real income enjoyed by a worker in a region depends first and foremost on the employment conditions prevailing in that region, for which real wages provide a convenient summary indicator.

As discussed previously, the assumptions of the factor-price equalization theorem must be invalid for wages to differ among regions of a country. Empirically, it is well-known that real wages can, indeed, differ among regions for specific types of labour. For example, prolonged net East-West migration in the United States (essentially during the entire 20th century) has resulted in a significant reallocation of labour from relatively low-wage to relatively high-wage regions. The 'great migration' of black workers from the southern United States to northern and mid-western cities during the period 1930-60 reflects a movement from low-wage agricultural employment to higher-wage manufacturing jobs. These major trends demonstrate the existence of real wage differentials and their fundamental importance for major demographic shifts through internal migration. They suggest that the productivity of specific types of labour can vary over time and among regions because of technological change (for example, changes in cotton-harvesting technology) and because of changes in domestic or world demand conditions that affect prices, desired output levels, and the associated derived demand for labour. Diminishing returns to labour inputs in a geographic area can arise because of the presence of locationally fixed or quasi-fixed factors. These include land and other natural resources, but also the stock of public infrastructure (highway systems, port facilities, water, gas and electricity distribution networks) which, even if variable in the long run, is often very slow to change. Some types of private fixed capital investments are also quite long-lived, as are quasi-public entities like major educational institutions and related research centres.

The presence of fixed or quasi-fixed inputs in the production process has far-reaching implications for the allocation of labour and the determination of wage rates. A simple and familiar diagrammatic illustration can convey the main relevant points. Let the horizontal axis of Figure 1 measure the quantity of labour of a particular type, i, in a particular region, j; for simplicity, and without loss of important generality, assume that each worker *inelastically* supplies one unit of labour, so that the quantity of labour is equivalent to the number of workers of the specified type. Suppose also that the region is small relative to the rest of the domestic economy, in the sense that an increase or decrease in employment in that region has only a small impact on the real incomes of workers of this type in the rest of the economy, given by w_i in Figure 1. The demand for labour of type i in region j, as given in equation (1), depends on the amounts of other inputs in the region, the technology of production and

FIGURE 1

ALLOCATION OF LABOUR AND DETERMINATION OF WAGE RATES

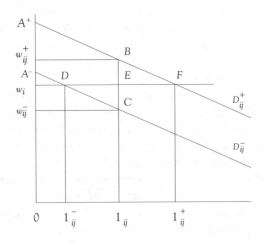

the price of the output produced by these workers, all of which generally vary over time.[6] Let l_{ij} denote the number of workers initially located in the region. If migration into or out of the region is costless, then the region will experience immigration or emigration of workers of type i depending on the values of local demand determinants. If migration is impossible (infinitely costly), then local demand conditions will determine the equilibrium local wage.

Figure 1 illustrates two possible cases, one with high demand for type i labour, represented by D_{ij}^+, and one with low demand, represented by D_{ij}^-. These demands may reflect different values of output prices on world markets, different degrees of protectionist trade policies (for example, a tariff on imports of goods produced with type i labour in the high-demand case, free trade in the low-demand case), different states of technology or different levels of complementary inputs such as public or private capital investment. When labour is costlessly mobile, the equilibrium level of employment reflects local demand conditions, shown as l_{ij}^+ and l_{ij}^- in Figure 1. The difference between local demand and the initial endowment of labour, $l_{ij}^+ - l_{ij}$, represents net immigration of type i labour in the high-demand situation, while $l_{ij} - l_{ij}^+$ represents the outflow of this type of labour in the low-demand situation. The equilibrium wage is fixed at w_i by external market conditions, independently of the level of local demand. When labour is completely immobile, the equilibrium level of employment is fixed at l_{ij} and no migration can occur, but the equilibrium local wage rate varies with local demand, for example from w_{ij}^+ in the high-demand situation to w_{ij}^- in the low-demand situation.

This simple diagram illustrates the crucial role of fixed or quasi-fixed inputs in giving rise to diminishing returns to labour in a particular location, and shows how factor mobility — in this case, the mobility of labour — is central in the equalization of factor prices among regions. Of course, migration costs may limit the extent to which local employment responds to varying local demand conditions, as indeed is illustrated most clearly in the case where migration costs are so high as to be prohibitive. In this case, local wages vary in accordance with local labour market demand conditions, rather than being determined entirely by external market conditions. But to the extent that labour can move among regions, wages — or, to be more accurate, real incomes — will tend to be equalized across space.

Note from this simple analysis that labour mobility contributes to the efficiency of resource allocation because workers move to regions where they are more productive and away from regions where they are less productive. In other words, labour mobility is *productivity enhancing*. This point is well-known. For example, Hamilton and Whalley (1984) use a computable general equilibrium (CGE) model of the world economy in which labour is treated as a homogeneous factor of production. They estimate that free international mobility of labour would increase world output and real income by an amount approximately equal to world gross domestic product (GDP). To this writer's knowledge, a similar calculation has not been made to illustrate how much labour mobility has contributed to the growth of U.S. or Canadian GDP, although, in principle, this is not a difficult exercise. There is every reason to think that labour mobility makes a major contribution to the efficient functioning of North American labour markets, especially when the heterogeneity of labour is taken into account.[7]

INTERNAL MIGRATION: WHY ARE GROSS FLOWS SO LARGE?

WHILE NET MIGRATION AMONG REGIONS OR COUNTRIES is often a focus of attention for policymakers and analysts, the net movement of labour among regions in Canada and the United States is the result of gross flows in opposite directions that are often much larger — frequently, by an order of magnitude — than the net flows.

Tables 1 to 3 draw on recent Canadian census data. Table 1 shows 5-year migration by province and for the country as a whole, for the census years 1991 and 1996.[8] Table 2 presents the same data expressed as percentages. Table 3 presents 1-year migration levels and rates for the year 1996.

Looking first at Tables 1 and 2 for 1996, we see that 43 percent of Canadians moved (i.e. changed addresses) during the period 1991-96. However, many of these movers stayed in the same municipal area (strictly speaking, the same census subdivision) and hence are classified as non-migrants. Most of these non-migrants presumably changed residences but, if in the workforce, continued to participate in the same local labour market. Migrants, on the other hand, lived in different municipal areas or outside of Canada five years earlier; of these, approximately 3 percent lived in a different province and thus are classified as interprovincial migrants. This means that gross interprovincial migration — the sum of in- and out-migration for all provinces excluding international migration — amounted to 6 percent of the national population. The level of migration varies substantially by province; unsurprisingly, in absolute terms, in-migration in the two largest provinces was larger than for any other province, but was comparatively modest in proportional terms, amounting to only 1 to 3 percent of the provincial population; corresponding figures for other provinces were generally in the 5 to 7 percent range. Of course, one would expect that the larger provinces would exhibit lower levels of interprovincial migration on account of their size. It is noteworthy, for example, that the proportion of all migrants to Ontario and Quebec is quite close to the national average, and that intraprovincial migration rates were relatively high for these two provinces; less-populous provinces generally exhibit higher rates of interprovincial migration and lower rates of intraprovincial migration.

TABLE 1

POPULATION FIVE YEARS AND OVER, MOBILITY STATUS BASED ON PLACE OF RESIDENCE FIVE YEARS AGO, CANADA, PROVINCES AND TERRITORIES, 1991 AND 1996

	CANADA	NEWFOUNDLAND	PRINCE EDWARD ISLAND	NOVA SCOTIA	NEW BRUNSWICK	QUEBEC
1991						
Total	24,927,870	524,845	117,490	823,850	664,585	6,319,430
Non-movers	13,290,690	375,885	76,915	510,660	436,200	3,564,470
Movers	11,637,180	148,955	40,570	313,190	228,385	2,754,960
Non-migrants	5,776,215	76,565	17,770	165,140	120,000	1,382,255
Migrants	5,860,970	72,390	22,805	148,050	108,385	1,372,710
Internal Migrants	4,947,645	69,710	21,825	139,410	102,990	1,230,860
Intraprovincial Migrants	3,970,595	48,975	13,035	86,150	67,155	1,148,865
Interprovincial Migrants	977,050	20,735	8,785	53,260	35,825	81,995
External Migrants	913,320	2,680	980	8,640	5,400	141,845
1996						
Total	26,604,135	516,455	123,790	843,750	685,045	6,588,580
Non-movers	15,079,410	378,840	84,150	539,825	461,660	3,962,295
Movers	11,524,725	137,615	39,640	303,925	223,385	2,626,285
Non-migrants	6,130,740	75,370	20,355	178,680	125,735	1,407,750
Migrants	5,393,985	62,240	19,285	125,245	97,650	1,218,535
Internal Migrants	4,465,295	59,560	18,595	115,810	92,215	1,078,625
Intraprovincial Migrants	3,575,025	43,335	9,650	68,355	58,155	1,009,725
Interprovincial Migrants	890,270	16,225	8,945	47,455	34,060	68,895
External Migrants	928,690	2,680	690	9,435	5,435	139,910

Table 1 (cont'd)

Population Five Years and over, Mobility Status Based on Place of Residence Five Years Ago, Canada, Provinces and Territories, 1991 and 1996

	Ontario	Manitoba	Saskatchewan	Alberta	British Columbia	Yukon	Northwest Territories
1991							
Total	9,225,700	984,125	891,255	2,291,065	3,011,330	24,785	49,400
Non-movers	4,797,795	557,525	544,015	1,081,105	1,320,285	8,775	17,045
Movers	4,427,905	426,595	347,240	1,209,965	1,691,050	16,010	32,355
Non-migrants	2,098,400	275,780	189,410	668,220	757,890	7,295	17,500
Migrants	2,329,505	150,815	157,830	541,745	933,160	8,715	14,855
Internal Migrants	1,831,825	126,305	149,235	466,860	786,125	8,270	14,235
Intraprovincial Migrants	1,561,840	82,255	111,015	296,840	547,945	1,810	4,695
Interprovincial Migrants	269,985	44,050	38,220	170,015	238,175	6,460	9,540
External Migrants	497,675	24,510	8,595	74,890	147,035	440	620
1996							
Total	9,904,595	1,019,590	906,355	2,474,850	3,456,245	28,310	56,560
Non-movers	5,635,420	612,580	556,695	1,244,925	1,570,900	11,805	20,320
Movers	4,269,180	407,010	349,660	1,229,925	1,885,345	16,505	36,240
Non-migrants	2,252,460	265,965	191,375	705,835	877,170	8,330	21,715
Migrants	2,016,725	141,050	158,285	524,090	1,008,170	8,170	14,530
Internal Migrants	1,561,110	121,565	148,580	453,845	793,650	7,795	13,945
Intraprovincial Migrants	1,367,090	78,350	101,055	291,200	541,025	1,840	5,230
Interprovincial Migrants	194,020	43,215	47,520	162,645	252,625	5,955	8,710
External Migrants	455,615	19,485	9,710	70,250	214,520	375	590

Source: Statistics Canada, 1996 Census national tables.

TABLE 2

POPULATION FIVE YEARS AND OVER, MOBILITY STATUS BASED ON PLACE OF RESIDENCE FIVE YEARS AGO, CANADA, PROVINCES AND TERRITORIES, 1991 AND 1996 (PERCENTAGE)

	CANADA	NEWFOUNDLAND	PRINCE EDWARD ISLAND	NOVA SCOTIA	NEW BRUNSWICK	QUEBEC
1991						
Total	100	100	100	100	100	100
Non-movers	53	72	65	62	66	56
Movers	47	28	35	38	34	44
Non-migrants	23	15	15	20	18	22
Migrants	24	14	19	18	16	22
Internal Migrants	20	13	19	17	15	19
Intraprovincial Migrants	16	9	11	10	10	18
Interprovincial Migrants	4	4	7	6	5	1
External Migrants	4	1	1	1	1	2
1996						
Total	100	100	100	100	100	100
Non-movers	57	73	68	64	67	60
Movers	43	27	32	36	33	40
Non-migrants	23	15	16	21	18	21
Migrants	20	12	16	15	14	18
Internal Migrants	17	12	15	14	13	16
Intraprovincial Migrants	13	8	8	8	8	15
Interprovincial Migrants	3	3	7	6	5	1
External Migrants	3	1	1	1	1	2

TABLE 2 (CONT'D)

POPULATION FIVE YEARS AND OVER, MOBILITY STATUS BASED ON PLACE OF RESIDENCE FIVE YEARS AGO, CANADA, PROVINCES AND TERRITORIES, 1991 AND 1996 (PERCENTAGE)

	ONTARIO	MANITOBA	SASKATCHEWAN	ALBERTA	BRITISH COLUMBIA	YUKON	NORTHWEST TERRITORIES
1991							
Total	100	100	100	100	100	100	100
Non-movers	52	57	61	47	44	35	35
Movers	48	43	39	53	56	65	65
Non-migrants	23	28	21	29	25	29	35
Migrants	25	15	18	24	31	35	30
Internal Migrants	20	13	17	20	26	33	29
Intraprovincial Migrants	17	8	12	13	18	7	10
Interprovincial Migrants	3	4	4	7	8	26	19
External Migrants	5	2	1	3	5	2	1
1996							
Total	100	100	100	100	100	100	100
Non-movers	57	60	61	50	45	42	36
Movers	43	40	39	50	55	58	64
Non-migrants	23	26	21	29	25	29	38
Migrants	20	14	17	21	29	29	26
Internal Migrants	16	12	16	18	23	28	25
Intraprovincial Migrants	14	8	11	12	16	6	9
Interprovincial Migrants	2	4	5	7	7	21	15
External Migrants	5	2	1	3	6	1	1

Source: Table 1.

TABLE 3

POPULATION ONE YEAR AND OVER, MOBILITY STATUS BASED ON PLACE OF RESIDENCE ONE YEAR AGO, CANADA, PROVINCES AND TERRITORIES, 1996 (NUMBER AND PERCENTAGE)

	CANADA	NEWFOUNDLAND	PRINCE EDWARD ISLAND	NOVA SCOTIA	NEW BRUNSWICK	QUEBEC
Number						
Total	28,155,225	541,630	131,050	888,835	721,070	6,958,710
External Migrants	228,695	1,000	275	2,890	1,510	37,275
Interprovincial Migrants	293,340	7,285	3,440	17,155	12,710	25,410
Intraprovincial Migrants	1,290,150	18,410	3,795	28,470	24,330	352,880
Non-migrants	2,540,400	32,440	8,890	77,920	55,760	537,505
Non-movers	23,802,645	482,490	114,650	762,395	626,760	6,005,650
Percentage						
Total	100.00	100.00	100.00	100.00	100.00	100.00
External Migrants	0.81	0.18	0.21	0.33	0.21	0.54
Interprovincial Migrants	1.04	1.35	2.62	1.93	1.76	0.37
Intraprovincial Migrants	4.58	3.40	2.90	3.20	3.37	5.07
Non-migrants	9.02	5.99	6.78	8.77	7.73	7.72
Non-movers	84.54	89.08	87.49	85.77	86.92	86.30

TABLE 3 (CONT'D)

POPULATION ONE YEAR AND OVER, MOBILITY STATUS BASED ON PLACE OF RESIDENCE ONE YEAR AGO, CANADA, PROVINCES AND TERRITORIES, 1996 (NUMBER AND PERCENTAGE)

	ONTARIO	MANITOBA	SASKATCHEWAN	ALBERTA	BRITISH COLUMBIA	YUKON	NORTHWEST TERRITORIES
Number							
Total	10,496,475	1,084,900	963,305	2,631,835	3,644,505	30,220	62,680
External Migrants	104,335	5,275	3,675	18,730	53,415	170	140
Interprovincial Migrants	67,080	15,615	18,255	54,690	66,205	2,360	3,130
Intraprovincial Migrants	479,750	30,220	40,300	112,285	196,280	745	2,670
Non-migrants	896,995	108,975	90,235	310,395	406,395	4,095	10,795
Non-movers	8,948,305	924,815	810,840	2,135,735	2,922,205	22,855	45,945
Percentage							
Total	100.00	100.00	100.00	100.00	100.00	100.00	100.00
External Migrants	0.99	0.49	0.38	0.71	1.47	0.56	0.22
Interprovincial Migrants	0.64	1.44	1.90	2.08	1.82	7.81	4.99
Intraprovincial Migrants	4.57	2.79	4.18	4.27	5.39	2.47	4.26
Non-migrants	8.55	10.04	9.37	11.79	11.15	13.55	17.22
Non-movers	85.25	85.24	84.17	81.15	80.18	75.63	73.30

Source: Statistics Canada.

The data for the 5-year period 1986-1991 are broadly similar but reveal somewhat higher levels of population movements than in the more recent period. Once again, while interprovincial migrants account for a comparatively small fraction of the populations of Ontario and Quebec, the total share of migrants in these provinces is quite close to the national average, again reflecting their larger size. Both in 1991 and 1996, immigration from outside the country was about as large as the total amount of interprovincial migration.

Table 3 presents similar figures for 1996, but showing only the level of migration taking place in a single year. Of course, all of the figures in this table are significantly smaller than for the 5-year data presented in Tables 1 and 2. Qualitatively speaking, however, the 1-year data are generally similar to those of the 5-year tables.

Tables 4 and 5 depict the migration to the United States. In this case, the information is presented at the level of the four census regions, each comprised of a number of individual states. The total populations of these regions are approximately two to three times the size of the total Canadian population. These tables show data on annual migration flows for selected years, and are therefore most comparable to Table 3. They indicate that the United States is also characterized by a high level of internal migration. The data explicitly separate in- and out-migration, as well as report net migration flows. Annual in- and out-migration rates are generally in the range of 1 to 1.75 percent, with gross migration rates (combined in- and out-migration rates) generally ranging from 2 to 3.25 percent. Of course, net migration rates are, by definition, smaller than gross migration rates, but the data in Table 5 show that the magnitude of the difference is quite substantial: gross flows often exceed net flows by a factor of 10 or more, and in almost no cases exceed them by less than a factor of 4.

In the United States as in Canada, this information could be reported at different levels of spatial aggregation, such as at the level of states or metropolitan areas. As one moves to smaller spatial units, migration rates rise. In 1999-2000, for instance, a total of 16 percent of the U.S. population changed location; of this total, only 0.6 percent were movers from abroad, 6.3 percent moved from one state to another, 9 percent moved to a different county within the same state, and 9 percent moved from one place to another within the same county. During the same year, the nation's metropolitan areas experienced internal in-migration of 2 million people, out-migration of 1.9 million, net internal in-migration of 0.1 million, and immigration from abroad of 1.6 million. Note, again, that net internal migration is very small relative to gross migration flows. No doubt much (but not all) relocation at the most disaggregated level (within counties) is accounted for by changes in residence rather than by changes in employment, and even at the level of census regions a certain proportion of moves may involve no change of employment. Nevertheless, it is evident from the data — which, as in the Canadian case, reflect

TABLE 4

INTERREGIONAL MIGRATION IN THE UNITED STATES, 1980-2000,
SELECTED YEARS (THOUSANDS)

MOBILITY PERIOD AND TYPE	NORTHEAST	MIDWEST	SOUTH	WEST
1999-2000				
In-migrants	363	722	1,258	763
Out-migrants	615	640	1,031	820
Net Internal Migration	−252	82	227	−57
Movers from Abroad	292	238	612	604
Net Migration (including from abroad)	40	320	839	547
Population	53,594	64,393	100,237	63,198
1989-90				
In-migrants	461	908	1,428	964
Out-migrants	758	1,024	1,198	781
Net Internal Migration	−297	−116	230	183
Movers from Abroad	328	169	500	562
Net Migration (including from abroad)	31	53	730	745
Population	50,809	59,668	85,446	52,786
1980-81				
In-migrants	464	650	1,377	871
Out-migrants	706	1,056	890	710
Net Internal Migration	−242	−406	487	161
Movers from Abroad	207	180	412	514
Net Migration (including from abroad)	−35	−226	899	675
Population	49,137	58,867	75,367	43,171

Source: U.S. Census Bureau.

long-standing migration patterns that have persisted at least since World War II — that there are high levels of internal migration in the United States involving changes either in employment status (school to work, work to retirement, etc.) or in the location of employment. Furthermore, and very importantly, the high levels of gross relative to net migration reveal that there is a great deal of *cross-hauling* of labour: workers in the East move to the West while workers from the West move to the East.

The high levels of gross internal migration in Canada and the United States show convincingly that *free internal trade has not eliminated internal migration*. In addition, they suggest that labour cannot be accurately characterized as a homogeneous factor of production over time horizons of years or decades. Large and largely offsetting flows of labour into and out of local labour markets are indicative of a sorting or matching process in which workers search for and find

TABLE 5

MIGRATION RATES IN THE UNITED STATES, 1980-2000, SELECTED YEARS

MOBILITY PERIOD AND TYPE	NORTHEAST	MIDWEST	SOUTH	WEST
1999-2000				
In-migrants	0.68	1.12	1.26	1.21
Out-migrants	1.15	0.99	1.03	1.30
Net Internal Migration	−0.47	0.13	0.23	−0.09
Movers from Abroad	0.54	0.37	0.61	0.96
Net Migration (including from abroad)	0.07	0.50	0.84	0.87
Gross Internal Migration Rates	1.82	2.12	2.28	2.50
Gross/Net Internal Migration Rates	−3.88	16.61	10.08	−27.77
1989-90				
In-migrants	0.91	1.52	1.67	1.83
Out-migrants	1.49	1.72	1.40	1.48
Net Internal Migration	−0.58	−0.19	0.27	0.35
Movers from Abroad	0.65	0.28	0.59	1.06
Net Migration (including from abroad)	0.06	0.09	0.85	1.41
Gross Internal Migration Rates	2.40	3.24	3.07	3.31
Gross/Net Internal Migration Rates	−4.10	−16.66	11.42	9.54
1980-81				
In-migrants	0.94	1.10	1.83	2.02
Out-migrants	1.44	1.79	1.18	1.64
Net Internal Migration	−0.49	−0.69	0.65	0.37
Movers from Abroad	0.42	0.31	0.55	1.19
Net Migration (including from abroad)	−0.07	−0.38	1.19	1.56
Gross Internal Migration Rates	2.38	2.90	3.01	3.66
Gross/Net Internal Migration Rates	−4.83	−4.20	4.66	9.82

Source: Table 4.

better — higher-productivity and higher-real-wage — jobs in other markets, a process which inevitably involves search and relocation costs that could be avoided if existing workers in local markets filled these jobs. The fact that this does not occur means that local workers are less satisfactory matches for local jobs, in many instances, than workers from other regions.[9] In turn, this implies that large labour markets are productivity-enhancing.

GROSS MIGRATION AND SKILL SPECIALIZATION

OF COURSE, MOBILITY IS NOT EQUALLY productivity-enhancing for all workers. Empirically, highly-educated workers (especially young ones) migrate with greater frequency than lower-skilled workers. This has long been known in the literature. Ehrenberg and Smith (1988, p. 360), for example, observe that age is the most important determinant of migration, with young people moving more than old, and that "education is the single best indicator of who will move *within* an age group. ... [C]ollege education ... raises the probability of migrating the most" (emphasis in original). A number of recent studies examine the movement of highly-educated workers. Bound, Groen, Kezki and Turner (2001) find that states with higher-education institutions that produce many graduates may employ such workers at a somewhat higher rate than other states, but that the rate of employment of highly-educated workers is not strongly linked to the number of such workers produced in a state. Kodrzycki (2001) finds that college graduates are more mobile than others, as expected, and that net migration in this group is substantially smaller than *gross* migration. As can be seen in Table 6, whereas over 6 percent of individuals with at least a college-level education move among census divisions (which divide the United States into nine areas) each year, the corresponding figure is just over 4 percent for high-school graduates and even lower for individuals with less than a high-school education. Table 7 shows that about 25 percent of college graduates move across census divisions within a 5-year period, with gross migration flows much higher than net migration flows. Interestingly, this is true whether migration is defined relative to high-school location (presumably an indicator of *home* region) or relative to college location (which, for some people, might be a 'sojourn' away from the home region), indicating that job-related moves are indeed of considerable importance among highly-educated people.

TABLE 6

FREQUENCY OF MOVES BETWEEN 1979 AND 1996,
BY EDUCATIONAL ATTAINMENT, NLSY SAMPLE

PERCENT MOVING PER PERIOD[a]	HIGH SCHOOL DROPOUT	HIGH SCHOOL ONLY	SOME COLLEGE	COLLEGE GRADUATE ONLY	MORE THAN COLLEGE GRADUATE
Between States	5.3	5.3	6.4	8.7	10.2
Between Non-contiguous States	3.6	4.0	4.7	6.0	7.6
Between Census Divisions	3.5	4.1	4.7	6.3	7.8

Note: a Annually, except for period 1994-1996.
Source: Kodrzycki (2001), Table 2, based on the *National Longitudinal Survey of Youth* (NLSY).

TABLE 7

FIVE-YEAR MIGRATION RATES ACROSS CENSUS DIVISIONS, COLLEGE GRADUATES, 1979 TO 1991, NLSY SAMPLE

CENSUS DIVISION	DOMESTIC IN-MIGRATION	DOMESTIC OUT-MIGRATION	DOMESTIC NET MIGRATION
High School Location			
New England	19.5	29.9	−10.4
Middle Atlantic	19.3	20.5	−1.2
East North Central	9.8	25.6	−15.9
West North Central	13.2	27.4	−14.2
South Atlantic	32.9	19.2	13.8
East South Central	23.5	35.3	−11.8
West South Central	23.6	19.4	4.2
Mountain	69.4	36.1	33.3
Pacific	52.6	10.5	42.1
United States	23.5	23.5	0
College Location			
New England	16.4	20.5	−4.1
Middle Atlantic	15.6	13.8	1.8
East North Central	17.3	23.2	−5.9
West North Central	14.7	25.5	−10.8
South Atlantic	27.5	15	12.6
East South Central	21.3	25.5	−4.3
West South Central	10.9	28.3	−17.4
Mountain	42.5	25	17.5
Pacific	26.3	11.6	14.7
United States	19.8	19.8	0

Note: Sample Size = 1,003.
Source: Adapted from Kodrzycki (2001), Table 3, based on the *National Longitudinal Survey of Youth* (NLSY).

Given the higher degree of specialization that is normally associated with high levels of education, this is perhaps not surprising. To take an example from higher education in economics, a university that seeks to hire a faculty member to teach (say) monetary economics may search over a large geographic area (possibly the entire world) in order to find a candidate with the desired skill attributes. Hiring a labour economist from a nearby university might save some moving costs, but a labour economist is not a good substitute for a monetary economist. In fact, a university that hires a monetary economist from another, distant university may at the same time find that another distant university, or perhaps even the same one, will successfully recruit a faculty member from its own history or physics department. The net migration flows among universities in a given year may thus be rather modest even while significant gross migration takes place. The explanation for the cross-hauling of labour, in this case, resides in the fact that employers are seeking workers to meet quite specialized demands, and that workers that can perform the required specialized tasks are not good substitutes for each other.

The notion that specialization is related to the size of a market is well known in economics (Smith, 1776, Book I, Chapter 3). Perhaps most commonly, economic analysis has focused on the size of goods markets (see, for example, Stigler, 1951) and its implications for industry structure, but the size of factor markets can in principle be also important. The *size* of a labour or capital market may be defined in different ways; presumably, the key characteristic of a *large* market is the presence of numerous buyers and sellers; and, as pointed out by Krugman (1991) and others, the creation of large markets may be one of the key underlying agglomerative forces leading to urbanization. However, the observed continuing migration flows of highly-skilled workers in offsetting directions indicate a possible link between the specialization of workers and labour markets that are large in a spatial sense. Indeed, it is quite possible that specialization in goods and services markets is complementary to specialization in the acquisition of skills, especially skills acquired early in life involving investments in human capital that are not readily reversible.

To illustrate this idea, consider the decision to invest in highly specialized medical training and facilities, such as those needed to carry out kidney-pancreas transplants. According to the Scientific Registry of Transplant Recipients, a total of 911 kidney-pancreas transplants were performed in the United States in 2000. These procedures took place at 91 different facilities throughout the country, only 30 of which performed 10 or more transplants. There were four facilities in California at which 10 or more transplants were performed; in no other state were there more than two such facilities.[10]

There are many risks associated with the assembly and utilization of the productive resources needed to provide such specialized medical services. Those who invest *non-human* capital in specialized medical facilities of this type clearly take some risk, since the ability to staff and use profitably such a facility over the investment planning horizon cannot be guaranteed.[11] Many of the risks confronting these investors can, however, be pooled through financial markets, within the organizational structure of a hospital or consortium of health-care providers, or by other means, thus reducing the cost associated with these risks and their deterrent to undertaking the investment in the first place.[12]

Because many institutions can help manage the risks facing those who invest non-human capital in specialized uses, the cost associated with these risks may be relatively small. By comparison, individuals contemplating investment in the *human* capital required to work at very specialized tasks face potentially much more costly risks, since their lifetime earnings streams cannot readily be insured. The ability to relocate may help to reduce some of this costly risk. For example, suppose that a pancreas-kidney transplant specialist's first job is at a transplant centre in (say) Missouri. Conceivably, this will be the best possible lifetime employment match for this specialist. However, over a working lifetime of three or four decades, it is possible that local employment conditions deteriorate (perhaps the transplant centre is mismanaged, funding is inadequate or local regulatory policies become excessively burdensome) or that new and better opportunities arise elsewhere. In the case of this specialized form of medical practice, as we have seen, "elsewhere" usually means "in a different state" (or country). For these and other specialized workers, restrictions on geographic mobility can magnify costly lifetime earnings risks.[13] Similarly, the opportunity to search for job openings in a large market over the entire life cycle affects the incentives for workers to develop their human capital over time. For instance, the prospect of searching for new jobs in a large market raises the incentive for medical (or other) specialists to hone their technical skills on an ongoing basis in occupations where these skills might otherwise depreciate quickly because of rapid technological change. It can also provide an incentive to acquire managerial and organizational skills that may be of greatest value in organizations elsewhere — either *start-up* facilities that need to assemble an entire team or existing ones looking to the outside market for 'fresh blood.'

For these and other reasons, the possibility of participating in a large, geographically-dispersed market affects the incentives to acquire, maintain, develop and utilize specialized skills. The timing and frequency with which any individual will find it advantageous to exercise the *exit* option may depend on many idiosyncratic factors, but a life-cycle pattern of employment characterized by occasional job switching and relocation would arise naturally in such an environment.[14]

The efficiency and distributional consequences of the workings of integrated labour markets are, in principle, rather complex. Fundamentally, however, integrated labour markets contribute to (i) more efficient utilization of existing stocks of specialized human capital, (ii) reduced costs associated with the risk of investing in the acquisition of specialized skills and thus (*ceteris paribus*) (iii) greater incentives to invest in such skills.[15] An *ex ante* reduction in risk corresponds to an *ex post* reduction in inequality within skill groups. The overall distributional effects of greater market integration, such as the impact on relative earnings of high- and low-skilled workers, on the returns to immobile natural resources or to capital are much more difficult to ascertain.

Many of these ideas are easily illustrated using Figure 1.[16] Suppose that the two demand curves shown represent the future demand for specialized labour of type i in region j in different states of the world. For example, consider a young person who has acquired specialized legal training in the field of intellectual property rights (labour of type i) and is initially employed in New York City (region j). In the future, the demand for this person's particular skills may be very high in New York City, but it may also be relatively low as greater demand arises in other locations, for example in Washington, D.C. (home of the Patent and Trademark Office), Silicon Valley in California, Redmond in Washington State, or the Research Triangle Park in North Carolina. If workers of this type could not move freely between New York and other locations, their specialized skills would produce high earnings (w_{ij}^+) in high-demand local labour markets, but low earnings (w_{ij}^-) in other cases — their future earnings would be risky. For their employers, income would also generally vary with the state of the world. As Figure 1 happens to be drawn, with demand curves that differ among states of the world solely by a vertical shift, the income accruing to the owners of the (other) immobile resources (for example, general partners in major New York law firms) would be state-invariant, given by the equal-sized triangles $A^+Bw_{ij}^+$ in the high-demand situation, and $A^-Cw_{ij}^-$ in the low-demand situation. In this admittedly special case, all income risk is borne by workers of type i, and no income risk is borne by the owners of other productive resources.

Now compare this with the polar opposite case where labour of type i is costlessly mobile among regions. To keep the example simple, suppose that the high- and low-demand states shown in Figure 1 are equally probable, that the wage facing type i workers in the rest of the economy is non-stochastic and is given by w_i, and that $w_i = 0.5w_{ij}^+ + 0.5w_{ij}^-$ is a simple average of the high and low wages shown in Figure 1.[17] It is easy to see that type i workers would move into region j in the high-demand state of the world, with employment increasing to l_{ij}^+; in this case, high demand produces a quantity adjustment but no price adjustment. In the low-demand state of the world, workers leave region j, with employment falling to l_{ij}^-. In both situations, workers receive the same income as that prevailing elsewhere in the economy, namely w_i. This is the same as the average or *expected* wage in the case where these workers are immobile. However, their income is now *state-invariant* whereas it varied previously with the state of the world. The owners of the immobile resources now receive income equal to A^+Fw_i in the high-demand state of the world and A^-Dw_i in the low-demand state. Note that the expected income of the immobile factor owners is now higher, by an amount corresponding to $DEC+BEF$, but their income, previously state-invariant, is now risky. In short, in this example, labour mobility completely shifts the distribution of income risk from workers to owners of immobile resources, it leaves unchanged the average income of workers and it raises the expected or average income of immobile resource owners.

Note that the high- and low-demand situations portrayed in Figure 1 can also illustrate a situation where there are differing demand conditions in two different regions. In one region, local industries using type i workers are flourishing, while in the other region such workers are in low demand. The movement of these workers from one region to the other gives rise to the efficiency gain represented by the two triangles DEC and BEF. While one region attracts workers of one type, it may be in the *opposite* situation with respect to workers of other types — as one or more local industries may be increasing their employment of workers with one type of skills (say, a particular type of legal services), others may be shedding workers with a different type of skills (say, a particular type of medical training). Such a region would exhibit a level of *gross* migration in excess of *net* migration; in fact, this region and others might experience no net migration whatsoever as workers of different types move from regions where their skills are in low demand to regions where the enjoy better employment opportunities. Note, however, that such *gross* migration is still efficiency-enhancing, even if it does not result in any net migration. For this reason, an analysis that treats all labour as homogeneous will underestimate the efficiency gains arising from labour mobility. Low levels of net migration would be estimated to yield little if any productivity gains, whereas the productivity gains from mobility could be very important if internal migration results in large but offsetting gross migration. This latter case seems to typify the Canadian and U.S. labour markets.

This simple analysis shows that (a) there are efficiency gains from the free mobility of labour (aggregate expected or average income going up), (b) free mobility tends to equalize real incomes within a given skill or occupational category across regions, (c) the distribution of these efficiency gains may accrue to resources other than mobile workers and (d) free mobility of labour can alter the *distribution of income risk* among different factors of production. In the example illustrated by Figure 1, free mobility of labour reduces (in fact, eliminates) the variability of earnings for type i workers without affecting expected earnings. It follows that acquisition of the specialized skills needed to become that type of worker is a more attractive investment for risk-averse individuals, assuming — as is reasonable — that they are not able to insure their future earnings. In other words, the mobility of specialized labour influences not only the efficiency of utilization of a labour force with *given* skills, but the incentives to invest in the acquisition of specialized human capital in the first place. Persistently high levels of internal migration by highly-educated workers within the Canadian and U.S. labour markets, with gross flows among regions going in opposite directions, suggest that local industries in these economies are subject to continuously changing conditions that result in shifting demands for workers of different occupational or skill categories. Highly-integrated markets providing relocation options over the life cycle affect both the expected life-cycle return on investment in specialized human capital and its riskiness, and thus the demand for higher education and other opportunities for skill acquisition.

HIGHER EDUCATION IN CANADA AND THE UNITED STATES

R IDDELL (2001) PROVIDES A USEFUL SURVEY of the educational systems of Canada, the United States and other Organisation for Economic Co-operation and Development (OECD) countries.[18] As one might have antici-pated, both Canada and the United States stand out as countries with high levels of education, at least measured by readily-quantifiable and comparable indicators. Of particular interest for the present discussion, expenditures on post-secondary education amount to about 2.5 percent of GDP in both countries (1995 data), as compared with the OECD average of 1.3 percent. Of people aged 25-64, 19 percent of Canadians and 27 percent of U.S. residents have com-pleted a university education, as compared with only 14 percent for OECD countries as a whole; Canada actually leads OECD countries with over 25 percent of its population having completed some form of postsecondary (in-cluding non-university) education.

In both Canada and the United States, subnational governments, princi-pally at the provincial and state levels, are heavily involved in the *provision* of higher education through public higher-education institutions. In both countries, the public sector is also involved in the *financing* of higher education, partly through direct and indirect subsidization of public institutions of higher learning, but also through direct and indirect subsidies to students (or their families).

Taking the United States first, note from Figures 2, 3 and 4 that the four most important sources of financing for degree-granting postsecondary institu-tions over the past two decades have been state governments, tuition and fees paid by students, sales and services, and revenues from the federal government (see National Center for Education Statistics, 2002, and Barbett and Korb, 1999, for further discussion). As shown in Figure 2, the first two account for about half of all revenues, with funding from state governments declining from 30.7 percent of the total in 1980 to 23.1 percent in 1995 as tuition and fees rose from 21.0 to 27.9 percent. (Both of these trends were monotonic.) Sales and services consistently accounted for approximately 20 percent of all revenues over this period; about half of this total represents revenue from university hospitals. The federal government provided 14.9 percent of university revenues at the be-ginning of this period, a share that had declined slightly to 12.1 percent by the end of the period. Figures 3 and 4 provide similar data for public and private institutions, respectively. The most noteworthy difference between the two is the role of state government funding, which declined from about 45 percent to about 35 percent of all revenues for public institutions during the period 1980-96, while constituting a tiny share of the financing of private institutions.

FIGURE 2

REVENUE OF U.S. DEGREE-GRANTING INSTITUTIONS, BY SOURCE, 1980-96

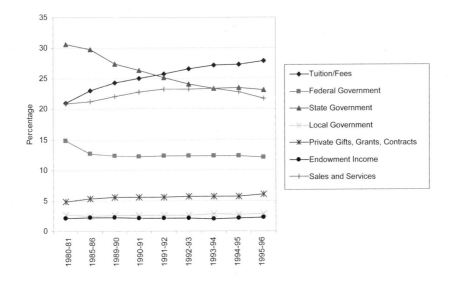

FIGURE 3

REVENUE OF U.S. PUBLIC DEGREE-GRANTING INSTITUTIONS, BY SOURCE, 1980-97

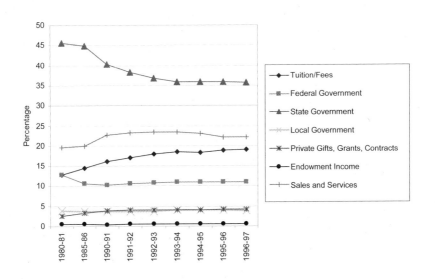

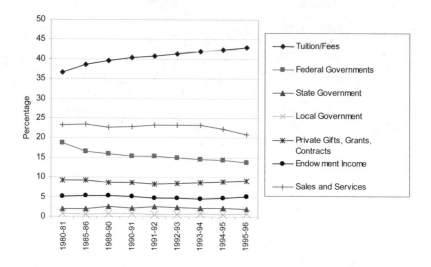

For public institutions, the (monotonically) falling share of state government funding was offset by the rising share of tuition and fees, which grew (monotonically) from 12.9 percent of revenues in 1980 to 19.0 percent in 1996. For private institutions, tuition and fees also rose over this period, from 36.6 to 43.0 percent; for these institutions, revenues from the federal government fell by about 5 percentage points while revenues from sales and services fell by about 2 percentage points.[19] The most important trend revealed by these figures is that direct public sector payments to colleges and universities, particularly outlays by state governments, are dwindling in relative importance. In 1980, the federal, state, and local governments together accounted for about 48 percent of the revenues of all higher-education institutions, but by 1995 this share had fallen to 38 percent. In this respect, public sector involvement in the *provision* of higher education has fallen substantially.

The fact that tuition and fees are rising in importance relative to direct support for higher-education institutions does not imply that public sector *financing* for higher education in general is declining. For instance, the federal and state governments provide grants and loans to students to defray the cost of higher education; these outlays account for a portion of tuition and fees. In addition, there are special provisions in the tax law, particularly at the federal level, that allow for tax-sheltered savings for higher education. The not-for-profit status of colleges and universities allows them to avoid direct taxation, and they generally qualify as institutions that can receive tax-deductible contributions from individuals or businesses. Government subsidization of health care for the poor, elderly, or other groups helps medical schools and hospitals managed by higher-education institutions. Finally, and presumably not least, the taxation of earnings provides some special advantages for investment in human capital. Once education is completed, the government captures a portion of the return to education through taxes on earnings and consumption, thus reducing the net return to investment in education. However, taxes also reduce the cost of investment in human capital, most notably because the cost of foregone earnings is expensed rather than depreciated, unlike the cost of investment in non-human capital. If earnings (or consumption) were taxed at a uniform rate at all points in the life cycle and if there were no other tax distortions in the economy, tax policy would be *neutral* in its impact on incentives to invest in human capital, and thus would be more favourable than the tax treatment of investment in non-human capital (at least investments in non-human capital that are not tax-sheltered or tax-favoured in some other way).[20] To this author's knowledge, no adequate measurements exist of the full extent of these subsidies to higher education, some of which are highly implicit. It appears, however, that the public sector's contribution to higher education has been shifting away from direct support to public *institutions*, toward support for *individuals* acquiring higher education, with federal support (especially through the tax system) growing in importance relative to support from state governments.

In very general terms, public sector involvement in Canada exhibits many of the same features as in the United States. In 1999-2000, total university expenditures in Canada amounted to about $14.1 billion. As shown in Table 8, the combined contributions of the federal, provincial and local governments accounted for more than half of all university revenues during the mid- to late-1990s, with provincial governments taking the lead role. A direct comparison with U.S. data is quite problematic because of possible differences in accounting conventions and in the population of institutions included in the data; for example, Sales of services and products amount to less than 10 percent of university revenues in Canada, but this may reflect (as one of several possibilities) differences in the accounting of revenues accruing to university-related health-care providers. For present purposes, it is of much greater interest to note that direct provincial government support to universities declined markedly in relative importance during the period 1994-99 — from 53.3 to 45.3 percent of revenues — bringing the total government share from 62.8 to 55.0 percent in a brief period of time. Student fees rose from 16.0 percent to 19.3 percent of revenues during the same period, a large increase in proportionate terms, though still well below the corresponding (if not fully comparable) figures for the United States.

TABLE 8

REVENUE OF CANADIAN UNIVERSITIES, 1994-2000

	1994-95	1998-99	1999-2000
Total revenue	100.0	100.0	100.0
Government grants and contracts			
Federal	9.1	8.3	8.9
Provincial	53.3	46.2	45.3
Municipal and other	0.4	0.7	0.7
Total	62.8	55.2	55.0
Student fees	16.0	20.3	19.3
Bequests, donations, non-government grants/contracts	8.0	9.7	9.5
Sales of services and products	8.6	8.4	9.1
Investment revenue	2.6	3.5	3.7
Miscellaneous	2.0	2.9	3.6

As in the United States, Canada's public sector contributes directly and indirectly to the financing of higher education in many ways other than through direct support to higher-education institutions. Publicly-financed loans and scholarships are available for students, tenable at private and public institutions; these may be located in Canada, but also may be foreign institutions.[21] Federal and provincial tax systems alter the incentives to invest in human capital in ways similar to those described above for the United States.

The key conclusions to draw from this brief review of education finances in Canada and the United States are the following. First, in both countries, subnational governments have played a very important role in direct support to institutions of higher education. However, this role is declining over time relative to other sources of financing. The change in the structure of financing partly reflects a change in the nature of the aid recipient — to a growing extent, the student or the student's family rather than the higher-education institution — and partly a change in the level of government providing the explicit and implicit assistance — a shift toward increased reliance on higher-level relative to lower-level governments.

LABOUR MARKET INTEGRATION AND FISCAL COMPETITION IN NORTH AMERICA

THE ECONOMIES OF CANADA AND THE UNITED STATES are highly internally integrated; both have been characterized by very liberal internal trade conditions for a long period of time. As the discussion in the third section makes clear, labour markets in Canada and the United States are also highly internally integrated, characterized, as they are, by persistent migration flows over large regions (provinces, states, census regions). Both countries have highly-educated labour forces by world standards, and the level of educational attainment has risen steadily over the course of the past century. Internal migration options seem to be particularly important for highly-educated individuals. Capital markets are also highly integrated in these countries.

The economies of Canada and the United States are also, to some degree, integrated with each other and with the rest of the world. There has long been a high volume of trade between the two economies, and recent policy initiatives — notably, NAFTA — have strengthened the opportunities to continue and expand trade. Mobility of capital and labour between Canada and the United States is also relatively high, and it is partly a matter of policy choice whether to increase or decrease the integration of labour and capital markets. Although flows of labour go in both directions across the Canada-U.S. border, Canada has experienced negative net migration *vis-à-vis* the United States, a fact that has led some, in Canadian policy debates, to express concern about a North-South *brain drain*. Borjas' (1993) analysis indicates that, during the 1970s and 1980s, Canada attracted migrants from the United States who tended to earn less than native Canadians, whereas Canadians migrating to the United States tended to enjoy higher earnings than U.S. natives. However, it is of interest to note that Borjas finds that migrants going in either direction tended to have higher levels of education than destination-country natives — another indication, perhaps, of the heterogeneity of high-skilled workers. Several analysts have observed that the level of North-South migration is now lower than in the past; Helliwell (1999), for instance, notes that the number of Canadians residing in the United States has steadily declined over time. Finnie (2001) notes that the movement of highly-skilled workers from Canada to the United States has been relatively modest, in some respects, and has also been concentrated in particular occupational groups (physicians, for example), suggesting that policy responses to such mobility, if any, might best be targeted at specific sectors of the economy. Coulson and DeVoretz (1993) find that immigrants to Canada have brought considerable amounts of human capital into the country, though restrictions on immigration reduced human capital inflows substantially between about 1970 and the late 1980s. Of course, the original brain drain literature (see, for example, Bhagwati and Partington, 1976) was concerned precisely with the fact that developed countries like Canada and the United States were net recipients of human capital from less-developed countries. Both Canada and the United States continue to be net immigration countries and attract both well- and poorly-educated migrants from the rest of the world.

Helliwell (1997, 1998) has argued convincingly that "borders matter" both for trade and for migration. The volume of interprovincial trade in Canada is very high relative to trade across the Canada-U.S. border. Furthermore, internal migration in each country is much larger than migration between the two. There are many reasons why this may be the case; attachment to home, language, custom, and familiarity with social norms may all contribute to greater degrees of economic integration within countries than among them. One could conclude that competition for highly-skilled human resources should not be a policy priority in Canada or, for that matter, in the United States. No doubt, fiscal, educational or other policy reforms cannot be driven solely by competition for human resources without full consideration of other policy dimensions. Still, competition for human and other productive resources does exist and it is worth considering its implications. The following remarks attempt to pull together some ideas from the discussion presented in previous sections, focusing on the analysis of tax and expenditure policies, including higher-education financing, in an integrated market environment.

EFFICIENCY AND DISTRIBUTIONAL EFFECTS OF INTEGRATION

THE POTENTIAL BENEFITS FROM TRADE IN GOODS AND SERVICES, both within and among countries, have been thoroughly discussed and do not require additional comment here. Aside from general gains from trade, benefits from greater product variety, economies of scale or greater competition, trade is also thought to affect factor prices and the distribution of income, as already mentioned. Trade is also perceived as contributing to widening inequality in the distribution of wages,[22] as well as increasing the riskiness of income: openness, it is argued, may expose an economy to more shocks from fluctuations in external markets. The effects of trade on the distribution and riskiness of income are important for fiscal policy because large fractions of government expenditures and major elements of the tax systems in both Canada and the United States, as in all other high-income countries, serve to alter the distribution of income and income risk. If trade contributes to greater earnings dispersion, then stronger redistributive interventions by the public sector would be needed to prevent increased inequality in the distribution of net income (see, for example, Rodrik, 1998, and Agell, 1999, 2000).

As observed above, factor mobility can contribute to more efficient utilization of existing resource stocks. Persistent internal migration in Canada and the United States has presumably generated significant efficiency gains in both economies. International mobility of labour and capital can likewise contribute to higher productivity. Like trade, factor mobility also affects returns to factors. In a classical two-factor production function $F(K, L)$ with output depending solely on capital and labour, factor prices are governed by the capital/labour ratio.

In a more general setting with many factors of production, factor prices, as shown in equation (1), depend in less predictable ways on factor proportions because of potentially complex substitution/complementarity relationships. As noted in the third section, the fact that gross labour flows far exceed net labour flows in Canada and the United States provides evidence that different types of labour are not highly substitutable for one another. In fact, the high degree of mobility of highly-educated individuals indicates both that high- and low-skilled labour are imperfect substitutes and that different types of high-skilled labour are also imperfect substitutes. For this reason, it is difficult to predict the distributional impact of factor flows. However, it may be reasonable to suppose as a first approximation that high-skilled labour, capital, low-skilled labour, and natural resources are generally complementary inputs. For any given type of labour, mobility reduces disparities in earnings (or, more precisely, in real income) among regions. This is true within countries and among countries. If integration of labour markets leads to higher levels of investment in human capital, it can be expected to lead to higher returns for complementary inputs, including low-skilled labour.

Increased labour mobility between Canada and the United States, and between North America and the rest of the world, can be mutually beneficial, in terms of allocative efficiency, for the same reason that internal migration in both countries contributes to more efficient resource utilization. Observed migration behaviour suggests that the efficiency gains from mobility are particularly important for highly-educated workers. The full general-equilibrium effects of greater factor-market integration for highly-skilled workers are complex, but, leaving aside for one moment the issue of education finance, greater opportunities to participate in *large* labour markets would generally be expected to enhance the lifetime earnings prospects of young people who invest in specialized skills by reducing their lifetime earnings risk. For both Canadian and U.S. university students, the option to search for employment in locations beyond state, provincial, or national boundaries is valuable and contributes to the incentive to acquire higher education.

FISCAL COMPETITION: EDUCATION FINANCE AND TAX POLICY

THE FISCAL SYSTEMS OF CANADA AND THE UNITED STATES are extremely complex and this should be borne in mind when attempting to assess the fiscal implications of household mobility. In short, these complexities arise (a) because households interact with fiscal systems over their entire life cycles, (b) they interact both with the expenditure and the revenue elements of fiscal systems, and (c) they interact simultaneously with the fiscal systems of national, state/provincial and local governments. For example, many types of public expenditures — on health, education, pensions — are directed either

toward children or toward elderly people. The bulk of tax and non-tax revenues are collected mainly from people in the middle part of their life cycle. The
distribution of the burdens of taxation and of the benefits of public services
varies not only with age but with income, household size and composition, as
well as many other attributes. This is true both for national and subnational
governments. The lifetime distribution of benefits and burdens of government
on different types of people is only imperfectly understood.[23]

Migration changes the demographic composition of a region, and adds yet
another dimension to the relationship between the individual and the public
sector over the life cycle. A young person may benefit from education provided
by local schools and by state or provincial governments, and then relocate either to another state or province or even to another country. This creates a
potentially serious problem for the financing of higher education, in particular.
A jurisdiction that attempts to use high levels of taxation to finance high levels
of education may find that the beneficiaries of spending on education then migrate to other jurisdictions, reducing the tax base with which education is to be
financed. Indeed, standard models of fiscal competition typically lead to the
conclusion that a small, open jurisdiction would optimally impose a zero *net
fiscal burden* on a freely-mobile resource.

The logic underlying this conclusion is easily illustrated with Figure 1.
Suppose that labour of type i earns an exogenously-fixed net return of w_i on the
external market, and that the demand for type i labour in region j is given by,
say, D_{ij}^+. In the absence of any taxes or subsidies, the equilibrium level of employment in this region would be l_{ij}^+ assuming that labour is freely mobile. If this
region imposes a tax of BE on each unit of labour, then the equilibrium employment level would be only l_{ij}, as the gross wage for this type of labour rises to
w_{ij}^+. Assuming that immobile resources in the region are owned by local residents, the loss in income to immobile resources, $w_{ij}^+ BFw_i$, is greater than the
tax revenue collected, $w_{ij}^+ BEw_i$, and the real income accruing to people in the
region would fall by BEF.[24]

Fundamentally, this result — which, of course, must be qualified when the
underlying assumptions are altered — can be viewed simply as a variant of the
standard optimal tariff argument. The same principles explain why it is also
optimal for a small jurisdiction not to subsidize mobile resources. Note that
these results obtain whether mobile resources flow into or out of a jurisdiction,
and whether the magnitude of observed flows is small or large, just as the standard optimal tariff argument applies equally to export taxes and does not depend on the volume of trade.

Although these observations are, from an analytical standpoint, immediately obvious, they depart quite significantly from many common policy prescriptions. For instance, in the context of the *brain drain* debate, the departure of highly-trained individuals from a jurisdiction is often viewed as self-evidently a bad outcome. One might then suppose that subsidies to retain highly-skilled individuals would be an appropriate policy response. In fact, a net subsidy to highly-skilled workers is not an optimal policy, unless one can show that there are positive externalities associated with the presence of such individuals. Note that this conclusion applies independently of the size of the local endowment of labour of type *i* and, thus, independently of whether labour flows into or out of the region — in large or in small amounts. That is, the policy conclusion follows independently of the observed level of in- or out-migration. The key question for determining the optimal policy is whether the jurisdiction is small or large relative to external markets, and whether it is open (or could be made open) to these markets. With reference to internal migration in Canada and the United States, or to migration between the two countries, the crucial issue is not whether there is positive or negative net migration into or out of any one province, state or country, but whether labour markets among regions are integrated or isolated. The high levels of gross internal migration in Canada and the United States testify to the fact that labour markets within these countries are significantly linked. Migration between Canada and the United States shows that there are linkages between the Canadian and U.S. labour markets, though the degree of integration is, at least in part, a matter of policy choice and could be enhanced or diminished by either or both countries, if desired.

The competition for mobile resources is often asserted to lead to a *race to the bottom*, which is usually interpreted to mean, for instance, that competition leads to reductions in taxes. In fact, this is not an accurate interpretation of the analysis. Many public services, especially those that relate to human resources (such as education, health and others) exhibit what is known as *congestibility*, which is to say that the cost of their provision depends partly on the size of the population being served. For example, the total cost of providing education to 1,000 students is far less than the cost of providing education to 20,000 students — that is, the incremental or marginal cost of educating one more student is not zero. Indeed, it is commonplace to measure education costs in terms of cost per student — a crude but useful first approximation that implicitly assumes that marginal cost and average cost are equal. What does the theory of fiscal competition suggest should happen to fiscal systems when public services exhibit congestibility? It does not imply that taxes are driven toward zero any more than perfect competition among firms implies that prices are driven toward zero. Rather, *net fiscal burdens*, the value of taxes paid by mobile resources net of the cost of providing them with public services, are driven toward zero. In particular, if the marginal cost of providing public services to those who use these services is high, then competition among jurisdictions should lead to high public sector charges for those users. In the case of higher education, if students or their parents are relatively highly mobile, fiscal competition is expected to lead to greater reliance on student fees and charges or on other revenue instruments that similarly link revenues with costs. Fiscal competition would be expected to limit the extent of *redistributive* financing for higher education — that is, the financing of higher education in ways that allow some to utilize scarce educational resources that are paid for by others. The most obvious way in which this can occur is through increased reliance on tuition and fees assessed by higher-education institutions on enrolled students.

Does this mean that higher education cannot or should not be financed with standard revenue instruments, such as income or consumption taxes, when skilled workers are mobile? Such a conclusion would be unwarranted, at least in an unqualified form, for at least three reasons.

First, if taxes are not used to finance higher education, what is the alternative? If students have or can obtain sufficient financial resources to pay the full cost of their own education, then indeed the case for tax financing of higher education is substantially weakened. It might still be argued that higher education provides spillover benefits to the rest of society and that it therefore warrants public sector support. But, as estimates of the education premium confirm, a very substantial part of the benefit of investment in higher education accrues to students in the form of higher earnings. If they are the principal beneficiaries of their own education, and if they enjoy relatively high lifetime incomes, there is little normative justification for the subsidization of higher education. This supposes, however, that students can, if necessary, borrow the money required to finance their education. If they are credit-constrained, the level of investment in higher education would be inefficiently low. The high level of public sector expenditure in support of higher education that has developed in Canada and the United States over the past century was undoubtedly predicated, at least in part, on the assumption that private capital markets would not provide sufficient resources for education. In the presence of such a capital market failure, reliance on public sector revenue sources, even ones that give rise to allocative distortions, may be part of an optimal policy. In effect, the government's revenue system offsets the misallocation that would otherwise result from a 'missing' market; the young who benefit from the provision of publicly-supported education in effect repay an implicit loan from the government through taxes later in life.[25]

Second, even if young and well-educated people are highly mobile, the same is not necessarily true of older people, including the parents of children who are using publicly-supported higher-education systems. Although students certainly benefit from being educated, so do their parents if they are altruistic toward their children. One can visualize a traditional Canadian or U.S. public university as an institution from which parents, through their payment of income and other taxes, purchase higher education for their children. Parents may be relatively immobile and thus relatively unresponsive, along the migration margin, to local taxes. Furthermore, if access to publicly-supported higher education is contingent on residence in a state or province (meaning, traditionally, the residence of a student's parents), then the net fiscal burden imposed on parents by publicly-supported higher education may be rather modest: the burden of taxes is offset by the benefit of education for one's children. In Figure 1, a tax of BE is properly interpreted not just as a tax in the strict sense, but as a net fiscal burden (i.e. as the burden of location-contingent taxes net of location-contingent benefits of public services to the individual). To the extent that the benefits of higher education (or other public services) offset the taxes paid by residents, the size of the 'wedge' in the diagram is reduced.

Third, as noted above, the degree of mobility of labour within Canada and the United States is greater than the degree of international mobility. Perhaps the competition for highly-skilled individuals by states or provinces means that these units of government will (or, from the perspective of their local constituencies, should) alter their revenue systems in ways that reduce the net fiscal burdens falling on those with high earnings. If these individuals are not particularly mobile internationally, then they can be taxed more heavily by national governments. The revenues accruing to the national government could then be used, if desired, to support higher education. This support could be directed at public higher-education institutions in the form of direct grants, or through grants to state and provincial governments on condition that these resources are used to support public universities. It could also be directed at students through national student loan or scholarship programs, or to their families, through tax-preferred savings vehicles, with students then able to use these public sector resources to defray the cost of their higher education at whatever institutions, public or private, they might choose to attend. Indeed, financial support of this latter type is found both in the United States and Canada. In other words, interprovincial or interstate fiscal competition could lead to an upward reassignment of public sector responsibility for higher-education financing — that is, to a restructuring of public sector financing roles among levels of government in a country.

While we should not exaggerate the importance of the competition for human resources for the structuring of education finance and for revenue systems, gradual changes in the degree of economic integration in North America as well as with the rest of the world may create pressures for policy change. By comparison with the period immediately following World War II, which saw a large expansion of the public sector role in higher education, the opportunities for purely private financing of higher education have certainly increased. Economic growth has led to growing wealth that leave many families much better equipped to pay for the higher education of their children. Financial institutions offer much better opportunities for many students to borrow the resources necessary to finance their education, especially with support from national (and sometimes subnational) governments in the form of loan guarantees or other incentives; in addition, as noted above, a variety of tax preferences and savings incentives help families to accumulate resources with which to finance their children's higher education. These developments presumably reduce the importance of keeping tuition and other fees at low levels.

Of course, the observed trends in higher-education finance also reflect underlying demand and supply conditions. The private return to human capital investment — often measured by the 'education premium,' that is, the higher earnings enjoyed by better-educated workers — affects the incentive for young people to pursue higher education and thus the market environment within which higher-education institutions operate. Freeman and Needels (1993) find that the education premium has risen markedly in United States and, to a lesser extent, Canada, during the 1980s. The ratio of college- to high-school-educated individuals fell somewhat in United States, a "lagged response to the decline in enrolments induced by the falling return to college of the 1970s," while rising in Canada. According to Riddell and Sweetman (1999, p. 28), referring to the Canadian experience over the past decade, "[d]espite the substantial growth in the number of well-educated workers, and the decline in the supply of those with low levels of education, the relative earnings of university and college graduates did not fall relative to the less well-educated groups. [...] We interpret this evidence to suggest that the demand for more educated workers has increased substantially over this period, sufficiently to absorb the large increase in their supply...".[26] In such an environment, it is perhaps not surprising to see increases in tuition and fees for higher education. This is true independently of any pressures arising from fiscal competition among provinces or states.

Changes in the demand for and supply of highly-skilled workers in Canada and the United States also affect earnings differentials between the two countries, and with respect to the rest of the world. *Ceteris paribus*, rising inequality in the United States relative to Canada would strengthen the incentives for highly-skilled Canadians to move to that country. What can we say about the international competition for human resources?

The *brain drain* debate often tends to view international migration as a zero-sum phenomenon and, without doubt, net migration flows are potentially important. However, as has been emphasized above, migration can be productivity-enhancing. The fact that higher education offers opportunities for employment on an international scale certainly increases the demand for higher education, even in countries that are net importers of highly-skilled workers. It is also worth noting that gross international migration flows are larger than net flows, though to a degree that is not easily measured. In general, resource flows across international boundaries suggest gains from trade. Furthermore, the possibility of return migration should not be underestimated. A series of recent studies on Irish migration by Barrett (2002), Barrett, Fitzgerald and Nolan (2000), and Barrett and O'Connell (2001) show that Ireland, a country that has traditionally lost many workers to emigration, including well-educated individuals, has recently experienced substantial return migration, especially of high-skilled workers. These workers have enjoyed substantial gains in earnings relative to those who have stayed in Ireland, suggesting that migration has been productivity-enhancing for people who moved.[27] Furthermore, their return to Ireland appears to have reduced the earnings premium enjoyed by high-skilled workers in that country. In the Irish case, at least, return migration has meant that the level of permanent international migration has turned out to be smaller than the level of temporary migration. Similar migration patterns across the Canada-U.S. border, as indeed is observed across state and provincial boundaries within Canada and the United States, can easily be imagined. Policy changes that liberalize migration across international borders presumably give rise to gains from trade even as they may increase the competitive pressures on national and subnational fiscal systems.

Although it is an issue with ramifications going well beyond the brain drain debate, the tax treatment of highly-skilled individuals is often discussed in this context. More definitive analysis must await further investigation, but there is no doubt that the tax treatment of high-income individuals provides potentially fertile ground for intergovernmental competition because these individuals have such a large impact on government revenues. By way of illustration, in 1999, the top 1.9 percent of taxpayers received 24.4 percent of total income,[28] while the top 0.16 percent of taxpayers received 11.2 percent of income. These figures testify to the degree of income concentration in the United States. The distribution of taxes is even more concentrated: the top 1.9 percent of taxpayers paid 43.4 percent of all personal income taxes (the main revenue source for the federal government, along with the social security payroll tax), while the top 0.16 percent of taxpayers paid 20.8 percent of these taxes. These very rich taxpayers paid an average income tax of almost $900,000. The jurisdiction that succeeds in attracting such taxpayers is sure to enjoy a huge fiscal benefit. As a simple back-of-the-envelope calculation, if half of the top 0.16 percent of taxpayers in the United States in 1999 (about 100,000 taxpayers) had located in, say, Monaco, the United States would have lost about 10 percent of all personal income tax revenues — about $90 billion, much more than the entire proceeds of the estate tax and equal to about half of all corporation income tax revenues. These figures are very rough but demonstrate clearly that the locational choices of high-income individuals are a matter of importance, in terms of fiscal policy, far out of proportion to their number, and it is thus not unreasonable to argue that governments at all levels (national and subnational) either will or should adapt their fiscal systems (or other policies) in order to attract high-income individuals.[29]

These competitive pressures exist both at the international and subnational levels. Insofar as households are more mobile within countries, fiscal competition may be more intense among subnational governments. One might accordingly expect to see *upward reassignment* of redistributive policies, with national governments playing an increased role in providing financial support to students of modest means in search of higher education, accompanied by reductions in the amount of financial aid offered by subnational governments.[30] The trends in higher-education financing described in the fourth section might be offered, tentatively, as evidence of this type of policy change.

SCOPE FOR ADDITIONAL RESEARCH

THE FOREGOING DISCUSSION HAS TOUCHED on a large number of interrelated issues, including trade in goods and services within and among countries and its implications for factor markets and incomes; internal migration in Canada and the United States and its implications for efficient resource allocation, the distribution of income and income risk; the incentives to invest in higher education and the financing of higher education by national and subnational governments as well as by private individuals; the possible effects of fiscal competition on the financing of higher education and on the allocation of human resources among regions, both within and among countries. Many theoretical and empirical studies have contributed to a better understanding of these issues, but very substantial gaps remain.

The preceding discussion has identified several of these gaps. Further analysis of the allocative and distributional effects of migration with heterogeneous workers would improve our understanding of the role of integrated labour markets. A fully satisfactory analysis cannot limit attention solely to the effects of migration on labour markets, but should also consider the impact of labour market integration on the allocation of and return to other factors of production, notably capital and natural resources. The implications of labour mobility for human capital investment are far from well understood. The interaction of labour markets and fiscal systems, including both tax systems and systems of higher-education financing, should be investigated more fully in light of a more complete understanding of the role of internal and international labour mobility. Progress in these areas would contribute substantially to a better foundation for the analysis of the very complex policy issues that both Canada and the United States must address as economic integration proceeds.

ENDNOTES

1   Trefler (1993) emphasizes the importance of international differences in productivity and their relevance for explaining trade patterns and testing for factor price equalization — a matter of considerable importance, since it is known that factor-price equalization can fail when production technologies differ. The discussion below is agnostic about differences in technologies among regions, but it should be noted that productivity-adjusted factor price equalization among regions is fully consistent with the possibility that workers (or other factors) could increase their incomes by moving from low- to high-productivity regions.

2   Each of these input variables may be interpreted, if desired, as a vector, thus allowing for any number of productive inputs.

3   See, for example, Bauer and Zimmermann (1999) for a recent overview of theoretical and empirical analyses of migration.

4   The "net rates of return" to which factor owners respond should be interpreted carefully: in cases where factor movements are not costlessly reversible, the rates of return in question should be understood as expected utilities over the relevant (possibly endogenously-determined) decision horizon, appropriately adjusted for taxes, benefits from public goods and services, environmental, cultural, and other amenities, regulatory treatment, etc. Only in the simplest cases does this reduce to equalization of instantaneous pecuniary factor returns.

5   This is a characterization of the standard theory in its pure form. Of course, many authors have modified the standard model in order to capture spatial factors. The specific-factors model can be interpreted in the context of geographically-fixed inputs; other studies distinguish regions within countries and analyze the implications of transportation costs and trade barriers for these regions; a notable example, relevant for the Canadian case, is Melvin, 1985. More recently, Helliwell (1998) discusses internal and external trade at length and provides many more references to the relevant literature.

6   The amounts of other *variable* inputs depend on their prices, and thus the demand for type i labour depends on other input prices as well as on the quantities of other fixed inputs. Assuming that the region is small in all relevant markets, prices of other inputs are parametrically given and thus can be subsumed within the other data on the problem.

7   Topel (1986) shows that migration behaviour is largely explained by the prospect of higher earnings. Topel (1991) shows that job mobility (i.e. job changes) accounts for a significant part of earnings growth over the life cycle. Job mobility is not identical to migration, but is certainly correlated with it. An analysis that links migration to earnings growth over the life cycle would provide considerable insight into the productivity gains generated by migration, and could provide the basis for an estimate of how much productivity and income the Canadian or U.S. economies would lose if internal migration were curtailed.

8   For further discussion and analysis of interprovincial migration by both native and immigrant Canadians, see Edmonston, 2002. The author finds that immigrants to Canada have higher rates of interprovincial migration than native Canadians, but that their migration patterns are otherwise broadly similar to that of natives.

9   Alternatively, the Canadian and U.S. economies are characterized by a large and persistent volume of costly and wasteful migration. Wildasin and Wilson (1996) develop a model in which local governments, acting in the interests of owners of immobile local resources (e.g. property owners), pursue policies that generate such migration in equilibrium. As noted in that analysis, profit-maximizing firms might well pursue wage policies that produce inefficient labour turnover in order to exercise dynamic monopsony power. This argument does not, however, provide a convincing explanation for *long-distance* relocation of workers.

10   The most performed at any one location was 47; those performing 10 or more accounted for 553, or approximately 60 percent, of all such procedures. Kidney transplants are considerably more common than combined kidney-pancreas transplants, which in turn are more common than transplantation of the pancreas alone. In these other cases, as well, a large proportion of procedures are carried out at comparatively few locations.

11   Even not-for-profit institutions face at least a long-run survival or break-even constraint.

12   One of the risks facing those who invest in specialized medical facilities — that of not being able to staff the facility adequately — is mitigated, to some degree, by the option to engage in a nationwide or even international search for new or replacement personnel.

13   A specialized worker with few outside employment options may confront monopsony exploitation, which, properly speaking, is not a risk but a type of hold-up problem (cf. Wildasin and Wilson, 1996). Intersectoral competition for young workers would still require the monopsonist to offer a lifetime earnings stream that is as attractive as any alternative. But the same basic obstacles to the insurance of lifetime earnings — costly verification, moral hazard as well as prohibitions on indenture — mean, in practice, that an irreversible investment in specialized skills faces a riskier return over the life cycle when the range of future employment opportunities is narrow.

14   Riddell and Sweetman (1999), analyzing a sample of Canadian workers, find that there is a substantial earnings premium for workers who assert that their job is closely related to their field of study. This suggests that workers whose specialized skills are well-matched with their employment are more productive, and that there is a substantial loss of productivity associated with working in jobs that do not require specific skills.

15   These ideas have been developed more formally in Wildasin, 2000.

16   The following discussion draws on Wildasin, 1995.

17   None of these specific assumptions is essential; the key point is that demand for labour of a particular type is not *perfectly* correlated across all regions. If it were, there would be no incentive for labour to move among regions; since we are now exploring the implications of observed internal migration, situations where such migration would not occur are not of interest.

18   See also Riddell and Sweetman, 1999.

19   No short statement about the financing of higher education can do justice to its many complexities. As just one example: while tuition and fees were increasing on the revenue side, so were university expenditures on financial aid to students —

though the latter less than fully offsets the former. Furthermore, while the rise in endowment income and unrestricted gifts clearly increases the resources at the disposal of universities, it is not at all clear that the same can be said for grants, contracts and restricted gifts. For example, a hypothetical $10 million grant from the government to build a $12 million cyclotron would require a $2 million contribution from other university resources and might thus conceivably be viewed as a net loss. How to draw the boundaries between revenues and expenditures and how to determine the net income from grants, contracts, hospital services, athletics, etc. are very difficult problems both at a conceptual and at a practical level.

20   It should be noted, however, that to the extent that earnings are taxed at progressive rates over the life cycle, this tax preference for investment in human capital is offset or possibly more than offset. On the other hand, sales taxes and especially the payroll tax are important components of the overall tax structure which do not have progressive rate structures.

21   For example, the Ontario Student Assistance Program (OSAP) provides assistance to students attending approved non-Canadian colleges and universities, such as the University of Kentucky.

22   The extent to which this is actually the case has been a matter of intense study; Zhu and Trefler (2001) characterize the current state of professional opinion on this topic as a "20-percent solution," according to which only about 20 percent of the recent increase in earnings inequality can be explained by trade.

23   Research on *generational accounting* (see, for example, Kotlikoff, 1993; and Auerbach, Kotlikoff and Leibfritz, 1999) highlights the importance of the life-cycle impact of both tax and expenditure policies. In general, trying to measure the distribution of benefits from public services over the life cycle presents a larger measurement challenge than for taxes and cash benefits such as public pensions.

24   See, for example, Cremer, Fourgeaud, Leite-Monteiro, Marchand and Pestieau (1996) and Wildasin (1998) for discussions and further references.

25   In practice, earnings are not taxed at a uniform rate over the life cycle, partly due to the progressivity of rate structures and partly because of ongoing tax reforms. Progressivity of the rate structure, by itself, tends to discourage investment in human capital, since education raises the lifetime variability of earnings by steepening the life-cycle earnings profile. As observed by Sturn and Wohlfahrt (2000), however, the *condensing* of earnings over the life cycle means that progressive taxation shifts tax burdens toward more educated members of the population, thus recouping some of the subsidies to education received earlier in the life cycle. They argue that progressive tax systems thereby recoup significant portions of the subsidies to education made available at early stages of the life cycle, meaning that publicly-supported higher education, in the presence of progressive tax systems, has smaller redistributive impacts than might otherwise appear to be the case.

26   For further discussion of Canadian and U.S. labour markets, see Riddell, 1999.

27   This contrasts with the findings reported by Finnie (2001) showing that internal migrants in Canada — especially young males — generally benefit from increased earnings, but that interprovincial return migration in Canada may actually be associated with earnings losses. These studies are not directly comparable in detail, however, but are not necessarily inconsistent.

28 Specifically, "adjusted gross income", which is related but certainly not identical to true economic income. These figures are drawn from the U.S. Treasury's *Statistics of Income.*

29 It should perhaps be emphasized in this context that the key issue concerns the location, for tax purposes, of the *incomes* of the rich, which may or may not be where they spend 180 or so days per year. However, discussion of fiscal competition in all of its aspects, including the tax treatment of not only high-income individuals but of corporations, and of expenditure policies that benefit different types of households and business activity, goes beyond the scope of the present study. For further discussion and references, see Wildasin, 2002.

30 Determining the degree of competition for mobile resources is a difficult task, both conceptually and empirically. In this writer's view, explicit dynamic modeling of factor reallocations may provide the most fruitful approach to this issue (see Wildasin, forthcoming). Decressin and Fatás (1995) provide an interesting empirical comparison of the degree of labour mobility between the United States and Europe, focusing on the speed of labour-market adjustment to changing demand conditions.

ACKNOWLEDGMENTS

A N EARLIER VERSION OF THIS STUDY was presented at a conference on Social and Labour Market Aspects of North American Linkages, sponsored by Human Resources Development Canada and Industry Canada, and held in October 2002, in Montreal. I am grateful especially to E. Beaulieu, M. Lovely, P. Poutvaara, M. Streams and conference participants for helpful comments, but retain of course responsibility for any errors.

BIBLIOGRAPHY

Agell, J. "On the Benefits from Rigid Labour Markets: Norms, Markets Failures, and Social Insurance." *Economic Journal* 109 (1999): 143-164.

——. "On the Determinants of Labor Market Institutions: Rent-Sharing vs. Social Insurance." 2000. Unpublished.

Auerbach, A.J., L.J. Kotlikoff and W. Leibfritz (eds). *Generational Accounting Around the World.* Chicago: University of Chicago Press, 1999.

Barbett, S., and R.A. Korb. "Current Funds Revenues and Expenditures of Degree-Granting Institutions: Fiscal Year 1996." Washington, D.C.: National Center for Education Statistics, 1999.

Barrett, A. "Return Migration of Highly-Skilled Irish into Ireland and their Impact on GNP and Earnings Inequality." In *International Mobility of the Highly-Skilled.* Paris: OECD, 2002, pp. 151-157.

Barrett, A., J. Fitzgerald and B. Nolan. "Earnings Inequality, Returns to Education and Immigration into Ireland." IZA Discussion Paper No. 167, 2000.

Barrett, A., and P.J. O'Connell. "Is There a Wage Premium for Returning Irish Migrants?" *Economic and Social Review* 32 (2001): 1-21.

Bauer, T., and K.F. Zimmermann. "Causes of International Migration: A Survey." In *Crossing Borders: Regional and Urban Perspectives on International Migration*. Edited by C. Gorter, P. Nijkamp and J. Poot. Aldershot: Ashgate Publishing Ltd., 1999, pp. 95-127.

Bhagwati, H.N., and M. Partington. *Taxing the Brain Drain I: A Proposal*. Amsterdam: North-Holland, 1976.

Borjas, G.J. "Immigration Policy, National Origin, and Immigrant Skills: A Comparison of Canada and the United States." In *Small Differences That Matter*. Edited by D. Card and R.B. Freeman. Chicago: University of Chicago Press, 1993, pp. 21-44.

Bound, J., J. Groen, G. Kezki and S. Turner. *Trade in University Training: Cross-State Variation in the Production and Use of College-Educated-Labor*. NBER Working Paper No. 8555, 2001.

Cremer, H., V. Fourgeaud, M. Leite-Monteiro, M. Marchand and P. Pestieau. "Mobility and Redistribution: A Survey." *Public Finance* 51 (1996): 325-352.

Coulson, B.G., and D.J. DeVoretz. "Human Capital Content of Canadian Immigrants: 1967-1987." *Canadian Public Policy* 29 (1993): 357-366.

Decressin, J., and A. Fatás. "Regional Labor Market Dynamics in Europe." *European Economic Review* 39 (1995): 1627-1655.

Edmonston, B. *Interprovincial Migration of Canadian Immigrants*. Research on Immigration and Integration in the Metropolis. Working Paper No. 02-10. Vancouver: Centre of Excellence, 2002.

Ehrenberg, R.G., and R.S. Smith. *Modern Labor Economics: Theory and Public Policy*. 3rd ed. Glenview, Ill.: Scott Foresman, 1988.

Finnie, R. *The Effects of Inter-Provincial Mobility on Individuals' Earnings: Panel Model Estimates for Canada*. Ottawa: Statistics Canada, Catalogue No. 163, 2001.

Freeman, R.B., and K. Needels. "Skill Differentials in Canada in an Era of Rising Labor Market Inequality." In *Small Differences That Matter*. Edited by D. Card and R.B. Freeman. Chicago: University of Chicago Press, 1993, pp. 45-68.

Hamilton, B., and J. Whalley. "Efficiency and Distributional Implications of Global Restrictions on Labour Mobility: Calculations and Policy Implications." *Journal of Development Economics* 14 (1984): 61-75.

Helliwell, J.F. *National Borders, Trade, and Migration*. NBER Working Paper No. 6027, 1997.

——. *How Much Do National Borders Matter?* Washington, D.C.: Brookings Institution Press, 1998.

——. "Checking the Brain Drain: Evidence and Implications, 1999." Unpublished.

Kodrzycki, Y.K. "Migration of Recent College Graduates: Evidence from the National Longitudinal Survey of Youth." *New England Economic Review* (2001).

Kotlikoff, L. *Generational Accounting*. New York: Free Press, 1993.

Krugman, P. *Geography and Trade*. Cambridge: MIT Press, 1991.

Melvin, J.R. "The Regional Economic Consequences of Tariffs and Domestic Transportation Costs." *Canadian Journal of Economics* 18 (1985): 237-257.

Mirrlees, J.A. "An Exploration in the Theory of Optimum Income Taxation." *Review of Economic Studies* 38 (1971): 175-208.

Mundell, R.A. "International Trade and Factor Mobility." *American Economic Review* 47 (1957): 321-335.

National Center for Education Statistics. *Digest of Education Statistics, 2001.* Washington, D.C.: NCES, 2002.

Riddell, W.C. "Canadian Labour Market Performance in International Perspective." *Canadian Journal of Economics* 32 (1999): 10-97.

——. "Education and Skills: An Assessment of Recent Canadian Experience." In *The State of Economics in Canada: Festschrift in Honour of David Slater.* Edited by P. Grady and A. Sharpe. Montreal and Kingston: McGill-Queen's University Press, 2001, pp. 485-517.

Riddell, W.C., and A. Sweetman. "Human Capital Formation in a Period of Rapid Change." 1999. Unpublished.

Rodrik, D. "Why Do More Open Economies Have Bigger Governments?" *Journal of Political Economy* 106 (1998): 997-1032.

Smith, A. *The Wealth of Nations.* Modern Library, 1776.

Solow, R.M. *Capital Theory and the Rate of Return.* Chicago: RandMcNally, 1963.

Stigler, G.J. "The Division of Labor Is Limited by the Extent of the Market." *Journal of Political Economy* 59 (1951).

Sturn, R., and G. Wohlfahrt. "Who Pays for Higher Education? A Note on the Neglected Role of Income Tax Progression." *FinanzArchiv* 57 (2000).

Topel, R.H. "Local Labor Markets." *Journal of Political Economy,* Part 2, 94, 3 (1986): 111-143.

——. "Specific Capital, Mobility, and Wages: Wages Rise with Job Seniority." *Journal of Political Economy* 99 (1991): 145-176.

Trefler, D. "International Factor Price Differences: Leontief Was Right!" *Journal of Political Economy* 101 (1993): 961-987.

Wildasin, D.E. "Factor Mobility, Risk, and Redistribution in the Welfare State." *Scandinavian Journal of Economics* 97 (1995): 527-546. (An expanded version appeared under the title "Factor Mobility, Risk, Inequality, and Redistribution." In *Topics in Public Economics.* Edited by D. Pines, E. Sadka and I. Zilcha. Cambridge: Cambridge University Press, 1997, pp. 314-339.)

——. "Factor Mobility and Redistributive Policy: Local and International Perspectives." In *Public Finance in a Changing World.* Edited by P.B. Sorensen. London: Macmillan Press Ltd., 1998, pp. 151-192.

——. "Labor Market Integration, Investment in Risky Human Capital, and Fiscal Competition." *American Economic Review* 90 (2000): 73-95.

——. "Tax Coordination: The Importance of Institutions." *Swedish Economic Policy Review* 9, 1 (Spring 2002): 171-194.

——. "Fiscal Competition in Space and Time." *Journal of Public Economics* 87, 11 (2003): 2571-2588.

Wildasin, D.E., and J.D. Wilson. "Imperfect Mobility and Local Government Behavior in an Overlapping-Generations Model." *Journal of Public Economics* 60 (1996): 177-198.

Zhu, S.C., and D. Trefler. *Ginis in General Equilibrium: Trade, Technology and Southern Inequality.* NBER Working Paper No. 8446, 2001.

P489:   537- 39

Comment

Canada
USA
NAFTA FIS JII F22
N   F16 J24

Mary E. Lovely
Syracuse University

DAVID WILDASIN HAS WRITTEN AN AMBITIOUS STUDY, covering a variety of theoretical and empirical concerns about the effects of deeper economic integration between Canada and the United States. The study is divided into four separate sections, each of which stands as a distinct contribution. The first section provides a theoretical treatment of internal labour migration. Wildasin asks what drives this migration and indicates how the forces behind migration influence the resulting welfare effects. Next, he presents empirical measures of interregional and international labour forces. He characterizes such flows as high, especially gross flows. In the third section, Wildasin turns his attention to trends in higher education finance. The picture that emerges from his investigation of the data is one of an increased role for national governments on both sides of the border. Finally, Wildasin discusses the efficiency implications of labour market integration and fiscal competition in education finance and in the tax treatment of highly skilled individuals. He has made many important contributions in these areas and his review offers both familiar and new insights into this complicated area of public finance.

Because the issues raised by this study are so varied and rich, I focus here on those aspects of the study that speak most directly to the conference theme. Wildasin correctly identifies the crucial question with respect to factor market integration between Canada and the United States as whether policies should inhibit or discourage such integration, not whether trade will make it superfluous. Evidence provided by the author and others at the conference shows that free trade has not eliminated labour and capital market flows. Indeed, in many respects, both the Canada-U.S. Free Trade Agreement and North American Free Trade Agreement promote such flows by easing and clarifying the rules that regulate them. The rest of my comment is devoted to exploring the answers to this policy question offered in Wildasin's study and to sketching directions for future research.

The first model used by Wildasin to understand the welfare effects of integration is one with competitive markets, free trade in goods, and homogenous labour. In this model, labour mobility is driven by interregional wage differentials. The production function exhibits a diminishing marginal product of labour.

Therefore, when workers cannot move across borders, local wages reflect local labour demand conditions. When labour mobility is permitted, however, only local employment levels, not local wages, reflect local demand conditions. The normative implication highlighted by Wildasin is that labour mobility is productivity enhancing; labour moves from the location where its marginal product is low to the location where its marginal product is higher. Consequently, the value of aggregate output must be higher with labour mobility than without it. The policy lesson is that labour mobility is welfare enhancing and should not be discouraged.

A second model sketched by Wildasin amends the basic model by adding a clever and useful characterization of specialized skill acquisition. It offers a rationale for the observed large, two-way, labour flows. The model assumes that firms achieve higher labour productivity when they employ a mix of skills. (In this regard, the model is similar to models of differentiated producer inputs in the trade and growth literatures.) Workers differentiate themselves by investing in specialized skill acquisition. However, such investment is risky due to idiosyncratic regional demand shocks. Workers are unable to diversify their human capital portfolio by acquiring multiple skills. Wildasin shows that, in this environment, interregional labour market integration reduces risk and raises investment in specialized human capital. The normative implication is that labour market integration allows a more efficient utilization of skills (as in the case of homogeneous labour, mobility equalizes marginal products across borders) and, additionally, reduces risk and raises the aggregate level of human capital. The clear policy lesson is that labour mobility should not be inhibited.

These models offer a stimulating starting point for thinking about the welfare effects of deeper labour market integration. They also raise a number of challenges for researchers interested in the normative dimensions of integration. The first main challenge is to clearly identify the relevant distributional issues. The second is to move beyond the standard competitive framework in thinking about these issues.

The first challenge forces us to grapple with the question: "Whose welfare do we care about?" Is it enough for us to consider the effect of deeper integration on the aggregate GDP of NAFTA countries? Canada alone? The United States alone? Mobile workers? Non-mobile workers? Many of the conference papers made little or no mention of capital owners or of Mexico, yet clearly these categories of interest also have much at stake with deeper integration. Are any of these various interests in conflict, and how will such conflict affect the political economy of deeper integration?

Even within the standard competitive framework, the distributional conflict inherent in deeper integration is apparent. Wildasin stresses the efficiency gains from integration, but these gains are not shared equally within or between countries. We learn that labour mobility is productivity enhancing, but we might usefully ask: "Whose productivity is enhanced?" In the standard model, labour flows from the low-wage location to the higher wage location. As Wildasin highlights, the value of aggregate output (both regions combined) must rise as a consequence. However, the total income of the sending location must fall while the total income of the receiving location must rise. Inside the sending location, the incomes of remaining mobile workers rise while those of non-mobile factors (fixed capital and non-mobile workers) fall. In the receiving location, the opposite factor price effects obtain: the incomes of mobile workers fall while those of non-mobile factors rise. Like freer goods trade, deeper labour market integration gives rise to a distributional conflict in the standard, competitive setting. Adding specialized skills to the model does not resolve the conflict. While it adds the possibility for new types of gains from integration, it also raises new questions. To whom is the risk of idiosyncratic demand shocks passed when that risk is reduced for workers?

The lesson for policy is that we do not presently have a basis for prescription. Are labour flows too large or too small? Should policy encourage or discourage them? Without a clear normative standard, we cannot define a reasonable counterfactual for assessing current labour market flows.

The second challenge is the wider adoption of richer models for analysis. Wildasin's model of skill acquisition takes us in a new and, potentially, quite important direction for understanding the effects of cross-border migration on the migrants themselves. Other elements of the model might also be usefully enriched. Product differentiation is one such element and it offers the possibility of gains for all groups, thereby lessening the distributional conflict of integration. Imperfect competition in goods markets is another direction for generalization. Industry-specific rents may explain much of the impulse to throw sand in the wheels of labour market integration, just as they have helped us to understand the prevalence of anti-dumping and countervailing duties. Finally, we must confront the questions posed by economic geography. Do scale economies and transport costs imply that integration will make rich, primary urban areas grow richer and larger? Can we somehow address the very real worries of fixed factors in secondary cities?

David Wildasin's study challenges us to address a wide array of issues concerning voters on the North American continent. Free trade has become foul language in some circles and deeper labour market integration can easily be painted with the same brush. Our answer to critics of economic integration between Canada and the United States must extend beyond the (almost certainly true but nonetheless banal) statement that aggregate GDP will increase. Our training permits us to address the genuine fears of those who will be left behind. Current circumstances demand that we do.

Richard G. Harris
Simon Fraser University

12

Productivity and North American Labour Market Integration: New Analytical Perspectives

INTRODUCTION

NORTH AMERICAN INTEGRATION HAS BEEN AT THE TOP of the Canadian policy agenda since the signing of the Canada-U.S. Free Trade Agreement (FTA) and of its successor, the North American Free Trade Agreement (NAFTA) in 1994. The steady increase in the degree of trade and investment integration of the Canadian and U.S. economies has led some observers to conclude that the next logical economic step in this arrangement would be the formation of a continental common market. Common markets differ significantly from free trade areas in a number of respects. One of the most important is that common markets are characterized by the free movement of labour. Not only are goods and capital markets integrated but so are labour markets. Harris and Schmitt (2003) discuss the various arguments — pro and con — as well as the relevant empirical evidence on the economic consequences of labour mobility. The bulk of the empirical work done in this area is based on the experience of the European Common Market.[1] The evidence thus far points to little significant impact from the labour mobility provisions. It appears that even if labour is free to move, it has no interest in moving for the most part. However, it may well be that it is too early to make a judgment on this. Within long established common markets, such as the U.S. states, there are much larger labour movements. While a North American common market may be someway off, there are certainly pressures to consider the issue further from a Canadian standpoint. These stem from at least three concerns. First, the significant *brain drain* of high-skilled Canadians during the U.S. technology boom of the 1990s has led to serious concerns about Canada's ability to retain its talent and to create economic opportunity for highly-skilled people on a par with the United States.

A common Canada-U.S. labour market could help, but it may also conceivably make matters worse. Second, the extensive trade and economic integration of Canada and the United States over the last 15 years has clearly been helped by the ability of business to move people across borders with relative ease, due in part to the NAFTA TN visa provisions that have facilitated these types of movements. To the extent that further commercial integration is possible, constraints on labour movements may prove to be important. Third, the terrorist attacks of September 11, 2001 have led the United States to increase security at its borders significantly. There is real concern that this may seriously hamper cross-border movements of both goods and people. One policy response to this initiative was the concept of a North American security perimeter, in which all security measures regarding persons and goods would be applied at the point of entry in North America. If the North American economies were to take this step, the idea of integrating labour markets would not be far behind. For these and other reasons, the role of labour market integration in North America will likely remain on the policy agenda. Even if NAFTA does not evolve into a common market, commercial pressures alone will push countries to increase the mobility of certain types of professionals and skilled trades in particular areas as economic integration proceeds.

The economic literature on the integration of labour markets pales in comparison to the equivalent literature on trade and foreign direct investment (FDI). There is a practical reason for this: almost all market liberalization initiatives, either multilateral or regional, have been concerned with trade, investment, and services to some extent. While the economics of immigration is a vast subject, the work done in this area is almost entirely cast within the tradition of labour economics, with very little concern for traditional economic integration issues. In the international economics literature, immigration or migration is treated as a factor movement problem. Labour is seen as moving from one country to another permanently, thus changing the relative factor supplies in both countries.[2] Moreover, the traditional treatment is usually set in a static neoclassical trade framework, quite unlike the modern treatment of trade and investment integration, where the emphasis is on economies of scale, imperfect competition, multinational enterprises, human capital accumulation, innovation and international knowledge spillovers. Clearly, the time has come for international economists' treatment of the labour market and labour market integration to catch up with both current reality and the theoretical innovations of the last two decades. One purpose of this study is to lay out some nontraditional arguments about the potential impact of labour market integration, or of the creation of a permanent regime of mobility rights, within a pre-existing free trade area — NAFTA being the obvious case of interest.

This shift in theoretical approach immediately brings to the fore a number of issues. First, within the traditional factor migration approach to labour, potential economic effects of labour movements are invariably small when expressed as a percent of gross domestic product (GDP) and compared to measured gains from trade liberalization. From a national welfare perspective, the role of labour mobility thus pales in comparison, for example, to the well-established benefits from free trade in goods and the liberalization of investment. Is this view correct? It almost certainly originates directly from the analytical framework within which 'labour mobility' has traditionally been viewed. Whether this view is correct or not is ultimately an empirical matter, but the basic theory one uses is an important prerequisite to appropriately framing the quantitative question. Second, there are perennial concerns raised by large versus small countries. As the small country, Canada is often fearful of increased integration with the United States, on grounds of reduced sovereignty in the exercise of control over its borders and the risk of losing in the economic competition for investment and people. The brain drain issue of the 1990s is a classic example in this respect.[3] The brain drain is parallel to de-industrialization and to the prospect of Canada becoming a regional North American economy peripheral to the U.S. core. To address this question adequately, traditional static factor-migration perspectives are entirely inadequate. Modern theory and evidence point to the overwhelming significance of the process of national productivity growth and the way in which economic integration impacts on this process in arriving at a correct answer to this question. Therefore, it is imperative that increasing the level of economic integration by integrating labour markets be viewed from the same analytical perspective. It may or may not lay to rest the fears of de-industrialization, but at least the question will be posed appropriately. Third, labour market integration is quite different from labour movements between one country and another, for example in response to a lessening of immigration controls. There are both geographic and intertemporal aspects to this difference. First, an integrated labour market would be regarded as a permanent institutional change in the set of rules governing rights of access to the labour markets of the integrating countries. This is quite different from a one-time shift in factor supplies. It would lead to differences in expectations, supply responses, the organization of work, and so forth that a one-time migration would not trigger. The geographic context of the Canada-U.S. and U.S.-Mexico borders is very important. Labour markets are usually regional in nature, and thus under full labour market integration we would expect to see substantial growth in two-way flows of labour in bordering areas. Second, there is the intertemporal dimension. A worker may move from Toronto to New York one year, and then move from there to Montreal two years later. Given that most jobs turn over at a relatively rapid pace, a fully integrated labour market would be characterized by cross-border job turnover, with reverse and multiple-reverse migrations for many workers. Neither of these features is present in the migration approach to the international movement of labour.

The primary purpose of the study is to re-think conceptually this set of issues regarding labour market integration using new analytical perspectives derived from the literature on economic growth, international trade and knowledge-based economies. It is worth mentioning that one analytical tradition not covered here is that associated with the field of urban and regional public finance. Often subsumed under the heading of the study of federalism, public finance economists have looked at a number of issues that derive from a perspective in which labour is mobile across cities and regions. Two classic issues are a) the welfare gains that mobility secures from a closer matching of individual tastes to the set of goods and services, including public goods, that are produced locally, and b) the role of mobility as a means to reduce income risk in the face of idiosyncratic shocks to local economies. Both of these issues and the related literature are discussed at length in David Wildasin's study presented in this volume.

The rest of the study proceeds as follows. The next section, entitled *Mobility, Factor Prices and Productivity*, reviews the reasons why traditional models of international trade and factor mobility predict that labour mobility is inconsequential from an efficiency point of view, and then goes on to discuss the Achilles heel of this approach — inattention to national productivity differences. The core of the study considers four analytical perspectives in which integration of labour markets might have significant effects. The third section, entitled *Human Capital-based Growth: Implications of Labour Mobility for Income Convergence*, looks at the role of human capital formation, using a multi-country extension of the class of endogenous growth theories developed by Robert Lucas. The fourth section, entitled *Global Mobility and Knowledge Flows*, takes up the issue of knowledge spillovers and how labour mobility impacts on the knowledge-based economy. The fifth section, entitled *Skill Specialization and Service Exports*, deals with the role of services, service market integration and how it interacts with labour market integration. This issue is of considerable importance given the overall size of the service sector in the economy. The sixth section, entitled *GPTs, Skill-biased Technological Change and Labour Mobility*, deals with the potential interaction between large-scale technological change, characterized as either skill-biased technological change (SBTC) or the emergence of a general purpose technology (GPT) based on information and communication technologies (ICTs) and the organization of goods and labour markets. Shifts in the organization of work could interact with labour market integration in ways that most traditional theories miss. Finally, the last section concludes with a summary and observations on policy and future research.

MOBILITY, FACTOR PRICES AND PRODUCTIVITY

IN THIS SECTION, THE BASIC STATIC WELFARE ARGUMENTS are reviewed and discussed in light of the literature that has emerged on the determinants and dynamics of productivity growth. The basic question to ask is: Under what circumstances might the efficiency gains from liberalizing the movement of labour prove to be high? One of the most important economic theories of international trade, the Heckscher-Ohlin model, produces a set of very strong predictions on the circumstances in which factor mobility will have no welfare or efficiency impact — a result due to Canadian Nobel economist Robert Mundell (1957). Understanding this argument clearly is of immense value in judging other theories that generate either net costs or benefits from labour mobility.[4]

The Heckscher-Ohlin model of long-run international trade presumes that a fixed set of goods, N, is produced using common international methods of production, as summarized by N sectoral production functions which use M factors of production. Factors of production are mobile between industries in a country but are not mobile across countries. Add to this the assumption of competitive markets, no trade distortions and constant returns to scale, and a predicted outcome of the theory is what is known as the Factor-Price Equalization (FPE) theorem, provided N is at least as large as M — the number of goods is at least as large as the number of factors. According to the FPE, countries facing common prices for internationally traded goods will have the same factor prices. For example, if one factor is skilled labour, the price of skilled labour will then be identical in all countries. The reason for this is that competition forces prices to equal unit or average costs of production for all goods produced. If there are two factors of production, skilled and unskilled labour, and two goods, 1 and 2, this equilibrium condition can be stated as:

$$p_1 = a_u W_w + a_s W_s$$
$$p_2 = b_u W_u + b_s W_s \quad,$$

where a and b are common technology coefficients. These conditions are independent of the factor supplies or of the quantities of goods produced or traded in an economy. With two equations, commodity prices determine uniquely the two wage rates, W. One implication of factor price equalization is that the value of the marginal product of each factor is the same in all countries, for all industries in which it is employed. Therefore, in equilibrium there are no unrealized efficiency gains to be achieved from a reallocation of factors from one country to another. If labour moves from a skilled labour-abundant country to another country, that merely re-arranges the patterns of outputs produced in different countries, but it does not increase total output. Moreover, as factor prices are equalized and the cost of purchasing goods is the same in all countries, there is no incentive to relocate due to cost-of-living differences.[5] Mundell's results provide a powerful intellectual basis for two policy positions. First, all efficiency gains at the international level can be secured through free trade; second, factor mobility does not increase national or global output. Thus, to the extent that there may be other reasons to limit labour mobility, they will not have negative consequences on efficiency.

If the real world was as depicted in the Heckscher-Ohlin model, there would not be much discussion about factor market integration within formal or informal common markets. As Trefler (1995) and others have documented, the major failing of the Heckscher-Ohlin model of international trade is the assumption that technology is common across countries. At any point in time, countries differ, often dramatically so, in their productivity levels. For some years now, there have been repeated concerns in Canada about the country's low productivity level relative to the United States. The debate was given added impetus by the increase in the labour productivity gap between Canada and the United States — which has accelerated after 1994 as discussed in Bernstein, Harris and Sharpe (2002). From 1977 to 1994, the Canada-U.S. gap in manufacturing output per hour averaged 14 percent. Subsequently, Canada's relative gap rose 20 percentage points — from 12 percentage points in 1994 to 32 percentage points in 2001. Output per hour in Canadian manufacturing fell from 88 percent of the U.S. level in 1994 to 68 percent in 2001. In Europe, integration of a poor South with a rich North has led to similar concerns about labour market integration.[6] When countries have different productivity levels, factor migration not only raises an issue of efficiency gains but is also inherently a question of distributional impacts across countries.

To illustrate the role of productivity differences, consider a simple two-country world in which each country produces the same good using skilled labour and unskilled labour. Suppose that one country, labelled U, has a higher level of total factor productivity than the other country, labelled C. Each country has as a production function for total output given by:

$$Y = A_i F(L_s, L_u)$$
$$i = U, C$$

The A term is the level of total factor productivity (TFP). If TFP is higher in U than in C if and the two countries start off with similar ratios of the supply of skilled to unskilled labour, then wages will be higher in U than in C. Suppose that one opens up the possibility of migration for skilled labour, with no such possibility for unskilled labour. If skilled labour migrates from C to U, this leads to 'skilled labour wage convergence' in that wages of skilled labour in C rise while those in U fall. With complete mobility of skilled labour and perfect arbitrage of wages, the outcome would be equality of skilled labour wages in the two countries. Moreover, this equilibrium would be efficient in that the marginal product of skilled labour would be the same in both countries. Labour mobility therefore raises total output but it now has important additional distributional consequences: unskilled labour in the country experiencing out-migration (C) has been made worse off while it has been made better off in the other country (U). Unlike the classical analysis of gains from trade, in which both countries gain from free trade, the question of factor mobility has first order impacts on distribution in which there are both winners and losers. Much of the brain drain discussion, and in particular the migration of skilled labour from developing to developed countries, is conducted within this frame of analysis. Rich countries with high productivity levels seek to attract more skilled labour. This raises the rich country's GDP but, at the same time, increases the income gap between the rich country and the poor country. Note, however, that if unskilled labour is given free access to the rich country's markets, the theory becomes unstable as all factors of production would want to move from the low- to the high-productivity country. Moreover, if the world as a whole is more abundant in unskilled labour and if that labour could migrate to the rich country, unskilled labour wages would be driven down in the rich country. This, of course, illustrates a powerful argument as to why industrial countries do not open their borders to unskilled labour.[7]

Despite the arguments against labour mobility, economists have long argued that mobility of capital is generally efficiency-enhancing, and the liberalization of capital movements along with trade have been a major force of economic growth over the last 50 years.[8] Capital mobility carries the same implications as labour mobility when national productivity differences persist. Capital would like to move from low-productivity locations to high-productivity locations. The overwhelming set of reasons offered to explain why this is beneficial for all countries has to do with the set of assumptions made about the determinants of productivity — productivity is not exogenous but, in fact, highly endogenous within any reasonable time frame. The productivity terms, A_i, respond to a variety of economic and policy related determinants — including education, learning by doing, R&D, technology transfers, knowledge spillovers, market competition, regulatory and tax policies, and others. In the case of FDI — the most important form of liberalized long-term capital movement in the modern period of globalization — a substantial list of studies show that high levels of FDI provide significant productivity benefits to the host and source countries.[9] If productivity levels increase in one or both countries as a result of liberalizing investment, they can more than offset any potential negative effects from the induced shift in relative factor supplies, as discussed in the above case. It is even conceivable that capital would flow in directions other than the initial rate of return comparisons would suggest, because of the induced productivity change. The balance of evidence on economic integration is that it tends to contribute to income and productivity convergence. But the bulk of this evidence pertains primarily to trade and investment.[10] However, we could make the case that economic integration can lead to divergence if market forces tend to exacerbate international productivity differences. For example, in the simple model above, suppose that as skilled labour moves from C to U, A_U/A_C increases — the Canada-U.S. productivity gap widens. This would be a case for divergence.

Mundell's argument against factor mobility can be turned on its head in a world where productivity differences are transitory but subject to endogenous convergence pressures. Suppose, for example, that regions are hit continuously with region-specific shocks to productivity, but that endogenous responses by firms and governments cause regions that are behind leaders to catch-up. In such a case then, regions subject to free trade of goods and factors would have, over time, similar average levels of productivity, with transitory periods in which they are above or below the average. There is some evidence provided by Barro and Sala-I-Martin (1995) that such a process describes the history of U.S. states, for example, that are specialized in goods production but whose productivity levels have generally not diverged significantly. Despite the fact that productivity differences are neither large nor permanent, a regime that ensures the arbitrage of returns to factors across regions, for example fully integrated labour and capital markets, provides a mechanism that continuously disciplines the processes leading to productivity differences, and therefore sets in motion decisions by firms and individuals that seek to restore long-run relative productivity. In this case, factor mobility becomes the disciplinary device which leads to a factor-price equalization outcome. In the long run, FPE requires both free trade in goods and factor mobility. FPE is the end of the process rather than the beginning. To dispense with factor mobility after achieving convergence would only lead to subsequent divergence as regions are hit with idiosyncratic shocks that then lead to permanent productivity differences.

These arguments can be brought to bear directly on the issue of labour market integration in a free trade area. If productivity convergence is a consequence of liberalizing factor movements, then the dynamics underlying policy on labour market liberalization should be quite different than the simple static analysis indicates. In each of the four theories discussed in subsequent sections of the study, moving to a regime of labour mobility has productivity consequences; it is these consequences that generate important quantitative differences for the cost-benefit analysis of moving to a labour mobility regime. Moreover, one has to make the case that these benefits are not achievable within the existing policy framework where trade and capital movements are substantially liberalized.

HUMAN CAPITAL-BASED GROWTH: IMPLICATIONS OF LABOUR MOBILITY FOR INCOME CONVERGENCE

IN THIS SECTION, AN IMPORTANT ARGUMENT about the role of labour mobility as a force leading to economic convergence in a dynamic endogenous growth model is developed.[11] The particular theory of economic growth used here is based on human capital spillovers developed by Robert Lucas (1988). In his theory, which described growth in a closed economy, income level differences are due to differences in the average level of human capital in an economy. The model was extended to an open economy context by Razin and Yuen (1997a) who examined the impact of labour mobility on growth and convergence in an economic union. It is the only published study explicitly looking at the role of international labour mobility within an endogenous growth framework. Lucas' (1988) framework shows how differences across countries in education and other human capital acquisition policies with immobile human capital can create differences in both growth rates and income levels. Razin and Yuen show that, in the Lucas framework, free mobility of labour is a necessary condition to achieve convergence of income levels. Labour market integration goes beyond migration, in that market forces must be allowed to continuously arbitrage the returns to human capital in alternative locations. What is extremely interesting in the Razin-Yuen model is the observation that free trade in goods and unrestricted capital mobility are insufficient to insure income convergence among regions in a free trade area. In the absence of free movement of labour, they show that permanent income differences will persist between economies whose growth is driven by human capital. This provides a compelling intellectual case for policies that improve international labour market integration. In this section, a simplified version of the Lucas-Razin-Yuen framework is presented to illustrate the intuition behind this fascinating result.

The Razin-Yuen model has the following structure. There are two countries, with aggregate output in each described by a two-factor production function in which GDP, denoted Y, is produced with two inputs: physical and human capital, K and H. h is the level of human capital of the representative workers in the economy and L is the number of workers. H measures total labour supply in efficiency units. The production function has a Cobb-Douglas form and is given by:

$$(1) \qquad Y = h^{\varepsilon} A K^{\alpha} H^{1-\alpha}.$$

This is fairly conventional except that there is a spillover term of average human capital, denoted by h^{ε}, which affects the level of TFP. All parameters of the production function are similar across countries. In the Lucas framework, growth in a country's total factor productivity hinges directly on increases in h. Private and social returns to education and training are different and increasing in the spillover parameter, ε. To abstract from some non-essentials, population growth is ignored and the number of workers, L, is set equal to one. Each worker is endowed with one unit of time, which is split between working and going to school. Let e denote the number of hours spent in school. The remainder of the time is spent on work, which implies that $H = (1-e)h$. Human capital dynamics are described by the following equation:

(2) $\qquad \dot{h} = B(e)h - \delta_h h$.

You can think of $B(e)h$ as the education production function.

Let y denote output per worker, c per capita consumption and k the physical capital stock per worker. The equation describing capital accumulation dynamics is then:

(3) $\qquad \dot{k} = y - c - \delta k$.

Human capital accumulation depends on the amount of time devoted to education. Households have identical preferences and choose a time path of consumption $c(t)$ that maximizes lifetime utility, V, given by:

(4) $\qquad V = \dfrac{1}{1-\sigma} \int_0^\infty e^{-\beta t} c^{1-\sigma} dt$,

where σ is the inverse of the intertemporal elasticity of substitution in consumption. First-order intertemporal optimization conditions give the traditional consumption growth equation relating the growth in the marginal utility of consumption to the real interest rate which, in turn, is given by the net marginal production of capital:

(5) $\qquad (\dfrac{\dot{c}}{c})^\sigma = r = MPK - \delta$.

The gross marginal product of capital, MPK is given by:

(6) $\qquad MPK = \alpha h^\varepsilon A (k/h)^{\alpha-1}$.

In this model, it turns out that the time devoted to education, e, and thus work is constant in a steady state. For the purposes of our analysis, there is little loss of generality by setting e constant. The growth rate of variable x is denoted by g_x. In a steady state with a constant growth rate of consumption, output and a constant capital/output ratio, y/k, the growth rates of these variables equal the common economic growth rate of per capita output:

$$(7) \qquad g_c = g_y = g_k \equiv g.$$

In a steady state, the real interest rate, which is constant, equals the net marginal product of capital; this, in turn, means that the marginal product of capital is constant. Using equation (5) with $g_c = g$ implies that:

$$(8) \qquad k^{-\alpha} h^{\varepsilon + \alpha} = const$$

for any feasible steady state. Equation (8) carries the implication that, in a steady state, the growth rate of h is given by:

$$(9) \qquad g_h = \frac{\alpha}{\alpha + \varepsilon} g_k.$$

If there is no external effect of human capital so that $\varepsilon = 0$, then the growth rate of h equals the growth rate of k. In general, the growth rate of h is less than the growth rate of k. In a steady state, the constant MPK condition can be written as:

$$(10) \qquad g^\sigma = \alpha A k^{\alpha - 1} h^{\varepsilon + 1 - \alpha} - \delta.$$

It is convenient to work with the trend-adjusted values of k and h. Let k^* and h^* denote the trend-adjusted values of k and h. They are defined as:

$$(11) \qquad \begin{aligned} k^*(t) &= e^{-g^t} k(t) \\ h^*(t) &= e^{-g_h t} h(t) \end{aligned}$$

From the condition of constant marginal product of capital, we can substitute the trend-adjusted values of k and h into equation (10) and use equation (9) to get a steady-state relation between k^* and h^*, which is, in log form:

$$(12) \qquad \log k^* = const + \frac{(\alpha + \varepsilon)}{\alpha} \log h^*.$$

This is depicted by the line SS' with a slope greater than unity in Figure 1. Economies with higher levels of h have an increasing ratio of physical to human capital; that is, k^*/h^* increases as we move to the right along the locus of constant MPK.

An initial value of $t = 0$ (for log k_0, log h_0) leads to a set of dynamics indicated by the arrows in Figure 1. Different initial conditions lead to different steady states. In the figure, two possibilities are indicated — one, a set of dynamics starting from a low initial point, Z_L, and another starting from a high initial point, Z_H. While countries with similar tastes and technology have identical long-run growth rates, interest rates, and marginal productivity of capital, they have different k^*/h^* ratios if ε is greater than zero and start from different initial conditions. Economies with different long-run k/h ratios will have different wage rates and thus different income levels. Wage income per unit of labour supply will be $W = w_h h$, where the wage rate per unit of human capital rises with the level of human capital along alternative steady states. Effectively, with increasing returns to scale in h, along a locus of constant marginal product of capital (MPK constant), Y (output) is proportional to k. Thus, Y/h varies with k/h. Economies with a higher h have a higher k/h ratio, and thus a higher income per unit of human capital. This is what leads to income diversity within the Lucas framework.

FIGURE 1

STEADY-STATE ANALYSIS OF RAZIN-YUEN MODEL, INCOME DIVERSITY

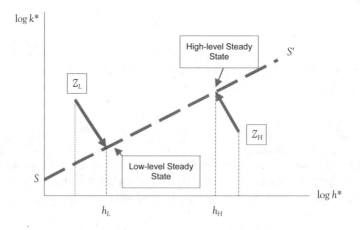

CAPITAL MOBILITY

WHAT IS THE IMPACT OF ALLOWING for the international mobility of capital? Consider two economies which, to simplify matters, have the same level of h but different levels of k, one high and one low. Since $L = 1$, $K = k$. The initial vertical point on the arrows corresponds to the level of the capital stock in each region prior to opening the international capital market. Upon opening the international market for physical capital, the high-K economy will have a lower marginal product of capital than the low-K economy. Capital will shift from the high-K economy to the low-K economy. With no adjustment costs to relocating capital, the equilibrium will jump to the new steady state where MPK is the same for both economies. As drawn, the allocation that equalizes the MPKs also happens to correspond to the steady-state MPK level. The implication is that by allowing capital mobility, the transition to the steady state is instantaneous. In the more general case, the impact of capital mobility is to increase the speed of convergence. In the general case, however, capital mobility *does not lead to income convergence*. Economies will differentiate themselves depending upon their initial levels of human capital, with high human capital economies also having a high physical capital stock and higher per capita incomes.

LABOUR MARKET INTEGRATION

THE INTRODUCTION OF LABOUR MOBILITY allows individuals to arbitrage the returns to human capital internationally. Let's start with a situation where we have a low-income country and a high-income country, corresponding to points A and B in Figure 2. The wage per efficiency unit of H will be higher in country B — the high-income country. If labour is mobile, individuals from country A will migrate to country B, increasing the supply of labour in B and driving down the efficiency wage in that country. This migration will also reduce initially the average level of human capital in B, as those migrating come with a lower h than those in A. Both countries start with steady states where growth rates and returns to capital are equal, but incomes and returns to human capital are different. As migration occurs, wages are equalized leading to a reduction in the level of h in B and an increase in A. The process ends at point E where incomes are equalized.

The major force at work in the low-income source country is the increased scarcity of labour which raises the returns to human capital, and thus the incentives to acquire additional human capital. The productivity spillover from a high h raises the returns to all factors leading to an increase in capital per worker. In the host country, wages fall as labour migrates in and average productivity (or TFP) falls. The process leads to a stable outcome in which incomes converge. It is important to note that there are no negative effects on

FIGURE 2

LABOUR MARKET INTEGRATION AND INCOME CONVERGENCE

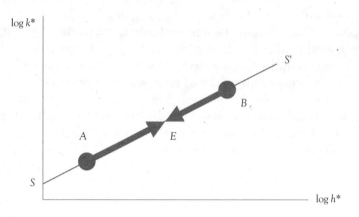

the productivity level of the country that is the source of the migration — the low-income country. People leaving do not change the average level of human capital in the economy and, therefore, the national total factor productivity (TFP) level. In this sense, there are no brain drain 'negatives'. The model would have quite different properties either if a) migration lowered average human capital levels, or b) there were international knowledge spillovers so that one country's level of human capital directly impacted on productivity in the other country.

While the model depicts a transition dynamic through which migration occurs from A to B, it is important to emphasize that for incomes to remain convergent despite other shocks — for example, terms-of-trade, factor-endowment or productivity shocks —, there must be a continuous arbitrage of human capital. Therefore, the model produces in the long run the type of convergence dynamics discussed in the second section.

Within the Lucas-Razin-Yuen framework, the equilibrium is not efficient either globally or nationally given the presence of the human capital externality. From a global point of view, there is underinvestment in human capital, which could be corrected by a subsidy to education. Both countries would have incentives to correct this particular market failure, for example by providing public education. There are divergent national incentives, however, in the initial pre-integration situation. The high-income host country will experience a reduction in the average quality of human capital when it allows free movement of labour. Workers in the high-income country thus have a transitional incentive to prevent or slowdown labour inflows by whatever means. A policy commitment not to do so should therefore be an explicit part of an integration agreement. The model highlights that, within a new economic union with substantial income differences across regions, there will be asymmetric national interests in terms of arriving at a common labour market. But once integration has been achieved, these asymmetries disappear.

The empirical relevance of this model is explored in Razin and Yuen (1997b) who look at the growth and convergence experience of nine U.S. regions and nine European countries between 1960 and 1988. The authors proxy the state of labour mobility by using the coefficient of variation of unemployment rates — an indicator commonly used in the literature. They find that labour mobility restrictions have a significant effect on level divergence. They interpret this result as strongly supporting their theory which claims that labour mobility promotes income-level convergence. From the Canada-U.S. perspective, this model has obviously some limitations. Probably most serious is the notion that external effects are national in scope, and other determinants of productivity beyond human capital externalities are excluded. Nevertheless, the theory provides a powerful intellectual case for the economic benefits of an integrated labour market.

GLOBAL MOBILITY AND KNOWLEDGE FLOWS

ONE OF THE COMPELLING FACTS on economic growth documented in the last decade is the importance of knowledge spillovers between nations. A wide range of studies using proxies for knowledge, such as R&D stocks or patent filings, show that knowledge created in one country, after diffusion to other countries, impacts on productivity. Knowledge 'spills over' in the sense that its benefits are not entirely appropriable by its creator. This raises the question of the means by which knowledge is diffused from one country to another. It has long been argued that trade facilitates international technological diffusion, or is an important means by which it is facilitated. Initially, this line of argument involved measuring the impact of R&D expenditures undertaken in one country on productivity growth in another country. For example, Coe and Helpman (1995) and Coe, Helpman and Hoffmaister (1997) construct an index of total knowledge capital in each industrial country and assume that trading partners get access to a country's stock of knowledge in proportion to their imports from that country. They find that access to foreign knowledge is a statistically significant determinant of the rate of total factor productivity growth in a country. The most obvious interpretation of this finding is that technological knowledge is diffusing from one country to another. The estimated effects are very large. In a widely cited study, Keller (2001) estimates that diffusion from the G-5 countries to nine other small OECD countries contributed almost 90 percent of the total effect of R&D on productivity growth. In a related study, Keller (2002) examines the role of distance, trade, FDI and language similarity as propagation mechanisms for international technological diffusion. Looking at the effects of distance, he finds that the average value of a dollar of U.S. R&D in Canada is 78 percent of the value of a dollar of Canadian R&D. Given that U.S. R&D spending is about 40 times that of Canada, U.S. technological development is thus of enormous importance for Canadian growth. However, the author goes on to measure the impact of other mediation channels — the combined roles of trade, FDI flows and language similarity — on technological diffusion. The level of technology in an industry is approximated by the level of total factor productivity. Keller measures the strength of bilateral technology diffusion across different country pairs by reporting the share of a sender country in a given technology recipient's total technology inflows. In the case of Canada, he estimates that 69 percent of total world technology diffusion originates from U.S. R&D, while the share originating from the United Kingdom, for example, is much lower, at 13.5 percent. The combined results show that distance and low trade volumes reduce dramatically technological diffusion spillovers.

However, the issue surrounding the exact channel by which knowledge diffuses from one country to another remains unresolved. One suspects that the trade channel is a proxy for some more fundamental causal mechanism. Given that knowledge resides in people, one is lead to think that interactions between people are the root source of these spillovers. If interactions between people in any two locations increase, it would be reasonable to assume that general transfers of knowledge would also increase. One consequence of globalization is that the pace of human interactions across borders has increased significantly. The reason people are so important, rather than, for example, a simple computer and web link, is that much useful knowledge is non-codified and tacit in nature. Recent work on the knowledge economy has drawn increased attention to the importance of tacit knowledge and the mechanisms by which it is created and distributed.[12] As tacit and non-codified knowledge becomes more important, person-to-person communication and interactions become relatively more important for the diffusion of knowledge. This is particularly evident in those segments of the economy where labour markets have become global in scope. The segments of the labour market that are now globalized (in the sense that the industry of employment is knowledge-based and global in scope) and that have a high degree of international mobility are still small. They include not only high-technology industries, but the management of most multinational enterprises, as well as scientific and technical professions. Knowledge workers facilitate knowledge transfers.

In thinking about the role of labour mobility and how it interacts with knowledge spillovers, it is useful to view the labour market as segmented between jobs that are part of the global knowledge economy, and jobs that are not.

Obviously, this classification is slightly artificial as some jobs could as easily be classified as both national and global in scope. The usefulness of this framework hinges on a twofold classification. First, with regard to the scope of knowledge spillovers across relevant organizations: are these largely national or global in scope? Second, the degree to which movements between jobs within the global knowledge sector — even if they involve a change of location — are subject to much less friction that a movement from the non-global sector to the global sector. The working assumption here is that most people would classify themselves in the second group — they would not routinely view alternative opportunities to their current job as being outside the national or even the local labour market. However, truly globally mobile workers are much more likely to take a job — be it in London, Hong Kong or Toronto — based on characteristics other than location. The emergence of global knowledge workers is a trend that became noticeable in the 1990s, driven by technology, the increased globalization of corporations and a long economic expansion.

A MODEL OF NATIONAL VERSUS GLOBAL KNOWLEDGE WORKERS[13]

LET'S START WITH THE ASSUMPTION that the decision to become a global knowledge worker involves considerable cost and foregone alternatives in the local economy. Typically, the types of people who are potential global knowledge workers are highly skilled both with respect to general human capital and to very specific skills. Let's assume also that there is, at a point in time, a supply curve for these individuals, citizens of a small open national economy like Canada. The supply curve is increasing in the way depicted as SS' in Figure 3. The elasticity of this supply curve reflects in part the propensity of individuals to shift from a local labour market to the global one. We take the geographic distribution of demand for these types of workers as given. There are jobs in Toronto, Montreal, New York, San Francisco and a number of other locations at home and abroad. To simplify, assume that there are only two locations, Canada and the United States. The presumption is that the demand for these workers in the United States is so large relative to the Canadian supply that the demand for workers originating in Canada is perfectly elastic at the wage W^*. This is the horizontal line D^*W^* in Figure 3. Demand in Canada for these workers is downward sloping, denoted by D_C. Given the complete mobility of these workers, wages are equalized across jobs in Canada and the United States. In practice, these wages would have to be appropriately adjusted for cost-of-living differences and non-wage perquisites, etc. Given the initial supply curve of Canadian-based globally mobile workers, OA find employment in Canada and the rest, AB, are employed abroad.

FIGURE 3

INTERNATIONAL MOBILITY OF GLOBAL KNOWLEDGE WORKERS

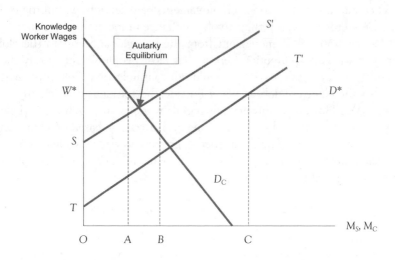

Imagine now a sudden lowering in the cost of becoming globally mobile. For example, lower airfares, better communication systems and a general willingness to seek employment opportunities abroad would result in a shift in the supply curve from SS' to TT'. We can refer to the source of these shifts as mobility-biased supply shifts. With unchanged demand, the number of people who end up working abroad rises from AB to AC. Given the high skill level of these individuals, such movement could be identified as a brain drain. An alternative driver would be better economic opportunities abroad, as reflected by an increase in wage W*. Given unchanged home demand and supply SS', this would result in an increase in the number of mobile workers employed abroad and a decrease in the global workforce employed at home, albeit at higher wages.

The analysis thus far ignores an important aspect of global mobility — the nature of knowledge spillovers between individuals within the global workforce and the impact this has on the productivity of other factors of production that are not globally mobile. The assumption made here is that knowledge spillovers in these types of jobs are not geographically limited. However, they are limited to the set of people who regularly interact in these global networks. To illustrate, assume that Canadian output, Y_C, is produced with the following production function:

$$Y_C = \Gamma(M_S, M^*)F(N, M_C).$$

The two immobile market-mediated factor inputs are Canadian workers, N, and global knowledge workers employed in Canada, M_C. The total number of knowledge workers supplied from Canada is denoted by M_S. Output depends on knowledge spillovers, which impact on the total factor productivity term, Γ, and the private production function, F.[14] However, total factor productivity is a function of the amount of global knowledge generated by the global knowledge workforce, M_C plus M^* — globally mobile workers supplied from both Canada and the United States.[15] Canadian-based knowledge workers serve two distinct functions in this framework. First, as captured within F, they facilitate privately appropriable technological diffusion valuable to an individual firm. Second, they facilitate the external non-appropriable knowledge transfer by interacting with global knowledge workers, as captured in the total factor productivity term. The important distinction here is that productivity depends on the total stock of global knowledge workers and not just on knowledge workers employed in Canada. For example, a brain drain caused by either a shift in the supply curve of mobile workers or an increase in external demand corresponds to an increase in M_S but not M_C. This increase in the stock of knowledge workers will lead to increased productivity at home and thus higher wages for all. A particularly favourable view of this process is the *brain circulation* hypothesis.[16] It posits that workers in the global knowledge pool cycle back and forth between domestic and foreign employment, in each case carrying back to the home economy the knowledge they acquired.

The assumption that global knowledge spillovers work in this way is simple, but it captures the basic idea. Increased global mobility can be viewed as a valuable attribute of a national labour force. Once individuals enter these global markets, they participate in networks through which knowledge is shared and transferred. These benefits accrue globally, but the benefits also fall on the economy from which knowledge workers originated. Knowledge workers abroad serve as preferential conduits for the reverse flow of knowledge. For very small economies, this can be quite important. Most ideas are developed in larger economies and expatriates may provide better access to those ideas and faster technology transfer than would otherwise be the case.

For an economy highly dependent on global knowledge, a pool of nationals who participate in global knowledge industries, whether located at home or abroad, is a valuable conduit for knowledge diffusion. Therefore, Canada's participation in global knowledge industries will likely be of growing importance for sustaining a high rate of productivity growth and, thus, living standards. The brain drain debate emphasized that the composition of Canadian emigration in the 1990s was heavily concentrated among two groups — Executives and Managers, and Engineers, Computer and Natural Scientists. In 1997, these two groups accounted for 37.5 and 18.4 percent, respectively, of the total number of emigrants. While viewed as evidence of a brain drain, it might also indicate a shift toward the globalization of knowledge-based industries.

If one views global knowledge workers as important mediators of international knowledge flows, then it is useful to determine the impact of establishing a permanent right of mobility for these workers versus one-time migration flows. The purpose of a common market with legal right of access is to create a stable and transparent policy regime governing cross-border labour movements. Modern labour markets are characterized by a high degree of turnover. Most people expect to work for a number of firms over the course of their careers. For those potentially involved in cross-border migration, the propensity both to leave and to return will be heavily conditioned by the risk they attach to any cross-border move. In the current situation, for example, Canadians who get a U.S. *green card* face a serious risk when returning to Canada, in that their subsequent rights of access to the U.S. market are not guaranteed. This risk effectively implies that after migrating to the United States, there is reduced probability of a return flow. As is well known to anyone who has made such a move, matters are further complicated when other family members are involved. There is no guarantee that one's spouse or children will be given similar right of access. This serves as an effective barrier both to emigration and to return migration. A common labour market with permanent right of access would change the entire structure of expectations regarding future possible employment and career choices. The current regime works to the disadvantage of the smaller country. Economic opportunity in the United States is a powerful short-term attraction for young Canadian knowledge workers to gain experience and access to international networks in their field. Firms facing the choice to locate in Canada versus the United States have a similar dilemma in that they risk reduced access to the pool of North American knowledge workers. In order to leverage the process of international knowledge diffusion, a common North American labour market could have a significant impact on total two-way flows.

SKILL SPECIALIZATION AND SERVICE EXPORTS

THE IMPORTANCE OF CURRENT AND FUTURE ECONOMIC INTEGRATION for the service economy cannot be understated. Manufacturing represents 18 percent of GDP while services represent 68 percent. In the 1990s, business services grew at an annual rate of 4.9 percent compared to a growth rate of 2.4 percent for the whole economy. Among other service industries, communications and wholesale trade grew at a rate of 4.5 percent and 5.4 percent, respectively. In general, service-producing industries are more labour intensive than their goods-producing counterparts. In 2001, service sector jobs accounted for 74 percent of total employment. Moreover, incomes are higher in services than in other sectors. Business services posted a 3.7 percent average annual earnings growth over the past five years while the overall growth rate of the economy was only 1.6 percent. Large parts of the service sector are subject to integration pressures through changes in technology and policy initiatives. Given the importance of geographic proximity in service transactions, this is particularly the case for Canada-U.S. economic integration, and of key importance in examining the labour market integration issue. In 2001, Canadian exports of services reached $55.1 billion, or 11.8 percent of total Canadian exports of goods and services; the same year, imports of services reached $61.9 billion, or 15 percent of total Canadian imports of goods and services. While free trade has resulted in substantial goods trade, service market integration is still relatively limited, although increasing quickly.

A distinctive characteristic of the 'New Economy' technological change based on information and communication technologies (ICT) is the *death of distance*, which has a large impact on the production and distribution of business services, many only recently traded across international borders. Examples include financial, accounting, market, engineering, media, telecommunication, and transport services. Partial liberalization of these areas has been attempted in most of the regional free trade agreements with mixed success. It is widely claimed that the next stage of liberalization will be all about services, both at the regional and multilateral levels.[17]

Many services associated with the New Economy are thought to be characterized by localization economies — that is, the physical proximity of buyers and sellers is a necessary feature for these to develop. In a large economy or city, these would usually be non-traded services. The same is true in isolated small economies. Most of these types of services can be viewed as highly specialized, involving close interaction between customer and provider. Moreover, they are invariably extremely labour-intensive — one might view many of these services as simply the provision of labour services by another name. However, one can argue that labour in the service sector is highly differentiated, particularly in the types of tasks it performs. The old Smithian adage of the 'division of labour limited by the extent of the market' is clearly relevant. Labour market integration ought to have some effects beyond wages and factor supplies — clearly, one of these effects must be the degree of task specialization. Therefore, specialization in the service export market can be thought of as equivalent at least in part to the specialization of labour.[18] In this section, we present a model built around this idea. Labour market mobility and service market integration thus go hand in hand. The link between service trade and factor mobility is common in the discussion of FDI. Producer services, such as managerial and engineering consulting services, can provide domestic firms with the substantial benefits of specialized knowledge that would be costly in terms of time and money for domestic firms to develop on their own. The key idea in that literature is that a diverse set (or higher quality set) of business services allows downstream users to purchase a quality-adjusted unit of business services at a lower cost. But these intermediate services are often non-traded, or costly to trade. With the high cost of trading services, foreign services are best transferred through FDI. Specialized service providers who have access to larger markets will earn higher returns. One response to this situation may be an increase in the number and diversity of these types of specialized service providers. In the Canada-U.S. integration case, given the geographic proximity of markets, it is entirely reasonable to expect that full labour mobility, together with free trade in services, would lead to joint integration of the service and skilled labour markets in these sectors for reasons similar to those found in the FDI literature.

A MODEL OF LABOUR MARKET SPECIALIZATION AND INTEGRATION

IN THIS SECTION, a variant of the monopolistic competition model of international services trade developed by Harris (1998) is amended to deal with labour market integration. With economies of scale in the production of services and specialization gains to labour, the effects of market integration are quite different than in traditional models of factor movements. Two regimes are considered. In the first one, there is free trade of goods, but no labour mobility in the service industries. In the second — the 'integrated market' regime —, there is mobility of labour and cross-border delivery of services. Business services in this model are treated solely as an intermediate input. There are two factors of production: skilled labour and unskilled labour. Skilled labour inputs are necessarily used in the service sector and, initially, all business services are non-traded.

The model focuses on the economic integration of two countries, labelled Home and Foreign, within a larger global economy, labelled ROW. We assume that both the Home and Foreign countries are geographically proximate and co-exist in an established free trade area. The Home and Foreign economies produce and trade two final goods and use two factors, skilled labour, S, and unskilled labour, L. The Home and Foreign economies are both small relative to the global markets for goods, and thus are price takers in these markets. They practice free trade in goods so there are no tariffs or quotas on imports of goods. Services are initially produced and consumed in each region. One good is referred to as M, or the manufacturing good (also denoted as sector 2); the production of this good uses both skilled and unskilled labour. Unskilled labour is a factor input specific to manufacturing; thus, we think of this sector as a catch-all for traditional traded goods industries. M is a competitive constant-returns sector with the following production function:

(13) $\qquad Y_M = F(L, S_M).$

There is a second sector, referred to as T, the technology sector; it is competitive, has constant returns and uses only business services inputs. Given an n-vector, z, of business services, sector T output, Y_T, is given by:

$$(14) \qquad Y_T = \left(\sum_{i=1}^{n} z_i^\rho \right)^{1/\rho}.$$

The third sector, Business services, is indexed with a b. It has a monopolistic competitive market structure: many firms, each producing a differentiated business service using non-differentiated skilled labour as sole input.

The production function for service i is given by:

$$(15) \qquad z_i = \begin{cases} \dfrac{1}{\beta} s_i \cdots if \cdots f > 0 \\ 0 \quad otherwise \end{cases},$$

where s_i is the variable input of skilled labour to service input i, and f is a fixed input of skilled labour independent of the scale of output. The basic idea here is that skilled labour undergoes a process of differentiation in order to deliver a specific service variety. The fixed input f denotes the time resources necessary for skilled labour to specialize itself in a particular niche. Output, z_i, can be thought of as the services of skilled labour after it has become specialized in task i. Note that skilled labour is used directly in business services, but only indirectly in sector T, as it is used to produce an intermediate input, business services.[19] A property of the production function in equation (14) is that, as labour specialization increases (that is, the number of service varieties rises), overall productivity increases in the producing sector T. This effect is external to upstream firms using and supplying business services, as well as to the downstream user and thus is a genuine type of externality.

Service firms are assumed to be in monopolistic competition. They transform homogenous skilled labour into specialized skilled labour and price by marking up their marginal costs which, in turn, depend on the wage of skilled labour. No two b-sector firms provide the same service. All service inputs are imperfect substitutes from the sector-T buyers' point of view. There is free entry in sector b so that a long-run equilibrium is characterized by zero excess profits on each specialized service. The mark-up on variable costs is just sufficient to cover the cost of producing specialized labour. One can think of this as a return on the service firm's training expenditures. If you think of a service firm as just being a partnership or group of skilled individuals offering a particular service, the firm as a whole produces a particular type of human capital service. Skilled labour is the input in the production of this differentiated human capital.

Consider a single country with an endowment L of unskilled labour and S of skilled labour engaged in goods trade but not in service trade. Both M and T goods are sold at fixed world prices, p_T and p_M. The price of specialized labour service i is q_i. The symmetric monopolistic competition equilibrium (MCE) has n business services produced in quantities $z_i = z$ and prices $q_i = q$. As price equals average cost in the constant-returns T sector, it can be shown, solving the cost-minimization problem, that the price-equal-cost condition can be written as:

(16) $\qquad p_T = c_T = qn^\lambda .^{20}$

Let v denote the wage paid to skilled labour before specialization. Under the assumption of symmetric monopolistic-competition equilibrium in Business services, the price mark-up rule in the representative service firm is:

(17) $\qquad q = \dfrac{1}{\rho}\beta v .$

As skilled labour is the only variable input to services, substituting in equation (16) gives:

(18) $\qquad p_T = \dfrac{1}{\rho}\beta v\, n^\lambda .$

Solving for service sector wages as a function of the price of T and of the degree of labour specialization gives an equation for the (log) skilled labour wage consistent with profit maximization and zero profits in the b and T sectors:

(19) $\qquad \log v_b = \log(\rho\, p_T/\beta) - \lambda\, \log n .$

This wage, v_b, is also the value of the average product of skilled labour in the integrated Technology and Business services sector. From equation (19), it follows that the average product of skilled labour in this integrated sector is raising the level of labour specialization. The zero-profit condition implies that the number of specialties, n, adjusts such that price equals average cost for each service input. Applying the mark-up rule and with price equal to average cost, the equilibrium scale, z, of the representative service firm is:

$$z = \dfrac{f}{\beta}\dfrac{\rho}{1-\rho} .$$

Total skilled labour requirements in sector b are given by $S_b = nf + n\beta z$. Solving for the number of service varieties as a function of the total amount of skilled labour used in services gives the following:

$$(20) \qquad n = \frac{S_b}{f}(1-\rho).$$

Note that the degree of labour specialization, n, is linear in the total quantity of skilled labour used in the Business services sector.[21] Substituting for n in equation (19), we have:[22]

$$\log v_b = k - \lambda \log S_b - \lambda \log f.$$

Given competitive goods, factor market wages in sector M are given by the values of the marginal products. Note that skilled labour working in sector M is non-specialized.

$$(21) \qquad \begin{aligned} v_M &= p_M F_s(L, S_M) \\ w &= p_M F_L(L, S_M) \end{aligned}.$$

Factor market clearing with skilled labour wages equalized across sectors M and b is depicted in Figure 4 (the traditional specific factors diagram), where the horizontal axis represents the total available supply of skilled labour in the country. On the left side, a downward sloping value of the marginal product of skilled labour in manufacturing is drawn (VMP_M), and on the right, a *rising* value of average product schedule for skilled labour in the integrated Technology and Business services sector (AP_b). The equilibrium allocation of skilled labour between the two sectors is determined by the intersection of two schedules. Given an allocation of skilled labour S_b to sector b, the total level of labour specialization is determined by equation (20). An increase in the quantity of skilled labour allocated to services raises the average product of skilled labour in that sector due to a Smithian effect of increasing labour specialization (larger n) in services.[23]

Some simple comparative statics illustrate the properties of the model. A decrease in the relative price of manufactured goods shifts the VMP_M curve down (left), increases skilled labour wages and increases the output of the Technology and Business services sector. A service-biased technological change defined as an increase in the productivity of service inputs raises the AP_b curve. This, in turn, implies an increase in skilled labour wages and a decrease in unskilled labour wages. There is also an increase in the output of services and a

FIGURE 4

SKILLED LABOUR MARKET EQUILIBRIUM

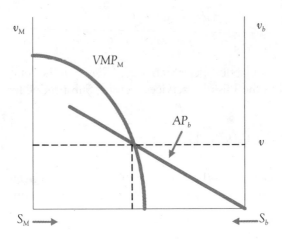

decrease in the output of manufactured goods. The model is generally consistent with the notion of SBTC and with the facts of increased wage inequality due to technological change specialized in the service and technology sectors. The model is also consistent with the more general observation that globalization has brought not only growing wage inequality, but continued growth in the relative size of the service sector. Both the Home and Foreign economies pre-integration can be separately analyzed in this manner. With free trade in goods between Home, Foreign and ROW, *factor prices are not equalized*. For example, if both countries have the same endowment of unskilled labour, L, the country with the larger endowment of skilled labour will have higher skilled labour wages and lower unskilled labour wages.

Thus far, we have assumed free trade in the two goods, M and T, but no trade in services. Suppose that there is a change in the integration agreement such that skilled labour employed in the service sector becomes fully mobile between the Home and Foreign countries and that service firms can now sell their specialized labour services in both markets. In the pre-integration situation, service firms — or more accurately the services they provide — are country-specific. Thus, due to the market constraints, they both sell their outputs and purchase their inputs in the same national market. Under an integration regime, two things happen. First, skilled labour can move between countries so that skilled labour wages are equalized; second, any sector-T firm can purchase a business service from either the Home or Foreign country. Given the CES production function in equation (14), which has a 'love of variety' property, sector-T firms will purchase all available business services.[24] It will also be true that each service firm will specialize in a unique and different task/variety. The number of business service varieties available in each country is now equal to $n*+n$.[25] Service firms will both produce and sell in the domestic market and will also sell in the export market. Specialization leads to two-way trade in business services. Skilled labour mobility ensures that skilled labour wages are equalized across countries and that service prices are equalized. Therefore, one effectively has a fully integrated business services and technology sector (T).

The net effect of this integration is an increase in the average product of labour in services due to a greater degree of labour market specialization within the free trade area. The average product of skilled labour is proportional to the total labour employed in the business services and technology sector as a whole and is given by:

$$\log v_b = k - \lambda \log S_{Tot} - \lambda \log f$$
$$S_{Tot} = S^*_b + S_b.$$

The effect of integration is to raise skilled labour wages and, thus, to reduce unskilled labour wages in both countries. The service and technology sectors expand in both countries while manufacturing contracts. In addition, each country now exports and imports business services with each other, whereas this was not previously possible. The reduction in manufactured exports is offset by an increase in exports of high-technology products to the ROW by both the Home and Foreign countries. In this model, the reduction in unskilled labour wages due to integration is very much a property of the factor-intensity assumption chosen — all unskilled labour is employed in traditional manufacturing and this sector receives no productivity benefits from market integration. Clearly, this particular result would change if either sector M used service sector output or if unskilled labour was employed in both sectors M and T. However, the results indicate that this type of market integration is very much like SBTC in terms of it distributive impact. Factors that are used intensively in sectors that do not benefit from integration-driven changes will lose.

Asymmetric Country Size

In the recent literature on the new economic geography following Krugman (1992), there is the theoretical possibility that free trade can lead to lower incomes in smaller regions given economies of scale and imperfectly competitive market structures. This effect tends to be stronger when factors employed in the increasing-returns sector are more mobile. Could the same effect arise in this model? Suppose that one allowed only labour market integration but not service market integration. In that case, the benefits of increased specialization from trade would be lost, as sector b output would remain non-traded. However, labour market integration would lead to equal wages across sectors, but changes in the supply of skilled labour to each country. This could potentially have very asymmetric effects. Take the case where the Home and Foreign countries are identical in all respects except that the latter has a larger initial endowment of skilled labour. As argued above, prior to opening up the labour market, skilled labour wages would be higher in the Foreign country. Upon removing barriers to movements of skilled labour, workers would move from the Home to the Foreign country. This, in turn, would generate an unstable set of dynamics with falling wages for skilled labour in the Home country and rising wages for skilled labour in the Foreign country, exacerbating the initial difference. The Home country would cease to produce in sectors b and T, with all labour employed in sector M. In this extreme case, the Home country would effectively be de-industrialized. This is a fairly natural consequence given that terms of trade are taken as exogenous, that there are no trade costs and, thus, that the large country can capture all the benefits of service specialization by concentrating all those activities on its territory. More realistically, if the model had a domestic service sector which was an essential input to all sectors or if terms of trade were endogenous, this extreme result from labour market liberalization could be avoided.

But under a simultaneous integration of both service and labour markets, the de-industrialization outcome is quite different — both large and small economies gain.[26] Moreover, smaller countries are disproportionately the largest gainers from integration. This happens because trade provides a mechanism through which productivity gains from size accrue to all firms within the free trade area and are not confined to national boundaries. In the larger country, similar conclusions apply but, quantitatively, the productivity effect is not as important. With respect to trade patterns, the smaller country shows a larger increase in high-technology exports and, as a proportion of total trade, intra-regional business services trade is relatively more important for that country.[27]

How Important is Labour Mobility to Services?

At least in theory, one can imagine a situation where service market integration occurs, but without labour mobility. This would clearly have benefits, if possible. With specialization in labour services and trade in services, much of the productivity benefits to sector T could be captured through trade in service inputs even without labour mobility. But for a wide range of services, it makes no practical sense to speak of exporting or importing without a mechanism through which people who provide a service could interact with their customers. While, in some cases, this can be partially done through electronic media, in a wide range of circumstances it requires the producer (in this case, specialized labour) to go to the location of the customer. If one were to extend this model to two types of services, those requiring proximity of the producer to the customer and those that do not, then prohibiting temporary labour mobility would effectively prohibit or severely limit trade in services requiring producer-customer interaction. In this case, the end result would be more limited international specialization and a larger service sector focused on the domestic market. Much of the gains from service trade would be foregone as a consequence of the restrictions imposed on labour mobility.

GPTS, SKILL-BIASED TECHNOLOGICAL CHANGE AND LABOUR MOBILITY

THE PHENOMENON OF SKILL-BIASED TECHNOLOGICAL CHANGE has received an enormous amount of attention by economists seeking an explanation for the increased wage inequality and growing skill premium. Together with the rapid gains in U.S. productivity being heavily concentrated in a few sectors, sometimes referred to as the New Economy, both are thought to be driven by large-scale and temporally concentrated shifts in the entire technological system based on innovations in ICTs. This type of systemic, economy-wide technological change associated with a few key innovations impacting on all sectors has been labelled by economists a 'general purpose technology' (GPT). The introduction of steam and railways in the last century, of electrification early in the 20th century and, later, of Fordism or mass-production methods are examples of past GPTs. The ICT revolution is also thought to be a key driver behind globalization through effective reductions in the cost of international exchange and business dealings. In this section, the influence of the current GPT on labour markets is reviewed, with some speculation on how these technological trends will impact on the economics of labour market integration in the Canada-U.S. context.

Promises of a new golden age of high productivity growth in the United States have focused considerable attention on the New Economy hypothesis over the last few years. The recent evidence is certainly impressive in the case of the U.S. economy. Average labour productivity grew at an annualized rate of 2.15 percent from 1995 through the first quarter of 1999, after increasing at just over 1 percent from 1972 to 1995. Does this herald the return of the golden age of productivity growth witnessed in the 1950-1970 period, in which productivity grew at a rate of more than 2.5 percent? Thus far, despite the burst in the technology equity bubble, productivity growth in the United States has remained solid.

The ICT-based GPT is also thought to be the principal factor behind the increase in the skill premium in the United States and in the residual wage inequality. In the labour market literature, this class of explanations is summarized as 'skill-biased technological change' (SBTC). In its simplest form, SBTC is an exogenous shift in the production function that raises the demand for skilled labour. The SBTC and GPT explanations have much in common, but the latter, emphasizing both creative destruction and the slow development of commercial innovations that are complementary to ICTs, has more dramatic implications.[28] Simple SBTC theories cannot account for the slowdown and acceleration in growth while GPT theories can. Their differences, however, are less important than their common features. At the popular level, they could all be subsumed under the heading of the New Economy.

We now realize that preceding the advent of the New Economy was the demise, in part, of the Old Economy. This entailed the obsolescence of skills and industries which, in the short term, lead to falling incomes, rising unemployment and painful structural adjustment — effects that figure prominently in modern Schumpeterian theories of endogenous growth.[29] The New Economy hypothesis stresses the causation running from technological change to both growth and wage inequality. More recently, a number of studies have attempted to model in greater detail the changing structure of labour demand resulting from the diffusion of the current ICT-based GPT throughout the economy.[30] These analyses have a number of features in common:

1. New technology increases learning opportunities. Skilled workers are best able to lever the potential benefits of the new technology and to take advantage of learning by doing. However, there is considerable randomness in the process, with some skilled workers switching to the new technology and others, who have substantial sunk investments in an existing technology, less willing to switch. As the diffusion of the GPT accelerates, there is naturally increased dispersion of wages amongst workers with similar education and experience.

2. The ICT-based GPT changes the nature of capital. Capital is generally more flexible than in the old production-line technology. This flexibility, evident for example in numerically-controlled machinery, quality manufacturing circles, just-in-time inventory systems, and so forth, has shifted the relative advantage of custom versus mass production. This has happened in the past. During the first half of the 20th century, the spread of mass production led to larger manufacturing plants. Assembly lines replaced the customizable batch production of skilled craft workers. Milgrom and Roberts (1990) argue that the recent experience of U.S. manufacturing shows that flexible, numerically-controlled machines have allowed plants to operate at a smaller scale. Production has

shifted from the traditional assembly line methods to batch processes using new machines.

3. The move to batch production and flexible manufacturing has changed the nature of labour demand and the organization of work. The early 20th century shift to mass production resulted in the *routinization* of many jobs that required little of the skills once needed to produce the same goods — the *deskilling* phenomenon. With flexible manufacturing and batch production, workers are no longer as highly specialized in a single routinized task. Each batch is highly customizable and requires a worker who can manipulate the modern machinery and make it perform a wide variety of tasks depending on the custom features of the batch. Labour must be able to work with this new type of equipment, which raises the general skill level. Skills make it easier for workers to do a variety of tasks (*multitasking*). At the turn of the century, a skilled craftsman could accomplish a wide variety of tasks needed to complete a given item. On the other hand, a worker on the assembly line has a repetitive and very specific task to perform. Because the work is focused on repeating a single task, problem-solving skills that allow a worker to do a variety of tasks are not required. As the Fordist factory has given way to batch production methods, the set of problems that a worker needs to solve has expanded, increasing the demand for skills. Traditional work arrangements, in which employees perform highly specialized and fragmented jobs, are increasingly giving way to ones where a substantial segment of the workforce performs several tasks. The resulting break-down of occupational barriers reverses a trend that began with the Industrial Revolution, in which efficiency improvements from new machinery were exploited through increasing labour specialization. These advances reinforce the incentives to move from extreme occupational specialization to multitasking. Evidence of these trends is found in a variety of business case studies.[31] In the wage inequality literature, Dunne, Foster, Haltiwanger and Troske (2000) find that investment in computers is an important determinant of wage dispersion across U.S. manufacturing plants during the post-1975 period. Specifically, there is a significant dispersion between wages at high-wage plants with high computer investment and wages at low-wage plants with low computer investment. Since the types of flexible machines that allow for batch methods are closely connected to computers, this suggests that organizational changes linked to these machines are precisely the sort of changes responsible at least in part for SBTC-induced wage inequality.

4. In the economic history literature, this process has been characterized in a variety of ways. A number of accounts emphasize that technological change increases *capital-skill complementary*, as first argued by Nelson and Phelps (1967). One major historical GPT that has received a considerable amount of scrutiny is electricity. Goldin and Katz (1998) provide strong evidence of technology-skill complementarity during the 1910s and 1920s due to the increased demand for skills coming from the introduction of electricity in most manufacturing processes. However, it is also clear that the deskilling consequences of technological change can occur at the same time as real wages grow and as the demand for skills falls over time. The combination of rapid productivity growth and increased skill premiums in recent decades indicates that deskilling has not a characteristic of recent technological change. The current ICT-based GPT has increased the degree of capital-skill complementarity. This, in turn, has raised the relative importance of investment as a source of productivity growth.

5. International trade has also expanded dramatically in recent decades, accompanied by an increasing specialization at the national, industry and plant levels. Feenstra (1998) argues that the rapid growth in outsourcing and trade in intermediate components is evidence of the global nature of this process. Part of this increasing specialization has been attributed to the growing importance of modern methods of production, increased flexibility of capital and the growing skill level of the modern labour force. This type of technology is most prevalent in certain parts of the value-chain, particularly at in the high value-added segments. Not surprisingly, this activity is concentrated in high-income, high-skill countries.

IMPLICATIONS FOR LABOUR MOBILITY

THESE TECHNOLOGICAL AND ORGANIZATIONAL CHANGES are having dramatic effects on the national and global economy. A natural question to ask is what impact will they have on pressures for or against economic integration, and more specifically on the cost-benefit calculation of labour market integration? There are two possible interpretations of the mobility implications of SBTC-GPT trends, depending upon which of the above factors one wishes to emphasize. One option is to focus on the link between flexible manufacturing and the shift from occupational specialization to multitasking. From the small country perspective, this trend ought to be welcome. Small economies are naturally disadvantaged by small domestic markets when economies of scale are important. The *home bias* debate in Canada, as summarized by Head and Ries (1999), suggests that the small-country bias has not been significant for Canada, but it has nonetheless raised some concern. Flexible manufacturing and batch production allow smaller economies to specialize for the purposes of international exchange; at the same time, serving home markets in final goods when either necessary or profitable can be done more efficiently using these methods. Baldwin and Sabourin (2001) and Baldwin, Beckstead and Caves (2001) have documented the increasing use of these types of technologies in Canada. In the labour market, the shift to multitasking carries with it greater demand for skills, but the demand for occupational specialization is reduced. This view takes us closer to a world that looks like the factor-price equalization universe — trade and labour mobility are substitutes, in which case the efficiency gains from labour market integration are reduced.

An alternative view is that globalization, with lower transport and communication costs, has accelerated the trend toward international specialization. Vertical country-specialization within industries implies an even greater interdependence than was the case when mass-assembly methods of production were standard. When countries specialize in particular segments of vertical production chains, their demand is basically determined by the nature of demand for the industry as a whole. Thus, a company supplying a particular type of engine parts in Canada would depend on the overall North American demand for autos, in addition to the fortunes of the specific customers it supplies. In a world of just-in-time inventory and flexible manufacturing, vertical customer-supplier relationships hinge on durability and reliability. These linkages provide powerful short- and medium-term constraints on how quickly a firm, and thus a nation, can re-orient itself in terms of markets. It is entirely possible that flexible manufacturing and vertical specialization are in fact complementary, as reduced scale and flatter organizational structures allow large firms to vertically disintegrate and create new, smaller firms. In labour markets, the existence of a larger number of more specialized firms may or may not increase the degree of occupational specialization in the aggregate, even if it appears to be diminishing at the firm level due to multitasking. New industries often lead to the creation of new job classifications. As the current GPT evolves, it remains uncertain which of these trends will dominate. For small industrial economies, product-line specialization within industries seems an overwhelming trend. Labour may be performing multiple tasks within a firm, but the firm itself, and thus the worker over time, will tend to be highly specialized.

Short of writing down a formal model of this process, we can sketch the general outline of a theory that integrates some of these factors. It is useful to characterize jobs along two dimensions. First, we think of jobs and people as being distinguished by the level of skill, defined as general human capital and the capacity to solve problems. In this sense, increased skill is complementary to flexible capital and ICTs. Workers with more of these types of skills are more likely to be involved in modern production than those with low skills. Jobs can also be distinguished by the degree of occupational specialization. An occupation can be thought of as a particular peg in the division of labour that hinges often on a) a specific skill to carry out a particular task or set of tasks, and b) a specific industry in which the task is performed. Experience, tacit knowledge, and firm-specific human capital are important aspects of this particular dimension of jobs and thus, labour demand. For the economy as a whole, as occupational specialization changes, the total range of occupations describing job opportunities also changes. Major technological changes shift the structure of goods and labour markets in ways that impact on both dimensions, which we can characterize in summary form as a) the general skill level and b) occupational diversity. In the case of small industrial countries, globalization has implications for both dimensions. It clearly has increased the general level of skill demand. However, increased international specialization has also increased the international and, thus, national division of labour.

We can describe this as an increase in the overall degree of occupational specialization in an economy using a two-dimensional diagram, as in Figure 5, where skill is represented on the vertical axis and occupational diversity on the horizontal axis. At a given point in time, an economy faces a potential range of economic structures consistent with its size, average level of development and trade opportunities. It offers a mix of jobs with varying characteristics along these dimensions. The frontier of this jobs mix is indicated in the figure by the curve labelled 'jobs frontier.' This curve slopes upward to the right — economies with a higher average level of occupational skill are able to sustain more diversified employment bases. Different economies face different job frontiers. The curve depicting a larger economy will generally be to the right of that of a smaller economy. Larger markets place fewer constraints on the range of occupations that an economy can support. For specific countries, economic integration and technological change shift the jobs frontier in particular ways, at different points in history. Most recently, these forces — often referred to as globalization — have shifted the jobs frontier in a north-west direction for countries like Canada, as shown in Figure 6. Average skill levels have gone up, but international specialization has brought reduced occupational diversity in smaller economies. One can view the overall globalization trend as a source of substantial economic benefits, but the increase in occupational specialization and skill requirements is a mixed blessing. Higher specialization increases dependency on external markets and the accompanying risk. Jobs become more heavily dependent on external developments. In addition, with more intense industry and occupational specialization, choices within a national labour market become more limited. If a country specializes to the point where entire industries disappear, then occupations that are specific to these industries also vanish.

FIGURE 5

THE SKILL-DIVERSITY FRONTIER

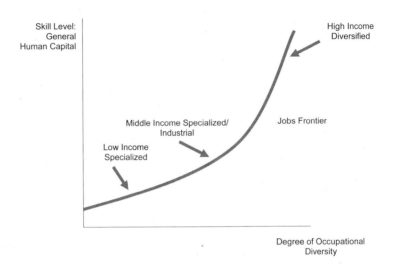

FIGURE 6

SHIFTS IN SKILL-DIVERSITY OPPORTUNITIES DUE TO GLOBALIZATION

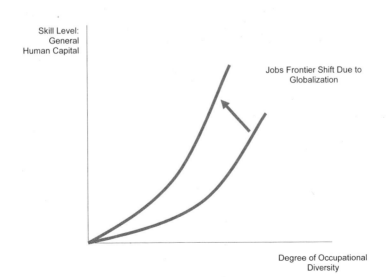

FIGURE 7

LABOUR MOBILITY: IMPACT ON FIRMS VERSUS WORKERS

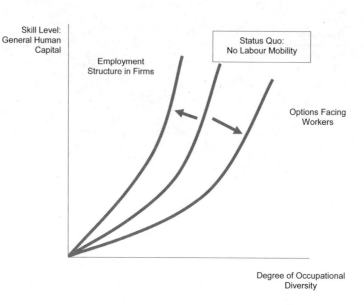

A change in the labour mobility regime by which a small country gains access to a large country labour market plays an important role in shifting the structure of incentives and options facing both firms and individuals. One can distinguish between the jobs frontier facing those supplying labour services from a given economy and the jobs frontier which describes the characteristics of employment in an economy. Increasing the size of the labour market implies reduced constraints on occupational choices imposed by the small domestic economy. An individual wishing to enter an occupation that is only available in the large-country market can do so if there is right of access to that market. Therefore, individual suppliers are faced with a jobs frontier which, from their perspective, has shifted to the right as a result of international labour mobility, as illustrated in Figure 7.

Overall market size for certain types of occupational specializations can be critical. It is difficult for small countries to offer markets that are deep enough to support even a few people in some areas. The need for experts to solve particular problems has created an extensive market for consultants in most industries. Labour mobility allows firms in small countries to access these consultants when necessary. On the other hand, citizens of small countries that wish to become experts are no longer constrained by the size of the domestic market if international consulting is a viable alternative. Therefore, labour mobility provides an effective counterbalance to the forces of occupational specialization that are brought to bear on small countries by globalization.

Firms and industries respond to technological change and the economic opportunities created by trade and market integration by re-arranging their organizational structure, including the nature of jobs within firms. Flexible manufacturing and outsourcing imply that firms can specialize more intensely in individual product lines. Labour mobility and international trade break in part the link between product specialization and occupational specialization. In the absence of a large labour market, firms operating in highly specialized sectors and seeking to expand face supply constraints. These constraints emerge because very specific labour skills are required in a particular niche of an industry. Sourcing by the firm of specialized labour from other regions would be possible if national labour markets were integrated. Therefore, individual firms are likely to become more specialized at some stage in the vertical structure of the industry. The overall increase in organizational and production flexibility places them at a lower risk of losing particular customers, while at the same time allowing them to quickly adjust production to meet the demands of new customers in the same industry. Overall, this may lead firms in the small country to become more specialized but also more human capital intensive. From the demand side, therefore, we can think of the jobs frontier or employment structure in a country's economy as shifting to the left in response to the change in mobility regime, as depicted in Figure 7.

Thus far, the SBTC-GPT literature has been entirely focused on the wage inequality issue with virtually no attention paid to either occupational specialization or the nature of labour adjustment mechanisms, including interregional labour mobility. Economists need to develop more formal theories to deal with the structure of work and link these to economic integration in order to provide policy relevant analyses along the lines indicated here. Increased specialization in product markets should lead to greater heterogeneity in labour market outcomes. Firms in industries that successfully find niches in global markets will provide high-paying jobs; for people employed in firms and industries displaced in the global chain of comparative advantage, the outcome will depend on the ability of the economy to provide new employment opportunities. One policy response would be to increase the overall multitasking skills of the labour force, in the hope that these skills will be valuable in most sectors of the economy and thus allow for greater ease in the process of labour adjustment. However, to the extent that occupational skills are industry- and product-specific, integrated Canada-U.S. labour markets would provide an important adjustment mechanism for Canadians trapped in occupations with few domestic opportunities. This, in turn, should help limit the extent to which inequality increases in response to SBTC.

CONCLUSION

THE ECONOMIC CASE FOR THE LIBERALIZATION of cross-border labour flows is still at an early stage of both theoretical and empirical investigation in the North American context. The essential point of this study is that new analytical frameworks are needed to deal with the key question of the productivity effects of taking NAFTA from a trade and investment agreement to a common market framework in which labour mobility, or more accurately labour market integration, is a legal and practical reality. Traditional static economic analysis focusing on shifts in factor supplies provides little comfort for those seeking to justify greater labour market integration based on economic efficiency criteria. Whatever efficiency gains might be obtained in a framework where national productivity differences are given, the flow of labour from one country to another almost certainly creates significant national losers. This fundamental difference between the case for liberalizing trade and the case for liberalizing labour movements remains an intellectual stumbling block to the rationale for a common market.

Developments in the economic theory of endogenous productivity growth provide an analytical avenue through which this objection might be overcome. In a framework where productivity levels are endogenous to the system, there are potential linkages between labour market integration and economic well-being that make the economic consequences of labour market integration both quantitatively significant and more likely to generate positive as opposed to negative net outcomes. In this study, four alternative ways of linking labour market integration to productivity were explored.

1. In the case of human capital-driven economic growth, labour market integration influences the growth process through its impact on investment in both physical and human capital. It was shown that, in an economic union, labour mobility can lead to an equalization of income levels by equalizing the returns on investment in human capital, when otherwise human capital externalities sustain permanent differences in income levels in a free trade area.

2. It is now widely recognized that international knowledge spillovers are an important determinant of national productivity levels. When knowledge workers participate in global networks, they can potentially mediate the diffusion of knowledge created in large markets to small-country markets. A model of global versus local knowledge workers was developed in which this effect was illustrated. A common labour market with secure and permanent rights of access would encourage greater participation by Canadians in global knowledge labour markets, and give Canadian firms greater access to foreign knowledge workers.

On both counts, this would contribute to faster rates of knowledge diffusion to Canada.

3. The service economy and service trade are of growing importance in all countries. Increases in the quality and variety of intermediate business services are an increasingly important determinant of productivity in downstream user industries, and consequently of national productivity levels. Economic integration of service markets could help or hinder this process. A two-country model of service market integration was developed in which integration-driven service specialization also leads to labour market specialization. In this case, an integrated service market is usefully complemented by labour market integration. While market size economies might potentially lead to the loss of the business services market for a small economy integrating with a large economy, labour mobility in conjunction with service market integration would limit this possible adverse effect. In the model, the smaller economy captures most of the productivity gains from increased specialization when service and labour markets are simultaneously liberalized. This is highly relevant to the Canadian case, where domestic firms are large users of services and the combination of geography and technology allows for increased sourcing of these inputs from the United States.

4. Large-scale technological change driven by ICTs has a significant impact on the distribution of income and economic growth. The emergence of flexible manufacturing and other information-based technologies is claimed to be responsible for higher skill requirements, increased multitasking by workers, and a shift away from highly specific tasks. This reversal in the trend toward greater occupational specialization is occurring at the same time as industries are increasingly specializing vertically within economies. A framework attempting to reconcile these two trends was developed. Individuals who would otherwise be constrained in their occupational choices in a specialized small industrial economy have a larger range of occupational options if labour markets are expanded through a common market. At the same time, firms in small economies that require specialized labour can source from the large-country market when necessary, without foregoing the benefits offered by a less specialized flexible manufacturing system. For both reasons, a small country could realize some significant productivity gains by joining a large country labour market.

At this point in time, significant obstacles remain toward further policy driven Canada-U.S. economic integration, including a possible common labour market. Nevertheless, the European 'grand experiment' will continue to stimulate academic and policy interest on the economic consequences of increased cross-border labour market integration in free trade areas. The linkages between productivity and labour market integration identified in this study should prove to be an important aspect of the overall case for or against policy initiatives aimed at greater Canada-U.S. economic integration.

ENDNOTES

1 Harris and Schmitt (2003) and Zimmermann (1996) provide overviews of the evidence available to date.

2 A useful textbook treatment of this approach is contained in Markusen, Melvin, Kaempfer and Maskus, 1995, chapter 21.

3 Finnie, 2001, provides a useful overview of the evidence on the Canadian brain drain debate.

4 A useful summary of this theory is provided in Markusen, Melvin, Kaempfer and Maskus, 1995, chapter 12.

5 This result extends to the important case of non-traded goods. If productivity in non-traded goods is the same in all countries, then FPE ensures that the prices of non-traded goods will be the same in all countries.

6 See Zimmermann, 1996.

7 When technological differences exist between countries, it is also the case that trade and factor movements are not necessarily substitutes. Holding productivity constant, shifts in factor supplies from one country to another can increase trade. See Markusen, 1983.

8 Some of these arguments have to do with the gains in intertemporal trade that are achieved by unlinking national investment from national saving — thus, by importing capital, poor countries raise investment levels and grow at rates higher than would be feasible if all investments were generated internally.

9 For example, see Caves (1974), Globerman (1979), Blomström and Persson (1983), Blomström and Wolff (1989) and Xu (2000).

10 Harris, 1996, contains a summary of this evidence as it pertains to Canada.

11 Topel, 1999, provides a useful survey of human capital-based growth theories and evidence to date.

12 See Harris, 2001, for a review and discussion.

13 This section is adapted from Harris, 2004.

14 The Canadian demand curve for knowledge workers would be given by the private marginal product of these workers. In this particular model, it would be equal to ΓF_M.

15 To keep the analysis simple, we ignore global knowledge workers who are not in Canada or the United States. This is obviously unrealistic and would need to be amended in any application of the model.

16 The *brain circulation* hypothesis would have been first advanced by Johnson and Regets (1998) in an analysis of the return migration of students who were studying science and engineering in the United States.

17 The next World Trade Organization (WTO) round was intended to deal with multilateral service liberalization with a possible extension of the General Agreement on Trade in Services (GATS). The Seattle 'failure' has cast considerable doubt on this process.

18 Some models that link the degree of specialization to market size include those of Baumgardner (1988), Kim (1989) and Stigler (1951).

19 This specification follows that of Ethier, 1979.

20 The parameter $\lambda = 1 - 1/\rho$ is a negative number. This follows from the requirement that the elasticity of substitution must be greater than one which in turn implies that $-1 < \rho < 0$.

21 For this model to make sense, n must be greater than 1, which places a lower bound on S_b. The diagrams are drawn on a scale that allows to ignore this problem, so the productivity curves for the integrated b-T sector are zero for $n = 0$. If f were very large, then productivity in services would only be positive for some positive finite value of S_b sufficient to cover more than the fixed cost of setting up at least one firm.

22 k is a constant equal to log $(\rho p_T/\beta)$.

23 An increase in the total amount of skilled labour will raise the price of skilled labour, v, and reduce the quantity of skilled labour used in sector M provided the economy produces both M and T. From the determination of w, this would necessarily reduce the wage of unskilled labour. The argument hinges upon assuming a diversified equilibrium, which requires that the VMP curve in sector M cuts the AP curve in sector b from above.

24 Under a CES production function [Equation (14)] with an elasticity of substitution between all pairs of inputs constant and greater than one, competitive firms will always purchase some quantity of all variable inputs. Any increase in the availability of the number of inputs will always lead to some positive demand.

25 Foreign-country variables are indexed with a * superscript.

26 In a geography-style goods trade model, Ludema and Wooton (1999) also find that the likelihood of de-industrialization for small economies can be reduced by factor market integration.

27 It is straightforward to extend the results to countries that differ in size as measured by the unskilled labour force, holding the skilled labour force constant. In this case, the results conform more closely to the neoclassical model. But as in the case analyzed above, integration leads to an expansion of high-technology exports, a rise in skilled labour wages and an increase in intra-regional business services trade.

28 Notably, GPT theories predict that measured productivity slowdowns precede productivity accelerations when a new GPT appears. See the essays in Helpman, 1998, for an elaboration.

29 This class of theories is a major focus of the book by Aghion and Howitt, 1998. The Schumpeterian perspective gives prominence to the process of 'creative destruction' that technological change induces. Other theories emphasizing the role

of investment in large-scale technological change include Greenwood, Hercowitz and Krusell (1997) and Greenwood and Yorukoglu (1997).

30 This literature is growing rapidly. Some of the early studies include Caselli (1999), Acemoglu (1998), Krusell, Ohanian, Rios-Rull and Violante (2000) and Mitchell (2001).

31 Examples are Hammer and Champy (1993), Pfeiffer (1994), Wikström and Norman (1994) and Womack, Jones and Roos (1991).

ACKNOWLEDGMENTS

THIS WORK WAS SUPPORTED BY INDUSTRY CANADA under the North American Linkages research program. The views expressed in the study are solely those of the author. I am grateful to Eugene Beaulieu for comments on an earlier draft. The author can be reached by e-mail at: rharris@sfu.ca.

BIBLIOGRAPHY

Acemoglu, D. "Why Do New Technologies Complement Skills? Directed Technical Change and Wage Inequality." *Quarterly Journal of Economics* 11, 3 (1998): 1055-1089.

Aghion, Philippe, and Peter Howitt. *Endogenous Growth Theory.* Cambridge, Mass.: MIT Press, 1998.

Baldwin, John, and David Sabourin. *Impact of the Adoption of Advanced Information and Communication Technologies on Firm Performance in the Canadian Manufacturing Sector.* MIE Paper No. 174. Statistics Canada, October 2001.

Baldwin, John, Desmond Beckstead and Richard Caves. *Changes in the Diversification of Canadian Manufacturing Firms and Plants (1973-1997): A Move to Specialization.* Research Paper No. 179. Statistics Canada, Analytical Studies Branch, 2001.

Barro, Robert J., and Xavier Sala-I-Martin. *Economic Growth.* New York: McGraw-Hill, 1995.

Baumgardner, James R. "The Division of Labor, Local Markets, and Worker Organization." *Journal of Political Economy* 96 (1988): 509-527.

Bernstein, Jeffrey, Richard Harris and Andrew Sharpe. "The Widening Canada-U.S. Manufacturing Productivity Gap." *International Productivity Monitor* 5, Fall 2002.

Blomström, Magnus, and Hakan Persson. "Foreign Investment and Spillover Efficiency in an Underdeveloped Economy: Evidence from the Mexican Manufacturing Industry." *World Development* 11, 6 (1983): 493-501.

Blomström, Magnus, and Edward Wolff. "Multinational Corporations and Productivity Convergence in Mexico." New York University, 1989. Mimeo.

Caselli, F. "Technological Revolutions." *American Economic Review* 89 (1999): 78.

Caves, Richard. "Multinational Firms, Competition and Productivity in Host Country Markets." *Economica* 41, 162 (1974): 176-193.

Coe, David T., and Elhanan Helpman. "International R&D Spillovers." *European Economic Review* 39, 5 (1995): 859-887.

Coe, D.T., E. Helpman and A.W. Hoffmaister. "The North-South R&D Spillovers." *Economic Journal* 107 (1997): 134-149.

Dunne, T., L. Foster, J. Haltiwanger and K. Troske. *Wage and Productivity Dispersion in U.S. Manufacturing: The Role of Computer Investment.* NBER Working Paper No. 7465. 2000.

Ethier, W. "Internationally Decreasing Costs and World Trade." *Journal of International Economics* 9 (1979): 1-24.

Feenstra, Robert C. "Integration of Trade and Disintegration of Production in the Global Economy." *Journal of Economic Perspectives* 12, 4 (Fall 1998): 31-50.

Finnie, Ross. *The Brain Drain: Myth and Reality — What It Is and What Should Be Done.* Working Paper No. 13. School of Policy Studies, Queen's University. Subsequently published by the Institute for Research on Public Policy in *Choices* 7, 6 (2001): 3-29.

Globerman, Steven. "Foreign Direct Investment and 'Spillover' Efficiency Benefits in Canadian Manufacturing Industries." *Canadian Journal of Economics* 12 (1979): 42-56.

Goldin, C., and L. Katz. "The Origins of Technology-Skill Complementarity." *Quarterly Journal of Economics* 11, 3 (1998): 693-732.

Greenwood, Jeremy, Zvi Hercowitz and Per Krusell. "Long-Run Implications of Investment-Specific Technological Change." *American Economic Review* 87, 3 (1997): 342-362.

Greenwood, Jeremy, and Mehmet Yorukoglu. "1974." *Carnegie-Rochester Conference Series on Public Policy* 46 (1997): 49-95.

Hammer, Michael, and James Champy. *Reengineering the Corporations.* New York, Harper Business, 1993.

Harris, Richard G. "Evidence and Debate on Economic Integration and Economic Growth." In *The Implications of Knowledge-Based Growth for Micro-Economic Policies.* Edited by Peter Howitt. Industry Canada Research Series. Calgary: University of Calgary Press, 1996, pp. 119-155.

———. "The Internet as a GPT: Factor Market Implications." In *General Purpose Technologies.* Edited by Elhanan Helpman. Cambridge, Mass.: MIT Press, 1998, Chapter 6.

———. "The Knowledge-based Economy: Intellectual Origins and New Economic Perspectives." *International Journal of Management Reviews* 3, 1 (2001): 21-40.

———. "Costing the Brain Drain." In *Brains on the Move.* Edited by R.G. Harris, S. Easton and N. Schmitt. Toronto: C.D. Howe Institute, 2004. Forthcoming.

Harris, Richard G., and Nicolas Schmitt. "The Consequence of Increased Labour Mobility within an Integrating North America." In *North American Linkages: Opportunities and Challenges for Canada.* Edited by Richard G. Harris. The Industry Canada Research Series. Calgary: University of Calgary Press, 2003, pp. 313-354.

Head, Keith, and John Ries. *Can Small-Country Manufacturing Survive Trade Liberalization? Evidence from the Canada-U.S. Free Trade Agreement.* Perspectives on North American Free Trade Series, Paper No. 1. Ottawa: Industry Canada, 1999.

Helpman, Elhanan, ed. *General Purpose Technologies*. Cambridge, Mass.: MIT Press, 1998.

Johnson, Jean M., and Mark C. Regets. "International Mobility of Scientists and Engineers to the United States: Brain Drain or Brain Circulation?" Issue Brief. Washington, D.C.: National Science Foundation, Directorate for Social, Behavioral, and Economic Sciences (Division of Science Resources Studies), 1998.

Keller, Wolfgang. *International Technology Diffusion*. NBER Working Paper No. 8573. 2001.

———. "Geographic Localization of International Technology Diffusion." *American Economic Review* 92, 1 (2002): 120-142.

Kim, Sunwong. "Labor Specialization and the Extent of the Market." *Journal of Political Economy* 97, 3 (1989): 692-705.

Krugman, Paul R. *Geography and International Trade*. Cambridge, Mass.: MIT Press, 1992.

Krusell, Per, Lee Ohanian, Jose-Victor Rios-Rull and Giovanni Violante. "Capital-Skill Complementarity and Inequality: A Macroeconomic Analysis." *Econometrica* 68 (2000): 1029-1053.

Lucas, Robert E. "On the Mechanics of Economic Development." *Journal of Monetary Economics* 22 (1988): 3-42.

Ludema, Rodney, and Ian Wooton. "Regional Integration, Trade and Migration: Are Demand Linkages Relevant for Europe?" In *Migration: The Controversies and the Evidence*. Edited by Ricardo Faini, Jaime de Melo and Klaus Zimmermann. Cambridge University Press and Center for Economic Policy Research, 1999.

Markusen, James. "Factor Movements and Commodity Trade as Complements." *Journal of International Economics* 14 (1983): 341-356.

Markusen, J., J. Melvin, W.H. Kaempfer and K. Maskus. *International Trade: Theory and Evidence*. McGraw-Hill, 1995.

Milgrom, Paul, and John Roberts. "The Economics of Modern Manufacturing: Technology, Strategy and Organization." *American Economic Review* 80 (1990): 511-528.

Mitchell, Matthew F. *Specialization and the Skill Premium in the 20th Century*. Research Department Staff Report 290. Federal Reserve Bank of Minneapolis, 2001.

Mundell, Robert A. "International Trade and Factor Mobility." *American Economic Review* 47 (1957): 321-335.

Nelson, Richard, and Edmund Phelps. "Investment in Humans, Technological Diffusion and Economic Growth." *American Economic Association Papers and Proceedings* 56 (1967): 69-75.

Pfeiffer, Jeffrey. *Competitive Advantage Through People*. Boston, Mass.: Harvard Business School Press, 1994.

Razin, Assaf, and Chi Wa Yuen. "Income Convergence within an Economic Union: The Role of Factor Mobility and Coordination." *Journal of Public Economics* 66, 2 (1997a): 225-245.

———. "Factor Mobility and Income Growth: Two Convergence Hypotheses." *Review of Development Economics* 1, 2 (1997b): 171-190.

Stigler, George J. "The Division of Labor is Limited by the Extent of the Market." *Journal of Political Economy* 59 (1951): 185-193.

Topel, R. "Labor Markets and Economic Growth." In *Handbook of Labor Economics*, vol. 3C. Edited by O.C. Ashenfelter and D. Card. Amsterdam: North-Holland, 1999.

Trefler, D. "The Case of the Missing Trade and Other Mysteries." In *American Economic Review* 85 (1995): 1029-1046.

Wikström, Solveig, and Richard Norman. *Knowledge and Value*. London: Routledge, 1994.

Womack, James, Daniel J. Jones and Daniel Roos. *The Machine that Changed the World.* Harper Perenniel, 1991.

Xu, Bin. "Multinational Enterprise, Technology Diffusion and Host Country Productivity Growth." *Journal of Development Economics* 62 (2000): 477-493.

Zimmermann, K.F. "European Migration: Push and Pull." *International Regional Science Review* 19, 1 and 2 (1996): 95-112.

Comment

Eugene Beaulieu
University of Calgary

INTRODUCTION

THE STUDY BY RICHARD HARRIS provides a much-needed overview of the analytical foundations for thinking about the impact of labour market integration between North American countries. Understanding the analytical foundations of labour market integration is an important aspect of the larger debate over deeper integration within North America. The study makes an important contribution because, in spite of the vast body of literature on North American integration, very little ink has been spilled considering the integration of the labour market. The lack of attention paid to issues raised by labour market integration is not just an artefact of the North American context but is pandemic in the economic literature on integration which focuses on international trade in goods and services, and on foreign direct investment (FDI) and international flows of capital.

Of course, there is an important strand of the economics literature focusing on the causes and consequences of one-time migrations. Migration is treated as a permanent movement of labour from one country to another, thus changing relative factor endowments in both countries. However, labour market integration is quite different from a one-time change in factor endowment. It implies that labour is able to migrate between countries in either direction, and that the direction of migration may change over time. Moreover, as the author points out, the traditional approach to migration is usually set in a static neoclassical trade framework.

There are three important reasons why relying on traditional static models is not sufficient. First, these models ignore salient and important aspects of the economy that determine how labour market integration affects economic growth and productivity. Second, the use of static neoclassical models leaves aside advances in theoretical and empirical economics that add a great deal of depth to the economist's tool kit. For example, the so-called *new trade theory* incorporates economies of scale, imperfect competition, multinational enterprises, human capital accumulation, innovation, and international knowledge spillovers. This theoretical approach has been widely used to examine trade in goods and investment integration, but it has not been applied to labour market integration. Finally, examining labour market integration within a static neoclassical model yields the implausible result that an integrated labour market within a free trade area will have no effect on economic welfare.

The most important message of the study is that labour market integration ought to be examined within the framework of dynamic endogenous growth models that incorporate human capital formation and international knowledge spillovers. The study makes three important points with respect to the welfare gains from labour market integration in a free trade area. First, traditional theory suggests that such gains are small or non-existent. Second, to get some additional welfare leverage, gains must come from some type of specialization effects in labour markets that cannot be achieved otherwise through trade in goods or capital. Third, recent work on skill-biased technological change offers some suggestions about the form of technological change that changes the way labour might endogenously choose to become skilled when the labour market is integrated, as opposed to when it is not. Therefore, this conceptual framework might yield some interesting and important consequences for human capital formation in Canada under the status quo, compared to an integrated North American labour market.

The study makes a significant contribution to the literature on economic integration because it forces the reader to consider a range of possible models that provide insight into how labour market integration will impact long-run economic growth. It raises many important questions and lays out a research agenda that should be of interest to academics and policy makers. Currently, the study of labour market integration is in the same intellectual space that international trade theory was 20 years ago — before the widespread adoption of the new trade theory. It is worth noting that Richard Harris was an important actor in the intellectual shift toward applying the new trade theory to trade in goods and services, and a primary catalyst in the adoption of that framework in academic and policy research.

In the following comments, we try to adopt the spirit of the study by bringing into the discussion additional issues and directions for further research. The main theme of the study is compelling, and I am sympathetic to the argument that North American labour market integration should be examined within a non-traditional framework — similar to the study of trade in goods and capital markets. The research agenda on North American integration needs to focus on the potential impact of labour market integration, that is, on the creation of a permanent regime of labour mobility rights within a pre-existing free trade area.

THE TRADITIONAL APPROACH

CLEARLY, THE TIME HAS COME for international economists to examine the labour market and labour market integration in a framework that has caught up with both current reality and the theoretical innovations of the last two decades. As mentioned above, the traditional approach to international labour market integration focuses on permanent migration in a static framework. Within that framework, research efforts have concentrated on examining the impact of one-time migration on factor supplies, and on the real wages and relative wages of skilled and unskilled workers. This framework is generally not suitable for examining the impact of an integrated labour market where workers can move between two countries within the same labour market, as is currently possible within a country. It is worth pointing out that the recent literature on capital mobility differs markedly from studies examining the impact of one-way and one-time capital flows. The capital market literature evolved from the traditional approach of considering one-way capital flows to considering two-way integrated capital markets, where FDI flows in both directions. Research on labour market integration has not, until now, undergone a similar evolution.

Richard Harris argues that a major shortcoming of the traditional theoretical approach is that the estimated economic welfare gain from labour market integration in a free trade area is zero. This is reminiscent of the free trade debate of the 1980s where the gains to Canada from a free trade agreement with the United States, estimated with traditional approaches, ranged from modest to zero. However, as Cox and Harris (1985) revealed in a famous article, the gains may be very large when scale economies and imperfect competition are incorporated into the model. Therefore, the study makes the key point that a conceptual argument for labour market integration within a free trade area must incorporate non-traditional approaches — commonly used in the study of international trade and capital markets. It is important to recognize that empirical evidence running counter to traditional trade models helped motivate and support the research and development of the new trade theory. Similarly, the empirical analysis of labour market integration must incorporate non-traditional conceptual frameworks and push the development of the theoretical modeling.

However, it is also important to realize that much can be learned about labour market integration from extending the traditional framework and focusing on different issues. Recent empirical analyses of labour market integration based on traditional frameworks provide very useful and important insights. In fact, the empirical literature supports Harris's premise that alternative frameworks need to be developed and explored. Perhaps the most well-known example of a traditional approach to migration is the widely cited study by David Card (1990) looking at the large, unexpected migration of Cubans to Miami in what is known as the 1980 Mariel boatlift. The beauty of this study is that it provides a classic natural experiment of the impact of a one-time migration. The 1980 Mariel boatlift of primarily unskilled workers from Cuba translated into a 7-percent increase in Miami's labour force. The pertinent result in Card's analysis is that this large migration of unskilled labour had a very small, if any, impact on the wages of unskilled workers in Miami. This could be interpreted as empirical evidence in support of the traditional approach to migration as depicted in the Heckscher-Ohlin model and summarized by Harris in his study. That is, in a small open *classical* economy with free trade in goods, a large labour migration should have no impact on relative wages.

However, a more recent re-examination of the lack of impact of the Mariel boatlift on wages provides a very different interpretation that is consistent with the alternative approaches discussed and examined by Harris. Lewis (2004) re-examines the Mariel boatlift using evidence on the manufacturing and technology mix in Miami compared to other metropolitan areas in order to shed light on two possible explanations: (i) interregional trade mitigates the local impact of supply shocks; and (ii) production technology rapidly adapts to the local mix of workers. The author tests these alternative explanations by estimating the effect of increases in the relative supply of particular skill groups on the relative growth rate of different industries and on the relative utilization of these skill groups within industries. He finds evidence that the mix of industrial output did not change in response to the migration, but the utilization of unskilled labour in Miami's industries rose proportionately to the increase in supply generated by the migration. Lewis's research implies that city-wide increases in the relative supply of unskilled labour lead to increases in relative factor intensity, with little or no effect on relative wages. That is, there is an endogenous reaction by industries — they adjust their production techniques to local supplies — as predicted by theoretical models of endogenous technological change. Consistent with this interpretation, Lewis also found that on-the-job computer use expanded most rapidly over the 1980s in cities where the relative supply of educated labour was growing fastest.

Other researchers have found similar results. Gandal, Hanson and Slaughter (2004) examine the impact of immigration in Israel. In the early 1990s, Israel experienced a surge of immigration from the former Soviet Union. These immigrants had high relative education levels. The authors look at the mechanisms through which Israel may have absorbed the labour-supply shock triggered by the Russian immigration. Similar to Lewis (2004), they find no evidence that changes in the production mix caused this result. Instead, they find that changes in production techniques more than offset Israel's change in relative factor supplies. Their results are also consistent with the notion of skill-biased technical change.

Additional evidence from Hanson and Slaughter (2002) based on U.S. states is somewhat mixed. These authors examine the mechanisms through which U.S. states absorb labour supply shocks. They find that changes in labour supplies are absorbed through changes in production techniques. However, they also find that changes in the output mix of traded goods helped absorb labour supply shocks. In this case, the authors find that changes in production techniques played a larger role.

Recent empirical evidence from extensions of the traditional framework suggests that this framework can be expanded to incorporate endogenous technological change. As Harris points out, this is a fundamental feature that must be taken into account to understand the consequences of North American labour market integration. However, before engaging in a discussion of endogenous growth models, it is useful to consider what lessons we have gleaned from the *brain drain* literature.

In his study, Richard Harris briefly mentions the brain drain literature, which examined the supposed departure of high-skilled Canadians to the United States during the U.S. technology boom of the 1990s. A number of questions remain unanswered and further research in this area may provide some insights into the effects of a fully integrated North American labour market. Here are some of the remaining questions: To what extent is the brain drain really a problem for Canada? How would a fully integrated labour market impact the brain drain? Harris correctly points out that the traditional static approach to migration is completely inadequate to answer these questions. However, using a dynamic framework to examine the current institutional arrangements may provide some important clues on labour market integration. For example, the impact and consequences of the TN visa program would provide a useful starting point to study some of these issues. This program encompasses a small share of the two countries' labour markets, but it has removed some barriers to migration. Similar research could try to determine whether the Canada Research Chairs Program of the Social Sciences and Humanities Research Council of Canada had an effect on the brain drain. As far as I know, there has been no empirical study of the impact of this program.

A related strand of the literature looking at micro-economic data on employer-to-employer (EE) labour market flows may shed some light on the integration of labour markets. A recent study by Fallick and Fleischman (2004) examines EE flows in the United States and shows that the number of such labour market transactions is large — in fact twice as large as the flow of workers from employed to unemployed status. The authors estimate that two fifths of the new jobs started in the United States between 1994 and 2003 were due to a change of employer. Although they do not explore issues of labour market integration per se, exploiting the Current Population Survey data used in their empirical analysis could provide important insights into these issues.

A further type of empirical evidence that is spawning a distinct strand of literature comes from studies using cities as a unit of analysis, rather than focusing on the growth and productivity of U.S. states and/or Canadian provinces. There are potentially large gains to be reaped from focusing research on cities. A wealth of comparable long-run data is available on a large number of cities in a large number of countries or states. These data have not been fully exploited and are well suited to an empirical examination of dynamic models of growth and productivity. A good example of research conducted along these lines is the recent work of Glaeser and Saiz (2004). These authors examine a panel of U.S. cities over time to explore the relationship between human capital and economic growth. They find that high-skill abundant cities grow faster than low-skill abundant cities because they are becoming more productive (relative to their lower-skilled counterparts). Although the study does not address issues of labour market integration, this type of data could be exploited to that end. Moreover, their results are consistent with the type of endogenous growth models discussed at length in Harris's study. It is worth mentioning that part of the explanation for the higher growth rates of high-skill cities is that they are better at adapting to economic shocks than low-skill cities. Harris does not discuss this possible mechanism in his study, but mentions it in reference to David Wildasin's study also published in this volume.

THE NON-TRADITIONAL FRAMEWORK

PERHAPS THE KEY POINT TO TAKE HOME from Harris's study is that productivity convergence is a likely consequence of liberalizing factor markets, and therefore the dynamics that drive labour market liberalization policy cannot be adequately understood from a simple static analysis. As we argued above, the growing literature based on modified traditional approaches provides compelling empirical evidence in support of this view.

The fundamental issue in considering a policy initiative toward labour market integration is the impact that such integration will have on productivity growth. As is well understood, productivity is an important determinant of economic growth. The productivity issue is particularly significant in the North American case because Canada has lagged behind the United States in terms of productivity. As Harris points out, the Canada-U.S. productivity gap has widened significantly over the last 20 to 30 years — the gap in output per hour went from 14 percentage points in 1977 to 32 percentage points in 2001.

The most relevant material on productivity and growth is the economic growth literature looking at convergence and divergence. A well-known and important contribution to this literature is that of Barro and Sala-I-Martin (1995). Their work was extremely prescient in the case of North American integration. They examine the economic growth and convergence of U.S. states over a long period — U.S. states have different productivity levels and are fully integrated in goods markets as well as in capital and labour markets. The historical analysis reveals that U.S. states do not diverge markedly over time. According to Harris, the important lesson to retain from this analysis is that fully integrated factor markets provide a mechanism that continuously disciplines the processes leading to productivity differences, and therefore set in motion decisions by firms and individuals that seek to restore long-run relative productivity (Harris, p. 548).

While there are no welfare consequences from labour market integration under free trade in goods in the standard static framework, there are such effects in a dynamic endogenous growth model. Harris provides a very useful overview of the Lucas (1988) closed economy endogenous growth model extended to an open economy by Razin and Yuen (1997). In this case, free trade in goods and free capital mobility are insufficient to bring income convergence among countries belonging to a free trade area — free mobility of labour is necessary for income convergence to occur. As Harris argues, these types of models and their extensions provide the correct framework to explore labour market integration in North America.

Other endogenous growth models also provide a useful framework for exploring labour market integration, productivity and growth. Lloyd-Ellis and Roberts (2002) present an endogenous growth model in which both skill acquisition by individuals and innovation by firms contribute to productivity growth. A key feature of this model is that neither skill acquisition nor innovation will, in isolation, drive productivity growth. While the authors do not consider labour market integration, the model could be extended to an open economy framework and used to examine trade and labour market integration. The value added from this would be to adapt the policy analysis capabilities of the model — focusing on the efficacy of growth-promoting measures — to a world characterized by free trade and labour market integration.

OMISSIONS AND THE POLITICAL ECONOMY

ALTHOUGH THE STUDY IS EXTREMELY VALUABLE and lays out an important research agenda, two important themes are absent from that agenda. First, the research program does not include the third North American and NAFTA partner, Mexico. Second, the research agenda excludes discussions of the political economy of labour market integration.

Considerations of labour market integration should include Mexico. This does not mean that research focusing exclusively on Canada and the United States is not valuable in its own right. In fact, for practical and political reasons deeper labour integration between Canada and the United States seems like a feasible and sensible approach. However, for conceptual reasons and to take a more ambitious and longer view of North American labour market integration, Mexico should be included. Moreover, it is worth noting that Mexico was not on the policy radar when Canada and the United States negotiated the FTA, but only five years later we had concluded the monumental NAFTA. Like trade liberalization with Mexico, it is conceivable that some form of labour market integration may become a reality, contrary to conventional wisdom. In any case, it would be useful to probe the consequences of labour market integration for academic and conceptual reasons.

A useful framework emerging from the literature on trade and wages could be extended and applied to issues of labour market integration. Beaulieu, Benarroch and Gaisford (2004b) examine the impact on the wage gap between skilled and unskilled labour of a decline in intra-industry trade barriers *within* a skill-intensive high-tech sector. They develop a simple model that blends the standard Heckscher-Ohlin-Samuelson analysis of inter-industry trade with a technology-driven Ricardian model of intra-industry trade involving varieties of skill-intensive high-tech goods. Trade barriers, in the form of tariffs, act as impediments to intra-industry trade. Within the high-tech sector, comparative advantage rests on international differences in the speed of adoption of new technology styled after Krugman (1985). While there is on-going technological progress in the background, the model generates a simple static equilibrium for all key variables. The model incorporates some features that Harris claims are important for understanding labour market integration. Zhu and Trefler (2004) present a similar model incorporating a continuum of goods based on factor intensity differences across product varieties, rather than technological differences. Their study focuses on how technological convergence or *Southern catch-up* affects wage differentials between skilled and unskilled labour. These models could play a useful role in understanding labour market integration in the

Canada-U.S. context or the Canada-U.S.-Mexico context. The reader is invited to consult Beaulieu, Benarroch and Gaisford (2004b) and Zhu and Trefler (2004) for summaries of this literature.

The work on *technological catch-up* within a differentiated products model — with wage inequality — is a natural segue into a discussion of the political economy dimension. One of the biggest political hurdles facing trade liberalization under FTA and NAFTA was the potential impact of liberalized trade on the labour market. The trade-and-wages debate has evolved toward an understanding that technological change played an important role in the observed growing wage inequality between skilled and unskilled workers. The evidence strongly supports the view that international trade contributed to the increased wage gap as it impacted technology through both trade channels and outsourcing. Beaulieu, Benarroch and Gaisford (2004a) provide a summary of this literature and present a theoretical framework showing how trade liberalization in the manufacturing sector based on intra-industry trade can increase the wages of skilled workers in both skill-abundant and skill-scarce countries. The increased demand for skilled workers in both poor and rich countries induces skill development among their populations.

Note that the key aspect of labour market integration is that it may have important distributional consequences across countries, and raise significant political economy considerations both within and between countries.

THE CHALLENGE OF SMALL NUMBERS

AS POINTED OUT IN THE STUDY and emphasized above, the traditional modeling approach shows no economic gain from labour market integration. This is a conceptual challenge for those who believe that labour market integration would bring large gains to Canada. There are additional hurdles to overcome before policy makers can be convinced to take the politically difficult initiative of promoting labour market integration. Existing empirical evidence would lead one to believe, a priori, that such gains are likely to be small. As the study points out, and Harris and Schmitt (2003) discuss in more detail, the empirical evidence from the European common market shows that labour market provisions have a very small impact. The conclusion from the European case is that even when labour is free to move between countries, very little international migration occurs. It may be too early to draw strong conclusions based on evidence from the European experiment. It is commonly argued that the labour force is much more mobile within long established common markets like the United States. So, one can conclude from existing empirical evidence that any economic gains from North American labour market integration will be very small, or might be larger but take several generations to materialize. This is an inauspicious beginning to a policy debate on a fundamental, and politically sensitive, policy prescription.

CONCLUSION

WHAT DO WE TAKE AWAY FROM THIS STUDY? The traditional approach to migration is not a sufficient framework for analyzing the economic consequences of labour market integration in North America. Research needs to focus on empirical and theoretical frameworks that incorporate dynamic endogenous growth, imperfect competition and scale economies. Within such frameworks, there are potentially large gains from North American labour market integration. Theoretical work should draw from endogenous growth models and macro-economic work on productivity, as well as labour market models and general equilibrium trade models. Empirical work should continue to examine which modeling features are salient and how large are likely to be the effects of labour market integration. The empirical strategy should be broad-based, drawing from computable general equilibrium (CGE) models, micro-economic labour models and macro-economic models. Research also needs to focus on the political economy issues surrounding labour market integration.

BIBLIOGRAPHY

Barro, Robert J., and Xavier Sala-I-Martin. *Economic Growth*. New York: McGraw-Hill, 1995.

Beaulieu, Eugene, Michael Benarroch and James Gaisford. "Intra-Industry Trade Liberalization, Wage Inequality and Trade Policy Preferences." University of Calgary, Mimeo, March 20, 2004a.

——. "Trade Barriers and Wage Inequality in a North-South Model with Technology-Driven Intra-Industry Trade." *Journal of Development Economics* 75, 1, (October 2004b): 113-136.

Card, David. "The Impact of the Mariel Boatlift on the Miami Labor Market." *Industrial and Labor Relations Review* 43, 2 (January 1990): 245-257.

Cox, David, and Richard Harris. "Trade Liberalization and Industrial Organization: Some Estimates for Canada." *Journal of Political Economy* 93 (1985): 115-145.

Fallick, Bruce, and Charles A. Fleischman. *Employer-to-Employer Flows in the U.S. Labor Market: The Complete Picture of Gross Worker Flows*. Finance and Economics Discussion Series, Board of Governors of the U.S. Federal Reserve System, 2004.

Gandal, Neil, Gordon H. Hanson and Matthew J. Slaughter. "Technology, Trade, and Adjustment to Immigration in Israel." *European Economic Review* 48, 2 (April 2004): 403-428.

Glaeser, Edward L., and Albert Saiz. *The Rise of the Skilled City*. Discussion Paper No. 2025, Harvard Institute of Economic Research, 2004.

Hanson, Gordon H., and Matthew J. Slaughter. "Labor-Market Adjustment in Open Economies: Evidence from U.S. States." *Journal of International Economics* 57, 1 (June 2002): 3-29.

Harris, Richard G., and Nicolas Schmitt. "The Consequences of Increased Labour Mobility within an Integrating North America." In *North American Linkages: Opportunities and Challenges for Canada.* Edited by Richard G. Harris. Industry Canada Research Series. Calgary: University of Calgary Press, 2003, pp. 313-354.

Krugman, Paul R. "A 'Technology Gap' Model of International Trade." In *Structural Adjustment in Advanced Economies.* Edited by K. Jungenfelt and D. Hague. London: Macmillan Press, 1985, pp. 35-49.

Lewis, Ethan. *Local, Open Economies within the U.S.: How Do Industries Respond to Immigration?* Working Paper No. 04-3, Federal Reserve Bank of Philadelphia, 2004.

Lloyd-Ellis, Huw, and Joanne Roberts. "Twin Engines of Growth: Technology and Skills as Equal Partners in Balanced Growth." *Journal of Economic Growth* 7, 2 (June 2002): 87-115.

Lucas, Robert E. "On the Mechanics of Economic Development." *Journal of Monetary Economics* 22 (1988): 3-42.

Razin, Assaf, and Chi Wa Yuen. "Income Convergence within an Economic Union: The Role of Factor Mobility and Coordination." *Journal of Public Economics* 66, 2 (1997): 225-245.

Zhu, Susan Chun, and Daniel Trefler. "Trade and Inequality in Developing Countries: A General Equilibrium Analysis." *Journal of International Economics* (2004). (Forthcoming).

Panel III

Assessing the Merit of Easing Further the Movements of Workers Between Canada and the United States

International Labour Mobility, Free Trade and Regional Integration: A Comparison of the European Union and NAFTA

Jean-Christophe Dumont
Organisation for Economic Co-operation and Development

A T A TIME WHEN THE EUROPEAN UNION (EU) is opening its ranks to 10 new countries and when the North American Free Trade Agreement (NAFTA) enters a new phase, this study assesses the consequences of these agreements in terms of international mobility. Using the European example, we explore the prospects for deepening NAFTA and related migration issues.

THE LINKS BETWEEN REGIONAL INTEGRATION AND MIGRATION

WORK CONDUCTED at the Organisation for Economic Co-operation and Development (OECD/WIFO, 1997), based on regional analyses (OECD, 1994, 1998a, 1998b and 2000), has highlighted the links between regional integration, economic development and international migrations. These studies could now contribute to shed light on some of the issues associated with a broadening of the European Union and a deepening of NAFTA.

Regional integration is interpreted here as a process of trade intensification within a *de jure* or *de facto* group of countries (Alba, Garson and Mouhoub, 1998). The creation of free trade areas, of areas where capital and/or people are free to move, and of monetary unions represents a succession of steps on the way to a complete economic integration. In the second half of the 20th century, OECD countries have taken many initiatives in this regard, seeking to benefit from the expected economic effects of a removal of customs barriers, and for the European Union in particular, to also modify in a sustainable way the geopolitical (dis)equilibriums that marked the history of European nations.

In this context, the link with international migratory movements is both direct and indirect. Even when regional integration agreements remain (almost) silent on the international mobility of individuals, as is the case, for example, of the Asian Free Trade Area (AFTA), Mercosur and the association agreements signed between the European Union and countries bordering the southern shore of the Mediterranean, we can theoretically expect a reduction in the incentive to emigrate.

The classical theory of international trade, as formulated in the HOS (Heckscher-Ohlin-Samuelson) model, shows effectively that international trade and factor movements are substitutable (Mundell, 1957).[1] A country where labour is relatively abundant, and thus relatively less expensive, could as easily export goods that have a high ratio of low-skilled labour as it could export its own workers. The removal of customs barriers between countries that have comparable production techniques reduces differences in the returns to factor and, consequently, the incentive to migrate between these countries.

However, such analyses have attracted a number of criticisms that relate to: i) the underlying hypotheses of the classical model of international trade (perfect competition, constant returns to scale, technological symmetry, lack of essential specific factors); and ii) the micro-economic foundations of factor mobility (solely determined by return differentials at a point in time). Several theoretical studies[2] have shown that, even with a marginal departure from the standard model, free trade does not necessarily result in factor-price equalization, and that trade and migration appear complementary. Unfortunately, empirical surveys or models do not provide a definitive answer to this question.[3]

FREEDOM OF CIRCULATION AND ESTABLISHMENT AT THE HEART OF THE EUROPEAN UNION CONSTRUCTION

WITH RESPECT TO THE CONSTRUCTION of the European Union, it is useful to recall first the implementation schedule of the arrangements that have led to the Common Market. In fact, while the principle of freedom of circulation and establishment was enshrined in the 1957 treaty that created the European Economic Community (EEC) and was integral to the philosophy underlying the construction of the European Union, trade-opening measures have systematically preceded the freedom of circulation for people. The latter only came in 1968 for the six founding states (Germany, Belgium, France, Italy, Luxembourg and the Netherlands), in 1988 for Greece, and in 1992 for Spain and Portugal. Thus, founding members had to wait 10 years, Greece 7 years, and the Iberian countries 6 years to have access to this provision. Indeed, the initial delay imposed on the six founding countries was essentially motivated by institutional obstacles related to the progressive nature of the European integration process.[4] However, in the case of subsequent member countries, this delay was a safeguard measure justified by a deteriorating employment situation in existing member countries and by the fact that the former were then countries of emigration. Such delays were not imposed on countries that joined the European Community at more favourable times.[5] Notwithstanding the constraints imposed on some candidate countries, the notion of establishing a regional integration area in order to limit potential migration flows was obviously not contemplated when the European project was initially conceived.[6]

In this context, what lessons can be learned from the process of European regional integration on relevant aspects of the freedom to circulate? In our view, five general observations emerge:

First Finding:
While European integration has made much progress, intra-European migration flows are limited...

Today, intra-European mobility is low, in spite of important and persistent differences in labour market conditions (for example, unemployment is relatively high in Spain, Germany and France, but much lower in the United Kingdom and the Netherlands). Intra-European migration flows represent less than 0.2 percent of the total EU population, while migratory movements between the nine census regions of the United States represent 1.5 percent of their total population. The low intra-European mobility is explained, in part, by a lack of incentives and the presence of linguistic, cultural and institutional barriers (Vandamme, 2000; Kendall, 2001). It is also due to structural labour-market rigidities in each member state. In fact, despite being higher than inter-state migration, interregional mobility within member countries is also low. Approximately 1.2 percent of employed persons changed residence in 1999 (European Commission, 2001).

In 2001, the proportion of nationals from EU member states in total immigration flows represented approximately 78 percent for Luxembourg, 45 percent for Belgium and 27 percent for Sweden and Portugal (see Table 1). In other EU countries, the levels are much lower. More than 34 percent of Europeans expatriated in another EU country were living in Germany, compared to 16 percent in the United Kingdom.

An analysis of intra-European mobility based on nationality shows a wide diversity reflecting primarily cultural and linguistic affinities (Germans in Austria and conversely, French and Dutch nationals in Belgium, Finns in Sweden and conversely). Historical links also play an important role, as in the case of Portuguese and Italian nationals in France, and of Italian nationals in Austria.

The European Union clearly intends to increase mobility between member states in order to reduce disparities among employment pools and to ensure a more efficient allocation of labour and skills. Various measures have already been taken, for example the freedom of movement for people not in the labour force, for students[7] and for retired persons, as well as a set of directives on the recognition of qualifications and access to public sector jobs, until now restricted to nationals. The European Commission recently launched an ambitious action plan to eliminate any remaining administrative and legal barriers, to increase the transferability of complementary pension entitlements of migrant workers, and to improve certification systems for regulated professions.

As can be seen, worker mobility in a barrier-free area is not automatic. In a monetary union — given the difficulties associated with using migration from third countries to respond to short-term labour market fluctuations (OECD, 2001a) — it is crucial to increase the internal mobility of human resources.[8] This has direct consequences for policy coordination and harmonization, particularly in the fields of education, employment and taxation.

Second Finding:
...but migration flows between member countries have virtually disappeared with the implementation of a freedom of circulation regime.

We cannot point to the principle of freedom of circulation, adopted in 1968, to explain Europe's convergence, even if we can show that Italian immigration during the 1950s and 1960s helped to close the gap in living standards between Italy and its European partners.[9] As can be seen in Figure 1, migration flows of Italian nationals to France ended as early as 1967, and shortly after in Germany, coinciding with the first oil shock. During the 1970s, the development of Northern Italy accelerated and the region was able to absorb the population ready to emigrate from the Mezzogiorno.

TABLE 1

INTRA-EUROPEAN MOBILITY, 2001
IMMIGRATION FLOWS BY NATIONALITY, AS A PROPORTION OF THE TOTAL FLOWS OF EUROPEAN UNION NATIONALS

	HOST COUNTRY														
	Austria	Belgium	Denmark	Finland	France (1998)	Germany	Greece (1998)	Italy (2000)	Luxembourg	Netherlands	Portugal	Spain	Sweden	United Kingdom	Total
Austria	—	0.7	1.7	1.4	1.0	9.6	3.6	3.9	0.6	1.6	1.0	1.0	1.1	1.8	4.1
Belgium	0.8	—	2.1	1.2	6.7	1.8	3.2	3.6	17.2	8.2	3.3	4.5	1.2	0.8	2.7
Denmark	1.0	1.3	—	4.2	1.4	2.1	3.6	2.1	2.1	1.7	1.2	1.2	21.3	6.1	3.0
Finland	1.3	1.3	5.4	—	1.1	2.2	4.1	2.0	1.0	1.9	0.9	1.6	28.9	0.9	2.6
France	3.7	27.1	8.7	7.7	—	11.2	14.7	21.4	24.5	9.6	12.9	9.9	5.6	28.4	14.8
Germany	61.9	9.7	20.0	13.5	10.7	—	26.2	23.9	7.6	22.6	15.7	21.4	13.8	28.2	15.3
Greece	2.5	1.9	1.5	2.3	1.4	13.4	—	5.1	0.8	3.8	0.3	0.3	2.9	9.8	7.0
Ireland	0.7	1.2	1.6	1.8	2.0	1.7	1.0	1.3	1.6	2.5	1.0	1.7	1.4	0.9	1.5
Italy	10.0	8.2	8.3	5.4	13.8	23.9	9.1	—	7.0	6.8	7.1	12.4	3.8	1.7	12.2
Luxembourg	0.4	0.7	0.0	0.1	0.3	0.6	0.1	0.1	—	0.1	0.3	0.1	0.0	0.0	0.3
Netherlands	3.8	27.5	7.1	4.2	3.1	7.0	6.6	4.7	2.3	—	7.8	4.7	4.2	4.5	6.9
Portugal	2.6	4.5	1.4	0.7	31.9	7.7	0.3	3.1	26.5	6.3	—	6.1	0.6	7.7	6.8
Spain	2.0	5.1	8.4	5.0	9.2	7.2	0.9	11.9	1.8	6.1	29.3	—	3.3	4.8	5.5
Sweden	3.1	1.7	17.5	37.5	2.5	2.5	7.1	3.5	1.6	2.4	1.6	3.2	—	4.5	3.3
United Kingdom	6.2	9.0	16.3	15.0	15.1	9.2	19.5	13.1	5.4	26.3	17.6	32.0	11.9	—	14.2
Total, Citizens of the EU	100.0	100.0	100.0	100.0	100.0	100.0	100.0	100.0	100.0	100.0	100.0	100.0	100.0	100.0	100.0
% of Total	4.7	8.5	2.1	0.5	1.8	34.4	0.8	3.0	2.5	6.4	1.5	14.3	3.4	16.3	100.0

TABLE 1 (CONT'D)

INTRA-EUROPEAN MOBILITY, 2001
IMMIGRATION FLOWS BY NATIONALITY, AS A PROPORTION OF THE TOTAL FLOWS OF EUROPEAN UNION NATIONALS

| | HOST COUNTRIES | | | | | | | | | | | | | | |
	AUSTRIA	BELGIUM	DENMARK	FINLAND	FRANCE (1998)	GERMANY	GREECE (1998)	ITALY (2000)	LUXEM-BOURG	NETHER-LANDS	PORTUGAL	SPAIN	SWEDEN	UNITED KINGDOM	TOTAL
Percentage of Total Inflows of Foreigners	22.1	45.0	22.0	16.3	6.1	17.6	22.9	5.5	78.3	23.7	26.8	12.7	27.0	21.4	26.2
Total Flows, 2001 (France, 1999)															
Foreigners from the EU (% of All Foreigners)	14.9	66.6	20.7	17.7	36.6	25.6	6.2	10.5	86.1	30.1	27.5	30.4	38.5	36.1	
Foreigners from the EU (% of Total Population)	1.3	5.5	1.0	0.3	2.0	2.3	0.4	0.3	31.8	1.3	0.6	1.0	2.1	1.6	

Source: Eurostat, *New Cronos*.

FIGURE 1

ITALIAN IMMIGRATION IN GERMANY AND FRANCE

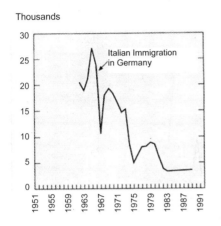
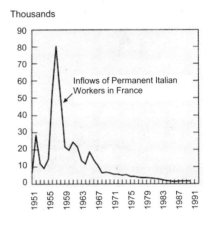

Source: Tapinos, 1994.

The case of other important emigration countries, such as Spain, Portugal and Greece, is similar. These countries had long-established links with Western European countries, especially through migration. Migration flows from Spain to France (Figure 2) began to reverse around the mid-1970s, long before this country signed an agreement to join the European Community. In fact, the incentive to emigrate fell substantially in the wake of the political changes that took place during the post-Franco era in Spain and as the country's economy was catching up and benefited from substantial inflows of foreign investment that bolstered job creation and closed the wage gap. Identical processes were at play in Greece and Portugal. Today, all of these countries are immigration destinations.

Third Finding:
Migration flows from third countries are still important...

Immigration from less-developed countries with strong migratory potential dominates the migration flows of most European countries (see Figure 3). The dawn of the colonial era[10] and the rising prosperity of Europe during the long postwar expansion stimulated job-related immigration from non-European countries. Migration flows to France and Belgium from the Maghreb

FIGURE 2

RELATIVE INTENSITY OF EXCHANGES AND OF
MIGRATION FLOWS BETWEEN SPAIN AND FRANCE

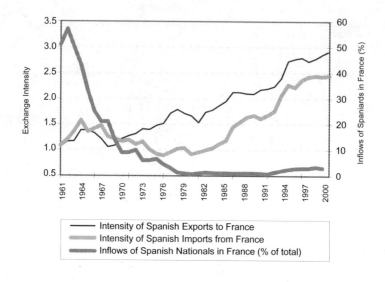

Source: Dumont and Garson, 2002.

and sub-Sahara regions of Africa, to Germany from Turkey and Yugoslavia, and to the United Kingdom from the Indian sub-continent were all part of this trend. Neither the European integration process nor the pro-active policies adopted to recruit foreign labour have substantially altered this pattern (Tapinos, 1994).

Immigrants from the southern region of the Mediterranean basin, and especially from the Maghreb, make up a large group in some EU countries (including the new immigration countries of Southern Europe). In spite of the long-standing nature of migratory movements and the geographic proximity of Europe, migration issues have not been tackled in regional integration agreements between the European Union and the three Maghreb countries (Barros and Garson, 1998).

FIGURE 3

EVOLUTION OF IMMIGRATION FLOWS BY COUNTRY OF ORIGIN IN SELECTED EUROPEAN OECD COUNTRIES, 1990-2000 AND 2001 (10 MOST IMPORTANT COUNTRIES OF ORIGIN IN 2001, AS A PERCENTAGE OF INFLOWS)[a]

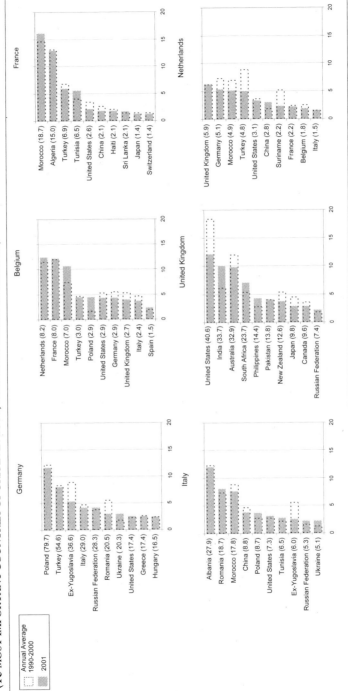

Note: a   Inflows for 2001, in thousands of persons, appear in parenthesis.
Source: *Tendances des migrations internationales*, OECD, 2003.

Fourth Finding:

... even from countries with which the European Union has signed free trade agreements.

Work undertaken for the OECD on the regional integration process of Mediterranean countries with the European Union (OECD, 1998a) have shown that the removal of customs barriers is not sufficient to reduce the incentive to emigrate in the short to medium term.[11] Recent migratory movements between Southern European countries and countries on the southern shore of the Mediterranean — with which the European Community has signed partial free trade agreements,[12] — are a case in point. Using a computable general equilibrium model, Cogneau, Dumont and Izzo (1998) show that only a more comprehensive regional integration, involving massive financial transfers for public expenditures having the potential to generate positive externalities (infrastructure and investment in human capital) could significantly alter migratory patterns in this area in the medium to longer term.[13] This is in fact what happened in the case of Portugal (Ramos, 2000).

Fifth Finding:

The impact on international mobility of expanding the European Union to include countries from Central and Eastern Europe.

The prospects for expanding the European Union[14] have re-activated the debate on the appropriate delay that should be imposed on new candidate countries, but the principle of freedom of circulation has not been challenged. Germany and Austria, among others, have expressed fears about potential massive inflows of labour from Central and Eastern European countries (CEEC). The European Commission signed an agreement with candidate countries providing for a transitory period of up to 7 years (2+3+2), during which access to the labour market of EU countries will be restricted. However, many countries have recently considered opening their border unilaterally to nationals from future EU member countries and giving them free access to their labour market as early as D-day. This is the case for Sweden and, under certain conditions, for the United Kingdom and Ireland. Specific quotas for nationals of new member countries are also expected in the Netherlands and Italy. However, these countries reserve the possibility of waiving these measures in light of the future evolution of their job markets.

Recent studies aimed at assessing the impact of EU expansion on the migration of workers all lead to the same conclusion: east-west flows will not have a major impact on the labour market of today's 15 member states; in the long term, these movements could fall, or even be reversed. Results of a report sponsored by the European Commission and published by the European Integration

Consortium indicate that the proportion of the population originating from the CEEC will rise significantly, but this increase will take place over many years (Boeri and Brücker, 2001). If the accession of new members occurred now, approximately 335,000 additional persons would settle in the EU-15, but this number would gradually fall in subsequent years. Based on these estimates, the contingent originating from CEEC would represent only 3.5 percent of the total EU population in 30 years. Another study estimated these flows at between 267,000 and 336,000 persons per year (Hille and Straubhaar, 2001). Assuming that Hungary, Poland and the Czech Republic would accede to the EU in 2005, the Austrian Economic Institute (WIFO) predicted that the number of migrants from the three countries would reach 144,000 that year but would fall afterwards (Breuss, 2001). However, these results largely depend on the efforts that EU member countries would be willing to make to quickly integrate candidate countries, especially through structural funds. In the case of Ireland and Portugal, an effective use of structural funds from the European Community has allowed these countries to modernize their infrastructure and increase investment in human capital from the day of entry into the Union. These two factors have largely contributed to attracting foreign capital, which has played a key role in the process of economic and technological catch-up that eventually reversed migration flows.[15]

However, the most important challenge associated with the free movement of people in the case of CEEC is perhaps improperly assessed: the lack of transitory measures could expose candidate countries to the impact of free mobility more directly than member countries. In effect, if international labour movements increasingly involve skilled workers, the prospect of extending freedom of circulation in the short to medium term could trigger a large increase in migration of skilled or highly skilled individuals from new member countries. These migrants could result in shortages of qualified labour in their countries of origin, when the latter are at a critical stage in their efforts to join the international trade community and to enter the process of regional economic integration.

TOWARDS A DEEPENING OF NAFTA

STUDIES CONDUCTED AT THE OECD on the effects of the North American Free Trade Agreement, which took effect in 1994, are generally in line with work conducted elsewhere. They have led to the conclusion that, on the one hand, the fears expressed when the free trade agreement came into force were essentially unfounded (Weintraub, 1998; Kirton, 1998; Venturini, 1998) and, on the other hand, that the gains expected would be moderate and, in any case, insufficient to fundamentally alter the incentive to migrate (Sobarzo, 1998; Hinojosa-Ojeda, McCleery and de Paolis, 1998).

Estimates of the impact of free trade from computable general equilibrium models generally show positive welfare effects, albeit very modest.[16] Similarly, gravitational models based on *ex post* econometric estimates show that NAFTA only had a limited impact on bilateral trade flows.[17] Krueger (1999) summarizes this work by concluding that data collected so far confirm the initial prediction of most economists: the impact of NAFTA was relatively modest in the United States, while for Mexico, the evolution of trade flows up until now do not provide a very strong basis to the argument that NAFTA had serious trade-diversion effects.

It seems however that Canada has benefited more from the liberalization of trade, and in particular from increased foreign direct investment, especially in terms of productivity gains in the manufacturing sector (Trefler, 2001). Similarly, Helliwell (1997), and Helliwell, Lee and Messinger (1999) show that the implementation of NAFTA substantially lowered the "border effect" between Canada and the United States by stimulating international trade.

Migratory movements between the three countries have been largely dominated by the flows from Mexico to the United States, which have not fallen to any extent with trade liberalization (see Table 2 for an illustration based on legal migration flows). In 1950, Mexican workers represented 0.5 percent of the labour force in the United States; in 1990, the proportion was close to 4 percent and, in 2000, it had almost doubled again. This proportion is clearly higher for specific geographic areas or economic sectors. In this case, it can be argued that migratory movements have already contributed to broadening the process of regional economic integration, but without sufficient impact to accelerate the convergence of economies and, more precisely, of the Mexican economy towards the other two NAFTA economies. It appears that migration flows alone cannot initiate a development process that will ensure greater convergence between the country of origin and the host country of migrants.

However, NAFTA allows some professionals to work temporarily in another member country (with a TN visa) if they have a *bona fide* job offer, without prior clearance based on the non-availability of local manpower resources. The visa application can be made directly at the border and is processed immediately. Entry visas are issued for a period of one year but can be renewed indefinitely. There are no quantitative quotas for Canadian nationals, but the number of Mexicans who can apply for a visa of this type is currently limited to 5,500 per year. This ceiling was to be abolished in January 2004, along with the provision governing wage conditions (wages must be comparable to those usually offered on the U.S. labour market). An increase in the emigration of skilled Mexican workers to the United States is thus expected. In 2000, close to 89,900 Canadians professionals (60,700 in 1999 and approximately 93,000 in 2001) and slightly less than 2,500 Mexicans entered the United States with a

TABLE 2

MEXICAN EMIGRATION TO THE UNITED STATES

YEAR	EMIGRATION OF MEXICANS TO THE UNITED STATES (THOUSANDS)	PERSONS WHO BENEFITED FROM THE 1986 REGULARIZATION UNDER THE IMMIGRATION REFORM AND CONTROL ACT (THOUSANDS)
1993	126.6	17.5
1994	111.4	4.4
1995	90.0	3.0
1996	163.7	3.6
1997	146.9	2.0
1998	131.6	0.7
1999	147.6	–
2000	173.9	0.3
2001	206.4	0.1

Source: *Tendances des migrations internationales*, OECD, 2003.

TN visa. Under this regime, the immigration of Mexicans and Americans in Canada is substantially smaller and totalled no more than 10,100 persons in 2000. On the other hand, migration to Mexico is quite strong: in 2000, more than 170,000 Canadian and U.S. nationals holding a NAFTA visa were registered in that country.

The issue of skilled labour mobility under NAFTA has raised fears in Canada about a *brain drain* to the United States. In the 1990s, Canada suffered a net loss of skills to its U.S. neighbour, especially in sectors linked to the new information and telecommunications technologies and in the health sector. However, the size of this loss must be interpreted in relative terms as the number of migrants to the United States is estimated at between 22,000 and 35,000 persons annually (Zhao, Drew and Murray, 2000), which represents approximately 0.1 percent of the Canadian population.[18] Nevertheless, there has been an acceleration of Canadian migration to the United States since the implementation of NAFTA (De Voretz and Laryea, 1998), primarily among highly-educated and well-paid young people. However, these losses are partly compensated by immigration to Canada from European and Asian countries. In addition, several studies tend to demonstrate that these outflows are likely of a temporary nature, representing a *brain exchange* phenomenon rather than strictly a *brain drain*.[19]

The mobility of skilled workers under NAFTA was envisaged as a means to expand trade between Mexico, the United States and Canada, and not to promote permanent immigration (Globerman, 2000). In other words, the intent was to facilitate the mobility of professionals (related to foreign direct investment flows) or employee transfers within multinational enterprises. The criteria governing TN visas were defined with this objective in mind, especially with regard to categories and qualification levels.[20] In this context, facilitating mobility between Canada, Mexico and the United States raises a number of questions. Work undertaken at the OECD and the European experience can shed some light on the three following questions:

First Question:
Deepening or extending NAFTA: Different challenges in terms of international labour mobility?

While an easing of some of the mobility conditions that apply to workers would be feasible in the context of NAFTA, e.g. for new professions (particularly those related to commercial activity), the simplification of border controls[21] or the transferability of retirement plans (Gunderson, 2001), in other cases a redefinition of the Agreement's objectives would be required. As such, the Agreement does not seek to promote social and political integration. Only the economic dimension is addressed, in a logical framework that differs significantly from the one that inspired the construction of the European Union — which involved a process of harmonization and financial transfers (structural funds) not found in NAFTA. Easing migration for medium-skilled professions would require, for example, a review of certification processes in both Canada and the United States. Moreover, a complete liberalization of borders for nonskilled workers would probably raise issues related to fiscal harmonization, social benefits and the functioning of the labour market.

While the European experience demonstrates that, with the required political will, it is possible to make quick progress in some of these areas, it is also clear that such widening of the regional integration process would focus attention on the asymmetry among partner countries — in terms of size, development stage and challenges. Again, it is useful to point to the key role played by structural funds in the European integration process.

On the question of matching national interests, while Canada may look primarily to its natural and most important trading partner, the United States,[22] the latter, with more than 35 million Hispanic residents — 20.6 million originating from Mexico — faces substantially different geopolitical and social challenges. This does not mean that concerns expressed in the three countries are incompatible; but if these concerns were naturally converging when NAFTA was first negotiated, it seems more difficult to reach a consensus now on the need to pursue the regional integration agenda involving a greater liberalization of labour movements.

Consequently, we think that expanding NAFTA to Central and Latin America is a more attainable and probable objective, notwithstanding all the progress that would have to be made before other countries join NAFTA, as was evident at the end of the third Summit of the Americas held in Quebec City, in April 2001.[23] Chile, which signed a free trade agreement with Canada in 1997[24] and with Mexico in 1998, and which has always expressed its interest in joining NAFTA, is a telling example. In this perspective, issues pertaining to the mobility of individuals will undoubtedly play an important role, even if the U.S. Congress has decided to exclude from upcoming trade talks any migration-related topics.

Conversely, implementing a limited process of deeper integration between Canada and the United States would probably contradict some of the initial objectives of NAFTA, especially in terms of the convergence of standards of living and its consequences on migration flows from Mexico in the long term.

Second Question:
What role could play the regional dimension of international migrations in the process of North American integration?

The process of regional integration in North America takes place in a fundamentally different institutional setting than the one characterizing the construction of the European Union, a difference linked to the future of federalism among participating states. In this case, the issue of international mobility takes a larger regional dimension. The main North American economic regions overlap national borders. This is the case, for example, of the region made up of Seattle and Vancouver (the *Cascadia* region), the region encompassing Michigan, Ontario and New York State (the *Golden Horseshoe* region) or even, to a lesser extent, the region covering California and Baja California.

To our knowledge, there has been no detailed assessment of the impact of NAFTA on regional development and on the international mobility of people.[25] However, given the level of industrial and technological concentration, we can infer that in the absence of compensating mechanisms, regional disparities are likely to increase (OECD, 2001b) and the attraction of economic centres will gradually intensify. To the extent that foreign labour is more mobile, it is more directly concerned by this trend (Borjas, 2001). In this context, even though it has not really happened yet, we could witness growing integration of transborder labour pools, which would encourage an adjustment of the practical conditions surrounding the international mobility of people to the specific needs of each region.

With 85 percent of its population living close to the U.S. border, Canada is directly affected by this evolution. The fact that Quebec now trades more with the United States than with the rest of Canada provides another illustration of the nature of issues raised by a deepening of NAFTA (Lisée, 2001).

In this perspective, the provinces will no doubt play an increasingly important role in multilateral negotiations on the deepening and broadening of NAFTA. This tendency is even more visible in regions that have a relative autonomy in dealing with migration flows, as is the case of many Canadian provinces. This process is generally symmetrical with the one observed in the construction of the European Union, where regionalization is an increasingly important issue and where transborder migration plays a predominant role in intra-European mobility.

Third Question:
What would be the effects of relaxing NAFTA's international mobility provisions on policies governing migration with third countries?

Migration policy in the United States is based on the principle of family preference, while remaining relatively open to the migration of skilled workers. Canada's migration policy is based on a selection process, although the family and humanitarian dimensions play an equally important role. A priori, the two systems tend to converge, and studies have shown that immigrants to Canada are not more skilled, on average, than those who settle in the United States.

The prospect of even a partial liberalization of migratory movements between the three partner countries beyond the categories currently considered would impact Canada and the United States differently.

Contrary to the situation that characterized the expansion of the European Community to include Southern European countries, it is clear that Mexico has not yet completed its "migratory transition." In fact, despite the restrictions imposed on mobility and the tightening of border controls, Mexican migration to the United States remains high. Part of this flow is linked to older migratory movements that predate the signing of NAFTA. However, unskilled labour needs, especially in the U.S. agricultural sector (attraction factor), the persistent poverty of part of Mexico's population, and a weak convergence process (incentive factor) are still driving Mexican migration dynamics (Thoreau and Paracini, 1998). In this context, we could expect that an "unconditional" opening of the North American labour market to Mexican workers would trigger significant population movements. Beyond issues of feasibility, such a scenario may have only a limited impact on the macro-economic equilibrium of the U.S. labour market (OECD, 2001a), but would probably have important social and budgetary consequences. Under this scenario, Mexico would probably be lead to reinforce its border controls, thereby limiting transitory labour movements from Central and Latin America to the United States.

In the event of a symmetrical opening of the North American market, it is unlikely that Canada would receive very large inflows of Mexican workers. In part, this assumption may be based on the characteristics of migrant networks or the nature of manpower needs. At any rate, two things could happen, one linked to an accelerating migration of skilled Canadian workers to the United States, especially in the intermediate skill categories, and the other linked to the inflow of less-skilled U.S. nationals who might be attracted by the level of social protection available in Canada. However, the magnitude of these trends is highly speculative, and could well remain limited. This is at least what the history of the formation of the European Union suggests.[26]

While more specific studies are required on this aspect, it seems that a greater opening of North American borders would have a significant and direct impact on Canadian migration policy and on the role that it could eventually play in support of the country's long-term economic development.

CONCLUSION

THE REGIONAL INTEGRATION PROCESSES in Europe and North America are fundamentally different for many reasons (OECD, 1998b), especially the role played by international migration. The philosophy underlying the construction of Europe promotes directly a multidimensional integration of member states; consequently, it has followed an adaptative policy that involved public upgrading investments in the less prosperous countries or regions, an effort to ensure progressive harmonization across the board, as well as freedom of circulation and establishment for people.

In the case of NAFTA, the objectives were fundamentally different, primarily oriented towards maximizing the expected economic benefits from a liberalization of trade and investments, while seeking to limit over time the incentive to emigrate for Mexican workers. Of course, the migration of skilled workers was facilitated, but the intent was primarily to expand economic exchanges. In this context, a deepening of the regional integration process would require a change of philosophy towards NAFTA that appears unlikely in the short term.

In a sense, and despite their differences, members of the European Union and NAFTA partners are more directly interested in the broader issues linked to the expansion of free trade areas and regional integration areas to new countries. On this aspect, lessons learned from past experiences show that concerns generally expressed, especially about the international mobility of individuals, are overestimated to a very large extent (OECD, 2001c).

Another obviously neglected issue is the regional dimension of the international mobility of people within regional integration areas. In this regard, regional authorities are expected to play an increasing role, particularly in multilateral talks and in the day-to-day management of the practical aspects of international mobility, two areas that are usually the prerogative of federal and central governments.

At the international level, the European experience has shown that regional integration does not necessarily reduce migration flows from third countries. For this reason, cooperation among member states in managing migratory movements is crucial, a fact further emphasized by recent security concerns. The fact that Mexico, a country of transit, receives a growing number of migrants from Central and Latin America reinforces this finding.

Finally, we should keep in mind that migration flows are very large in the NAFTA space, notwithstanding the restrictions imposed on the mobility of persons. This situation is much like the one observed during the construction of the European Union, i.e. migratory movements preceded the process of regional integration, even if access to freedom of circulation for individuals came after free trade. This leads us to stress the importance of migrations in initiating the process of regional integration. All considered, the historical examples of Canada and the United States, on the one hand, and of Mexico and the United States, on the other, do not contradict this analysis.

ENDNOTES

1   The notion of complementarity/substitutability has two distinct meanings (Wong, 1995):
    - Quantitative aspect: movements of goods and factors are said to be substitutes if an increase in international trade reduces factor movements and/or if an increase in factor movements reduces international trade.
    - Equalization of factor prices: movements of goods and factors are said to be substitutes if free trade of goods leads to an equalization of factor prices and/or if the free movement of factors leads to an equalization of prices for goods.
2   See, among others, Markusen (1983), Schiff (1994, 1995), Markusen and Venables (1996), and Lopez and Schiff (1995). See also Simon (1989) for a discussion of the relevance of a symmetrical treatment between exchanges of goods and migration.
3   Some have attempted to assess empirically the nature of the relationship between free trade and migration. For example, Abowd and Freeman (1991) show that in the United States, the proportion of foreign workers has a positive correlation with the level of sectoral protection, regardless of the sector. Straubhaar (1988) and Molle (1994) analyze the linkages between trade in the European Community (which was expanding between 1958 and 1980) and migrations between countries

of that area (which were decreasing over the period) and conclude that movements of goods have gradually replaced movements of workers. However, the results presented in Faini and Venturini (1993) show that protectionist policies in industrialized countries have increased the incentive to migrate. The authors conclude that trade liberalization in industrialized countries could make a significant contribution towards reducing migratory pressures. Conversely, Wong (1988) shows that, in the U.S. case, the inflow of immigrants stimulates imports and exports. Similarly, Collins, O'Rourke and Williamson (1997), using historical data on a large number of western OECD countries for the period 1870-1940, reject significantly the substitutability hypothesis between migration and trade. For detailed reviews of these studies, see Assous (2000) and Schiff (2000).

4   We should remember that, at the time and until at least the mid-1970s, European countries were quite open to migration and had proactive policies to recruit foreign workers. Germany signed bilateral agreements to recruit workers in Italy (1955), Spain and Greece (1960), Turkey (1961), Morocco (1963), Portugal (1964), Tunisia (1965) and Yugoslavia (1968). Switzerland signed an agreement with Italy in 1948 and, subsequently, with Spain and Portugal. France received mainly African nationals, while the United Kingdom accepted people originating from India and Pakistan.

5   Citizens from the United Kingdom, Ireland and Denmark, countries that entered the EEC in 1972, benefited immediately from the freedom of circulation and establishment regime. The same could be said of Austria, Finland and Sweden upon their entry in the European Union in 1995. Note, however, that free mobility areas already existed between Ireland and the United Kingdom, as well as between the Scandinavian countries (Denmark, Finland, Iceland, Norway and Sweden — the passport agreement between Nordic countries). In 1996, when Denmark, Finland and Sweden entered the Schengen area, Iceland and Norway, who are not members of the European Union, negotiated cooperation agreements with the Schengen member states, but the Nordic free mobility area was maintained. Most of the countries mentioned (except Ireland) had not been countries of immigration for some time when they joined the European Union. They were also closer to the European average than the countries of Southern Europe.

6   In contrast, it is true of the association agreements signed by the European Union, which are thus more directly comparable to the situation prevailing under the North American Free Trade Agreement.

7   Intra-European mobility for students has increased substantially over the past few years, particularly through the influence of numerous specific programs such as Erasmus, Socrate (I and II) and Leonardo.

8   However, Puhani (1999) indicates that given low intra-European mobility and the inertia of migration flows, it is unlikely that international mobility within the European Union will provide a response to asymmetric shocks in *Euroland*.

9   International migrations have played a dominant role in intra-European convergence at the end of the 19th century and the beginning of the 20th century (see O'Rourke and Williamson, 1995; and Taylor and Williamson, 1997).

10　Relatively important flows were observed during the decolonization period with, for example, the return to France of more than one million persons from Algeria, or the return to Portugal of 800,000 persons from Angola and Mozambique.

11　Note, however, that free trade agreements did not initially include the agricultural sector.

12　See Channawi (1998) for a description of the free trade agreement between the EU and Morocco, and Mahjoub (1998) for the Tunisian case.

13　In the short term, we can even contemplate a surge in migration linked to a less stringent budgetary constraint for some potential migrants (Cogneau and Tapinos, 1995).

14　In 1993, the European Council held in Copenhagen developed the principles governing the extension of the European Union to several Central and Eastern Europe countries (CEEC). Negotiations were undertaken with the five most economically advanced countries in 1998 (Poland, the Czech Republic, Hungary, Estonia and Slovenia — the Luxembourg Group) and, in February 2000, with five other countries (Bulgaria, Lithuania, Latvia, Romania and the Slovak Republic, — the Helsinki Group). Malta (1990), Cyprus (1990) and Turkey (1987) also expressed their intention to join the European Union. The most recent initiative to expand the European Union, which is restricted to 10 new member countries (Estonia, Latvia, Lithuania, the Czech Republic, the Slovak Republic, Hungary, Slovenia, Poland, Cyprus and Malta), became effective on May 1st, 2004.

15　See Cogneau, Dumont and Mouhoub (2000) for a theoretical discussion of the linkages between migration, convergence and foreign direct investment.

16　However, departing from the neoclassical framework may produce more significant results. See Robinson and Thierfelder (1999) for a review of the literature.

17　See, for example, the overview given in Burfisher, Robinson and Thierfelder (2001).

18　The average number of workers emigrating to the United States in 1996 and in 1997 as a percentage of the total workforce shows that the most affected occupation is that of medical doctors, whose rate of emigration was around 0.8 percent (approximately one quarter of new graduates); however, the ratio does not exceed 0.3 percent for engineers and 0.07 percent for computer scientists (see Zhao, Drew and Murray, 2000).

19　The phenomenon was highlighted for Canadian graduates in 1995 (Frank and Bélair, 1999). The study shows that of a total of 300,000 graduates, 4,600 emigrated to the United States (1.5 percent) but after four years, almost one quarter of these migrants had come back. Among those who emigrated, 57 percent went to the United States to find employment, 23 percent to continue their studies, and 17 percent to get married or pursue a personal relationship. Of these emigrants, 57 percent held a TN visa.

20　The groups involved were:
- Investors: a) who wish, in a supervisory or executive capacity or for the performance of tasks requiring essential skills, to conduct significant goods or services trade primarily between the territory of the Party of which they are citizens and the territory of the Party specified in the application for admission, or b) who wish, in a supervisory or executive

capacity or for the performance of tasks requiring essential skills, to establish, develop or administer an investment, or to provide advice or technical services that are essential to the operation of the investment to which they or their firms have committed, or are committing, a significant sum of money;

- Employees transferred within a multinational firm;
- Professionals: people who provide a predetermined professional service as salaried employees of a firm in their country of origin, as defined in a list (www.nafta-sec-alena.org/english/nafta/chap-162.htm#Ap1603.D.1), and who have completed four years of university education or hold a bachelor's degree (licence). Under certain conditions, three years of professional experience may be equivalent to one year of university studies.

21 In December 2001, Canada and the United States signed a joint declaration to implement a *smart border* between the two countries. Among expected improvements, this should facilitate border movements for people who have already been cleared, through the use of electronic systems.

22 Helliwell (2001) offers an interesting analysis of the asymmetry of perceptions between Canada and the United States.

23 Earlier summits took place in Miami in 1994, and in Santiago in 1998.

24 Like NAFTA, this agreement foresees the possibility for Chilean professionals and employees of multinationals to work temporarily in Canada. However, quotas remain extremely low: in 2000, only 26 Chilean nationals obtained a work visa of this type (compared to eight in 1998 and 1999).

25 See Richardson (2002) for an analysis of the special case of the Vancouver-Seattle area.

26 However, one can argue that, in the North American context, cultural and linguistic barriers to international mobility are lower, and in the absence of harmonization, the supply of social services — particularly in the health sector — and fiscal structures will eventually become more dissymmetrical.

ACKNOWLEDGMENTS

OPINIONS EXPRESSED IN THIS STUDY are the sole responsibility of the author and do not necessarily reflect those of the OECD or of its member countries. I would like to thank Jean-Pierre Garson and Georges Lemaître for their helpful comments on an earlier version of this document.

BIBLIOGRAPHY

Abowd, J.M., and R.B. Freeman. *Immigration, Trade and the Labour Market*. University of Chicago Press, 1991.

Alba, F., J.-P. Garson and E.M. Mouhoub. "Migration Policies in a Free Trade Area: The Issue of Convergence with the Economic Integration Process." In *Migration, Free Trade and Regional Integration in North America*. Paris: OECD, 1998.

Assous, L. "Intégration régionale et flux migratoires : revue critique de la littérature récente." In *Mondialisation, migrations et développement*. Paris: OECD, 2000.

Barros, L., and J.-P. Garson. "L'Union européenne face aux pays tiers du bassin méditerranéen." In *Migrations, libre-échange et intégration régionale dans le bassin méditerranéen*. Paris: OECD, 1998.

Boeri, T., and H. Brücker. *The Impact of Eastern European Enlargement on Employment and Labour Markets in the EU Member States*. DIW, CEPR, FIEF, IGIER, HIS, Berlin and Milano, 2001.

Borjas, G. *Does Immigration Grease the Wheels of the Labour Market?* Presentation to a meeting of representatives of the Instituts nationaux de recherche économique (NERO). Paris: OECD, July 6, 2001.

Breuss, F. *Macroeconomic Effects of EU Enlargement for Old and New Members*. WIFO, Working Paper No. 143, April 2001.

Burfisher, M., S. Robinson and K. Thierfelder. "The Impact of NAFTA on the United States." *Journal of Economic Perspectives* 15, 1 (Winter 2001).

Channawi, L. "Les enjeux du libre-échange pour l'emploi et les migrations au Maroc." In *Migrations, libre-échange et intégration régionale dans le bassin méditerranéen*. Paris: OECD, 1998.

Cogneau, D., and G. Tapinos. "Libre-échange, répartition du revenu et migrations au Maroc." *Revue d'économie du développement* 1 (1995).

Cogneau, D., J.-C. Dumont and P. Izzo. "Intégration régionale, investissements directs et migrations dans l'espace euro-méditerranéen : enseignements d'un modèle d'équilibre général calculable." In *Migrations, libre-échange et intégration régionale dans le bassin méditerranéen*. Paris: OECD, 1998.

Cogneau, D., J.-C. Dumont and E.M. Mouhoub. "Intégration régionale, migrations, croissance et investissements directs étrangers." In *Mondialisation, migrations et développement*. Paris: OECD, 2000.

Collins, W., K. O'Rourke and J. Williamson. *Were Trade and Factor Mobility Substitutes in History?* NBER Working Paper No. 6059. 1997.

DeVoretz, D., and S. Laryea. "Migration and the Labour Market: Sectoral and Regional Effects on Canada." In *Migration, Free Trade and Regional Integration in North America*. Paris: OECD, 1998.

Dumont, J.-C., and J.-P. Garson. *Migration et échange international*. La Documentation française, Cahier français n° 307, 2002.

European Commission. *Employment in Europe. Recent Trends and Prospects*. Brussels, 2001.

Faini, R.J., and A. Venturini. "Trade, Aid and Migration: Some Basic Policy Issues." *European Economic Review* 37 (1993): 435-442.

Frank, J., and E. Bélair. *South of the Border. Graduates From the Class of 95 Who Moved to the United States*. Ottawa, Statistics Canada, 1999.

Globerman, S. "Trade Liberalization and the Migration of Skilled Professionals and Managers: The North American Experience." *The World Economy* 23, 7 (2000).

Gunderson, M. "North American Economic Integration and Globalization." In *The State of Economics in Canada: Festschrift in Honour of David Slater*. Montreal and Kingston: McGill-Queen's University Press, 2001.

Helliwell, J. *National Borders, Trade and Migration*. NBER Working Paper No. 6027. 1997.

——. "Canada: Life Beyond the Looking Glass." *Journal of Economic Perspectives* 15, 1 (Winter 2001).

Helliwell, J., F.C. Lee and H. Messinger. *Effects of the Canada-United States Free Trade Agreement on Interprovincial Trade*. Perspectives on North American Free Trade Series, Paper No. 5. Ottawa: Industry Canada, 1999.

Hille, H., and T. Straubhaar. *The Impact of the EU Enlargement on Migration Movements and Economic Integration: Results of Recent Studies in Migration Policies and EU Enlargement*. Paris: OECD, 2001.

Hinojosa-Ojeda, R., R. McCleery and F. de Paolis. "Economic Effects of NAFTA: Employments and Migration Modelling Results." In *Migration, Free Trade and Regional Integration in North America*. Paris: OECD, 1998.

Kendall, V. *Labour Mobility: It Is Not That Easy*. London: The Economist Intelligence Unit, 2nd quarter 2001.

Kirton, J. "NAFTA Foreign Direct Investment and Economic Integration: A Canadian Approach." In *Migration, Free Trade and Regional Integration in North America*. Paris: OECD, 1998.

Krueger, A. *Trade Creation and Trade Diversion Under NAFTA*. NBER Working Paper No. 7429. 1999.

Lisée, J.-F. "Is Quebec a North American Region-State?" *Policy Options* (December 2001).

Lopez, R., and M. Schiff. *Migration and the Skill Composition of the Labour Force: The Impact of Trade Liberalisation in LDCs*. The World Bank, Policy Research Paper No. 1493. August 1995.

Mahjoub, A. "La zone de libre-échange entre la Tunisie et l'Union européenne." In *Migrations, libre-échange et intégration régionale dans le bassin méditerranéen*. Paris: OECD, 1998.

Markusen, J.R. "Factor Movements and Commodity Trade as Complements." *Journal of International Economics* 14 (1983): 341-356.

Markusen, J.R., and A. Venables. *The Theory of Endowment, Intra-industry, and Multinational Trade*. NBER Working Paper No. 5529. April 1996.

Molle, W. *The Economics of European Integration: Theory, Practice, Policy*. Aldershot: Darmouth Publishing Company, 1994. Chapter 9.

Mundell, R.A. "International Trade and Factor Mobility." *American Economic Review* 47 (1957): 321-335.

OECD. *Migration et développement : un nouveau partenariat pour la coopération*. Paris: OECD, 1994.

——. *Migrations, libre-échange et intégration régionale dans le bassin méditerranéen*. Paris: OECD, 1998a.

——. *Migration, Free Trade and Regional Integration in North America*. Paris: OECD, 1998b.

——. *Mondialisation, migrations et développement*. Paris: OECD, 2000.

——. *Perspectives de l'emploi dans les pays de l'OCDE, juin 2001*. Paris: OECD, 2001a.

——. *OECD Territorial Outlook*. Paris: OECD, 2001b.

——. *Migration Policies and EU Enlargement*. Paris: OECD, 2001c.

——. *Tendances des migrations internationales.* Paris: OECD, 2003.

OECD/WIFO. *Migration, Free Trade and Regional Integration in Central and Eastern Europe.* Paris: OECD, 1997.

O'Rourke, K., and J. Williamson. *Around the European Periphery 1870-1913: Globalization, Schooling and Growth.* NBER Working Paper No. 5392. 1995.

Puhani, P. *Labour Mobility an Adjustment Mechanism in Euroland?* IZA Discussion Paper No. 34. 1999.

Ramos, M. "L'intégration économique du Portugal dans l'Union européenne : effets sur les investissements directs, les migrations et l'emploi." In *Mondialisation, migrations et développement.* Paris: OECD, 2000.

Richardson, K. *Sieve or Shield? NAFTA and its Influence Within Canada,* RIM Working Paper No. 02-16. 2002.

Robinson, S., and K. Thierfelder. *Trade Liberalization and Regional Integration: The Search for Large Numbers.* Institut international de recherche sur les politiques alimentaires, Document de discussion TMD No. 34. 1999.

Schiff, M. *How Trade, Aid and Remittances Affect International Migration.* The World Bank, Policy Research Paper No. 1376. November 1994.

——. "Politique commerciale et migration internationale à court terme." *Revue d'économie du développement* 1 (1995): 3-5.

——. "Migration Nord-Sud et commerce : une revue de la littérature." *Revue d'économie du développement* 3 (2000): 3-54.

Simon, J. *The Economic Consequences of Immigration.* Oxford: Basic Blackwell, 1989.

Sobarzo, Fimbres H. "Applied General Equilibrium: The Mexican Experience of NAFTA." In *Migration, Free Trade and Regional Integration in North America.* Paris: OECD, 1998.

Straubhaar, T. "International Labour Migration Within a Common Market: Some Aspects of EC Experience." *Journal of Common Market Studies* 27, 1 (1988): 44-62.

Tapinos, G. "L'intégration économique régionale et ses effets sur l'emploi et les migrations." In *Migration et développement : un nouveau partenariat pour la coopération.* Paris: OECD, 1994.

Taylor, A., and J. Williamson. "Convergence in the Age of Mass Migration." *European Review of Economic History* 1 (1997).

Thoreau, C., and T. Paracini. "Demographic Situation, Employment and Economic Performance in North America." In *Migration, Free Trade and Regional Integration in North America.* Paris: OECD, 1998.

Trefler, D. *The Long and Short of the Canada-US Free Trade Agreement.* NBER Working Paper No. 8293. 2001.

Vandamme, F. "Labour Mobility Within the European Union: Findings, Stakes and Prospects." *International Labour Review* 139, 4 (2000).

Venturini, F.M. "NAFTA Foreign Direct Investment and Economic Integration: A Mexican Approach." In *Migration, Free Trade and Regional Integration in North America.* Paris: OECD, 1998.

Weintraub, S. "NAFTA Foreign Direct Investment and Economic Integration: A United States Approach." In *Migration, Free Trade and Regional Integration in North America.* Paris: OECD, 1998.

Wong, K.-Y. "International Factor Mobility and Volume of Trade: An Empirical Study." In *Empirical Methods For International Trade*. Edited by Robert C. Feenstra, Cambridge, Mass.: MIT Press, 1988.

——. *International Trade in Goods and Factor Mobility*. London and Cambridge, Mass.: MIT Press, 1995.

Zhao, J., D. Drew and S.T. Murray. "Exode et afflux de cerveaux : migration des travailleurs du savoir en provenance et à destination du Canada." *Revue trimestrielle de l'éducation* 6, 3 (2000).

Transborder Mobility of Highly-Qualified Labour

Robert Lacroix
University of Montreal

I WOULD LIKE TO DISCUSS THE BROAD ISSUE of transborder mobility between Canada and the United States using an example with which I am familiar: the mobility of highly qualified workers. This example might be of some interest to you as this type of mobility will represent a key challenge for Canada over the next decade.

In the area of university research and education, the mighty United States is a powerful catalyst that today attracts more Canadian researchers and professors than Canada is able to attract from that country. But contrary to what we may think, things have not always been that way.

In the 1960s and 1970s, the baby-boom generation was massively entering university and it became necessary to recruit large numbers of new teachers. During the 1960s, the number of faculty positions more than tripled in Canada, and 19 new universities were created. New university departments were then created entirely on the strength of academics recruited in the United States. The Vietnam War caused serious tensions and many U.S. university professors chose to pursue their career in Canada.

At the same time, a large number of Europeans, primarily from Britain and France, entered the scientific and academic fields in Canada, attracted by better research and working conditions than those offered in their countries.

This migration from abroad was so important that, for a while, it was perceived as a threat. In 1981, the Canadian government even considered it necessary to impose quotas on the immigration of foreign academics in Canada. For open teaching positions, the law gave preferential treatment to Canadian candidates, requiring universities that wanted to recruit foreign candidates to prove that no Canadians could meet the selection criteria.

Looking at future growth and needs, Canadian universities will experience between now and 2010 a situation similar in all respects to the one prevailing in the 1960s and 1970s. First, they will face again a tremendous surge in the student population. As in the 1960s, universities will have to adjust to strong demographic pressures, which will be exacerbated by an ever rising proportion of young people — especially young women — enrolled in higher education. A university curriculum has become a pre-requisite for a wide spectrum of jobs, and the structure of the labour market creates strong incentives to pursue graduate studies. For these reasons, it is estimated that university enrolment will have grown by almost 30 percent by the end of the decade.

To accommodate this large increase in the student population, universities will be forced, as in the 1960s, to allocate a significant portion of their resources to their teaching staff. This task will be complicated by the fact that universities will not only have to create new faculty positions, but also replace approximately 20,000 professors who will retire between now and 2011. Moreover, Canadian universities are expected to play a key role in the federal innovation strategy, a role they will not be able to fulfill without increasing substantially their research staff. In total, universities may have to recruit between 30,000 and 40,000 new academics over the next 10 years.

While the demand conditions on the labour market are quite similar to those that universities faced 40 years ago, the international context is entirely different and clearly less favourable now. In fact, the university landscape has changed dramatically, and candidates to faculty positions can now literally choose the institution where they would like to work.

And their options extend well beyond the borders of their native country. Today, Canada is just one of many countries where foreign researchers and professors could pursue their career. Why move to Vancouver, Montreal or Toronto, rather than Tokyo, Lyon or Los Angeles? While Canada remains a country of immigration, it will not be able to rely, as in the past, on a providential inflow of foreign academics eager to leave their country.

This assessment applies directly to the select group of Ph.D. holders — the main pool of recruitment for universities. The knowledge economy attracts an increasingly qualified workforce out of graduate studies programs. Of the 4,000 persons who receive a Ph.D. in Canada each year, almost 60 percent find employment in the private sector or in the civil service — that is, outside the university environment. Even if we doubled the number of Ph.Ds. granted,

Canadian universities would not be able to train a sufficient number of candidates to fill the large number of positions that will be opened in coming years.

In addition to the non-university labour market, U.S. universities are also attracting Ph.D. graduates. The Institute of International Education indicated recently that the number of Canadians who pursue studies in the United States has increased by 38 percent over the last 10 years. And, a study by the National Science Foundation shows that, between 1996 and 1999, 55 percent of Canadian students who received a Ph.D. in the United States subsequently stayed in that country.[1]

Without waving the threat of a brain drain, as we are too often inclined to do, we can insist on the increasing demand for highly-skilled people in Canada, and on the need to take appropriate action to meet this demand. Failing to do so, the academic community could face a serious skill shortage, which would compromise the quality of teaching and research work.

How can we avoid the expected skill shortage? What strategy could we adopt to retain Canadian academics, or to attract foreign academics? I can only see one answer to these questions: Our universities must become competitive on the international scientific market and they must become more attractive for Canadian and foreign students and professors.

There are numerous and varied ways to increase the attractiveness of our institutions. Working conditions, compensation and taxation levels are all potential incentives, but they are not the only factors at play, and more importantly, they are not the most decisive. For a researcher whose life has essentially been dedicated to science, an innovative and challenging research environment often represents a more important advantage than compensation or working conditions. As for knowledge development, a generous compensation does not mean much if one is not well supported and well equipped. Only projects with an international scope can create an ideal research environment. Without mobilizing projects, there can be no competitive research environments and no international visibility.

Theses projects necessarily require a critical mass of high-level researchers who can work in a highly collaborative climate. This is particularly true in scientific fields such as engineering or biomedicine, where a concentration of human and technical resources is a pre-requisite to innovation.

I will give here one example: the *Institut de recherche en immunovirologie et en cancérologie*, recently created by the University of Montreal. This innovative project will bring together an outstanding group of researchers, offering them a high-technology platform to which they would not otherwise have access. This initiative is made possible through a strategic combination of resources provided by the University of Montreal and the Quebec government, in addition to input from some visionary Canadian government programs, such as the Canada Research Chairs Program and the Canada Foundation for Innovation.

A new facility, equipped with scientific instrumentation whose value rivals the cost of the building ($48M), will open its doors to researchers a year from now. Eventually, 400 graduated students, postdoctoral trainees and research professionals will work together under the guidance of 30 professor-researchers, 18 of whom hold a Canada Research Chair. Students will benefit from an unparallel coaching system, and will be constantly exposed to state-of-the-art biomedical research.

As this example illustrates, we must have something to offer in order to attract or retain academics and graduates students: well-equipped laboratories, competent teachers and motivated students.

But in the case of foreign graduates and professors, we must also be in a position to effectively recruit candidates. The restrictive legislation mentioned earlier on the hiring of foreign professors was adopted in a context that no longer exists today, where we are witnessing a globalization of university programs. Human Resources Development Canada has recently undertaken to relax these legislative provisions by allowing simultaneous posting — in Canada and abroad — of positions to fill. This bold initiative is a first step towards a faster integration of foreign candidates in the Canadian academic community.

The attractiveness of an institution is measured by two criteria: its scientific capital, inherited from the past, and its projects, which are future-oriented. Reputations rest on the first criteria, but they expand through the second. Canadian universities have a scientific and institutional heritage that is the envy of their counterparts all over the world. But it is through the research projects they undertake that Canadian universities will be able to consolidate their favourable position on the international scene and to supply the country with the highly-skilled manpower needed to participate fully in the knowledge-based economy.

ENDNOTE

1   The same study reports on a survey, conducted among foreign Ph.D. holders enrolled in U.S. university institutions, on the country where they are expecting to pursue their career. For the last 10 years, the ratio of graduating students from Canada who have indicated their intention to take up residence in the United States has steadily increased: from 45.6 percent in 1990 to 65 percent in 1999. The students were also asked to indicate if they had the "firm intention" to stay in the United States. Here again, the percentage of positive answers among graduating students from Canada has steadily increased — from 36.5 percent in 1990 to 50 percent in 1999. (Source: www.nsf.gov.)

Border Regulations and Migratory Flows

Marc A. Van Audenrode
Laval University, and Analysis Group, Boston

VAN AUDENRODE STARTED HIS PRESENTATION from his own personal experience as a child living in Belgium. Border effects were very important then because of high border costs and the fact that cross-country labour mobility was very limited. Going back in that region recently, he noted that things have changed quite a bit and borders are almost non-existent. Cross-border movements are much more prevalent than they were 25 years ago.

In the case of Canada and the United States today, the first thing to ask is whether the rules and regulations governing mobility are actually limiting migration flows. In his view, since the introduction of TN visas, professionals and business people are essentially free to move, so that observed flows of skilled workers are not unduly restricted by existing rules.

Van Audenrode does not have a definitive answer to the question of whether we should seek to extend this kind of mobility opportunities to other groups of lesser-skilled workers. However, he noted the importance of overall economic activity in the decision to move, and linked some specific outflows of Canadians to the United States to poor economic conditions in Canada. The cost of changing countries is higher than we can imagine and the situation has to be very bad for people to decide to leave. He also made references to specific cases where new businesses were created in Canada by U.S. firms to take advantage of the lower costs of skilled labour in Canada. The relative strength of the demand for labour between Canada and the United States is a major determinant of migratory flows, and this must condition our thinking on policy related to labour migration.

Another factor that may be important for mobility policy is the diverging population trends in Canada and the United States. It is not clear what this divergence will imply for migration flows between the two countries, but it may be an important consideration for Canada if, for example, the national tax burden imposed on working individuals increases more in Canada than in the United States.

Conference Program

SOCIAL AND LABOUR MARKET ASPECTS OF NORTH AMERICAN LINKAGES

WORKSHOP ORGANIZED
BY
HUMAN RESOURCES DEVELOPMENT CANADA
AND
INDUSTRY CANADA

November 20-22, 2002
Delta Hotel
Montreal, Quebec

WORKSHOPS

DAY 1

OPENING REMARKS BY CO-HOSTS
Renée St-Jacques, Industry Canada
Thomas Townsend, Human Resources Development Canada

PANEL – NORTH AMERICAN LINKAGES: SOCIAL AND
LABOUR MARKET ISSUES FOR CANADA

FACILITATOR
Jean-Pierre Voyer, Policy Research Initiative

PANELISTS
Stephen Clarkson, University of Toronto
Keith G. Banting, Queen's University
Daniel Schwanen, Institute for Research on Public Policy

DAY 2

SESSION 1 – THE EXTENT AND EVOLUTION OF ECONOMIC INTEGRATION
BETWEEN CANADA AND THE UNITED STATES

CHAIR
Alan V. Deardorff, University of Michigan

PAPER
Border Effects and North American Integration: Where Are We Up To?
Serge Coulombe, University of Ottawa

DISCUSSANT
Mark Brown, Statistics Canada

PAPER
**Border Effects: Assessing Their Implications for Canadian Policy in a
North American Context**
John F. Helliwell, University of British Columbia

DISCUSSANT
James E. Anderson, Boston College

SESSION 2 – NORTH AMERICAN INTEGRATION AND THE LABOUR MARKET

CHAIR
    Peter Kuhn, University of California, Santa Barbara

PAPER
    Trade Liberalization and the Labour Market
    Thomas Lemieux, University of British Columbia

DISCUSSANT
    W. Craig Riddell, University of British Columbia

PAPER
    The Political Economy of North American Integration,
    Labour Market Adjustments and Plant Closures in Canada
    Eugene Beaulieu, University of Calgary and
    Christopher D. Joy, University of Calgary

DISCUSSANT
    Richard G. Harris, Simon Fraser University

SESSION 3 – NORTH AMERICAN INTEGRATION AND ADJUSTMENTS BY WORKERS AND FIRMS

CHAIR
    Don J. DeVoretz, Simon Fraser University

PAPER
    A New Look at the Out-migration of Canadian Workers in the
    1980s and 1990s
    Ross Finnie, Queen's University

DISCUSSANT
    Jennifer Hunt, University of Montreal

PAPER
    Innovation and Response in Industrial Relations and Workplace Practices
    under Increased Canada-U.S. Economic Integration
    Richard P. Chaykowski, Queen's University and
    George A. Slotsve, Northern Illinois University

DISCUSSANT
    Peter Kuhn, University of California, Santa Barbara

PANEL – ASSESSING THE EXTENT OF CURRENT CANADA-U.S. ECONOMIC LINKAGES AND THEIR COSTS AND BENEFITS

FACILITATOR
Thomas Townsend, Human Resources Development Canada

PANELISTS
Glen Hodgson, Export Development Canada
Andrew Jackson, Canadian Labour Congress
Jayson Myers, Canadian Manufacturers & Exporters

DINNER SPEAKER
Carl Grenier, Free Trade Lumber Council, Montreal

DAY 3

SESSION 4 – NORTH AMERICAN INTEGRATION: IMPLICATIONS FOR SOCIAL POLICY

CHAIR
Richard P. Chaykowski, Queen's University

PAPER
Does Economic Integration Lead to Social Policy Convergence? An Analysis of North American Linkages
Rafael Gomez, London School of Economics and Morley Gunderson, University of Toronto

DISCUSSANT
Michael R. Smith, McGill University

PAPER
Redistribution, Social Protection and North American Linkages: Assessing the Long-term Latitude for Social Policy Distinctiveness under Increased Labour Mobility
Gerard W. Boychuck, University of Waterloo

DISCUSSANT
Alain Noël, University of Montreal

Session 5 – Modeling Labour Mobility Decisions and the General Equilibrium Effects on the Economy

CHAIR
David E. Wildasin, University of Kentucky

PAPER
Labour Mobility Between Canada and the United States: Quo Vadis 2002?
Don J. DeVoretz, Simon Fraser University and
Diane Coulombe, Simon Fraser University

DISCUSSANT
Dwayne Benjamin, University of Toronto

PAPER
A Simple General Equilibrium Model with International Labour Market Linkages
Jean Mercenier, Cergy-Pontoise University and
Nicolas Schmitt, University of Geneva and Simon Fraser University

DISCUSSANT
Alan V. Deardorff, University of Michigan

Session 6 – The Implications of Increased Labour Mobility on Human Capital Formation and Selected Canadian Policies

CHAIR
Jean Mercenier, Cergy-Pontoise University

PAPER
The Implications of Labour Mobility on Fiscal Competition and Higher Education Policy in Canada
David E. Wildasin, University of Kentucky

DISCUSSANT
Mary E. Lovely, Syracuse University

PAPER
Productivity and North American Labour Market Integration: New Analytical Perspectives
Richard G. Harris, Simon Fraser University

DISCUSSANT
Eugene Beaulieu, University of Calgary

PANEL – ASSESSING THE MERIT OF EASING FURTHER THE MOVEMENTS OF WORKERS BETWEEN CANADA AND THE UNITED STATES

FACILITATOR
Renée St-Jacques, Industry Canada

PANELISTS
Jean-Christophe Dumont, Organisation for Economic Co-operation and Development
Robert Lacroix, University of Montreal
Marc A. Van Audenrode, Laval University

CLOSING PANEL – THE WAY FORWARD: IDENTIFYING ISSUES, KNOWLEDGE GAPS AND RESEARCH PRIORITIES

FACILITATOR
W. Craig Riddell, University of British Columbia

PANELISTS
Richard G. Harris, Simon Fraser University
John F. Helliwell, University of British Columbia
Thomas Lemieux, University of British Columbia

About the Contributors

James E. Anderson is the William B. Neenan, S.J. Professor of Economics at Boston College and a Research Associate at the National Bureau of Economic Research. His main research interests include international trade, political economy, economic history and economic development. Dr. Anderson is the author of many academic publications and he has written for periodicals such as the *American Economic Review*, the *International Economic Review*, the *Journal of International Economics* and the *World Bank Economic Review*. He currently serves on the editorial board of the *Review of International Economics* and has recently served on the editorial boards of the *American Economic Review* and the *Journal of International Economics*.

Keith G. Banting is a Professor in the School of Policy Studies and in the Department of Political Studies at Queen's University. He holds the Queen's Research Chair in Public Policy and was the Director of the School of Policy Studies from 1992 until July 2003. Recognized internationally for his expertise on the politics of the welfare state, his research interests focus on federalism, multiculturalism and social policy in Canada and other Western countries. Dr. Banting holds a Ph.D. from Oxford University. He has been a visiting scholar at various institutions, including the London School of Economics, the Brookings Institution and Harvard University. Professor Banting has edited and/or authored numerous books and has contributed articles to many prestigious journals.

Eugene Beaulieu is an Associate Professor in the Department of Economics at the University of Calgary, which he joined after completing his Ph.D. at Columbia University in 1997. Before, he worked as an economist for the government of Kenya and the Bank of Canada. Dr. Beaulieu's research focuses on the political economy and distributional consequences of international trade policy in Canada and the United States. He was awarded the 1998 Petro-Canada Young Innovators Award to study the impact of the FTA and NAFTA on manufacturing plant closures in Canada and the United States. In 2003, he held a Killam Resident

Scholarship and, more recently, he was awarded a three-year Social Sciences and Humanities Research Council (SSHRC) grant to conduct research on the evolution of the political economy of Canada's trade policy. Dr. Beaulieu serves on the Academic Advisory Council to the Deputy Minister of International Trade, in the Department of International Trade of the Government of Canada.

Dwayne Benjamin is a Professor of Economics at the University of Toronto, where he teaches courses in econometrics and labour economics. He completed his Ph.D. in economics at Princeton University. Professor Benjamin's research interests include development and labour economics, with an emphasis on labour markets, both in the Canadian context and in developing countries. He is the author of many academic papers and articles. His texts have appeared in periodicals such as the *Journal of Labor Economics*, the *American Economic Review* and the *Canadian Journal of Economics*.

Gerard W. Boychuk is an Associate Professor in the Department of Political Science at the University of Waterloo. He is the author of *Patchworks of Purpose: The Development of Provincial Social Assistance Regimes in Canada*, published in 1998. He is co-investigator, with Debora VanNijnatten, in a SSHRC-sponsored multi-year project comparing the public policies of Canadian provinces and U.S. states in the areas of environmental protection and social policy. He has also been a consultant to Human Resources Development Canada on public policy comparisons between Canada and the United States. He currently holds the 2004-2005 Fulbright-Michigan State University Visiting Chair.

Mark Brown is a Senior Research Economist in the Micro-Economic Analysis Division of Statistics Canada. He holds a Ph.D. in Geography from McMaster University, specializing in economic geography, and was a faculty member in the Department of Geography and the Department of Agricultural Economics at McGill University prior to taking his current position at Statistics Canada.

Richard P. Chaykowski is currently a faculty member in the Master of Industrial Relations Program at the School of Policy Studies, Queen's University. His research interests include labour policy, especially employment relations and workplace equity, labour market issues, including skills development and the impact of unions, and workplace issues, such as innovation in the workplace and the impact of technological change. Dr. Chaykowski received his Ph.D. from Cornell University. He was co-founder and is currently Co-chair of the Canadian Workplace Research Network, which facilitates national networking between human resources and industrial relations researchers. His work has appeared in leading scholarly journals and he has published over 40 papers in edited volumes, periodicals, academic proceedings, and other professional and technical reports. He has been a guest co-editor of special issues for *Relations industrielles* and *Canadian Public Policy*.

Stephen Clarkson is a Professor of Political Science at the University of Toronto. His research interests include Canadian statistics, globalization and North American integration. He completed his graduate studies at Oxford University as a Rhodes Scholar, and at the Sorbonne as a Ford Foundation foreign area scholar. Dr. Clarkson won the John Porter Prize for his book on the political economy of Canada's relationship with the United States, entitled *Canada and the Reagan Challenge: Crisis and Adjustment 1981-85*. He was also awarded the Governor General's Prize in 1990 for a non-fiction book he co-authored, entitled *Trudeau and Our Times. Volume one: The Magnificent Obsession*. He was subsequently granted the John W. Dafoe Prize for *Trudeau and Our Times. Volume two: The Heroic Delusion*.

Diane Coulombe is currently senior researcher, librarian and translator at the Vancouver Centre of Excellence for Research on Immigration. Her research interests include the mobility of immigrants and language learning among newcomers. She has taught languages in post-secondary institutions and schools in Canada, Europe and the United States. She received a doctorate in second-language acquisition from Laval University.

Serge Coulombe is a Professor of Economics at the University of Ottawa. His current research interests include economic growth and regional economic development, North American economic integration, trade, human capital and growth, monetary theory, and migration. Professor Coulombe received his Ph.D. in Economics from Laval University. Previously, he was Director of the M.A. Program in the Department of Economics at the University of Ottawa, President of the National Congress of l'Association des économistes québécois (ASDEQ), and Vice-President of the Société canadienne de science économique. Dr. Coulombe has presented his work at numerous conferences and seminars and has published papers in periodicals such as the *Canadian Journal of Economics*, *Regional Studies* and *Canadian Public Administration*.

Alan V. Deardorff is the John W. Sweetland Professor of Economics, and a Professor of Economics and Public Policy at the University of Michigan. His current research interests include the role of labour standards in international trade policy, the interactions among domestic economic policies in an international setting and the determinants of bilateral trade patterns. With Robert Stern, he developed the Michigan Model of World Production and Trade, which is used to estimate the effects of trade agreements. He has been a consultant to the U.S. departments of Commerce, Labor, State, and Treasury, and to international organizations such as the Overseas Economic Development Council and the World Bank. He has published numerous articles on various aspects of international trade theory and policy. He received his Ph.D. from Cornell University.

Don J. DeVoretz is Co-director of the Centre of Excellence for the Study of Immigration and a Professor of Economics at Simon Fraser University. He received his Ph.D. in Economics from the University of Wisconsin. Professor DeVoretz's main research interests include the economics of immigration with special emphasis on the employment, income and saving effects of Canadian immigration flows. Dr. DeVoretz served on the Academic Advisory Board of Employment and Immigration Canada from 1987 to 1991 and chaired the economic section of Canada's Ten-year Strategic Immigration Review, in 1994. Recently, he was an adjunct scholar at the C. D. Howe Institute. His work has appeared in periodicals such as the *Canadian Journal of Economics* and *Policy Options*.

Jean-Christophe Dumont is an economist in the Employment, Labour and Social Affairs Directorate (Division of Non-member Economies and International Migration) at the OECD, in Paris. He joined the OECD Secretariat in 2000 to work on international migration issues. He has authored several publications on the economic impact of the international mobility of persons. He holds a Ph.D. in Development Economics from the University of Paris IX-Dauphine and has worked as a Research Fellow at Laval University, in Quebec City. Previously, he was a research assistant at DIAL, a European centre for research on development economics, based in Paris.

Ross Finnie is an Adjunct Professor in the School of Policy Studies at Queen's University since 1997, and a Visiting Fellow at Statistics Canada since 1993. His research focuses in income inequality and income dynamics, postsecondary graduates and the postsecondary education system. Dr. Finnie studied at Queen's University, the London School of Economics and the University of Wisconsin, at Madison. On the *brain drain* topic, Dr. Finnie has also written "The Brain Drain: Myth and Reality – What It Is and What Should Be Done?" (with comments by Peter Kuhn, John Helliwell, Daniel Schwanen, Peter Barrett and David Stewart-Patterson), published in *Choices* by the Institute for Research on Public Policy in 2001.

Rafael Gomez is a Lecturer in the Interdisciplinary Institute of Management at the London School of Economics, in the United Kingdom. His research interests include labour market analysis, human resource management, comparative industrial relations, growth and economic performance, consumer behaviour and strategic marketing. Professor Gomez obtained his Ph.D. in Industrial Relations from the University of Toronto. He is affiliated with several professional associations, namely the Canadian Economics Association, the Royal Economic Society and the Society for the Advancement of Socio-economics. Previously, he held positions with the Canadian Department of Finance as a research consultant, and was a senior consultant and board member for Isolon Ltd, a company based in London, United Kingdom. Dr. Gomez has been widely published and his research has appeared in publications such as the *Canadian Journal of Economics*, the *British Journal of Industrial Relations* and *Canadian Public Policy*.

Morley Gunderson is a Professor in the Centre for Industrial Relations (CIR) and the Department of Economics at the University of Toronto, where he also holds the CIBC Chair in Youth Employment. His current research interests include labour market impacts of trade liberalization and globalization, youth unemployment, retirement and pension issues, and workers' compensation. Dr. Gunderson earned his Ph.D. at the University of Wisconsin. He is presently a member of the editorial boards of the *International Journal of Manpower* and the *Journal of Labor Research*, and of the editorial committee of the Canadian Policy Research Network. In 1997, the Morley Gunderson Prize was established as a tribute to Professor Gunderson's 10-year tenure as Director of the CIR. Dr. Gunderson is a widely published author and his research has appeared in publications such as the *Canadian Journal of Economics*, the *Journal of Labor Economics* and *Canadian Public Policy*.

Richard G. Harris is the Telus Professor of Economics at Simon Fraser University, and a Senior Fellow of the C.D. Howe Institute. His main area of specialization is international economics, particularly the economics of integration. During the 1980s he worked extensively on the modelling of the economic impact of the Canada-U.S. Free Trade Agreement and, subsequently, of NAFTA. He has served as a consultant to numerous Canadian government departments, international organizations and corporations in the area of international economics. In addition to technical articles, he has published policy-oriented books and articles on Canada-U.S. free trade, international macro-economics, economic growth, the Asia-Pacific region and Canadian public policy.

John F. Helliwell is a Professor of Economics at the University of British Columbia and a member of the National Statistics Council. Dr. Helliwell was the 2003-04 Special Advisor to the Bank of Canada. Earlier in 2003, he was a Visiting Research Fellow at Merton College, Oxford University. Dr. Helliwell has also held other visiting appointments, including the Christensen Visiting Fellowship at St. Catherine's College, Oxford University, and the Mackenzie King Visiting Professorship in Canadian Studies at Harvard University. Dr. Helliwell is widely published and his research has appeared in many leading periodicals such as the *Review of Economic Studies,* the *Journal of Economic Perspectives* and the *European Economic Review.* He has also written several books on trade-related issues, including *Globalization and Well-Being,* which won the prestigious Donner Prize for best book in Canadian public policy, in the spring of 2003.

Glen Hodgson is Vice-President and Chief Economist of The Conference Board of Canada. Prior to his current post, he was Vice-President and Deputy Chief Economist of Export Development Canada (EDC), Canada's export credit agency. He co-lead the group that assesses political, environmental and other risks pertinent to EDC's business. He also served as Vice-President of Policy and International Relations at EDC. Prior to joining EDC, Mr. Hodgson worked at the Canadian Department of Finance, where his positions included Assistant Director of International Finance and Development, and Departmental Secretary to the Deputy Minister of Finance. He also represented Canada at the International Monetary Fund in Washington from 1984 to 1988.

Jennifer Hunt is Associate Professor in the Department of Economics at McGill University. She previously held positions as an assistant professor (1992-1997) and associate professor (1997-2001) at Yale University, and as an associate professor at the University of Montreal (2001-2004). She received a Ph.D. in Economics from Harvard University in 1992, and a Bachelor's degree in Electrical Engineering from the Massachusetts Institute of Technology in 1987. Dr. Hunt is affiliated with the National Bureau of Economic Research in Cambridge (Mass.) and several other research institutions. She has done research in the areas of employment and unemployment policy, immigration, wage inequality, and transition economics. She is currently investigating the determinants of crime and corruption.

Andrew Jackson is Senior Economist at the Canadian Labour Congress since 1989 and a Research Associate with the Canadian Centre for Policy Alternatives. His areas of interest include the labour market and the quality of jobs, income distribution and poverty, macro-economic policy, tax policy and the impacts of globalization on workers and on social-democratic economic policy.

He served as Director of Research at the Canadian Council on Social Development. Mr. Jackson was educated at the London School of Economics and at the University of British Columbia. He has written numerous articles for academic publications and has co-authored three books, including *Falling Behind: The State of Working Canada 2000*.

Christopher D. Joy is a market analyst at the Alberta Market Surveillance Administrator (MSA). The MSA oversees electricity trading on the Alberta market. Mr. Joy is responsible for real-time market analysis and provides analytical support on energy trading and market issues. Prior to joining the MSA, he worked as an economist at the Canadian Energy Research Institute (CERI), focusing on long-term energy and environmental modeling and forecasting. Mr. Joy holds an M.A. in Economics from the University of Calgary and teaches economics at Mt. Royal College, in Calgary.

Peter Kuhn is a Professor of Economics at the University of California, Santa Barbara. His research interests include trade unions, immigration, displaced workers, unemployment, comparative labour markets, labour market impacts of information technology, and trade unions. Professor Kuhn received his Ph.D. in Economics from Harvard University in 1983. He has held faculty positions at the University of Western Ontario and McMaster University, and visiting faculty positions at the London School of Economics, University College, London, and Princeton University. Dr. Kuhn is a widely published author and his research has appeared in publications such as the *American Economic Review*, the *Canadian Journal of Economics* and the *Journal of International Economics*.

Robert Lacroix has been the Rector of the University of Montreal since 1998 and a Professor of Economics at the University since 1970. Prior to his appointment as Rector, he has held several positions at the University, including Chair of the Department of Economics, Director of the Centre for Research and Development in Economics (CRDE) and Dean of the Faculty of Arts and Sciences. He founded the Centre for Interuniversity Research and Analysis of Organizations (CIRANO) and served as its Chair and Director General from 1994 to 1998. Professor Lacroix obtained his Ph.D. in Economics from the University of Louvain, in Belgium. He has done extensive research into the economics of labour and human resources, and the economics of technological progress and innovation. Dr. Lacroix was elected a member of the Royal Society of Canada in 1989, named a Member of the Order of Canada in 2000, and an Officier de l'Ordre national du Québec in 2001.

Thomas Lemieux is a Professor of Economics and Distinguished University Scholar at the University of British Columbia, and a Research Associate of the National Bureau of Economic Research. He is also the director of the Team for Advanced Research on Globalization, Education, and Technology (TARGET). His research interests include changes in the wage distribution, the role of education in the labour market, and the impact of labour market institutions on wages and employment. Professor Lemieux earned his Ph.D. at Princeton University. In 1998, he received the John Rae Prize of the Canadian Economics Association, which is awarded every other year to the economist who has been most productive in research over the previous five years. Dr. Lemieux is a co-editor of the *Berkeley Electronic Journal of Economic Analysis and Policy*, and an associate editor of the *American Economic Review*, the *Review of Economics and Statistics*, and the *Journal of the European Economic Association*. He has published articles in books and journals, including the *American Economic Review*, the *Quarterly Journal of Economics* and the *Canadian Journal of Economics*.

Mary E. Lovely is an Associate Professor of Economics in the Maxwell School of Citizenship and Public Affairs, at Syracuse University, where she combines interests in international economics and public economics. Her current research projects examine the determinants of foreign direct investment flows to Chinese provinces and their relation to provincial differences in environmental policy and labour conditions. She has recently completed work on the geographic concentration of exporting firms and the welfare effects of free trade areas. Dr. Lovely's earlier work emphasizes the income and distributional effects of policies designed to foster industries that provide positive spillovers to the domestic economy. She has written on the measurement of labour market effects of increased international trade and on the welfare effects of smuggling. She has studied the optimal design of commodity taxes when consumers cross borders to shop in lower-taxing jurisdictions as well as the benefits and costs of restricting this activity. Dr. Lovely earned her Ph.D. in Economics at the University of Michigan, Ann Arbor.

Jean Mercenier is a Professor at Théorie Économique, Modélisation et Applications (THEMA), at Cergy-Pontoise University, in France. His research interests include macro-economics, international trade and development, and applied general equilibrium. He has been a visiting scholar and a professor at a number of institutions worldwide, including in Canada, Uruguay, the United States, Belgium and Turkey. Professor Mercenier has written numerous articles for academic publications, and his research has appeared in periodicals such as the *International Economic Review*, the *Journal of Policy Modelling*, *Econometrica*, and the *European Journal of Political Economy*.

Jayson Myers is Senior Vice President and Chief Economist of Canadian Manufacturers & Exporters (CME) and is in charge of CME's national policy office in Ottawa. Dr. Myers is a well-known economic commentator and is widely published in the fields of Canadian and international economics, and technological and industrial change. He serves on the Special Advisory Councils to the Minister for International Trade, the Minister of Industry, and the Bank of Canada. Dr. Myers studied at Queen's University and the University of British Columbia, and at the London School of Economics and Oxford University in the United Kingdom. He has held appointments as a research fellow at Nuffield College, Oxford, and as a lecturer in international studies at Warwick University, also in the United Kingdom. He is currently the Canadian affairs analyst for Oxford Analytica, an international consulting group based at Oxford University.

Alain Noël is a Professor in the Department of Political Science and the Director of the Centre de recherche interuniversitaire sur les transformations économiques et sociales (CRITÈRES), at the University of Montreal. He is also a Research Fellow of the Institute for Research on Public Policy, and is a member of the Advisory Council of the Institute of Intergovernmental Relations at Queen's University. Professor Noël has worked as an expert consultant for the Secrétariat aux affaires intergouvernementales canadiennes and for the Ministère de l'emploi et de la solidarité of the Quebec government. He is the author of several studies on federalism and social policy in Quebec and Canada. His work has been published in various books and periodicals, including the *American Political Science Review, Comparative Political Studies*, the *Revue française des affaires sociales* and the *Canadian Journal of Political Science*. In 2004-05, he will spend the year as a visiting scholar at the Université de Grenoble.

W. Craig Riddell is a Professor in the Department of Economics and currently holds a Royal Bank Faculty Research Professorship at the University of British Columbia (UBC). His research interests include labour economics, labour relations and public policy. His current work focuses on unemployment and labour market dynamics, experimental and non-experimental approaches to the evaluation of social programs, unionization and collective bargaining, unemployment insurance and social assistance, and skill formation, education and training. Professor Riddell is the former Head of the Department of Economics at UBC, and past President of the Canadian Economics Association. He obtained his Ph.D. from Queen's University. Dr. Riddell has published papers in numerous academic journals such as the *American Economic Review*, the *Canadian Journal of Economics, Econometrica*, and the *Journal of Labor Economics*.

Nicolas Schmitt is a Professor of Economics at the University of Geneva and on leave from Simon Fraser University, where he teaches mainly in industrial organization, international trade and micro-economics. He completed his Ph.D. in Economics at the University of Toronto. His research is currently focused on the role of vertical restraints in international markets, trade liberalization and on the economics of brain circulation. His published work includes papers on non-tariff barriers, trade liberalization and market integration, which have appeared in periodicals such as the *International Economic Review*, the *Journal of Development Economics* and the *Journal of International Economics*.

George A. Slotsve is an Associate Professor in the Department of Economics at Northern Illinois University. His research focuses on labour economics, income distribution, the economics of poverty, and industrial relations. Professor Slotsve received his Ph.D. from the University of Wisconsin, at Madison. Prior to joining Northern Illinois University in 1996, he held a position at Vanderbilt University. He has authored and co-authored articles that have appeared in publications such as the *Canadian Journal of Economics*, the *North American Journal of Economics and Finance*, the *Bell Journal of Economics* and *Public Policy*, which is published by the John Deutsch Institute at Queen's University.

Michael R. Smith is a Professor in the Department of Sociology at McGill University. His research interests include organizational structures, industrial disputes, the politics of macro-economic policy, the functioning of labour markets, and economic security and its consequences. Professor Smith obtained his Ph.D. from Brown University. He recently completed a report for the Government of Canada's Policy Research Secretariat on the effects of technology on employment levels and on the demand for skills, and on the implications for the training needs of those affected. He is a member of the editorial board of the *Canadian Journal of Sociology* and he serves on the Program Committee of the Quebec Ministry of Education. Dr. Smith is a widely published author and his research has appeared in periodicals such as *Canadian Public Policy*, the *Canadian Journal of Sociology* and the *Review of Social Economy*.

Marc A. Van Audenrode is a Professor at Laval University and a vice-president with Analysis Group. His research interests focus on the role of institutions in labour markets, and his current work deals with unemployment insurance and the dynamics of labour markets, employment protection laws and job creation, and wage-setting mechanisms. Dr. Van Audenrode obtained his Ph.D. from the University of California, at Berkeley. He has contributed articles to many academic journals, including *Canadian Public Policy*, the *Journal of Economic Theory* and the *Canadian Journal of Economics*.

David E. Wildasin is the Endowed Professor of Public Finance at the Martin School of Public Policy and Administration, and a Professor of Economics at the University of Kentucky. His current research focuses on fiscal policy, the integration of labour and capital markets, and intergovernmental fiscal relations in developing and transition countries. He received his Ph.D. from the University of Iowa. Professor Wildasin serves on the editorial boards of the *National Tax Journal*, *International Tax and Public Finance*, the *Journal of Regional Science*, the *Journal of Urban Economics*, and other professional journals. Dr. Wildasin's published research has appeared in the *American Economic Review*, the *Journal of Public Economics*, the *Canadian Journal of Economics*, the *Oxford Economic Papers*, and numerous other books and journals.